Model Stock Purchase Agreement with Commentary

Second Edition

Volume II: Exhibits, Ancillary Documents, and Appendices

Mergers and Acquisitions Committee

AMERICAN BAR ASSOCIATION
Business Law Section

The materials contained herein represent the opinions of the authors and editors and should not be construed to be the action of either the American Bar Association or the Business Law Section, unless adopted pursuant to the bylaws of the Association.

Nothing contained in this book is to be considered as the rendering of legal advice for specific cases, and readers are responsible for obtaining such advice from their own legal counsel. This book is intended for educational and informational purposes only.

The Prefaces, Preliminary Notes, Appendices, and Commentary in both Volume I and Volume II of the Second Edition of the *Model Stock Purchase Agreement*, Exhibits, and Ancillary Documents are protected under United States copyright law and may not be reproduced in any manner without express permission. The Model Stock Purchase Agreement itself and it Exhibits and Ancillary Documents, as they appear in the printed publication and on its accompanying CD-ROM, may be freely reproduced by the reader.

The set of files on the CD-ROM accompanying the *Model Stock Purchase Agreement*, Second Edition, may only be used on a single computer or moved to and used on another computer unless modified by the user. Under no circumstances may the set of files be used on more than one computer at one time. For permission, contact the ABA Copyrights and Contracts Department at copyright@americanbar.org or via fax at 312-988-6030, or complete the online form at http://www.americanbar.org/utility/reprint.html.

Cover design by ABA Publishing.

Page composition by Quadrum.

Library of Congress Cataloging-in-Publication Data

Model stock purchase agreement / by Murray Perelman, editor. — 2nd ed.
    p. cm.
  ISBN-13: 978-1-60442-998-5
  ISBN-10: 1-60442-998-4
  1. Stock purchase agreements (Close corporations)—United States. I. Perelman, Murray. II. American Bar Association. Committee on Mergers and Acquisitions. III. Title.
  KF1466.M64 2010
  346.73'0922—dc22

                    2010026842

Volume II: Exhibits, Ancillary Documents, and Appendices

Discounts are available for books ordered in bulk. Custom covers are also available for bulk orders. Special consideration is given to state and local bars, CLE programs, and other bar-related organizations. Inquire at Book Publishing, American Bar Association, 321 North Clark Street, Chicago, Illinois 60654-7598.

www.ShopABA.org

23 22   6 5

Summary Table of Contents

Contents

Exhibits, Ancillary Documents, and Appendices
(Volume II)

Introduction

The Exhibits, Ancillary Documents, and Appendices volume is comprised of the following:

(i)   various exhibits to the Model Agreement;

(ii)   ancillary documents, which although not exhibits, may be useful in a stock acquisition; and

(iii)   appendices describing unique issues in purchasing the stock of a subsidiary, reviewing the use of stock as consideration for an acquisition, outlining considerations in drafting employment agreements, analyzing nine hypothetical scenarios that illustrate the operation and interaction of certain provisions of the Model Agreement, and discussing the option of including binding arbitration as a means of dispute resolution.

The exhibits and ancillary documents are usually drafted by buyer's counsel, but some may be drafted by seller's counsel. In drafting or reviewing ancillary agreements, consideration might be given to achieving consistency between the miscellaneous provisions (such as governing law, notices, severability, assignment, and counterparts) in these agreements and those in the Model Agreement. Differences in wording or in what is included or excluded in these agreements might create confusion if they become subject to disputes among the parties. Often, consistency is lacking because of time pressures, the use of different precedents, or their preparation by different attorneys.

That is not to say that the miscellaneous provisions must be identical. For example, the Model Agreement has extensive miscellaneous provisions, as is customary, and it is usually not considered necessary or appropriate to include all such detailed provisions in each exhibit and ancillary document. In addition, some agreements may require additional miscellaneous provisions that are unique to the subject matter, as, for example, with employment agreements and covenants not to compete. Even where two agreements contain the same types of miscellaneous provisions, the substance may differ, as, for example, with regard to the remedies that are available and the method of dispute resolution.

EXHIBITS

EXHIBIT 2.2(b)

Nonnegotiable Promissory Note

PRELIMINARY NOTE

The commentary to Section 2.2 of the Model Agreement briefly describes Buyer's Promissory Notes to be delivered to Sellers. It discusses the principal reason why Buyer will want the Promissory Notes to be in nonnegotiable form: the protection of Buyer's setoff rights. Nonnegotiable notes will enable Buyer to exercise its right to a setoff provided in the Model Agreement by withholding payments due under the Promissory Notes in circumstances that entitle Buyer to make a claim against Sellers under the Model Agreement. Buyer's right to a setoff is a particularly potent remedy since, in addition to affording Buyer control over the funds, a good-faith exercise of the right will not constitute an Event of Default under Paragraph 2(a) of the Promissory Notes, even if such exercise is ultimately determined to be unjustified. *See* commentary to Section 11.7 of the Model Agreement for a more detailed discussion of setoff rights.

The requirements for a negotiable instrument are set out in Section 3-104 of the Uniform Commercial Code (UCC). The "magic words" needed for negotiability are missing in at least two respects: the Promissory Note designates the named Seller as the sole payee, thereby failing to meet the requirement of UCC Section 3-104(1)(d) of being "payable to order or to bearer," and the Promissory Note states, in the second paragraph, that it is subject to the terms and conditions of the Model Agreement, thereby rendering Buyer's promise conditional and making the Promissory Note nonnegotiable. *See* UCC §§ 3-104(1)(b), 3-105(2)(a).

Paragraph 3(a) of the Promissory Note contains limitations on assignment or transfer by the named Seller. Assignment and transfer (essentially the transfer of title to an instrument, with the transferee getting no more than the rights of the transferor) should be distinguished from negotiation, which ordinarily involves endorsement and transfer to a holder.

The terms of the Promissory Note will be influenced by the relative bargaining power of the parties to the transaction. Sellers usually want the Promissory Notes to be negotiable so that they might be sold or pledged to a bank or financial institution to obtain immediate liquidity. If the Promissory Notes are nonnegotiable, by definition there cannot be a holder in due course. *See* UCC § 3-302. However, if the Promissory Notes are negotiable and a Seller negotiates the notes to a holder in due course, Buyer would be unable to make any claims against the Promissory Notes arising out of a breach of warranty by Sellers. *See* UCC § 3-305.

Buyer and its senior lender will sometimes insist that the Promissory Notes be subordinated to any senior indebtedness of Buyer. If that is the case, the Promissory Notes will typically be titled "Nonnegotiable Subordinated Promissory Notes." The terms of subordination can be lengthy and complex and are often heavily negotiated. Given their complexity, such terms are often contained in a separate subordination or intercreditor agreement with the senior lender, and such an agreement is in turn referenced in the Promissory Note itself with language such as the following:

> Notwithstanding anything in this Note to the contrary, the Payee's right to any payments under this Note and the exercise by Payee of any right or remedy under, or in connection with, this Note are expressly subject to the provisions of that certain Subordination and Intercreditor Agreement dated as of _____ by and among Payee, Maker, and [name of senior lender] as the same may be amended, restated, supplemented, or otherwise modified from time to time in accordance with its terms (the "Intercreditor Agreement"). In the event of any conflict between the terms of the Intercreditor Agreement and this Note, the terms of the Intercreditor Agreement will control.

Among the topics that an intercreditor or subordination agreement may address are the circumstances under which Sellers may receive any payments on the Note while the senior indebtedness is outstanding, whether the Promissory Note may be secured (and the relative priority of such security), whether and for how long the senior lender may impose a payment or enforcement standstill period with respect to the Promissory Note, and the relative rights of Sellers and the senior lender to seek enforcement as well as their rights in the event of Buyer's bankruptcy.

This Note has been issued without registration or qualification under the Securities Act of 1933, as amended, and applicable state securities laws and may not be sold, transferred, or otherwise disposed of without (A) such registration and qualification, or (B) an opinion of counsel reasonably satisfactory to the issuer in form and substance that such sale, transfer, or disposition may lawfully be made without registration or qualification.

COMMENT

This legend is consistent with Sellers' representation in Section 3.25 of the Model Agreement regarding the Notes under the Securities Act. As discussed in the commentary to Section 3.25 of the Model Agreement, the Notes are not necessarily securities.

Exhibit 2.2(b) Nonnegotiable Promissory Note

NONNEGOTIABLE PROMISSORY NOTE

$_____

FOR VALUE RECEIVED, _____, a _____ corporation ("Maker"), promises to pay to _____ ("Payee"), in lawful money of the United States of America, the principal sum of $_____, together with interest in arrears on the unpaid principal balance at an annual rate of _____%, in the manner provided below. Interest will be calculated on the basis of a year of 365 or 366 days, as applicable, and charged for the actual number of days elapsed.

This Note has been executed and delivered pursuant to, and is subject to the terms and conditions of, a Stock Purchase Agreement (the "Purchase Agreement") dated _____, among Maker and Sellers named therein, including Payee, which is, by this reference, incorporated in, and made a part of, this Note. Capitalized terms used in this Note without definition have the respective meanings given to them in the Purchase Agreement.

1. PAYMENTS

(a) The principal amount of this Note will be payable in _____ equal consecutive [annual] [quarterly] installments commencing on _____, [and on _____ of each year thereafter] [and on _____, _____ and _____ of each year thereafter] until paid in full. Accrued and unpaid interest on the unpaid principal balance of this Note will be due and payable [annually] [quarterly], together with each payment of principal.

(b) All payments of principal and interest on this Note will be made by [certified or bank cashier's] check at _____, _____, _____, or at such other place in the United States of America as Payee may designate to Maker in writing [or by wire transfer of immediately available funds to an account as Payee may designate to Maker in writing]. If any payment of principal of, or interest on, this Note becomes due on a day that is not a Business Day, such payment will be due on the next succeeding Business Day, and such extension of time shall be taken into account in calculating the amount of interest payable under this Note.

(c) Maker may, without premium or penalty, at any time and from time to time, prepay all or any portion of the outstanding principal balance due under this Note, provided that each such prepayment is accompanied by accrued interest on the amount of principal prepaid calculated to the date of such prepayment. Any partial prepayments will be applied to installments of principal in inverse order of their maturity.

(d)   Maker may withhold and set off against any amount due on this Note, the amount of any claim for indemnification, payment, or reimbursement to which Maker may be entitled arising from the Purchase Agreement, any other agreement entered into pursuant to the Purchase Agreement, or otherwise.

2.   DEFAULTS

(a)   The occurrence of any one or more of the following events with respect to Maker will constitute an event of default under this Note ("Event of Default"):

   (i)   If Maker fails to pay when due any payment of principal of, or interest on, this Note and such failure continues for 15 days after Payee notifies Maker of such failure to pay in writing; provided, however, that the exercise by Maker in good faith of its right of setoff pursuant to Paragraph 1(d), whether or not ultimately determined to be justified, will not constitute an Event of Default.

   (ii)   If, pursuant to or within the meaning of the United States Bankruptcy Code or any other federal or state law relating to insolvency or relief of debtors (a "Bankruptcy Law"), Maker (A) commences a voluntary case or proceeding; (B) consents to the entry of an order for relief against it in an involuntary case; (C) consents to the appointment of a trustee, receiver, assignee, liquidator, or similar official; (D) makes an assignment for the benefit of its creditors; or (E) admits in writing its inability to pay its debts as they become due.

   (iii)   If a court of competent jurisdiction enters an order or decree under any Bankruptcy Law that (A) is for relief against Maker in an involuntary case; (B) appoints a trustee, receiver, assignee, liquidator, or similar official for Maker or substantially all of Maker's assets; or (C) orders the liquidation of Maker, and in each case the order or decree is not dismissed within 60 days.

(b)   Upon the occurrence of an Event of Default under Paragraph 2(a)(i) (unless all Events of Default have been cured by Maker or waived by Payee), Payee may, at its option, (i) by written notice to Maker, declare the entire unpaid principal balance of this Note, together with all accrued and unpaid interest thereon, immediately due and payable regardless of any prior forbearance, and (ii) exercise any and all rights and remedies available to it under applicable law, including the right to collect from Maker all amounts due under this Note. Upon the occurrence of an Event of Default under Paragraph 2(a)(ii) or (iii) of this Note, the entire unpaid principal balance of this Note, together with all accrued and unpaid interest thereon, will become immediately due and payable.

Exhibit 2.2(b) Nonnegotiable Promissory Note

3. MISCELLANEOUS

(a) **Assignments and Successors. This Note may not be assigned or transferred by Payee without the prior written consent of Maker. Any purported assignment or transfer without such prior written consent will be void. Subject to the foregoing, this Note will inure to the benefit of the heirs, executors, administrators, legal representatives, successors, and permitted assigns of Payee.**

(b) **Governing Law. All matters relating to or arising out of this Note will be governed by and construed and interpreted under the laws of the State of _____, without regard to conflicts-of-laws principles that would require the application of any other law.**

(c) **Notices. Any notice required or permitted to be given under this Note shall be given in accordance with Section 12.18 of the Purchase Agreement.**

(d) **Severability. If any provision of this Note is held invalid or unenforceable by any court of competent jurisdiction, the other provisions of this Note will remain in full force and effect. Any provision of this Note held invalid or unenforceable only in part or degree will remain in full force and effect to the extent not held invalid or unenforceable.**

IN WITNESS WHEREOF, Maker has executed and delivered this Note as of the date first written above.

[BUYER]

By: _____

Name: _____

Title: _____

COMMENT

Terms of the Promissory Notes will include the interest rate, the amortization schedule, the manner of payment (Buyer's company check if Sellers will accept it; possibly wire transfer if the amount warrants it), events of default (note, however, that nonpayment as a result of Buyer's good faith exercise of its setoff rights is excluded from the definition of "Event of Default"), and remedies. An aggressive Buyer might not even include a default section, requiring that Sellers bargain for acceleration, or might delete the acceleration provision.

In jurisdictions where usury may be an issue, a usury savings provision might be included in the Promissory Note. Such a provision would provide that, in the event the rate of interest provided for in the Promissory Note is determined to exceed the maximum rate of interest permitted by the applicable usury or similar law, the application of such rate will be suspended and there will be charged instead the maximum rate of interest permitted by such law.

SELLERS' RESPONSE

The express setoff rights may be troubling to Sellers. They may argue that the Escrow Agreement was created as a source of payment for claims under the Model Agreement. Alternatively, they may argue for the reduction of the amount of, or elimination of, the Escrow Agreement. In any event, they would probably insist that Buyer establish its right to a setoff, before asserting it, or that the payments on the Note be escrowed until the right to a setoff is established.

In addition to concerns about Buyer's creditworthiness, Sellers may have concerns about the Promissory Notes' lack of security, the lack of covenants, whether there should be additional events of default, and the prepayment provisions. Sellers may want the Promissory Notes to contain representations and warranties as though issued under a credit agreement. Sellers may want the Sellers' Representative to coordinate all remedies, much like a trustee under a trust indenture. In fact, Sellers may insist on providing the first draft of the Promissory Note.

Sellers may also have other concerns. Buyer will be able to treat Sellers differently: it can pick and choose which Sellers get paid if it is otherwise unable to fully honor all Promissory Notes. There is no forum for suing on the Promissory Notes. If Buyer is located in a distant jurisdiction, and Sellers are unable to gain personal jurisdiction in their home state, Sellers will be required to sue in Buyer's home state. Sellers might suggest adding provisions such as the following:

> Maker waives presentment, notice of dishonor, protest, and notice of protest.

> If this Note is not paid when due, Maker agrees to pay all costs of collection, including reasonable attorneys' fees.

> At the option of Payee, this Note may be enforced in any federal court or state court sitting in _____, _____; and Maker consents to the jurisdiction and venue of any such court and waives any argument that the venue in such forum is not convenient. If Maker commences any action in another jurisdiction or venue under any tort or contract theory arising directly or indirectly from the relationship created by this Note, Payee at its option shall be entitled to have the case transferred to one of the jurisdictions and venues above-described, or, if such transfer cannot be accomplished under applicable law, to have such case dismissed without prejudice.

Exhibit 2.2(b) Nonnegotiable Promissory Note

Neither any failure nor any delay by Payee in exercising any right, power, or privilege under this Note will operate as a waiver of such right, power, or privilege, and no single or partial exercise of any such right, power, or privilege will preclude any other or further exercise of such right, power, or privilege or the exercise of any other right, power, or privilege. To the maximum extent permitted by applicable Legal Requirements, (i) no claim or right arising out of this Note can be waived by Payee, in whole or in part, unless made in a writing signed by Payee; (ii) a waiver given by Payee will only be applicable to the specific instance for which it is given; and (iii) no notice to, or demand on, Maker will (A) waive or otherwise affect any obligation of Maker, or (B) affect the right of Payee to take further action without notice or demand as provided in this Note.

With regard to all dates and time periods set forth in this Note, time is of the essence.

Sellers may also want to add additional events of default, include a provision whereby Buyer gives them notice upon the occurrence of an event of default, and bargain for an increase in the interest rate upon default.

EXHIBIT 2.4(a)(v)

Release

PRELIMINARY NOTE

The Model Agreement requires a separate Release of each Seller. Providing for separate releases may facilitate preparation where different Sellers may be asked to sign variations or when not all Sellers are expected to be present at the Closing.

Buyer will be seeking the maximum effectiveness of the Release. Sellers may be tempted to regard the Release as an ordinary piece of boilerplate, but they should carefully consider its implications. It may release in some unexpected way rights of one or more of Sellers. For example, Sellers release each Acquired Company and its affiliates. While "affiliates" is not defined, the term might include the shareholders, officers, and directors of the Acquired Companies. In Born v. Berg, 2007 WL 4472478 (Minn. App. 2007), a corporation's CEO made a personal loan to the CFO, who signed a note to evidence the loan. In connection with the transfer of control of the corporation, the CEO released the corporation and "each of its officers." The court held that the CFO was discharged on the note. As for unexpected consequences, *see* Knight v. Caremark Rx, Inc., 2007 WL 143099 (Del. Ch. 2007) (general release covering "all claims" extinguished stock options).

See the Introduction to this Volume I and the commentary to Article 12 of the Model Agreement for further discussion relevant to the miscellaneous provisions of the Release.

RELEASE

This Release is made as of _____ by _____ ("Seller"). This is one of the Releases referred to in the Stock Purchase Agreement (the "Purchase Agreement"), dated _____, among _____, a _____ corporation ("Buyer"), and Seller and the other sellers named therein (the "Other Sellers"). Capitalized terms used in this Release without definition have the respective meanings given to them in the Purchase Agreement.

Seller acknowledges and agrees that execution and delivery of this Release is a condition to Buyer's obligation to purchase the outstanding capital stock of the Company pursuant to the Purchase Agreement and that Buyer is relying on this Release in consummating such purchase.

Seller, for good and valuable consideration, the receipt and sufficiency of which is hereby acknowledged, and intending to be legally bound, in order to induce Buyer to purchase the outstanding capital stock of the Company pursuant to the Purchase Agreement, agrees as follows:

Seller, for himself or herself and on behalf of each of his or her Related Persons, hereby unconditionally and irrevocably releases and forever discharges Buyer, each Acquired Company, each of their Employee Plans, and each of their respective individual, joint or mutual, past, present, and future Representatives, affiliates, shareholders, controlling persons, Subsidiaries, successors, and assigns (individually, a "Releasee" and collectively, "Releasees") from any and all claims, counterclaims, setoffs, demands, Proceedings, causes of action, Orders, obligations, contracts, agreements, debts, damages, and liabilities whatsoever, whether known or unknown, suspected or unsuspected, both at law and in equity (collectively, "Claims"), which Seller or his or her Related Persons now has, has ever had, or may hereafter have against the respective Releasees arising contemporaneously with or prior to the Closing Date or on account of or arising out of any matter, cause, or event occurring contemporaneously with or prior to the Closing Date, including any right to indemnification, reimbursement from, or payment by any Acquired Company, whether pursuant to their respective Organizational Documents, contract, or otherwise and whether or not relating to Claims pending on, or asserted after, the Closing Date (collectively, the "Released Claims"); provided, however, that nothing contained in this Release will operate to release (a) any obligation of Buyer arising under the Purchase Agreement or any agreement or instrument being executed and delivered pursuant to the Purchase Agreement, or (b) any obligation of any Acquired Company listed on Schedule A.

Seller represents and warrants to each Releasee that Seller has not transferred, assigned, or otherwise disposed of any part of or interest in any Released Claim.

Seller hereby irrevocably covenants not to, directly or indirectly, assert any claim or demand, or commence, institute, or voluntarily aid in any way, or cause to be commenced or instituted, any Proceeding of any kind against any Releasee based upon any Released Claim.

Without in any way limiting any rights and remedies otherwise available to any Releasee, Seller, jointly and severally with the Other Sellers, shall indemnify and hold harmless each Releasee from and against and shall pay to each Releasee

Exhibit 2.4(a)(v) Release

the amount of, or reimburse each Releasee for, all loss, liability, claim, damage (including incidental and consequential damages), or expense (including costs of investigation and defense and reasonable attorneys' and accountants' fees), whether or not involving third-party claims, arising directly or indirectly from or in connection with (a) the assertion by or on behalf of Seller or any of his or her Related Persons of any Released Claim, and (b) the assertion by any third party of any claim or demand against any Releasee which claim or demand arises directly or indirectly from, or in connection with, any assertion by or on behalf of Seller or any of his or her Related Persons against such third party of any Released Claim.

Seller acknowledges and agrees that the execution of this Release does not constitute in any manner whatsoever an admission of liability on the part of any Releasee for any Released Claim, and that such liability is specifically denied.

Seller agrees to (a) execute and deliver such other documents, and (b) do such other acts and things, as Buyer may reasonably request for the purpose of carrying out the intent of this Release.

This Release may not be amended, supplemented, or otherwise modified except in a writing signed by the person against whose interest such change will operate.

All matters relating to or arising out of this Release will be governed by and construed and interpreted under the laws of the State of _____, without regard to conflicts of laws principles that would require the application of any other law.

If any provision of this Release is held invalid or unenforceable by any court of competent jurisdiction, the other provisions of this Release will remain in full force and effect. Any provision of this Release held invalid or unenforceable only in part or degree will remain in full force and effect to the extent not held invalid or unenforceable.

IN WITNESS WHEREOF, the undersigned has executed and delivered this Release as of the date first written above.

_____
Seller [1]

Schedule A

[All obligations to which the Release does not apply to be listed.]

COMMENT

By its terms, the Release covers all claims that Sellers, including their Related Persons, have against any of the Releasees, which includes not only Buyer, but also the Acquired Companies. It includes claims that the releasing parties may have for indemnification, employee benefits, or reimbursement from any Acquired Company.

Without such a Release, if Buyer asserts claims against Sellers, Sellers might assert that Buyer's claims relate to actions taken by them in their capacities as directors and officers of an Acquired Company and present a claim for indemnification and advancement of costs of defense to the Acquired Companies against Buyer's claims.

This instrument does not release any claims that Sellers have under the Model Agreement (such as a claim under Buyer's Promissory Note). It does not release an obligation of any Acquired Company that may have been listed on Schedule A.

The Release contains a representation that no Seller has transferred any interest in a Released Claim. Such a representation is appropriate when known claims are being released. If the Release is more general in nature, then this representation may be omitted.

The Release also includes a covenant not to sue with respect to any matter purported to be released. In addition to the affirmative defense of the Release, the covenant may give a released party a cause of action for breach of covenant.

Additional language or formalities (such as conspicuousness) may be required under applicable state law. For example, if the Release is subject to California law, it should contain an express waiver of Section 1542 of the California Civil Code (to the effect that a general release does not extend to claims that a creditor does not "know or suspect to exist" in his favor, which if known by him would have materially affected his settlement with the debtor). The Release contains a severability provision reflecting the parties' intention that if a provision of the Release is held invalid or unenforceable, the remaining provisions are separated from the invalid or unenforceable provision and remain in effect.

SELLERS' RESPONSE

Sellers may be concerned that the Release, perhaps inadvertently, releases obligations that are not intended to be released. The definition of "Related Persons," used in the Model Agreement and the Release, utilizes vague concepts, such as "control" and "Material Interest" (by reference to the Exchange Act). As a result,

Exhibit 2.4(a)(v) Release

Sellers, as among themselves, the Company, and other entities and persons may all be "Related Persons." Sellers will need to identify possible problems and negotiate appropriate savings clauses in the Release.

At the same time, Sellers may want to be explicit about their own relationships, probably by means of Ancillary Document E—Contribution Agreement. The Contribution Agreement could include releases as among Sellers.

If Buyer is a public company or a large, diversified private company, Sellers might consider reducing the breadth of the definition of Releasees so that claims that are unrelated to the acquisition of the Acquired Companies are not released. In addition, Sellers might consider only releasing the identified persons (agents, representatives, employees, officers, directors, affiliates, shareholders) for actions they have taken while acting in such capacities.

While Sellers will be concerned about inadvertent release of rights that they may have, such as loans, rights of indemnification as directors, officers, and employees under contract, statute, or common law, existing contracts (such as leases), employee benefits, and otherwise, they might want to consider the other provisions. For example, while Buyer might have a legitimate interest in ensuring that Sellers have no claim against an Acquired Company, it may have no interest in extinguishing claims against Representatives of Buyer (which includes advisors, accountants, financial advisors, and legal counsel) that may be wholly unrelated to the transaction.

Sellers may insist that claims arising under standard indemnification provisions (such as director and officer indemnification) not be released. This would be accomplished by adding as another exception in the fourth paragraph: "any Claim against any Acquired Company that arises as a result of, or is related to, Seller's capacity as an officer, director or employee of the Acquired Company." If the Acquired Companies have D&O insurance (which is usually written on a claims-made basis), Sellers may want to assure that they have continuing coverage, requiring the purchase of "tail" coverage. In that event, they will want to assure that the Release does not inadvertently alter the scope of coverage of any insurance.

EXHIBIT 2.4(a)(vii)

Escrow Agreement

PRELIMINARY NOTE

The Escrow Agreement provides that a portion of the Purchase Price is to be held in escrow as a source for funding any claim by Buyer under Article 11 of the Model Agreement. The relationship between the Model Agreement and the Escrow Agreement is referred to in Sections 11.7, 11.8(g), and 11.9 of the Model Agreement. The Escrow Agreement provides an escrow only for indemnification claims, not for purchase price adjustment (true-up) claims. Inclusion of such a provision complicates drafting because often a portion of the escrow is released after the purchase price adjustment is agreed to and before the escrow for indemnification claims would be released. Nevertheless, providing an escrow for the purchase price adjustment is often done and the Escrow Agreement could be modified accordingly. The determination of the purchase price adjustment often utilizes a different dispute resolution mechanism (involvement of accountants), which is not reflected in the Escrow Agreement. *See* "Escrow Agreement" in commentary to Section 2.2.

The sample Escrow Agreement contemplates an institutional escrow agent. The institutional escrow agent would take the view that its duties are purely ministerial in nature and that it is not being paid to accept any duty to exercise judgment or liability for anything but the most egregious of its errors. Counsel will normally find that negotiation of the escrow agreement is expedited if the escrow agent is invited to supply its own preferred version of the exculpatory provisions to be included in the escrow agreement. The substance of these provisions tends to be fairly consistent, although the style varies widely. It may be easier to use a form provided by the escrow agent or one that counsel has previously negotiated with the escrow agent.

Occasionally, a party may propose that its counsel act as escrow agent. State bar opinions vary on whether such a role is permitted. Many professional liability insurers discourage the practice.

ESCROW AGREEMENT

This Escrow Agreement ("Agreement") is made as of _____, by _____, a _____ corporation ("Buyer"), those individuals who have executed the signature page to this Agreement (collectively "Sellers"), _____ as Sellers' Representative, and _____ a [national banking association] [bank organized under the laws of _____], as escrow agent (together with its successors in such capacity, the "Escrow Agent"). This is the Escrow Agreement referred to in the Stock Purchase Agreement (the "Purchase Agreement"), dated _____, between Buyer and Sellers. Capitalized terms used in this Agreement without definition have the respective meanings given to them in the Purchase Agreement.

The parties, intending to be legally bound, agree as follows:

1. ESTABLISHMENT OF ESCROW

(a) Buyer is depositing with Escrow Agent $_____ by wire transfer (as increased by any income thereon and as reduced by any disbursements, amounts withdrawn under Paragraph 5(j), or losses on investments, the "Escrow Fund"). Escrow Agent acknowledges receipt of the Escrow Fund.

(b) Escrow Agent agrees to act as escrow agent and to hold, safeguard, and disburse the Escrow Fund pursuant to the terms and conditions of this Agreement.

COMMENT

Interest and other earnings on the funds held in escrow are retained by the Escrow Agent and are thus available to satisfy claims. Sellers may seek to provide that these amounts are to be paid to them currently, although they need to understand any tax implications. *See* commentary to Paragraph 7. Buyer may request that it be paid earnings, since it is paying taxes on the earnings. *See* Paragraph 7.

2. INVESTMENT OF ESCROW FUND

Except as Buyer and Sellers' Representative may from time to time jointly instruct Escrow Agent in writing, the Escrow Fund shall be invested from time to time, to the extent possible, in United States Treasury bills having a remaining maturity of 90 days or less and repurchase obligations secured by such United States Treasury bills, with any remainder being deposited and maintained in a money market deposit account with Escrow Agent, until disbursement of the entire Escrow Fund. Escrow Agent is authorized to liquidate, in accordance with its customary procedures, any portion of the Escrow Fund consisting of investments to provide for payments required to be made under this Agreement. Escrow Agent is authorized to execute purchases and sales of any such investments through the facilities of its own trading or capital markets operations or those of any affiliated entity.

Exhibit 2.4(a)(vii) Escrow Agreement

COMMENT

An escrow agreement customarily provides that funds held in escrow will be invested only in highly liquid, high-grade, short-term investments. The nature of those investments often depends upon the size of the fund. If the amount is modest, a deposit account at the Escrow Agent may be appropriate. If the amounts are larger, investment in short-term U.S. Treasury securities may be preferable in order to avoid exposure to the credit risks inherent in uninsured deposits with the Escrow Agent. The parties may also instruct the Escrow Agent to invest the Escrow Fund in other investments, such as certificates of deposit, mutual funds, or publicly traded securities. There is often a default security specified if the Escrow Agent does not receive instructions, often the Escrow Agent's own collective investment fund. The parties will have to strike a balance on the risk they are each willing to bear with respect to the investment of the Escrow Fund, since Buyer will seek to ensure that the Escrow Fund remains available to satisfy any potential claims it may have under the Escrow Agreement, while Sellers may be willing to bear more risk in exchange for a possible greater growth in the Escrow Fund.

3. CLAIMS

(a) **From time to time on or before _____, Buyer may give notice (a "Notice") to Sellers' Representative and Escrow Agent specifying in reasonable detail the nature and dollar amount of any claim (a "Claim") it may have under Article 11 of the Purchase Agreement. Buyer may make more than one Claim with respect to any underlying state of facts. If Sellers' Representative gives notice to Buyer and Escrow Agent disputing any Claim (a "Counter Notice") within 30 days of the effectiveness of the Notice regarding such Claim, such Claim shall be paid as provided in Paragraph 3(b). If no Counter Notice is effective within such 30-day period, the dollar amount of the Claim as set forth in the Notice shall be deemed established for purposes of this Escrow Agreement and the Purchase Agreement, and Escrow Agent shall promptly pay to Buyer the dollar amount claimed in the Notice from (and only to the extent of) the Escrow Fund. Escrow Agent shall not inquire into or consider whether a Claim complies with the requirements of the Purchase Agreement.**

(b) **If a Counter Notice is given disputing any Claim, Escrow Agent shall make payment with respect to such Claim only in accordance with (i) joint written instructions of Buyer and Sellers' Representative, or (ii) a final nonappealable order of a court of competent jurisdiction. Escrow Agent shall act on such written instructions or court order without further question.**

COMMENT

Paragraph 3 provides the procedures for making claims against the Escrow Fund. If a Claim for indemnification is made and not disputed within 30 days, it is treated as admitted and paid by the Escrow Agent. If disputed, the funds are held until ultimate resolution of the Claim by the parties or litigation. If the Model Agreement were to provide for resolution of claims through arbitration or other forms of alternative dispute resolution, the Escrow Agreement should be modified to provide for release of funds on the basis of the arbitral award. Buyer may want the Escrow Agreement to provide an express right to immediately recover the funds pending resolution of any claim, but as noted above, the Escrow Agent will likely freeze disbursement in the event of a dispute anyway.

The Escrow Agreement only covers claims arising under Article 11 of the Model Agreement; it does not pertain to other claims that Buyer might have arising out of the transaction, such as tort-based claims or contract claims that are not brought under Article 11. Buyer may want to broaden the Escrow Agreement.

Paragraph 3(a) provides that if no Counter Notice is received within the applicable period, "the dollar amount of the Claim . . . shall be deemed established for purposes of . . . the Purchase Agreement." This provision does not consider what happens in the unlikely event that the Counter Notice disputes only a portion of the Claim. The procedures of Paragraph 3 are independent of the Model Agreement.

4. TERMINATION OF ESCROW

On _____, and from time to time thereafter, Escrow Agent, in accordance with instructions delivered by Sellers' Representative, shall pay and distribute the Escrow Fund to Sellers' Representative in accordance with (i) joint written instructions of Buyer and Sellers' Representative, or (ii) a final nonappealable order of a court of competent jurisdiction. Escrow Agent shall act on such written instructions or court order without further question.

COMMENT

Escrowed funds are generally released to the seller after a specified period of time, which is often the same as the general time limit provided for the assertion of claims in the acquisition agreement (*see* Section 11.5 of the Model Agreement). However, such release requires the buyer to join in the instructions; if the buyer has a pending claim, it presumably will not so join.

Sellers often negotiate for a scale down, such that a portion of the escrow is paid out after, for example, one year and a portion after two years, with the balance paid out when the escrow terminates at three years. The periods and portions are highly negotiable.

Exhibit 2.4(a)(vii) Escrow Agreement

5. DUTIES OF ESCROW AGENT

COMMENT

While this Paragraph is captioned "Duties of Escrow Agent," it is largely a limitation on those duties. What is specified in this series of disclaimers varies and, as stated in the Preliminary Note to this agreement, many escrow agents have their own preferred versions of these provisions. Examples of additional clauses are:

- The Escrow Agent may do nothing if it senses a dispute between the parties.
- There are no implied duties of the Escrow Agent.
- The Escrow Agent has no responsibility for investment returns.

(a) **Escrow Agent shall not be under any duty to give the Escrow Fund any greater degree of care than it gives its own similar property and shall not be required to invest any funds held under this Agreement except as directed in this Agreement. Uninvested funds held under this Agreement shall not earn or accrue interest.**

(b) **Escrow Agent shall not be liable for actions or omissions under this Agreement, except for its own gross negligence or willful misconduct and, except with respect to claims based upon such gross negligence or willful misconduct that are successfully asserted against Escrow Agent. The other parties shall jointly and severally indemnify and hold harmless Escrow Agent (and any successor Escrow Agent) from and against, and shall pay to Escrow Agent the amount of, and reimburse Escrow Agent for, any and all losses, liabilities, claims, actions, damages, and expenses, including reasonable attorneys' fees and disbursements, arising out of and in connection with this Agreement. Without limiting the foregoing, Escrow Agent shall in no event be liable in connection with its investment or reinvestment of any cash held by it in good faith in accordance with the terms of this Agreement, including, without limitation, any liability for any delays (not resulting from its gross negligence or willful misconduct) in the investment or reinvestment of the Escrow Fund, or any loss of interest incident to any such delays.**

(c) **Escrow Agent shall be entitled to rely upon any order, judgment, certification, demand, notice, instrument, or other writing delivered to it pursuant to this Agreement without being required to determine the authenticity or the correctness of any fact stated therein or the propriety or validity of the service thereof. Escrow Agent may act in reliance upon any instrument or signature believed by it to be genuine and may assume that the person purporting to give the receipt or advice or make any statement or execute any document in connection with the provisions hereof has been duly authorized to do so.**

Escrow Agent may conclusively presume that the representative of any party to this Agreement has full power and authority to instruct Escrow Agent on behalf of that party unless written notice to the contrary is delivered to Escrow Agent.

(d) Escrow Agent may act pursuant to the advice of counsel with respect to any matter relating to this Agreement and shall not be liable for any action taken or omitted by it in good faith in accordance with such advice.

(e) Escrow Agent does not have any interest in the Escrow Fund but is serving as escrow holder only and has only possession thereof. Any payments of income from the Escrow Fund shall be subject to withholding regulations then in force with respect to United States taxes. The parties will provide Escrow Agent with appropriate Internal Revenue Service Forms W-9 for tax identification number certification or nonresident alien certifications.

(f) Escrow Agent makes no representation as to the validity, value, genuineness, or the collectability of any security or other document or instrument held by or delivered to it.

(g) Escrow Agent shall not be called upon to advise any party as to the wisdom in selling or retaining or taking or refraining from any action with respect to any securities or other property deposited under this Agreement.

(h) Escrow Agent may at any time resign as such by delivering the Escrow Fund to any successor Escrow Agent jointly designated by Buyer and the Sellers' Representative in writing, or to any court of competent jurisdiction, whereupon Escrow Agent shall be discharged of and from any and all further obligations arising in connection with this Agreement. The resignation of Escrow Agent will take effect on the earlier of (i) the appointment of a successor (including a court of competent jurisdiction), or (ii) the day which is 30 days after the date of delivery of its written notice of resignation to the other parties. If at that time Escrow Agent has not received a designation of a successor Escrow Agent, Escrow Agent's sole responsibility after that time shall be to retain and safeguard the Escrow Fund until receipt of a designation of successor Escrow Agent or a joint written disposition instruction by the other parties or a final nonappealable order of a court of competent jurisdiction.

COMMENT

The parties may wish to include a provision permitting them to remove and replace the escrow agent.

(i) In the event of any disagreement among the other parties resulting in adverse claims or demands being made in connection with the Escrow Fund or in the

Exhibit 2.4(a)(vii) Escrow Agreement

event that Escrow Agent is in doubt as to what action it should take under this Agreement, Escrow Agent shall be entitled to retain the Escrow Fund until Escrow Agent shall have received (i) joint written instructions of Buyer and Sellers' Representative, or (ii) a final nonappealable order of a court of competent jurisdiction. Escrow Agent shall act on such written instructions or court order without further question.

(j)   Buyer and Sellers shall pay Escrow Agent compensation (as payment in full) for the services to be rendered by Escrow Agent under this Agreement of $_____ at the time of execution of this Agreement and $_____ annually thereafter, and agree to reimburse Escrow Agent for all reasonable expenses, disbursements, and advances incurred or made by Escrow Agent in the performance of its duties (including reasonable fees, expenses, and disbursements of its counsel). Any such compensation and reimbursement to which Escrow Agent is entitled shall be borne 50% by Buyer and 50% by Sellers' Representative in its representative capacity. Any fees or expenses of Escrow Agent or its counsel that are not paid as provided for in this Agreement may be taken from any property held by Escrow Agent under this Agreement.

COMMENT

To avoid any dispute, the Escrow Agent may prefer that joint and several responsibility be placed on Buyer and Sellers and that the 50/50 split be as between the parties. The allocation of responsibility for the Escrow Agent's fees and expenses between Sellers and Buyer is the subject of negotiation. *See* Section 12.1 of the Model Agreement.

(k)   No printed or other matter in any language (including prospectuses, notices, reports, and promotional material) that mentions Escrow Agent's name or the rights, powers, or duties of Escrow Agent shall be issued by the other parties or on such parties' behalf unless Escrow Agent shall first have given its specific written consent thereto.

(l)   The other parties authorize Escrow Agent, for any securities held under this Agreement, to use the services of any United States central securities depository it reasonably deems appropriate, including the Depository Trust Company and the Federal Reserve Book Entry System.

(m)   In the event that (i) any dispute shall arise between the parties with respect to the disposition or disbursement of any of the assets held under this Agreement, or (ii) Escrow Agent shall be uncertain as to how to proceed in a situation not explicitly addressed by the terms of this Agreement, whether because of conflicting demands by the other parties or otherwise, Escrow Agent shall be permitted to interplead all of the assets held under this Agreement into a court of competent jurisdiction and thereafter be fully relieved from any and all liability or obligation with respect to such interpleaded assets. The parties other than Escrow Agent further agree to pursue any redress or recourse in connection with such a dispute without making Escrow Agent a party to same.

(n)   Escrow Agent shall have only those duties as are specifically provided in this Agreement, which shall be deemed purely ministerial in nature, and shall under no circumstance be deemed a fiduciary for any of the other parties. Escrow Agent shall neither be responsible for, nor chargeable with, knowledge of the terms and conditions of any other agreement, instrument, or document between the other parties in connection herewith, including the Purchase Agreement. This Agreement sets forth all matters pertinent to the escrow contemplated by this Agreement, and no additional obligations of Escrow Agent shall be inferred from the terms of this Agreement or any other agreement. IN NO EVENT SHALL THE ESCROW AGENT BE LIABLE, DIRECTLY OR INDIRECTLY, FOR (i) DAMAGES OR EXPENSES ARISING OUT OF THE SERVICES PROVIDED UNDER THIS AGREEMENT, OTHER THAN DAMAGES WHICH RESULT FROM THE ESCROW AGENT'S FAILURE TO ACT IN ACCORDANCE WITH THE STANDARDS SET FORTH IN THIS AGREEMENT, OR (ii) SPECIAL OR CONSEQUENTIAL DAMAGES, EVEN IF THE ESCROW AGENT HAS BEEN ADVISED OF THE POSSIBILITY OF SUCH DAMAGES.

(o)   This Paragraph 5 shall survive notwithstanding any expiration or termination of this Agreement or the resignation of Escrow Agent.

6.   LIMITED RESPONSIBILITY

This Agreement expressly sets forth all the duties of Escrow Agent with respect to any and all matters pertinent to this Agreement. No implied duties or obligations shall be read into this Agreement against Escrow Agent.

7.   OWNERSHIP FOR TAX PURPOSES

For purposes of federal and other taxes based on income, Buyer will be treated as owner of the Escrow Fund and shall report all income, if any, that is earned on, or derived from, the Escrow Fund as its income and in the taxable year or years in which such income is properly includible, and pay any taxes attributable thereto.

COMMENT

Many escrow agreements contain provisions that seek to treat the seller as the owner of the escrowed funds for tax purposes. From a tax standpoint, many sellers

Exhibit 2.4(a)(vii) Escrow Agreement

prefer to treat the contingent payments from escrow on an installment tax basis. In order to qualify for such treatment, though, a seller cannot be deemed the owner of the escrowed funds until the conditions for release to the seller actually occur. In addition, federal income tax regulations proposed in 1999 under Code Section 468B(g) would allocate income tax liability on escrowed funds income to the buyer in all cases anyway (unless such funds come into dispute, in which event they are taxed as a separate entity). *See* Prop. Reg. § 1.468B-8 (Jan. 29, 1999). If the buyer is the deemed owner of the escrowed funds, and some or all of such funds are ultimately released to the seller, for tax purposes such amounts are discounted from the date of the stock sale based on the imputed interest rules of Code Section 483 and 1274 (unless a higher rate is provided in the escrow agreement). The interest portion is taxable to the seller and deductible by the buyer. The remaining principal portion of the payment increases the buyer's basis in the purchased stock. Conversely, if any amounts are paid out of escrow to the buyer, such amounts are merely deemed a nontaxable return of the buyer's capital.

On the other hand, if the seller is considered the owner of the escrowed funds, then the seller must recognize the entire amount at the time of the sale without benefit of the installment method. The buyer should be able to include such escrowed funds in its basis for the purchased stock when the escrow is established. Furthermore, the seller would be taxed on the income earned by the escrowed funds. In such circumstances, if escrowed funds are released to the seller, no tax consequences arise on release, since such amounts were already included in seller's proceeds from the sale. If any portion of the escrowed funds were paid to the buyer, such amounts would be deemed a reduction in the purchase price paid for the stock, thus being available as capital loss to the seller and a reduction in basis to the buyer. If the seller has no offsetting capital gains, its value is diminished. *See* Gerson and Alioto, *The Taxation of Escrow Funds*, 15 M&A Tax Report No. 12 (July 2007), 16 M&A Tax Report No. 1 (August 2007).

The question of who owns the escrowed funds prior to release also has implications in a bankruptcy context. This issue is addressed more fully in commentary to Paragraph 8.

8. No Transfer or Encumbrance; Security Interest

(a) **Neither the Escrow Fund nor any beneficial interest therein may be pledged, encumbered, sold, assigned, or transferred (including any transfer by operation of law) by Sellers, or be taken or reached by any legal or equitable process in satisfaction of any debt or other liability of Sellers, prior to the delivery of such Escrow Fund to Sellers' Representative by the Escrow Agent in accordance with this Agreement. The Escrow Agent shall have no responsibility for determining or enforcing compliance with this Paragraph 8(a), except that the Escrow Agent shall retain possession of the Escrow Funds pursuant to Paragraph 1(b).**

(b)   The parties acknowledge and agree that Sellers' interest in the Escrow Fund is merely a contingent right to payment from the Escrow Fund, and that neither a voluntary or involuntary case under any applicable bankruptcy, insolvency, or similar law nor the appointment of a receiver, trustee, custodian, or similar official in respect of any Seller (any of which, a "Bankruptcy Event") shall increase such Seller's interest in the Escrow Fund or affect, modify, convert, or otherwise change any right such Seller or its estate may have to the Escrow Fund. Accordingly, in order to assure the foregoing result even if it is determined by a court of competent jurisdiction (whether or not in connection with a Bankruptcy Event) that a Seller has an interest in the Escrow Fund that is greater than a contingent right of payment from the Escrow Fund payable only in accordance with the provisions of this Agreement, each Seller hereby grants to Buyer, jointly and severally, effective as of the date of this Agreement, a security interest in, and hereby pledges and assigns to Buyer, all of such Seller's right, title, and interest in the Escrow Fund (except for such Seller's contractual rights thereto under this Agreement) to secure Buyer's rights in such Seller's obligations under this Agreement. Escrow Agent acknowledges that Buyer has a security interest in the Escrow Fund, and all funds and instruments comprising the Escrow Fund from time to time, and Escrow Agent is maintaining the Escrow Fund subject to such security interest. The parties agree that this Paragraph 8(b) shall establish "control," as defined in Sections 9-104 and 8-106 of the Uniform Commercial Code (the "UCC"), as enacted in the State of _____, and as amended from time to time, of the Escrow Fund, which control is effective to perfect Buyer's security interest in the Escrow Fund. For purposes of giving effect to such control, the parties agree that if Escrow Agent shall receive any instruction from Buyer regarding disposition of the Escrow Fund after Buyer has failed to receive any payment required to be made to it pursuant to Paragraph 3, Escrow Agent shall comply with such direction without further consent by Sellers or any other person, provided that this provision shall in no way diminish or affect any rights which Sellers may have or be entitled to pursue against Buyer for taking action in violation of other provisions of this Agreement or the Purchase Agreement. Escrow Agent and each Seller shall take all actions as may be reasonably requested in writing of it by Buyer to perfect or maintain the security interest created by Sellers in the Escrow Fund. Buyer is authorized by the other parties to file UCC financing statements to perfect Buyer's security interest, with or without execution by the other parties, to the extent permitted by applicable law. Such security interest shall automatically be released with respect to any funds properly distributed from the Escrow Fund pursuant to the terms of this Agreement. Buyer agrees to execute such instruments of release and termination of the security interest granted under this Agreement with respect to any funds properly distributed from the Escrow Fund received by Sellers' Representative pursuant to the terms hereof, as may be reasonably requested.

Exhibit 2.4(a)(vii) Escrow Agreement

COMMENT

In the event that Buyer or one of the Sellers should file for bankruptcy after the escrow is established but before the escrowed funds are released, the bankruptcy estate of such persons may attempt to claim the escrowed funds as part of the bankrupt's assets available to creditors. Generally, state law will determine whether a debtor has an equitable or legal interest in property for purposes of including it in the bankruptcy estate. *See, e.g.,* Dickerson v. Central Florida Radiation Oncology Group (In re Central Florida Radiation Oncology Group), 225 B.R. 241 (M.D. Fla. 1998). Under the law of many states, legal title to property placed in escrow remains with the grantor until release conditions occur, and the other party has only a contingent interest until such conditions occur. Apart from the tax considerations discussed in the commentary to Paragraph 7, an escrow agreement could establish either party as the grantor by providing either that the Sellers are deemed to establish the escrow after constructive receipt of the escrowed funds or that the Buyer pays the escrowed funds directly into the escrow account. In such an event, if the deemed legal owner declares bankruptcy prior to the expiration of the escrow period, the other party runs the risk that the bankruptcy estate will try to claim the escrowed funds. On the other hand, a bankruptcy estate of the party that possesses only a contingent interest will not likely be able to pull the funds into the estate absent the satisfaction of the requisite release conditions in its favor. Note that pursuant to the language of Paragraph 1 of the Escrow Agreement, Buyer is establishing the escrow and may be deemed the legal owner of the escrowed funds. Paragraphs 7 and 8 are consistent with that view.

9. MISCELLANEOUS

COMMENT

See the Introduction to this Volume II and commentary to Article 12 of the Model Agreement for further discussion relevant to the miscellaneous provisions of the Escrow Agreement.

(a) **Entire Agreement. This Agreement supersedes all prior agreements, whether written or oral, between the parties with respect to its subject matter and constitutes a complete and exclusive statement of the terms of the agreement between the parties with respect to its subject matter.**

(b) **Modification. This Agreement may only be amended, supplemented, or otherwise modified by a writing executed by the parties.**

(c) **Assignments and Successors. No party may assign any of its rights or delegate any of its obligations under this Agreement without the prior consent of the other parties, except that Buyer may assign any of its rights and delegate any of its obligations under this Agreement to any Subsidiary of Buyer and to the purchaser of all or substantially all [a substantial part of] of the equity** securities or business of the Acquired Companies and may collaterally assign its rights under this Agreement to any financial institution providing financing in connection with the purchase of the Shares. Any purported assignment of rights or delegation of obligations in violation of this Paragraph 9(c) will be void. Subject to the foregoing, this Agreement will apply to, be binding in all respects upon, and inure to the benefit of the heirs, executors, administrators, legal representatives, successors, and permitted assigns of the parties.

(d) **No Third-Party Rights.** No Person other than the parties will have any legal or equitable right, remedy, or claim under or with respect to this Agreement. This Agreement may be amended or terminated, and any provision of this Agreement may be waived, without the consent of any Person who is not a party to this Agreement.

(e) **Governing Law.** All matters relating to or arising out of this Agreement and the rights of the parties (whether sounding in contract, tort, or otherwise) will be governed by and construed and interpreted under the laws of the State of _____, without regard to conflicts of laws principles that would require the application of any other law.

COMMENT

The Escrow Agent will often require that the governing law of the state in which its office is located be chosen and that the forum specified in Paragraph 9(g) be in the same state, even if different from the governing law and forum specified in the Model Agreement.

(f) **Remedies Cumulative.** The rights and remedies of the parties are cumulative and not alternative.

(g) **Jurisdiction; Service of Process.** Except as otherwise provided in this Agreement, any Proceeding arising out of or relating to this Agreement shall be brought in the courts of the State of _____, County of _____, or, if it has or can acquire jurisdiction, in the United States District Court for the _____ District of _____, and each of the parties irrevocably submits to the exclusive jurisdiction of each such court in any such Proceeding, waives any objection it may now or hereafter have to venue or to convenience of forum, agrees that all claims in respect of such Proceeding shall be heard and determined only in any such court, and agrees not to bring any Proceeding arising out of or relating to this Agreement in any other court. Each party acknowledges and agrees that this Paragraph 9(g) constitutes a voluntary and bargained-for agreement between the parties. Process in any Proceeding referred to in the first sentence of this Paragraph 9(g) may be served on any party anywhere in the world. Any party may make service on any other party by sending or delivering a copy of the process to the party to be

Exhibit 2.4(a)(vii) Escrow Agreement

served at the address and in the manner provided for the giving of notices in Paragraph 9(k). Nothing in this Paragraph 9(g) will affect the right of any party to serve legal process in any other manner permitted by law or at equity.

COMMENT

The Escrow Agent will often require that the forum for any litigation be where it is located (and the governing law specified in Paragraph 9(e) be the location of its primary business).

(h) **Waiver of Jury Trial. EACH PARTY, KNOWINGLY, VOLUNTARILY, AND INTENTIONALLY, WAIVES ITS RIGHT TO TRIAL BY JURY IN ANY PROCEEDING ARISING OUT OF OR RELATING TO THIS AGREEMENT, WHETHER SOUNDING IN CONTRACT, TORT, OR OTHERWISE.**

(i) **Attorneys' Fees.** In the event any Proceeding is brought in respect of this Agreement, the prevailing party will be entitled to recover reasonable attorneys' fees and other costs incurred in such Proceeding, in addition to any relief to which such party may be entitled.

(j) **No Waiver.** Neither any failure nor any delay by any party in exercising any right, power, or privilege under this Agreement or any of the documents referred to in this Agreement will operate as a waiver of such right, power, or privilege, and no single or partial exercise of any such right, power, or privilege will preclude any other or further exercise of such right, power, or privilege or the exercise of any other right, power, or privilege. To the maximum extent permitted by applicable Legal Requirements, (i) no claim or right arising out of this Agreement or any of the documents referred to in this Agreement can be waived by a party, in whole or in part, unless made in a writing signed by such party, (ii) a waiver given by a party will only be applicable to the specific instance for which it is given, and (iii) no notice to or demand on a party will (A) waive or otherwise affect any obligation of that party, or (B) affect the right of the party giving such notice or demand to take further action without notice or demand as provided in this Agreement or the documents referred to in this Agreement.

(k) **Notices.** All notices and other communications required or permitted by this Agreement will be in writing and will be effective, and any applicable time period shall commence when (i) delivered to the following address by hand or by a nationally recognized overnight courier service (costs prepaid), addressed to the following address, or (ii) transmitted electronically to the following facsimile numbers or e-mail addresses, in each case marked to the attention of the Person (by name or title) designated below (or to such other address, facsimile number, e-mail address, or Person as a party may designate by notice to the other parties):

Sellers:

[Name of Sellers' Representative]
Attention:
[Street]
[City, state, and zip code]
Fax no.:
E-mail address:

with a copy to:

_____

Attention:
[Street]
[City, state, and zip code]
Fax no.:
E-mail address:

Buyer:

_____

Attention:
[Street]
[City, state, and zip code]
Fax no.:
E-mail address:

with a copy to:

_____

Attention:
[Street]
[City, state, and zip code]
Fax no.:
E-mail address:

Escrow Agent:

_____

Attention:
[Street]
[City, state, and zip code]
Fax no.:
E-mail address:

with a copy to:

_____

Exhibit 2.4(a)(vii) Escrow Agreement

Attention:
[Street]
[City, state, and zip code]
Fax no.:
E-mail address:

(l)   Severability. If any provision of this Agreement is held invalid or unenforceable by any court of competent jurisdiction, the other provisions of this Agreement will remain in full force and effect. Any provision of this Agreement held invalid or unenforceable only in part or degree will remain in full force and effect to the extent not held invalid or unenforceable.

(m)   Time of Essence. With regard to all dates and time periods set forth or referred to in this Agreement, time is of the essence.

(n)   Counterparts/Electronic Signatures. This Agreement and other documents to be delivered pursuant to this Agreement may be executed in one or more counterparts, each of which will be deemed to be an original copy and all of which, when taken together, will be deemed to constitute one and the same agreement or document, and will be effective when counterparts have been signed by each of the parties and delivered to the other parties. A manual signature on this Agreement or other document to be delivered pursuant to this Agreement whose image is transmitted electronically will constitute an original signature for all purposes. The delivery of copies of this Agreement or other document to be delivered pursuant to this Agreement, including executed signature pages where required, by electronic transmission will constitute effective delivery of this Agreement or such other document for all purposes.

IN WITNESS WHEREOF, the parties have executed and delivered this Agreement as of the date first written above.

BUYER: SELLERS:

_____   _____

By: _____   [1]

Name: _____   _____

Title: _____   [2]

31

ESCROW AGENT:

_____   . . .

By: _____

Name: _____   _____

Title: _____   [8]

SELLERS' REPRESENTATIVE:

_____

Schedule A
Pro Rata Shares

Seller 1

Seller 2

. . .

Seller 8

ALTERNATIVE PROVISIONS—ESCROW FUND THAT INCLUDES SECURITIES

In some circumstances, the escrowed funds may consist of property other than just cash. The following provisions may be used as a base for drafting modifications to the sample Escrow Agreement to provide for a situation where the Escrow Fund includes securities issued by Buyer.

Those provisions are conceptually at odds with Paragraphs 7 and 8, which postulate that Sellers' interest in the Escrow Fund is merely an expectancy. Therefore, the tax and bankruptcy issues raised by those paragraphs will need to be addressed if these alternative provisions are used.

Exhibit 2.4(a)(vii) Escrow Agreement

1. ESTABLISHMENT OF ESCROW

(a) **Deposit. Buyer is depositing with Escrow Agent: (i) $_____ by wire transfer (the "Escrow Cash"); and (ii) _____ shares of _____ stock of Buyer (the "Escrow Securities," and together with the Escrow Cash, as increased by any earnings, dividends, interest, or distributions thereon and as reduced by any disbursements, or losses on investments, the "Escrow Fund"). Escrow Agent acknowledges receipt thereof. The Escrow Securities are represented by a certificate or certificates representing the total number of Escrow Securities, together with a stock power executed in blank, and Escrow Agent may elect to retain such certificates and stock power in blank or may transfer the Escrow Securities into its name or the name of its nominee, noting on the applicable transfer instruments that, subject to this Agreement, Sellers are the owners of such Escrow Securities proportionate to their pro-rata share as set forth on Schedule A.**

(b) **Escrow Securities. All cash dividends, stock dividends, and other dividends paid upon any of the Escrow Securities and all other securities received as additions to or in exchange, substitution, or replacement for any of the Escrow Securities, including through any conversion into a different number of shares or a different class of shares by reason of any reclassification, recapitalization, split-up, combination, exchange of shares, or readjustment of the Escrow Securities, shall be the property of Sellers but shall become part of the Escrow Fund and shall be deposited with Escrow Agent. Prior to deposit with Escrow Agent, the Escrow Securities shall be issued by Buyer in the name of Sellers, and the Escrow Securities shall be accordingly reflected as issued and outstanding on the books and records of Buyer, subject to the terms and conditions of this Agreement. During such time as Escrow Agent may hold the Escrow Securities pursuant to this Agreement, Sellers shall have all rights, powers, privileges, and preferences pertaining to the Escrow Securities, including, without limitation, all voting and dividend rights with respect to the Escrow Securities, subject to the terms of this Agreement.**

COMMENT

In this example, the securities are issued to Sellers at the closing rather than at the time of release from escrow in order to start the applicable holding period for tax and securities laws purposes. However, as discussed above in the commentary to Paragraphs 7 and 8, deemed ownership has important tax and bankruptcy ramifications. On the other hand, a transaction structured as a tax-free reorganization will have consequences not described in Paragraph 7.

(c)   **Power to Transfer Escrow Fund. Subject to the terms and conditions of this Agreement, Escrow Agent is hereby granted the power to effect any transfer of the Escrow Fund contemplated by this Agreement. Each Seller hereby irrevocably appoints and constitutes Escrow Agent as its true and lawful attorney with full power of substitution to complete and fill in any blank endorsements and resignations, to file the same and to take such further action as Escrow Agent may deem necessary to carry out and perform its obligations and rights under this Agreement, whether or not such resignation or transfer is effected. The power-of-attorney appointment made in this Paragraph 1(c), being coupled with an interest, shall be deemed irrevocable until the release of the Escrow Fund pursuant to the terms and conditions of this Agreement.**

To be Added to Paragraph 3:

(c)   **Subject to the last two sentences of this Paragraph 3(c), any release of Escrow Funds pursuant to Paragraph 3 shall be effected from either the Escrow Cash or the Escrow Securities (at a value of \$_____ per share), at the discretion of Buyer, provided that if Buyer has not delivered instructions to Escrow Agent for the payment out of the Escrow Funds at least two Business Days prior to the Claim payment date, any release pursuant to Paragraph 3 shall be accomplished as follows: (i) _____ % of the amount of any release of the Escrow Fund shall be by delivery from Escrow Agent to Buyer of certificates, together with executed stock powers in blank, representing an amount of Escrow Securities equivalent to the released amount based on a per share value of \$_____ for each Escrow Security, adjusted as applicable to reflect any conversion into a different number of shares or a different class of shares by reason of any reclassification, recapitalization, split-up, combination, exchange of shares or readjustment of the Escrow Securities, and (ii) _____ % of the amount of any release of the Escrow Fund shall be by delivery from Escrow Agent to Buyer of Escrow Cash in accordance with wire transfer instructions delivered by Buyer. Promptly upon receipt of the certificates and stock powers representing the applicable released Escrow Securities, Buyer shall deliver to the Escrow Agent or its designee a replacement certificate or certificates representing the amount of Escrow Securities that have not been released to Buyer.**

COMMENT

In the event a claim is paid out of the escrowed funds, the mix of cash and securities released may become an issue, depending on the value and liquidity of the escrowed securities. The parties may negotiate the issue as to which of them chooses the mix of released escrow funds, or they may decide to avoid the issue by providing that the mix is a predetermined percentage. Note that the release of the escrowed funds could have tax consequences to either party. The sample language

Exhibit 2.4(a)(vii) Escrow Agreement

keeps things simple by ascribing a dollar value to each escrowed share, although the value of the escrowed securities could be a significant factor to the parties. Alternative valuation mechanisms could include using current market prices if the security is publicly traded, and the agreement could specify whether to apply the last sales, "bid" or "asked" price on the day before release, or the average of such prices over a short range prior to such release if trading in such securities is volatile. If circumstances warrant, the parties may also agree upon a third-party appraisal.

A dispute mechanism for disagreements in valuation may be provided, such as the following:

> If the parties do not agree with the values established for the Escrow Securities pursuant to Paragraph 3(c), such value shall be determined by appraisal by an independent investment banking firm or other suitable independent appraiser with expertise in the type of property being valued ("Appraiser") selected by Buyer and reasonably acceptable to Sellers' Representative; provided, however, if the parties cannot agree on an Appraiser, such appraised value shall be determined by averaging the appraised values calculated by (a) an Appraiser selected by Buyer, (b) an Appraiser selected by Sellers' Representative, and (c) an Appraiser selected by the Appraisers selected by Buyer and Sellers' Representative. Each party shall bear the expense of any appraisal by the party it selects and the parties shall share the expense of any appraisal performed in accordance with clause (c) of the immediately preceding sentence.

EXHIBITS 8.6(a) and 9.5(a)

Legal Opinions

PRELIMINARY NOTE

Stock purchase agreements sometimes (but far less frequently than in the past) provide as a condition to closing that each party deliver to the other party an opinion letter prepared by the delivering party's lawyer. Delivery of opinion letters is rare when the target is a public company.

Opinion letters delivered in an acquisition by counsel for the sellers and the target (which sometimes are different counsel) generally cover the following:

- valid existence of the target and its corporate power to enter into the transaction;
- authorization, execution, and delivery of the transaction documents by the opinion giver's client;
- the transaction does not violate the target's organizational documents (i.e., corporate charters and bylaws) or breach or result in a default under specific agreements to which the target is a party;
- no governmental consents or filings are required in connection with the transaction;
- the transaction documents are valid, binding, and enforceable obligations of the opinion giver's client;
- the capitalization of the target and certain characteristics of its issued and outstanding stock; and
- less frequently, the effect of the receipt of the target stock by the buyer (but not as to title to that stock).

Counsel for buyers in acquisitions deliver opinion letters even less frequently than counsel for sellers and targets, and rarely when the buyer is paying all cash at the closing. When counsel for a buyer does deliver an opinion letter, the opinions it gives usually do not address all of the subjects described above. *See* preliminary note to Exhibit 9.5(a). There is a trend away from "no litigation confirmations" in opinion letters, even when they are limited to the opinion giver's knowledge, and certainly away from those addressing litigation generally affecting the client.

The illustrative opinion letters and commentary set forth below are intended to provide a guide for M&A lawyers to basic considerations in giving opinions in the context of acquisitions. A much more thorough discussion of opinion practice is contained in reports of the ABA and other bar associations and treatises referenced in the commentary below.

At times, this commentary uses nomenclature from ABA and other opinion literature to describe lawyers in the opinion process. The term "opinion giver" refers to the lawyer or law firm in whose name the opinion letter is signed. The term "opinion recipient" refers to the addressee of the opinion letter and others, if any, granted permission by the opinion giver to rely on the opinion letter. The term "opinion preparers" refers to the lawyers in a law firm who prepare the opinion letter.

Whether to Request—Applying a Cost-Benefit Analysis. Rather than automatically requiring opinion letters as a closing condition, the parties should consider at the outset whether the opinions being requested provide sufficient value to the recipient to justify the time and expense of preparing and negotiating them. This cost-benefit analysis is treated as a fundamental consideration in legal opinion reports, including Section 1.2 of the ABA Business Law Section's Legal Opinions Committee's *Guidelines for the Preparation of Closing Opinions* found in 57 Bus. Law. 875 (Feb. 2002) (the "ABA Legal Opinion Guidelines") and Section 1.3 of the TriBar Opinion Committee's *Third Party "Closing" Opinions: A Report of the TriBar Opinion Committee,* 53 Bus. Law. 592 (Feb. 1998) ("TriBar '98"). *See also* Lipson, *Cost-Benefit Analysis and Third-Party Opinion Practice,* 63 Bus. Law. 1187 (Aug. 2008), and Opinions Committee of the California State Bar Business Law Section, *Toward a National Opinion Practice*: *The California Remedies Opinion Report,* Part II.B., 60 Bus. Law 907 (May 2005).

In an increasing number of acquisitions, parties are willing to dispense with the condition that the other party's lawyer deliver a closing opinion, and rely instead upon their own diligence, the representations of the other party, and the remedies in the acquisition agreement. Nontax legal opinions are rarely given in public company acquisitions, and even in private company acquisitions, the percentage is declining. The Deal Points Studies in 2004, 2006, and 2009 showed a continuing decline in the number of deals requiring closing opinions from 73% to 70% to 58%.

Notwithstanding the decline in closing opinions in private target acquisitions, many buyers still *see* value in obtaining an opinion regarding the sellers and the target and may view the following as benefits:

- Opinions on subjects such as legal status of an entity, corporate power, due authorization, and governmental consents are all within the special competence of the sellers' or target's lawyer, and, although representations from the sellers or target provide comfort and protection on these topics, the legal opinion provides additional comfort.

- In some transactions, the buyer may have more confidence in the thoroughness, sophistication, and integrity of the lawyer or firm delivering the legal opinion than in the individual officers of the party providing the representations and warranties; that is, the buyer may fear that the other party is making representations without the requisite care or based on a business risk analysis and that its lawyers will likely be more focused and careful.

- When target's counsel has a long-standing relationship with the target and, as is often the case, also serves as sellers' counsel, the opinion provides a buyer with additional assurance that representations on some topics that the target or sellers may not be capable of making without legal advice have, in fact, been carefully considered.

- A buyer may anticipate the need for an opinion regarding the target for the benefit of a lender that is providing acquisition financing.

- Tradition and habit – "we always get an opinion."

Some buyers take the position that at the very least the remedies (enforceability) opinion is appropriate when the sellers insist that the transaction documents be governed by the law of the target's jurisdiction and that is not a jurisdiction in which the buyer's lawyer practices. Even in those instances, however, the advice of buyer's local lawyer may be more valuable to buyer than a legal opinion of sellers' counsel.

"Customary Practice" Governs Opinion Letters. The scope and meaning of, and diligence required to support, third-party opinion letters are governed by "customary practice." Customary practice is addressed in many sources, including (1) the ABA Business Law Section's Legal Opinions Committee's *Legal Opinion Principles,* 57 Bus. Law. 882 (Feb. 2002) (the "ABA Legal Opinion Principles"), specifically its introductory paragraphs, (2) TriBar '98 §§ 1.1 and 1.14, and (3) more recently, *Statement of the Role of Customary Practice in the Preparation and Understanding of Third-Party Legal Opinions,* 63 Bus. Law. 1277 (Aug. 2008) (a brief statement approved by the ABA Business Law Section's Legal Opinions Committee, the TriBar Opinion Committee, and numerous other bar and legal groups listed in the statement). All these cite Restatement (Third) of the Law Governing Lawyers § 52 as confirming the role of customary practice.

Opinion Resources. What constitutes customary practice has become increasingly clear in recent years. Third-party closing opinions are the subject of relatively few court decisions. (For a list of court decisions, *see* ABA Business Law Section's Legal Opinions Committee's *Annual Review of the Law on Legal Opinions,* 60 Bus. Law. 1057 (May 2005)). The principal sources of guidance are the ABA, TriBar, and state bar association reports, most of which are reproduced in Glazer, FitzGibbon & Weise, Glazer & FitzGibbon on Legal Opinions: Drafting, Interpreting and Supporting Closing Opinions in Business Transactions (3d ed. 2008) ("Glazer & FitzGibbon"). *See also* Field and Smith, Legal Opinions In Business Transactions (2d ed. 2009).

The bar association reports with the broadest following, particularly among firms with a multi-jurisdictional practice, are those issued by the ABA Business Law Section's Legal Opinions Committee and by the TriBar Opinion Committee. In addition, opinion preparers should be aware of any opinion committee or similar reports of the state bar association of the opinion giver's jurisdiction.

<u>ABA Business Law Section's Committee on Legal Opinions Reports</u>. The ABA LEGAL OPINION GUIDELINES and ABA LEGAL OPINION PRINCIPLES are together a concise statement of the basic approach to customary practice to be followed in preparing and interpreting third-party closing opinions. The ABA LEGAL OPINION PRINCIPLES apply to closing opinions, whether or not they are expressly incorporated. Nevertheless, some firms expressly incorporate them by reference.

<u>TriBar Opinion Committee Reports</u>. The TriBar Opinion Committee (consisting of representatives of the New York County Lawyers' Association, the Association of the Bar of the City of New York, the New York State Bar Association, and many other bar associations, including Atlanta, Boston, California, Chicago, Delaware, Washington, D.C., Georgia, North Carolina, Pennsylvania, Texas, and Ontario) has published a series of very well regarded reports, including (1) the TRIBAR '98 report and (2) a report titled *Special Report of The TriBar Opinion Committee: The Remedies Opinion – Deciding When to Include Exceptions and Assumptions,* 59 BUS. LAW. 1483 (Aug. 2004) ("TRIBAR '04 (Remedies Supp.)").

<u>Supplemented by State Bar Association Reports</u>. As to specific issues under applicable state law, the bar association reports of the opinion giver's jurisdiction are important tools, particularly with regard to corporate status, authorization, and valid issuance of stock and legal issues that may require a qualification to the remedies/enforceability opinion.

<u>Access to the ABA, TriBar, and Certain Other Reports</u>. The various ABA and TriBar reports are collected in an ABA Business Law Section publication titled *The Collected ABA and TriBar Legal Opinion Reports 2009,* and can also be accessed at the Joint ABA/TriBar Legal Opinion Resource Center website www.abanet.org/buslaw/tribar. That website also provides access to other opinion letter-related articles and publications, including selected reports of state bar associations.

The Illustrative Opinion Letters are Intended to be Reasonable First Drafts— Reflecting the "Golden Rule." Unlike the Model Agreement (which is drafted from the perspective of a buyer's first draft), the illustrative opinion letters set forth below are designed to serve as opinion letters that both a reasonable recipient is willing to accept and a reasonable opinion giver is willing to deliver, subject to qualifications appropriate to the particular jurisdiction, target and transaction. This approach reflects the "golden rule" admonition of ABA LEGAL OPINION GUIDELINES § 3.1 and TRIBAR '98 § 1.3. The illustrative opinion letters follow the format and language of the "Illustrative Legal Opinion" attached to TRIBAR '98 as Appendix B-1 (Outside Counsel—Stock Purchase Agreement).

Requested Opinions Should be Limited to Opinion Giver's Professional Judgment as to Legal Matters and Not Overly Broad. Legal opinions reflect the opinion giver's professional judgment as to legal matters based on facts that are represented by the client or certified by an appropriate officer of the client or that are confirmed by the opinion giver's customary diligence. This concept—that an opinion is limited to the lawyer's professional judgment on legal matters—is supported by all the recognized authorities. *See* ABA Legal Opinion Guidelines § 1.2; ABA Legal Opinion Principles § I.D.; and TriBar '98 § 1.2(a). In other words, *"an opinion is not a guaranty."*

Opinion givers should not be asked for opinions on broad-ranging topics regarding the client's general business. ABA Legal Opinion Guidelines § 4.3 (titled "Comprehensive Legal or Contractual Compliance") states that an opining lawyer should not give *"an opinion that its client is not in violation of any applicable laws. . . ."* TriBar '98 § 6.6, n.162 states: *"In addition, opinion givers should not be asked to render an opinion that covers compliance by the Company with laws generally. . . . Such an opinion would require a detailed understanding of a Company's business activities and could almost never be rendered (assuming it could be rendered at all) without great expense."* ABA Legal Opinion Guidelines § 4.4 (titled *"Lack of Knowledge of Particular Factual Matters"*) states as follows: *"An opinion giver normally should not be asked to state that it lacks knowledge of particular factual matters. Matters such as the absence of prior security interests or the accuracy of the representations and warranties in an agreement or the information in a disclosure document (subject to section 4.5 below [discussing 'Negative Assurance']) do not require the exercise of professional judgment and are inappropriate subjects for a legal opinion even when the opinion is limited by a broadly worded disclaimer."* [Emphasis added.] Finally, TriBar '98 § 1.3 states: *"No opinion letter should be sought that is so broad that it seeks to make the opinion giver responsible for its client's factual representations or the legal or business risks inherent in the transaction."*

Legal Opinions as a Closing Condition. Receipt of the opinions specified in an acquisition agreement is often a condition to a party's obligation to close the acquisition, as provided in §§ 8.6(a) and 9.5(a) of the Model Agreement. This may have the effect of making matters covered by those opinions a closing condition, typically without the materiality standard that would apply to the same matter if cast solely as a representation required to be affirmed at closing. Lawyers should be sensitive to the interplay between the opinions that are to be given and the representations. Parties are cautioned against making receipt of opinions a contractual requirement rather than just a closing condition because, if the opinion giver is unable to deliver the specified opinions, even for valid reasons, the opinion giver's client may be found to have breached the agreement.

Matters Covered by Other Lawyer's Opinions. Sometimes, opinions are obtained from local or specialist lawyers (such as opinions on tax treatment or regulatory issues) in addition to the basic transaction opinion. The illustrative opinion letters neither state that counsel is relying on nor otherwise comment in any way on a separate local counsel opinion (that is, neither that it is reasonable for the recipient to rely on it or that it is in form and scope satisfactory). This approach of "unbundling" opinions is supported by ABA Legal Opinion Guidelines § 2.2 and TriBar '98 §§ 5.2 and 5.5. In addition, if another lawyer is giving an opinion on existence, power, and authorization and/or other matters that are necessary for the opinions covered by the opinion giver's opinion letter, the opinion letter should expressly assume the legal conclusions in that other lawyer's opinion letter and not comment on them.

Limited Liability Companies. Special issues are raised by legal opinions involving target LLCs because they are governed in many, and frequently most, respects by a contract (often referred to as an operating agreement) that overrides the default provisions of the applicable LLC statute. An excellent discussion of legal opinion issues involving LLCs is contained in the TriBar Opinion Committee's "Third Party Closing Opinions: Limited Liability Companies," 61 Bus. Law. 679 (Feb. 2006).

Preferred Stock. Issues relating to preferred stock are not specifically addressed in the illustrative opinion letters, but if a target has preferred stock or the buyer is issuing its preferred stock, the opinion preparers should consider the special issues involved. *See*, TriBar Opinion Committee, *Special Report of the TriBar Opinion Committee: Duly Authorized Opinions on Preferred Stock,* 63 Bus. Law. 921 (May 2008). *See also* Glazer & FitzGibbon §§ 10.4.2, 10.4.5, 10.6.4.2 (2009 Supplement).

Caveat Regarding Not Misleading Opinion Recipients. Above and beyond the specific language of the opinions and qualifiers, an opinion giver should not give an opinion that the opinion giver knows will mislead the recipient with regard to the matters addressed. This overriding concept is covered in the ABA and TriBar reports (*see* ABA Legal Opinion Guidelines § 1.5 and TriBar '98 § 1.4(d)). Examples of matters that may mislead an opinion recipient are: (1) a "no litigation" confirmation that is limited to claims asserted in writing, but does not point out that the opinion giver (and not the recipient) knows of a substantial and serious claim made orally with sufficient formality, and (2) an opinion ignoring adopted legislation that is not yet effective. TriBar '98 §§ 1.4(d) and 1.2(a), n.11.

The Illustrative Opinion Letters Are Not "Accord" Opinions. In 1991, the Section of Business Law of the American Bar Association published the *Third-Party Legal Opinion Report*, which includes the *Legal Opinion Accord* (the "Accord") (47 Bus. Law. 167 (Nov. 1991)). The Accord proposed a different approach to establishing the meaning of legal opinion letters. Instead of attempting to describe customary practice, the Accord was designed to be adopted by the opinion giver and agreed to by the opinion recipient by incorporating the Accord by reference. The Accord, however, has not been generally accepted, and it is not commonly used in current opinion practice. The Model Agreement provides only non-Accord illustrative opinion letters.

EXHIBIT 8.6(a)

Opinion Letter—
Counsel to Sellers

[Opinion Giver's Letterhead]

[Date]

[Name and Address of Buyer]

Re: Acquisition of _____ (the "Company") by
_____ (the "Buyer") pursuant to the Stock Purchase
Agreement dated _____ __, ____ (the "Stock Purchase
Agreement")

Ladies and Gentlemen:

We have acted as counsel for Sellers (as identified and defined in the Stock Purchase Agreement) in connection with their execution and delivery of the Stock Purchase Agreement.

COMMENT

The reference line and this introductory paragraph are stated in a manner to avoid an argument or claim, no matter how implausible, that counsel is giving an implicit opinion either that "the Company" is a corporation or Sellers have title to the shares being sold—that is, the Company is not identified in the reference line as an XXXX corporation and Sellers are not referred to in the reference line as shareholders. More properly, the opinion as to the Company's status is addressed in opinion number 1 and, as discussed in the commentary to opinion numbers 6 and 7, an opinion should not be given as to Sellers' stock ownership. Even if the reference

43

line and this paragraph did identify the Company as a corporation and identify Sellers as shareholders, an opinion should not be inferred on either the Company's status as a corporation or Sellers' title to the shares being sold.

Some opinion givers add "special" before counsel in the introductory sentence, particularly when the opinion giver does not regularly represent that client. Adding that qualification is less common than in the past, and merely using the term "special counsel" without describing how the opinion giver has limited the investigation required by customary practice does not change the standard of care to which the opinion giver is subject. GLAZER & FITZGIBBON § 2.5.2.

This opinion letter is delivered to you pursuant to Stock Purchase Agreement § 8.6(a).

COMMENT

The fact that the Model Agreement contemplates the delivery of a legal opinion letter to the other party as a condition to closing constitutes the client's consent to the delivery of the opinion letter. *See* ABA LEGAL OPINION GUIDELINES § 2.4 and TRIBAR '98 § 1.7.

Although the second sentence states that the opinion letter is delivered "pursuant to Stock Purchase Agreement § 8.6(a)," the opinion letter only says what it says. Thus, if the opinions given at the closing differ from the opinions required as a condition to closing in the stock purchase agreement, the opinions given (and not the opinions required by the stock purchase agreement) establish the matters covered. *See* TRIBAR '98 § 1.6. The penultimate paragraph of this opinion letter is included to eliminate any doubt as to that conclusion.

Each capitalized term in this opinion letter that is not defined in this opinion letter but is defined in the Stock Purchase Agreement is used herein as defined in the Stock Purchase Agreement.

COMMENT

This is a common provision of an opinion letter, but, as discussed in the context of the "no breach or default" opinion (opinion number 3), the opinion giver may want to avoid using defined terms in some opinions. Accordingly, some opinion givers do not include this sentence but rather define terms in the opinion letter to avoid an inadvertent use of a term that is intended to have a different meaning in the opinion letter than in the Model Agreement.

Exhibit 8.6(a) Opinion Letter—Counsel to Sellers

In acting as counsel to Sellers, we have examined [copies of] the following documents and instruments (collectively, the "Transaction Documents"):

1. The Stock Purchase Agreement;

2. The Escrow Agreement; and

3. The Releases.

In addition to the Transaction Documents, we have examined:

4. The Articles [Certificate] of Incorporation of each Acquired Company, as in effect on the date hereof, certified by the Secretary of State of its jurisdiction of incorporation;

5. The other Organizational Documents of each Acquired Company, certified to be true and correct by the Secretary of the Company;

6. Certificates from the Secretary of State of the state of incorporation of each Acquired Company with regard to each Acquired Company's existence and good standing;

7. Copies of resolutions adopted by the board of directors of the Company with respect to the authorization of the execution, delivery, and performance of those Transaction Documents to which the Company is a party and certified to be true and correct by its secretary;

8. Certificate of [title of officer] of the Company, dated the date hereof, certifying as to certain factual matters (the "Company Certificate");

9. Documents listed in the Company Certificate; and

10. Such other documents as we have deemed appropriate in order to give the opinions expressed below.

COMMENT

The definition of Items (1) through (3) as "Transaction Documents" is intended to limit the documents covered by some opinions (for example, due authorization, execution and delivery, and enforceability) to the specified documents. Many lawyers eliminate Items (4) through (9) on the basis that review of those documents (as well as others) is covered by Item (10). Some lawyers eliminate Item (10) in the belief that doing so narrows the opinion letter's scope. That belief, however, is mistaken because, even without Item (10), a recitation of documents reviewed for purposes of giving the opinion is understood as a matter of customary practice not to excuse the opinion preparers from reviewing all documents customarily required to be reviewed. Unless expressly stated otherwise in the opinion letter, the opinion preparers are expected to have conducted customary diligence whether or not stated in the opinion letter. See TriBar '98 §§ 1.4 and 2.6.1.

As to certain matters of fact relevant to the opinions in this opinion letter, we have relied on certificates of officers of the Company and on factual representations made by the Sellers in the Stock Purchase Agreement. We also have relied on certificates of public officials. We have not independently established the facts or, in the case of certificates of public officials, the other statements so relied upon.

COMMENT

An opinion letter typically states the source of the facts relied upon in giving the stated opinions. Many opinions are an interplay between facts and law. For example, an opinion that a corporation "duly authorized" an agreement relies on the shareholder and/or board resolutions certified to in an officer's certificate, with the opinion preparers determining whether those resolutions comply with the corporation's articles and bylaws and with applicable law. Although implicit even if not included, language along the lines of the last sentence of the above boldface paragraph is frequently included in opinion letters.

Limits on Permitted Reliance. An opinion giver cannot rely on factual certificates or representations if either (1) *"reliance is unreasonable under the circumstances in which the opinion is rendered or the information is known to the opinion givers to be false"* (TRIBAR '98 § 2.1.4; *see* also § 2.2.1(c)) or (2) *"the factual information on which the lawyers preparing the opinion letter are relying appears irregular on its face or has been provided by an inappropriate source"* (ABA LEGAL OPINION PRINCIPLES § III.A). In addition, the opinion giver cannot rely on certificates that make statements or certifications that are tantamount to the legal conclusion in an opinion (other than in limited respects on a certificate of a governmental official). ABA LEGAL OPINION PRINCIPLES § III.C; TRIBAR '98 § 2.2.1(b). For example, an opinion that the entering into and the consummation (or performance) of the Transaction Documents does not breach or result in a default under specified agreements cannot be made solely on the basis of an officer's certificate to that effect, but rather must be made on the basis of the opinion preparers' review of the specified agreements.

No Knowledge Definition in These Illustrative Opinion Letters. Because (1) the illustrative opinion states that the no breach or default opinion should be given with respect to listed agreements and not those "known to us" and (2) the recommended approach for a "no litigation confirmation" does not require a knowledge definition, the illustrative opinion letters do not contain a general "knowledge" definition. This approach reflects in part concern over a court decision that interpreted knowledge qualifiers (that the opinion giver thought were knowledge limitations) as assertions of superior knowledge. *See* the ABA Business Law Section Legal Opinion Committee's *Annual Review of the Law on Legal Opinions*, 63 BUS. LAW. 1057 (May 2005). However, if a knowledge limitation is included, then opinion givers should consider one of the following or a similar approach:

Exhibit 8.6(a) Opinion Letter—Counsel to Sellers

Alternative 1:   The words "to our knowledge" or "known to us" in this opinion letter limit the statements to which they apply to the actual knowledge, without any investigation except as set forth herein, of the lawyers in this firm involved in representation of Sellers in connection with their execution and delivery of the Stock Purchase Agreement.

Alternative 2:   When used in this opinion letter, the phrase "to our knowledge" or an equivalent phrase limits the statements it qualifies to the actual knowledge of the lawyers in this firm responsible for preparing this opinion letter after such inquiry as they deemed appropriate. Boston Bar Association, *Streamlined Form of Closing Opinion*, 61 Bus. Law. 389, at 397 n.21 (Nov. 2005).

Under either formulation, the opinion recipient might request that the opinion giver include within the definition of the opinion giver's "knowledge" the knowledge of the lawyer or lawyers in the firm having principal responsibility for representation of the target or sellers.

No Statement of Scope of Investigation. These illustrative opinion letters do not state that "For purposes of this opinion letter, we have made such investigation as we have deemed appropriate" (although the optional and expanded listing of documents examined by the opinion givers states that they have examined "Such other documents as we have deemed appropriate in order to give the opinions expressed below.") No statement of "such investigation" is included because the opinion giver has this obligation, even if not stated, and thus not only is no advantage gained by stating it, but a court could construe that statement as imposing some unintended obligation to investigate. *See* footnote 10 of Dean Foods Co. v. Pappathanasi, 2004 WL 3019442 (Mass. Super. Ct. Dec. 3, 2004). The second paragraph of TriBar '98's Illustrative Opinion B-1 does include such a statement, but TriBar '98 § 1.4(c) states that it "merely emphasizes that the opinion letter is given in accordance with customary practice and its omission is not sufficient, by itself, to indicate that customary practice is not being followed."

Based upon and subject to the foregoing and the other qualifications and limitations stated in this opinion letter, our opinions are as follows:

1.   **Each of the Company and its Subsidiaries is validly existing as a corporation [and in good standing] under the law of the State of _____.**

COMMENT

Validly Existing. This "validly existing" opinion reflects the view expressed in TriBar '98 § 6.1.3(b) that the "validly existing" opinion is increasingly accepted in lieu of a "duly incorporated" opinion. *See* also the related Illustrative Opinion Letter (TriBar '98 Appendix B-1). TriBar '98 § 6.1.3(b) states that the "validly existing" opinion is customarily based on the opinion giver's review of the subject corporation's charter documents and a good-standing certificate updated to the opinion date but not a review of the "corporate record books." The opinion preparers should review any applicable report of a state bar association to determine if further diligence is necessary.

Many opinion recipients accept the narrower "validly existing" opinion in the M&A context. If a "duly incorporated" opinion is required, then further diligence will be necessary, essentially confirming that the incorporation documents and procedures complied with the corporation law in effect at the time. Although this is generally not a burdensome undertaking for a recently incorporated corporation, it could be quite burdensome for one incorporated under a now superseded corporation statute.

Duly Organized. Occasionally a buyer may request a further opinion that the entities are "duly organized." However, "due organization" opinions are rarely requested or given and should be avoided (*see* TRIBAR '98 § 6.1.3(b)). Giving a "due organization" opinion entails costs that are rarely justified. What "due organization" means will depend on the law in effect at the time of incorporation and organization, which law could be quite different from current law and will not always be clear. In some states, giving the opinion would require such steps as reviewing actions of the incorporators and initial directors, obtaining evidence of advertising, and confirming receipt of specified capital before commencing business.

Good Standing and Qualification as a Foreign Corporation. If given, an opinion as to "good standing" usually is limited to the company's jurisdiction of incorporation. Buyers will sometimes request an opinion that the target is qualified to do business in specified jurisdictions, but because that opinion will be given solely on the basis of good-standing certificates issued by state officials, it is of little value, and thus ABA LEGAL OPINION GUIDELINES § 4.1 and TRIBAR '98 § 6.1.4 recommend omitting it altogether. Even more inappropriately, buyers may request an opinion that *"The Company is qualified in all jurisdictions where the nature of its business requires it to be so qualified."* Sometimes the formulation is limited to only those jurisdictions *"where the failure to so qualify would have a material adverse effect on the Company and its operations."* However stated, requests for this opinion are not appropriate. Not only does this opinion require the opinion preparers to analyze state laws with which the opinion preparers are not familiar and to undertake extensive diligence (the cost of which is not justified by the benefit of this opinion), but also requires lawyers to make difficult materiality judgments—and thus the materiality qualifier does not cure the inappropriateness of this opinion. As a further reason that requests for this opinion are inappropriate, it improperly (as stated in TRIBAR '98 § 1.3) " . . . *seeks to make the opining lawyer responsible for its client's factual representations or the legal or business risks inherent in the transaction.*" Finally, if the Company has numerous subsidiaries that are not individually significant to its overall operations, the parties should consider dispensing with this opinion as applied to those subsidiaries due to the likely cost in relation to the value of the opinion.

Exhibit 8.6(a) Opinion Letter—Counsel to Sellers

2. **Each of the Transaction Documents has been [duly authorized,] executed, and delivered by the Sellers. [OPTIONAL: Include if the target is a party to any Transaction Documents: The Company (a) has the corporate power to execute and deliver, and to perform its obligations under, each Transaction Document to which it is a party, (b) has taken all necessary corporate action to authorize the execution and delivery of, and the performance of its obligations under, each Transaction Document to which it is a party, and (c) has duly executed and delivered each Transaction Document to which it is a party.]**

COMMENT

The due authorization, execution and delivery opinion (or "action" opinion) is often stated separately from the remedies/enforceability opinion (*see* opinion number 5), even though a remedies/enforceability opinion could not, of course, be given unless the execution, delivery, and performance of the Transaction Documents had been duly authorized and the Transaction Documents had been duly executed and delivered.

The due authorization language is bracketed in the first sentence of this opinion as to the Sellers because that opinion is not appropriate in the circumstances of the Fact Pattern for the Model Agreement because each Seller is an individual of legal majority, and individuals are not required to authorize transactions. To the extent sellers in a transaction are corporations or other entities, a due authorization opinion is customary.

The illustrative opinion as to the Company also includes an optional opinion on the target's corporate power and authorization. Even though the Company is not a party to the Model Agreement, these opinions are included on the assumption that the Company is a party to other ancillary agreements that may be defined as Transaction Documents.

3. **Neither the execution and delivery by each Seller of each Transaction Document to which it is a party nor the consummation of the Contemplated Transactions by each Seller (a) violates any provision of the Organizational Documents of any Acquired Company; (b) breaches or constitutes a default (or an event that, with notice or lapse of time or both, would constitute a default) under, or results in the termination of, or accelerates the performance required by, or excuses performance by any Person of any of its obligations under, or causes the acceleration of the maturity of any debt or obligation pursuant to, or results in the creation or imposition of any lien or other security interest upon any property or assets of any Acquired Company under, any agreements or commitments listed in Part 3.17(a) of the Disclosure Letter; (c) violates any judgment, decree, or order listed in Part 3.15(b) of the Disclosure**

Letter; or (d) violates any federal law of the United States or any law of the State of [the state whose law is covered by the opinion letter].

COMMENT

This opinion, which is regularly requested and given, is stated in terms of no "violation," "breach" or "default." Opinion givers are cautioned to avoid the use of *"no conflict with"* because of the imprecision of that phrase. *See* TRIBAR '98 § 6.5.2. The opinion would have greater significance if the Company were a party to the agreement and not just the Sellers.

Also, this opinion avoids adopting the broad meaning of certain defined terms in the Model Stock Purchase Agreement by not capitalizing those terms (e.g., "breach" or "law").

Consummation v. Performance. The opinion only covers breaches or defaults related to performance of the Stock Purchase Agreement through the closing when the opinion letter is delivered ("... *consummation of the Contemplated Transactions by Sellers* ...."). Buyer may seek to broaden the opinion to include required post-closing performance, in which event the opinion should cover *"execution, delivery, and performance* ....", and the language relating to consummation should be deleted. However, if the latter approach is taken, then a potentially difficult analysis is required. *See* TRIBAR '98 §§ 1.2(f), 6.5.4 and 6.7. The discussion in TRIBAR '98 § 6.5.4 addresses one aspect of this potentially difficult analysis, distinguishing between: (1) Obligations: actions that the Company is "obligated" to take (or not take) in the future under a Transaction Document (such as the Company's obligation to issue shares if an investor exercises warrants) that will result in a breach or default of its articles, bylaws, or an agreement that prohibits the action—and thus that "obligation" prevents the opinion giver from giving this opinion (unless a consent is obtained); and (2) Rights: actions that the Company has the "right" (but not the obligation) to take in the future, but such permitted action will result in a breach or default of its articles, bylaws or an agreement only if taken (such as the exercise of a repurchase right for outstanding shares in violation of a prohibition on stock repurchases in a Transaction Document)—and thus the existence of that "right" does not prevent the opinion giver from giving this opinion. As a further illustration, TRIBAR '98 § 6.5.4 also states that breaches or defaults under listed agreements that will occur only if specified events or circumstances occur or exist in the future ordinarily do not prevent giving this opinion—but if such events or circumstances exist at the time the opinion is given (and are not otherwise excepted out of the opinion), then this opinion should not be given.

Listing of Covered Agreements. This opinion covers only those agreements and commitments that are listed in the applicable disclosure schedule or, if that disclosure schedule includes agreements that do not justify being covered by this opinion, to some other list (e.g., a list of agreements attached to the opinion letter or exhibits to an SEC filing). This approach of utilizing a specific list requires that

Exhibit 8.6(a) Opinion Letter—Counsel to Sellers

the parties define the selection criteria in a way that satisfies Buyer's legitimate interest in having the opinion preparers review those agreements and commitments of the Company and the Sellers likely to present significant issues while limiting the scope of that review to one that is feasible and does not involve disproportionate costs in the context of the transaction. Lawyers should carefully consider the consequences before giving an opinion as to *"any agreement or commitment known to us to which any Acquired Company is a party or by which any assets of an Acquired Company are bound"* [emphasis added] because, as discussed under "No Knowledge Definition in These Illustrative Opinion Letters," use of "known to us" introduces the uncertainties inherent in a knowledge standard.

Agreements Governed by the Law of Another State. Companies typically are parties to agreements governed by the law of states whose law is not covered by the opinion letter. In giving the no breach or default opinion above, TRIBAR '98 § 6.5.6 states the opinion giver may *"assume, without so stating in the opinion letter, that those contracts would be interpreted in accordance with their plain meaning (unless the . . . [opining lawyer] identif(ies) a possible problem, in which event they may want to obtain an opinion from local counsel)."* Further, *"[i]n the case of technical terms, their meaning would be what lawyers generally understand them to mean in the jurisdiction (or principal jurisdiction if more than one) whose law is specified for coverage in the opinion letter)."* Nevertheless, some lawyers add a parenthetical to address this point expressly: (*"interpreting each such agreement as if the law of the State of XXX were_____ . . ."*) with the "State of XXX" being the state whose law is being covered generally in the opinion letter (*see* the governing law paragraph below).

Acceleration Events; Expanding the Opinion Language to Cover Other Adverse Consequences. This opinion is stated so that it expressly covers "acceleration" events. This is important, particularly from the recipient's viewpoint, because TRIBAR '98 § 6.5.3 states that the "no breach or default opinion" does not cover "adverse consequences" unless the opinion specifically states that it does – and then notes that the following "adverse consequences" are not automatically covered by the "no breach or default opinion": (1) termination of a credit facility commitment; (2) increase in royalty rate or interest rate; (3) creation of a lien; (4) requirement to provide additional collateral; (5) creation of "puts" resulting from a change of control; and (6) creation of right to accelerate or require prepayment by existing debt holders. The recipient may want the opinion to cover adverse consequences (1) through (5) in addition to (6), which is the only acceleration event.

Possible Exceptions for Financial Covenant Analysis. Some opinion preparers take an exception for compliance with financial covenants or similar provisions requiring financial calculations or determinations to ascertain compliance. Others consider it appropriate for lawyers to cover compliance based on certificates of officers with the requisite knowledge. They note that financial covenants often require legal interpretation as to their meaning. Also, opinion preparers sometimes take an exception for provisions tied to a "material adverse event" or terms of similar import when there is uncertainty as to what is essentially a factual determination.

These exceptions are not addressed by either the ABA or TriBar reports but are sometimes included and accepted. *See* GLAZER & FITZGIBBON § 16.3.5.

4.   **Except for requirements of the HSR Act, no consent, approval, or authorization of, or declaration, filing, or registration with, any governmental authority of the United States or the State of [the state whose law is covered by the opinion letter] is required in connection with the execution and delivery of any Transaction Document by Sellers or the Company or the consummation by Sellers [or Company] of any of the Contemplated Transactions.**

COMMENT

This opinion is limited to consents required through the Closing. Some buyers may seek to broaden the opinion to include consents required to perform the Model Agreement after the Closing. *See* the discussion of opinions addressing post-closing matters in the commentary to the immediately prior "no breach or default" opinion in opinion number 3 above. This opinion may be difficult for an opinion giver who has not previously represented the Company (see GLAZER & FITZGIBBON Ch. 15), but it is often requested and given. If no Transaction is to be consummated by Company, the language in the second bracket should be deleted.

5.   **Each of the Transaction Documents is a valid and binding obligation of Sellers, enforceable against Sellers in accordance with its terms; *provided, however*, that this opinion does not cover _____ [*Note to Drafter*:   identify any particular clauses in the Transaction Documents to be excluded, such as the noncompetition provisions of § 7.1 of the Model Agreement].**

COMMENT

The opinion that each of the Transaction Documents is a *"valid and binding obligation of Sellers, enforceable against Sellers in accordance with its terms"* is referred to as the "remedies opinion" (it is also commonly referred to as the "enforceability opinion"). Subject to exceptions express and implied, this opinion is generally understood to mean as to each Transaction Document: (1) that an agreement has been formed; (2) that the remedies specified in the agreement will be given effect by the courts; and (3) that each provision unrelated to the concept of breach (such as a choice of law provision or specified amendment procedures) will be given effect by the courts. The determination of whether a provision is enforceable is based on the opinion giver's professional judgment as to whether the highest court of the jurisdiction whose law governs the agreement would enforce a particular provision. *See* TRIBAR '98 §§ 1.2(a) and 3.1; GLAZER & FITZGIBBON §§ 9.6, 9.7 and 9.8.

Exhibit 8.6(a) Opinion Letter—Counsel to Sellers

Often lawyers use all or a combination of the words *"valid," "binding,"* and *"enforceable"* to express the remedies opinion. Today, however, as a matter of customary practice, the words *"valid," "binding,"* and *"enforceable"* are considered to provide the same opinion, and any of those words is sufficient for purposes of the remedies opinion. In the past, in addition to the words *"valid," "binding,"* and *"enforceable,"* the word *"legal"* was used in the formulation. The word *"legal,"* however, adds nothing and no longer is commonly used. *See* GLAZER & FITZGIBBON § 9.1.1, n.10.

Exceptions—Bankruptcy and Equitable Principles. Courts may not give effect to a party's contractual obligations in the context of bankruptcy or because of the application of equitable principles. Exceptions for bankruptcy and equitable principles are generally accepted and should not be a matter of controversy. As is done in the illustrative opinion letters (in a single, combined paragraph below), stating these exceptions is common (for example, the TriBar illustrative opinions expressly include them), but they are understood to be implicit even if not stated.

Exceptions—Certain Transaction Documents and Provisions. This opinion's proviso contemplates excluding specified provisions. For example, noncompetition agreements are often expressly excluded from the remedies opinion.

Determining whether to include other exceptions to the remedies/enforceability opinion—which are generally listed separately towards the end of the opinion letter (as is the case in the illustrative opinion letters)—requires that the opinion giver review the Transaction Documents to identify provisions that are potentially unenforceable. Exceptions commonly include provisions relating to choice of law and forum (at least in some jurisdictions), broad waivers, and particular indemnification provisions that may violate public policy. TRIBAR '04 (Remedies Supp) Part II suggests the following questions, modified for the Model Agreement Fact Pattern, to aid the opinion giver in deciding whether to include an exception:

(1) Do any of the provisions of any of the Transaction Documents raise legal issues of concern as to enforceability?

(2) Does the legal issue arise under the law covered by the opinion letter (taking into account that certain "bodies of law" are either expressly excluded by the coverage limitation or deemed excluded without so stating as described in the TriBar reports)?

(3) Is the legal issue addressed by the opinion letter in some other way—such as either (a) by an assumption otherwise included or deemed included in the opinion letter (for example, the genuineness of signatures) or (b) by the bankruptcy and equitable principles limitation? For example, with respect to the provision requiring that amendments to the Model Agreement be in writing, TRIBAR '04 (Remedies Supp) Part III.D states that one of the bases for not enforcing the provision is excluded

from the opinion's coverage by the equitable principles limitation and the other—creation of a new contract— is not covered by the opinion. *See also* TRIBAR '98 at 597 § 1.2(c).

(4) Can the legal issue be resolved by factual inquiry?

(5) Can the legal issue be avoided by restructuring the transaction or revising the agreement (for example, can issues as to enforceability of a waiver of rights be resolved by making the waiver more explicit)?

Thus, giving the remedies/enforceability opinion involves an analysis of the exceptions applicable to and assumptions underlying the opinion and the law covered by the opinion letter. In addition, in some cases, revisions to the Transaction Documents will eliminate an issue. *See* ABA LEGAL OPINION GUIDELINES § 1.3, TRIBAR '98 § 3.2, and TRIBAR '04 (Remedies Supp) § I.

> **6. The authorized capital stock of the Company consists of _____ shares of common stock, _____ par value, [of which _____ shares] [all of which] are outstanding. The Shares have been duly authorized and validly issued and are fully paid and nonassessable.**

COMMENT

The parties should consider whether the benefit of giving this opinion to the recipient justifies its cost. For example, after considering the cost, a decision might be made to cover only the authorized capital of the Company and not the number or status of outstanding shares. *See* ABA LEGAL OPINION GUIDELINES § 4.2, TRIBAR '98 § 6.2 and GLAZER & FITZGIBBON § 10.16.

If an opinion is given on the number of outstanding shares, many opinion givers qualify it by the following introductory clause because it is based solely on the corporate records reviewed and not on any further independent investigation by the opinion preparers:

> Based solely upon our review of the Company's [articles] [certificate] of incorporation and the Company's shareholders' list maintained pursuant to [statutory cite]:

If an opinion on the due authorization and valid issuance of outstanding shares is given, then the applicable state bar association's reports should be consulted for information about specific issues with regard to the issuance of stock under that state's laws.

Shares Authorized by Articles/Certificate of Incorporation. This opinion as to the shares authorized by the articles/certificate of incorporation is frequently not given because it generally provides little benefit—it involves only reading straightforward provisions of the corporate charter and that can just as easily be done by the

Exhibit 8.6(a) Opinion Letter—Counsel to Sellers

buyer's lawyer. If this opinion is given and covers more than one class of stock, the opinion giver needs to confirm that both the applicable corporation law and the corporate charter permit the attributes the stock purports to have.

Number of Outstanding Shares. The reasons for resisting giving the "outstanding shares" opinion range from the lack of any cost-justified benefit to the actual inappropriateness of giving this "opinion" because it does not involve any professional legal judgment. GLAZER & FITZGIBBON § 10.10 n.5 states: *"The Revised ABA Guidelines state that opinions 'should be limited to . . . matters that involve the exercise of professional judgment by the opinion giver' . . . .* <u>*The number of outstanding shares is not a matter requiring professional judgment.* . . ."</u> [Emphasis added].

Due Authorization and Valid Issuance. The "duly authorized" opinion addresses the proper creation of the shares in the charter documents under state law, and the "validly issued" opinion addresses whether the proper steps to approve a particular stock issuance have been taken. *See* TRIBAR '98 §§ 6.2.1 and 6.2.2. "Validly issued" also addresses whether the issuance of the shares violated preemptive rights under the applicable corporation law and company charter but does not address, unless expressly stated, contractual preemptive-type rights.

Fully Paid and Nonassessable. Generally, the phrase *"fully paid and nonassessable"* means what the applicable corporation law says it means. This opinion has legal substance. Legal judgment is involved as to what was proper consideration for the issuance of shares; however, as it relates to the receipt of that consideration, the opinion ordinarily is based on an officer's certificate. The "fully paid and nonassessable" opinion is often given in stock acquisitions, assuming it is cost-justified when the difficulties of giving it are considered.

No Opinion as to Ownership of Shares. An opinion as to registered (record) ownership of stock—which is not included in this illustrative opinion—is rarely given because it is primarily a factual issue. Any broader opinion (including an opinion on beneficial ownership) could not be given in the absence of a title system such as one that exists for motor vehicles. The TriBar reports do not specifically address the issue of opinions on share ownership, and such an opinion is not included in any of their illustrative opinion letters. In support of this, GLAZER & FITZGIBBON § 11.4.2 states: *"The Seller's status as a registered owner is a purely factual question, and the Buyer has the burden of making that determination . . . ."* and § 11.4.2, n.8 states: *"Sometimes, recipients ask for an 'opinion' that the Seller is the registered owner. This is not really an opinion but simply a statement of fact based solely on an examination of the stock record book or, for a public company, a certificate of the transfer agent."*

7. **Upon the delivery of certificates to Buyer indorsed to Buyer or indorsed in blank by an effective endorsement and the payment to Sellers being made at the Closing, and assuming Buyer has no notice of an adverse**

claim to the Shares within the meaning of Uniform Commercial Code § 8-105, Buyer will acquire the Shares free of any adverse claims within the meaning of Uniform Commercial Code § 8-303.

COMMENT

Title opinions should not be requested and, if requested, should be strongly resisted. As an alternative to a title opinion, buyers will sometimes ask for a "protected purchaser" opinion that the buyer is acquiring the shares free of adverse claims. This opinion can usually be given on the basis of UCC §§ 8-302 and 8-303. Note that this opinion is based on an assumption that buyer does not have notice of any adverse claim; that assumption should be acceptable to buyer because sellers' lawyer has no way to know what the buyer knows.

A request by buyer that this opinion state that the ownership passes *"free and clear"* of adverse claims should not be given, because the *"and clear"* language is not used in the UCC.

8. **All of the outstanding shares of capital stock of each Subsidiary have been duly authorized and validly issued and are fully paid and nonassessable. The outstanding capital stock of each of the Subsidiaries is owned of record by one or more of the Acquired Companies.**

COMMENT

See the commentary to opinion number 6 as to the meaning and value of these opinions.

Except as set forth in Part 3.15(a) of the Disclosure Letter, we are not representing any of the Acquired Companies or Sellers in any pending litigation in which any of them is a named defendant [or in any litigation that is overtly threatened [in writing] against any of them by a potential claimant] that challenges the validity or enforceability of, or seeks to enjoin the performance of, the Transaction Documents.

COMMENT

A Confirmation and Not a Legal Opinion. This paragraph is set apart from the numbered opinion paragraphs because it is not a legal opinion but rather a confirmation of fact concerning pending or threatened legal proceedings relating to the contemplated transactions. It is not a general "no litigation" confirmation as to litigation in which the Company is involved, but is limited to matters potentially affecting the consummation of the transaction. The illustrative confirmation paragraph is taken from the Boston Bar Association's *Streamlined Form of Closing Opinion,* 61 Bus. Law 389, 396–397 (Nov. 2005). A similar opinion is recommended in the Supplement to Report of the Legal Opinion Committee of the Business

Exhibit 8.6(a) Opinion Letter—Counsel to Sellers

Law Section of the North Carolina Bar Association. GLAZER & FITZGIBBON (2009 Supplement at App. 38A:13).

No Litigation Confirmations Are Less Frequently Given. For reasons discussed below, many lawyers refuse to give a no litigation confirmation, even one that is limited to litigation involving the transaction. In the past, buyers often requested broad confirmations that no material proceedings of any nature were pending or threatened against the Company either (1) by reason of its operations or (2) by reason of the proposed transaction. Recent decisions – specifically Nat'l Bank of Canada v. Hale & Dorr, LLP, 17 Mass. L. Rptr. 681, 2004 WL 1049072 (Mass. Super. Ct. Apr. 28, 2004) and Dean Foods Co. v. Pappathanasi, 2004 WL 3019442 (Mass. Super. Ct. Dec. 3, 2004) – together with the "no misleading opinion" admonition of ABA LEGAL OPINION GUIDELINES § 1.5 and TRIBAR '98 § 1.4(d) – have heightened concerns of increased exposure from no litigation confirmations. *See* Glazer & Field, *No Litigation Opinions Can Be Risky Business*, 14 BUSINESS LAW TODAY (July/Aug. 2005) for a more detailed account of *Dean Foods* and cautions regarding no litigation confirmations. TRIBAR '98 § 6.8 states that "*. . . in most cases the no litigation opinion could be omitted with no real loss to opinion recipients . . . .*" The TriBar Opinion Committee reached that conclusion before *Nat'l Bank of Canada* and *Deans Foods* were decided.

As a further caution, TRIBAR '98 § 1.4(d) specifically discusses a no litigation confirmation that is limited to written claims and concludes that an opinion would be "misleading" and thus should not be given if it does not disclose a substantial and apparently serious claim made orally in a formal manner (*e.g.*, at a lawyers' conference at which a draft complaint was discussed but not delivered) but not yet threatened in writing on the date of the opinion letter.

    Our opinions are limited in all respects to the law of the State of _____ and the federal law of the United States.

COMMENT

The opinion letter should identify the law that it covers. This will generally be federal law and the law of a state in which the opinion preparers practice.

Opinions under the Law of Other Jurisdictions – Generally. The opinion recipient may ask for an opinion on the law of a jurisdiction other than the jurisdiction in which the opinion preparers practice. Whether a lawyer can give an opinion on the law of such other jurisdiction is principally an issue of competence with regard to that law (*see* the discussion following as to opinions on Delaware's and other states' corporation statutes). When an opinion is requested on the law of a jurisdiction on which the opinion preparers do not regard themselves as competent, the opinion recipient should be furnished an opinion of local counsel. Ordinarily, local counsel's opinion letter should be addressed to the recipient and the primary opinion giver need not make reference to or comment on the local counsel opinion. This approach of "unbundling" opinions is supported by ABA LEGAL OPINION GUIDELINES § 2.2 and TRIBAR '98 §§ 5.2 and 5.5.

Opinions on Delaware and Other State Corporations. Given the large number of corporations incorporated in Delaware, many lawyers in states other than Delaware give opinions on issues governed by the Delaware General Corporation Law ("DGCL"). *See* TRIBAR '04 (Remedies Supp), § II, n.25. However, non-Delaware lawyers usually are unwilling (without at least conferring with Delaware counsel) to give opinions involving particularly difficult issues under the DGCL (such as issues raised by some complex preferred stock provisions). When giving an opinion on the DGCL, some opinion givers add the following to the coverage limitation:

> In addition, our opinions in numbered paragraphs 1 [status], 2 [due authorization, execution and delivery] and 3(a) [no breach of articles/bylaws] are limited to the Delaware General Corporation Law, as amended.

A reference to the DGCL, such as the foregoing, does not exclude coverage of applicable reported cases interpreting that statute.

Some lawyers may regard themselves as competent to give opinions on the corporate law of states other than Delaware in which they do not practice. The same analysis with regard to opinions on the DGCL by non-Delaware lawyers should apply to opinions on the corporate law of other states.

We express no opinion with respect to the law of any other jurisdiction [OPTIONAL—if applicable: (or the law of the State of [XXX] other than the [XXX corporate statute] as provided above) END OF OPTION]. We express no opinion as to any matters arising under, or the effect of any of, the following [bodies of law]:

COMMENT

The first sentence is implicit in all opinions and does not need to be stated — the opinion covers only what it says that it covers.

ABA LEGAL OPINION PRINCIPLES § II.D states that some laws are not covered by opinions even *"when generally recognized as being directly applicable."* Also, TRIBAR '98 §§ 1.2(e), 3.5.1, 3.5.2 and 6.6 discuss and list bodies of law *"that lawyers would recognize as being applicable to the transaction, but that are customarily not covered [by a legal opinion] unless specifically addressed."* Thus, opinion letters that follow the TriBar approach generally do not include a long list of excluded laws.

However, because ABA LEGAL OPINION PRINCIPLES § II.D expressly refers only to local laws and to securities, tax and insolvency laws, some opinion givers expressly exclude other laws from the coverage of their opinion letters.

The 2005 Report on Legal Opinions in Business Transactions of the State Bar of California, Part V, § C.4.c, includes the following example:

Exhibit 8.6(a) Opinion Letter—Counsel to Sellers

Furthermore, we express no opinion with respect to compliance with any law, rule or regulation that as a matter of customary practice is understood to be covered only when an opinion refers to it expressly. Without limiting the generality of the foregoing [and except as specifically stated herein,] we express no opinion on local or municipal law, antitrust, environmental, land use, securities, tax, pension, employee benefit, margin, insolvency, fraudulent transfer or investment company laws or regulations, nor compliance by the Company's board of directors or shareholders with their fiduciary duties.

If a standard list of excluded laws is included in an opinion letter, those laws that are clearly not covered by any of the opinions being given should be deleted.

Our opinions above are subject to bankruptcy, insolvency, reorganization, receivership, moratorium, and other similar laws affecting the rights and remedies of creditors generally and to general principles of equity (including without limitation the availability of specific performance or injunctive relief and the application of concepts of materiality, reasonableness, good faith and fair dealing).

COMMENT

As noted in the discussion of the remedies/enforceability opinion, courts may not give effect to a party's contractual obligations (a) in the context of bankruptcy and (b) because of the application of equitable principles. As in TRIBAR '98's illustrative legal opinions, the illustrative paragraph applies to all the opinions in the opinion letter, not simply the remedies/enforceability opinion. (*See also* TRIBAR '98 §§ 1.2(c) and 3.3.1). These exceptions are understood to be implicit even if not stated. TRIBAR '98's illustrative legal opinions use the following shorter version of this qualification: "Our opinions above are subject to bankruptcy, insolvency and other similar laws affecting the rights and remedies of creditors generally and general principles of equity." A similar shorter statement of this qualification — but one that includes references to "fraudulent transfer, reorganization and moratorium" — is used in the Boston Bar Association's *Streamlined Form of Closing Opinion*, 61 BUS LAW 389, 397 (Nov. 2005). All these formulations have the same meaning. TRIBAR '98 § 3.3.2.

For the purposes of the opinions expressed in this opinion letter, we have assumed: (a) the genuineness of all signatures on all documents; (b) the authenticity of all documents submitted to us as originals; (c) the conformity to the originals of all documents submitted to us as copies; (d) the correctness and accuracy of all facts set forth in all certificates and reports; (e) the due authorization, execution, and delivery of and the validity and binding effect of the Transaction Documents with regard to the parties to the Transaction Documents other than Sellers; and (f) the legal capacity of Sellers to enter into and perform the Transaction Documents.

COMMENT

TRIBAR '98 § 2.3(a) and ABA LEGAL OPINION PRINCIPLES § III.D take the position that "assumptions of general application" (such as those set forth above) are implicit whether or not stated expressly. They also state that omitting the assumptions set forth above is common practice.

If another lawyer is giving an opinion on existence, power and authorization and/or other matters that are necessary for the opinions in the opinion letter, the opinion letter (1) should expressly assume the legal conclusions in that other lawyer's opinion letter and (2) not comment on them. *See* ABA LEGAL OPINION GUIDELINES § 2.2 and TRIBAR '98 §§ 5.2 and 5.5.

We express no opinion as to any of the following [add any necessary exceptions]:

COMMENT

This clause provides for the list of provisions in the Transaction Documents or the legal issues they raise that are expressly excluded from the coverage of the opinion letter. No exceptions are included in the illustrative opinion letters, but the stated exceptions frequently include provisions relating to choice of law and forum (at least in some jurisdictions), broad waivers and particular indemnification provisions that may violate public policy. Although a broad public policy exception along the lines of *"or to the extent otherwise contrary to or against public policy"* is sometimes seen in opinion letters, the illustrative opinion letters do not contain that exception. TRIBAR '98 § 1.9(i) states that *"[g]eneral unspecified 'public policy' exceptions are not used because they make the entire opinion unacceptably vague, requiring the opinion recipient to guess at the opinion giver's source of concern."* ABA LEGAL OPINION GUIDELINES § 4.8 is to the same effect.

When to Include an Exception. *See* comments to the remedies/enforceability opinion for a discussion of how to determine what exceptions to include.

Include Only Applicable Exceptions (a/k/a "Avoiding the Kitchen Sink"). Only those exceptions that are applicable should be included. Some opinion givers include a voluminous list of exceptions and qualifications, many of which have nothing to do with the transaction at hand. This "kitchen sink" approach is inappropriate, and opinion givers should limit exceptions to relevant issues. *See* ABA LEGAL OPINION GUIDELINES § 1.3 (*"Closing opinions should not include assumptions, exceptions, and limitations that do not relate to the transaction and the opinions given"*), TRIBAR '98 § 3.2 (particularly its last sentence), and TRIBAR '04 (Remedies Supp) § I's penultimate paragraph. *See also* Field, *One Size Doesn't Fit All: Reject 'Kitchen-Sink' Responses in Opinion Letters,* BUSINESS LAW TODAY, 61–62 (May/June 2002). Commentators have expressed concern that, if an opinion letter inadvertently omits a necessary exception from a long list of exceptions, the opinion giver will have more difficulty convincing a court that the exception was

Exhibit 8.6(a) Opinion Letter—Counsel to Sellers

implicit than if the opinion giver had relied on customary practice and avoided stating those exceptions.

This opinion letter shall be interpreted in accordance with the Legal Opinion Principles issued by the Committee on Legal Opinions of the American Bar Association's Section of Business Law as published in 57 Bus. Law. 75 (2002) [a copy of which is attached].

COMMENT

The paragraph above is taken from the Boston Bar Association's *Streamlined Form of Closing Opinion* 61 Bus. Law. 389, 397 (Nov. 2005), which states that "many firms" include language expressly incorporating the ABA Legal Opinion Principles (which are only three pages long). The ABA Business Law Section's Committee on Federal Regulation of Securities' Subcommittee on Securities Law Opinions *No Registration Opinions,* 63 Bus. Law. 187 (Nov. 2007), confirms that some lawyers are referring to the ABA Legal Opinion Guidelines in their opinion letters. By doing so, the opinion recipient is put on notice that (1) the opinions are expressions of professional judgment and not guarantees of a particular result and (2) the opinion letter was prepared and is to be interpreted in accordance with customary practice, which means, among other things, that words and phrases in the opinion letter are not always meant to be interpreted in accordance with their literal meaning (that is, an unqualified reference to "law" literally must mean "all law") but with the meaning that customary practice has given them (in the case of "law," a significantly narrower definition). These principles are applicable even if that reference is not included. The TriBar reports (and to a lesser extent the ABA Legal Opinion Principles) helpfully set forth matters that need not be stated in opinion letters, such as (a) assumptions (particularly "assumptions of general application"such as that copies are identical to originals and signatures are genuine) and (b) exclusions from covered bodies of laws (such as tax and local laws). Accordingly, incorporation of the ABA Legal Opinion Principles not only puts the opinion recipient on notice regarding the application of customary practice, but in the unfortunate circumstance that a judge is analyzing an opinion letter, doing so makes clear to the judge that "as a matter of customary practice" many assumptions and qualifications are implicit even though not explicitly stated.

The opinions expressed in this opinion letter (a) are limited to the matters stated in this opinion letter, and, without limiting the foregoing, no other opinions are to be inferred and (b) are only as of the date of this opinion letter, and we are under no obligation, and do not undertake, to advise Buyer or any other person or entity either of any change of law or fact that occurs, or of any fact that comes to our attention, after the date of this opinion letter, even though such change or such fact may affect the legal analysis or a legal conclusion in this opinion letter.

COMMENT

Although not necessary, a provision such as this is common and generally accepted. ABA LEGAL OPINION PRINCIPLES § IV and TriBar '98 § 1.2(b) state that an opinion giver has no obligation to update even if the limitation is not expressly stated in the opinion letter. If a no litigation confirmation is given, some opinion givers add "and confirmations" to the above boldfaced paragraph.

This opinion letter: (1) is delivered in connection with the consummation of the sale of stock pursuant to the Stock Purchase Agreement, may be relied upon only by Buyer in connection with its purchase of stock pursuant to the Stock Purchase Agreement and may not be relied upon by Buyer for any other purpose; (2) may not be relied on by, or furnished to, any other person or entity without our prior written consent; and (3) without limiting the foregoing, may not be quoted, published, or otherwise disseminated, without in each instance our prior written consent.

COMMENT

If the acquisition is being financed, Buyer's lender will often seek to have the benefit of the opinion letter delivered by Sellers' counsel. Absent a consent in the opinion letter (or separately given by the opinion giver), lenders would not have the right to rely on the opinion letter. Opinion givers frequently agree to such an extension to the lenders, in which event the last sentence would be appropriate to limit reliance. If reliance by lenders is to be permitted, the following should be added:

> Notwithstanding the foregoing sentence, we understand that you are delivering a copy of this opinion letter to [identify lenders to Buyer] in connection with the financing of the transactions contemplated by the Agreement, and we agree that [those lenders] may rely on this opinion letter as if it were addressed to them.

Permitting successor lenders to rely is generally permitted only if the circumstances in which they can rely are set forth in considerable detail in an additional sentence to this paragraph, essentially restricting reliance to the same extent as if the opinion letter had been addressed and delivered to them at the date the opinion letter was issued and that their reliance is otherwise reasonable. *See* GLAZER & FITZGIBBON § 2.3.1, n.3.

Very truly yours,

[LAW FIRM]

COMMENT

The form of the signature block will be determined by the opinion giver's policies.

EXHIBIT 9.5(a)

Opinion Letter—
Counsel to Buyer

PRELIMINARY NOTE

As is the case with Buyer's representations in the Model Agreement, the scope of the opinion letter required to be delivered to Sellers by Buyer's lawyer is often limited to matters affecting the validity of the Transaction Documents. Where, as here, Buyer is delivering the Promissory Notes for a significant portion of the purchase price, however, Sellers may require additional representations from Buyer and, correspondingly, additional opinions from Buyer's lawyer. Still other opinions might be required from Buyer's lawyer if Buyer is issuing its stock as part of the purchase price.

It may be appropriate in some acquisitions for Sellers to ask Buyer's lawyer for opinions on corporate status, power and authority, the need for consent or approval, and other opinions in the opinion letter of counsel to the seller or target. The appropriateness of these additional requests should turn on the nature and size of Buyer, the cost-effectiveness of the opinion, and whether consideration other than cash is being paid. Where Buyer is paying all cash at closing, little or no purpose is usually served in requiring an opinion from Buyer's lawyer.

Reference is made to general discussions in the commentary to the various opinions in the Opinion of Counsel to Seller form, which are not repeated in this illustrative opinion letter form.

[Opinion Giver's Letterhead]

[Date]

[Names and Addresses of Sellers]

Re: Acquisition of _____ (the "Company") by _____ (the "Buyer") pursuant to the Stock Purchase Agreement dated _____ __, 20__ (the "Stock Purchase Agreement")

Ladies and Gentlemen:

We have acted as counsel for the Buyer in connection with its execution and delivery of the Stock Purchase Agreement.

This opinion letter is delivered to you pursuant to Stock Purchase Agreement § 9.5(a).

Each capitalized term in this opinion letter that is not defined in this opinion letter but is defined in the Stock Purchase Agreement is used herein as defined in the Stock Purchase Agreement.

In acting as counsel to Buyer, we have examined [copies of] the following documents and instruments (collectively, the "Transaction Documents"):

1. The Stock Purchase Agreement;

2. The Escrow Agreement; and

3. The Promissory Notes.

In addition to the Transaction Documents, we have examined:

4. The Articles [Certificate] of Incorporation of Buyer, as in effect on the date hereof, duly certified by the Secretary of State of [state];

5. The Bylaws of Buyer, certified to be true and correct by its Secretary;

6. A certificate from the Secretary of State of [state] indicating that Buyer is in good standing in the State of [state];

7. Copies of resolutions adopted by the board of directors of Buyer authorizing the execution, delivery, and performance of the Transaction Documents and certified to be true and correct by its Secretary;

Exhibit 9.5(a) Opinion Letter—Counsel to Buyer

8. Certificate of [title of officer] of Buyer, dated the date hereof, certifying as to certain factual matters (the "Buyer Certificate");

9. Documents listed in the Buyer Certificate; and

10. Such other documents as we have deemed appropriate in order to render the opinions expressed below.

As to certain matters of fact relevant to the opinions in this opinion letter, we have relied on certificates of officers of Buyer and on factual representations made by the Buyer in the Stock Purchase Agreement. We also have relied on certificates of public officials. We have not independently established the facts, or in the case of certificates of public officials, the other statements, so relied upon.

Based upon and subject to the foregoing and the other qualifications and limitations stated in this opinion letter, our opinions are as follows:

1. Buyer is validly existing [and in good standing] as a corporation under the law of the State of _____.

2. Buyer (a) has the corporate power to execute and deliver, and to perform its obligations under, each Transaction Document to which it is a party, (b) has taken all necessary corporate action to authorize the execution and delivery of, and the performance of its obligations under, each Transaction Document to which it is a party, and (c) has duly executed and delivered each Transaction Document to which it is a party.

3. Neither the execution and delivery by Buyer of each Transaction Document to which it is a party nor the consummation of the Contemplated Transactions by Buyer (a) violates any provision of the Articles [Certificate] of Incorporation or Bylaws of Buyer; or (b) violates any judgment, decree, or order listed in Part ___ of the Disclosure Letter; or (d) violates any federal law of the United Sates or any law of the State of [the state under which the remedies/enforceability opinion is given].

4. Each of the Transaction Documents is a valid and binding obligation of Buyer, enforceable against Buyer in accordance with its terms [identify any particular clauses to be excluded].

Our opinions are limited in all respects to the law of the State of _____ and the federal law of the United States.

We express no opinion with respect to the laws of any other jurisdiction [OPTIONAL—if applicable: (or the laws of the State of [XXX] other than the [XXX corporation statutes] as provided above) END OF OPTION] [or as to any matters arising under, or the effect of any of, the following [bodies of laws]: [list bodies of law to be specifically excluded].

Our opinions above are subject to bankruptcy, insolvency, reorganization, receivership, moratorium, and other similar laws affecting the rights and remedies of creditors generally and to general principles of equity (including without limitation the availability of specific performance or injunctive relief and the application of concepts of materiality, reasonableness, good faith, and fair dealing), regardless of whether considered in a proceeding at law or in equity. [*See* an alternate version in the Comment to the comparable provision of the illustrative Sellers' Counsel form.]

For the purposes of the opinions in this opinion letter, we have assumed: (a) the genuineness of all signatures on all documents; (b) the authenticity of all documents submitted to us as originals; (c) the conformity to the originals of all documents submitted to us as copies; (d) the correctness and accuracy of all facts set forth in all certificates and reports; and (e) the due authorization, execution, and delivery of and the validity and binding effect of the Transaction Documents with regard to the parties to the Transaction Documents other than Buyer.

We express no opinion as to any of the following [add any necessary exceptions]:

This opinion letter shall be interpreted in accordance with the Legal Opinion Principles issued by the Committee on Legal Opinions of the American Bar Association's Section of Business Law as published in 57 Bus. Law. 875 (Feb. 2002) [, a copy of which is attached].

The opinions expressed in this opinion letter (a) are strictly limited to the matters stated in this opinion letter, and without limiting the foregoing, no other opinions are to be implied and (b) are only as of the date of this opinion letter, and we are under no obligation, and do not undertake, to advise the Sellers or any other person or entity either of any change of law or fact that occurs, or of any fact that comes to our attention, after the date of this opinion letter, even though such change or such fact may affect the legal analysis or a legal conclusion in this opinion letter.

This opinion letter: (1) is delivered in connection with the consummation of the sale of stock pursuant to the Stock Purchase Agreement, may be relied upon only by the Sellers in connection with the sale of stock pursuant to the Stock Purchase Agreement, and may not be relied upon by the Sellers for any other purpose; (2) may not be relied on by, or furnished to, any other person or entity without our prior written consent; and (3) without limiting the foregoing, may not be quoted, published, or otherwise disseminated, without in each instance our prior written consent.

Very truly yours,

[LAW FIRM]

ANCILLARY DOCUMENTS

ANCILLARY DOCUMENT A

Confidentiality Agreement

PRELIMINARY NOTE

A confidentiality agreement, also referred to as a "nondisclosure agreement" or "NDA," is usually the first agreement entered into in connection with a potential transaction. There may have been some level of discussion, and the target may even have provided some information, whether inadvertently or by design, prior to executing the confidentiality agreement.

The first draft of the confidentiality agreement is usually prepared by the target's counsel or the target's financial advisor, since the principal focus is protection of confidential information regarding the target. The recipient also has a stake in maintaining the confidentiality of information provided by the target to other parties, as disclosure of trade secrets or competitively significant confidential information could impair the value of the target. Similarly, as a prospective owner of the target, the recipient will want to preserve any attorney-client or other privilege that may be asserted with respect to the target's information.

While confidentiality agreements are most often focused on protecting the confidentiality of the target's information, the recipient may want to protect information that it supplies to the target, particularly where the recipient's stock or notes will be issued in the transaction. This might include, for example, information relating to its future business plans that is intended to demonstrate the business fit or to provide assurance of its financial capacity to complete the transaction and develop the business of the target. Providing confidentiality protection for the recipient may be achieved either by preparing a separate confidentiality agreement or by preparing a single, reciprocal confidentiality agreement. The following sample form of confidentiality agreement has been prepared only to protect target materials.

Confidentiality agreements are commonly prepared in the form of a letter agreement. While largely a matter of convention, this format may reflect the desire of business people to be less formal at this early stage. For similar reasons, the business people may urge that the confidentiality agreement be as brief as possible and often have little patience for extensive negotiation of this preliminary document. Properly prepared confidentiality agreements, however, cover a number of important subjects. Considerations of positioning, negotiation strategy, and the client's desire to proceed quickly must be balanced by counsel against the importance of assuring that the confidentiality agreement adequately protects the client's interests in a specific transaction. Not infrequently, clients proceed with a confidentiality agreement prior to consulting with counsel.

If a letter of intent and a confidentiality agreement are executed at the same time, the parties sometimes consider consolidating them into one document. Because the confidentiality agreement is intended to be enforceable and major portions of the letter of intent are intended to be unenforceable, however, combining these documents could result in one or the other being more or less enforceable than intended or, in any event, ambiguous. Also, because the letter of intent is normally a recipient-oriented document, the confidentiality provisions in the letter of intent would likely need to be revised to protect the discloser's confidential information.

For helpful resources on confidentiality agreements in acquisitions, *see* the M&A PROCESS ch. 6; KLING & NUGENT ch. 9; Berick & Boredo, *Confidentiality Agreements for the Sale of a Business (With Form)*, 48 PRAC. LAW. 11 (Dec. 2002); Krus, *Annotated Confidentiality Agreement*, 10 M&A LAW. 17 (March 2001).

TYPICAL PROVISIONS

A confidentiality agreement normally covers the following points:

- the definition of the information that will be subject to the terms of the agreement (usually stated very broadly as covering all information that is provided) and exceptions to the definition or to the confidentiality obligations imposed by the agreement (such as information that is already publicly available);

- the obligation to preserve the confidentiality of the information that is provided, together with provisions for enforcement of that obligation;

- the obligation to limit use of the information to evaluation and negotiation of a possible transaction;

- a disclaimer of any obligation to negotiate or complete a transaction;

- an obligation to return or destroy the information that has been provided (and related notes and analyses), to the extent the information is in tangible, electronic, or other retrievable form, if discussions are terminated; and

- a disclaimer of any representation or warranty as to the accuracy or completeness of the information that is being provided, deferring any such representations to a definitive acquisition agreement between the parties.

While less common, depending upon the circumstances, provisions prohibiting or limiting the solicitation of the disclosing company's employees and provisions granting a period of exclusivity for the recipient may be also included in a confidentiality agreement.

PROTECTING TRADE SECRETS AND OTHER GOALS

In addition to protecting the confidentiality of the parties' important nonpublic information, confidentiality agreements can assist a disclosing party in preserving the protected nature of proprietary information that it believes constitute "trade secrets" under the Uniform Trade Secrets Act and other applicable law. Under the Uniform Trade Secrets Act, for information to be treated as a trade secret, it must be subject to efforts that are reasonable under the circumstances to maintain its secrecy or confidentiality. *See* Uniform Trade Secrets Act §1(4), 14 U.L.A. 438.

Confidentiality agreements seldom require that the parties provide any specific information. Instead, they are directed toward protecting any confidential information that is provided. Further, as noted above, confidentiality agreements typically state that the provider of the information makes no representation or warranty, and assumes no liability, regarding the accuracy or completeness of the information it furnishes.

[Date]

[Buyer]
[Address]

Attention:

Ladies and Gentlemen:

In connection with your consideration of a possible negotiated transaction ("Transaction") with _____ (the "Company"), we may provide information to you concerning our business, financial condition, operations, assets, and liabilities. As a condition to any such information being furnished to you or your Representatives, you agree to treat any such information in accordance with, and to otherwise comply with, the terms and conditions set forth in this agreement.

COMMENT

Reflecting the preliminary stage of discussions and the desire not to imply that there is any agreement regarding whether there will be a transaction, confidentiality agreements typically do not describe in any detail the type of transaction that may result. This agreement refers only to a "possible negotiated transaction" and does not even identify that the transaction may consist of the acquisition of the target by the recipient. To provide some greater definition of the subject matter without any commitment as to the form of, or consideration for, the transaction, reference could be made to a "mutually beneficial business combination" or some other generally descriptive phrase.

This sample agreement is prepared as a unilateral obligation of confidentiality. It would be possible to make all or only some of these provisions mutual.

1. CERTAIN DEFINED TERMS

As used in this agreement,

(a) **the term "Representative" means, as to any person, such person's affiliates, and its and their directors, officers, managers, general partners, members, employees and agents, advisors (including without limitation, financial advisors, legal counsel, and accountants), and controlling persons; the term "affiliate" has the meaning given to that term in Rule 12b-2 of the General Rules and Regulations under the Securities Exchange Act of 1934, as amended (the "Exchange Act"); and the term "person" means natural persons and all legal persons, including, without limitation, any corporation, general or limited partnership, limited liability company, trust, or other entity or company.**

COMMENT

The term "Representative" is defined broadly to encompass a wide range of persons associated in some fashion with the recipient or the target, including persons who may be advisors to the parties but who do not have any agency or other actual representative capacity. Lenders and other financing sources are not included within the defined category of Representatives. While the recipient may need to provide information it receives to its financing sources, they would not be within the category of persons commonly considered as representatives. The target would likely want to have greater control over whether its information will be disseminated to the broader category of potential financing sources. If a recipient will need to obtain financing, specific provision can be made for sharing Evaluation Material for that purpose, subject to prior approval by the target and other safeguards.

(b) **the term "Evaluation Material" means all information concerning the Company or its subsidiaries (whether furnished before or after the date hereof, whether prepared by the Company, its Representatives, or otherwise, whether or not marked as being confidential and regardless of the form of communication, including oral as well as written and electronic communications) that is furnished to you or to your Representatives by or on behalf of the Company. The term "Evaluation Material" also includes all notes, analyses, compilations, studies, interpretations, and other documents prepared by you or your Representatives that contain, reflect, or are based** upon, in whole or in part, the information that the Company or the Company's Representatives furnish to you or your Representatives. The term "Evaluation Material" does not include information that (i) has become generally known to the public other than as a result of a disclosure by the Company or the Company's Representatives, (ii) was within your possession prior to its being furnished to you by or on behalf of the Company, provided that the source of such information was not bound by a confidentiality agreement with, or other contractual, legal, or fiduciary obligation of confidentiality to, the Company or any other person with respect to such information, or (iii) has become available to you on a nonconfidential basis from a source other than the Company or any of the Company's Representatives if such source was not bound by a confidentiality agreement with, or other contractual, legal, or fiduciary obligation of confidentiality to, the Company or any other person with respect to such information.

COMMENT

The key term "Evaluation Material" is defined broadly to include all information provided by the target or on its behalf, with few exceptions. Thus, Evaluation Material includes any information whether or not marked as confidential and regardless of the form in which it is communicated. Oral communications as well as written and electronic communications are included. Evaluation Material is also defined to include notes, analyses, and other materials that contain, reflect, or are based upon information provided by a target, even information that was provided prior to the signing of the agreement. This is so that all items of information will be subject to a requirement that they not be disclosed and to the further requirement that they be returned or destroyed if discussions relating to a transaction are terminated.

The definition of Evaluation Material includes material that is not marked as confidential. Prospective recipients of the Evaluation Material may argue that this is overinclusive and places too great a burden on the recipient to determine what information actually is confidential and contend that the confidentiality obligations should apply only to information that is marked or otherwise specifically indicated as being confidential. The target, on the other hand, would likely argue that requiring it to mark each document as confidential is too burdensome—especially considering that at some point the recipient may be given broad access to the target's books, records, and corporate files—and that its need for the protection of a confidentiality agreement would apply to all confidential information even if there were an inadvertent failure to mark it as such. The recipient is also protected by exclusions to the definition of confidential information. A possible compromise, though one generally favoring the recipient, would be a provision stating that all information provided will be deemed confidential, and therefore within the definition of "Evaluation Material," if it is either designated as confidential at the time it is provided or is so designated by the target within a specified number of days thereafter.

The exclusions from the definition of Evaluation Material in this example include those most commonly found in confidentiality agreements. These exceptions share the common characteristic that they identify situations in which specific information, even though provided by the target, could not properly be described as being within the target's legitimate claim to confidentiality. Whether particular information falls within one or more of the excluded categories is not always easy to determine. Greater protection can be extended to the provider of information by specifying that the recipient bears the burden of proof on whether a particular exception applies. For example, the phrase "which the recipient demonstrates" can be added immediately prior to the listing of exceptions.

A possible additional exclusion is for information that the recipient can demonstrate was independently developed by the recipient without reference to any confidential information disclosed by the target. Other changes to these exclusions are also sometimes requested. For example, in some cases the recipient will add the words "known to the recipient to be" before "bound" in the exceptions in clauses (ii) and (iii). The target might object to the addition of these words, claiming that if the recipient receives Evaluation Material from a source other than the target, it should assume that such source has a confidentiality obligation to the target unless it is certain that no such obligation exists.

Some drafters prefer that there be no exceptions to the definition of "Evaluation Material" and choose instead to state exceptions to the obligation to maintain the information provided in confidence. This form of agreement takes the approach that the material described in the exceptions is, in fact, not confidential and that there would therefore be no purpose in purporting to impose any confidentiality obligations on the recipient with respect to that information.

There may be information that is particularly sensitive to the target as a business matter, particularly where the recipient and the target are competitors. *See* commentary to Section 5.1 of the Model Agreement. There also may be contracts that by their terms, or pursuant to confidentiality agreements, must be maintained in confidence. In the first situation:

- disclosure may be provided at a later stage when it is more likely that a transaction will be agreed upon or completed;
- information that is particularly sensitive, including from an antitrust perspective, may be disclosed only to specified persons (such as outside counsel) and not be permitted to be shared with others in the recipient's organization who could use it for competitive purposes; and
- disclosure of such information may be made to a neutral third party for analysis in a controlled manner that assures its unavailability to parties who could use it improperly.

In some situations, a recipient may prefer not to receive any confidential information at all or only certain specified categories of confidential information. Prospective purchasers who are direct competitors of a target company will want to be particularly cautious in receiving target company information of a confidential and proprietary nature, particularly pricing information. Such information could be compartmentalized and its internal dissemination restricted to lessen the possibility of any claim that the recipient inappropriately used such information in violation of the antitrust laws. In addition to antitrust concerns, a recipient may want to avoid receiving certain types of information so as to avoid any question of whether it has obtained any trade secrets or other proprietary information that might form the basis for legal actions if a transaction is not completed.

2. USE OF EVALUATION MATERIAL AND CONFIDENTIALITY

You will use the Evaluation Material solely for the purpose of evaluating and negotiating the terms of a Transaction, will keep the Evaluation Material strictly confidential, and will not disclose any of the Evaluation Material in any manner whatsoever without the prior written consent of the Company; provided, however, that you may disclose the Evaluation Material to your Representatives who agree to use the Evaluation Material solely for the purpose of evaluating and negotiating the terms of a Transaction, to keep the Evaluation Material strictly confidential, and not to disclose any of the Evaluation Material in any manner whatsoever without the prior written consent of the Company; provided, further, that such Representatives are provided with a copy of this Agreement and agree to be bound by the terms of this Agreement to the same extent as if they were parties hereto. In any event, you will be responsible for any breach of this agreement by any of your Representatives and you agree, at your sole expense, to take all reasonable measures to assure that your Representatives do not make any prohibited or unauthorized disclosure or use (including in legal proceedings) of the Evaluation Material.

COMMENT

Paragraph 2 states the limited purpose for which the information is being provided. Paragraph 2 further states the basic obligation of the recipient to maintain the information in strict confidence and not disclose it in any manner subject to the exception that the information may be provided to the recipient's Representatives who agree to the same conditions. This limited exception is only available if the Representatives also agree to maintain it in confidence and are provided with a copy of the confidentiality agreement (so that they will have notice of its requirements) and agree to be bound by its terms to the same extent as if they were direct parties to the agreement. Some confidentiality agreements specify that the Representatives must also sign a copy of the confidentiality agreement, in which case they would have direct contractual obligations to the target. Representatives are normally reluctant to accept such direct obligations, however, and it often would not be practical to seek signed agreements from all of the Representatives who may properly receive Evaluation Material.

Paragraph 2 contains an agreement by the recipient to be responsible for any breach of the confidentiality agreement by any of its Representatives and to take reasonable measures to assure that they comply with the agreement. The recipient may object to being exposed to potential liability for breaches of the confidentiality agreement by its Representatives. The recipient may argue that the recipient does not ultimately have control over their actions. The recipient might suggest that an acceptable compromise would be to delete the concept of responsibility of the recipient for actions of its Representatives, but to retain the obligation to take reasonable steps to assure compliance by its Representatives. The recipient might also suggest that if any of its Representatives sign an agreement directly with the target, the recipient should no longer remain responsible for that Representative.

The recipient may be concerned that the procedural aspects of Paragraph 2 are out of touch with its acquisition practices, which may include entering into similar confidentiality agreements and initiation of reviews of dozens of targets each month utilizing a range of advisors, both external and internal. The recipient may feel comfortable that its policies, professional obligations, and general engagement agreements are sufficient protection. It may, therefore, propose striking the second proviso on the basis that it does not show the form of every agreement to each of its Representatives, and does not require that they agree to its terms. The recipient may also attempt to simplify the proviso.

Some drafters prefer to state explicitly the additional restriction (implicit in the prohibition of use of the Evaluation Material for any purpose other than consideration of the proposed transaction) that the information contained in the Evaluation Material may not be used by the recipient for any competitive purpose. This prohibition is important to the target for the purpose of protecting its business and competitive position. It is also important to both the target and the recipient for purposes of evidencing their intention to comply with applicable antitrust laws. A provision such as the following could be added for this purpose: "Without limiting the foregoing, neither you nor your Representatives will use any information obtained from the Evaluation Material to divert or attempt to divert any business or customer of the Company or its subsidiaries, or otherwise use any such information competitively against the Company or its subsidiaries, or for any anticompetitive purpose."

A recipient might point out that the information contained in the Evaluation Material will undoubtedly become stale and negotiate for an end to the confidentiality restriction after some period of time.

A recipient may be concerned, in the event a transaction does not occur, that, despite its best efforts, its employees who receive Evaluation Material will not be able to purge the information received fully from their memory and that it will be difficult or impossible to prove that they did not use the information in some fashion in the course of the recipient's subsequent business operations. To deal with this concern, the recipient may propose adding a provision such as the following:

This agreement will not be deemed breached by you in the event Residual Knowledge is used by your employees unintentionally, subject to any valid patents, copyrights, or other intellectual property rights of the Company. "Residual Knowledge" means ideas, concepts, know-how, or techniques that are retained in the unaided memories of your employees who have had access to the Evaluation Material. An employee's memory will be considered unaided if the employee has not intentionally memorized the Evaluation Material for the purpose of retaining and subsequently using or disclosing it.

In response to this proposal, the target might point out that while this provision may be included in some confidentiality agreements relating to intellectual property license negotiations, it is not appropriate for inclusion in M&A-related confidentiality agreements because significantly more information is typically disclosed in the M&A context than in the licensing context. Also, the target may be concerned that this provision would make it too easy for the recipient to circumvent the important use restrictions contained in the confidentiality agreement.

3.   NONDISCLOSURE OF TRANSACTION

Except as set forth in Paragraph 4, you agree that without our prior written consent, neither you nor any of your Representatives will disclose to any other person the fact that the Evaluation Material has been made available, the fact that discussions or negotiations concerning any Transaction are or may be taking place, or have taken place, or any of the terms, conditions, or other matters discussed with respect thereto. Without limiting the generality of the foregoing, you agree that neither you nor any of your Representatives will enter into any discussions or any agreement, understanding, or arrangement with any person regarding participation by that person or others in any Transaction.

COMMENT

Paragraph 3 expands the scope of required confidentiality to impose an obligation on the recipient not to disclose the fact that any discussions are or may be taking place between the parties or that any information has been provided. The target is concerned that disclosure of this information would disturb its employees, cause uncertainty among its customers, and provide potential advantage to its competitors who may use the possibility of a transaction to recruit employees and to persuade customers that they can no longer rely on the target. The target may also be concerned that if word of a possible transaction leaks out and is not followed by an actual transaction, other potential buyers would conclude that there may be some problem with the target that prevented the transaction from happening.

The second sentence of Paragraph 3 would most commonly be included in the case of an auction or other multiple potential buyer situation in which the target seeks to avoid the lessening of competition among potential buyers. Sometimes exceptions are provided when the recipient may need to obtain financing to complete the transaction. Language of this sort may be tailored to fit the particular facts, such as by specifically limiting the language to potential institutional lenders or by expanding it to include potential providers of equity financing as well.

4.   LEGALLY COMPELLED DISCLOSURE

If you or any of your Representatives is required, in the written opinion of its legal counsel who has been informed of the relevant facts, by law or the rules of any securities exchange to which you or any such Representative is subject, or in any judicial, administrative, or other legal proceeding, or pursuant to subpoena, civil investigative demand, or other compulsory process, to disclose any of the Evaluation Material or any Transaction, you and your Representative shall provide the Company with prompt written notice of any such requirement, to the extent you and it may legally do so, so that the Company may seek a protective order or other appropriate remedy, and will consult with the Company with respect to the Company or you (or such Representative) taking steps to resist or narrow the scope of such required disclosure. If, in the absence of a protective order or other remedy or the receipt of a waiver by the Company, you or any of your Representatives are nonetheless, in the further written opinion of legal counsel, legally compelled to disclose Evaluation Material to any tribunal or other authority or else stand liable for contempt or suffer other censure or penalty, you (or such Representative) may disclose only that portion of the Evaluation Material that such counsel advises is legally required to be disclosed, provided that you (or such Representative) exercise best efforts to preserve the confidentiality of the Evaluation Material, including, without limitation, by cooperating with the Company to obtain an appropriate protective order or other reliable assurance that confidential treatment will be accorded the Evaluation Material by such tribunal or other authority.

COMMENT

Paragraph 4 recognizes that notwithstanding the contractual obligation under the confidentiality agreement not to disclose information contained in the Evaluation Material, such disclosure may nonetheless be compelled by the securities laws or stock exchange rules (which laws and rules would normally be relevant only in the context of the recipient possibly becoming obligated to disclose that a transaction is being considered), or by judicial, administrative, or other legal proceedings. Paragraph 4 provides that if the recipient believes, based on the written opinion of its legal counsel, that it is required to disclose any information constituting part of the Evaluation Material or the possibility of a transaction, it must promptly notify and consult with the target with respect to efforts the target may desire to make to either resist or narrow the scope of the required disclosure. The recipient may object to the requirement that the opinion of its legal counsel be in writing on the basis that obtaining a written opinion would likely involve unnecessary delay and expense. The target, on the other hand, may respond that maintaining the confidence of its information is sufficiently important, that the question of whether disclosure is required would normally be sufficiently easy to determine, and that the balance of cost and benefit weighs in favor of the target's requirement of a written legal opinion. Paragraph 4 further requires that the recipient only disclose the minimum amount of information required to be disclosed and that it cooperate with the target to obtain a protective order or other assurance that the legal authority requiring disclosure will maintain the confidential nature of the information to the extent possible. The recipient might argue that all these steps impose an undue burden on it when it has been advised by legal counsel that it must disclose the information.

5. TERMINATION OF DISCUSSIONS; RETURN OF EVALUATION MATERIAL

(a) **If you determine that you do not wish to proceed with a Transaction, you will promptly inform the Company of that determination. In that case, or at any time upon the request of the Company for any reason, you will promptly, and in any event no later than 30 days after the request, deliver to the Company or, at the Company's option, destroy all Evaluation Material (and all copies, extracts, or other reproductions thereof), whether in paper, electronic, or other form or media. In the event of such a determination or request, all Evaluation Material prepared by you or your Representatives will be destroyed within such 30-day period and no copy, extract, or other reproduction thereof will be retained, whether in paper, electronic, or other form or media.**

(b) **Notwithstanding the foregoing, you may retain data or electronic records containing Evaluation Material for the purposes of backup, recovery, contingency planning, or business continuity planning so long as such data or records, to the extent not permanently deleted or overwritten in the ordinary course of business, are not accessible in the ordinary course of business and are not accessed except as required for backup, recovery, contingency planning, or business continuity purposes. If such data or records are restored or otherwise become accessible, you agree to permanently delete them.**

(c) **Through an authorized supervising officer, you shall certify in writing to the Company the destruction of the Evaluation Material, including that prepared by you or your Representatives, promptly after such destruction occurs. Notwithstanding the return or destruction of the Evaluation Material, you and your Representatives will continue to be bound by obligations of confidentiality and other obligations hereunder.**

COMMENT

The recipient is required under this provision to return to the target, or destroy, all the Evaluation Material it has received upon the recipient's decision not to proceed with a Transaction or any time when so requested by the target. Since the recipient may have written notes on documents included in the Evaluation Material that it does not wish the target to *see*, and the term "Evaluation Material" includes notes, analyses, and other work products prepared by the recipient or its Representatives that contain, reflect, or are based upon information furnished by the target or its Representatives, the recipient will often elect to destroy rather than return the Evaluation Material. In addition, it may simply be easier as an administrative matter to destroy the material than to return it. Paragraph 5(a) gives the recipient the right to destroy Evaluation Material, but Paragraph 5(c) requires that the fact of destruction of all of the Evaluation Material that is not returned be certified in writing by an authorized officer of the recipient who supervised such destruction. Bearing in mind that the knowledge gained from having reviewed the Evaluation Material will continue in the minds of the persons who did so, Paragraph 5(c) further explicitly states that the recipient and its Representatives must continue to maintain the confidentiality of all such information. Due to the difficulties in destroying certain materials because of a recipient's electronic data management system, Paragraph 5(b) specifically permits the retention of such materials for the purposes of backup, recovery, contingency planning, or business continuity planning, subject to the stated limitations.

Recipients will sometimes request that they be permitted to retain one copy of the Evaluation Material received, or possibly portions of it, for "compliance," "evidential," or "archival" purposes—such as for purposes of being able to prove, if later called upon, what information they did and did not receive. For companies engaged in some regulated industries, there may be specific regulatory requirements supporting this request as well. Outside of those industries, this request may be resisted by the target, especially where the recipient is a direct competitor. If the target does agree to this request, it should attempt to be more specific as to the reasons for such retention (and subsequent permitted use of the retained material) and should require that any such copy be maintained in a confidential and secure location and not be available to the recipient's personnel generally. For example, the target might require that any such material be maintained by outside counsel, or perhaps in separate, restricted-access files in the legal department of the recipient, and only be available for limited purposes that do not include use for competitive purposes or future acquisition activity.

Paragraph 5(a) gives the recipient up to 30 days to return or certify the destruction of all Evaluation Material it has received. This time period may be the subject of negotiation, but a short time frame may impose unreasonable burdens on the recipient.

6. PRIVILEGED INFORMATION

Neither party intends that the provision of any Evaluation Material will be deemed to waive or in any manner diminish any attorney-client privilege, attorney work product protection, or other privilege or protection applicable to any such Evaluation Material. The parties acknowledge and agree that they (a) share common legal, as well as commercial, interests in all of the Evaluation Material, (b) are or may become joint defendants in legal proceedings to which such Evaluation Material relates, and (c) intend that all such privileges and protections remain intact should either party become subject to any legal proceedings to which such Evaluation Material is relevant. In furtherance of the foregoing, each party agrees not to claim or contend that the other party has waived any attorney-client privilege, attorney work product protection, or other privilege or protection by providing information pursuant to this agreement, or any subsequent definitive agreement regarding a Transaction into which the parties may enter.

COMMENT

This provision is intended to deal with the difficult, and not uncommon, occurrence that important information relating to the target is information to which an attorney-client or other privilege or protection from disclosure is applicable, which would be jeopardized by disclosure to anyone outside the target or its legal counsel. Such information may be of great importance to the recipient in its evaluation of the target but, as the prospective owner of the target, the recipient will not want to jeopardize any privilege or protection that may apply to the information and to other information (whether or not disclosed) that relates to the same subject matter. Moreover, since there is seldom assurance that a transaction will be agreed upon and completed, the target runs the dual risk of having forfeited the attorney-client privilege and not having the benefit of a transaction. Paragraph 6 seeks to deal with this problem by relying on a form of the "joint defense" doctrine under which disclosure of confidential information among joint defendants having the same interests in litigation may be permitted without destroying the attorney-client privilege that applies to such information and that would normally be lost if the information is provided to a third party. *See* King, *The Common Interest Doctrine and Disclosure During Negotiations for Substantial Transactions*, 74 U. Chi. L. Rev. 1411 (2007).

The effectiveness of this provision is not certain. Compare Hewlett-Packard Co. v. Bausch & Lomb Inc., 115 F.R.D. 308 (N.D. Cal. 1987) (stating that parties having a common commercial interest, but not a common legal defense strategy, may share information without destroying the attorney-client privilege, although the court also noted that the prospective buyer and target referred to in the case could reasonably have expected to be subject to similar litigation from the same plaintiff), with Libbey Glass Inc. v. Oneida, Ltd., 197 F.R.D. 342 (N.D. Ohio 1999) (joint defense doctrine does not apply if the parties have only a shared commercial interest and not a shared legal defense strategy). The court in *Hewlett-Packard* reasoned that even though parties to a business transaction may never have a need to formulate a joint defense strategy, removing the attorney-client privilege from information shared in connection with consideration of a proposed business transaction could have the societal disadvantage of discouraging parties from entering into transactions. The court further noted that the parties in the case were not attempting to selectively provide only information that would be favorable in future litigation while withholding information that would be harmful. The courts in both cases stated that providing information without a confidentiality agreement would result in waiver of the privilege (great care was taken to preserve the confidentiality of the information in *Hewlett-Packard*; according to the court, none was taken in *Libbey Glass*). The *Libbey Glass* case suggests that parties seeking to rely on the joint defense doctrine should articulate in their confidentiality agreement any potential joint litigation defense concerns they may have to support the effectiveness of this type of provision. This may be most effectively done in a separate confidentiality agreement entered into at the time the privileged information is provided.

The applicability of the joint defense doctrine in this context is not certain and the effectiveness of this provision will depend upon the law of the jurisdiction involved and the facts of the particular case. The approach taken in this agreement is to include the provision as an efficient means of establishing a basis for the applicability of the joint defense doctrine should it become necessary to disclose privileged information. As suggested above, an alternative approach is to enter into a specific separate agreement with respect to particular subsets of the Evaluation Material. The separate agreement might, for example, be entered into only at a later stage in the parties' discussions regarding the possible transaction and might limit disclosure to certain persons, such as outside counsel. Some drafters also believe that dealing with the issue in this manner gives greater credibility to the position that the joint defense doctrine should apply. This would be particularly true if specific circumstances can be referred to in the separate agreement that support the conclusion that the parties have, or reasonably expect that they will have, the same or similar interests as defendants in litigation.

A further potential difficulty in dealing with attorney-client privileged information is that the recipient may have a legitimate business interest in disclosing that information for evaluation by its financial advisor or for other nonlitigation purposes. In such cases, consideration should be given to whether the disclosure of the attorney-client privileged information for the nonlitigation purpose would be permitted under the case law of the relevant jurisdiction without jeopardizing the attorney-client privilege.

Other approaches to the problem of disclosing privileged or otherwise protected information include deferring any disclosure of the relevant information until a very late stage in the discussions when a more careful evaluation of the benefits and detriments of disclosure can be made, or attempting to convey the general character of the potential liability or other issue to which the information relates without disclosing the specific information that is subject to the relevant privilege or protection in such a way as to destroy that privilege or protection.

7.   COMPLETENESS AND ACCURACY OF EVALUATION MATERIAL

We reserve the right, in our sole discretion, to determine what information we will provide or withhold, as well as the times at which we will make such information available. Neither we nor any of our Representatives have made or will make any representation or warranty, express or implied, as to the accuracy or completeness of the Evaluation Material. You agree that none of the Company, its subsidiaries, or any of their respective Representatives will have any liability to you or to your Representatives relating to or resulting from the use of the Evaluation Material or any errors therein or omissions therefrom. You also agree that you are not entitled to rely on the accuracy or completeness of any Evaluation Material and that you will be entitled to rely solely on such representations or warranties regarding the Evaluation Material or the subject matter thereof as may be made in any definitive agreement relating to a Transaction, when, as, and if entered into by the parties, and subject to such limitations and restrictions as may be specified therein.

COMMENT

The parties to a confidentiality agreement are normally not under an obligation to provide any information and are usually not willing to accept any responsibility for the accuracy or completeness of the information they do provide. The target will want to reserve the right to stage the information it provides, deferring to a later point information that is especially sensitive from a competitive or other standpoint. While each party should endeavor to provide relevant and accurate information, the nature of the typical due diligence process—often involving a large number of persons reading through voluminous files and collections of documents under tight time constraints—may make it difficult for the target to be certain of the accuracy or continuing relevance of the information that is provided and whether the recipient properly understands the information it receives. The target will also argue that it is only willing to represent the accuracy of information it supplies and to accept liability for breach of such representations in the context of a definitive acquisition agreement in which the parties can articulate with precision the factual statements being made through representations and warranties and qualifying schedules.

The effectiveness of this type of disclaimer or nonreliance provision may be subject to challenge, depending on the facts. *See* "Noncontract Remedies" in preliminary note to Article 11 and commentary to Section 11.2 of the Model Agreement. Sellers should note that the Third Circuit Court of Appeals refused to give preclusive affect to a similar clause and recognized an implied cause of action based upon Rule 10b-5 with regard to disclosures in due diligence in AES Corp. v. The Dow Chem. Co., 325 F.3d 174 (3d Cir.), *cert denied*, 540 US 1068 (2003).

As noted above, the recipient will usually agree with this provision. Nonetheless, the recipient may argue for at least some general indication that the target is using reasonable efforts to provide relevant information. The target may agree to accommodate the recipient by adding at the beginning of Paragraph 7 a phrase such as "Although we will endeavor to include in the Evaluation Material information that we believe to be relevant for the purpose of your initial evaluation, ..."

8. EFFECT OF AGREEMENT

No agreement providing for any Transaction currently exists and none will be deemed to exist between the parties unless and until a definitive written agreement with respect to a Transaction is negotiated, executed, and delivered with the intention of legally binding the parties and any other necessary parties. The parties agree that, unless and until a definitive agreement between them with respect to a Transaction has been executed and delivered by them and any such other parties with the intention of being legally bound, neither party nor any of their respective affiliates will be under any obligation of any kind with respect to a Transaction, including any obligation to commence or continue negotiations, by virtue of this agreement or any other written or oral expression with respect to such a Transaction by the parties or any of their Representatives.

COMMENT

This provision is intended to forestall any argument that the parties have already reached an agreement regarding a transaction or any of its terms, or that either party is obligated to reach such an agreement, or even to negotiate. In the absence of such a provision, a party might argue that even though the parties have not reached actual agreement on a transaction, the other party has at least an obligation to negotiate in good faith to reach such an agreement. *See* general discussion in preliminary note to Ancillary Document B—Letter of Intent.

If the confidentiality agreement is entered into in connection with an auction process in which the target is exploring the possibility of a sale to multiple potential buyers, the target's financial advisor, or the target, normally establishes the auction process procedures (required timing and procedures for submitting proposals, selection of potential buyers with whom further negotiations may be conducted, and similar matters) by means of a separate letter to the potential buyers. Such letters normally state that the procedures may be changed at any time by the target without notice and that the target retains the absolute right to terminate the process at any time. This portion of the confidentiality agreement should be coordinated with the provisions of any such auction process letter. *See* M&A PROCESS 102–15.

9. DESIGNATED CONTACT PERSON

All communications regarding any Transaction, requests for additional information, requests for facility tours or management meetings, and discussions or questions regarding procedures will be directed exclusively to _____, and neither you nor any of your Representatives will initiate or cause to be initiated any communication with any director, officer, or employee of the Company or its subsidiaries, or their Representatives, other than _____, concerning the Evaluation Material (including any requests to obtain or discuss any Evaluation Material) or any Transaction.

COMMENT

The requirement stated in this Paragraph that the recipient must communicate only with a designated contact person serves two principal purposes. First, it reduces the possibility that word of the discussions and the possibility of a transaction may leak out among the target's employees or third parties. Second, it assists in maintaining an orderly process of disclosure of information by giving greater control to the target over process and timing and by permitting it to keep a more accurate record of what information it has provided. The parties should consider whether a provision is practical in the particular circumstances. Recipients may resist this provision on the basis that it would unduly hinder their due diligence efforts.

10. NONSOLICITATION

You agree that, for a period of __ years from the date hereof, neither you nor any of your affiliates will, directly or indirectly, solicit or hire for employment any person who is currently, or at any time during the period commencing on the date hereof through the date you inform the Company that you do not wish to proceed with a Transaction becomes, an officer or employee of the Company or any of its subsidiaries.

COMMENT

The target may be concerned that in the course of consideration of a possible transaction, the recipient will develop knowledge of, and a relationship with, the target's key employees and will seek to hire those employees away if a transaction does not take place. This is most likely in the case of technology companies or other companies where there are key employees who have valuable knowledge and skills or who are especially important to the company's customer relations. Many recipients will object to nonsolicitation provisions, particularly ones that purport to apply to employees of the target who do not even know about the possible transaction. Recipients might also seek to have the nonsolicitation provisions not apply at an early stage in the process before they begin to receive information

85

about the target's employees. Even if a recipient agrees with the basic concept, it may have a number of comments to the particular provision. For example, the recipient may wish to:

- reduce the nonsolicitation period;
- limit the provision to the employees or other representatives of the recipient who are involved in (or likely to be aware of) the possible transaction;
- limit the provision to a specific subset of the target's employees defined by a specific list or category (e.g., officers, employees at the level of vice president or above, key technical or sales persons);
- specify that the prohibition does not apply to general hiring efforts of the recipient (such as advertisements in trade publications) that are not directed to the target's personnel or to situations in which a target employee seeks employment by the recipient on his or her own volition and not in response to a solicitation from the recipient.

Particularly with very large companies, the recipient may be concerned that the necessity of alerting parts of the recipient's organization other than the directly affected unit (that proposes to make an acquisition) could have the counterproductive result of endangering the confidentiality of the transaction discussions. A more extensive delineation of the permitted circumstances under which the recipient may hire employees may be stated by adding a clause along the following lines:

> ; provided, however, that the foregoing does not preclude you or your affiliates from: (a) soliciting employees through, or hiring employees who respond to, general job advertisements or similar notices that are not targeted specifically at the employees of the Company or its subsidiaries; or (b) engaging any recruiting firm or similar organization to identify or solicit persons for employment or soliciting the employment of any employee who is identified by any such recruiting firm or organization, as long as such recruiting firm or organization is not instructed to target any employees of the Company or its subsidiaries; or (c) soliciting or hiring persons who have not been employed by the Company or its subsidiaries during the previous 90 days.

Private equity firms may further be concerned to assure that the operation of this type of provision does not result in any limitations being placed on the recruitment efforts of their portfolio companies as a result of the private equity firm agreeing to the provision during the course of its due diligence investigation of an acquisition target.

Depending upon the nature of the target's business and the type of information it will be providing to the potential buyer, it may be appropriate to include other restrictive covenants in a confidentiality agreement. For example, if the target operates retail stores and is providing information regarding store-level profitability and lease terms, it might want to restrict the ability of the recipient to contact the target's landlords until after its leases expire.

11. REMEDIES

You acknowledge and agree that money damages would not be a sufficient remedy for breach of this agreement by you or any of your Representatives and that the Company will be entitled to equitable relief, including injunctions and specific performance, as a remedy for any such breach without the necessity of posting any bond or other security and without proof of irreparable harm or of any actual damages. Such remedies will nonetheless not be deemed to be the exclusive remedies for a breach of this agreement and will be in addition to all other remedies available at law or in equity.

COMMENT

The most important remedy for a breach or threatened breach of the terms of a confidentiality agreement is an injunction prohibiting disclosure of confidential information and requiring compliance with the terms of the confidentiality agreement. This Paragraph is intended to support a request for such relief by stating the parties' agreement that such relief would be appropriate and may be sought without necessity of proof of irreparable harm or actual damage or any requirement of posting a bond or other security. The Company cannot assume that such relief will be available when requested since the granting of such relief is in the discretion of the court to which the question is presented. The absence of an adequate remedy at law is one element that must be proved to obtain such relief. In addition, the possibility of injunctive relief may be of little use or comfort in view of the fact that the target often would not obtain advance knowledge of the possibility of breach of the confidentiality agreement. In some cases, such as the disclosure to the recipient of information constituting trade secrets, there may, in fact, be a substantial money damage claim that the target may pursue in the event of its improper disclosure by the recipient or its Representatives. Even in such cases, however, it may be argued that the substantial monetary damages claim would not provide an adequate remedy because the full loss suffered includes lost profits that may not be provable with sufficient certainty to be recoverable.

12. MISCELLANEOUS

COMMENT

See the Introduction to this Volume II and the commentary to Article 12 of the Model Agreement for further discussion relevant to the miscellaneous provisions.

The confidentiality agreement has no "sunset" provision and is silent on the topics of the duration of obligations of confidentiality and to what extent the obligations continue if the acquisition closes (such as in Section 12.7 of the Model Agreement) or does not close. Absent such a provision, the discloser may take the position that they continue forever. The recipient, on the other hand, will argue that at some point in time even the discloser's proprietary know-how will eventually become obsolete. Thus, a recipient will argue that all obligations of confidentiality should come to an end at some early point. The parties may wish to consider if their interests are served by "sunsetting" the confidentiality agreement as a whole or by providing different survival periods for the various obligations. Private equity funds, banks, and other financial institutions are particularly resistant to confidentiality agreements with no termination dates.

(a)   **Entire Agreement. This agreement supersedes all prior agreements, whether written or oral, between the parties with respect to its subject matter and constitutes a complete and exclusive statement of the terms of the agreement between the parties with respect to its subject matter.**

(b)   **Modification. This agreement may only be amended, supplemented, or otherwise modified by a writing executed by the parties.**

(c)   **Governing Law. All matters relating to or arising out of this agreement or any Transaction and the rights of the parties (sounding in contract, tort, or otherwise) will be governed by and construed and interpreted under the laws of the State of _____, without regard to conflicts of laws principles that would require the application of any other law.**

(d)   **Jurisdiction; Service of Process. Any proceeding arising out of or relating to this agreement or any Transaction shall be brought in the courts of the State of _____, County of _____, or, if it has or can acquire jurisdiction, in the United States District Court for the _____ District of _____, and each of the parties irrevocably submits to the exclusive jurisdiction of each such court in any such proceeding, waives any objection it may now or hereafter have to venue or to convenience of forum, agrees that all claims in respect of such proceeding shall be heard and determined only in any such court, and agrees not to bring any proceeding arising out of or relating to this agreement in any other court. Each party acknowledges and agrees that this Paragraph 12(d) constitutes a voluntary and bargained-for agreement between the parties. Process in any proceeding referred to in the first sentence of this paragraph may be served on any party anywhere in the world.**

(e)   **No Waiver. Neither any failure nor any delay by any party in exercising any right, power, or privilege under this agreement will operate as a waiver of such right, power, or privilege, and no single or partial exercise of any such right, power, or privilege will preclude any other or further exercise of such right, power, or privilege or the exercise of any other right, power, or privilege. To the maximum extent permitted by applicable law, (i) no claim or right arising out of this agreement can be waived by a party, in whole or in part, unless made in a writing signed by such party; (ii) a waiver given by a party will only be applicable to the specific instance for which it is given; and (iii) no notice to or demand on a party will (A) waive or otherwise affect any obligation of that** party or (B) affect the right of the party giving such notice or demand to take further action without notice or demand as provided in this agreement or the documents referred to in this agreement.

(f)   Severability. If any provision of this agreement is held invalid or unenforceable by any court of competent jurisdiction, the other provisions of this agreement will remain in full force and effect. Any provision of this agreement held invalid or unenforceable only in part or degree will remain in full force and effect to the extent not held invalid or unenforceable.

(g)   Counterparts/Electronic Signatures. This agreement may be executed in one or more counterparts, each of which will be deemed to be an original copy and all of which, when taken together, will be deemed to constitute one and the same agreement and will be effective when counterparts have been signed by each of the parties and delivered to the other parties. A manual signature whose image shall have been transmitted electronically will constitute an original signature for all purposes. The delivery of copies of this agreement, including executed signature pages, by electronic transmission will constitute effective delivery of this agreement for all purposes.

Please confirm your agreement with the foregoing by signing and returning one copy of this letter to the undersigned, whereupon this letter will become a binding agreement between you and us.

Very truly yours,

[TARGET]

By: _____

Name: _____

Title: _____

Accepted and agreed as of
the date first written above.

[RECIPIENT]

By: _____

Name: _____

Title: _____

ANCILLARY DOCUMENT B

Letter of Intent

PRELIMINARY NOTE

A letter of intent is often entered into between a buyer and a seller following the successful completion of the first phase of negotiations of an acquisition transaction. The letter generally, but not always, describes the purchase price (or a formula for determining the purchase price) and certain other key economic and procedural terms that form the basis for further negotiations. In most cases, the buyer and the seller do not yet intend to be legally bound to consummate the transaction and expect that the letter of intent will be superseded by a definitive written acquisition agreement. Alternatively, buyers and sellers may prefer a memorandum of understanding or a term sheet to reflect deal terms.

Although the seller and the buyer will generally desire the substantive deal terms outlined in a letter of intent to be nonbinding expressions of their then current understanding of the shape of the prospective transaction, letters of intent frequently contain some provisions that the parties intend to be binding. As discussed more fully below, the binding provisions of a letter of intent generally relate to the process of conducting the negotiations and proceeding towards a definitive agreement.

A client should have the benefit of its lawyer's advice before entering into a letter of intent. What portions of the letter of intent should be binding or nonbinding and the risks of entering into a letter of intent at all are important issues with a heavy legal overlay. The level of detail in the letter of intent and which issues should be addressed or deferred are key strategic questions that should be discussed with the client, and their likely impact on the negotiation of the acquisition should be fully explored.

There are several reasons why letters of intent are used. A buyer and a seller frequently prefer a letter of intent to test the waters before incurring the costs of negotiating a definitive agreement and performing due diligence. The parties may also feel morally, if not legally, obligated to key terms once they are set down in writing. Sometimes the deal terms are sufficiently complicated that it is helpful to put them down in writing to ensure that the buyer and seller have consistent expectations.

Signing a letter of intent at an earlier stage of the acquisition process, rather than waiting for the definitive agreement, can facilitate compliance with regulatory requirements. For example, a premerger notification form can be filed under the HSR Act upon entering into a letter of intent, thereby starting the clock on the applicable waiting period. *See* the discussion of the HSR Act in Section 1.1 of the Model Agreement. A signed letter of intent may also assist the buyer in convincing prospective lenders or investors to evaluate the transaction for the purpose of providing financing. The letter of intent often provides an outline for the transaction that can be used as the basis for drafting the definitive agreement.

Letters of intent are also used to define the rights and obligations of the parties while a definitive agreement is being negotiated. For example, an exclusivity provision is often included, which prohibits the seller from negotiating with another party while negotiations with the buyer are ongoing. A letter of intent, either alone or in conjunction with a separate confidentiality agreement, will usually permit the buyer to inspect the target's properties and to review its operations and books and records while simultaneously restricting the buyer's ability to disclose and use the target's trade secrets and other proprietary information received during the negotiations. A letter of intent often covers how expenses of the acquisition and negotiations, such as fees and expenses of brokers, attorneys, and other advisors, will be paid and limits the rights of each party to publicize the acquisition or negotiations without the consent of the other party. A letter of intent may establish the time frame for conducting due diligence and closing the acquisition and certain other milestones and pre-conditions prior to the execution of a definitive agreement or the closing of the transaction.

Many commentators and business lawyers believe that the effect of a letter of intent is generally more favorable to the buyer than to the seller. An exclusivity provision in the letter of intent may prevent the seller from introducing other interested parties to the acquisition to enhance its negotiating position with the buyer. In those cases where a letter of intent is not used, the buyer might consider entering into a separate exclusivity agreement with the seller. If actual or suspected problems are uncovered during due diligence, the buyer may try to use that information to negotiate a lower purchase price or more favorable terms. A signed letter of intent, even if not binding, together with the buyer's inspection of the target's properties and review of its operations and books and records, often will create an expectation on the part of the target's employees, vendors, customers, lenders, or investors that a sale to the buyer will occur. Buyer's investigation of the target may also uncover information that can be used by the buyer to compete with the target if the sale is not consummated, even if the target receives protection against the disclosure or use by the buyer of the target's trade secrets and other proprietary information.

Notwithstanding these considerations, a seller is often as insistent as a buyer that a letter of intent be executed before work on a definitive agreement is begun. One reason may be that the negotiation of a letter of intent provides the seller with an excellent opportunity to negotiate certain key acquisition issues at a time when the seller possesses maximum leverage. The seller may also feel pressure to show some evidence of a prospective transaction to lenders or other interested persons. If the seller is not bound by an exclusivity provision, it may want to use the letter of intent to prompt other potential buyers to compete for the business transaction opportunity.

A controlled auction process (*see* M&A PROCESS ch. 6) may or may not include a letter of intent, depending on how the process is conducted, the completeness of documentation, and other timing issues.

Although letters of intent are common, no consensus exists among business lawyers regarding their desirability. Many lawyers advise their clients that the great disadvantage of a letter of intent is that provisions intended by the parties to be nonbinding may be later found by a court to be binding. There is often an inherent conflict between the goals of the parties in negotiating a letter of intent. The buyer generally is most interested in securing exclusivity or other standstill types of provisions from the seller while seeking to maintain great flexibility regarding the purchase price and other key provisions that may be impacted by the results of the buyer's acquisition review of the target. The seller, on the other hand, generally will attempt to define more clearly the purchase price, limitations on its exposure with respect to the representations that will be part of the definitive agreement, and key terms of employment agreements, noncompete covenants, and other ancillary arrangements. If possible, the seller will prefer to avoid altogether, or to limit the scope of, any exclusivity commitment. The negotiation of a letter of intent can sometimes become bogged down in detailed discussions that are generally reserved to the negotiation of the definitive agreement. Because of these twin concerns of the possible, but unintended, binding nature of the letter of intent and the risk that the negotiation of the letter of intent will become mired in endless detail, lawyers often advise their clients to forgo a letter of intent and commence negotiation of a definitive agreement.

It is helpful at the outset to determine the client's desires as to whether a letter of intent is binding. For example, the acquisition may be so economically or strategically attractive that the client is willing, as a business decision, to risk being bound at this initial stage. The parties might also intend to be bound if the acquisition review has been completed and all economic issues have been settled. However, a fully binding letter of intent can lead to problems and unexpected results if the parties later are unable to agree to the terms of a definitive agreement. In that event, a court may impose upon the parties its interpretation of commercially reasonable terms for any unresolved issues.

At the stage in the transaction when the letter of intent is signed, the transaction itself usually is still conditional in nature. Most often, many terms have not even been considered, much less discussed or settled. Moreover, due diligence is rarely completed at this stage and quite often not even commenced, and both parties may be oblivious to many potential pitfalls. Accordingly, the buyer may want to avoid specifics on many business deal points. This strategy may enhance the buyer's negotiating position by deferring discussions on these key issues until after the buyer has completed its due diligence and the seller's negotiating position has been compromised by executing a letter of intent. The seller, on the other hand, will want in most cases to resolve all important issues at the letter of intent stage when the seller may have its greatest negotiating leverage. For example, the seller may want to negotiate limitations with respect to its indemnification obligations in the letter of intent by providing for a cap, a basket, an expiration of the indemnification obligations, reliance on the indemnity provisions as the buyer's exclusive remedy, or some combination of these concepts. The seller may also seek to avoid guaranties and draconian escrows at the outset by facing these issues at the letter of intent stage.

LEGAL PRINCIPLES

The legal principles for determining whether a letter of intent is binding are fairly easy to state, although often difficult to apply:

- If the parties intend not to be bound to each other prior to the execution of a definitive agreement, the courts will give effect to that intent, and the parties will not be bound until the agreement has been executed. This is true even if all issues in the negotiations have been resolved. *See* R. G. Group, Inc. v. Horn & Hardart Co., 751 F.2d 69 (2d Cir. 1984); V'Soske v. Barwick, 404 F.2d 495 (2d Cir. 1968).

- On the other hand, if the parties intend to be bound prior to the execution of a definitive agreement, the courts will also give effect to that intent and the parties will be bound even though they contemplate replacing their earlier understanding with a definitive agreement at a later date. *See* Texaco, Inc. v. Pennzoil Co., 729 S.W.2d 768 (Tex. App. 1987), *cert. denied*, 485 U.S. 994 (1988); *but see* Durbin v. Dal-Briar Corp., 871 S.W.2d 263 (Tex. App. 1991); *cf.* Isern v. Ninth Court of Appeals, 925 S.W.2d 604 (Tex. 1996) (superseded by statute), *cert. denied*, Watson v. Isern, 117 S. Ct. 612 (1996); R. G. Group, 751 F.2d at 74; V'Soske v. Barwick, 404 F.2d 495 (2d Cir. 1968).

- Parties intending to be bound prior to the execution of a definitive agreement will be bound even if there are certain issues that have not been resolved. Depending upon the importance of the open items, the courts will either supply commercially reasonable terms for those unresolved issues or impose a contractual duty on the parties to negotiate the resolution of those issues in good faith. *See* Itek Corp. v. Chicago Aerial Indus., Inc., 248 A.2d 625 (Del. 1968). When the courts impose a duty to negotiate open terms in good faith, they will impose liability if one party acts in bad faith. *See* Fickes v. Sun Expert, Inc., 762 F. Supp. 998 (D. Mass. 1991). On the other hand, if the parties do negotiate in good faith, the fact that a final agreement is not reached will not result in liability. *See* Feldman v. Allegheny Int'l, Inc., 850 F.2d 1217 (7th Cir. 1988). *See also* Copeland v. Baskin Robbins U.S.A., 117 Cal. Rptr. 2d 875 (Cal. App. 2002) (contract may constitute agreement to negotiate in good faith).

In determining whether the parties intend to be bound, the courts generally examine the following factors:

- the actual words of the document;
- the context of the negotiations;
- whether either or both parties have partially performed their obligations;
- whether there are any issues left to negotiate; and
- whether the subject matter of the discussions concerns complex business matters that customarily involve definitive written agreements.

See Teachers Ins. and Annuity Ass'n v. Tribune Co., 670 F. Supp. 491 (S.D.N.Y. 1987); Arcadian Phosphates, Inc. v. Arcadian Corp., 884 F. 2d 69 (2d Cir. 1989); Texaco, 729 S.W.2d at 768; R. G. Group, Inc. v. Horn & Hardart Co., 751 F.2d 69 (2d Cir. 1984).

Courts have consistently stated that the most important factor in determining whether or which provisions in a letter of intent are binding is the language used by the parties in the document. The language of the letter of intent should, therefore, be definite and precise. A lawyer might advise the client, however, to avoid factual situations and subsequent communications that have led some courts to find provisions of a letter of intent to be binding despite language seemingly to the contrary in the document. There are many things that can overcome the carefully crafted words in a letter of intent purporting to make a document or certain provisions in a document nonbinding. Loosely worded e-mails, oral communications, and other actions are often given great weight by courts in interpreting the intent of the parties. Oral statements such as "Looks like we have a deal!" or handshakes can indicate an intent to be bound. *See* American Cyanamid Co. v. Elizabeth Arden Sales Corp., 331 F. Supp. 597 (S.D.N.Y. 1971); Computer Sys. of Am., Inc. v. IBM Corp., 795 F.2d 1086 (1st Cir. 1986). *But see* Reprosystem, B. V. v. SCM Corp., 727 F.2d 257 (2d Cir. 1984), *cert. denied*, 469 U.S. 828 (1984); R. G. Group, 751 F.2d 75–76 (2d Cir. 1984); Seaman's Direct Buying Serv., Inc. v. Standard Oil Co., 686 P.2d 1158 (Cal. 1984).

When parties to a letter of intent have clearly identified that certain provisions are binding (such as exclusivity) and others are not, courts will enforce the binding provisions as bargained-for agreements and not lightly read in unstated exceptions such as fiduciary outs. *See* Global Asset Capital, LLC vs. Rubicon US Reit, Inc., C.A. No. 5071-VCL (Del. Ch. Nov. 16, 2009).

SAMPLE LETTERS OF INTENT

Two illustrative letters of intent are provided below. The first ("Long Form") is a much more comprehensive and legally precise form, designed to flush out many of the pertinent issues and to make very clear which elements of the letter are binding and which are not. The second illustrative letter of intent ("Short Form") is a much shorter, less formal, and less legalistic form that might be used when one or both of the parties are very anxious to sign a letter of intent on short notice at an early stage of discussion, while preserving protections against later litigation if negotiations break off.

Both illustrative letters of intent contemplate the proposed acquisition by a single corporate buyer of all the outstanding capital stock of a privately held company from its shareholders. The purchase price would be payable with a combination of cash and notes, and a portion of the cash payment due at closing would be escrowed. This fact pattern is consistent with the Fact Pattern for the Model Agreement.

Both illustrative letters of intent have been prepared as a buyer's first draft, recognizing the custom that the buyer or its counsel will generally prepare the first draft of a letter of intent.

Letters of intent such as the Short Form that are less formal and comprehensive can also be effective, and many clients prefer a less comprehensive approach. The primary advantages of a comprehensive, longer letter of intent, such as the Long Form, are: (a) issues that are deal-breakers can be identified early in the negotiation process before substantial expenses are incurred in due diligence and the drafting of a definitive agreement with any accompanying disclosure letter or schedules, (b) resolution of difficult issues at the letter of intent stage facilitates the negotiation of a definitive agreement, permitting the buyer more time and energy to prepare for the transition to its ownership of the target, and (c) legal counsel for both parties are sometimes more successful in prompting their clients to focus on and understand important issues that might otherwise be lost or misunderstood in the much more complex, definitive documents. The primary disadvantage of a comprehensive letter of intent such as the Long Form is that it may burden the negotiations with too many difficult issues too early in the process and may impede the deal's momentum or even cause a breakdown in the negotiations that may have been avoided if certain issues had been deferred. Consideration should be given to the strategic impact of a comprehensive letter of intent on the negotiating dynamics of a deal before a letter of intent based upon the Long Form is prepared.

The Long Form is divided into two parts: provisions intended not to be binding and provisions intended to be binding. The nonbinding provisions consist primarily of the business deal points, such as a description of the proposed transaction, the purchase price, and key ancillary agreements. The binding provisions focus on the regulation of the negotiation process, including access for the buyer to conduct its due diligence, exclusivity, payment of the parties' expenses, and termination provisions. The nonbinding and binding portions of the Long Form are clearly delineated to assist a court in determining the intent of the parties, if that becomes necessary. Another common format is to set out binding and nonbinding provisions without grouping them in separate parts and to include a general statement that the entire letter of intent is nonbinding, except for certain provisions that are specifically itemized by paragraph number. This is the format used in the Short Form. Care should be taken where the itemization is by reference to paragraph numbers or letters that redrafting changes do not result in inadvertent reference to the wrong paragraphs.

Given the many considerations involved in negotiating a letter of intent, it cannot be overemphasized that virtually everything in a letter of intent is subject to variation based upon the particular context of the proposed acquisition. There is no such thing as a standard letter of intent applicable to all proposed acquisitions.

With respect to letters of intent in general, *see* M&A PROCESS ch. 8; Kling & Nugent Ch. 6; Spreen, *Ten Practice Tips for Negotiating the Letter of Intent*, DEAL LAW. 13 (May-June 2008).

LONG FORM LETTER OF INTENT

[Date]

Seller [1]

Seller [2]

. . .

Seller [8]

Ladies and Gentlemen:

This letter will confirm that _____ ("Buyer") is interested in acquiring all the outstanding capital stock (the "Shares") of _____ (the "Company") from you ("Sellers"), all the Company's shareholders. In this letter, (a) the Company and its subsidiaries are called the "Acquired Companies," and (b) Buyer's possible acquisition of Shares (or other acquisition of the Company) is sometimes called the "Possible Acquisition."

PART ONE—NONBINDING PROVISIONS

The parties wish to commence negotiating a definitive written acquisition agreement providing for the Possible Acquisition (a "Definitive Agreement"). To facilitate the negotiation of a Definitive Agreement, the parties request that Buyer's counsel prepare an initial draft. The execution of any Definitive Agreement would be subject to the satisfactory completion of Buyer's ongoing investigation of the Acquired Companies' business and would also be subject to approval by Buyer's board of directors.

Based upon the information currently known to Buyer, it is proposed that the Definitive Agreement would include the following terms:

COMMENT

The introductory paragraphs of Part One make explicit the customary practice that the buyer and its counsel prepare the initial draft of the definitive agreement. This allows the buyer to control the drafting process and the timing of negotiations. Sellers may counter, requesting that the Letter of Intent contain specific dates by which drafts will be prepared, comments received, new drafts prepared, and similar deadlines.

The introductory paragraphs put Sellers on notice that the form of any definitive agreement must be approved by Buyer's board of directors. In addition, this provision may provide Buyer with some protection if the nonbinding provisions are determined to be binding and enforceable. *See* A/S Apothekernes Laboratorium v. LM.C. Chemical Group, Inc., 873 F.2d 155 (7th Cir. 1989). Sellers may object to this provision and instead insist that the Letter of Intent contain a specific confirmation that Buyer's board has approved the Letter of Intent.

The initial phrase of the last paragraph of this introductory section ("Based on the information currently known to Buyer. . . .") is intended to provide Buyer with a defensible moral and legal (if the provisions of Part One are construed to be binding) position that its due diligence of the target may result in Buyer offering a lower purchase price or different terms than those contained in the Letter of Intent.

1. BASIC TRANSACTION

Sellers would sell all the Shares to Buyer at the price (the "Purchase Price") set forth in Paragraph 2 at the closing of the Possible Transaction (the "Closing"), which is expected to be no later than _____.

COMMENT

Paragraph 1 and each of the other paragraphs of Part One state the business deal points of the proposed acquisition. As mentioned in the Preliminary Note, these deal points correspond to the assumptions underlying the Model Agreement, which contains commentary that may also be applicable to Part One.

In Paragraph 1 and throughout Part One, the word "would" is used This word is intended to convey the conditional nature of the proposed acquisition and to contrast with the more definite words used in the binding provisions of Part Two, such as "will." Other conditional terms may also be used, such as "prospective buyer," "prospective seller," and "proposed transaction." While the conditional language of Part One may appear awkward and stilted at times, it provides another indication of the parties' intent that the provisions of Part One are not be binding.

2. PURCHASE PRICE

The Purchase Price would be $_____ (subject to adjustment as described below) and would be paid in the following manner:

(a)   at the Closing, Buyer would pay Sellers $_____ in cash;

(b)   at the Closing, Buyer would deposit with a mutually acceptable escrow holder $_____, which would be held in escrow for a period of at least _____ years in order to secure the performance of Sellers' obligations under the Definitive Agreement; and

(c)   at the Closing, Buyer would execute and deliver to each Seller an unsecured nonnegotiable promissory note. The promissory notes to be delivered to Sellers by Buyer would have an aggregate principal amount of $_____, bear interest at the rate of _____ % per annum, mature on the _____ anniversary of the Closing, and provide for _____ equal [annual] [quarterly] payments of principal along with [annual] [quarterly] payments of accrued interest.

The Purchase Price assumes that the Acquired Companies have consolidated shareholders' equity of at least $_____ as of the Closing. The Purchase Price would be adjusted based on changes in the Acquired Companies' consolidated shareholders' equity as of the Closing on a dollar-for-dollar basis.

COMMENT

If Buyer expects to require an escrow or other holdback of a portion of the proposed purchase price, it may be important to include a specific provision to that effect. At the letter of intent stage, Buyer typically may not be able to determine or defend a specific amount to be escrowed. Buyer will be better able to do so following its due diligence. Even if the amount of the escrow or holdback is not yet determined, a statement that one will be required will put Sellers on notice and should make the subsequent negotiation of that issue easier. Obtaining Sellers' agreement to an escrow or holdback is difficult if the issue has not been raised prior to signing a letter of intent and the due diligence fails to reveal any compelling new reasons for one.

Buyer may also want to describe known areas of potential liability, such as environmental clean-up and pending litigation, that will affect the purchase price. By putting Sellers on notice at an early stage that such liabilities will affect the purchase price, escrowed amount, or other amounts held back, Buyer's position to negotiate these issues in the definitive agreement should be enhanced.

There are a variety of purchase price adjustment mechanisms that may be included in any particular transaction. For example, the purchase price adjustment may include limitations in the form of caps, collars, and floors. The parties may desire the letter of intent to include detailed provisions describing the timing, method, and process of calculating the purchase price adjustment, although such details are usually subject to heavy negotiation that might be more appropriate to the negotiation of the definitive agreement. The parties should be sensitive to the fact that post-closing purchase price adjustments can be the subject of considerable dispute and contention, especially if they are complex or include criteria that can be manipulated by one of the parties. The parties may wish to reference in general terms a specific type of dispute resolution mechanism that would be contained in the definitive agreement to address the possibility of disagreement on the purchase price adjustment. The parties may also agree to place a portion of the purchase price in a separate escrow to facilitate payment of the adjustment amount. For further discussion on purchase price adjustments, *see* Sections 2.5 and 2.6 of the Model Agreement and related commentary.

3. EMPLOYMENT AND NONCOMPETITION AGREEMENTS

At the Closing:

(a) **the Company and _____ would enter into a _____ -year employment agreement pursuant to which he/she would agree to continue to serve as the Company's _____ and would be entitled to receive a salary of $_____ per year; and**

(b) **each Seller would execute a _____ -year noncompetition agreement in favor of Buyer.**

COMMENT

The noncompetition provisions may be included within the definitive acquisition agreement or, as provided in this sample letter of intent, as a separate agreement. Paragraph 3 does not contemplate separate consideration for the noncompetition covenants. The parties should consult qualified tax advisors on the tax consequences of allocating (or failing to allocate) a portion of the purchase price to noncompetition obligations. *See* the commentary to Sections 2.2 and 7.2 of the Model Agreement.

If more than one transaction document contains noncompetition provisions, care should be taken to ensure that they are consistent and do not cause unnecessary tax risks. *See* Appendix C—Considerations Regarding Employment Agreements in Connection with Sale of Stock and commentary to Section 7.2 of the Model Agreement for further discussions of these and other issues.

4. OTHER TERMS

Sellers would make comprehensive representations and warranties to Buyer and would provide comprehensive covenants, indemnities, and other protections for the benefit of Buyer. The consummation of the Possible Acquisition by Buyer would be subject to the satisfaction of various conditions required to be satisfied prior to Closing, which would include, but not be limited to, the following:

(a) Sellers will own 100% of the outstanding capital stock of the Company, and the Shares will be free and clear of all liens and encumbrances;

(b) There will have been no material adverse change in the business or financial condition of any Acquired Company;

(c) Buyer's satisfactory environmental audit of all real properties owned or occupied by each Acquired Company;

(d) Between the date of the Definitive Agreement and the Closing, Sellers will cause the Acquired Companies to operate their business in the ordinary course and to refrain from any extraordinary transactions;

(e) The truth and accuracy of the representations and warranties of Sellers set forth in the Definitive Agreement;

(f) Sellers will have performed or complied in all material respects with all agreements required by the Definitive Agreement to be performed or complied with by them; and

(g) Such other conditions as are customary in transactions of this type.

COMMENT

Specific representations and covenants may be added to Paragraph 4, as well as the survival period of representations, indemnification limits, and related provisions. Unless Buyer has specific concerns prior to signing the Letter of Intent, Buyer will generally prefer to defer discussions regarding these provisions to negotiation of the definitive agreement until its due diligence of the target is more advanced and Sellers' negotiating position may be weaker. The absence of specific provisions in the letter of intent, however, may encourage Sellers to request a full discussion of the representations and covenants that will be required. Moreover, Sellers may recognize that the negotiation of the letter of intent affords it an opportunity to establish limits on representations, covenants, and indemnities that may be subsequently difficult to obtain. Usually, the extent of representations and indemnities given by Sellers in a particular transaction will depend on the circumstances surrounding the transaction. For example, the sale of a distressed company may result in a lower purchase price, but be made with limited or no warranty protection or strict limitations on Sellers' liability. It may benefit the parties to use the letter of intent as an opportunity to establish a common expectation with respect to the scope of representations, covenants, and indemnities.

While many specific conditions to the acquisition may be omitted from a letter of intent and included in the definitive agreement, vital, "deal-breaking" terms and conditions are often included at this stage. If the letter of intent gives rise to an obligation to negotiate in good faith, the introduction of new terms and conditions not included may constitute bad-faith negotiations. In one extreme example, a buyer's good-faith attempt, albeit unsuccessful, to obtain financing was held to be bad-faith negotiating because the letter of intent did not make the acquisition contingent on obtaining financing. *See* Bruce v. Marcheson Implementos E. Maquinos Agriculas Tatu, S.A., 1990 U.S. Dist. LEXIS 18527 (S.D. Iowa 1990).

Buyer may want to list in Paragraph 4 all conditions precedent to the acquisition that will eventually appear in the definitive agreement to ensure that Sellers are fully aware at an early stage of what will be required. An alternative and more often used strategy would be to include only those conditions that differ from the standard conditions precedent that commonly appear in acquisition agreements and otherwise state that the agreement would contain conditions customarily included in agreements of this type.

Any other key terms or assumptions of the proposed acquisition should be added to Paragraph 4 or elsewhere in the nonbinding provisions of Part One.

PART TWO—BINDING PROVISIONS

The parties, intending to be legally bound, agree to the following legally enforceable paragraphs of this letter.

5. ACCESS

Sellers will cause the Company to afford Buyer and its duly authorized representatives full and free access to each Acquired Company, its personnel, properties, contracts, books and records, and all other documents and data, subject to the Confidentiality Agreement referred to in Paragraph 8.

COMMENT

Paragraph 5 specifies Sellers' binding obligation to cooperate in Buyer's due diligence investigation. Sellers must not only provide Buyer and its representatives access to each Acquired Company's properties and books and records but also access to their personnel.

Sellers may be reluctant to disclose certain information about the Acquired Companies' customers, marketing strategies, new products, and other sensitive areas until after the definitive agreement is executed or later. Sometimes staged access to such information is negotiated in the letter of intent.

Sellers may object to "full and free" access, which may mean regardless of the time of day and regardless of the disruption caused. *See* commentary to Section 5.1 of the Model Agreement for a discussion of reasonable access.

In the event that a significant portion of the purchase price is to be paid with promissory notes or Buyer securities, Sellers will likely request certain information from, and due diligence rights with respect to, Buyer. In most cases, Buyer may seek to limit its disclosure obligations to financial information and developments that may materially and adversely affect its business.

6. EXCLUSIVE DEALING

(a)   **Sellers will not, and will cause the Acquired Companies not to, directly or indirectly, through any representative or otherwise, solicit or entertain offers from, negotiate with or in any manner encourage, discuss, accept, or consider any proposal of any other person relating to the acquisition of the Shares or the Acquired Companies, their assets or business, in whole or in part, whether directly or indirectly, through purchase, merger, consolidation, or otherwise (other than sales of inventory in the ordinary course); and**

(b)   **Sellers will immediately notify Buyer regarding any contact between Sellers, any Acquired Company, or their respective representatives and any other person regarding any such offer or proposal or any related inquiry and if made in writing furnish a copy thereof.**

COMMENT

Paragraph 6 restricts Sellers from soliciting or considering other offers to acquire the target until the letter of intent is terminated. This provision is commonly known as an exclusivity provision and is often the primary goal of Buyer in entering into a letter of intent. *See* Section 5.6 of the Model Agreement for a more detailed discussion of these provisions and the issues they raise. This Paragraph, which also provides that Sellers will immediately notify Buyer of any third-party overture, should better enable Buyer to react to a competing offer.

Buyer might require, in the event of breach, an obligation to pay fees such as the following:

(c) In the event of Sellers' breach of this Paragraph 6, Sellers will jointly and severally reimburse Buyer's reasonable out-of-pocket costs and expenses incurred in the course of pursuing the Possible Acquisition (including, without limitation, reasonable legal and financial advisor fees) and incurred up to and including the Termination Date or 90 days after the date of this letter, whichever is earlier.

Even if Sellers were to agree to such a provision, they might suggest: "The remedy provided in this Paragraph 6(c) will be Buyer's sole and exclusive remedy for

Sellers' breach of its obligations under this Paragraph 6." Sellers also may request a cap on any amounts reimbursable under this provision. In the alternative, the parties often agree upon a specific liquidated damages amount in lieu of or in addition to expense reimbursement.

An aggressive Buyer may also require that Sellers pay a break-up fee or topping fee as recompense for the Buyer serving as a stalking horse that results in Sellers receiving a more attractive offer for the target. A topping fee is typically computed by reference to the amount by which a successful third-party offer exceeds the offer made by the Buyer. These types of fees are unusual in private transactions, generally being limited to public company acquisitions and bankruptcy sales, and Buyer may face considerable resistance from Sellers with respect to this type of provision. The actual formulation of this provision is highly variable.

7. CONDUCT OF BUSINESS

Sellers shall cause the Acquired Companies to operate in the ordinary course and to refrain from any transactions outside the ordinary course of business.

COMMENT

Buyer will want to restrict Sellers from shifting assets or otherwise affecting the operations of the Acquired Companies in a way that may reduce Acquired Companies' value before specific provisions are put in place in a definitive agreement. This sample provision could be modified to require Sellers only to notify Buyer in advance of any extraordinary transactions or conduct outside the ordinary course of business, thereby providing Buyer with the opportunity both to learn promptly of such activities and to alert Sellers if Buyer believes such activities will have a negative effect on their negotiations toward a definitive agreement. Sellers may object to these levels of restraint on the operation of the Acquired Companies' business in the absence of any binding agreement on the terms of a sale or earnest money payments by Buyer. The sample provision may also be modified to detail more specific prohibitions or exclusions based on the particular concerns of the parties.

Sellers may be concerned about the overly restrictive nature of this covenant, particularly considering its duration. *See* commentary to Section 5.2 of the Model Agreement.

In any event, Buyer should take care not to involve itself too directly in the operation of the Acquired Companies' business prior to the signing of a definitive agreement. Such involvement may be a factor used by the court to determine that the parties intended the letter of intent to bind them to the proposed acquisition. *See* Computer Systems of America, Inc. v. IBM Corp., 795 F.2d 1086 (1st Cir. 1986). *But see* Skycom Corp. v. Telstar Corp., 813 F.2d 810 (7th Cir. 1987).

Buyer, particularly if a competitor of the target, would also be concerned about the antitrust implications of such involvement. *See* commentary to Sections 5.1 and 5.2 of the Model Agreement.

8. CONFIDENTIALITY

Except as expressly modified by the Binding Provisions, the Confidentiality Agreement entered into by the Company and Buyer on _____ (the "Confidentiality Agreement") shall remain in full force and effect.

COMMENT

Parties commonly enter into a confidentiality agreement prior to negotiating a letter of intent. If a confidentiality agreement between the parties was previously entered into and continues in effect, Paragraph 8 can be used. If not, the parties might deal with confidentiality by a binding provision in the letter of intent or by means of a separate agreement. *See* Ancillary Document A—Confidentiality Agreement.

9. HART-SCOTT-RODINO

Buyer and Sellers shall proceed, as promptly as is reasonably practical, to prepare and to file any notifications required by the Hart-Scott-Rodino Antitrust Improvements Act of 1976 ("HSR Act").

COMMENT

Paragraph 9 adds a contractual obligation for both parties to jointly make appropriate Hart-Scott-Rodino filings, if required. Such filings will start the clock on the applicable waiting period, thereby reducing the time between the execution of the definitive agreement and the closing of the acquisition.

10. COSTS

Buyer and each Seller will be responsible for and bear all of its respective costs and expenses (including any broker's or finder's fees and the expenses of their representatives) incurred at any time in connection with pursuing or consummating the Possible Acquisition. Notwithstanding the preceding sentence, Buyer will pay one-half and Sellers will pay one-half of the HSR Act filing fees.

COMMENT

Paragraph 10 establishes how the parties will allocate the legal and other fees and expenses in the transaction and the Hart-Scott-Rodino filing fee prior to the execution of a definitive agreement. The definitive agreement, if one is executed, will generally include a provision dealing with such fees and expenses. The division of the Hart-Scott-Rodino filing fee is pro-Buyer, since the fee is imposed on Buyer absent agreement to the contrary. Sometimes one of the parties has the leverage to have its fees covered by the other party (or the target) up to some specified maximum amount. *See* commentary to Section 1.1 of the Model Agreement.

Buyer may want to require a sharing arrangement, or otherwise address the cost of a Phase I or Phase II environmental audit, if one or more will be commenced prior to the execution of a definitive agreement.

11. TERMINATION

The Binding Provisions will automatically terminate upon the earliest of the following (the "Termination Date"): (i) _____, (ii) execution of the Definitive Agreement by all parties, (iii) the mutual written agreement of Buyer and Sellers, or (iv) written notice of termination by Buyer, for any reason or no reason, with or without cause, at any time; provided, however, that the termination of the Binding Provisions will not affect the liability of a party for breach of any of the Binding Provisions prior to the termination. Upon termination of the Binding Provisions, the parties will have no further obligations under this letter, except Paragraph 13 will survive such termination.

COMMENT

Buyer's unilateral termination right could result in a demand by Sellers that the parties agree to negotiate in good faith toward the execution of a definitive agreement. If the parties specifically intend to require good-faith negotiations, they should so state. Such a provision has its dangers, though. Some commentators have suggested that the inclusion of a good-faith requirement in the binding provisions may encourage a court to construe a binding element to the nonbinding provisions as well. *See* Farnsworth, *Precontractual Liability and Preliminary Agreements: Fair Dealing and Failed Negotiations*, 87 COL. L. REV. 217 (1987). Accordingly, it may be advisable (as has been done in the sample letter of intent) to avoid the good-faith requirement language and rely on a break-up or topping fee or some other protection for Buyer. The letter of intent could specifically exclude a duty of either party to negotiate any aspect of the transaction in good faith. Such a provision is unusual, however, since the language could be interpreted by business persons as equivalent to indicating an intent to operate in bad faith.

Sellers would negotiate for the shortest possible date to be filled in the blank, while Buyer would insert a later date.

Sellers may negotiate for their own termination right. In that event, Buyer might negotiate for the survival of certain Binding Provisions, e.g., Paragraph 6. Such a survival may be intended to discourage Sellers from terminating the Binding Provisions if Sellers' objective is to take another offer.

12. EFFECT OF LETTER

The provisions of Paragraphs 1 through 4 of this letter are intended only as an expression of interest on behalf of Buyer, are not intended to be legally binding on any party or Acquired Company, and are expressly subject to the negotiation and execution of an appropriate Definitive Agreement. In addition, nothing in this letter should be construed as an offer or commitment on the part of Buyer to submit a definitive proposal. Except as expressly provided in Paragraphs 5 through 13 (or as expressly provided in any binding written agreement that the parties may enter into in the future), no past or future action, course of conduct, or failure to act relating to the Possible Acquisition, or relating to the negotiation of the terms of the Possible Acquisition or any Definitive Agreement, will give rise to or serve as a basis for any obligation or other liability on the part of the parties or any of the Acquired Companies.

COMMENT

Paragraph 12 makes it clear that the parties do not intend to create a legally binding obligation with respect to Part One. A clear expression of this intent is desirable and, as noted in the preliminary note, courts have on occasion refused to give less precise words a nonbinding effect. For example, some cases have held language that the letter of intent is "subject to" a definitive agreement merely states a condition subsequent rather than the requisite intent not to be bound. *See, e.g.,* Computer Systems of America, Inc. v. IBM Corp., 795 F.2d 1086 (1st Cir. 1986); Teachers Ins. & Annuity Ass'n v. Tribune Co., 670 F. Supp. 491 (S.D.N.Y. 1987); Texaco, Inc. v. Pennzoil Co., 729 S.W.2d 768 (Tex. App. 1987), *cert. denied,* 485 U.S. 994 (1988). One of these cases also found that the parties had entered into a contract of preliminary commitment binding one another to negotiate in good faith, an obligation arising from the "subject to" language. *See* Teachers Insurance & Annuity Ass'n., 670 F. Supp. at 500. The phrase "no past or future action, course of conduct, or failure to act relating to the Possible Acquisition . . . will give rise to or serve as a basis for any obligation or other liability on the part of any of the parties or any of the Acquired Companies" is an attempt to remove the possibility that oral communications or other actions can give rise to a binding obligation. The broad exculpatory language to relieve parties of any liability, should the other party claim that the nonbinding provisions are binding, is intended to allow a party to withdraw from the acquisition at any stage prior to the execution of a definitive agreement. Notwithstanding this precise language regarding future conduct and lack of liability, there will remain some risk that a court may give effect to oral communications and other actions in interpreting the intent of the parties. *See* the discussion in the Preliminary Note.

13. MISCELLANEOUS

COMMENT

See the Introduction to this Volume II and commentary to Article 12 of the Model Agreement for further discussion relevant to the miscellaneous provisions.

(a)   **Entire Agreement. The Binding Provisions supersede all prior agreements, whether written or oral, between the parties with respect to its subject matter and constitute a complete and exclusive statement of the terms of the agreement between the parties with respect to its subject matter.**

COMMENT

Paragraph 13(a) is intended to prevent any prior writings, understandings, discussions, or conduct from being integrated into or otherwise affecting the letter of intent.

(b)   **Modification. The letter may only be amended, supplemented, or otherwise modified by a writing executed by the parties.**

(c)   **Governing Law. All matters relating to or arising out of a Possible Acquisition and the rights of the parties (sounding in contract, tort, or otherwise) will be governed by and construed and interpreted under the laws of the State of _____, without regard to conflicts of laws principles that would require the application of any other law.**

(d)   **Jurisdiction; Service of Process. Any proceeding arising out of or relating to a Possible Acquisition shall be brought in the courts of the State of _____, County of _____, or, if it has or can acquire jurisdiction, in the United States District Court for the _____ District of _____, and each of the parties irrevocably submits to the exclusive jurisdiction of each such court in any such proceeding, waives any objection it may now or hereafter have to venue or to convenience of forum, agrees that all claims in respect of such proceeding shall be heard and determined only in any such court, and agrees not to bring any proceeding arising out of or relating to a Possible Acquisition in any other court. Each party acknowledges and agrees that this Paragraph 13(d) constitutes a voluntary and bargained- for agreement between the parties. Process in any proceeding may be served on any party anywhere in the world.**

(e)   **Counterparts. This letter may be executed in one or more counterparts, each of which will be deemed to be an original copy and all of which, when taken together, will be deemed to constitute one and the same document, and will be effective when counterparts have been signed by each of the parties and** delivered to the other parties. **A manual signature on this letter whose image shall have been transmitted electronically will constitute an original signature for all purposes. The delivery of copies of this letter, including executed signature pages, by electronic transmission will constitute effective delivery of this letter for all purposes.**

If you are in agreement with the foregoing, please sign and return one copy of this letter, which thereupon will constitute our understanding with respect to its subject matter and a binding agreement with respect to the Binding Provisions.

COMMENT

The signatures are intended only to indicate agreement to the binding provisions and preserves the argument that the signatories never intended to be bound by the nonbinding provisions of Part One.

Very truly yours,

BUYER:

By: _____

Name:_____

Title:_____

Agreed to as to the Binding Provisions
on _____ .

SELLERS:

_____
[1]

_____
[2]

. . .

_____
[8]

SHORT FORM LETTER OF INTENT
[DATE]

Seller [1]

Seller [2]

. . .

Seller [8]

Ladies and Gentlemen:

This will set forth the preliminary intention of the parties as to general terms upon which _____ ("Buyer") would consider acquiring from you ("Sellers") all the outstanding capital stock of _____ ("Company").

1.   Upon the closing of the sale, Buyer would acquire all of the capital stock of Company from the shareholders of Company in exchange for an aggregate payment at closing of $_____ in cash, subject to adjustment, and promissory notes of Buyer in the aggregate principal amount of $_____. Each Seller would receive cash equal to $_____ per share owned, subject to adjustment, and a promissory note in the principal amount of $_____ per share. Our willingness to consider this proposed transaction is conditioned on the willingness and eventual agreement of all shareholders of the Company to sell on terms acceptable to Buyer.

2.   As promptly as practicable and in any event by _____, Buyer's counsel will prepare an initial draft of a definitive stock purchase agreement ("Purchase Agreement") and other related agreements for review by you and your counsel. The draft Purchase Agreement will provide for customary representations and warranties, covenants, conditions to closing, escrows, and indemnities. The parties will endeavor to negotiate and execute a final definitive Purchase Agreement on or before _____, and to close the sale on or before _____. The parties anticipate that prior to the execution of any definitive Purchase Agreement, Buyer will have the opportunity to conduct due diligence of the Company and you will have the opportunity to conduct due diligence of Buyer.

3.   It is understood that before the parties would consider entering into a definitive Purchase Agreement, (a) Buyer shall have been satisfied with the results of

its due diligence investigation of Company, and (b) Buyer shall have become satisfied that it is able to borrow $__ million of the cash portion of the purchase price on terms acceptable to Buyer.

4. It is agreed that each party shall bear its own legal, accounting, investment banking, and other expenses in connection with the negotiation, documentation, and closing of the acquisition, whether or not a closing occurs. Any expenses borne by Company would be deducted from the purchase price in the event of a closing. Each party represents that it has not engaged any broker or finder in connection with the acquisition.

5. The parties agree that this letter is merely an expression of intent and neither party is under any legal obligation to the other unless and until a definitive Purchase Agreement is executed, except for (a) the provisions of paragraph 4, this paragraph 5, and paragraph 6 and (b) the confidentiality agreement executed by Buyer with respect to the confidential information of Company.

6. It is agreed that any party may cease pursuit of the contemplated transaction at any time for any or no reason. No party is obligated to negotiate in good faith.

    If the foregoing is in accordance with your understanding, please execute and return the enclosed copy of this letter.

Very truly yours,

_____
Buyer

Agreed to as to Paragraphs 4, 5 and 6.

_____
Seller 1

. . .

_____
Seller 2

COMMENT

The Short Form is intended to satisfy a preference of the parties to document the status of their negotiations in a simpler, less formal writing than the more comprehensive Long Form. The Short Form could be prepared and negotiated upon very short notice. The Short Form could easily be expanded to include more details on nonbinding provisions or to add binding provisions such as exclusivity. This form also may appear to be more user-friendly and less intimidating to a target in the early stages of its first exposure to the acquisition process than the Long Form.

Some lawyers, rather than using a signed letter format of any kind, prefer a term sheet or "heads of agreement" which may or may not be signed or initialed by the parties and simply lists the principal business terms upon which the parties are in agreement and are to be the bases for further negotiation of a definitive purchase agreement. Even if unsigned, the parties should include on the term sheet a disclaimer of intention to be bound or legal obligation to each other of the sort contained in paragraph 12 of the Long Form or paragraph 5 of the Short Form, as there is a possibility that a court might otherwise view the points of agreement on the term sheet as written evidence of a meeting of minds sufficient to form a binding agreement, particularly when supported with oral testimony or e-mails or other informal writings.

ANCILLARY DOCUMENT C

Disclosure Letter

PRELIMINARY NOTE

The form and content of the Disclosure Letter is typically negotiated concurrently with the Model Agreement, and the two documents are usually executed contemporaneously. Where this is not practicable and the Disclosure Letter will be finalized after the Model Agreement is signed, or it is contemplated that the disclosures in the Disclosure Letter may be supplemented or amended, modifications of both the Model Agreement and the Disclosure Letter would be appropriate. For example, Buyer may request that the information in the Disclosure Letter be subject to acceptance by Buyer evidenced by Buyer's execution of the Disclosure Letter, and that Buyer be given a specified period after receipt of the Disclosure Letter to terminate the Model Agreement.

Rather than a separate Disclosure Letter, parties often will append schedules to the Model Agreement referencing the appropriate sections of the Model Agreement. The net effect is the same: the Disclosure Letter or the schedules serve to limit, modify, complete, or possibly expand the representations and warranties of Sellers set forth in Article 3 of the Model Agreement. Unlike situations where a buyer may have assisted in the preparation of the schedules, one benefit of a Disclosure Letter is that the seller clearly takes responsibility for the information provided. Buyers should be wary of broad disclosures, whether in a Disclosure Letter or schedules, that essentially rewrite or largely vitiate the representations in the agreement.

Sellers typically prepare the first draft of the disclosure schedules, and are often tempted to limit the effect of the schedules, as reflected in Sellers' Response below. The form of Disclosure Letter in this Ancillary Document C would be presented by a Buyer. As such, it attempts a preemptive strike against such variances. *See* Section 12.3 of the Model Agreement.

Although Buyer in the Model Agreement Fact Pattern is not a publicly held company, a buyer that is publicly held may be concerned whether the Model Agreement is required to be publicly filed. Item 601(b)(2) of Regulation S-K prohibits filing of schedules unless material to an investment decision. *See* Report of Investigation Pursuant to Section 21(a) of the Securities Exchange Act of 1934 and Commission Statement on potential Exchange Act Section 10(b) and Section 14(a) liability. Release No. 51283 (March 1, 2005). A full discussion of filing requirements and Freedom of Information Act (FOIA) susceptibility is beyond the scope of this Appendix.

Unlike the Disclosure Letter, schedules are not signed and are often transmitted electronically, often as drafts. Unless there exists a hard copy of the final acquisition agreement with all schedules attached, issues may arise as to which versions are the particular schedules referred to in the acquisition agreement because several drafts may exist. To avoid this problem, drafts could be identified by watermarking or a similar technique. *See* the M&A Process Ch. 11— Preparing the Acquisition Agreement and Related Documents—Schedules to the Agreement—Delivering the Schedules.

See generally Kling & Nugent Ch. 10 and the M&A Process Ch. 11—Preparing the Acquisition Agreement and Related Documents—Schedules to the Agreement.

[Date]

[Buyer]

[Address]

      We refer to the Stock Purchase Agreement (the "Purchase Agreement") to be entered into today between the undersigned individuals ("Sellers") and _____ ("Buyer") pursuant to which Sellers are to sell and Buyer is to purchase all the issued and outstanding capital stock of _____ as provided in the Purchase Agreement.

      Terms defined in the Purchase Agreement are used with the same meaning in this Disclosure Letter.

      By reference to Article 3 of the Purchase Agreement (using the numbering in such Article), the following is disclosed:

[describe particularly any required listings and exceptions]

Very truly yours,

SELLERS:

_____

[1]

_____

[2]

. . .

_____

[8]

Buyer acknowledges receipt of this Disclosure Letter.

BUYER:

By: _____

Name: _____

Title: _____

SELLERS' RESPONSE

Sellers may want to include the following: "Inclusion of information in any one or more sections of this Disclosure Letter shall also be deemed to constitute inclusion of such information in all other sections of this Disclosure Letter." This would introduce an ambiguity because Section 12.3(b) of the Model Agreement provides just the opposite. Perhaps Sellers would suggest a modification to Section 12.3(b) instead. Buyer may resist inclusion of this provision and insist that all relevant disclosures be made in the context of each relevant section. This would avoid disputes later whether disclosure in the context of a particular representation is relevant to some other representation where no mention is made of it in the Disclosure Letter.

On the other hand, Sellers may suggest specific cross-references to other Parts of the Disclosure Schedule. This is often done without explicit permission in the documents. Buyers will usually have no objection to this practice so long as the cross reference is to a single document or perhaps a section of the Disclosure Letter with a small number of exceptions listed.

Sellers might want to include the following three additional paragraphs after the second paragraph:

> This Disclosure Letter is qualified in its entirety by reference to the specific provisions of the Purchase Agreement and is not intended to constitute, and shall not be construed as constituting, representations or warranties of Sellers.

> Inclusion of information in this Disclosure Letter shall not be construed as an admission that such information is material to the business, assets, financial condition, or operations of the Company. Furthermore, matters reflected in this Disclosure Letter are not necessarily limited to matters required by the Purchase Agreement to be reflected in this Disclosure Letter. Such additional matters are set forth for information purposes only and do not necessarily include other matters of a similar nature.

> Where documents or provisions in documents have been summarized, reference must be made to the actual documents for complete information.

Buyer may resist the first suggestion. There are undoubtedly representations made in the Disclosure Letter. Section 11.2(a) of the Model Agreement in fact provides indemnification with respect to those representations.

The second suggestion deals with the fact that, although Sellers will probably over-disclose because of their wish to avoid any possible liability, that should not be evidence of what "material" means. Thus, if Sellers are to schedule "material contracts," which in the context of a particular transaction reasonable parties ought to agree means at the $50,000 dollar level, disclosure of $5,000 contracts is not a concession that $5,000 is "material." Buyer may not necessarily object to this paragraph.

Buyers may resist the third suggestion, insisting that Sellers should be obliged to ensure that they have accurately and completely summarized the particular document or provision in question.

Language covering some of these subjects, worded somewhat differently, is suggested in commentary to Section 12.3 of the Model Agreement.

ANCILLARY DOCUMENT D

Earnout Agreement

PRELIMINARY NOTE

In an earnout, payment of a portion of the purchase price is made contingent upon achievement of certain negotiated financial or nonfinancial measurement standards during a specified period of time after closing. The contingent amount is typically "earned" and paid when the acquired business achieves the measurement standards. There may be no earnout payment if these measurement standards are not fully achieved, or a partial payment based on the extent to which the standards have been met.

Earnouts differ from purchase price adjustments. A purchase price adjustment is normally designed to adjust the purchase price after closing to reflect changes in the amount of assets, liabilities, net working capital, or other financial metrics of the target between the date of an earlier balance sheet and closing. As a result, a purchase price adjustment may increase or decrease the purchase price. By contrast, an earnout will, if and to the extent the measurement standards are met, only increase the amount of the purchase price received by the seller.

Earnouts are not suitable for every transaction. They are most often used when there is a particular hurdle to overcome in the price negotiations and consequently the frequency of their use tends to vary with the cyclicality of M&A transactions. They can serve to bridge the gap between a seller's perception of the value of a business and a buyer's desire to reduce the risk of overpaying for the business. This valuation gap is often exacerbated when the seller values the business based on an optimistic projection of future results and the buyer values the business based on limited or lackluster historical results or on a more conservative projection of future results. Valuation gaps often arise in situations involving:

- development-stage companies (entrepreneurs often have an inflated perception of the value of their businesses, notwithstanding limited operating history);
- companies financially dependent on new product lines or technologies that have not been proven in the market;

- turnaround acquisitions where the sellers will likely argue that historical financial information is not an accurate measure of the value of the business; and

- fast-growing market sectors where differences in valuation may be heightened.

Earnouts are most often used when the target is privately held. If the target is publicly held, earnouts are commonly called contingent payment rights. Structuring these rights in a public trading market can become very complicated.

Earnouts become more difficult to draft when the acquired business will be fully integrated into the buyer's business or when the product lines of the buyer and the target are essentially the same, because it will be harder to measure the financial performance of the acquired business accurately.

The percentage of the purchase price represented by earnouts varies widely. If an earnout is to represent only a minor percentage of the purchase price, it may not be worth the time and effort to negotiate the terms or warrant the risk of future litigation if a dispute arises. On the other hand, if an earnout is to represent a significant portion of the purchase price, the risk to a seller of not achieving the measurement standards may be unacceptable.

If an earnout might be used in a transaction, a party retaining an investment banker or financial advisor will want to consider how it would be treated in calculating the purchase price and thus its effect on the investment banker's or financial advisor's compensation. Many engagement agreements use a very broad definition of the purchase price and include the maximum amount of potential earnout payments for purposes of determining the success fee, regardless of whether they are actually earned. The party negotiating the success fee may want to specify that the calculation only includes earnouts to the extent they are actually paid.

For more information about earnouts in general, *see* M&A Process 147–51; Kling & Nugent § 17.03; Fuerst, San Filippo IV & Ornstein, *Farn-Outs; Bridge the Gap, With Caution*, 12 M&A L. Rep. 581 (BNA June 15, 2009); Gunderson, *Seller Beware: In an Earnout, the Buyer Has Doubts, the Seller Has Hopes*, 14 Bus. Law Today 49 (March/April 2005); Section of Business Law, Earnouts in Business Acquisitions—A Practical Solution or a Trap for the Unwary? (2005).

Accounting Treatment

In December 2007, the Financial Accounting Standards Board revised Statement of Financial Accounting Standards No. 141, "Business Combinations" (SFAS 141(R)) (FASB Accounting Standards Codification 805), which applies to all business combinations closed on or after December 15, 2008. SFAS 141(R) requires a buyer to record an earnout at its fair value as of the acquisition date and record it as part of the purchase price. Although uncertainty typically exists at closing as to whether, and how much of, an earnout will eventually be paid, a buyer under FAS 141(R) must nonetheless make a determination of the closing date fair value. The methods of making such an estimate might include applying a probability-weighted percentage or a risk-adjusted discount rate to the projected amounts of the earnout. Except in a bargain purchase, this will typically result in additional goodwill being recognized by the buyer. The value of the earnout is then remeasured annually until all potential payments are made, and any corresponding changes will result in a gain or loss on the buyer's income statement. SFAS 141(R) represents a dramatic change from prior accounting practice under which the additional purchase price was not recognized at closing, but only when payment of the earnout was reasonably assured. This valuation can become a point of contention between a buyer and seller. A seller may want to require that it be advised of the methodology used by the buyer, as well as the actual periodic computations of the fair value, but a buyer may be reluctant to provide that information.

Tax Treatment

A seller in a taxable transaction will generally expect that the earnout will be treated similarly to deferred purchase price payments, resulting in tax at the capital gains rate at the time of receipt. However, the application of the federal tax law to earnouts may be more complicated, and can significantly affect the structuring and drafting of the earnout provisions.

The first issue is to confirm that the earnout will be respected as a debt obligation of the buyer for tax purposes. For example, if the earnout affords the seller a significant degree of continued participation in the enterprise that is inconsistent with having terminated all interest in the target, the arrangement might be characterized as an equity interest or a partnership with respect to the buyer or acquired business.

Earnouts can also be considered additional compensation for ongoing management, in which case the recipients may be required to recognize ordinary income and the buyer will be entitled to a deduction rather than including this amount in the tax basis of the purchased stock. This result is more likely if earnout payments are made to only those shareholders who are required to manage the acquired business or if the right to receive earnout payments is forfeited on termination of employment.

In the case of taxable transactions, an earnout will generally be characterized as a debt obligation of the buyer. Most earnouts can be reported using the installment method under Section 453 of the Internal Revenue Code. Under this method, a portion of the seller's stock basis is allocated to the earnout payments and gain is recognized only in the year in which each payment is received. The amount of stock basis allocable to each payment is determined under Temp. Regs. §15A.453-1(c), and depends on whether the earnout payment is limited as to amount or timing. A seller can elect out of the installment method, in which case the fair value of the earnout is recognized in the year of sale.

Because an earnout will generally be characterized as a debt obligation, if it does not accrue interest at the applicable federal rate published by the Internal Revenue Service (IRS), a portion of each earnout payment will be characterized as imputed interest. The amount of imputed interest may be deductible to the buyer, and the seller must recognize the interest as ordinary income rather than capital gain.

DRAFTING ISSUES

Structure of Transaction. In a sale of stock, the earnout will be payable directly to the selling shareholder or shareholders as additional consideration for their stock. One or more of the shareholders may wish to exercise some control over the acquired business during the earnout period to protect their interests.

Measurement Standard. Earnouts can be based on a variety of measurement standards. These standards can be financial, such as revenues, gross profit (revenues less cost of goods sold), operating profit (revenues less cost of goods sold and operating expenses), EBIT (earnings before interest and taxes), EBITDA (earnings before interest, taxes, depreciation, and amortization), or net income, as well as related metrics, such as the number of units sold. The earnout payments can be determined on an all-or-nothing or a graduated basis depending on the level of performance achieved, which is often the amount by which the performance of the acquired business surpasses a threshold. In addition, earnouts can be structured as fixed or variable amounts payable upon the occurrence of certain events or the achievement of nonfinancial milestones, such as regulatory approval of drug applications, entering into post-closing contracts, or the launch of products.

From a buyer's standpoint, using revenues as the performance standard means that the related cost of sales or other operating expenses are not being taken into account in the earnout calculation. The seller may argue for a revenues-based approach on the ground that revenues are the only readily determinable, externally driven amount, this approach is most likely to avoid a dispute, and the buyer may be in the best position to manage the cost of sales and other expenses. In addition, a revenues-based approach often allows integration into the buyer's business with less impact on the earnout mechanics.

If the measurement standard is profit-based and if the seller will not be managing the business after the closing, it may be possible to structure a series of "not to exceed" percentages to be applied to the revenues to determine the cost of goods sold, operating expenses, and the like for purposes of calculating the earnout in an effort to minimize disputes and prevent manipulation of the performance standard.

The use of EBITDA or some variation will permit a seller to realize an earnout payment based upon an earnings measure that does not reflect increased interest expense associated with post-closing working capital. EBITDA is often considered to be a good indicator of the true post-closing financial success of an acquired business, but the parties will need to consider other items that should be specifically included or excluded in the calculation.

A number of drafting and business issues will arise depending on the measurement standards used, and the negotiations will likely become more complex the further down the income statement the chosen standard is found.

Business to be Measured. The measurement standards may be applied to the acquired business as a whole, a portion of it, a single product, or may be blended over several entities. A blended standard can reduce the risk that revenues are not shifted artificially by the buyer from the acquired business to the buyer's affiliates.

A seller may request a provision preventing the buyer from making subsequent acquisitions that would affect the acquired business. For example, a seller may want a provision that requires the buyer to maintain the acquired business in a separate subsidiary during the earnout period. The buyer will resist such a provision where it would substantially interfere with its business strategy. If acquisitions are to be permitted, the parties will want to document how the operations will be integrated and dealt with in connection with any performance standards.

Integrating the Acquired Business. If the business being acquired is substantially unrelated to the business activities of the buyer, there may be no dispute as to the allocation of revenues between these operations. However, where it is anticipated that the acquired business will provide a synergistic effect on the buyer's operations, there may be disputes as to allocation of additional revenues to the total enterprise. New orders in the same product line from customers of the target are readily allocated to the acquired business. Orders for products from prior customers of buyer that were not serviced by the target and orders from new customers need to be addressed. Notwithstanding any attention given to these potential problems in the agreement, disputes can also arise over failed or deferred deliveries at the end of the earnout term.

Control Over the Acquired Business. An earnout can complicate the transition of the business from the seller to the buyer. A buyer will generally focus on changing certain aspects of the acquired business in order to integrate it into its business. On the other hand, the seller has a desire to control operation of the business to maximize the earnout or to make the computation easier. These disparate incentives that can be created by an earnout are frequently not taken into account during the earnout negotiations. Attention of the seller to short-term targets that can support or increase the earnout may be inconsistent with the long-term goals and objectives of the buyer, thereby creating an environment in which the seller's objectives conflict with those of the buyer. The buyer and the seller must examine the earnout performance standards not only for the financial impact on both parties, but also within the context of the buyer's overall goals and objectives and whether the earnout performance standards are consistent or in conflict with these overall goals.

A seller may want to include various affirmative and negative covenants in the agreement governing the continuing operation of the acquired business during the earnout period. If the buyer is to operate the business, the seller may ask for provisions stipulating that it will be operated as a separate corporation and consistent with past practice or that the buyer will operate it in such a way as to maximize the earnout. If the seller is to continue to operate the business, it might want control over significant strategic and operational decisions, such as making capital expenditures and hiring, firing, and directing employees, as well as determining their incentive compensation. In that case, an employment agreement for the seller during the earnout period is frequently negotiated and entered into at the closing. In addition, the buyer might be required to retain the name of the target, provide sufficient working capital for operation of the business, and be precluded from consolidating the acquired business with its other operations, selling the business, or buying another business.

If the seller will continue managing the business, it may be desirable to set up a dispute-resolution mechanism regarding the effect of operational changes on meeting the performance standards. Although the buyer may, in any event, want to implement the changes from an overall business standpoint, a seller may be in a better position to identify and deal with those changes that might affect the earnout.

One way for the buyer to attempt to mitigate against the litigation risk is to include a provision whereby the seller acknowledges that the buyer has the right to control the acquired business in its sole discretion and waives any implied fiduciary duty or implied duty of good faith and fair dealing. The following is an example of such a pro-buyer provision that might be added to the Model Agreement or Earnout Agreement:

> Sellers acknowledge that (i) upon the Closing, Buyer has the right to operate the business of the Acquired Companies and Buyer's other businesses in any way that Buyer deems appropriate in Buyer's sole discretion, (ii) Buyer has no obligation to operate the Acquired Companies in order to achieve or to maximize any Earnout Amount, (iii) Buyer is under no obligation to continue to manufacture the Acquired Companies' product line(s), (iv) the Earnout Amount is speculative and is subject to numerous factors outside Buyer's control, (v) there is no assurance that Sellers will receive any Earnout Amount and Buyer has neither promised nor projected any Earnout Amount, (vi) Buyer owes no fiduciary duty or express or implied duty to Sellers, including any implied duty of good faith and fair dealing, and (vii) the parties solely intend the express provisions of this Agreement to govern their contractual relationship relating to the earnout. Sellers hereby waive any fiduciary duty or express or implied duty of Buyer to Sellers, including any implied duty of good faith and fair dealing.

Some of these clauses will be more objectionable to a seller than others. By including this type of provision, a buyer runs a significant risk that the seller will not only reject it, but will demand extensive covenants regarding control over operation of the acquired business after closing. In some jurisdictions, an implied duty of good faith and fair dealing may not be recognized under all circumstances and, even if recognized, it may not be clear whether the parties are free by contract to negate its application. The seller may want to explore the possibility of challenging the enforceability of this provision insofar as it purports to disclaim or waive the implied duty of good faith and fair dealing.

Earnout Period. The time period for earnouts varies. An earnout becomes more risky to a seller as the time for measuring performance increases since unforeseen changes in circumstances may make it more difficult to achieve the measurement standards. Most earnouts extend for a period of between one to three years, and in many cases a one- to two-year period will be sufficient to demonstrate the ongoing earning capacity of the business.

When a performance standard is used, the earnout might be calculated and paid on a periodic basis over several accounting periods or on a one-time basis for one accounting period. If multiple periods are used, the agreement may provide for interim payments and take into account shortfalls and possible overpayments at the time the final earnout payment is calculated. Accounting periods can also be aggregated to determine whether a performance standard has been achieved.

Acceleration or Early Termination. The earnout may be subject to acceleration or termination upon the occurrence of certain specified events, and sometimes the buyer has a right to terminate the earnout and pay the seller a predetermined amount if the buyer, for example, finds that the earnout would interfere with an acquisition or reorganization that it would like to accomplish. This could be based on the then present value of the earnout discounted at a specified rate or determined by a valuation professional.

The seller may have developed a good working relationship with, and degree of trust of, the buyer's management during the negotiations and subsequent operation of the acquired business. This relationship could be jeopardized if the buyer experiences a change in control. Accordingly, a seller may insist on acceleration and full vesting of the earnout upon a change in control. In addition, certain liquidity events, such as an IPO, a leveraged recapitalization, or other events that change the resources, lines of business, or management of the buyer may justify the seller, buyer, or both in accelerating the final earnout, in anticipation of which, it may be best to negotiate the circumstances triggering an acceleration in advance.

The earnout might also be accelerated upon a sale of the acquired business by the buyer before the earnout period ends. In some cases, the seller may be permitted to share in a portion of the proceeds when the buyer sells the acquired business within a specified period of time after closing at a significantly higher price than it paid.

A buyer might also consider negotiating early termination of the earnout if, for example, the acquired business suffers significant losses, faces a significant liability, performs substantially below expectations, or becomes subject to legal restrictions that adversely affect its operations.

Industry-Specific Legal Issues. The structure of an earnout should take into account any legal issues pertaining to the target's specific industry or type of business. For example, in the healthcare industry, federal fraud and abuse laws are designed to prevent certain activities under Medicare and Medicaid, including improperly receiving remuneration for patient referrals or the provision of items or services. If an earnout is linked to the undertaking of such activities, it would be prudent to confirm that it does not pose these concerns.

Escrowing Payments. If earnout payments are to be made over time with an eventual adjustment (plus or minus) at the end of the term, a buyer may be more comfortable in providing for an annual (or other periodic) earnout payment to be set aside in escrow until the end of the term with a one-time settlement. This structure would obviate a need for the buyer to call upon the seller to refund money that had previously been paid on the earnout if the final payment were to be insufficient to make up for the shortfalls.

Form of Consideration. Most earnouts provide for cash payments. Using a buyer's stock rather than cash raises a number of issues, including the date or method for determining the per share price at which the stock is valued, taxability of the transaction, whether the shares will (or need be) registered under federal or state securities laws, voting and control issues, approval of the issuance of the stock by the buyer's shareholders, and listing on stock exchanges on which the stock is traded. *See* Appendix B—Receipt of Stock of a Public Company as Purchase Consideration.

RISKS ASSOCIATED WITH EARNOUTS

Although the concept of an earnout based upon future performance or achievement of other milestones may seem simple, drafting an agreement that adequately addresses the parties' interests and concerns often proves to be difficult, particularly given the precision that is required and the difficulty in anticipating all the issues that might arise in the future. The parties may have to document, among other things, who has control over operations, what resources the buyer will be required to provide to the acquired business, and the duties and efforts of the buyer and the seller to achieve the earnout. While seemingly innocuous, clauses that provide that a buyer will use reasonable efforts to maintain the acquired business as a separate enterprise within the corporate structure or reasonably cooperate with the seller in achieving the earnout may create problems for the buyer. Without such a clause, a seller might still seek recourse by claiming a breach by the buyer of an implied duty of good faith and fair dealing to the extent that it might apply to the earnout.

Even where earnouts are drafted with considerable thought and care, disputes can and often do arise. Although some practitioners believe that earnouts are invitations to future litigation, many have still resulted in significant additional purchase price payments to a seller. In acquisitions that a seller believes are fully priced, the earnout might be considered simply as an added bonus.

The following cases highlight some of the litigation issues that have arisen involving earnouts in acquisitions:

- Sonoran Scanners, Inc. v. PerkinElmer, Inc., 2009 WL 3466048 (1st Cir. 2009) (acquired business operated by the buyer was a failure, but the court remanded the case to the district court, holding that the buyer was bound by an implied covenant to use reasonable efforts to develop and promote the technology and products of the acquired business)

- Comet Systems Inc. v. MIVA Inc., 2008 WL 4661829 (Del. Ch. 2008) (bonuses triggered by acquisition should not have been deducted as "operating costs" in determining earnout, and court awarded interest due to delay in payment)

- Chabria v. EDO Western Corp., 2007 WL 582293 (S.D. Ohio 2007) (motion to dismiss denied where sufficient facts pled to support claims that buyer failed to use reasonable efforts to sell products of business acquired and induced the seller to sell the business by representing that it had the capability and intent to generate earnout payments)

- Woods v. Boston Scientific Corp., 2007 WL 2471744 (2d Cir. 2007) (affirmed injunction against buyer from terminating co-chief executive officers of subsidiary where agreement contained provisions outlining a system of joint control to protect interests of earnout recipients)

- Vaughan v. Recall Total Information Management, Inc., 217 Fed. Appx. 211 (4th Cir. 2007) (revenues of other businesses acquired during the earnout period treated as revenues of the acquired business for purposes of an earnout)

- LaPoint v. AmerisourceBergen Corp., 2007 WL 2565709 (Del. Ch. 2007) (buyer failed to "exclusively and actively" promote the target's products and miscalculated agreed-upon adjustments to EBITDA)

- Instrument Industries Trust v. Danaher Corporation, 2005 WL 704817 (Mass. Super. Ct. 2006) (integration of operations by buyer triggered acceleration of earnout as constituting the business being "merged or consolidated" without seller's consent)

- O'Tool v. Genmar Holdings, Inc., 387 F.3d 1188 (10th Cir. 2004) (affirmed judgment based on finding that buyer changed known brands, shifted production priority to benefit its original brands, required new subsidiary to bear cost of design and new production, failed to give sellers necessary operational control, and shut down facility)

Even where buyers are found to have breached an earnout agreement, some courts have determined that the damages are speculative or the sellers have had difficulty proving damages. In some acquisitions, the parties have agreed to liquidated damages in the event of a breach of a fundamental covenant in order to avoid having to prove damages. While this could provide some leverage, it may not adequately compensate a seller for the lost earnout amount.

The indefiniteness of earnout agreements may pose risk not only to the parties, but also to their counsel. *See* Harrison v. The Proctor & Gamble Co., 2009 U.S. Dist. LEXIS 9114 (N.D. Tex. Feb. 9, 2009) (dismissal of a malpractice claim for alleged negligent negotiation of an earnout).

STRUCTURE OF THE EARNOUT AGREEMENT

Earnouts can be included as part of an acquisition agreement or set forth in a separate agreement with a reference in the acquisition agreement to the earnout being part of the purchase price. If an earnout were to be part of the Model Agreement, the body of the earnout could follow Section 2.6, it would be referred to in Section 2.2 as being part of the purchase price, and the related definitions would be included in Section 1.1. Some practitioners prefer to cover earnouts in a separate agreement, primarily because they are heavily negotiated and the changes can be made without continually revising the acquisition agreement.

The sample Earnout Agreement that follows is based on the Fact Pattern for the Model Agreement (although the Fact Pattern does not include an earnout) and is integrated with portions of the Model Agreement by making cross references where appropriate and using some of the same defined terms. The terms of any earnout are largely dictated by the specific facts and circumstances of the situation. This sample Earnout Agreement therefore is intended only to provide a basic framework for an earnout and to address some related issues in the commentary.

The earnout in this Earnout Agreement is based upon a percentage of Adjusted EBITDA of the acquired business in excess of a specified threshold for a one-year period. This is a rather simple arrangement, as earnouts frequently cover longer or multiple periods. Some parties prefer an uncomplicated mathematical approach, while others prefer the specificity of precise and fairly complex formulas.

EARNOUT AGREEMENT

This Earnout Agreement ("Agreement") is made as of _____ by _____, a _____ corporation ("Buyer"), those individuals who have executed the signature page to this Agreement (collectively "Sellers"), and _____, as Sellers' Representative. This is the Earnout Agreement referred to in the Stock Purchase Agreement (the "Purchase Agreement"), dated _____, between Buyer and Sellers. Capitalized terms used in this Agreement without definition have the respective meanings given to them in the Purchase Agreement.

RECITALS

Sellers have this date sold to Buyer all the Shares of _____, a _____ corporation (the "Company"), pursuant to the Purchase Agreement.

The Purchase Agreement provides that a portion of the Purchase Price is to be calculated and paid as an earnout.

Buyer and Sellers have agreed that the determination and payment of the earnout contemplated by the Purchase Agreement is to be in accordance with the terms of this Agreement.

The parties, intending to be legally bound, agree as follows:

1. DEFINITIONS

For purposes of this Agreement, the following terms have the meanings specified or referred to in this Paragraph 1:

"Adjusted EBITDA"—EBITDA, adjusted as described in the last sentence of this definition and by excluding the effects of any of the following to the extent otherwise included in consolidated earnings from operations:

(a) gains, losses or profits realized by the Acquired Companies from the sale of assets other than in the ordinary course of business and any "extraordinary items" of gain or loss (as determined in accordance with GAAP);

(b) any management fees, general overhead expenses, or other intercompany charges, of whatever kind or nature, charged by Buyer to the Acquired Companies, [except that Buyer may charge interest on any loans or advances made by Buyer or its Affiliates to any of the Acquired Companies in connection with their business operations at a rate of _____ percent per annum];

(c) any legal or accounting fees and expenses incurred in connection with this Agreement, the Purchase Agreement or the Contemplated Transactions; and

(d) [Add any other items to be excluded].

In determining consolidated earnings from operations, the purchase and sales prices of goods and services sold by the Acquired Companies to Buyer or its Affiliates, or purchased by the Acquired Companies from Buyer or its Affiliates,

shall be adjusted to reflect the amounts that the Acquired Companies would have received or paid if dealing with an independent party in an arm's-length commercial transaction.

COMMENT

The exclusions and adjustments for the calculation of Adjusted EBITDA are for illustrative purposes only and should not be viewed as standard provisions. Any adjustments to the calculation of a financial metric will depend on the specific facts and circumstances. SFAS 141(R) (business combinations) (FASB Accounting Standards Codification 805), as well as Statement of Financial Accounting Standards Nos. 142 and 144 (impairment of goodwill) (FASB Accounting Standards Codification 350 and 360), are among the accounting requirements that may impact EBITDA.

"Affiliate"—with respect to any entity, an entity that directly or indirectly controls or is controlled by, or is under common control with, as the case may be, the relevant entity.

"Computation Notice"—as defined in Paragraph 3(a).

"EBITDA"—consolidated earnings from operations of the Company and its Subsidiaries, as determined in accordance with GAAP as consistently applied by the Company, before consolidated interest, taxes, depreciation, and amortization of the Company, in each case, as determined in accordance with GAAP as consistently applied by the Company.

COMMENT

This definition provides that the consolidated earnings from operations will be determined in accordance with GAAP as consistently applied by the Company, which is often the way this type of provision is worded. As discussed in commentary to the definition of "GAAP" in Section 1.1 of the Model Agreement, GAAP permits different accounting methods and requires many estimates and judgments. For example, a change in the method of accounting for inventory to bring the Company's accounting into line with Buyer's accounting (e.g., changing between first-in,-first-out (FIFO) and last-in, first-out (LIFO)) would be recognized as a change in accounting method. While changes of this nature would still be in accordance with GAAP, they would not be permitted under the consistently applied language. Calculation of an earnout can also be affected by accounting "method and related judgment" changes. For example, changes in the method and related judgments for bad debts, allocating corporate overhead, or obsolete inventory are not changes in accounting principles but, instead, reflect accounting judgments and estimates. Other areas that involve accounting judgments include estimating reserves for inventory markdowns, warranty claims, product returns, product liabilities, environmental claims, litigation claims, and accrued contingent liabilities. In addition, there could be different judgments surrounding the timing of revenue and expense recognition. The application of these methods and judgments to the calculation of an earnout can lead to disputes between the parties.

In an effort to minimize such accounting disputes, it may be helpful for the parties to reach agreement on the specific accounting principles and policies to be applied post-closing, rather than leaving it to a broad statement referring to GAAP as consistently applied. This would be particularly important if Buyer wants to utilize some of its accounting principles and policies rather than those consistently applied by the Company. *See also the commentary to Section 2.6 of the Model Agreement.* Sometimes the parties will prepare and attach an example of the method by which EBITDA is to be calculated.

"Earnout Amount"—an amount equal to (a) Adjusted EBITDA for the Earnout Period, less (b) the Threshold Amount.

"Earnout Payment"—as defined in Paragraph 2(a).

"Earnout Period"—the fiscal year ending _____.

COMMENT

Using a period other than a complete fiscal year may be problematic.

"Income Statement"—as defined in Paragraph 3(a).

"Independent Accountants"—as defined in Paragraph 3(d).

"Objection Notice"—as defined in Paragraph 3(c).

"Payment Rate"—_____ percent.

COMMENT

The payment rate is a percentage that is to be applied in Paragraph 2 to the Earnout Amount, which is Adjusted EBITDA less the Threshold Amount. Whether the parties want to use a percentage of Adjusted EBITDA or some other method of determining the amount of the earnout will depend on the specific transaction. Since purchase prices are often negotiated on the basis of a multiple of EBITDA, this may already have been factored in when the potential amount of the earnout is determined. Buyer may counter that the success of the acquired business will also be attributable in large measure to its direction and support, including its financial resources, management, and marketing.

"Threshold Amount"—the amount of $_____.

COMMENT

The threshold amount is often EBITDA of the acquired business for a period prior to the closing of the acquisition, but it could be a greater or lesser amount. Since the purchase price already reflects historical EBITDA, the earnout would reward Sellers for any increase post-closing.

2. EARNOUT PAYMENT

(a) Buyer shall pay to Sellers' Representative on behalf of Sellers an amount equal to (i) the Earnout Amount, multiplied by (ii) the Payment Rate, but only if the Earnout Amount is a positive number (the "Earnout Payment"). If the Earnout Amount is a negative number, no Earnout Payment shall be made. The Earnout Payment will be paid by Buyer within 30 days after the final determination of the Earnout Amount. Notwithstanding any provision in this Agreement to the contrary, in no event will the Earnout Payment exceed $\$\underline{\hspace{2cm}}$.

COMMENT

Sellers may want to provide that payment will initially be made of the amount of the earnout as originally computed by Buyer, with any remaining amount being subject to the procedure set forth in Paragraph 3. A maximum is provided so that the earnout will not exceed the parties' reasonable expectations and over-reward Sellers. Sellers may object to a maximum being imposed as unreasonably limiting their upside potential.

It is contemplated that the Sellers' Representative will act for Sellers under the Earnout Agreement in the same manner as under the Model Agreement. This would require either the addition in this Agreement of language giving authority to the Sellers' Representative much like that in Section 12.5 of the Model Agreement, or modifying Section 12.5 to refer to the Earnout Agreement.

(b) Sellers shall not be entitled to any interest on the Earnout Payment under this Agreement.

COMMENT

No interest is included on the Earnout Payment. Sellers may wish to bargain for interest from the Closing Date on the basis that the earnout payment represents deferred purchase price, or for default interest if an earnout payment is not timely made. In the event that the determination of the earnout is delayed and becomes subject to an objection by the Sellers' Representative under Paragraph 3(c), Sellers may want interest from that time until payment is finally made. For associated tax issues, *see* the discussion on tax treatment in the Preliminary Note.

(c) Upon notice to Sellers' Representative specifying in reasonable detail the basis therefor, Buyer may set off any amount to which it claims to be entitled from any Seller, including any amounts that may be owed under Article 11 of the Purchase Agreement or otherwise, against amounts otherwise payable under this Agreement. The exercise of such right of setoff by Buyer in good faith, whether or not ultimately determined to be justified, will not constitute a default under this Agreement, regardless of whether any Seller disputes such setoff claim, or whether such setoff claim is for a contingent or unliquidated amount. Neither the exercise of, nor the failure to exercise, such right of setoff will constitute an election of remedies or limit Buyer in any manner in the enforcement of any other remedies that may be available to it.

COMMENT

The setoff rights in Paragraph 2(c) provide Buyer a broad right to set off any claim for indemnification under the Model Agreement against any amounts due Sellers under the Earnout Agreement. Sellers may object to the setoff rights for a variety of reasons, including that they permit setting off of nonfinal claims for indemnification against amounts then due under the earnout. For a complete discussion of setoff rights and related issues, *see* Section 11.7 of the Model Agreement and related commentary.

3. PROCEDURE

COMMENT

Paragraph 3 is derived from the adjustment procedure for the post-closing adjustment in Section 2.6 of the Model Agreement and much of the commentary to that Section applies to this Paragraph.

(a) Buyer shall maintain separate accounting books and records for the Acquired Companies during the Earnout Period. Promptly following the end of the Earnout Period, Buyer shall prepare (i) a consolidated income statement of the Company and its Subsidiaries for the Earnout Period, which shall be prepared in accordance with GAAP as consistently applied by the Company (the "Income Statement"), and (ii) a computation of EBITDA and Adjusted EBITDA, showing separately each of the adjustments made to EBITDA to arrive at Adjusted EBITDA (the "Computation Notice"). Buyer shall deliver the Income Statement and the Computation Notice to Sellers' Representative within 45 days following the end of the Earnout Period.

COMMENT

Unlike the post-closing adjustment that is determined with reference to a closing balance sheet, the earnout requires the delivery of both a consolidated income statement of the Company and Subsidiaries for the earnout period and a computation of both EBITDA and Adjusted EBITDA, as defined in Paragraph 1. EBITDA will be derived from the income statement as determined in accordance with GAAP, which is the starting point for the determination of Adjusted EBITDA. Sellers might have an objection to the manner in which GAAP was applied to the income statement, as well as to whether the income statement reflects accounting principles consistently applied by the Company.

Sellers will generally want separate accounting books and records to be maintained by Buyer, which would require that the acquired business be kept separate from Buyer's other businesses. The time period for delivery of a consolidated income statement will often depend upon the ease of closing the books and the complexity of the financial accounting for the acquired business. It should be noted that, unless otherwise agreed, information during this period can be, and often is, used to evaluate the judgments behind the accounting estimates reflected in an income statement, but not information that becomes known after this period.

Paragraph 3 could be revised to require a separate audit of the income statement. There are practical issues to dealing with such an audit, especially if the acquired business is insignificant to Buyer. Because financial results of the acquired business may be immaterial for purposes of the scope of a normal audit of Buyer's financial statements, an audit would require significant additional work by Buyer's accountants.

(b) **Upon execution of such access letters as may be reasonably required by Buyer, Sellers' Representative and its Representatives shall be given reasonable access during reasonable business hours to (and copies of) all Buyer's and its Representatives' books, records, and other documents, including work papers, worksheets, notes, and schedules used in preparation of the Income Statement and its computation of EBITDA and Adjusted EBITDA in the Computation Notice for the purpose of reviewing the Income Statement and the Computation Notice, in each case, other than work papers that Buyer considers proprietary, such as internal control documentation, engagement planning, time control and audit sign off, and quality control work papers.**

COMMENT

Consideration might be given by Sellers to providing that the Sellers' Representative and its Representatives also be given reasonable access to key management and accounting personnel, including those who made the judgments and developed the estimates used in preparation of the income statement, as well as access to the site where the financial records are maintained and to the actual accounting/financial systems.

(c)   If, within 45 days following delivery of the Income Statement and the Computation Notice to Sellers' Representative, Sellers' Representative has not given Buyer notice of an objection as to any amounts set forth on the Income Statement or the computation of EBITDA or Adjusted EBITDA in the Computation Notice (which notice shall state in reasonable detail the basis of Sellers' Representative's objection) (the "Objection Notice"), the Adjusted EBITDA as computed by Buyer will be final, binding, and conclusive on the parties.

(d)   If Sellers' Representative timely gives Buyer an Objection Notice, and if Sellers' Representative and Buyer fail to resolve the issues raised in the Objection Notice within 30 days after giving the Objection Notice, Sellers' Representative and Buyer shall submit the issues remaining in dispute for resolution to [name of individual] in the [location] office of [name of accounting firm] (or, if [name of individual or name of accounting firm] is providing accounting services to Buyer or is otherwise unable or unwilling to serve in such capacity, a recognized national or regional independent accounting firm mutually acceptable to Buyer and Sellers' Representative) (the "Independent Accountants").

COMMENT

The Earnout Agreement provides that any dispute be submitted to an accounting firm for resolution. Consideration might be given to broadening this to include consultants, so that the parties have more flexibility. For example, valuation firms or other consultants might also be capable of dealing with the issues presented by the income statement and earnout calculation.

(e)   The parties shall negotiate in good faith in order to seek agreement on the procedures to be followed by the Independent Accountants, including procedures with regard to the presentation of evidence. If the parties are unable to agree upon procedures within 10 days of the submission to the Independent Accountants, the Independent Accountants shall establish such procedures giving due regard to the intention of the parties to resolve disputes as promptly, efficiently, and inexpensively as possible, which procedures may, but need not, be those proposed by either Buyer or Sellers' Representative. The Independent Accountants shall be directed to resolve only those issues in dispute and render a written report on their resolution of disputed issues with respect to the Income Statement and the Computation Notice as promptly as practicable but no later than 60 days after the date on which the Independent Accountants are engaged. The determination of Adjusted EBITDA by the Independent Accountants will be based solely on written submissions of Buyer, on the one hand, and Sellers' Representative, on the other hand, and will not involve independent review. Any determination by the Independent Accountants will not be outside the range established by the amounts in (i) the

Income Statement and the computation of EBITDA and Adjusted EBITDA in the Computation Notice proposed by Buyer, and (ii) Sellers' Representative's proposed adjustments thereto. Such determination will be final, binding, and conclusive on the parties.

COMMENT

Paragraph 3(e) provides that the resolution is limited to only the issues in dispute and the determination will be based solely on the written submissions of the parties and will not involve an independent review. Limiting the Independent Accountants to the issues in dispute is intended to avoid their delving into other accounting issues or the manner in which the calculation was made with respect to other adjustments. However, limiting the Independent Accountants to the written submissions could preclude them from having access to other information that they believe would be pertinent to arriving at their determination. Of course, additional access could be provided for in the engagement agreement when the precise issues in dispute are known.

The last sentence of Paragraph 3(e) provides that the determination is final, binding, and conclusive. Sometimes, the words "in the absence of manifest error" are added to provide some flexibility to the parties to appeal the determination.

(f)   If the computation of Adjusted EBITDA is submitted to the Independent Accountants for resolution:

  (i)   Sellers' Representative and Buyer shall execute any agreement required by the Independent Accountants to accept their engagement pursuant to this Paragraph 3;

  (ii)   Sellers' Representative and Buyer shall promptly furnish or cause to be furnished to the Independent Accountants such work papers and other documents and information relating to the disputed issues as the Independent Accountants may request and are available to that party or its accountants or other Representatives, and shall be afforded the opportunity to present to the Independent Accountants, with a copy to the other party, any other written material relating to the disputed issues;

  (iii)   the determination by the Independent Accountants, as set forth in a report to be delivered by the Independent Accountants to both Sellers' Representative and Buyer, will include all the changes in the Income Statement and the computation of EBITDA and Adjusted EBITDA in the Computation Notice required as a result of the determination made by the Independent Accountants; and

(iv) **Sellers and Buyer shall each bear one-half of the fees and costs of the Independent Accountants; provided, however, that the engagement agreement referred to in clause (i) above may require the parties to be bound jointly and severally to the Independent Accountants for those fees and costs, and in the event Sellers or Buyer pay to the Independent Accountants any amount in excess of one-half of the fees and costs of their engagement, the other party(ies) agree(s) to reimburse Sellers or Buyer, as applicable, upon demand to the extent required to equalize the payments made by Sellers and Buyer with respect to the fees and costs of the Independent Accountants.**

COMMENT

Paragraph 3(f)(iii) sets forth the content of the report to be delivered by the Independent Accountants. It could provide that the Independent Accountants render a "reasoned report," which would include the rationale and basis for the determination and, some might say, could result in a more disciplined approach to the determination.

Paragraph 3(f)(iv) provides for sharing responsibility for the fees and costs of the Independent Accountants. As an alternative, the fees and costs could be awarded by the Independent Accountants or apportioned between the parties based on the extent to which each prevails in the dispute. Sellers may want to set up an expense fund with the Sellers' Representative to cover these types of expenses.

4. MISCELLANEOUS

COMMENT

See the Introduction to this Volume II and commentary to Article 12 of the Model Agreement for further discussion relevant to the miscellaneous provisions.

(a) **Entire Agreement. This Agreement, together with the other agreements among the parties executed and delivered concurrently herewith, supersedes all prior agreements, whether written or oral, between the parties with respect to its subject matter and constitutes a complete and exclusive statement of the terms of the agreement between the parties with respect to its subject matter.**

(b) **Modification. This Agreement may only be amended, supplemented, or otherwise modified by a writing executed by the parties.**

(c) **Assignments and Successors. No party may assign any of its rights or delegate any of its obligations under this Agreement without the prior consent of the other parties. Any purported assignment of rights or delegation of obligations in violation of this Paragraph 4(c) will be void. Subject to the foregoing, this**

Agreement will apply to, be binding in all respects upon, and inure to the benefit of the heirs, executors, administrators, legal representatives, successors, and permitted assigns of the parties.

COMMENT

An earnout is normally structured as a nontransferable contract right. This is typically one of the factors that is taken into account in determining whether the earnout right might be considered a security for purposes of federal and state securities laws.

(d) **Governing Law. All matters relating to or arising out of this Agreement and the rights of the parties (whether sounding in contract, tort or otherwise) will be governed by and construed and interpreted under the laws of the State of _____ without regard to conflicts of laws principles that would require the application of any other law.**

(e) **Remedies Cumulative. The rights and remedies of the parties are cumulative and not alternative.**

(f) **Jurisdiction; Service of Process. Except as otherwise provided in this Agreement, any Proceeding arising out of or relating to this Agreement shall be brought in the courts of the State of _____, County of _____, or, if it has or can acquire jurisdiction, in the United States District Court for the _____ District of _____, and each of the parties irrevocably submits to the exclusive jurisdiction of each such court in any such Proceeding, waives any objection it may now or hereafter have to venue or to convenience of forum, agrees that all claims in respect of such Proceeding shall be heard and determined only in any such court, and agrees not to bring any Proceeding arising out of or relating to this Agreement in any other court. Each party acknowledges and agrees that this Paragraph 4(f) constitutes a voluntary and bargained-for agreement between the parties. Process in any Proceeding referred to in the first sentence of this Paragraph 4(f) may be served on any party anywhere in the world. Any party may make service on any other party by sending or delivering a copy of the process to the party to be served at the address and in the manner provided for the giving of notices in Section 12.18 of the Purchase Agreement. Nothing in this Paragraph 4(f) will affect the right of any party to serve legal process in any other manner permitted by law or at equity.**

(g) **Waiver of Jury Trial. EACH PARTY, KNOWINGLY, VOLUNTARILY, AND INTENTIONALLY, WAIVES ITS RIGHT TO TRIAL BY JURY IN ANY PROCEEDING ARISING OUT OF OR RELATING TO THIS AGREEMENT, WHETHER SOUNDING IN CONTRACT, TORT, OR OTHERWISE.**

(h)   **Attorneys' Fees.** Except as provided in clause (iv) of Paragraph 3(f), in the event any Proceeding is brought in respect of this Agreement, the prevailing party will be entitled to recover reasonable attorneys' fees and other costs incurred in such Proceeding, in addition to any relief to which such party may be entitled.

(i)   **No Waiver.** Neither any failure nor any delay by any party in exercising any right, power, or privilege under this Agreement or any of the documents referred to in this Agreement will operate as a waiver of such right, power, or privilege, and no single or partial exercise of any such right, power, or privilege will preclude any other or further exercise of such right, power, or privilege or the exercise of any other right, power, or privilege. To the maximum extent permitted by applicable Legal Requirements, (i) no claim or right arising out of this Agreement or any of the documents referred to in this Agreement can be waived by a party, in whole or in part, unless made in a writing signed by such party; (ii) a waiver given by a party will only be applicable to the specific instance for which it is given; and (iii) no notice to or demand on a party will (A) waive or otherwise affect any obligation of that party or (B) affect the right of the party giving such notice or demand to take further action without notice or demand as provided in this Agreement or the documents referred to in this Agreement.

(j)   **Notices.** All notices and other communications required or permitted by this Agreement shall be given in accordance with Section 12.18 of the Purchase Agreement.

(k)   **Severability.** If any provision of this Agreement is held invalid or unenforceable by any court of competent jurisdiction, the other provisions of this Agreement will remain in full force and effect. Any provision of this Agreement held invalid or unenforceable only in part or degree will remain in full force and effect to the extent not held invalid or unenforceable.

(l)   **Time of Essence.** With regard to all dates and time periods set forth or referred to in this Agreement, time is of the essence.

(m)   **Counterparts/Electronic Signatures.** This Agreement may be executed in one or more counterparts, each of which will be deemed to be an original copy and all of which, when taken together, will be deemed to constitute one and the same agreement, and will be effective when counterparts have been signed by each of the parties and delivered to the other parties. A manual signature on this Agreement, which image is transmitted electronically, will constitute an original signature for all purposes. The delivery of copies of this Agreement, including executed signature pages where required, by electronic transmission will constitute effective delivery of this Agreement for all purposes.

IN WITNESS WHEREOF, the parties have executed and delivered this Agreement as of the date first written above.

BUYER: **SELLERS:**

By: _____   _____

Name: _____   [1]

Title: _____   _____

                                                    [2]

                                                    . . .

                                                    _____

                                                    [8]

SELLERS' REPRESENTATIVE:

_____

ANCILLARY DOCUMENT E

Contribution Agreement

PRELIMINARY NOTE

Often, as in the case of the Model Agreement, each Seller is jointly and severally liable for many, if not all, obligations under the acquisition agreement. In such a case, a contribution agreement may be appropriate to assure that each Seller bears his or her fair share of liabilities if post-closing claims by the Buyer must be satisfied by one or more of the Sellers. Because each Seller is jointly and severally liable, a particular seller could be forced to make a disproportionate payment to the Buyer. A contribution agreement seeks to avoid that result by requiring a Seller who did not make a payment to the buyer (or otherwise satisfy a liability) to reimburse those Sellers who made such a payment. While such reimbursement is usually made to assure that each Seller bears his or her pro rata share, another basis of reimbursement could be selected. Common law (or statutory) rights of contribution or subrogation may also be available, without the need for an express agreement.

From the perspective of the Sellers, a better result may be to persuade the Buyer to hold each Seller responsible for only his or her pro rata share of any liability. This would protect the Sellers with deep pockets from the credit risk and litigation expense of enforcing a contribution agreement against the other Sellers; the cost of multiple enforcement actions against individual Sellers might also discourage the Buyer from seeking to enforce a relatively minor claim. Buyer is likely to resist such a pro rata limitation on Seller liability. *See* "Joint and Several Liability" in commentary to lead-in to Section 11.2 and commentary to Section 12.4 of the Model Agreement.

There is no standard form of contribution agreement. The following contribution agreement should not be viewed as a standard form that each Seller should be willing to sign. Rather, it should be viewed only as an example of such a form in conjunction with the discussion of the various issues set forth below.

Other Possible Provisions. As drafted, the Contribution Agreement has a limited objective: adjusting the respective obligations of Sellers if one or more is called upon to make a payment under the Model Agreement. But they might also agree to adjust their other relationships. Many of those would be fact-specific. For example, under the Model Agreement, Sellers are required to repay indebtedness to the

Acquired Companies (Section 5.5). Because that might fall disproportionately on some Sellers, those affected might seek some makeup from the other Sellers; that could be handled in an agreement among the Sellers (the Contribution Agreement or some other agreement).

Buyer has included the concept of a "Sellers' Representative" in the Model Agreement for Buyer's own convenience. Rather than dealing with eight Sellers, it need deal only with the Sellers' Representative. Thus the Purchase Price is paid to the Sellers' Representative in stages—at Closing, after the Adjustment Amount is determined, and when the Escrow Fund is paid out. The Sellers' Representative stands in for Sellers with respect to Closing, for example, in setting the date (Section 2.3), receiving the purchase consideration (Section 2.4), waiving conditions (beginning of Article 9), and receiving closing documents (Sections 9.3–9.5). It receives (where applicable) and negotiates with Buyer with respect to the Adjustment Amount (Sections 2.5 and 2.6), and receives claims for indemnification (Section 11.5), notices of setoff (Section 11.7), notices of Third-Party Claims (Section 11.8), and notices of other claims (Section 11.9). Sellers' Representative is appointed by Section 12.5, and has broad authority. The Sellers' Representative is exculpated for conduct and is held harmless for any liability as long as it acts in good faith (Section 12.5).

Sellers may want to control the Sellers' Representative in some fashion. While Buyer probably has a legitimate position that it should be able to deal with one person, it should not expect that the Sellers' Representative will ignore the interests of Sellers when acting. Nowhere in the Model Agreement are limitations on the Sellers' Representative, either procedurally or substantively, imposed. Depending on the relationship of Sellers, there may be complete trust in the discretion of the Sellers' Representative. For instance, where virtually all the stock of the Company is owned by a private equity fund that will act as Sellers' Representative, all Sellers may feel protected by the self-interest and negotiating experience of the private equity fund. On the other hand, where the Company is owned by warring family factions, there may be little appetite for allowing the Seller's Representative to act with unbridled authority. In that instance, one of a number of control techniques could be used: the Sellers' Representative could be controlled by a committee of all Sellers or some actions could be subject to further approval by Sellers.

Sellers may want to appoint (and limit the authority of) the Sellers' Representative before the Model Agreement is signed since the Sellers' Representative will make decisions relating to Closing. They would want to scale back Section 12.5, probably appointing the Sellers' Representative in a document of their making, although confirming in the Model Agreement such appointment and Buyer's authority to deal exclusively with the Sellers' Representative. They would want to provide how the funds received by the Sellers' Representative would be paid out—presumably pro rata, but other choices could be made. They might want to limit the authority of any Seller to settle claims under the Model Agreement.

Sellers might want to create a separate fund out of the proceeds to allow the Sellers' Representative to discharge its duties. For example, the Adjustment Amount may be contested, and in that event Sellers' Representative would need a source of funds to hire accountants, attorneys, and other experts. Because the Sellers remain liable if indemnification or other claims exceed the Escrow Fund (and because there is no holdback or escrow for the Adjustment Amount), they may feel more comfortable if a backup fund is held by the Sellers' Representative to make investigations and defend against the Buyer's claims (and pay any amount owed for the Adjustment Amount).

When the Sellers' Representative in fact exercises no discretion and is directed by the Sellers, broad indemnification and exculpation may be important. When the Sellers' Representative enjoys broad discretion (and, in fact, is a Seller, perhaps with the major ownership interest), Sellers may be reluctant to grant such broad relief, and may want to provide expressly for the standard of care applicable to Sellers' Representative. If the Sellers' Representative is independent, their agreement may address compensation. Rather than reciting that appointment is coupled with an interest (an attempt to make it irrevocable), the Sellers may want to rely on state statutes to create a durable power of attorney.

The representations made by individual Sellers are made for the benefit of Buyer. Sellers might want their agreement to be clear that they are entitled to rely on the representations (as well as covenants) of the other Sellers.

CONTRIBUTION AGREEMENT

This Contribution Agreement ("Agreement") is made as of _____, among [1], [2], . . . and [8], who are sometimes referred to individually as a "Seller" and collectively as the "Sellers."

RECITALS

This Agreement relates to a Stock Purchase Agreement, dated the date hereof (the "Purchase Agreement"), among _____, a _____ corporation ("Buyer"), and the Sellers. All capitalized terms used and not defined in this Agreement have the meanings specified in the Purchase Agreement.

In the Purchase Agreement, the Sellers have agreed jointly and severally to indemnify Buyer and certain other Persons. In this Agreement, the Sellers agree to reimburse each other (pro rata based on their respective shareholdings) against certain joint and several liabilities arising under the Purchase Agreement.

The Sellers, intending to be legally bound, agree as follows:

1. OWNERSHIP

Part 3.3(a) of the Disclosure Letter lists Sellers and the number of Shares held by each Seller.

2. REIMBURSEMENT

Subject to the terms of this Agreement, each Seller shall be liable for his or her "Pro Rata Share" (as defined below) of any obligation arising out of Section 11.2 or 11.3 of the Purchase Agreement or otherwise pertaining to the sale of the Shares to Buyer (an "Indemnity Claim"). "Pro Rata Share" means a fraction, the numerator of which is the number of Shares owned by such Seller as shown in Part 3.3(a) of the Disclosure Letter and the denominator of which is the total number of issued and outstanding Shares as shown in Part 3.3(a) of the Disclosure Letter. Any amount payable by a Seller to another Seller pursuant to this Agreement shall be paid within thirty (30) days of receipt by such Seller of due notice given by a Seller to the effect that such Seller has made or will become obligated to make a payment in respect of an Indemnity Claim.

COMMENT

By making each Seller liable only for his or her pro rata share, the first Seller from whom Buyer seeks indemnification alone takes the entire risk of a nonpayment by one or more of the other Sellers. The Contribution Agreement could be modified to provide that each nondefaulting Seller bears his or her share of the portion left unpaid by any Seller.

The reimbursement obligation of each Seller goes beyond claims under Article 11 of the Model Agreement, to include other claims under the Model Agreement.

The Sellers' reimbursement obligation does not include another Seller's costs of defense.

Sometimes Sellers agree that liabilities under the acquisition agreement should not be shared proportionately. For example, Sellers who are active in the business may be willing to accept full responsibility for the representations made, regardless of whether a particular breach of representation is known or knowable. This Contribution Agreement does not deal with that possibility, other than in Paragraph 3, which denies contribution for certain instances of fault.

Exhibit 2.4(a)(vii)—Escrow Agreement does not address whether certain Sellers should bear some disproportionate liability. Because Sellers contribute proportionately to the Escrow Agreement (by means of a proportionate deduction from proceeds of sale), the Escrow Agreement (if the amount held thereunder is adequate to fund all Buyer claims or if the liability of Sellers is limited to the Escrow Agreement) effectively requires each nondefaulting Seller to bear his or her share of a liability of the

Sellers. However, the Escrow Agreement does not adjust the obligation of Sellers when their responsibilities are other than proportionate. Paragraph 3(a) below deals with this to some extent, requiring that if the Escrow Fund is used to pay a claim that is a particular Seller's responsibility, the Escrow Fund is reimbursed by the Seller responsible.

3. **RESPONSIBILITY FOR CERTAIN INDEMNITY CLAIMS**

(a) **Notwithstanding any provision of this Agreement, no Seller shall be entitled to any payment from any other Seller with respect to an Indemnity Claim relating to, arising or resulting from, or otherwise attributable to any of the following eventualities:**

> **(i)** **A Breach by such Seller of any covenant other than an obligation under Article 11 of the Purchase Agreement;**

> **(ii)** **A Breach of any representation or warranty that such Seller actually knew to be false at the time he or she made it; or**

> **(iii)** **The Breach of Section 3.2 or 3.3 of the Purchase Agreement with respect to such Seller;**

and each Seller agrees to pay any such Indemnity Claim personally, and to the extent the Escrow Fund is used to pay any such Indemnity Claim, to promptly reimburse the Escrow Fund the full amount of such payment.

COMMENT

Paragraph 3(a) sets forth exceptions to the scope of coverage set forth in Paragraph 2. The most controversial issue raised by these exceptions may be whether a Seller may seek contribution in an instance where he or she knew that the representation was false when made. On one hand, Sellers may argue that such an exclusion is too narrow and that they should not have to contribute where another Seller should have known that the representation was false at the time it was made. On the other hand, a Seller may argue both that the burden of even an intentional falsehood that results in the Sellers receiving a better price should be borne equally by all the Sellers and that the standard "knew" is unfair to him or her because he or she might have to defend against a claim that he or she "knew" when he or she did not and could be unable to receive contribution where a finder of fact incorrectly decides that Sellers "should have known" of the falsehood.

A Breach of covenant is an exception to contribution because normally a particular Seller should be responsible for his or her Breach. The exception for Sections 3.2 or 3.3 with respect to a particular Seller is because, to the extent a representation affecting a particular Seller is untrue, that particular Seller should be responsible.

(b)   **Each Seller agrees to use his or her best efforts to cause any Indemnity Claim to be satisfied out of funds held by the Escrow Agent, to the extent it is then available, rather than by Sellers.**

COMMENT

Perhaps the best way to avoid many of these issues and the need for a Contribution Agreement entirely is to agree among Sellers to keep an adequate reserve to cover both indemnification claims and the costs of defending and/or resolving such claims for an adequate period of time. Sellers, however, will often (if not usually) be anxious to have the escrow end as soon as possible.

Use of the Escrow Fund for the purpose of paying claims under Article 11 of the Model Agreement only goes part of the way. Sellers will still need to defend the claim, particularly if it is a Third-Party Claim, and the Contribution Agreement has no provision for that purpose.

Sellers might propose a partial solution by setting up an independent fund, perhaps held by Sellers' Representative, for use in defending claims. They might also provide that the remaining proceeds of the Escrow Fund be moved into that fund for that purpose.

For a discussion of "best efforts," *see* commentary to Section 5.7 of the Model Agreement.

4.   MISCELLANEOUS

COMMENT

See the Introduction to this Volume II and commentary to Article 12 of the Model Agreement for further discussion relevant to the miscellaneous provisions.

(a)   **Entire Agreement.   Other than the Purchase Agreement, this Agreement supersedes all prior agreements, whether written or oral, between the parties with respect to its subject matter and constitutes a complete and exclusive statement of the terms of the agreement between the parties with respect to its subject matter.**

COMMENT

Sellers have agreed to joint and several liability under Section 12.4 of the Model Agreement (which creates the need for the Contribution Agreement) and appointed Sellers' Representative in Section 12.5 of the Model Agreement. The entirety of Article 11, dealing with Sellers' obligations of indemnification, might also be thought of as relating to their agreement. Accordingly, this paragraph recognizes the Model Agreement as another agreement among the Sellers that is not superseded.

(b) **Modification.** This Agreement may only be amended, supplemented, or otherwise modified by a writing executed by the parties.

(c) **Assignments and Successors.** No party may assign any of its rights or delegate any of its obligations under this Agreement without the prior consent of the other parties. Any purported assignment of rights or delegation of obligations in violation of this Paragraph 4(c) will be void. Subject to the foregoing, this Agreement will apply to, be binding in all respects upon, and inure to the benefit of the heirs, executors, administrators, legal representatives, successors, and permitted assigns of the parties.

(d) **Governing Law.** All matters relating to or arising out of this Agreement and the rights of the parties (whether sounding in contract, tort, or otherwise) will be governed by and construed and interpreted under the laws of the State of _____, without regard to conflicts of laws principles that would require the application of any other law.

(e) **Remedies Cumulative.** The rights and remedies of the parties are cumulative and not alternative.

(f) **Jurisdiction; Service of Process.** Any proceeding arising out of or relating to this Agreement shall be brought in the courts of the State of _____, County of _____, or, if it has or can acquire jurisdiction, in the United States District Court for the _____ District of _____, and each of the parties irrevocably submits to the exclusive jurisdiction of each such court in any such proceeding, waives any objection it may now or hereafter have to venue or to convenience of forum, agrees that all claims in respect of such proceeding shall be heard and determined only in any such court, and agrees not to bring any proceeding arising out of or relating to this Agreement. Each party acknowledges and agrees that this Paragraph 4(f) constitutes a voluntary and bargained-for agreement between the parties. Process in any proceeding referred to in the first sentence of this Paragraph 4(f) may be served on any party anywhere in the world. Any party may make service on any other party by sending or delivering a copy of the process to the party to be served at the address and in the manner provided for the giving of notices in Paragraph 4(j). Nothing in this Paragraph 4(f) will affect the right of any party to serve legal process in any other manner permitted by law or at equity.

(g) **Waiver of Jury Trial.** EACH PARTY, KNOWINGLY, VOLUNTARILY, AND INTENTIONALLY, WAIVES ITS RIGHT TO TRIAL BY JURY IN ANY PROCEEDING ARISING OUT OF OR RELATING TO THIS AGREEMENT, WHETHER SOUNDING IN CONTRACT, TORT, OR OTHERWISE.

(h) **Attorneys' Fees.** In the event any Proceeding is brought in respect of this Agreement, the prevailing party will be entitled to recover reasonable attorneys' fees and other costs incurred in such Proceeding, in addition to any relief to which such party may be entitled.

(i)   No Waiver. Neither any failure nor any delay by any party in exercising any right, power, or privilege under this Agreement will operate as a waiver of such right, power, or privilege, and no single or partial exercise of any such right, power, or privilege will preclude any other or further exercise of such right, power, or privilege or the exercise of any other right, power, or privilege. To the maximum extent permitted by applicable Legal Requirements, (i) no claim or right arising out of this Agreement can be waived by a party, in whole or in part, unless made in a writing signed by such party; (ii) a waiver given by a party will only be applicable to the specific instance for which it is given; and (iii) no notice to or demand on a party will (A) waive or otherwise affect any obligation of that party or (B) affect the right of the party giving such notice or demand to take further action without notice or demand as provided in this Agreement.

(j)   Notices. All notices and other communications required or permitted by this Agreement will be in writing and will be effective, and any applicable time period shall commence when (i) delivered to the following address by hand or by a nationally recognized overnight courier service (costs prepaid) addressed to the following address or (ii) transmitted electronically to the following facsimile numbers or e-mail addresses, in each case marked to the attention of the Person (by name or title) designated below (or to such other address, facsimile number, e-mail address, or Person as a party may designate by notice to the other parties):

    Seller [1]:
    [Street]
    [City, state, and zip code]
    Fax no.:
    E-mail address:

    Seller [2]:
    [Street]
    [City, state, and zip code]
    Fax no.:
    E-mail address:

    . . .

    Seller [8]:
    [Street]
    [City, state, and zip code]
    Fax no.:
    E-mail address:

(k) **Counterparts/Electronic Signatures. This Agreement may be executed in one or more counterparts, each of which will be deemed to be an original copy and all of which, when taken together, will be deemed to constitute one and the same agreement, and will be effective when counterparts have been signed by each of the parties and delivered to the other parties. A manual signature on this Agreement, which image is transmitted electronically, will constitute an original signature for all purposes. The delivery of copies of this Agreement, including executed signature pages where required, by electronic transmission will constitute effective delivery of this Agreement for all purposes.**

IN WITNESS WHEREOF, the parties have executed and delivered this Agreement as of the date first written above.

_____

[1]

_____

[2]

. . .

_____

[8]

APPENDICES

APPENDIX A

The Purchase of a Subsidiary

While the Model Agreement can be used as a form for the purchase of a subsidiary out of a consolidated group, there are aspects of this type of transaction that will require significant changes or even the use of another form, such as the Model Asset Purchase Agreement. For example, not all the businesses, product lines, and assets wanted by a buyer may be in the subsidiary being purchased, but rather may be in the parent or in other subsidiaries. In that case, a contribution of assets might be made to the subsidiary prior to or at the closing, or the transaction might be structured as the purchase by the buyer of stock of the subsidiary and assets of the parent or the other subsidiaries. In some transactions, the subsidiary being purchased may operate a business or product line or have assets that are not wanted by a buyer or that a seller wishes to retain, so that they will have to be transferred out of the subsidiary prior to or at the closing.

Subsidiaries are seldom capable of operating as self-contained businesses and are dependent to some extent on their parents or affiliates. The following are examples of interrelationships that are common in subsidiary purchases and must be negotiated and provided for to the extent they continue after the closing:

- Various support functions may be supplied at the parent level, such as human resources, employee benefits, and legal services.
- Intellectual property may be owned by the parent or in a separate entity and licensed to the operating subsidiaries.
- Software may be licensed by, and used under, an enterprise-wide arrangement.
- A subsidiary may obtain products, components, or raw materials from, or sell them to, the parent or another subsidiary.

There are also other matters peculiar to subsidiary purchases that a buyer must address in conducting its due diligence and drafting an acquisition agreement, including the following:

- The subsidiary may have liabilities under ERISA as a member of a common group.
- The subsidiary may have income tax liabilities as part of a consolidated group.

- The subsidiary may lack complete business and financial records, and its financial statements will most likely not have been audited by independent accountants.

A buyer must ensure that it has adequately considered and dealt with these special circumstances.

This Appendix discusses some of the issues associated with a subsidiary purchase. While many of these issues may apply to the purchase of interests in a limited liability company or other noncorporate entity, the discussion will focus on the purchase of corporate subsidiaries.

SALE PROCESS

The sale process in these transactions, commonly called "divestitures," is generally not unlike that for the sale of any privately held company. There may be a greater tendency, however, to conduct the sale of a subsidiary in an auction process in which the seller prepares and asks bidders to mark up a form of acquisition agreement. For a discussion of the auction process, *see* M&A PROCESS 102–07. That process reduces the likelihood of substitution of a buyer-friendly draft, such as the Model Agreement, and may restrict a bidder's flexibility in marking up the form, lest it will be disadvantaged in the bidding process. However, because many of the issues discussed below are structural in nature, raising them may be less objectionable to a seller than in other bidding situations. For example, if a buyer has determined not to purchase a product line of the subsidiary that is unrelated to its primary business, appropriate carveouts in the acquisition agreement will be necessary, but will most likely be an expected part of the bid. Furthermore, corporate sellers may be less troubled than individual sellers in providing more adequate remedies to buyers for breaches of their representations.

DUE DILIGENCE

Business due diligence may be more difficult with respect to a subsidiary purchase. Often, accounting records and other historical business data are lacking. Accounting adjustments may have been taken at the parent level. Other businesses may have been contributed to the subsidiary with no thought of how the history of those other businesses could be tracked. Even if available, the records may not reflect all necessary adjustments, such as the allocation of overhead, particularly where the subsidiary is only a portion of a business segment. A significant part of the due diligence will involve understanding the subsidiary's financial statements, and determining what adjustments might be appropriate to give a true picture of its financial condition and results of operations. For example, related-party transactions, such as transfer pricing and support services, can significantly affect the reported results of a subsidiary.

In many respects, legal due diligence will be conducted just as in any stock acquisition. There may, however, be two significant differences. The first relates to the review of arrangements that will not be continued once the subsidiary is sold.

For example, participation in benefit plans of a parent would often be terminated at the time of sale and replaced with either the buyer's plans or newly established plans. While a buyer would be interested in any liabilities that participation in those benefit plans might have created and would have a general interest in understanding the level of benefits provided, it may have limited interest in understanding the intricacies of plan design and operation. It is not uncommon for incentive awards for employees of a subsidiary, such as options, to be based on the parent's stock price or performance. These awards will most likely terminate on a sale even though employment by the subsidiary continues after the sale.

The second is an understanding of the interrelationships that exist between the subsidiary being purchased and its parent and affiliates. A buyer will normally assume that, in the purchase of a stand-alone company, it has whatever it needs to operate its business, but in the purchase of a subsidiary a buyer will start with the opposite assumption (i.e., that the subsidiary has nothing that is required to operate its business). Due diligence must identify all support functions that will not be available after the closing, as well as all arrangements for the purchase and sale of products, components, and raw materials between the subsidiary and the parent and its affiliates. For example, insurance coverage may be provided on a blanket basis by the parent for all its affiliates, and letters of credit or surety bonds may depend on the credit of the parent and its consolidated operations. This will become important information in negotiating the final form of acquisition agreement and the ancillary agreements.

Special diligence may be required for a newly created subsidiary. A seller will sometimes take an unincorporated business and contribute its assets to a newly created subsidiary for purposes of sale. Often the reason is tactical—it is easier to negotiate and close a stock purchase than an asset purchase. The seller has inertia on its side if the buyer proposes to change what is in the new subsidiary. The buyer will be justifiably concerned about the adequacy of the creation of the subsidiary. All the considerations that go into negotiating an asset purchase agreement must be brought to bear on the newly created subsidiary. There will be concern about the assumption of liabilities and obligations and the failure to receive all the assets and contracts necessary to conduct the business.

FORM OF TRANSACTION

As discussed in the preliminary note to the Model Agreement, it is always appropriate to consider whether a stock purchase is the appropriate form. A buyer has the usual concerns about unknown liabilities that might be avoided through an asset purchase. If the purchase involves otherwise carving up the business of the subsidiary by requiring that the parent contribute or remove assets, certain aspects of an asset transfer are already involved and a buyer may prefer to deal with all the assets in a coordinated manner as an asset transaction. The structure of the transaction will also affect the tax consequences. Many sellers of stock of subsidiaries volunteer a Section 338(h)(10) election, which allows the seller and the buyer to treat the transaction as an asset sale for federal income tax purposes.

If the subsidiary being sold is a disregarded entity for tax purposes, it is otherwise treated as an asset sale in any event. There is, of course, the normal concern about nontax aspects of the transaction, such as the assignability of contracts. All these factors can affect a determination as to the form of the transaction.

NORMALIZING THE SUBSIDIARY

There may be a series of actions required so that the subsidiary will be able to operate as a self-contained business after the closing. These actions may address concerns such as the following:

- Some support services provided by the parent or its affiliates may need to be continued for a transition period. The types of services that will be provided and length of the transition period are highly variable.

- Intercompany arrangements may need to be terminated or modified. Intercompany receivables and payables may be eliminated or netted against each other. Often a subsidiary is capitalized through intercompany loan arrangements. A buyer may want outstanding borrowings converted to capital and the level of working capital normalized. A seller may want to remove all cash from the business. Tax-sharing agreements are usually eliminated or modified to apply only to periods prior to the closing. If an existing tax-sharing agreement does not address the ability to carryback post-acquisition operating losses of the subsidiary into pre-acquisition consolidated taxable years of the seller's consolidated group, a buyer may want the acquisition agreement to provide for such a carryback. The buyer and seller may also address continuation of arrangements between the subsidiary and its affiliates for the purchase or sale of products, components, and raw materials.

- To the extent intellectual property is not owned, it may need to be contributed or licensed to the subsidiary. This gets sorted out in various ways, depending on whether the intellectual property is used in other businesses of the parent, whether it is an important part of its licensing strategy with third parties, and whether it may be pursuing or be subject to infringement claims. If intellectual property owned by the subsidiary is used by the seller's other businesses, a license by the subsidiary would be expected.

- Other assets (and perhaps related liabilities) may be contributed to the subsidiary, either because this is simply part of the business arrangement or because assets used in the business of the subsidiary are held by the parent or its affiliates. Similarly, assets used by the parent or its affiliates in their other businesses may reside in the subsidiary or the buyer may not want a particular business or product line. A seller may also insist that certain additional liabilities that relate to the business being sold be assumed by the buyer.

Attached as Exhibit 1 is a fairly extensive checklist of issues to be considered in the purchase of a subsidiary. These can be covered in the acquisition agreement as covenants or conditions to closing, or in ancillary agreements to be delivered at closing, such as long-term supply agreements, licenses of intellectual property, assignments (with applicable consents) of software, and transition services agreements.

TAX ISSUES

The sale of a subsidiary out of a consolidated group presents special tax considerations:

- The transaction can be taxed as a sale of stock or an asset sale, depending on whether the parties make a Section 338(h)(10) election. If an election is made, the transaction would be treated for corporate law purposes as a sale of stock but for tax purposes as if the subsidiary had sold all its assets and then distributed the proceeds to the parent in liquidation. The buyer receives a step-up in basis as in any asset sale, with the purchase price reflecting the price paid for the stock and the liabilities of the subsidiary. For a discussion of a Section 338(h)(10) election as applied to the sale of S corporations, *see* commentary to Section 3.11 of the Model Agreement. The state tax treatment of the election will also be pertinent.

- While for federal tax purposes the sale will create a short year for the subsidiary, requiring the payment of taxes for the short year, the sale may not have a similar effect under the income tax laws of some states and particularly not for such things as sales tax returns. A method will have to be agreed upon for allocating taxes between buyer and seller and determining responsibility for preparing appropriate returns.

- A buyer will be concerned that a tax audit of the seller may affect the subsidiary, either because there is additional joint and several liability or because of the precedent-setting effect of any settlement. The seller may insist that it control any audit of its consolidated returns that include the subsidiary.

- Various tax records pertaining to the subsidiary may be held by the parent (which would normally be asked to retain them for the benefit of the buyer) or by the subsidiary (which would normally be asked to retain them for the benefit of the parent).

- Because a subsidiary is jointly and severally liable for all federal taxes of its consolidated group, this liability is often dealt with separately in the indemnification provisions, as well as being covered by the representations.

For a more detailed discussion of the special tax considerations applicable to these transactions, *see* KLING & NUGENT §19.02.

AGREEMENTS SIGNED AT CLOSING

The negotiated solution to normalizing the subsidiary may be provided in covenants and pre-closing conditions to the acquisition agreement, which may also involve documents to be delivered at closing. In addition, if there are ongoing business relationships between the subsidiary and the parent or its other affiliates that are to continue, they are often represented by ancillary agreements delivered at the closing. It is possible, of course, that the substance of those arrangements could simply become additional post-closing covenants in the acquisition agreement. However, some of these arrangements may be between entities that are not parties to the acquisition agreement.

Agreements representing a commercial or special relationship may take the form of ancillary agreements, the forms of which are usually attached as exhibits to the acquisition agreement. For example, a supply agreement may be long-term, involve unique remedies, and contain particular commercial limitations and provisions that may not be familiar to the transactional lawyer. It may be preferable to incorporate these terms in a self-contained agreement, which then can easily be terminated, modified, and enforced without affecting the entire acquisition agreement. Another example is the licensing of patents (and other intellectual property) that can run either way (a license from the seller or an IP entity to the subsidiary or a license by the subsidiary back to the parent and its affiliates for use in their businesses).

The continuation of services after the closing is usually covered in a separate document commonly called a transition services agreement (TSA). In addition to the factors set forth above, particularly the flexibility in making modifications, it is often kept separate simply because the parties seldom have enough facts to negotiate the terms at the time the acquisition agreement is signed. In addition, the details of the ongoing operations are often known only to a different set of business people from those negotiating the acquisition. A more complete discussion of TSAs is set forth below under "Transition Services Agreements" and a form is attached as Exhibit 3.

NEGOTIATED MODIFICATIONS TO THE MODEL AGREEMENT

The adjustments to be made in connection with the purchase of a subsidiary are always responsive to due diligence, the concerns of the parties, and other factors. How these are handled varies. If the Model Agreement is to be used as the form, changes will be required. There would be only one seller, and the references to the sellers as individuals, and portions of the acquisition and ancillary agreements that contemplate that the sellers are individuals, would need to be modified.

Economic Terms. For some sellers, price may not be as significant as its desire to close quickly and with a minimum of contingencies. Seller financing and earnouts are generally not in favor in these types of transactions. Moreover, a buyer will often rely on the general credit of the seller for indemnification and not insist on an escrow.

Examples of issues that might be covered as economic terms in the acquisition agreement include:

- Forgiveness of intercompany debt (including accounts payable and receivable) and extinguishment of agreements. However, some intercompany obligations may be expressly preserved, such as the obligation to make a profit-sharing plan contribution to the extent of participation by the subsidiary's employees.

- Working capital adjustments, including the contribution of cash or a dividend of cash to achieve some specified level. (Note that the Model Agreement's shareholders' equity purchase price adjustment is more often a working capital purchase price adjustment in subsidiary purchases.)

- Releases by the subsidiary of claims against its officers and directors (on the basis that such persons would seek indemnification against the seller).

- Releases by the seller of claims against the subsidiary. (A seller might expect a mutual release.)

- Allocation of benefits and burdens under shared contracts.

Because these items tend to be part of the basic economic terms of the transaction, they might be included in Article 2 of the Model Agreement or dealt with in ancillary agreements to be delivered at the closing and listed in Article 2.

Particular Representations. The representations will need to be adjusted to the particularities of the seller and of the transaction.

Initially, representations as to the status of the seller and due authorization for the transaction would be inserted, modeled on Buyer's representations in Article 4 of the Model Agreement.

If assets are held outside the subsidiary, but will be contributed to it before closing, the representations will need to be modified.

A representation about financial statements would be expected. A subsidiary will usually not have separately audited financial statements or even financial statements prepared in accordance with GAAP. The financial statements that are available may not have been subject to the same degree of scrutiny as the financial statements of the parent. Many sellers will take the position that the financial statements cannot be audited after the fact because the auditor failed to carry out the usual procedures at year-end (such as observing inventories of the subsidiary), although the auditors might be able use alternate procedures in lieu of what is customarily done. The financial statements may not even be capable of being prepared because there is no basis on which to determine the amount of expense appropriately allocated to the business. There can often be lengthy discussions about whether financial statements can be audited or any representations about them can be made, and sometimes whether they can even be prepared. If the buyer is a publicly held company, it may require audited financial statements to satisfy SEC requirements for financial statements of businesses acquired or to be acquired. *See* commentary to Section 3.4 of the Model Agreement regarding these financial statement requirements. The absence of audited financial statements can also affect the exit prospects for a buyer, particularly a financial buyer.

A representation about the adequacy of the assets may be particularly important. It would need to give effect to the assets to be contributed and any licenses to be entered into at closing. An exception with respect to services to be performed pursuant to the TSA might be expected.

The tax representation might be extended to include representations pertinent to the subsidiary as a part of a consolidated group.

There might be an expansion of the scope of the ERISA representations. Representations might be added that would help the buyer assess whether there is any substantial risk of group liability for which the subsidiary could have responsibility.

Since intercompany arrangements take on increasing importance, identification of these arrangements in the representations may be appropriate.

Pre-Closing Covenants. While the usual pre-closing covenants, designed to assure the maintenance of a business being purchased, may be satisfactory for the purchase of a subsidiary, it may be necessary to qualify certain negative covenants to give effect to the normalizing that is expected to occur prior to closing. A covenant with respect to clean-up items to be accomplished prior to closing, such as isolation of corporate records, might be considered. It may also be appropriate to assure that the separation is not complicated by actions taken in the interim. For example, in ordering new packaging, catalogs, or brochures for the subsidiary after the acquisition agreement is signed, identification of the seller might be omitted.

Closing Conditions/Deliverables. Most normalizing transfers can be adequately covered by the delivery of documents, such as bills of sale and assignments, at closing. The need for third-party consents may be heightened. Not only must change-in-control provisions in agreements to which the subsidiary is a party be considered, but also consents to some normalizing transfers may be required. For example, some software vendors are quite rigid in not allowing the subdivision of software licenses, often imposing new fees. Consents may also be required in order to permit some services to be provided under the TSA, such as from software vendors.

The need for consents at the parent level is likely. For example, covenants in credit agreements may prohibit a substantial sale without consent or the stock in the subsidiary may be pledged. Depending on the relative size of the subsidiary within the corporate group, there also may be a need for approval by the parent's directors and shareholders. For a discussion of shareholder approval requirements, *see* KLING & NUGENT § 4.09.

Post-closing arrangements subject to separate ancillary agreements, such as TSAs, supply agreements, and license agreements, might be among the deliverables at closing.

Post-Closing Covenants. Some post-closing covenants will be similar to those typically required when purchasing the stock of a company from individuals. These might include:

- Covenant not to compete—the scope of this agreement will be carefully crafted by the seller because it is often the case that some of its remaining businesses currently or prospectively overlap with the business of the subsidiary. Furthermore, a seller will be concerned that the covenant could preclude future acquisitions of companies that conduct, at least in part, a competing business. Most buyers are willing to allow the purchase of a competing business that is incidental to an entire business being purchased, perhaps with a proviso that the business be disposed of promptly or that it not be expanded. Since the members of management of a subsidiary are not shareholders, it might be more difficult to obtain enforceable covenants not to compete from them.

- Nonraiding provisions—these provisions are far more important than in the case of a purchase of a business from individuals because the seller will still conduct its remaining business after the sale and will want to retain its employees, some of whom may have had some involvement with the operations of the subsidiary. Similarly, the buyer may want assurances that the employees of the subsidiary will not be offered employment by the seller.

- Confidentiality—information pertaining to the subsidiary may be scattered throughout the seller's organization in hard and electronic form. A buyer may attempt to collect or have this information destroyed prior to the closing, rather than relying simply on a confidentiality agreement.

- Preservation and access to corporate records—a seller may have been responsible for filing consolidated income tax returns that include the subsidiary or tax returns on behalf of the subsidiary. Various state income tax, sales tax, and other returns may have been filed separately for the subsidiary. The subsidiary may need that information to defend itself against audits and to prepare subsequent returns. Other financial information of the seller may be pertinent to the subsidiary.

- Cooperation—because of mutual dependencies, there may be a broad cooperation clause. Defense of tax audits, litigation, and other governmental proceedings may require the involvement of personnel of seller and the subsidiary.

- Pending litigation—while the possible exposure or recovery for pending litigation is a subject for negotiation, the responsibility for defense or prosecution is also normally addressed. The general defense provisions under the indemnification sections of the Model Agreement could be tailored for the specifics.

- Change of names—the subsidiary's name or similar names used by affiliates may have to be changed.

- Benefit plans—participation in employee benefit plans maintained by a seller is usually terminated effective at the closing. Buyers may sometimes request that the seller continue to include the subsidiary's employees in those plans for some period of time while there is a transition to buyer's plans or to the subsidiary's new plans, particularly in the case of a financial buyer. Sellers usually resist this because of state insurance issues and other technical reasons. Sellers often negotiate for a minimum level of benefits for some period of time and some assurance of continued employment for the subsidiary's employees.

- Tax matters—because the tax issues can be fairly complicated, they are often addressed in a separate article of the acquisition agreement. This article would usually cover preparation and filing of tax returns, handling tax audits, allocating between split periods, and making a Section 338(h)(10) election.

- License—a limited license to continue to use the seller's name on brochures, signage, and other promotional materials for some limited period of time may be appropriate. This could be a post-closing covenant or in a separate license agreement delivered at closing. A seller may have a concomitant need when its materials include the name of the subsidiary.

It may be appropriate to include some (or all) post-closing arrangements in separate documents delivered at closing to better assure ease of enforcement. It may be easier to deal with and enforce a six-page covenant not to compete than one contained in a 100-page acquisition agreement. In addition, these arrangements may be among entities that are not parties to the acquisition agreement.

Remedies. There will be a concern that the remedies provision of the acquisition agreement sweeps in ancillary agreements that should have their own remedies, and that certain remedies are not inadvertently made subject to baskets and caps in the indemnification provisions. Sometimes indemnification is expressed as the exclusive remedy and covers all agreements contained in or entered into pursuant to the acquisition agreement, producing, at best, an ambiguity when those agreements have their own remedies and, at worst, unexpected limitations. Similarly, a buyer that has negotiated for a seller to assume certain liabilities of the subsidiary does not expect that this assumption would be subject to the basket.

A buyer may expect indemnification against certain liabilities, often without reference to proving a breach by the seller of a representation. This would normally apply to liabilities arising as a matter of law, such as liabilities as a member of a consolidated group or claims under ERISA as a member of a control group.

Sample Provisions. Attached as Exhibit 2 are certain provisions that might be inserted in the applicable articles of the Model Agreement to deal with some of the issues raised in this Appendix.

TRANSITION SERVICES AGREEMENTS

As the name implies, a TSA relates to services to be rendered and is for a limited period of time. While practices vary, anything relating to the use of an asset (rather than services) is often covered by a more traditional form of agreement, such as a limited license for a name or trademark or a lease or sublease for real property. A vendor-vendee relationship between the subsidiary and the parent or its affiliates, particularly those that are long-term, is often covered by a separate agreement.

The need for transition services is driven by the capabilities and circumstances of the buyer, the capabilities of the subsidiary, and what is being purchased. A financial buyer may need the seller to continue a whole range of corporate support services for an extended period, while a large strategic buyer may be able to begin supplying all or a substantial portion of support services on the day of closing. Driving forces may include whether the subsidiary remains physically a part of seller's business premises, training issues for employees, short-term issues where the support to be provided will change (such as when a buyer's benefit plans will not be put in place until the beginning of a new year), and where there is truly a technology transfer (such as a move to new software or hardware requiring conversion).

The seller is usually an unwilling participant in the process. After all, it is disposing of the business and wants to avoid any ongoing responsibilities after the sale. While most sellers understand that agreeing to provide some transition services may be necessary for a sale, they will attempt to limit the period of time during which the services will be provided, including inducements to encourage a prompt transition, such as escalating prices. A seller will normally seek broader limitations on its legal responsibilities than would be expected in a commercial setting because the service is being provided as an accommodation to the buyer.

There may be significant limitations on a seller's ability to provide these services. For example, a seller's software licenses may prohibit use of the software to provide service-bureau or server-based services to third parties. To the extent services are provided by third parties, a partial assignment of the underlying contract may be prohibited.

Services Covered. A buyer, in its due diligence, will need to consider whether the subsidiary being purchased has the internal capability of providing the various services required for its ongoing operations. In addition, if the subsidiary is being disaggregated by the transfer of certain assets or employees to the seller or other affiliates, certain services may need to be replaced. The following suggests a classification of services that may result in differing durational and pricing arrangements:

- Proximity services—general services for the physical operation of a business, such as loading dock, distribution, and procurement, as contrasted to general corporate services. These are usually services that a buyer would be able to quickly put in place. It may involve dedicated (rather than shared) employees, and in some cases employee leasing.

- Property services—services or usage rights involving real or personal property. An agreement to make real estate available is normally documented in a more conventional manner, such as a lease, sublease, or license. The same is true for the use by the subsidiary of personal property that it does not own. Intellectual property is normally dealt with in a separate license agreement, although the use of the seller's name and logo for a short period of time may be covered in the acquisition agreement.

- Support services—administrative services to be provided by the parent or its affiliates, such as data processing, billing, collections, employee benefits, and accounting services. Regardless of the resources of the buyer, a number of these functions typically cannot be taken over at closing. Because time may be required to train employees, transition computer software, and build infrastructure, the duration of these transitional arrangements may be fairly long.

The type of service may drive differing pricing mechanisms. For example, support services are often charged to a business unit without any attempt to determine the actual cost. Buyers are often willing to accept a continuation of that practice, but in some cases an effort is made to determine the cost of outsourcing the same or comparable services. On the other hand, proximity services are most likely to be on the basis of actual cost—corporations internally allocate these types of costs to particular business units on this basis. Property services often are based on an approximation of fair market value. None of this is to suggest that any single method is preferable or always the most appropriate.

Limitations. There are several situations where a seller's agreements with third parties restrict whether it will be able to provide some services. Too often, insufficient analysis is done on the underlying agreements, or perhaps the parties, due to the short-term nature of the TSA, implicitly acknowledging this risk.

Some of these issues will get sorted out in connection with closing the acquisition agreement. A buyer will insist that software licenses necessary for the subsidiary (which are often licensed on an enterprise basis) be assigned to the subsidiary. This may work for shrink-wrapped licenses used on individual PCs or where server-based software runs on a server belonging to the subsidiary. But it may not work when server-based software runs off a seller-owned server, even when subsidiary personnel are performing any necessary data input. These arrangements may be subject to the TSA, but software vendor consents are often required. Careful review of software licenses and skillful negotiation of consents is often required.

Sometimes services by third parties will be covered by the TSA. This might involve a partial assignment of the contract for those services, which may be prohibited by the underlying contract. A seller receiving the services and then providing them to the target may be less of a problem than instructing a third party to provide the services directly to the subsidiary.

Seller Concerns. A seller's concerns will be both practical and legal. It will normally seek to avoid devoting its internal resources to another's business. Accordingly, it will usually negotiate for short-term arrangements and will attempt to limit rights to extend the services. When it does grant extension rights, they often will be limited, require appropriate advance notice, and provide for additional fees. Once a TSA is in place, however, the parties often agree to informal terminations or extensions of various services.

A seller will also want legal protection. Most TSAs provide that the standard of service is the same as that previously provided and contain a force majeure clause. Some sellers will want limitations on liability for actionable conduct (e.g., only for gross negligence or willful misconduct) and on damages (e.g., limited to the payments made and excluding consequential damages), indemnification for third-party claims, and dispute resolution mechanisms.

Elements of the TSA. Many TSAs fall into the following scheme: there is a short agreement, providing specified services listed in an appendix, a price and term, a limitation on remedies, sometimes a confidentiality provision, a termination right, and miscellaneous provisions. A short form TSA that might be presented by a buyer is attached as Exhibit 3.

The services to be provided, the pricing of the services, and the duration of particular services may be relegated to an appendix. Services are often priced on a service-by-service basis, rather than a flat fee for all services, because they are to be provided for varying periods of time and can sometimes be extended on a service-by-service basis.

Some standard of performance may be provided for the services. A buyer may want to specify that the subsidiary will be treated the same as the parent and its affiliates, particularly as to timeliness and quality.

Termination rights will be of concern. A buyer might not agree to aggressive termination rights since performance of the TSA could be crucial to the subsidiary's operations. In fact, a buyer may negotiate for a right to continue receiving the services despite a payment breach.

Many TSAs contain confidentiality provisions. The acquisition agreement may also contain a mutual confidentiality provision that could cover the TSA as well, but it would be necessary to include post-closing information that is shared within the scope of confidential information to be protected. Consideration should also be given to providing for access to the information necessary to perform the services.

TSAs normally contain a clause indicating that seller or its affiliates are acting as independent contractors in providing the services to the subsidiary.

EXHIBIT 1

Checklist of Shared Services in the Purchase of a Subsidiary

Assets			
Office space—dedicated or shared			
Plants (owned or leased)			
Transportation/warehouse space and equipment			
Copiers, telecopiers, mailing equipment			
Shared systems—hardware, servers			
Furniture and fixtures			
Intellectual property, including domain names			
Contracts			
People			
Benefits continuation			
Payroll processing			
Human resources			
Operations/Sales			
Shared supply agreements			
Shared customer agreements			
Insurance			
Distribution			
Intercompany supplier/customer			
Obligations/Liabilities			
Funded debt			

Release/Indemnity			
Upstream guaranties			
Downstream guaranties			
Bonds/letters of credit			
Intellectual Property/Telecommunications			
Telecommunications			
Voice communications			
Data network			
Systems network architecture			
Personal computers			
Servers			
Mainframes			
Phone numbers and listings			
Leased lines/trunks			
Voicemail			
Switches			
Software			
Operating software			
Personal computer-based software			
Server-based software			
Mainframe-based software			
National/master/affiliate/enterprise software license issues			
Proprietary software			
Services			
Information services			
LAN and WAN systems support			
Help desk			
Intranet			
Transition Issues			
Offsite storage			

Exhibit 1—Checklist of Shared Services in the Purchase of a Subsidiary

Warehousing and distribution			
Brochures/marketing materials			
Microfiche/imaging			
Mail services—delivery, overnight, regular outgoing			
Purchasing—supplies, etc.			
Intellectual property/telecommunications			
Mainframe processing and storage			
Data center operations			
Systems security			
Technical services			
Backup			
Disaster recovery			
Host database administration			
Internet access			
Websites			
Hosting administration, domain names			
Financial			
Accounts receivable—who collects			
Accounts payable—who pays			
Billing			
Accounting services			
Legal services			
Contracting/sales support			
Signage, letterhead			
Insurance claims processing			

EXHIBIT 2

Alternative Provisions

Below are certain provisions that might be inserted in the applicable sections of the Model Agreement to deal with some of the issues raised in this Appendix. These provisions are merely illustrative. Most of these suggestions are structural in nature; no attempt has been made to revise the various representations contained in the Model Agreement. It is assumed that there is only one seller (although within a consolidated group it is possible that the Acquired Companies may be owned by several members of the consolidated group), and that revisions would be required in other portions of the Model Agreement.

The following would be added to Section 2.4(b) (Buyer's deliveries):

    (v) **[for itself and its affiliates, including the Acquired Companies,] a release [of Seller and its affiliates] in the form of Exhibit 2.4(b)(v), executed by Buyer.**[1]

    . . .

A new Section 2.4(c), relating to mutual agreements to be signed at closing, rather than listing the same agreements twice, might be constructed as follows:

(c) **Seller and the Company (or the Buyer, as the case may be) will enter into:**

    (i) **an escrow agreement in the form of Exhibit 2.4(c)(i) (the "Escrow Agreement") with _____;**

    (ii) **a transition services agreement in the form of Exhibit 2.4(c)(ii) (the "Transition Services Agreement");**

    (iii) **a license in the form of Exhibit 2.4(c)(iii) (the "License");**

    (iv) **a sublease in the form of Exhibit 2.4(c)(iv) (the "Sublease");**

    (v) **an assignment of Software in the form of Exhibit 2.4(c)(v) (the "Assignment"); and**

---

[1]   This is the analog of Seller's release of the Acquired Companies, which is intended to assure that any claims against the parent are released.

(vi)   **an assumption of [specified indebtedness/capitalized leases] in the form of Exhibit 2.4(c)(vi) (the "Assumption");**

. . .

The purchase price adjustment found in Sections 2.5 and 2.6 might be based on working capital, which is often used in these types of transactions in lieu of shareholders' equity. In that event, the definition of "Adjustment Amount" in Section 2.5(a) would have to be revised, taking into account any normalizing transactions that are to occur, and corresponding changes would be made to the rest of Section 2.5 and to Section 2.6.

The following are examples of provisions that might be used to reflect the agreement of the parties with respect to normalizing transactions. They could be added to Article 2, included among the covenants in Articles 5 and 7, or covered in an ancillary agreement.

2.__ INTERCOMPANY ACCOUNTS

[First Alternate] Net Intercompany Accounts shall be forgiven on the Closing Date.

[Second Alternate] After Closing, Buyer shall cause the Acquired Companies to pay to Seller the then-current balance of Net Intercompany Accounts (each as it becomes due in the ordinary course of business consistent with the Acquired Companies' past practices of paying Intercompany Accounts to Seller; provided that profit-sharing accounts and tax accounts shall be paid within 30 days after the Closing Date). On the day immediately before the Closing Date, Seller shall provide to Buyer a statement (certified as accurate by Seller's chief financial officer or chief executive officer) listing all Intercompany Accounts and estimating the balance for each expected to be outstanding on the Closing Date (which may include such accrual, if any, necessary to show such balance as of the Closing Date). If Buyer so requests, Seller shall provide to Buyer, not later than the fifth day before the Closing Date, an advance copy of such statement accurately reflecting the amount of each Intercompany Account as of the latest practicable date.

[Third Alternate]   On the Closing Date, Seller will cause the Acquired Companies to pay Seller an aggregate amount equal to the cash of the Acquired Companies as of the Closing in the form of a dividend. In the event that on the Closing Date the cash of the Acquired Companies is a negative amount, Seller will pay to the Acquired Companies, by wire transfer, an amount equal to such negative amount as of the Closing in the form of a capital contribution. Immediately prior to the Closing, (a) all amounts owed by the Acquired Companies to Seller or any of its affiliates, for any reason, shall be converted to capital and considered a capital contribution to the Acquired Companies, and (b) all amounts owed by Seller or any

Exhibit 2—Alternative Provisions

of its affiliates to the Acquired Companies shall be paid to the Acquired Companies in cash.

These alternatives will have tax effects, particularly for state tax purposes where the seller and its subsidiaries may not be consolidated. Forgiveness of debt may trigger income in the subsidiary, while the payment of dividends may trigger income in the parent. As discussed in the commentary to Section 2.3 dealing with when the Closing is effective, Seller and Buyer might consider whether the timing of the effectiveness of these transactions satisfies their tax objectives.

The following definitions would be added to Section 1.1:

"Intercompany Accounts"—means the accounts maintained by Seller and the Acquired Companies (in accordance with their customary practices) in which there are recorded the amounts owed (plus interest, if any, accrued through the Closing Date) by Seller or any of its Subsidiaries (other than the Acquired Companies) to the Acquired Companies or by the Acquired Companies to Seller or any of its Subsidiaries (other than the Acquired Companies), attributable to intercompany transactions through the Closing Date in respect of cash advances, current federal and state taxes payable and receivable, intercorporate expense allocations, and other corporate charges or transactions in goods or services, whether provided by Seller or any of its Subsidiaries (other than the Acquired Companies) to the Acquired Companies or by the Acquired Companies to Seller or any of its Subsidiaries (other than the Acquired Companies).

"Net Intercompany Accounts"—means the amount of the Intercompany Accounts owing to Seller and its Subsidiaries (other than the Acquired Companies) by the Acquired Companies, net of the Intercompany Accounts owing to the Acquired Companies by Seller and its Subsidiaries (other than the Acquired Companies).

2.___ INTERCOMPANY CONTRACTS

(a) **[First Alternate] All Contracts between the Company or a Subsidiary, on the one hand, and Seller or any of its Subsidiaries (other than the Acquired Companies), on the other hand, may be terminated at the option of Buyer at any time after the Closing Date, at no liability to the Acquired Companies, except for those Contracts listed on Exhibit ____.**

   [Second Alternate] The agreements listed on Exhibit __ shall terminate as of the Closing Date.

(b) **Effective upon the Closing, Seller shall assign to the Acquired Companies all of Seller's and its Subsidiaries' right, title, and interest in and to any confidentiality agreements to which Seller or the agent of Seller may be a party pertaining to the confidentiality of information pertaining to the Acquired Companies, the** hiring of employees of the Acquired Companies or other matters. Seller will request the return or destruction of information covered by such agreements within two Business Days of the date of this Agreement to the broadest extent permitted by such confidentiality agreements.

2.___ INTERCOMPANY TRANSACTIONS[2]

(a) Immediately prior to the Closing, Seller will cause the Company to transfer to Seller all outstanding capital interests in X, Y, and Z [subsidiaries].

(b) Immediately prior to the Closing, Seller will retire all funded debt of the Company and its Subsidiaries, after giving effect to the transfers made pursuant to Section 2.__.

(c) Immediately prior to the Closing, Seller shall cause its Subsidiaries (other than the Acquired Companies), pursuant to forms reasonably acceptable to Buyer, (i) to assign any Intellectual Property Rights listed on Exhibit ___ owned by them to the Acquired Companies, and (ii) to contribute the domain name "_____" to the Acquired Companies.

2.___ NONTRANSFERRED ASSETS

Buyer acknowledges that it will not be acquiring the Nontransferred Assets, and that Seller may cause the Acquired Companies to transfer and assign on or before the Closing Date all right, title, and interest of the Acquired Companies in and to the Nontransferred Assets to Seller or one of its Subsidiaries.

The following definition would be added to Section 1.1:

"Nontransferred Assets"—means (a) the assets and the claims and rights under the Contracts listed on Exhibit __, pursuant to which certain benefits, goods, services, or products arc available to the Acquired Companies prior to the Closing; (b) claims, rights, or benefits to be received from an Affiliate of the Acquired Companies relating to any corporate overhead or other services or accommodations, including, without limitation, treasury (including working capital and cash advances), accounting, Tax, legal or group purchase or leasing programs or arrangements; (c) the Acquired Companies' confidential business records and policies which relate generally to them, such as accounting procedures, instructions, organization materials, and strategic plans, but not including any strategic plans necessary or related to the Acquired Companies' business in any material respect; (d) other than the trademarks owned by the Acquired Companies, all names, trademarks, service marks, and logos of the Acquired Companies, or any registrations, derivations, or variations thereof; (e) all rights and claims of the Acquired Companies against their counsel, accountants, or financial advisors.

---

[2]   Any other transactions designed to restructure the Company before the sale would be included in the list.

Exhibit 2—Alternative Provisions

. . .

Many of the representations in Article 3 will probably have to be revised to deal specifically with the subsidiary and to take into account the corporate parent and its other affiliates.

. . .

The following are examples of additional post-closing covenants that might be added:

7.__ CHANGE OF NAME

Seller shall cause [name of subsidiary sharing common name] to change its name to "_____" promptly after the Closing Date.

While it may appear that the following covenants limit Buyer's flexibility, the subject matter will undoubtedly be negotiated. Buyer may want to get its formulation on the table first.

7.__ EMPLOYEE MATTERS

Employees of the Acquired Companies shall continue as employees of the Acquired Companies on the Closing Date, subject to the right of the Acquired Companies, as the case may be, to terminate the employment of such employees in accordance with law. Buyer represents that it expects that the employment of each such employee will be continued for at least 30 days after the Closing Date.

7.__ BENEFIT MATTERS

(a)   **[First Alternative—Under this provision, employees would remain under Seller's plans] Seller shall, to the extent necessary, take all appropriate action to continue each employee of the Acquired Companies as of the Closing Date as a participant in each Employee Plan that is not exclusive to the Acquired Companies through December 31, _____, and to treat each employee of the Acquired Companies as a terminated employee under the terms of each such Employee Plan at the close of business on December 31, _____. Buyer shall reimburse Seller for the costs associated with the continuing participation pursuant to this Section based on annualized costs through the date of this Agreement, not to exceed Seller's actual costs.**

[Second Alternative—provides for participation in Buyer's plans] Each employee employed by the Acquired Companies after the Closing Date shall be eligible for participation in the following employee welfare benefit plans of Buyer, as the case may be, subject to any eligibility requirements

applicable to such plans (with full credit for years of past service to Seller and its Subsidiaries) as of the first day after the Closing Date: health plan, dental plan, group life insurance plan, and disability plan. For purposes of vacation accrual, Buyer shall give the employees full credit for all accrued but unused vacation as of the Closing Date.

[Third Alternative—provides for participation in Buyer's plans] Each employee employed by the Acquired Companies after the Closing Date shall be eligible for participation in the medical, dental, life insurance, and disability plans maintained by Buyer for similarly situated employees of Buyer, subject to any eligibility requirements applicable to such plans (with full credit for years of past service to Seller and its Subsidiaries from the employee's most recent date of hire, and not subject to pre-existing condition exclusions that are not applicable under Seller's plans), and shall be eligible to enter each such plan (or Buyer's interim welfare benefits program providing similar benefits to new employees) on the first day after the Closing Date under the procedures normally applied by Buyer to similarly situated employees. For purposes of vacation accrual and severance payments under Buyer's plans, Buyer shall give the employees full credit for years of past service for Seller and its Subsidiaries since the employee's most recent date of hire, and for all accrued but unused vacation as of the Closing Date.

(b) Each employee employed by the Acquired Companies after the Closing Date shall be eligible for participation in the 401(k) Plan maintained by Buyer for similarly situated employees (the "401(k) Plan"), subject to any eligibility requirements applicable to the 401(k) Plan (with full credit for years of past service with Seller and its Subsidiaries for the purpose of satisfying any eligibility and vesting periods applicable to such plan, to the extent credited under Seller's 401(k) Plan in which the Acquired Companies participated), but not until the earliest date following the Closing Date that is administratively possible under the procedures normally applied by Buyer to similarly situated employees. Employees will not receive credit for service prior to the Closing Date for purposes of determining benefit accruals or rate of benefit accruals under Buyer's qualified and nonqualified pension plans.

(c) [First Alternative] Prior to the Closing Date, Seller shall take all necessary actions to cause the Acquired Companies and any Subsidiary to cease to be participating employers in all Employee Plans (other than the severance-pay agreements referred to in Part _____ of the Disclosure Letter) as of the Closing Date. Seller shall cause all participating Employees to become 100% vested and eligible to receive a cash payout amount reflecting the benefit amounts under Seller's 401(k) Plan with the option to keep vested benefit amounts in Seller's 401(k) Plan, to roll over such amounts to the 401(k) Plan, or to receive a cash payout. As of the Closing Date, all amounts contributed to the Profit-

Exhibit 2—Alternative Provisions

Sharing Plan for the accounts of employees shall become fully vested. Seller shall make a final pro rata contribution to such Profit-Sharing Plan for the portion of the plan year preceding the Closing Date for the participants in that Plan who are employees of the Acquired Companies or any Subsidiary (and will waive any requirement for employment on the last day of the plan year, and prorate any hour of service requirement, for receiving such contribution), such contribution to be at the same rate as that ultimately approved by Seller for that Plan year for Seller's other employees. Seller shall not be obligated to make additional contributions to such plan for any period of service after the Closing Date.

[Second Alternative] Except as provided in this Section _____, Seller shall take all actions (i) so that the employees cease to participate in its Employee Plans (other than the Acquired Companies' Employee Plans) after the Closing Date and (ii) to terminate the Acquired Companies' participation in the [Name] Profit-Sharing Plan (the "Profit-Sharing Plan"). As of the Closing Date, all employees shall be treated as if they terminated or severed employment or separated from service under the Profit-Sharing Plan. The accounts of such employees shall become fully vested and distributable in accordance with the terms of the Profit-Sharing Plan. Seller shall provide (or continue to provide) COBRA continuation coverage, as described in Section 4980B of the Code, to all former employees who are receiving COBRA continuation coverage as of the Closing Date with respect to its Employee Plans (other than the Acquired Companies' Employee Plans) that constitute health plans under Code Section 4980B, and the appropriate insurance carrier shall remain responsible for any long-term disability benefit for which there is a vested obligation as of the Closing Date.

(d)   On and after the Closing Date, Buyer shall be responsible with respect to all employees of the Acquired Companies and their beneficiaries for compliance with the Worker Adjustment and Retraining Notification Act of 1988 ("WARN") and any other applicable Legal Requirements, including any requirement to provide for and discharge any and all notifications, benefits, and liabilities to the Acquired Companies' employees and Governmental Bodies that might be imposed as a result of the consummation of the Contemplated Transactions. Seller agrees not to take any action, and to cause the Acquired Companies not to take any action, that would be attributable to Buyer for purposes of determining whether a "plant closing" or a "mass layoff" has occurred.

. . .

The following might be added to Section 11.2 to provide additional indemnification:

(g)   any liability of the Acquired Companies arising by virtue of its status as a member of a consolidated group or as a member of a controlled group; or

(h)   failure of Seller to assume, pay, and discharge the obligations of the Acquired Companies assumed by Seller pursuant to Section _____.

. . .

The agreement of the parties regarding tax matters might be added as a separate article at the end of the Model Agreement or to the post-closing covenants in Article 7. The following is an example of a separate article covering these matters:

13. ALLOCATION OF TAXES; TAX RETURNS

13.1 Allocation of Tax Liabilities

(a)   Seller will be responsible for all Taxes of each of the Acquired Companies regardless of when due and payable, (i) with respect to all Tax periods ending on or prior to the Closing Date and (ii) with respect to all Tax periods beginning before the Closing Date and ending after the Closing Date, but only with respect to the portion of such period up to and including the Closing Date; provided, however, Seller will not be responsible for the foregoing Taxes to the extent such Taxes are accrued on the books of any Acquired Company in the Ordinary Course of Business through the Closing Date.

(b)   Buyer will be responsible for all Taxes of each of the Acquired Companies, regardless of when due and payable, (i) with respect to all Tax periods beginning after the Closing Date, (ii) with respect to all Tax periods beginning before the Closing Date and ending after the Closing Date, but only with respect to (A) the portion of such period commencing after the Closing Date or (B) to the extent such Taxes are accrued on the books of any Acquired Company in the Ordinary Course of Business through the Closing Date.

(c)   All transfer, documentation, sales, use, stamp, registration, conveyance, or similar Taxes and any penalties and interest with respect thereto ("Transfer Taxes") imposed as a result of the Contemplated Transactions shall be borne by Seller. Seller and Buyer agree to cooperate in the filing of any returns with respect to the Transfer Taxes, including promptly supplying any information in their possession reasonably requested by the other party that is reasonably necessary to complete such returns.

Exhibit 2—Alternative Provisions

13.2 Tax Returns

(a) Seller will include the income or loss of the Acquired Companies for all Tax periods ending on or before the Closing Date on Seller's timely filed income Tax Returns and will file all such Tax Returns when due (including extensions). Seller will cause to be prepared, and will cause to be filed when due (including any extensions), all other Tax Returns of the Acquired Companies for all Tax periods ending on or before the Closing Date for which Tax Returns have not been filed as of such date. Where such other Tax Returns must be filed by any Acquired Company, upon the request of Seller, Buyer will cause such Tax Returns to be filed when due (including any extensions). Seller will submit copies (in the case of consolidated Tax Returns the consolidating portion thereof applicable to the Acquired Companies) to Buyer at least 30 days prior to the extended due date for Buyer's review and approval, and thereafter file, all federal, state, county, local, and foreign Tax Returns required to be filed by the Acquired Companies after the Closing Date for all Tax periods ending on or before the Closing Date. Seller will cause all such Tax Returns to be accurate and complete in accordance with applicable Legal Requirements and to be prepared on a basis consistent with the Tax Returns filed by or on behalf of the Acquired Companies for the preceding Tax period.

(b) Buyer will prepare and file when due (including any extensions) all Tax Returns of the Acquired Companies for Tax periods ending after the Closing Date; provided, however, that Seller will have the right to review and approve prior to filing all Tax Returns for any Tax period that includes the Closing Date or any period prior to the Closing Date.

13.3 Income and Loss Allocation

For purposes of this Article 13, in the case of any Taxes that are imposed on a periodic basis and are payable for a Tax period that includes (but does not end on) the Closing Date, the portion of such Tax related to the Tax period ending on the Closing Date will (a) in the case of Taxes other than Taxes based upon or related to income, sales, gross receipts, wages, capital expenditures, expenses, or any similar Tax base, be deemed to be the amount of such Tax for the entire period multiplied by a fraction, the numerator of which is the number of days in the Tax period ending on the Closing Date and the denominator of which is the number of days in the entire Tax period and (b) in the case of any Tax based upon or related to income, sales, gross receipts, wages, capital expenditures, expenses, or any similar Tax base, be deemed equal to the amount that would be payable if the relevant Tax period ended on the Closing Date. All determinations necessary to give effect to the foregoing allocations will be made in a manner consistent with prior practice of the Acquired Companies.

13.4 Cooperation

After the Closing Date, Buyer and Seller will make available to the other, as reasonably requested, all information, records, or documents (including state apportionment information) relating to Tax liabilities or potential Tax liabilities of any Acquired Company with respect to (a) Tax periods ending on or prior to the Closing Date and (b) Tax periods beginning before the Closing Date and ending after the Closing Date, but only with respect to the portion of such period up to and including the Closing Date. Buyer and Seller will preserve all such information, records, and documents until the expiration of any applicable statute of limitations thereof. Buyer will prepare and provide to Seller any information or documents reasonably requested by Seller for Seller's use in preparing or reviewing the Tax Returns referred to in Section 13.2(a). Notwithstanding any other provision hereof, each party will bear its own expenses in complying with the foregoing provisions.

13.5 Audits

Each party will promptly notify the other in writing upon receipt by such party of notice of any pending or threatened Tax liabilities of any Acquired Company for any (a) Tax period ending on or before the Closing Date or (b) Tax Period ending after the Closing Date but which includes the Closing Date. Seller will have the sole right to represent the interests of the Acquired Companies in any Proceeding related to Taxes for Tax periods ending on or prior to the Closing Date and to employ counsel of its choice at its expense, and Buyer and Seller agree to cooperate in the defense of any claim in such Proceeding. Seller will have the right to participate at its expense in representing the interests of the Acquired Companies in any Proceeding related to Taxes for any Tax period ending after the Closing Date, if and to the extent that such period includes any Tax Period before the Closing Date, and to employ counsel of its choice at its expense. Seller and Buyer agree to cooperate in the defense of any claim in such Proceeding.

13.6 Tax Refunds

(a) All refunds of Taxes relating to any Acquired Company received by Seller or any of its affiliates with respect to Tax periods ending on or before the Closing Date and involving Seller's consolidated returns will be for the account of Seller. At Seller's request, Buyer will pay over to Seller any such refunds that Buyer may receive immediately upon receipt of such request.

(b) All other refunds of Taxes with respect to any Acquired Company will be for the account of Buyer. At Buyer's request, Seller will take such action as reasonably requested by Buyer to obtain such refunds and will pay over to Buyer any such refunds immediately upon receipt thereof.

Exhibit 2—Alternative Provisions

13.7 Section 338(h)(10) Election

(a)   Seller and Buyer shall make, or cause to be made, a joint election under Section 338(h)(10) of the Code (and any corresponding election under state, local and foreign Tax law) (a "Section 338(h)(10) Election") with respect to the purchase and sale of the Shares hereunder. Seller and Buyer shall sign prior to or at the Closing all federal and state forms used to make a Section 338(h)(10) Election (the "Section 338(h)(10) Election Forms") requiring its signature which forms shall be held by Buyer pending filing. Buyer and Seller shall be jointly responsible for preparing and timely filing any forms used to make a Section 338(h)(10) Election, including the joint preparation and filing of IRS Form 8023 and related schedules. Such forms shall be filed promptly following the final determination of the Purchase Price, assumed liabilities, other relevant items, and the Allocation, but in no event later than the due date for the filing of any such forms. Promptly after the Closing Date, each party shall provide to the other party any information (including Tax elections made by or on behalf of the Acquired Company) reasonably requested by the other party in connection with its filing of a Section 338(h)(10) Election. Seller will pay all Taxes attributable to the making of the Section 338(h)(10) Election, including any federal, state, local, or foreign Tax attributable to an election under federal, state, local or foreign law similar to the election available under Section 338(h)(10) of the Code.

(b)   Buyer shall prepare an allocation of the Purchase Price for the Shares, the assumed liabilities, and other relevant items among the assets of the Company in accordance with Section 338(b)(5) of the Code and the Treasury Regulations thereunder (the "Allocation"). Within 60 days following the Closing but prior to the due date of the Section 338(h)(10) Election Forms, Buyer shall provide a copy of the Allocation to Seller. The Allocation shall be reasonable and shall be prepared in accordance with Section 338(h)(10) of the Code and the Treasury Regulations thereunder. The Allocation shall be deemed to be accepted by and shall be conclusive and binding on Seller except to the extent, if any, that Seller shall have delivered within 20 days after the date on which the Allocation is delivered to Seller, a written notice to Buyer stating each and every item to which Seller takes exception (it being understood that any amounts not disputed shall be final and binding). If a change proposed by Seller is disputed by Buyer, then Seller and Buyer shall negotiate in good faith to resolve such dispute. If, after a period of 20 days following the date on which Seller gives Buyer notice of any such proposed change, any such proposed change still remains disputed, then an independent accounting firm of recognized national standing (the "Allocation Arbiter") selected jointly by Buyer and Seller shall resolve any remaining disputes. The Allocation Arbiter shall act as an arbitrator to determine, based solely on presentations by Buyer and Seller, and not by independent review, only those issues still in dispute with respect to the Allocation, and Seller and Buyer shall reasonably cooperate to develop a schedule whereby such presentations are made within 15 days following the appointment of the Allocation Arbiter and a decision shall be rendered by the Allocation Arbiter within 30 days following such presentations. The decision of the Allocation Arbiter shall be final and binding. All of the fees and expenses of the Allocation Arbiter shall be equally paid by Buyer, on the one hand, and Seller, on the other hand. Buyer and Seller each agrees that promptly upon receiving the final and binding Allocation it shall return an executed copy thereof to the other party. The Acquired Company, Seller and Buyer shall file all Tax Returns and forms, including IRS Form 8883, consistent with the final Allocation and shall not take any position inconsistent with the final Allocation in any audit or other tax proceeding. The Acquired Company, Seller and Buyer shall cooperate with one another in order to properly prepare and timely file all documents required with respect to a Section 338(h)(10) Election. The Allocation shall be revised to reflect any adjustments to the Purchase Price pursuant to this Agreement.

(c)   Buyer and Seller shall take all actions as are necessary to make effective the Section 338(h)(10) Election, including the timely execution, delivery, and filing of all Tax Returns (including IRS Form 8883) in respect thereof. Seller will file its Tax Returns consistently with the Section 338(h)(10) Election.

(d)   Seller will cause each partnership or limited liability company that is at least 50% owned, either directly or indirectly, by the Acquired Company, to make an election under Section 754 of the Code and Treasury Regulations Section 1.754-1(b) to adjust the basis of the partnership or limited liability company property in the manner provided in Sections 734(b) and 743(b) of the Code to be effective for the tax year that includes the deemed asset sale under Section 338(h)(10) of the Code.

Exhibit 3

Transition Services Agreement

This Transition Services Agreement ("Agreement") is made as of _____ by _____, a _____ corporation ("Seller"), and _____, a _____ corporation (the "Company"). This is the Transition Services Agreement referred to in the Stock Purchase Agreement (the "Purchase Agreement"), dated _____, between Seller and _____, a _____ corporation ("Buyer"). Capitalized terms used in this Agreement without definition have the respective meanings given to them in the Purchase Agreement.

RECITALS

Seller has this date sold to Buyer all the Shares of the Company.

Seller has agreed to provide certain transition services to the Company on the terms and conditions set forth in this Agreement.

The parties, intending to be legally bound, agree as follows:

1. TRANSITION SERVICES

Seller shall provide the services described below (the "Transition Services") to the Company during the term of this Agreement:

(a) Seller Services. On the terms and subject to the conditions of this Agreement, Seller shall provide the services to the Company listed on Schedule A ("Seller Services"), in substantially the same scope, nature, and manner as was provided to the Company immediately prior to the Closing Date, and for the compensation set forth opposite each of such Seller Services on Schedule A.

(b) Third-Party Services. On the terms and subject to the conditions of this Agreement, Seller shall use commercially reasonable efforts to cause the services listed on Schedule B to be provided to the Company ("Third-Party Services"), in substantially the same scope, nature, and manner as was provided to the Company immediately prior to the Closing Date by the providers that provided such services to the Company immediately prior to the Closing Date, and for the compensation set forth opposite each of such Third-Party Services on Schedule B. The Company acknowledges that the provision of Third-Party Services may require the consent of the relevant providers. If Seller is unable to obtain such consent with respect to a particular Third-Party Service, Seller and the Company will use commercially reasonable efforts to arrange for an alternative person or an alternative methodology to provide the Third-Party Service.

(c) **Other Services.** During the term of this Agreement, Seller shall provide to the Company any other transition services not referenced in subparagraph (a) or (b) above consistent with the types of services discussed herein and at levels consistent with the past operation of the Company and reasonably requested by the Company in writing with reasonably sufficient detail as to the services requested. Any fee to be charged by Seller for any services provided pursuant to this Paragraph 2(c) shall be equal to Seller's actual cost to provide such Transition Services, including allocable overhead and Seller's reasonable out-of-pocket expenses consistent with past practice ("Seller's Costs"). At the Company's request, Seller shall furnish the Company with reasonable supporting documentation evidencing Seller's Costs hereunder.

(d) **Pricing.** The Company shall pay the respective amounts listed on Schedule A, Schedule B, and Seller's Costs for the Transition Services. Seller shall invoice the Company monthly for services rendered through the end of each month. The Company shall pay all invoices in full within 30 days of receipt thereof.

2. STANDARD OF PERFORMANCE

For Seller Services, Seller will perform such Transition Services in a timely, competent, and workmanlike manner and in a nature and at levels consistent with the Company's past conduct of its business. For Third-Party Services, Seller shall use commercial reasonably efforts to ensure that such services are provided by such third parties in a timely, competent, and workmanlike manner and in a nature and at levels consistent with the Company's past conduct of its business.

COMMENT

Seller may insist on a limitation on damages and indemnification from Buyer since it is performing these services as an accommodation to Buyer, such as the following:

Seller shall not be liable for actions or omissions under this Agreement, except for its own gross negligence or willful misconduct. Except with respect to claims based upon such gross negligence or willful misconduct that are successfully asserted against Seller, the Company shall indemnify and hold harmless Seller

Exhibit 3—Transition Services Agreement

from and against and shall pay to Seller the amount of, and reimburse Seller for, any and all losses, liabilities, claims, actions, damages, and expenses, including reasonable attorneys' fees and disbursements, arising out of and in connection with this Agreement and the services provided hereunder.

3. TERM AND TERMINATION

(a) The term of this Agreement shall commence on the date of this Agreement and continue until all Transition Services are completed, unless earlier terminated in accordance with this Paragraph 4.

(b) Seller shall provide or cause to be provided the Transition Services for the duration specified on Schedules A or B, as the case may be, except that the Company may direct Seller to discontinue any one or more Transition Services at any time without cause upon 10 days' written notice, whereupon Seller shall discontinue or cause to be discontinued the Transition Services for which such notice is given. Such discontinuance shall not extinguish the Company's obligation for payment of Transition Services actually rendered under this Agreement and, subject to Paragraph 4(a), this Agreement shall continue in full force and effect with respect to any Transition Services not discontinued.

(c) If either party hereto becomes bankrupt or insolvent, or makes an assignment for the benefit of creditors, or if a receiver is appointed to take charge of its property and such proceeding is not vacated or terminated within 30 days after its commencement or institution, the other may immediately terminate this Agreement by written notice. Any such termination shall be without prejudice to accrued rights of the terminating party, and to other rights and remedies for default.

4. MISCELLANEOUS

COMMENT

See the Introduction to this Volume II and commentary to Article 12 of the Model Agreement for further discussion relevant to the miscellaneous provisions.

(a) Force Majeure. Neither party shall be liable in any manner for failure or delay of performance of all or part of this Agreement (other than the payment of money), directly or indirectly, owing to acts of God, applicable orders or restrictions by a governmental authority, strikes or other labor disturbances, riots, embargoes, power failures, telecommunication line failures, revolutions, wars, fires, floods, or any other causes or circumstances beyond the reasonable control of either party, whether similar or dissimilar to those listed above. The affected party, however, in the case of such delay or failure, shall give prompt

notice to the other party and shall exert commercially reasonable efforts to remove the causes or circumstances of nonperformance with reasonable dispatch.

(b) Sales Taxes. Any sales, use, transaction, excise, or similar tax imposed on or measured by the rendering of the Transition Services shall be the responsibility of the Company. All other taxes arising from Transition Services shall be paid by Seller.

(c) Relationship of Parties. Seller shall perform the Transition Services under this Agreement as an independent contractor and as such shall have and maintain exclusive control over all its own employees, agents, subcontractors, and operations. Neither party shall be, act as, purport to act as, or be deemed to be the other's agent, representative, employee, or servant. Nothing in this Agreement shall be construed or interpreted as creating an agency, partnership, co-partnership, or joint venture relationship between the parties.

(d) Expenses. Except as otherwise expressly provided for herein, each party will pay its own expenses (including brokers', finders', attorneys', and accountants' fees) in connection with the negotiation of this Agreement, the performance of its respective obligations hereunder, and of the services contemplated by this Agreement.

(e) Entire Agreement. This Agreement (including the schedules hereto) supersedes all prior agreements, whether written or oral, between the parties with respect to its subject matter and constitutes a complete and exclusive statement of the terms of the agreement between the parties with respect to its subject matter.

(f) Modification. This Agreement may only be amended, supplemented, or otherwise modified by a writing executed by the parties.

(g) Assignments and Successors. Neither party may assign any of its rights or delegate any of its obligations under this Agreement without the prior consent of the other party. Any purported assignment of rights or delegation of obligations in violation of this Paragraph 4(g) will be void. Subject to the foregoing, this Agreement will apply to, be binding in all respects upon, and inure to the benefit of the heirs, executors, administrators, legal representatives, successors, and permitted assigns of the parties.

(h) Third-Party Benefit. Other than the parties, no Person will have any legal or equitable right, remedy, or claim under or with respect to this Agreement.

(i) Governing Law. All matters relating to or arising out of this Agreement and the rights of the parties (whether sounding in contract, tort, or otherwise) will be governed by and construed and interpreted under the laws of the State of

Exhibit 3—Transition Services Agreement

_____, without regard to conflicts of laws principles that would require the application of any other law.

(j)   **Jurisdiction and Venue.** Except as otherwise provided in this Agreement, any Proceeding arising out of or relating to this Agreement shall be brought in the courts of the State of _____, County of _____, or, if it has or can acquire jurisdiction, in the United States District Court for the _____ District of _____, and each of the parties irrevocably submits to the exclusive jurisdiction of each such court in any such Proceeding, waives any objection it may now or hereafter have to venue or to convenience of forum, agrees that all claims in respect of such Proceeding shall be heard and determined only in any such court, and agrees not to bring any Proceeding arising out of or relating to this Agreement in any other court. Each party acknowledges and agrees that this Paragraph 4(j) constitutes a voluntary and bargained- for agreement between the parties. Process in any Proceeding referred to in the first sentence of this Paragraph 4(j) may be served on any party anywhere in the world. Any party may make service on any other party by sending or delivering a copy of the process to the party to be served at the address and in the manner provided for the giving of notices in Paragraph 4(n). Nothing in this Paragraph 4(j) will affect the right of any party to serve legal process in any other manner permitted by law or at equity.

(k)   **Waiver of Jury Trial.** EACH PARTY, KNOWINGLY, VOLUNTARILY, AND INTENTIONALLY, WAIVES ITS RIGHT TO TRIAL BY JURY IN ANY PROCEEDING ARISING OUT OF OR RELATING TO THIS AGREEMENT OR ANY CONTEMPLATED TRANSACTION, WHETHER SOUNDING IN CONTRACT, TORT, OR OTHERWISE.

(l)   **Enforcement of Agreement.** Seller acknowledges and agrees that the Company would be irreparably harmed if any of the provisions of this Agreement are not performed in accordance with their specific terms and that any Breach of this Agreement by Seller could not be adequately compensated in all cases by monetary damages alone. Accordingly, Seller agrees that, in addition to any other right or remedy to which the Company may be entitled at law or in equity, the Company shall be entitled to enforce any provision of this Agreement by a decree of specific performance and to obtain temporary, preliminary, and permanent injunctive relief to prevent Breaches or threatened Breaches of this Agreement, without posting any bond or giving any other undertaking.

(m)   **No Waiver.** Neither any failure nor any delay by any party in exercising any right, power, or privilege under this Agreement will operate as a waiver of such right, power, or privilege, and no single or partial exercise of any such right, power, or privilege will preclude any other or further exercise of such right, power, or privilege or the exercise of any other right, power, or privilege.

To the maximum extent permitted by applicable Legal Requirements, (i) no claim or right arising out of this Agreement can be waived by a party, in whole or in part, unless made in a writing signed by such party; (ii) a waiver given by a party will only be applicable to the specific instance for which it is given; and (iii) no notice to or demand on a party will (A) waive or otherwise affect any obligation of that party or (B) affect the right of the party giving such notice or demand to take further action without notice or demand as provided in this Agreement.

(n) **Notices.** All notices and other communications required or permitted by this Agreement will be in writing and will be effective, and any applicable time period shall commence when (i) delivered to the following address by hand or by a nationally recognized overnight courier service (costs prepaid) addressed to the following address or (ii) transmitted electronically to the following facsimile numbers or e-mail addresses, in each case marked to the attention of the Person (by name or title) designated below (or to such other address, facsimile number, e-mail address, or Person as a party may designate by notice to the other parties):

  Seller:

  Attention:
  [Street]
  [City, state, and zip code]
  Fax no.:
  E-mail address:

  with a copy to:

  _____

  Attention:
  [Street]
  [City, state, and zip code]
  Fax no.:
  E-mail address:

  Company:

  _____

  Attention:
  [Street]
  [City, state, and zip code]
  Fax no.:
  E-mail address:

  with a copy to:

  _____

Exhibit 3—Transition Services Agreement

Attention:
[Street]
[City, state, and zip code]
Fax no.:
E-mail address:

(o) Severability. If any provision of this Agreement is held invalid or unenforceable by any court of competent jurisdiction, the other provisions of this Agreement will remain in full force and effect. Any provision of this Agreement held invalid or unenforceable only in part or degree will remain in full force and effect to the extent not held invalid or unenforceable.

(p) Time of Essence. With regard to all dates and time periods set forth or referred to in this Agreement, time is of the essence.

(q) Counterparts/Electronic Signatures. This Agreement may be executed in one or more counterparts, each of which will be deemed to be an original copy and all of which, when taken together, will be deemed to constitute one and the same Agreement, and will be effective when counterparts have been signed by each of the parties and delivered to the other parties. A manual signature on this Agreement, which image shall have been transmitted electronically, will constitute an original signature for all purposes. The delivery of copies of this Agreement, including executed signature pages where required, by electronic transmission will constitute effective delivery of this Agreement for all purposes.

IN WITNESS WHEREOF, the parties have executed and delivered this Agreement as of the date first written above.

SELLER: _____

By: _____

Name: _____

Title: _____

COMPANY:

By: _____

Name: _____

Title: _____

Schedule A
(Seller Services)

Transition Service	Compensation	Duration

Schedule B
(Third-Party Services)

Transition Service	Compensation	Duration

APPENDIX B

Receipt of Stock of a Public Company as Purchase Consideration

PRELIMINARY NOTE

The use of securities of a public company as consideration in an acquisition involves a variety of considerations, for both a buyer and a seller, that are not present in an all-cash acquisition. The buyer needs to comply with its obligations under the federal and state securities laws and has a desire to minimize the associated time, expense, and management effort. The buyer also has a desire to minimize the impact the issuance of its securities will have on the trading price of its existing securities. In the case of a transaction involving the issuance of a substantial percentage of a buyer's voting securities, the buyer may have a concern with respect to control issues arising from that issuance. If the buyer's shares are listed on a national securities exchange, it must also take into account the shareholder approval requirements of that exchange. The sellers will want to obtain the contractual protections associated with their investment in the buyer's securities and have a desire to maximize the value and liquidity of that investment. Finally, the buyer and the seller have a mutual desire to protect the benefit of their bargain from the volatility of the buyer's share price from the time the acquisition agreement is signed until the time the transaction is closed. The following is a summary of these considerations, followed by some suggested contractual provisions for inclusion in an acquisition agreement.

BUYER CONSIDERATIONS

Registration Requirements. The use of securities as consideration in an acquisition results in an offer and sale of securities subject to the registration requirements of the Securities Act of 1933, as amended (the "Securities Act"), and state securities laws, unless an exemption can be found. If an exemption is available, the buyer will generally want to satisfy the requirements of the exemption to avoid the extra expense, time, and management effort required to register the offer and sale of its securities.

At the federal level, the registration of securities requires the preparation and filing of a registration statement with the Securities and Exchange Commission ("SEC"). In the event the SEC elects to review the registration statement, additional time to complete the transaction may be required. In addition, the preparation of a registration statement will add to the cost of the transaction and require additional management attention.

Some buyers have prepared shelf registration statements for making a series of acquisitions using shares, avoiding the time and expense of individual registration statements.

The most commonly employed exemption from the registration requirements of the Securities Act is the "private placement" exemption provided by Section 4(2) of the Securities Act and SEC Regulation D.[1] Section 4(2) provides an exemption for transactions by an issuer not involving any public offering. While there is a long-standing body of case law interpreting the statutory exemption provided by Section 4(2), the SEC has promulgated Regulation D to provide issuers with a safe harbor.[2] In most transactions, it will be possible to satisfy the requirements of Regulation D, but there may be difficulties if there are a large number of sellers who do not qualify as "accredited investors" under Regulation D.[3] In those circumstances, the buyer will have to either rely upon the statutory exemption provided by Section 4(2), register the issuance of the securities, or restructure the transaction. While the presence of 35 or fewer sellers who are not accredited investors will not prevent the use of the Regulation D exemption, the presence of even one seller who is not an accredited investor will increase substantially the disclosure requirements that the buyer must satisfy to comply with the exemption.

In most cases, a buyer will want to utilize the exemption provided by Rule 506 of Regulation D because its use will preempt the varying restrictions imposed on private placements by state blue sky laws, as discussed below. In addition, Rule 506 imposes no limitations on the aggregate offering price of the securities sold.

Under Rule 506, the number of purchasers may not exceed 35 nonaccredited investors, but there is no limit on accredited investors. The Rule imposes an additional sophistication standard for nonaccredited investors. Each purchaser who is not an accredited investor must have, either alone or with his or her purchaser representative(s), such knowledge and experience in financial and business matters that he or she is capable of evaluating the merits and risks of the prospective investment, or the issuer must reasonably believe immediately before any sale that the purchaser comes within that description. Often some

---

1 17 CFR § 230.501 *et seq.* ("Regulation D"). Individual sections of the rules under the Securities Act are referred to by the rule number without further citation.

2 Regulation D provides three separate exemptions from registration. Rule 504 provides an exemption for sales having an aggregate offering price not exceeding $1 million. Rule 505 provides an exemption for sales having an aggregate offering price not exceeding $5 million. Rule 506 provides an exemption without regard to the dollar amount involved.

3 The term accredited investor is generally defined by reference to minimum levels of net worth or income or relationship to the issuer in the case of individuals and certain types of organizations. Rule 501(a).

stockholders of a target are quite sophisticated in these matters and others, such as nonmanagement employees who have received stock over the years, are not. In those situations, a purchaser representative[4] might be retained on behalf of those who do not meet this standard.

Rule 502(b) sets forth the type of information that must be provided by an issuer in a Rule 506 offering. If only accredited investors are involved, no information need be furnished. If there are nonaccredited investors, the issuer must provide the information specified in Rule 502(b)(2). In addition, each purchaser must have the opportunity to ask questions and receive answers concerning the transaction. The applicable resale limitations must also be disclosed to any purchaser, as well as any terms or arrangements of the proposed transaction that are materially different from those for all other security holders. Finally, Rule 503 provides that a notice must be filed with the SEC on Form D not later than 15 days after the sale.

States may also require the registration of the offer and sale of securities which are subject to their jurisdiction. Many states have their own statutory or regulatory version of the private placement exemption. However, many state versions of the private placement exemption have requirements that are more restrictive than the requirements of Regulation D. To address this situation, Section 18 of the Securities Act preempts state securities regulation of an offering and sale that qualifies for the exemption provided by Rule 506 of Regulation D. However, the state securities administrators can still require the filing of a notice of the exempt transaction and the payment of a fee.[5]

Disclosure Requirements. A buyer that does not have to register the securities being issued as consideration in an acquisition because of an exemption must still comply with the antifraud requirements of the federal and state securities laws. At the federal level, the issuance of securities by the buyer will be subject to the antifraud provisions of Section 17 of the Securities Act and Section 10(b) of the Exchange Act and Rule 10b-5 promulgated by the SEC thereunder.

Trading Restrictions. A buyer may be concerned that the securities issued as consideration in an acquisition will have an effect on the market for the buyer's securities. If the acquisition will result in the issuance of a relatively large amount of the buyer's securities, the subsequent sale of those securities into the market by the sellers could adversely affect the trading price of the buyer's securities. To alleviate these concerns, a buyer may seek to impose restrictions on the sellers' ability to sell the securities received in the acquisition. These restrictions may be included in the stock purchase agreement or embodied in a separate lock-up agreement.

Control Considerations. If the securities to be issued by the buyer represent a substantial percentage of the outstanding voting securities of the buyer, the buyer

---

4   Rule 501(h) sets forth the qualifications one must satisfy to act as a purchaser representative.

5   Section 18(c)(2)(A) of the Securities Act.

may have a concern with the control position the sellers may have resulting from that issuance or any further acquisitions of the buyer's securities. In such cases, a buyer may want to consider imposing a contractual restriction on any further acquisition of the buyer's voting securities. In addition, a buyer may want to require the sellers to agree to vote the shares being issued by the buyer in a specific manner.

Shareholder Approval Requirements. The New York Stock Exchange and the Nasdaq Stock Market each require shareholder approval if a buyer is issuing a number of shares of common stock, or securities convertible into common stock, in an acquisition that equals or exceeds 20% of the number of shares of common stock outstanding prior to the issuance.[6] A buyer needs to either structure the transaction in a manner to avoid the issuance of this level of securities or plan for shareholder approval as part of the transaction.

State Securities Laws. The buyer will also need to satisfy state securities (Blue Sky) laws unless those laws are preempted by federal requirements.

Sellers' Considerations. Since sellers are making an investment in the buyer when they receive securities as consideration in an acquisition, they will want to have many of the same protections as provided to the buyer in the stock purchase agreement with respect to the target's outstanding securities. These will include more extensive representations and warranties than would be provided by a buyer in an all-cash transaction. In addition, to assure the liquidity of the value tied up in the buyer's securities and to be able to preserve that value against market fluctuations, sellers will want the maximum flexibility to sell the securities received from the buyer. Since in most cases the shares received by the sellers will be restricted securities and not freely tradable, sellers will have an interest in negotiating certain rights to have the securities registered for resale by the buyer.

Resale Restrictions. Restricted securities received by sellers are subject to restrictions on resale. As in the case of the offering and sale of the securities by the buyer, any sale by sellers will have to be registered under the Securities Act and state securities law unless an exemption is available. The two exemptions available to a seller at the federal level are the Section 4(1) exemption and the exemption recognized in practice as the Section 4(1-1/2) exemption.

Rule 144, which was promulgated by the SEC under the Securities Act, affords a seller a "safe harbor" for purposes of the Section 4(1) exemption if certain requirements are met.[7] It is assumed for purposes of this discussion that no seller is an affiliate of the buyer and that the buyer is a public reporting company. Reliance on the Rule is conditioned upon the issuer of the securities having filed with the SEC all reports required to be filed by it under the Exchange Act (other than Form 8-K) within the preceding 12 months, although this limitation disappears after

---

6   New York Stock Exchange Listed Company Manual Section 312.03 and Nasdaq Manual, Marketplace Rule 5635(a).
7   Securities Act Rule 144(b).

12 months.[8] Sellers will have to hold the buyer's securities for a period of six months after the closing.[9] Once restricted securities are sold under Rule 144, they are freely tradable in the public market without registration.

Because Rule 144 is conditioned upon the issuer of the securities having filed its Exchange Act reports during the preceding 12 months, a seller intending to rely on Rule 144 to resell a buyer's securities may want to impose a contractual obligation upon the buyer to file all those reports.

The Section 4(1-1/2) exemption does not have a statutory basis, but has developed in practice. It is commonly recognized to provide an exemption for the private resale of restricted securities by a holder who follows all the precautions used by an issuer in a private placement under Section 4(2) of the Securities Act. While such a transaction does not involve a public distribution of securities, it does not qualify for the exemption under Section 4(2) because that exemption is not available to anyone other than an issuer. Unlike a resale under Rule 144, securities sold under the Section 4(1-1/2) exemption remain restricted securities in the hands of a purchaser and should, as a result, result in a lower price than a resale under Rule 144. *See* commentary to Section 4.3 of the Model Agreement.

Registration Rights. Since the restrictions on the resale of unregistered securities can prevent sellers receiving securities in an acquisition from taking advantage of fluctuations in the market price of the buyer's securities, sellers will often negotiate for the right to have the buyer's shares registered under the Securities Act. Registration rights can take a variety of forms, which impose different levels of burden on the buyer and provide different levels of benefit for sellers.

From the sellers' perspective, the most valuable registration right is an obligation on the part of the buyer to register the securities issued to sellers within a specified time period after the closing. From the buyer's perspective, the least burdensome form of registration right is to provide sellers with the opportunity to include its securities in a registration statement being filed by the buyer to register other securities, commonly referred to as a "piggy-back" registration right. In between these two extremes are "demand" registration rights—the right of sellers (or a minimum number of sellers) selling a negotiated minimum number of shares to require the buyer to register the securities issued as consideration.

In addition to being obligated to register the buyer securities held by sellers under the Securities Act, the sellers may want the buyer to maintain the effectiveness of the registration statement for a specified time, to keep the prospectus in the registration statement current, to register or qualify the securities under state securities laws, and to list the securities on any exchange or trading system on which its other securities are listed.

---

8   Rule 144(b)(1).

9   Rule 144(d)(1)(i).

Since the obligation to register its securities will require a buyer to disclose all material information at a time when there may be a proper business reason not to make such a disclosure, the buyer may want to include in any registration rights provision the ability to delay filing a registration statement for a limited period of time or suspend its use.

See Jacob, Gelfond, Levitt & Kanarek, *Key Considerations in Drafting a Registration Rights Agreement from the Company's Perspective*, REV. SEC. & COMM. REG. (May 21, 2008).

PRICING MECHANICS TO ALLOCATE MARKET RISK

The market price for a buyer's publicly traded securities may fluctuate from the time the acquisition agreement is executed until the time the transaction is closed. These changes can result from market conditions, industry conditions, market reaction to the transaction itself (and related arbitrage activity), or a combination of these factors. The buyer and sellers must assess the market risk in the valuation of the buyer's securities and should discuss allocating the risk between them.

A common formula for addressing market risk is for buyer and sellers to establish a fixed exchange ratio based solely on market and other conditions as they exist at the time the acquisition agreement is signed. With a fixed exchange ratio, the buyer and sellers agree that sellers' shares will be converted into buyer securities at a specified ratio. A fixed exchange ratio enables both buyer and sellers to know exactly how many buyer shares will be issued at closing. Because the price for the buyer's securities may move up before closing, the fixed exchange ratio exposes the buyer to the risk it may pay more value than it anticipated when it signed the acquisition agreement. Alternatively, if the stock price declines, sellers have a risk that they will receive less value than they were expecting at closing. To protect the expectations of the buyer and sellers, the parties may provide for "collars" with specified "floor" and "ceiling" share values for the buyer's securities. If a defined "average" price of the buyer's securities during a defined "pricing period" ending prior to the closing has fallen below a specified level, the exchange ratio is increased to maintain a specified floor market value. The buyer's concern for a significant increase in its share value may be addressed by a "ceiling" on the value of the shares the buyer is obligated to issue. The application of the floor value could result in significant dilution to the buyer. The buyer, therefore, may negotiate for an absolute cap on the amount the exchange ratio can be increased.

An alternative approach to the fixed exchange ratio is a fixed market value formula. Under this approach the sellers' shares are converted into the buyer shares at whatever exchange ratio is necessary to provide the sellers with the agreed value per buyer share based on the market value of the buyer's shares during a defined "pricing period" before closing. A fixed value approach protects the sellers against a decline in the buyer's share value between the time the acquisition agreement is signed and closing. The buyer, on the other hand, is exposed to the risk that it will have to issue additional shares because of downward pressure on its market price.

The sellers may also have a concern that a short-term increase in the buyer's share price may result in inadequately reflecting the inherent value of the sellers' shares. Similar to the fixed exchange ratio, the fixed market value formula may also utilize "floor" and "ceiling" collars.

Some of the risks inherent in stock price fluctuations may be addressed by a walk right, which gives the sellers the right to terminate the acquisition agreement if the market value of the buyer's shares during a specified period before closing falls below an agreed price that is substantially below the buyer's stock price on the day the acquisition agreement was signed. In the face of a demand for a walk right, the buyer may negotiate for a right to top up the exchange ratio with a value equal to the value that the sellers had initially agreed to at the time the acquisition agreement was signed. A walk right only provides limited protection to the sellers because by the time the walk right is exercised, the sellers may have had substantial expense and will have conducted the target's business for some period of time in anticipation of the transaction being closed. Sellers may also have turned down other alternative transactions that may no longer be available. The buyer will sometimes also insist on a walk right permitting it to terminate the acquisition agreement if its stock price exceeds an agreed upon price such that by reason of the fixed exchange ratio or the fixed value formula it would be required to issue shares having a total market value above a threshold amount.

SUGGESTED PROVISIONS

Additional definitions (Section 1.1).

Buyer Stock—the common stock, $1.00 par value per share, of Buyer.

Additional documents for delivery at Closing (Section 2.4)

Sellers' deliverables:

(viii) **lock-up agreements in the form of Exhibit 2.4(a)(viii), executed by Sellers (collectively "Lock-up Agreements"); and**

(ix) **registration rights agreement in the form of Exhibit 2.4(a)(ix), executed by Sellers (the "Registration Rights Agreement").**

Buyer's deliverables:

(i) **a certificate for the shares of the Buyer Stock to be issued to each Seller, registered in the name of such Seller and containing the legend set forth in Section 3.__(e);**

. . .

(v) **the Lock-up Agreements, executed by Buyer;**

(vi)   the Registration Rights Agreement, executed by Buyer.

Additional Seller representations and warranties:

3.__ BUYER STOCK

(a)   The Buyer Stock to be acquired by each Seller will be acquired for investment for such Seller's own account and not with a view to the distribution thereof within the meaning of Section 2(11) of the Securities Act.   Each Seller understands that the Buyer Stock has not been, and will not be, registered under the Securities Act by reason of a specific exemption from the registration provisions of the Securities Act, which depends upon, among other things, the bona fide nature of the investment intent and the accuracy of such Seller's representations as expressed in this Agreement.

(b)   Each Seller has received all the information it considers necessary or appropriate for deciding whether to acquire the Buyer Stock.   Seller has reviewed the quarterly, annual, and periodic reports of Buyer that have been filed with the United States Securities and Exchange Commission ("SEC").   Each Seller has been given the opportunity to obtain any information or documents relating to, and ask questions and receive answers about, Buyer, Buyer's Stock, and the business and prospects of Buyer which it deems necessary to evaluate the merits and risks related to its investment in such shares and to verify the information received.

(c)   Each Seller has such knowledge and experience in financial and business matters that such Seller is capable of evaluating the merits and risks of its investment in the Buyer and has the capacity to protect its own interests.   Each Seller is able to bear the economic risks of its investment in the Buyer Stock for an indefinite period of time, including the risks of a complete loss of such Seller's investment in such securities.

(d)   Each Seller understands that the Buyer Stock is characterized as "restricted securities" as defined in Rule 144 promulgated under the Securities Act because they are being acquired from the Buyer in a transaction not involving a public offering and that, under the Securities Act, the Buyer Stock may be resold without registration under the Securities Act only in certain limited circumstances.   Each Seller acknowledges that the Buyer Stock must be held indefinitely unless subsequently registered under the Securities Act and under applicable state securities laws or an exemption from such registration is available.   Each Buyer is aware that the provisions of Rule 144 promulgated under the Securities Act, which permit limited resale of shares purchased in a private placement are subject to the satisfaction of certain conditions, including, among other things, the availability of certain current public information about the Buyer and the resale occurring not less than six months after a party has purchased and paid for the security to be sold.

(e)   Each Seller understands that the Buyer Stock and any securities issued in respect thereof or exchanged therefor, may bear, substantially, one or all of the following legends:

> THESE SECURITIES HAVE NOT BEEN REGISTERED UNDER THE SECURITIES ACT OF 1933, AS AMENDED, AND MAY NOT BE SOLD, TRANSFERRED, ASSIGNED, OR HYPOTHECATED UNLESS (A) THERE IS AN EFFECTIVE REGISTRATION STATEMENT UNDER SUCH ACT COVERING SUCH SECURITIES, (B) THE SALE IS MADE IN ACCORDANCE WITH RULE 144 UNDER THE ACT OR (C) THE COMPANY RECEIVES AN OPINION OF COUNSEL FOR THE HOLDER OF THE SECURITIES REASONABLY SATISFACTORY TO THE COMPANY STATING THAT SUCH SALE IS EXEMPT FROM THE REGISTRATION AND PROSPECTUS DELIVERY REQUIREMENTS OF SUCH ACT.

Any legend required by the securities laws of any state to the extent such laws are applicable to the shares represented by the certificate so legended.

(f)   Each Seller is an accredited investor as defined in Rule 501(a) of Regulation D promulgated under the Securities Act.

Additional representations and warranties of Buyer:

4.__ SEC FILINGS; FINANCIAL STATEMENTS

(a)   Buyer has furnished or made available to Sellers a correct and complete copy of Buyer's Annual Report on Form 10-K filed with the SEC with respect to the fiscal year ended _____, and each Quarterly Report on Form 10-Q, Current Report on Form 8-K, other report, schedule, registration statement, and definitive proxy statement filed by Buyer with the SEC on or after the date of filing of the Form 10-K which are all the documents (other than preliminary material) that Buyer was required to file (or otherwise did file) with the SEC in accordance with Sections 13, 14 and 15(d) of the Exchange Act on or after the date of filing with the SEC of the Form 10-K (collectively, the "Buyer SEC Documents"). As of their respective filing dates, or in the case of registration statements, their respective effective times, none of the Buyer SEC Documents (including all exhibits and schedules thereto and documents incorporated by reference therein) contained any untrue statement of a material fact or omitted to state a material fact required to be stated therein or necessary in order to make the statements therein, in light of the circumstances under which they were made, not misleading, and the Buyer SEC Documents complied when filed, or in the case of registration statements, as of their respective effective times, in all material respects with the then applicable requirements of the Securities Act or the Exchange Act, as the case may be, and the rules and regulations promulgated by the SEC thereunder.

(b)   Each set of consolidated financial statements (including, in each case, any related notes thereto) contained in the Buyer SEC Documents was prepared in accordance with GAAP applied on a consistent basis throughout the periods involved (except as may be indicated in the notes thereto or, in the case of unaudited statements, do not contain footnotes as permitted by Form 10-Q of the Exchange Act) and each fairly presents the consolidated financial position of Buyer and its subsidiaries at the respective dates thereof and the consolidated results of its operations and cash flows for the periods indicated, except that the unaudited interim financial statements were or are subject to normal year-end adjustments (the effect of which will not, individually or in the aggregate, be materially adverse).

4.__ ORGANIZATION AND GOOD STANDING

(a)   Buyer is a corporation duly organized, validly existing, and in good standing under the laws of its jurisdiction of incorporation, with full corporate power and authority to conduct its business as it is being conducted, and to own or use its assets. Buyer and each of its subsidiaries is duly qualified to do business as a foreign entity and is in good standing under the laws of each jurisdiction that requires such qualification.

(b)   Buyer has delivered to Sellers copies of its Organizational Documents.

4.__ CAPITALIZATION

The authorized common stock of Buyer consists of _____ (___) shares of common stock, par value $_____ per share, of which _____ (_____) shares are issued and outstanding. All of the outstanding common stock of Buyer has been duly authorized and validly issued, and is fully paid and nonassessable. The Buyer Stock, when issued pursuant to terms of this Agreement, will be validly issued, fully paid, and nonassessable.

Additional condition for Buyer:

8.__ STOCK EXCHANGE LISTING

The Buyer Stock shall have been accepted for listing on the principal national securities exchange on which securities of the same class or series issued by Buyer are then listed.

Considerations Regarding Employment Agreements in Connection with Sale of Stock

PRELIMINARY NOTE

The Model Agreement contemplates that an employment agreement will be entered into between the Company and one of the Sellers who intends to remain employed by the Company (the "Executive"). The employment agreement contemplates an ongoing relationship in which the Company continues to benefit from the knowledge and talents of the Executive, while at the same time allowing the Executive to remain active with the Company. In most instances, the buyer will negotiate the terms of an employment agreement. Because many core provisions of employment agreements, especially those relating to duties, compensation, and termination, must be tailored to the individual circumstances of the transaction to which they relate, this Appendix provides an explanation of various components of acquisition-related employment agreements and how they may affect the negotiations surrounding the transaction. Consideration is also given to various ramifications of the continuing relationship between the Executive and the Company.

Consideration should be given to the nature of the proposed relationship between the Company and the Executive after the transaction has been consummated. While employment may be one relationship, consideration may also be given to a consulting relationship between the Executive and the Company, depending upon tax and other business considerations, as well as the intentions and desires of the parties. This Appendix does not address all the issues in determining whether the relationship between the Executive and the Company should be that of statutory employee or independent consultant. Rather, it addresses various basic components of an employee relationship and also includes references to consulting alternatives as appropriate. In drafting the employment agreement, distinctions that may be relevant between an entrepreneur and a professional manager should be considered. The mindset and anticipated role of the employee will significantly affect the terms of the employment agreement.

SUBSTANTIVE PROVISIONS

Duties. One of the first provisions of the Employment Agreement will set forth the scope of the Executive's position and the capacity in which the Executive is being engaged, his or her title, his or her duties, and the person or body to whom he or she will report. Although it is advisable to clearly lay out this information in the agreement, the scope of the Executive's position and the Company's activities may evolve over time and therefore appropriate flexibility should be incorporated into the agreement. Specifically, the Company may want to retain some ability to modify the Executive's duties and responsibilities in the future.[1] Further, the Company may want to retain the right to assign the Employment Agreement in the event of a merger, acquisition, corporate reorganization, or other business combination in which an assignment would be appropriate. Conversely, the Executive will be wary of granting to the Company broad rights to change or modify the party with whom he or she has an employment or consulting relationship. The Executive will also seek to limit the substantive changes which the Company may institute during the term of employment or engagement to ensure that the duties remain familiar and attainable.

The duties section of the Employment Agreement will also specify whether the Executive will be employed exclusively by the Company, or whether he or she will be able to also pursue other outside employment or consulting interests. In the latter case, the Employment Agreement might explicitly state how much time the Executive will be expected to spend on the job.[2]

The Executive's authority within the Company may also be a significant issue in the negotiation of the Employment Agreement. This is especially the case where some or all of the Executive's compensation will be incentive-based. In such situations, the Executive will not wish to be placed in a position in which he or she does not have the power to achieve the goals upon which the Executive's wages and other compensation are predicated. For this reason, the Executive will likely seek

---

[1] For example, if the Company acquires other businesses, it may wish to expand the Executive's scope of activities. Similarly, if the Company should add additional facilities, it may want to relocate the Executive. Additionally, the Company must retain sufficient flexibility to allow for transition and for the growth of other personnel to ultimately assume the role and duties performed by the Executive. Both the Company and the Executive must consider their short-term and long-term intentions and needs.

[2] When the Executive is permitted to provide services to others, issues relating to the protection of proprietary information, and the development of intellectual property and other advancements, become more difficult to define and require additional negotiations to ensure that the interests of the parties are adequately protected. If the Executive is not going to provide services exclusively to the Company, a consulting arrangement may be more appropriate. A consulting relationship may provide greater flexibility with respect to duties and time commitment, while relieving the Company of certain financial and tax obligations. *See* "Compensation Tax Issues" below. The ramifications of the relationship selected, including the economic and control consequences, must be thoroughly addressed.

decision-making authority within the scope of his or her activities, and may also seek a position as an officer and/or member of the Company's board of directors to bolster his or her ability to influence the Company's direction. The Executive may also seek to include terms in the Employment Agreement which commit certain resources of the Company for specific business activities.

It is not uncommon for a prospective executive employee, especially one who is accustomed to operating his or her own business, to want a prestigious title (even if the position actually has little actual authority).[3] Along with the grant of titles, the extent of authority actually or apparently vested in the Executive should be considered. Even if the title is solely intended to be honorific, a level of apparent authority will likely result. In such an event, it may be important to address the likely consequences of the Executive's apparent authority and to spell out the limits of the Executive's rights, including consideration of the adverse consequences to the Executive in the event those boundaries are exceeded.

Term. The term of the Employment Agreement and the scope of the Executive's duties depend upon the nature of the transaction and the negotiating leverage of the Executive. If the Executive's duties will be limited or on a part-time basis, the time that the Executive must devote to the Company's business may be stated as a certain minimum or maximum number of hours per week or month. On the other hand, if the Company has a continuing need for the Executive's services in order to maintain the business as a successful ongoing concern (for example, because of his or her technical knowledge, knowledge of the business, or relationships with customers, suppliers, or other employees, or if the buyer is a financial purchaser who will not be involved in the operation of the business), the buyer will want a covenant in the Employment Agreement requiring the Executive to spend all of his or her business time (and a minimum of normal and ordinary working hours for the employees of the Company generally) in the performance of his or her duties pursuant to the Employment Agreement. In addition to the amount of time that must be spent, consideration may be given to whether the Employment Agreement will have a fixed term or be terminable at will by the parties. Where the Company is dependent upon the Executive in order to maintain the business, the buyer will insist on a fixed term (of years) over an at-will arrangement. In the same vein, if the Executive is depending upon the continuing stream of income as an employee with the Company, he or she will seek a fixed term (of years).[4] In instances in which a fixed term is desired, the issue of termination of the employment relationship by the Company or by the Executive is increasingly important (*see* "Termination" below).

---

3   In the event the parties enter into a consulting relationship rather than an employment relationship, the granting of titles may imply something other than a consulting relationship. In all instances, the parties will want to ensure that the "message" conveyed by the titles is consistent with the understanding of the parties.

4   To the extent the compensation to be paid to the Executive is dependent upon reaching certain sales goals over a period of time, or if the Model Agreement provides for an earnout amount which may increase the ultimate consideration paid for the stock, the Executive will insist upon a fixed term to ensure that he or she will have the ability to influence the success of the Company.

In considering the term of the Employment Agreement, the extent of control granted to the Executive over the operation of the business of the Company and the flexibility which the Company desires to retain for continuing management must also be considered. Where an Employment Agreement includes a fixed term, the term may also include an evergreen clause that allows the term of the Employment Agreement to renew automatically for an unlimited number of one-year or multiple-year periods after the initial term, unless terminated by either party before the beginning of a renewal term (or with appropriate advance notice).

Compensation. Compensation under the Employment Agreement may include a variety of components, including base salary, bonuses (formulaic and discretionary), fringe benefits, and participation in various employee benefit plans and insurance policies.[5] In the acquisition context, the parties to the Employment Agreement often will seek creativity in structuring the Executive's compensation for a variety of tax and other reasons.

The core component of the Executive's compensation will be his or her base salary. This salary usually is comparable to other similarly situated executives of the Company. In some transactions, the parties enhance the Executive's compensation package to help bridge the gap between buyer and seller with respect to the purchase price negotiations. In certain instances, this increased compensation to the Executive may be a disguised increase in the purchase price. This issue, when present, creates potential conflicts of interest between the Executive and the other former shareholders of the Company, because the Executive is the only party benefiting from the enhanced compensation, and it is presumably at the expense of the shareholders generally.[6]

Once a base salary is established, a mechanism may be used to calculate increases in the salary over time.[7] These increases are most often found in two forms: (a) automatic increases, and (b) discretionary increases. If increases in base salary are to be automatic, the formula upon which it is to be based should be set forth clearly in the Employment Agreement. If the increases are to be discretionary, the Employment Agreement should carefully stipulate who has the authority to grant increases and what rights, if any, the Executive may have if no increase is granted. In either instance, the Executive will want assurance the Company will not make the criteria for the increases unattainable. Obviously, this issue dovetails with the control issue discussed above.

---

[5] These components are indicative of the employment relationship. The compensation components in a consulting relationship may likely provide for a retainer and/or base compensation, bonuses which are determined based upon certain formulae, possible discretionary bonuses, reimbursement for out-of-pocket expenses, and possible commission-based or performance-based compensation, but excluding fringe benefits.

[6] In instances in which the compensation package to the Executive is not offered to other selling shareholders on a basis which is pro rata with their shareholding interests, the buyer may factor such compensation into its calculation of the purchase price in the underlying transaction. Where the compensation can be justified as a result of expertise, relationships, or other benefits that are to be enjoyed by the buyer, the bases for such disparate treatment should be appropriately documented and supported. Such a proposal exacerbates the potential conflict in counsel's representation of multiple shareholders in the transaction.

[7] This may enable the parties to more easily accept an extended term for the Agreement.

The Executive's fringe benefits are often as important to him or her as the base salary. This is especially the case in instances where the Executive previously had significant control over the granting of fringe benefits to himself or herself. If the Executive had attractive perquisites in his or her former position, including expense accounts, company cars, generous vacations, and club memberships, the Executive may expect to be accorded the same treatment in his or her new job. The buyer, on the other hand, may have a different view of such perquisites, especially if the buyer believes that the full price has already been paid in the transaction. Very often the economic analysis conducted by the buyer includes a normalization of the compensation paid to executives. Consideration should also be given to whether the granting of significant perquisites to the Executive will have an adverse affect on other key employees or create dissension.

Also important and deserving of consideration are continuing participation in employee benefit plans. It may be presumed that the Executive was a participant in a variety of plans, ranging from profit-sharing, employee stock option, pension, or 401(k) plans to medical, life, and disability insurance plans. The Executive will likely expect to participate in plans comparable to the ones he or she previously enjoyed. Also, the Executive will want his or her seniority (and vested status, if applicable) in his or her current plans to be credited. In contrast, the buyer may have plans in place throughout its organization that are inferior to the Company's or that have longer vesting periods and may want the Company to change its plans accordingly. While the entity does not change, this does not mean that the plans and other benefits offered by the Company are not subject to revision. These issues can cause a great deal of friction both during and after the transaction, when the Executive is trying to integrate himself or herself within the larger organization of the buyer. Obviously, if the Company is a standalone entity and is not part of a larger concern, several of these issues may be minimized or inapplicable. However, in all instances, care should be given to precisely define those elements of compensation, including salary, bonuses, fringe benefits, and participation employee benefit plans to which the Executive will be entitled.[8]

Compensation Tax Issues. Just as the income tax consequences to the buyer and to the sellers are important considerations in determining the structure of an acquisition transaction, there likewise are income tax considerations with an employment agreement as contrasted with a consulting agreement. Initial consideration must be given to whether the relationship should be an employment-based relationship or an independent contractor relationship. In an independent contractor relationship, the Executive would be providing independent consulting services to the Company and the consulting agreement should be based upon those principles. Generally speaking, whether or not the parties call the relationship independent consulting, the IRS applies a multi-factor test to determine whether the individual is truly an independent contractor or, alternatively, is a statutory

---

8   In the context of a consulting agreement, fringe benefits and participation in employee benefit plans are generally not offered to the consultant. Rather, the consultant, on his or her own, or by forming a consulting entity, may establish fringe benefit policies and employee benefit plans that are outside the scope of the relationship with the Company.

employee. Of the various factors considered, the degree of control and direction over the activities of the Executive is the most important.

For income tax purposes, the payments received by the Executive as an employee or as a consultant will be ordinary income to the Executive and deductible to the Company, while sales proceeds (on the stock sold by the Executive), to the extent of gain on the sale, will be taxable to the Executive (seller) at the lower capital gain rates. In addition, if the Executive is an employee, the Company will be subject to employment taxes (FICA (Social Security)) and (FUTA (unemployment) taxes)) with respect to the compensation paid. The Company is required to provide the Executive with a W-2 at the end of each year to indicate the compensation paid as well as taxes paid to the government on behalf of the Executive.[9]

From the buyer's tax perspective, it would be preferable to make payments to the Executive under an Employment Agreement because the Company would then be permitted generally to deduct such payments under Section 162 of the Internal Revenue Code, while payments made under the Model Agreement will not be deductible. Conversely, from a tax standpoint only, the Executive would rather have the value attributed to the sale of the stock in order to receive capital gain treatment in respect of the consideration, rather than in the form of employment compensation and be required to pay tax at ordinary income rates and applicable employment taxes. It is this disparate tax treatment which will often be the subject of significant negotiations in allocating the amounts to be paid. It is also for this reason that returning to the true character of the compensation paid (and the purpose for which each amount is being paid) is important.

In instances where the purchase price appears not to reflect the true character of the consideration, the IRS has the ability to challenge and reallocate the purchase price. While this is the exception rather than the rule, the IRS is most likely to scrutinize a contractual allocation where the interests of the parties are not truly adverse as, for instance, where the additional tax costs to the Executive of compensation income is substantially less than the benefits of the deductions to the buyer. This is the case only when there is a small rate differential between ordinary income and capital gains. An allocation to an Employment Agreement will likely be respected where value is attributable to the personal knowledge, skill, or reputation of the Executive and to the services to be rendered.[10] Accordingly, employment agreements or consulting agreements may be more appropriately used in connection with acquisitions of businesses where the prior owners have had personal involvement with the business. Indeed, even in the context of a capital-intensive business, if the Executive, as a prior owner, has special knowledge of the

---

9   In contrast, if the Executive is an independent contractor, such compensation is considered to be outside the scope of FICA and FUTA as between the Executive and the Company, and the Executive is required to report the income as self-employment income and to pay self-employment tax in respect of this income. In such a context, the Company is required to report to the IRS the payment of independent contractor income to the Executive on a Form 1099.

10   Value may also be attributed to covenants of noncompetition and nondisclosure.

business or of the customers or of a particular challenge facing the Company, an allocation to an Employment Agreement is more effectively supported.

Restrictive Covenants. One of the most important as well as contentious sections of the Employment Agreement deals with the noncompetition, nonsolicitation, and nondisclosure covenants.[11] On their most basic terms, these provisions provide that, so long as the Executive is employed by the Company and for a certain period of time after his or her employment ends, he or she will not compete with the Company or attempt to take away the Company's customers, suppliers, or employees, or disclose confidential information. These provisions are necessary even if the Model Agreement or the ancillary documents contain similar language, because the Executive's obligations under those other documents may expire at a different point in time than the employment relationship.[12] Noncompetition provisions should be consistent and clear. Also, because courts generally disfavor restrictions on the ability of an individual to engage in economic activities, care should be given to tailor any restrictive covenants to meet the reasonable goals and needs of the Company. Duration, geographic scope, and the scope of businesses restricted are the three components that must be thoroughly assessed and considered. The more special knowledge an individual has, and the more proprietary information and goodwill a business possesses, the more likely the restrictive covenants are to be enforceable if challenged. In each instance, one should consult the law of the jurisdiction in which the Executive is to be employed for more specific direction regarding the permissible scope of such limitations and the enforceability of such limiting provisions. The law in this area can vary significantly from state to state.

Courts disfavor noncompetition covenants, especially the context of employment. Obviously, these restrictions and limitations are industry and case specific. It is often difficult, if not impossible, to determine or predict with certainty whether a given restrictive covenant will be enforceable. However, research into similarly situated transactions may be instructive. Further, consideration might be given to including a "blue pencil" clause, providing that if the restrictive covenants are found to be unenforceable, their scope will be reduced to the extent necessary to render the modified covenants valid and enforceable.[13] While this may appear as an invitation to the court to reduce the time, geographic scope, or scope of business contained in a restrictive covenant, it is generally viewed as a method to try to ensure that these restrictive covenants will be enforced at least to a reasonable extent.

Because restrictive covenants in the Employment Agreement may come under scrutiny by a court or arbitrator, it is advisable to provide recitations linking the legitimate interests of the Company in protecting its customer and client base and goodwill to its need to impose restrictive covenants on the Executive.

---

11 This discussion is equally applicable in the consulting agreement context.

12 This section does not discuss noncompetition covenants given by sellers in the sale of stock but rather focuses only on the noncompetition covenant in the employment context.

13 Not all jurisdictions have adopted or recognize a "blue pencil" doctrine.

With respect to nonsolicitation, this restriction may involve both an agreement not to solicit the customers or clients of the Company during the period of employment and for a period thereafter, as well as an agreement to refrain from soliciting employees of the Company during the term of employment and for a period thereafter. In service-based industries and technology-based industries, the human capital component of the Company is often of substantial value. For this reason, nonsolicitation provisions can be especially important.

In addition to the preservation of human capital as assets of the Company, to the extent the Company depends upon intangible assets, intellectual property, and other proprietary and confidential information such as trade secrets, the Company may want to include a nondisclosure provision in the Employment Agreement with the Executive. The Company would usually seek a broad definition of the confidential and other proprietary information to be protected. Often the employees of the Company will be asked to execute a separate confidentiality agreement. Employees may also be asked to grant assignments of inventions and intellectual property. In all instances, attention should be paid to dovetail all confidentiality provisions contained in the Model Agreement, the Employment Agreement, and the confidentiality agreement. *See also* commentary to Section 7.2 of the Model Agreement.

Setoff Rights. Under the Model Agreement and related documents, the Executive may owe the buyer monies relating to purchase price adjustments, indemnifications, and other obligations. It is often useful for the buyer to create a mechanism in the Employment Agreement to set off these amounts against any future payments that the Company would otherwise be required to make to the Executive under the Employment Agreement. In drafting such a provision, particular attention should be paid to which of the Executive's obligations under the Model Agreement are subject to the setoff, what type of notice is required prior to setoff, and what cure period, if any, the Executive will be entitled to prior to the setoff taking place. In addition, the buyer must check the laws of the jurisdiction in which the Executive is to be employed to ensure that such setoffs are permissible. Generally, a company is not entitled to setoff or deduct from ordinary wages and salaries without first obtaining the written consent of the employee. Whether or not the Employment Agreement provisions are sufficient to allow such setoff rights should be confirmed. *See also* commentary to Section 11.7 of the Model Agreement.

Termination. The Company generally will want to terminate the employment of the Executive "for cause." In contrast, the Executive will want to limit the Company's right to terminate his or her employment for cause and to have an opportunity to cure any breach that may occur. If the Employment Agreement favors the Company, it may consist solely of a clause permitting the Company to terminate for any Executive behavior or conduct that, in the judgment of the Company's Board of Directors, is detrimental or harmful to the business interests of the Company. The Executive usually will resist such a clause vigorously, particularly in the context of an acquisition in which the Executive may feel especially vulnerable to adverse action by the buyer. Alternatively, the parties could stipulate that failure of the

Executive to achieve mutually agreed upon business goals constitutes cause for termination. In addition, the Company will often reserve the right to terminate the employment relationship without cause but with a severance provision that will vary depending upon the Executive's position, the industry, and the timing of the termination. Such terminate-and-pay provisions may satisfactorily bridge the gap between the interests of the parties.

In considering the definition of "for cause" in an Employment Agreement, the parties should consider the legitimate interests of the Company (including the potential for embarrassment to the Board if the Company must pay severance, notwithstanding Executive wrongdoing), the expectations of the parties with respect to the employment relationship, the degree of flexibility to be maintained by the Company in conducting its business, and the short-term and long-term goals of the parties. Additionally, in order to obtain the intended performance, the parties may wish to include strong financial and other disincentives for breach of the Employment Agreement by the Executive. In instances where the Company is relying upon the continued efforts of the Executive, the Company may find using bonus and incentive compensation tools to be more beneficial than retaining a broad "for cause" provision. The Company would usually retain the right to terminate the Employment Agreement without paying severance benefits in the event the Executive becomes unable to perform his or her duties as a result of death, disability, or other such circumstances.

Conversely, the Executive may insist upon the right to terminate the Employment Agreement for good reason. This provision is intended to cover instances where the Company constructively terminates the Executive's employment by taking certain actions without the Executive's consent that result in lesser status, reduced responsibilities, or hardships for the Executive. Thus, if the Company takes actions which make it impossible for the Executive to succeed in his or her role, the Executive may seek to terminate the Employment Agreement. Generally, if the Executive terminates the Employment Agreement for good reason, he or she will be entitled to compensation and benefits for a specified period of time or for the balance of the term of the Employment Agreement. As discussed below, the employer usually desires flexibility to change terms and conditions of employment, particularly before a change in control. Severance benefits payable upon a termination by the Executive for good reason are typically the same as those severance benefits the Executive would receive upon a termination by the Company without cause. If the Company is required to pay the Executive's salary and benefits for an extended period of time after the termination of the employment relationship by the Executive for good reason, it may wish to provide, as a condition to the Executive's receipt of such continued compensation, that the Executive continue to abide by all the restrictive covenants contained in the Employment Agreement and release claims that the Executive may otherwise have against the Company or the buyer. In any event, severance payments should be carefully structured to ensure exemption from, or compliance with, Section 409A of the Internal Revenue Code (the "Code"), which deals with nonqualified deferred compensation payments.

The disability and death provisions of an Employment Agreement are another subject for negotiation by the parties. To determine whether the Executive is disabled, the Company may seek to have its Board of Directors or a physician selected by the Company make the determination. The Executive will often object to a determination of disability by the Company (or its representative) and seek the right to have an independent physician make this determination. Generally, in instances of disability, the focus is on the inability of the Executive to continue to perform under the Employment Agreement for a stipulated period of time. The Employment Agreement should also consider the consequences of termination in the event of the Executive's death, address what payments will become due, and the timing of such payments.

Change of Business Activities. An increasingly important subject to consider in the Employment Agreement context is the ability of the Company to change the Executive's role in the event of a major change in the business (e.g., loss of business, change in principal products, or changes in underlying technology and business methods, business combinations, divestitures, acquisitions, or other amalgamations). While the intent of the parties may be well understood at the time the Employment Agreement is executed, the business conditions and plans for the buyer are likely to change over time. To the extent the Company can retain some degree of flexibility with respect to these issues, it may serve to alleviate business planning constraints. Conversely, the Executive will seek some modicum of protection from having his or her duties materially altered. In such events, the Executive will seek the right to terminate the employment relationship for good reason, and obtain the benefit of his or her initial contractual bargain similar to that applicable in the change of control context discussed below.

Change of Control Provisions. The Employment Agreement may provide for payments that are contingent on a change in the ownership or effective control of the Company or in the ownership of a substantial portion of the Company's assets ("change in control") or a qualifying employment termination after a change in control (so-called "golden parachute" payments).[14] The Executive may hope to negotiate a provision that permits him or her to terminate employment in the event of a change in control and to receive vesting of incentive compensation

---

14   A golden parachute payment is any compensatory payment made to a "disqualified individual" (in general, an officer, highly compensated employee, or greater than 1% shareholder) that is contingent upon a change in control. If these payments constitute "excess parachute payments" within the meaning of Section 280G of the Code, then such payments will be nondeductible to the payor and the Executive may be subject to a 20% excise tax under Code Section 4999. Code Section 280G, however, includes an exemption for parachute payments, payable by a private company, if the Executive's right to the golden parachute payments is approved by persons who own more than 75% of the voting power of the company as determined immediately prior to the change in control (excluding the votes of any disqualified individuals), and the shareholders receive full disclosure of the material facts relating to those payments. (It should be noted that an automatic exemption without the need for a vote is available for S corporations.) It may also be possible to reduce or eliminate adverse tax consequences by conditioning payments on a compliance with a noncompetition agreement. The Employment Agreement should also address whether (1) the Executive will receive a "gross-up" payment to compensate the Executive for the impact of any excise tax (and other income tax on such gross-up payment) or (2) the golden parachute will be cut back to avoid triggering Code Section 280G. The foregoing is only a high-level overview of certain aspects of Code Section 280G and the extensive regulations thereunder, and does not purport to be a complete description of Code Section 280G and the related regulations which should be read and in their entirety in analyzing any given situation.

and severance benefits ("single triggers"). Permitting the Executive to terminate his or her employment in the event of a change in control and receive these enhancements is viewed by many investors to be poor corporate governance, and potentially create an incentive to sell the company for reasons contrary to shareholder interests. An alternative is a "double trigger" requiring a change in control and another event—the passage of time or some form of constructive termination after the passage of time. As an alternative to single trigger or double trigger golden parachute provisions, the Company could also insert a "cut back" provision which would limit the Executive payments to an amount that would not exceed the statutory threshold for "excess parachute payments" under Section 280G of the Code. Before including any golden parachute provisions in executive employment or other agreements, a company should, based on knowledgeable advice, fully understand the tax and other consequences of such a provision.

Dispute Resolution—Arbitration. Increasingly, the use of arbitration or some other form of alternative dispute resolution or ADR short of litigation is included in employment agreements. While alternative dispute resolution continues to grow and become more favored in many quarters, some remain skeptical and resist including ADR dispute resolution provisions in the context of employment agreements.

Miscellaneous. As with all contracts, the miscellaneous provisions relating to jurisdiction, choice of law, modification, and the like, must be considered and addressed in the Employment Agreement context. Consideration should be given to the detail included in these provisions to avoid unintended consequences and inconsistencies between the Employment Agreement and the Model Agreement itself.

APPENDIX D

Nine Hypothetical Scenarios

The following hypothetical scenarios illustrate the operation and interaction of:

- the Sellers' representations in Section 3 of the Model Agreement;

- the Sellers' pre-closing covenants in Section 5.4 of the Model Agreement (which contemplates the delivery of supplements to the Sellers' Disclosure Letter) and in Section 5.7 of the Model Agreement (which provides that each Seller will use its best efforts to cause the conditions in Article 8 to be satisfied);

- the closing conditions in Sections 8.1(a) and 8.3 of the Model Agreement (relating to the accuracy of the Sellers' representations and the delivery of a "bring down" certificate);

- the termination provisions in Section 10.1 of the Model Agreement (and the preservation of rights under Section 10.2); and

- the indemnification provisions in Article 11 of the Model Agreement.

Each of the hypothetical scenarios is based upon a lawsuit brought by a third party against the Company prior to the scheduled Closing Date. In Scenarios 1 through 4, it is assumed that the lawsuit is brought *before* the Model Agreement is signed, while in Scenarios 5 through 9, it is assumed that the lawsuit is brought *after* the Model Agreement is signed. Various assumptions are also made about whether the lawsuit is "material" and about when the lawsuit is first disclosed to Buyer.

In each scenario, it is assumed that:

- the Company received no threat of litigation before the lawsuit was brought;

- the lawsuit does not relate to any product manufactured by the Acquired Companies or any other matter covered by the express indemnities in Sections 11.2(c), 11.2(d), 11.2(e), or 11.2(f) of the Model Agreement;

- except for inaccuracies resulting from the lawsuit, there are no inaccuracies in the Sellers' representations as of the signing date or as of the scheduled Closing Date;

- Sellers have used their best efforts to cause the Company to settle the lawsuit prior to the scheduled Closing Date (although that would not be required when the litigation has been disclosed prior to the signing of the Model Agreement) and have otherwise complied fully with their pre-closing covenants in the Model Agreement;

- all of the conditions to the Buyer's obligation to consummate the acquisition are satisfied in full as of the scheduled Closing Date, except to the extent that the lawsuit results in a failure to satisfy the closing condition in Section 8.1(a) of the Model Agreement (and the related delivery of a "bring down" certificate as provided in Section 8.3);

- to the extent applicable, settlement of the lawsuit and payment of the settlement amounts are not prohibited by the pre-closing covenants;

- to the extent applicable, settlement of the lawsuit will only require payment of the settlement amounts and will have no other collateral effect;

- the End Date specified in Section 10.1(d) is the same as the scheduled Closing Date; and

- Buyer is not in material Breach of the Model Agreement.

With respect to each scenario, two key questions are posed:

1. ***Can Buyer refuse to consummate the acquisition and terminate the Model Agreement without incurring liability to Sellers (in other words, does Buyer have a "walk right")?***

2. ***If Buyer proceeds with the acquisition, will Sellers be required to indemnify Buyer and the Acquired Companies against any damages arising from the lawsuit?***

In a number of scenarios discussed below, question 2 is answered in the affirmative. It is possible, however, that notwithstanding the unambiguous language in the Model Agreement, Sellers may argue that the cases discussed in the Preliminary Note to Article 11 effectively override the Buyer's right to "close and sue" under theories of substituted performance, lack of reliance on the representation, or some other theory. That having been said, because Section 12.11 of the Model Agreement preserves all remedies, Buyer may be able to sue for breach of contract in tort, or otherwise, instead of claiming indemnification. Further analysis of these possible recovery scenarios is beyond the scope of this Appendix.

In addition, in scenarios where Buyer has, and elects to exercise, a "walk right" as a result of the lawsuit by terminating the Model Agreement, it is appropriate to pose a further question:

3. ***Can Buyer terminate the Model Agreement and recover damages from Sellers by reason of the lawsuit (in other words, can Buyer "terminate and sue")?***

In the scenarios discussed below where question 2 or 3 is answered in the affirmative, this Appendix does not in every case address the quantum of damages, if any, the Buyer may have suffered, especially where the disclosure results in a purchase price adjustment or the lawsuit is not material (effect of the lawsuit in the case of question 2; loss of the bargain in the case of question 3).

For additional discussions of the issues addressed in this Appendix, see the commentary to Sections 5.4 and 5.7, Sections 8.1 and 8.3, Sections 10.1 and 10.2, and Sections 11.1 and 11.2 of the Model Agreement.

SCENARIO 1
(MATERIAL PRE-SIGNING LITIGATION DISCLOSED IN ORIGINAL DISCLOSURE LETTER)

ASSUMED FACTS:

- A few days before the signing of the Model Agreement, a material lawsuit is brought against the Company.
- Sellers disclose the lawsuit in their Disclosure Letter (which is furnished to Buyer at the time the Model Agreement is signed).
- The lawsuit is not settled and remains pending on the scheduled Closing Date.
- Sellers deliver an unqualified "bring down" certificate pursuant to Section 8.3.

1. *Can Buyer refuse to consummate the acquisition (i.e., does Buyer have a "walk right")?*

   NO. Because the lawsuit was disclosed in the Disclosure Letter at the time of the signing of the Model Agreement, the Sellers' "absence of litigation" representation in Section 3.15(a) was accurate as of the signing date and remains accurate as of the scheduled Closing Date. Thus, the condition in each of the two clauses in Section 8.1(a) (and Section 8.3) is satisfied and the Buyer does not have a "walk right."

2. *Will Sellers be required to indemnify Buyer and the Acquired Companies against any damages arising from the lawsuit?*

   NO. Because the lawsuit was disclosed in the Disclosure Letter, the Sellers' "absence of litigation" representation was accurate as of the signing date, and the representation remains accurate as "brought down" to the Closing Date. Thus, neither the Model Agreement nor the Sellers' "bring down" certificate contains an inaccurate representation, and Sellers will have no indemnification obligation under Section 11.2(a) with respect to the lawsuit.

SCENARIO 2
(MATERIAL PRE-SIGNING LITIGATION NOT DISCLOSED IN ORIGINAL DISCLOSURE LETTER, BUT DISCLOSED BEFORE THE SCHEDULED CLOSING DATE IN SUPPLEMENT TO DISCLOSURE LETTER)

ASSUMED FACTS:

- A few days before the signing of the Model Agreement, a material lawsuit is brought against the Company.
- Sellers fail to disclose the lawsuit in their original Disclosure Letter (which is furnished to Buyer at the time the Model Agreement is signed). Sellers subsequently disclose the lawsuit in a supplement delivered to Buyer (pursuant to Section 5.4) a few days after the signing of the Model Agreement.
- The lawsuit is not settled and remains pending on the scheduled Closing Date.
- Sellers deliver a qualified "bring down" certificate disclosing the lawsuit.

1. ***Can Buyer refuse to consummate the acquisition (i.e., does Buyer have a "walk right")?***

   YES. Because a material lawsuit was not disclosed in the Sellers' original Disclosure Letter, the Sellers' "absence of litigation" representation in Section 3.15(a) was materially inaccurate as of the signing date. Thus, the condition in the first clause of Section 8.1(a) is not satisfied, and Buyer can terminate the Model Agreement under Section 10.1. (Under Section 8.1(a), no effect is given to the supplement to the Sellers' Disclosure Letter for purposes of determining the accuracy of the Sellers' representations.)

   If Buyer elects to exercise its "walk right" in these circumstances, Buyer may also seek damages from Sellers for their breach of the "absence of litigation" representation as of the signing date (in other words, Buyer may "walk and sue").

2. ***If Buyer proceeds with the acquisition, will Sellers be required to indemnify Buyer and the Acquired Companies against any damages arising from the lawsuit?***

   YES. Under Section 11.2(a), Sellers are required to indemnify Buyer and the Acquired Companies against all damages suffered as a result of any inaccuracy in the Sellers' representations. Because the Sellers' "absence of litigation" representation was inaccurate as of the signing date, Sellers will be required to indemnify Buyer and the Acquired Companies with respect to the lawsuit. (Under Section 11.2(a), no effect is given to the supplement to the Sellers' Disclosure Letter for purposes of determining the accuracy of the Sellers' representations.) The final sentence in Section 11.6(a) results in the "basket" in Section 11.6 probably not being applicable because the Breach of Section 3.15(a) was likely known to a Seller.

Under the terms of Section 11.2(a), Buyer retains its post-closing indemnification right even though Buyer was advised of the lawsuit before the closing and had the right to refuse to proceed with the acquisition. In other words, Buyer is expressly permitted to "close and sue."

SCENARIO 3
(MATERIAL PRE-SIGNING LITIGATION NOT DISCLOSED IN ORIGINAL DISCLOSURE LETTER, BUT DISCLOSED IN SUPPLEMENT TO DISCLOSURE LETTER AND SETTLED BEFORE THE SCHEDULED CLOSING DATE)

ASSUMED FACTS:

- A few days before the signing of the Model Agreement, a material lawsuit is brought against the Company.

- Sellers fail to disclose the lawsuit in their original Disclosure Letter (which is furnished to Buyer at the time the Model Agreement is signed). Sellers subsequently disclose the lawsuit in a supplement delivered to Buyer (pursuant to Section 5.4) a few days after the signing of the Model Agreement.

- Before the scheduled Closing Date, the Company settles the lawsuit by making a cash payment to the plaintiff. The settlement payment will be taken into account in calculating the Purchase Price Adjustment under Section 2.5.

- Sellers deliver a "bring down" certificate accurately describing both the misrepresentation and the settlement.

1. ***Can Buyer refuse to consummate the acquisition (i.e., does Buyer have a "walk right")?***

    YES. Because a material lawsuit was not disclosed in the Sellers' original Disclosure Letter, the Sellers' "absence of litigation" representation in Section 3.15(a) was materially inaccurate as of the signing date. Thus, the condition in the first clause of Section 8.1(a) is not satisfied, and Buyer has a "walk right." (Under Section 8.1(a), no effect is given to the supplement to the Sellers' Disclosure Letter for purposes of determining the accuracy of the Sellers' representation.)

Although the Sellers' "absence of litigation" representation is accurate as of the scheduled Closing Date due to the settlement of the lawsuit, Buyer nonetheless has a "walk right" under the Model Agreement in this situation.

If Buyer elects to exercise its "walk right" in these circumstances, it may also seek damages from Sellers for their breach of the "absence of litigation" representation as of the signing date (in other words, Buyer may "walk and sue"). However, in light of the settlement of the lawsuit before the closing and what would have been a reduction of the purchase price, there may be a question whether Buyer would have actually suffered any damages as a result of Sellers' initial failure to disclose the lawsuit. A court might not award loss of the bargain damages where Buyer would not have suffered any damages had it closed with a purchase price adjustment and thus could have avoided a loss.

2.   ***If Buyer proceeds with the acquisition, will Sellers be required to indemnify Buyer and the Acquired Companies against any damages arising from the lawsuit?***

NO. Under Section 11.2(a), the Sellers are required to indemnify the Buyer and the Company against all damages suffered as a result of any inaccuracy in the Sellers' "absence of litigation" representation. This representation was inaccurate as of the signing date. However, because the lawsuit has been settled, and because under Section 2.5 there will be a reduction in the purchase price to reflect the amount of the settlement payment made by the Company, neither Buyer nor any Acquired Company will suffer any damages as a result of the lawsuit, assuming there are no collateral effects of the lawsuit. Thus, Sellers will not be required to make any indemnification payment under Section 11.2 with respect to the lawsuit.

SCENARIO 4
(IMMATERIAL PRE-SIGNING LITIGATION NOT DISCLOSED IN ORIGINAL DISCLOSURE LETTER, BUT DISCLOSED BEFORE THE SCHEDULED CLOSING DATE IN SUPPLEMENT TO DISCLOSURE LETTER)

ASSUMED FACTS:
- A few days before the signing of the Model Agreement, a lawsuit is brought against the Company. The lawsuit is not "material"—the Company's anticipated liability in the lawsuit is relatively small.

- Sellers fail to disclose the lawsuit in their original Disclosure Letter (which is furnished to Buyer at the time the Model Agreement is signed). Sellers subsequently disclose the lawsuit in a supplement delivered to Buyer (pursuant to Section 5.4) a few days after the signing of the Model Agreement.
- The lawsuit is not settled and remains pending on the scheduled Closing Date.
- Sellers deliver a "bring down" certificate describing the inaccuracy.

1. *Can Buyer refuse to consummate the acquisition (i.e., does Buyer have a "walk right")?*

NO. Because the lawsuit is not material, the Sellers' "absence of litigation" representation in Section 3.15(a) was accurate as of the signing date in all *material* respects and is likewise accurate as of the Closing Date in all *material* respects. Thus, the conditions in each clause of Section 8.1(a) are satisfied, and Buyer must proceed with the closing.

2. *If Buyer proceeds with the acquisition, will Sellers be required to indemnify Buyer and the Acquired Companies against any damages arising from the lawsuit?*

YES. Under Section 11.2(a), Sellers are required to indemnify Buyer and the Acquired Companies against all damages suffered as a result of *any* inaccuracy (even an immaterial inaccuracy) in the Sellers' representations. Because the Sellers' "absence of litigation" representation was inaccurate as of the signing date, Sellers will be obligated under Section 11.2(a) to indemnify the Buyer and the Acquired Companies with respect to the lawsuit. Under Section 11.2(a), no effect is given to the supplement to the Sellers' Disclosure Letter for purposes of determining the accuracy of the Sellers' representations. The final sentence in Section 11.6(a) results in the "basket" in Section 11.6 probably not being applicable because the Breach of Section 3.15(a) was likely known to a Seller. However, given that the lawsuit is immaterial, any resulting damages are likely to be modest.

SCENARIO 5
(MATERIAL POST-SIGNING LITIGATION DISCLOSED BEFORE THE SCHEDULED CLOSING DATE IN SUPPLEMENT TO DISCLOSURE LETTER)

ASSUMED FACTS:

- A few days after the signing of the Model Agreement, a material lawsuit is brought against the Company.

- Sellers disclose the lawsuit in a Disclosure Letter supplement delivered to Buyer (pursuant to Section 5.4) promptly after the commencement of the lawsuit.
- The lawsuit is not settled and remains pending on the scheduled Closing Date.
- In the "bring down" certificate delivered by Sellers to Buyer on the scheduled Closing Date (in accordance with Section 8.3), Sellers expressly note the failure of a condition.

1. **Can Buyer refuse to consummate the acquisition (i.e., does Buyer have a "walk right")?**

   YES. Because a material lawsuit that was not disclosed in the original Disclosure Letter is pending against the Company on the scheduled Closing Date, the Sellers' "absence of litigation" representation in Section 3.15(a) is inaccurate as "brought down" to the Closing Date. Thus, the "bring down" condition in the second clause of Section 8.1(a) is not satisfied, and Buyer can terminate the Model Agreement under Section 10.1. (Under Section 8.1(a), no effect is given to the supplement to the Sellers' Disclosure Letter for purposes of determining the accuracy of the Sellers' representations.) Sellers have conceded in their bring down certificate that the condition in Section 8.1(a) has not been satisfied. If Buyer elects to exercise its "walk right" in these circumstances, Buyer has no claim under the bring down of the "absence of litigation" representation in Section 3.15(a) because that is applicable only if there is a closing.

2. **If Buyer proceeds with the acquisition, will Sellers be required to indemnify Buyer and the Acquired Companies against any damages arising from the lawsuit?**

   YES. Under Section 11.2(a), Sellers are required to indemnify Buyer and the Acquired Companies against any damages resulting from any inaccuracy in the Sellers' representations as "brought down" to the Closing Date. Section 11.2(a) provides that the determination of the accuracy of the Sellers' representations as of the Closing Date is to be made without giving effect to any supplement to the Disclosure Letter. Therefore, for purposes of Section 11.2(a), the "absence of litigation" representation is deemed to be inaccurate as brought down to the Closing Date and Sellers will be required to indemnify Buyer and the Acquired Companies with respect to the lawsuit.

SCENARIO 6

(MATERIAL POST-SIGNING LITIGATION DISCLOSED IN SUPPLEMENT TO DISCLOSURE LETTER AND SETTLED BEFORE THE SCHEDULED CLOSING DATE)

ASSUMED FACTS:

- A few days after the signing of the Model Agreement, a material lawsuit is brought against the Company.
- Sellers disclose the lawsuit in a Disclosure Letter supplement delivered to Buyer (pursuant to Section 5.4) promptly after the commencement of the lawsuit.
- Before the scheduled Closing Date, the Company settles the lawsuit by making a cash payment to the plaintiff. The settlement payment will be taken into account in calculating the Purchase Price Adjustment under Section 2.5.
- Sellers deliver a bring down certificate accurately describing the settlement.

1. *Can Buyer refuse to consummate the acquisition (i.e., does Buyer have a "walk right")?*

   NO. Because the lawsuit was not pending when the Model Agreement was signed, the Sellers' "absence of litigation" representation in Section 3.15(a) was accurate as of the signing date. Thus, the condition in the first clause of Section 8.1(a) is satisfied. Likewise, because the lawsuit is not pending on the Closing Date, the "absence of litigation" representation is accurate as "brought down" to the Closing Date. Therefore, Buyer has no "walk right" and must proceed with the closing. (If the agreement and bring down certificate were worded differently so that the representations had to be true at all times between signing and closing, the answer would be different.)

2. *Will Sellers be required to indemnify Buyer and the Acquired Companies after the closing against any damages arising from the lawsuit?*

   NO. Because the lawsuit was not pending when the Model Agreement was signed, the Sellers' "absence of litigation" representation was accurate as of the signing date. Likewise, because the lawsuit is not pending on the Closing Date, the "absence of litigation" representation is accurate as "brought down" to the Closing Date. Thus, the Sellers will have no indemnification obligation under Section 11.2 with respect to the lawsuit.

SCENARIO 7
(*MATERIAL POST-SIGNING LITIGATION NOT DISCLOSED IN SUPPLEMENT TO DISCLOSURE LETTER*)

ASSUMED FACTS:

- A few days after the signing of the Model Agreement, a material lawsuit is brought against the Company.
- Sellers fail to disclose the lawsuit in a supplement to their Disclosure Letter.
- The lawsuit is not settled and remains pending on the scheduled Closing Date.
- Sellers deliver a qualified bring down certificate disclosing the lawsuit.

1. ***Can Buyer refuse to consummate the acquisition (i.e., does Buyer have a "walk right")?***

   YES. Because a material lawsuit that was not disclosed in the original Disclosure Letter is pending on the scheduled Closing Date, the Sellers' "absence of litigation" representation in Section 3.15(a) is materially inaccurate as "brought down" to the scheduled Closing Date. Thus, the "bring down" condition in the second clause of Section 8.1(a) is not satisfied, and Buyer has a "walk right." By neglecting to disclose the material lawsuit in a Disclosure Letter supplement, Sellers have breached their pre-closing notification covenant in Section 5.4, and Buyer may also have a "walk right" under Section 8.2 and may also be able to recover damages from the Sellers for their breach of the notification covenant.

2. ***If Buyer proceeds with the acquisition, will Sellers be required to indemnify Buyer and the Acquired Companies against any damages arising from the lawsuit?***

   YES. Under Section 11.2(a), Sellers are required to indemnify Buyer and the Acquired Companies against all damages suffered as a result of any inaccuracy in the Sellers' representations as "brought down" to the Closing Date. Because the Sellers' "absence of litigation" representation is inaccurate as of the Closing Date, Sellers will be required under Section 11.2(a) to indemnify the Buyer and the Acquired Companies with respect to the lawsuit. The final sentence in Section 11.6(a) results in the "basket" in Section 11.6 probably not being applicable because the Breach of Section 3.15(a) was likely known to a Seller.

SCENARIO 8
(IMMATERIAL POST-SIGNING LITIGATION NOT DISCLOSED IN SUPPLEMENT TO DISCLOSURE LETTER)

ASSUMED FACTS:

- A few days after the signing of the Model Agreement, a lawsuit is brought against the Company. The lawsuit is not "material"—the Company's anticipated liability in the lawsuit is relatively small.
- Sellers fail to disclose the lawsuit in a supplement to their Disclosure Letter.
- The lawsuit is not settled and remains pending on the scheduled Closing Date.
- Sellers deliver an unqualified bring down certificate.

1. *Can Buyer refuse to consummate the acquisition (i.e., does Buyer have a "walk right")?*

   NO. Because the lawsuit was not pending when the Model Agreement was signed, the Sellers' "absence of litigation" representation in Section 3.15(a) was accurate as of the signing date. Thus, the condition in the first clause of Section 8.1(a) is satisfied. Because the lawsuit is not material, the "absence of litigation" representation is accurate as of the scheduled Closing Date in all material respects, and the bring down condition in the second clause of Section 8.1(a) is also satisfied. Therefore, Buyer has no "walk right" and must proceed with the closing. Sellers' failure to disclose the lawsuit in a Disclosure Letter supplement is a breach of their pre-closing notification covenant in Section 5.4. However, because the lawsuit is not material, this covenant has been complied with in all material respects. Therefore, Buyer has no "walk right" under Section 8.2.

2. *Will Sellers be required to indemnify Buyer and the Acquired Companies after the closing against any damages arising from the lawsuit?*

   YES. Under Section 11.2(a), Sellers are required to indemnify Buyer and the Acquired Companies against all damages suffered as a result of any inaccuracy (even an immaterial inaccuracy) in the Sellers' representations as "brought down" to the Closing Date. Because the Sellers' "absence of litigation" representation is inaccurate as of the Closing Date, the Sellers will be required under Section 11.2(a) to indemnify Buyer and the Acquired Companies with respect to the lawsuit. The final sentence in Section 11.6(a) results in the "basket" in Section 11.6 probably not being applicable because the Breach of Section 3.15(a) was probably known to a Seller. However,

223

Sellers will likely have difficulty pursuing damages of any consequence arising from an immaterial lawsuit.

SCENARIO 9
(*IMMATERIAL POST-SIGNING LITIGATION DISCLOSED BEFORE THE SCHEDULED CLOSING DATE IN SUPPLEMENT TO DISCLOSURE LETTER*)

ASSUMED FACTS:

- A few days after the signing of the Model Agreement, a lawsuit is brought against the Company. The lawsuit is not "material"—the Company's anticipated liability in the lawsuit is relatively small.

- Sellers disclose the lawsuit in a Disclosure Letter supplement delivered to Buyer (pursuant to Section 5.4) promptly after the commencement of the lawsuit.

- The lawsuit is not settled and remains pending on the scheduled Closing Date.

- Sellers deliver an unqualified "bring down" certificate.

1. ***Can Buyer refuse to consummate the acquisition (i.e., does Buyer have a "walk right")?***

NO. Because the lawsuit was not pending when the Model Agreement was signed, the Sellers' "absence of litigation" representation in Section 3.15(a) was accurate as of the signing date. Thus, the condition in the first clause of Section 8.1(a) is satisfied. Because the lawsuit is not material, the "absence of litigation" representation is accurate as of the Closing Date in all material respects, and the "bring down" condition in the second clause of Section 8.1(a) is also satisfied. Therefore, Buyer has no "walk right" and must proceed with the closing.

2. ***Will Sellers be required to indemnify Buyer and the Acquired Companies against any damages arising from the lawsuit?***

YES. Under Section 11.2(a), Sellers are required to indemnify Buyer and the Acquired Companies against any damages resulting from any inaccuracy (even an immaterial inaccuracy) in the Sellers' representations as "brought down" to the Closing Date. Section 11.2(a) provides that the determination of the accuracy of the Sellers' representations as of the Closing Date is to be made without giving effect to any supplement to the Disclosure Letter. Therefore, for purposes of Section 11.2(a), the "absence of litigation" representation is deemed to be inaccurate as brought down to the Closing

Date and Sellers will be required to indemnify Buyer and the Acquired Companies with respect to the lawsuit. The final sentence in Section 11.6(a) results in the "basket" in Section 11.6 probably not being applicable because the Breach of Section 3.15(a) was likely known to a Seller.

APPENDIX D

Hypothetical Scenarios Illustrating the Effect of a Lawsuit Against the Company on the Buyer's "Walk Rights" and Indemnification Rights

	Scenario #1	Scenario #2	Scenario #3	Scenario #4	Scenario #5	Scenario #6	Scenario #7	Scenario #8	Scenario #9
Was the lawsuit brought before the signing of the stock purchase agreement?	*Yes*—brought *before* signing	*Yes*—brought *before* signing	*Yes*—brought *before* signing	*Yes*—brought *before* signing	*No*—brought *after* signing	*No*—brought *after* signing	*No*—brought *after* signing	*No*—brought *after* signing	*No*—brought *after* signing
Was the lawsuit disclosed in the original version of the Sellers' Disclosure Letter?	*Yes*—disclosed in original DL	*No*—not disclosed in original DL	*No*—not disclosed in original DL	*No*—not disclosed in original DL	*Not applicable* (lawsuit not yet brought)	*Not applicable* (lawsuit not yet brought)	*Not applicable* (lawsuit not yet brought)	*Not applicable* (lawsuit not yet brought)	*Not applicable* (lawsuit not yet brought)
Was the lawsuit disclosed in a supplement to the Sellers' Disclosure Letter?	*Not applicable* (lawsuit already disclosed in original DL)	*Yes*—disclosed in supplement	*Yes*—disclosed in supplement	*Yes*—disclosed in supplement	*Yes*—disclosed in supplement	*Yes*—disclosed in supplement	*No*—not disclosed in supplement	*No*—not disclosed in supplement	*Yes*—disclosed in supplement
Was the lawsuit "material" at the time of the signing of the stock purchase agreement?	*Yes*—material as of signing	*Yes*—material as of signing	*Yes*—material as of signing	*No*—not material as of signing	*Not applicable* (lawsuit not yet brought)	*Not applicable* (lawsuit not yet brought)	*Not applicable* (lawsuit not yet brought)	*Not applicable* (lawsuit not yet brought)	*Not applicable* (lawsuit not yet brought)
Was the lawsuit settled prior to the scheduled Closing Date?	*No*—not settled	*No*—not settled	*Yes*—settled	*No*—not settled	*No*—not settled	*Yes*—settled	*No*—not settled	*No*—not settled	*No*—not settled
Is the lawsuit "material" as of the scheduled Closing Date?	*Yes*—material as of Closing Date	*Yes*—material as of Closing Date	*No*—not material as of Closing Date (lawsuit previously settled)	*No*—not material as of Closing Date	*Yes*—material as of Closing Date	*No*—not material as of Closing Date (lawsuit previously settled)	*Yes*—material as of Closing Date	*No*—not material as of Closing Date	*No*—not material as of Closing Date
"WALK RIGHT"—Can Buyer refuse to close and terminate because of the lawsuit?	NO	YES	YES	NO	YES	NO	YES	NO	NO
INDEMNIFICATION RIGHT—If the closing occurs, are Buyer and the Acquired Companies entitled to be indemnified by Sellers (subject to any applicable "basket") against any loss relating to the lawsuit?	NO	YES	NO (no indemnifiable damages)	YES	YES	NO	YES	YES	YES

APPENDIX E

Alternative Dispute Resolution

PRELIMINARY NOTE

The Model Agreement contains three provisions directed at influencing the manner in which disputes are resolved. Section 12.12 provides for selection of the laws of a single jurisdiction as the basis for adjudication of disputes, Section 12.13 provides a choice of venue in which disputes must be resolved, and Section 12.14 provides for waiver of the right to jury trial. The Model Agreement does not provide for mandatory arbitration of disputes.

The drafters of the Model Agreement concluded that there does not exist a sufficient consensus on the use of mandatory arbitration clauses in acquisition agreements to warrant including an arbitration provision. The following materials are provided for those who may want to provide for dispute resolution by means of binding arbitration. Some of the pros and cons of providing for binding arbitration of disputes are outlined in commentary following Section 13.4 of MAPA. Even with the passage of time since the publication of MAPA, the M&A bar remains divided on the wisdom of using mandatory arbitration.

It is often difficult to determine conclusively whether binding arbitration is a good idea until a dispute arises. The decision might become apparent in hindsight when, for example, litigation costs start to mount or when the client has received an unfortunate result in arbitration that is nonappealable. Some factors weighing on the advisability of arbitration are more predictable, such as the greater likelihood that a seller will be sued than a buyer and the fact that a court might be less able to understand complex business transactions than a qualified business arbitrator (not necessarily true of some courts, such as the Delaware Chancery Court), but there remains a risk that the decision to litigate or arbitrate can have substantial impact on the eventual outcome for the client. Neither litigation nor arbitration generates consistently preferable results, and consequently the ramifications of this decision should be the subject of careful communications between lawyer and client during the drafting process.

The sample language that follows leads off with three alternative clauses. One is a blanket agreement to arbitrate all matters other than the purchase price adjustment, and the other two adopt narrower scopes of arbitration. The clauses that follow subsection (a) are applicable to all three approaches.

(a)   *[Agreement to arbitrate all matters other than the purchase price adjustment]*— **Other than for matters contemplated by Section 2.6, for which the procedures in that Section shall be applicable, any dispute arising out of or relating to this Agreement will be settled by binding arbitration and, except as specifically stated otherwise in this Agreement, in accordance with the [rules of selected arbitration body] then in effect (the "Arbitration Rules") of [name of arbitration body] (the "Arbitration Body"). Matters to be arbitrated shall specifically include actions sounding in tort as well as contract claims and those arising out of any other principle of law.**

[Agreement to arbitrate all matters other than the purchase price adjustment and other than post-closing covenants]—**Other than for matters contemplated by Section 2.6, for which the procedures in that Section shall be applicable, and other than any matter arising out of or relating to the covenants in Sections 7.__ through 7.__ after the Closing, for which all legal and equitable remedies are preserved, any dispute arising out of or relating to this Agreement will be settled by binding arbitration and, except as specifically stated otherwise in this Agreement, in accordance with the [rules of selected arbitration body] (the "Arbitration Body") then in effect. Matters to be arbitrated shall specifically include actions sounding in tort as well as contract claims and those arising out of any other principle of law.**

[Agreement only to arbitrate breach of representation/indemnification claims]— **Any claim arising under Articles 3, 4, or 11, including the interpretation of those Articles, will be settled by binding arbitration and, except as specifically stated otherwise in this Agreement, in accordance with the [rules of selected arbitration body] (the "Arbitration Body") then in effect. Matters to be arbitrated shall specifically include actions under said Articles sounding in tort as well as contract claims and those arising out of any other principle of law.**

COMMENT

Subsection (a) deals with the scope of arbitration. Arbitration need not be binary. Some buyers may feel more comfortable when arbitration is used only in areas with a highly factual content, such as indemnification, rather than the entirety of the acquisition agreement. Even if arbitration is intended to be plenary, it is still appropriate to carve out specific procedures, such as the purchase price adjustment. Because arbitration is a creature of contract, virtually any arbitration provision can be included. The phrase "arising out of or relating to" is intended to pick up tort- or statutory-based remedies. Because of recent judicial interpretation seeking to limit arbitration clauses to contract matters, language is included at the end of each clause further confirming the intention to include tort claims. If there is an intention to preclude noncontract theories of recovery, the last sentence should be deleted and language making clear that limitation should be added.

There are a number of arbitration associations, including the following: CPR (The International Institute for Conflict Prevention and Resolution), JAMS (Mediation, Arbitration and Alternative Dispute Resolution Services), and AAA (the American Arbitration Association). Note that neither JAMS nor the AAA appear to have an appeal procedure, so subsection (e) would need to be addressed if the rules of those organizations are utilized. It is not clear that appeal to a CPR panel from a non-CPR arbitration is permitted. It is not necessary to specify a particular organization's rules. The applicable rules could be set forth in the acquisition agreement or the default statutory provisions would be applicable. Even when particular rules are incorporated by reference, a negotiated rule could override particular provisions.

In addition, under a Delaware statute adopted in 2009 (10 Del. C. §349), parties can, if certain pre-existing requirements are met, agree to have a member of the Delaware Court of Chancery arbitrate a dispute, or agree to have a matter adjudicated before a Master of the Court of Chancery, with the same force and effect as a decision of a member of the Court of Chancery. In either case, the parties can also agree that the adjudication, whether before a member of the Court of Chancery or a Master, is final and nonappealable to the Supreme Court of Delaware.

Whatever approach is followed for ADR, utilizing one of the arbitration associations or one of the alternatives set forth in the Delaware statute, the parties should ensure that the sample language is modified to be compatible with that approach.

None of the alternatives includes a limitation on when the action can be commenced. The indemnification provisions would normally include such a provision. A buyer would normally not want to suggest in its draft a limitation on its rights.

(b) **Any party proposing to arbitrate a matter pursuant to this Agreement shall serve notice on the other party, specifying in reasonable detail the facts giving rise to the claim and the relief sought. For a period of one month, the parties shall engage in discussions of the dispute with the objective of resolving it prior to further proceedings. After such one-month period, the party proposing to arbitrate a matter may commence arbitration by a demand for arbitration served on the other party as provided in Section 12.18. [*Another form without mediation*—Any party proposing to arbitrate a matter may commence arbitration by a demand for arbitration served on the other party as provided in Section 12.18.]**

(c) **Such arbitration will be conducted before a single arbitrator selected by the parties who shall be an admitted lawyer knowledgeable in the negotiation of agreements for the purchase of businesses who has not performed services for any party. If the parties cannot agree on an arbitrator by the end of the 14th day after the notice of demand for arbitration is given, the Arbitration Body shall select the arbitrator upon request of either party from a list of at least**

five potential qualified arbitrators that it shall develop. The Arbitration Body shall establish procedures by which each potential arbitrator shall furnish information on his or her qualifications and any relationship to either party. A party may object to the qualifications of any potential arbitrator, and the Arbitration Body shall disqualify any potential arbitrator not qualified. The Arbitration Body shall choose the arbitrator from the remaining potential arbitrators. The arbitrator will be paid a fee or rate determined by the parties. If the parties cannot agree, the fee will be determined by the Arbitration Body based on the reasonable hourly or daily rates. The parties agree to execute an engagement letter in the customary form required by the arbitrator.

Many agreements propose three arbitrators, one selected by each side and a third selected by other two. Such an approach seems to contemplate that the arbitrators selected by each side will advocate that side's position. Given that likelihood, the parties may consider simplifying the process by selecting a mutually acceptable single arbitrator. Other times, it is contemplated that there are three neutrals, presumably to alleviate concern about a wild card arbitrator.

The qualifications of the arbitrator are key to making this provision work. These procedures for selecting an arbitrator are not provided by the rules of any arbitration association. The idea is that the parties should try to select someone first, but there always needs to be a default procedure if they cannot agree.

(d)   **The parties intend that the arbitrator will have the power to conduct an arbitration procedure to the greatest extent provided by law, including the determination of the scope of arbitration. Except as specifically provided by the Rules of the Arbitration Body or this Agreement, the arbitrator shall establish all rules for the arbitration. The arbitration will be conducted in _____. Each party shall bear the portion of any deposit, advance, or other expense as determined by the arbitrator. A record shall be kept of all hearings and all evidence (including exhibits, deposition transcripts, and affidavits admitted into evidence) in the arbitration proceeding. The award of the arbitrator shall be based on a preponderance of the evidence. The arbitrator shall reach a decision in compliance with the applicable law and shall render a written decision setting forth the factual and legal bases of the award. The arbitrator may award any type of relief, including monetary damages and equitable relief (including any provisional relief). [*Alternate*—The arbitrator may award only monetary damages and not equitable or provisional relief.] The arbitrator will award to the prevailing party all costs, fees, and expenses related to the arbitration. Judgment upon the award may be entered in any court of competent jurisdiction.**

Courts generally hold that arbitrators have the power to determine whether a particular matter is within the scope of agreed arbitration. This clause makes that clear. If another result is intended, it should be expressly provided.

Often a neutral site is chosen. In doing so the parties should consider the possibility that application to the courts of the selected venue may be necessary to aid in arbitration.

The burden of proof is inserted to avoid Vice Chancellor Strine's struggle in *IBP, Inc. v. Tyson Foods, Inc.*, 789 A.2d 14 (Del. Ch. 2001), and to avoid any argument if at some time the Delaware courts adopt some sort of burden-shifting procedure to contracts, as they do for fiduciary duties.

The sentence dealing with the form of relief need not be stated, although judicial enforcement would be required. If the opposite result is desired, it will be necessary to so provide; just striking this sentence would be insufficient. Where the scope of arbitration is confined to monetary damages, then a denial of other forms of relief would be appropriate.

Note there is no limitation imposed on the award of punitive or other forms of damages since those limitations should be part of the substantive agreement developed elsewhere. Parties frequently exclude liability for punitive or consequential damages in the remedies Section of the agreement.

It is not necessary to include the last sentence. The Federal Arbitration Act ("FAA") provides that the parties can agree where the award may be entered. Since broadly any award could be against any party, it is not clear what the parties would specify. If the relief is narrow such that only one party may pay (such as for breach of representations), an appropriate court could probably be determined and inserted in this sentence if so desired.

[(e) **An appeal may be taken under the Arbitration Appeal Procedure of CPR from any final award of the arbitration panel. Unless otherwise agreed by the parties and the appeal tribunal, the appeal shall be conducted at the place of the original arbitration.]**

This provision takes advantage of an appeal panel established by CPR. The right to appeal is more limited than an appeal from a determination by a trial court, but may address the concern of many clients of the total lack of appeal right, except for the very limited appeal rights under the FAA. In order to take advantage of this, it is required that a written record be kept and a written award be made, both of which are provided in the prior subsection. It is not clear that the CPR appeal procedure can be used from a non-CPR arbitration. The inclusion of an appeal right in the CPR rules represents a major departure from the arbitration procedures of the other arbitration organizations and addresses what can be a major client concern about the use of arbitration.

(f) **Neither party nor the arbitrator shall disclose to any person any information about the arbitration, including the fact of arbitration, the status thereof, or any documents or other information disclosed in connection therewith, except that the award itself may be made public by any of the parties, whether or not**

entered as a judgment by a court pursuant to subsection (d). The parties and the arbitrator will take reasonable precautions to keep all such information confidential.

This subsection does not provide an exception for responding to subpoenas or other judicial process. As the provision is now drafted, it would be incumbent on the person compelled to provide information to seek an appropriate court order.

While the series of clauses set forth above would seem to address all major issues that may arise in terms of arbitration procedures, drafters of ADR provisions should nonetheless check for case law and statutes governing arbitration in the jurisdiction selected as the site of the arbitration to avoid unintended outcomes. For example, in California, an agreement to arbitrate claims relating to a contract creates authority to arbitrate "tort claims" and an agreement to arbitrate "any controversy" creates authority to award punitive damages. *See* Tate v. Saratoga Savings & Loan Association, 261 Cal. App. 3d 843 (1989).

Model Stock Purchase Agreement with Commentary

Second Edition

Volume I: Stock Purchase Agreement

**Mergers and Acquisitions
Committee**

AMERICAN BAR ASSOCIATION
Business Law Section

The materials contained herein represent the opinions of the authors and editors and should not be construed to be the action of either the American Bar Association or the Business Law Section, unless adopted pursuant to the bylaws of the Association.

Nothing contained in this book is to be considered as the rendering of legal advice for specific cases, and readers are responsible for obtaining such advice from their own legal counsel. This book is intended for educational and informational purposes only.

The Prefaces, Preliminary Notes, Appendices, and Commentary in both Volume I and Volume II of the Second Edition of the *Model Stock Purchase Agreement*, Exhibits, and Ancillary Documents are protected under United States copyright law and may not be reproduced in any manner without express permission. The Model Stock Purchase Agreement itself and it Exhibits and Ancillary Documents, as they appear in the printed publication and on its accompanying CD-ROM, may be freely reproduced by the reader.

The set of files on the CD-ROM accompanying the *Model Stock Purchase Agreement*, Second Edition, may only be used on a single computer or moved to and used on another computer unless modified by the user. Under no circumstances may the set of files be used on more than one computer at one time. For permission, contact the ABA Copyrights and Contracts Department at copyright@americanbar.org or via fax at 312-988-6030, or complete the online form at http://www.americanbar.org/utility/reprint.html.

Cover design by ABA Publishing.

Page composition by Quadrum.

Library of Congress Cataloging-in-Publication Data

Model stock purchase agreement / by Murray Perelman, editor. — 2nd ed.
    p. cm.
 ISBN-13: 978-1-60442-998-5
 ISBN-10: 1-60442-998-4
 1. Stock purchase agreements (Close corporations)—United States. I. Perelman, Murray. II. American Bar Association. Committee on Mergers and Acquisitions. III. Title.
 KF1466.M64 2010
 346.73'0922—dc22

2010026842

Volume I: Stock Purchase Agreement

Discounts are available for books ordered in bulk. Custom covers are also available for bulk orders. Special consideration is given to state and local bars, CLE programs, and other bar-related organizations. Inquire at Book Publishing, American Bar Association, 321 North Clark Street, Chicago, Illinois 60654-7598.

www.ShopABA.org

23 22   6 5

Summary Table of Contents

Committee Chair's Preface

The *Model Stock Purchase Agreement with Commentary*, second edition, is the result of the monumental efforts of the Committee on Mergers and Acquisitions' Task Force charged with updating our seminal publication. The work was produced during nine years of work by hundreds of practitioners from dozens of international jurisdictions and lawyers from most U.S. states. Participation and comment were also sought from specialists in substantive areas such as taxation, labor, intellectual property, employee benefits, environmental, and antitrust law, as well as from leading academics.

The first edition of the *Model Stock Purchase Agreement* was published by our Committee in 1995. More than 6,100 copies of the original work are in circulation, making it one of the Business Law Section's most popular publications. It has proven to be an invaluable resource to practitioners and students of the craft of structuring and documenting business transactions. Because it has captured the many developments that have occurred in the deal world since 1995, the revised work will, we believe, similarly enlighten practitioners around the world of best practices in the acquisition field. In addition to well-crafted contractual provisions, the second edition of the *Model Stock Purchase Agreement* contains extensive commentary that explicates the purpose and meaning of the provisions, and often suggests alternative approaches that could be employed in negotiating the particular facet of the deal. Among the groups we believe will benefit from this work are M&A deal lawyers who structure sophisticated, often international, transactions; lawyers who only occasionally engage in transactional practice and want to hone their skills; and law professors desiring a comprehensive vehicle for introducing law students to the subject of business transactions.

In providing sample language for the provisions that customarily appear in an acquisition agreement, the Task Force has crafted provisions that are comprehensive in scope. It recognizes that in less complex and relatively straightforward transactions, many of the operative provisions contained in this edition of the *Model Stock Purchase Agreement* either will not apply or may be scaled back substantially. The result is a model document that is intended to serve buyer's counsel as a starting point from which to fashion a fully negotiated acquisition agreement.

I hope you find this edition of the *Model Stock Purchase Agreement with Commentary* to be a valuable resource for your practice, law department, or law school.

> Leigh Walton
> Nashville, TN
> Chair, Committee on Mergers and Acquisitions

Task Force Chair's Preface

When the Negotiated Acquisitions Committee (our Committee's former name and now called the Mergers and Acquisitions Committee) was about to complete the *Model Asset Purchase Agreement* in 2001, the Committee determined that it would be appropriate to revise and update the *Model Stock Purchase Agreement*, published in 1995. Samuel S. Friedman and I were asked to be the Co-Chairs of the Revised Model Stock Purchase Agreement Task Force.

The Task Force commenced this project using the *Model Stock Purchase Agreement* as its base and the *Model Asset Purchase Agreement* as a guide for changes in practice and the law since the publication of the first edition of the *Model Stock Purchase Agreement*.

We continued the *Model Stock Purchase Agreement* approach of using comprehensive sample provisions and explanatory commentary as a teaching mechanism. We recognize, however, that practitioners will tailor the provisions of the Model Agreement to deal with particular transactions and, in the process, will change, add, or omit provisions. Most significantly, we also added additional commentary (with some sample alternative provisions) written from the point of view of a seller responding to a buyer's draft.

The second edition of the *Model Stock Purchase Agreement* represents the cumulative effort of many merger and acquisition practitioners, from law firms and corporations, large and small, practicing in financial centers as well as in smaller communities in the United States and Canada. Participation and comments were also sought from lawyers in practice areas such as tax, labor, employee benefits, environmental, intellectual property, and antitrust law, as well as from leading academics. We particularly want to acknowledge the valuable input we received from Thomas B. Hyman and members of the American Bar Association Business Law Section's Committee on Legal Opinions who provided helpful comments on the forms of legal opinions. Members of the American Institute of Certified Public Accountants' Task Force on Merger and Acquisition Disputes also provided useful input on the post-closing adjustment provisions in the Model Agreement and on the Earnout Agreement included in Volume II.

The hypothetical Fact Pattern around which the second edition of the *Model Stock Purchase Agreement* was created—the acquisition of all the capital stock of a private company—is one commonly encountered by counsel. This Fact Pattern also provided the Task Force with the best opportunity to discuss in the accompanying commentary the intent and purpose of the terms and conditions contained in the Model Agreement as well as how a seller might respond. In providing sample language for the provisions that customarily appear in a stock purchase agreement, the Task Force selected provisions that are comprehensive in scope. It recognized that in less complex and relatively straightforward transactions, many provisions contained in the Model Agreement will either not apply or may be scaled back substantially. The result is a Model Agreement that is intended to serve buyer's counsel as a starting point from which to fashion a fully negotiated acquisition agreement. It should also serve as an effective educational tool for four distinct groups: lawyers who deal with acquisitions on an occasional basis and who wish to sharpen their skills; less experienced lawyers seeking to gain greater insight into the acquisition process and documentation; law professors desiring a more comprehensive vehicle for introducing law students to the subject of mergers and acquisitions; and experienced counsel seeking to reflect on the intent and purpose of provisions that have become commonplace and familiar.

To accommodate the scope of the Revised Model Stock Purchase Agreement project, the work of the Task Force was divided into two groups: one working on the Model Agreement itself and related commentary, and the other focused on the exhibits, ancillary documents, and appendices to the Model Agreement. Samuel S. Friedman and I served as Co-Chairs of the first group and Murray J. Perelman served as Chair of the second group. Although Sam Friedman retired from the practice of law some years ago, he played a pivotal role in developing the project and moving it forward until he ceased playing an active role on our Task Force. Murray J. Perelman subsequently served as my Co-Chair to help complete our project.

Well over 100 lawyers served as members of the Revised Model Stock Purchase Agreement Task Force (a list too long to include in this Preface). Our Task Force members submitted drafts, conducted research, and met on numerous occasions to discuss the proposed language of the Model Agreement, as well as the commentary, exhibits, ancillary documents, and appendices. They also called upon their respective firms or corporations to access the broad expertise and other resources needed for a project of this magnitude, for which we are all thankful and indebted.

Once the full Task Force had assembled a working document, we formed an editorial group to complete the project. Our editorial group spent a great many hours at meetings and in Saturday morning conference calls editing and re-editing the Task Force's and each other's work. We want to especially acknowledge William Payne, who played a very significant role in that process by, among other things, collecting the submissions, applying the conventions, challenging us with questions and keeping us on track.

The members of our editorial group were:

David I. Albin	Stamford, CT
Martha Anderson	Buffalo, NY
Neal H. Brockmeyer	Los Angeles, CA
Bruce A. Cheatham	Dallas, TX
John F. Corrigan	Providence, RI
Warren M. Goodman	Montreal, Quebec
David Ley Hamilton	Wilmington, DE
Robert T. Harper	Pittsburgh, PA
John P. Lowe, Jr.	Rochester, NY
Alan MacEwan	Portland, ME
William B. Payne	Minneapolis, MN
Murray J. Perelman	Toronto, Ontario
Carl M. Ravinsky	Montreal, Quebec
William B. Rosenberg	Montreal, Quebec
George M. Taylor, III	Birmingham, AL
Thomas M. Thompson	Pittsburgh, PA
Dennis J. White	Boston, MA
Scott T. Whittaker	New Orleans, LA

While not a member of the Task Force, Joel Greenberg read the final drafts and made a number of helpful comments and suggestions.

Finally, our thanks to those who have served as Chairs of the Mergers and Acquisitions Committee during this project, to the American Bar Association Publication Staff for ongoing editorial support and encouragement to the Task Force, and to my assistant Jennifer W. Patterson for her dedication and countless hours seeing this project through to its end.

Robert T. Harper
Chair
Revised Model Stock Purchase Agreement Task Force

Preliminary Note

The second edition of the *Model Stock Purchase Agreement with Commentary* ("Model Agreement") revises and updates the first edition of the *Model Stock Purchase Agreement with Commentary* (1995), which was prepared by the Committee on Negotiated Acquisitions (now known as the Committee on Mergers and Acquisitions) of the Section of Business Law of the American Bar Association. The first edition of the *Model Stock Purchase Agreement* was used as a guide for the *Model Asset Purchase Agreement with Commentary* (2001). The Model Agreement is intended for use as a reference in acquisitions structured as a stock purchase.

PERSPECTIVE

The Model Agreement has been prepared as a resource for a buyer's first draft of a stock acquisition agreement. In a buyer's first draft, the provisions generally favor the buyer and are not necessarily typical of the final language in a fully negotiated agreement and consummated transaction. A buyer ordinarily would not include all the provisions of the Model Agreement in a first draft, but would instead tailor the document to the size and nature of the business to be acquired. Sellers usually will not agree to all the proposed provisions, and their counsel can be expected to negotiate for language more favorable to them. The commentary identifies some sections of the Model Agreement that are likely to prompt objections by a seller, but most, if not all, provisions are negotiable.

The buyer's counsel usually prepares the first draft unless the seller is conducting an auction with multiple potential buyers. The buyer's counsel may have rather superficial information regarding the target at the time the acquisition agreement is drafted. The inclusion of extensive representations and warranties in the first draft forces the seller to disclose significant information about the target. This will aid the buyer in assessing the benefits and risks of the acquisition and in pricing the transaction. In this respect, the buyer's first draft also serves as a request for information and a disclosure device.

The first draft will also deal with the allocation of risk among the parties for such contingencies as environmental, pension, and tort liability. The buyer typically will ask the seller to bear most of the risk associated with discoveries that directly or indirectly relate to the target's business prior to the closing—issues that may be material to pricing the acquisition. The seller may counter that unknown contingencies are inherent in operating any business and should be borne by the owner of the business at the time they arise.

No form of acquisition agreement is "standard" or suitable for all transactions, and every provision in the Model Agreement is subject to change, reflecting the facts and circumstances of the particular transaction. The Fact Pattern was developed so that a host of issues could be covered by the Model Agreement and discussed in the accompanying commentary. Because it is unlikely that all these issues would be presented in any single acquisition, the Model Agreement is more comprehensive than most stock acquisition agreements. Factors that may influence the scope and content of an acquisition agreement include the following:

- the size of the transaction (The acquisition agreement will likely be shorter and far less comprehensive for a smaller transaction.)

- the relative negotiating positions of the parties (Where the target is highly sought-after and there are competing offers, a seller may view some of the provisions of the Model Agreement as too aggressive or otherwise inappropriate. If the buyer anticipates delicate negotiations with the seller, the buyer's counsel may not use some of these stronger provisions or may temper them with qualifying language, even in the first draft. On the other hand, if the target is financially distressed or the seller is otherwise in a weak bargaining position, the buyer might be even more demanding in the draft it presents to the seller.)

- whether the target is a subsidiary of another corporation or is owned by individual shareholders.

Given the numerous variations in the facts and circumstances involved in any acquisition, the Model Agreement should not be considered as establishing any standards of general practice or constitute legal advice. The Model Agreement is not a substitute for a lawyer's careful exercise of judgment in a specific transaction and does not purport to measure the reasonableness of a lawyer's judgment in any situation. While the commentary to the Model Agreement includes a discussion of some U.S. federal and state tax considerations in structuring and negotiating a stock purchase transaction, the discussion is not intended to constitute tax advice. Tax statutes and regulations are subject to amendment and their application is fact-sensitive, and so the discussion in the commentary is no substitute for tax advice from a qualified tax advisor familiar with the then current tax law and the facts at hand. In no event is the tax discussion intended to be used, nor should it be used, for the purpose of (i) avoiding penalties under the Internal Revenue Code or (ii) promoting, marketing, or recommending to another party any transaction or matter discussed in the commentary to the Model Agreement.

CONSIDERATIONS IN SELECTING A STOCK PURCHASE

There are three basic structures for business acquisitions: a statutory business combination, a purchase of shares, and a purchase of assets. A statutory combination usually is structured as a merger, but, as permitted by applicable law in some jurisdictions, might be a consolidation or a "share exchange," whereby all shareholders can be bound to exchange their shares under a plan of exchange approved by holders of the requisite percentage of shares.

An acquisition might be structured as an asset purchase for a variety of reasons. It may be the only structure that can be used where the buyer is interested in purchasing only a portion of the company's assets or assuming only certain of its liabilities. If the stock of a company is widely held or it is likely that one or more of the shareholders will not consent, a sale of stock (except perhaps by way of a statutory merger or share exchange) may be impractical. In many cases, however, an acquisition can be structured as a merger, a purchase of stock, or a purchase of assets.

From tax and liability perspectives, it will often be in the buyer's best interests to purchase assets, but in a seller's best interests to sell stock or to merge. Because of these competing interests, it is important that counsel for both parties be involved at the outset in weighing the various legal and business considerations in an effort to arrive at the optimum, or at least a mutually acceptable, structure. Some of these considerations are specific to the business in which a company engages, some relate to the particular corporate or other structure of the buyer and the seller, and others are more general in nature.

The following are some of the matters to be addressed in evaluating a stock purchase as an alternative to an asset purchase or a statutory combination.

Assets. Asset transactions are typically more complicated and time-consuming than stock purchases and statutory combinations. In contrast to a stock purchase, the buyer in an asset transaction will acquire only the assets described in the acquisition agreement. Accordingly, the assets to be purchased are often described with specificity in the agreement and the transfer documents.

A purchase of assets also is cumbersome because the transfer of the target's assets to the buyer must be documented, and separate filings or recordings may be necessary to effectuate the transfer. This often will involve separate real property deeds, lease assignments, patent, trademark, and other intellectual property assignments, motor vehicle registrations, and other evidences of transfer that cannot simply be covered by a general bill of sale and assignment. Moreover, these transfers may involve assets in a number of jurisdictions, each with different forms and requirements for filing and recording.

Contractual Rights. Among the assets to be transferred are the target's rights under contracts pertaining to its business. These contractual rights often cannot be assigned without the consent of other parties. The most common examples are leases that require consent of the lessor and joint ventures or strategic alliances that require consent of the joint venturer or partner. A required consent can afford the third party an opportunity to request confidential information regarding the acquisition and the financial or operational capability of the buyer and to extract concessions in return for granting its consent. Although this can sometimes be avoided by a purchase of stock or statutory combination, many leases and other agreements require consent to any change in ownership or control, however accomplished. Many government contracts cannot be assigned and require a novation with the buyer.

Governmental Authorizations. Transfers of licenses, permits, or other authorizations granted to a target by governmental or quasi-governmental entities may be required in an asset transaction. In some cases, an application for a transfer or, if the authorization is not transferable, for new authorization may involve hearings or other administrative delays in addition to the risk of losing the authorization. Many businesses may have been "grandfathered" under regulatory schemes and thereby be exempt from any need to make costly improvements to their properties; the buyer in an asset purchase may forfeit the grandfathered benefits and be subject to additional compliance costs.

Liabilities. In a stock transaction, the buyer takes ownership of the target subject to all of its liabilities. An important reason for structuring an acquisition as an asset transaction is a buyer's desire to limit its responsibility for liabilities of the target, particularly unknown or contingent liabilities. Unlike a stock purchase or statutory combination, where the target retains all its liabilities and obligations, known and unknown, the buyer in an asset purchase has an opportunity to determine which liabilities of the target it will contractually assume. Accordingly, one of the most important issues to be resolved is what liabilities incurred by the target prior to the closing are to be assumed by the buyer.

Income Taxes. In most acquisitions, the income tax consequences to the buyer and the seller are among the most important factors in determining the structure of the transaction. A seller will prefer a structure that will generate the highest after-tax proceeds, whereas the buyer will seek ways to minimize taxes after the acquisition. The ability to reconcile these goals will depend largely upon whether the target is a C or an S corporation or is an entity taxed as a partnership.

In a taxable asset purchase, the buyer's tax basis in the purchased assets will be equal to the purchase price (including assumed liabilities). An important advantage to the buyer of an asset purchase is the ability to allocate the purchase price among the purchased assets on an asset-by-asset basis to reflect their fair market value, often increasing the tax basis from that of the target. This "step-up" in basis can allow the buyer greater depreciation and amortization deductions in the future and less gain (or greater loss) on subsequent disposition of those assets.

A C corporation will generally recognize gain on a sale of assets to a third party. Thus, if a buyer purchases assets, the selling corporation will recognize gain or loss on an asset-by-asset basis, which will be treated as ordinary income or loss or capital gain or loss, depending upon the character of each asset. Unlike individuals, corporations do not receive the benefit of a lower rate on long-term capital gains. Upon subsequent liquidation of the corporation, its shareholders will be taxed as if they had sold their stock for the proceeds received in liquidation. Gain or loss to a shareholder is measured by the difference between the cash received and the tax basis of that shareholder's stock.

A sale of stock would avoid this double tax. A buyer purchasing stock of a C corporation, however, will obtain a stepped-up basis only in the stock, which is not an asset it will be able to amortize or depreciate for tax purposes, and the buyer generally will not want to succeed to the seller's presumably low tax basis in the underlying assets.

If the target is an S corporation, a buyer's purchase of stock can be treated for tax purposes as a purchase of assets by making a joint election with the selling shareholder under Section 338(h)(10) of the Internal Revenue Code. The same result can be achieved in a purchase of stock out of a consolidated group through a joint election with the seller under Section 338(h)(10), as well as in other contexts but often is not cost effective.

The tax treatment to the target and its shareholders in an S corporation's sale of assets will depend upon the form of consideration, the relationship of the tax basis in the target's assets (the "inside basis") to the tax basis of its shareholders in their stock (the "outside basis"), whether there is "built-in gain" (i.e., fair market value of assets in excess of tax basis at the effective date of the S corporation election) and whether the target's S status will terminate. Generally, the amount and character of the gain or loss at the corporate level will pass through to the shareholders and be taken into account on their individual tax returns, thereby avoiding a double tax. However, the purchase price will be allocated among the S corporation's assets and, depending upon the relationship of the inside basis and the outside basis, the amount of the gain or loss passed through to the shareholders for tax purposes may be more or less than if the same price had been paid for the stock of the S corporation. An S corporation that was formerly a C corporation also must recognize built-in gain at the corporate level, generally for tax years beginning after 1986, on assets it held at the time of its election of S status, unless 10 years have elapsed since the effective date of the election.

The preceding discussion relates to federal income taxes under the Internal Revenue Code. Consideration should also be given to state and local tax consequences of the proposed transaction.

Transfer Taxes. Many state and local jurisdictions impose sales, documentary, or similar transfer taxes on the sale of certain types of assets. For example, a sales tax might apply to the sale of tangible personal property, other than inventory held for resale, or a documentary tax might be required for recording a deed for the transfer of real property. In some jurisdictions, these taxes are imposed even in a sale of stock where there is a change of control. Some states impose a stamp tax on the sale of stock (or interests in other forms of entities).

Employment Issues. A sale of assets may have more employment or labor issues than a stock sale or statutory combination because the target will typically terminate its employees, who may then be re-employed by the buyer. Both the target and the buyer run the risk that employee dislocations from the transition will result in litigation or adversely affect employee morale. The financial liability and risks associated with employee benefit plans, including funding, withdrawal, excise taxes, and penalties, may differ depending upon the structure of the transaction. Responsibility under the Worker Adjustment and Retraining Notification Act ("WARN Act") can vary between the parties, depending upon whether the transaction is structured as an asset purchase, stock purchase, or statutory combination. In a stock purchase or statutory combination, any collective bargaining agreements generally remain in effect. In an asset purchase, the status of collective bargaining agreements will depend upon whether the buyer is a "successor," based upon the continuity of the business and work force or on the provisions of the target's collective bargaining agreement. If it is a successor, the buyer must recognize and bargain with the union, but may not be subject to existing collective bargaining agreements.

ETHICAL CONSIDERATIONS

A stock acquisition, like many other legal transactions involving multiple parties with differing goals and interests, can raise ethical issues for the lawyers involved. For a discussion of these issues, *see* Chapter 2 of the Committee on Negotiated Acquisitions, *The M&A Process—A Practical Guide for the Business Lawyer* (2005).

MODEL AGREEMENT

The structure of the Model Agreement generally reflects prevailing practice. The text follows the Fact Pattern, which assumes a fairly straightforward sale of stock involving a single buyer and multiple sellers. No attempt has been made to give effect in the text of the Model Agreement to, or to discuss in the commentary, practice outside the United States, or changes that might be proposed in cross-border transactions.

Article 1 contains a glossary of defined terms as well as general guides to construction and interpretation. This article enhances ease of usage and organization of the Model Agreement and includes cross references to definitions in various sections in the Agreement.

Article 2 contains the economic and operative terms of the acquisition, including the consideration to be paid and the mechanics of the closing.

Articles 3 and 4 set forth the representations and warranties of Sellers and Buyer, respectively. The representations and warranties are statements of fact that existed, exist at the date of signing of the Model Agreement, and/or will exist at the time of the closing. Sellers' representations and warranties, which contain detailed statements about the business of the target, are often much more comprehensive than Buyer's and include extensive provisions regarding such matters as environmental concerns, employee benefits, and intellectual property, which could result in significant liabilities for Buyer after the closing if not covered by adequate representations and warranties (and the corresponding indemnification obligations) by Sellers. Buyer's representations and warranties deal mainly with its ability to enter into the Model Agreement and to consummate the acquisition. They may be more extensive if all or part of the consideration consists of Buyer's obligations or securities.

Articles 5 and 6 contain covenants in which the parties commit to perform (affirmative covenants) or not to perform (negative covenants) certain acts during the period between signing the Model Agreement and closing the acquisition. The heaviest burden of the covenants falls on Sellers, who, after signing, must take steps to consummate the acquisition and operate the business in the manner provided until the closing.

Article 7 contains post-closing covenants of the parties, including restrictive covenants.

Articles 8 and 9 contain conditions precedent to the obligations of Buyer and Sellers, respectively, to consummate the acquisition. These articles specify what each party is entitled to expect from the other at the closing. If a condition is not satisfied by one party, the other party may be able to elect not to complete the acquisition.

Article 10 outlines the circumstances in which each party may terminate the Model Agreement and the effects of such termination.

Article 11 contains indemnification provisions which afford each party specific remedies for the other's breach of certain representations and obligations under the acquisition agreement. These provisions cover such matters as calculation of damages, recovery of expenses and costs, including legal fees, in addition to damages and procedures for claiming damages.

Article 12 contains general provisions such as notice, severability, and choice of law.

In some transactions, the parties do not sign a binding agreement until closing. If a letter of intent has been executed that includes an exclusivity provision and provides the buyer adequate opportunity to conduct due diligence, the buyer may resist becoming contractually bound until it is ready to close. Conversely, the seller has an interest in not permitting extensive due diligence until the buyer is contractually bound. This is especially so in circumstances where the buyer is a competitor or where the seller is concerned that the due diligence process will necessitate or risk disclosure to employees, customers, or competitors that the business is for sale.

Occasionally, a seller is reluctant to sign before closing. This may be the case, for example, if the seller has announced that the business is for sale and does not want to preclude talking to other prospective buyers until it is certain that the transaction will close.

Sometimes, a simultaneous signing and closing occurs because the transaction simply evolves that way. The parties may be negotiating an agreement that contemplates a period between signing and closing, but the due diligence may proceed more rapidly than the negotiations, and it may develop that a waiting period would be pointless or even harmful to the transaction. In such circumstances, counsel should consider whether it is appropriate to remove from the agreement the pre-closing covenants, conditions to the parties' obligations to close, and other provisions that are rendered unnecessary by the decision to sign and close simultaneously. Care must be taken to ensure that no post-closing contractual obligation is affected by these changes.

COMMENTARY

The commentary to the Model Agreement consists of preliminary notes, general comments, comments, and sellers' responses. Preliminary notes present an overview of the Articles of the Model Agreement, with, in some cases, a separate sellers' perspective, and general comments serve the same function for many of the sections. Most of the sections include comments that describe the provisions, provide some background of the subjects covered, and set forth some of the considerations that could apply to drafting. The sellers' responses are an attempt to separately discuss some concerns and objections that a seller might have regarding the sections or other provisions as drafted. In many cases, alternative language is suggested to deal with particular issues discussed. All cross-references to the commentary are intended to include any sellers' responses that pertain to that same section or provision of the Model Agreement. The absence of a seller response for a particular provision should not be taken to mean that there is no possible seller response to that section or clause.

EXHIBITS, ANCILLARY DOCUMENTS, AND APPENDICES

The Exhibits to the Model Agreement are forms of the promissory notes, legal opinions, and other documents to be delivered at closing. The Ancillary Documents include various agreements that may be executed before or in conjunction with a stock purchase agreement, such as a confidentiality agreement and a letter of intent.

Appendices A through C discuss special considerations that arise in stock transactions. Appendix A treats special problems that arise when a transaction involves the purchase of a subsidiary. Appendix B deals with the receipt of publicly traded stock in the sale of a company. Appendix C deals with negotiations of employment agreements. Appendix D contains nine hypothetical scenarios, demonstrating the operation of the Model Agreement in certain circumstances. Appendix E contains alternative dispute resolution language that might be added to Article 12 in lieu of Sections 12.13 and 12.14.

RELATED RESOURCE MATERIALS

Texts. Lawyers engaged in acquisitions may want to consult the following texts, which are cited throughout the commentary to the Model Agreement and supplemental materials. For ease of reference, a short citation form is specified:

- COMMITTEE ON NEGOTIATED ACQUISITIONS, MODEL ASSET PURCHASE AGREEMENT WITH COMMENTARY (2001) ("MAPA").

- COMMITTEE ON NEGOTIATED ACQUISITIONS, THE M&A PROCESS—A PRACTICAL GUIDE FOR THE BUSINESS LAWYER (2005) ("M&A PROCESS").

- COMMITTEE ON NEGOTIATED ACQUISITIONS, MANUAL ON ACQUISITION REVIEW (1995) ("MANUAL ON ACQUISITION REVIEW").

- KLING & NUGENT, NEGOTIATED ACQUISITIONS OF COMPANIES, SUBSIDIARIES AND DIVISIONS (2009) ("KLING & NUGENT").

- FREUND, ANATOMY OF A MERGER: STRATEGIES AND TECHNIQUES FOR NEGOTIATING CORPORATE ACQUISITIONS (1975) ("FREUND").

- NEGOTIATING AND DRAFTING CONTRACT BOILERPLATE (STARK, ED., 2003) ("STARK").

Deal Points Studies. The Private Target Deal Points Studies produced by the M&A Market Trends Subcommittee of the Committee on Mergers and Acquisitions provide a statistical breakdown of the use of certain provisions in publicly available acquisition agreements that involved private targets being acquired by public companies. The 2009 Study, for example, covered a sample of 106 of these acquisition agreements for U.S. transactions completed in 2008, with estimated values ranging from $25 million to $500 million. Previous Studies published in 2007 and 2006 analyzed agreements from transactions completed in 2006 and 2004, respectively. Much of the data in the 2009 Study is compared with data from these earlier Studies. The Subcommittee also published Studies in 2008 on continental European and Canadian agreements for the acquisition of private targets.

The 2009 Study is available to members of the Committee and is posted on the Subcommittee's webpage, http://www.abanet.org/dch/committee. cfm?com=CL56003. It is anticipated that future Studies will also be made available to Committee members in this manner. The Subcommittee has usually posted on its extranet site the full text of the acquisition agreements that were reviewed in producing its Studies.

These Studies can be a useful resource for determining the extent to which certain provisions are used, the language of those provisions, and various exceptions and carve-outs. A comparison of the data from the Studies also provides helpful insight into evolving trends. The data points, however, should be viewed with a critical eye in negotiations. In considering whether the data reflects "market," it should be kept in mind that there are many factors that can affect the data, including the sample from which the agreements are drawn, the economic and business climate at the time, the relative bargaining power and size of the parties, the size of the transactions, and the types of businesses and industries in which the parties are engaged. In addition, only the final, fully negotiated agreements were reviewed, so the Studies do not reflect the starting points in the drafts or the tradeoffs in the evolution of the changes negotiated.

Annual Survey of Judicial Developments. The Annual Survey of Judicial Developments Pertaining to Mergers and Acquisitions is prepared by the Annual Survey Task Force of the M&A Jurisprudence Subcommittee of the Committee on Mergers and Acquisitions and is published in the February issue of the Business Lawyer. The primary charge of the Annual Survey Task Force is to summarize annually significant judicial decisions in the area of mergers and acquisitions ("M&A") and to publish the summary as a service to American Bar Association members who practice in the M&A area. The Annual Survey is written from the perspective of the practicing M&A lawyer. The summarized cases are limited to those believed to be of greatest interest and significance to a wide range of M&A practitioners. Cases discussed in the Annual Survey are frequently cited in the commentary to the Model Agreement.

Fact Pattern

The following facts, and certain of Buyer's intentions with respect to the acquisition, are assumed as background for the *Model Stock Purchase Agreement*:

Sellers. The target (the "Company") is a closely held corporation with two principal shareholders (the "Principal Shareholders"). Both have been active in the business. One will remain so after the closing (the "Continuing Principal Shareholder"), and the other will retire. There are also eight other shareholders who are employees of the Company or relatives of the Principal Shareholders and who hold, in the aggregate, 10 % of the issued and outstanding stock of the Company. The employee shareholders have been involved in the business, but not at the top decision-making levels. The family shareholders have never been involved in running the business. All the shareholders (collectively, "Sellers") will sign the agreement.

Capitalization of the Company. Sellers collectively own all the outstanding common stock of the Company. The Company has no other capital stock, options, warrants, or securities convertible into capital stock outstanding.

Subsidiaries. The Company has two wholly owned subsidiaries.

Buyer. Buyer is a strategic buyer (one that anticipates the Company's business will complement or otherwise fit into its own long-range business plans and objectives), but does not intend to be active in the day-to-day operations of the Company's business.

Nature of the Company's Business. The Company is a manufacturing concern with a full range of business activities, including the design and manufacture of products and the furnishing of advisory and consulting services to customers.

Purchase Price. The purchase price will be a combination of cash and nonnegotiable promissory notes. Sellers have agreed that Buyer will have the right to offset any claims for indemnification against amounts due under the promissory notes.

Real Estate and Environmental Issues. The business is conducted from two sites. The principal site is owned by the Company outright and the other is leased from an unrelated third party. These are industrial properties, but neither site has been the subject of any governmental investigation or action.

Taxes. The Company is a C corporation for tax purposes.

Regulatory Matters. The closing will be subject to compliance with the Hart-Scott-Rodino Antitrust Improvements Act and with any other applicable laws and regulations.

Liens. The stock of the Company will be conveyed free and clear of all encumbrances. The assets of the Company and its subsidiaries are free and clear of all encumbrances, except certain liens arising by operation of law in the ordinary course of business or identified in Sellers' Disclosure Letter.

Licensing and Intellectual Property. A number of the Company's products are manufactured pursuant to licensing agreements with unrelated third parties. These licensing agreements are not assignable (including an indirect transfer by way of a change in control of the Company), without the respective licensor's consent. The Company has patented a number of the products it manufactures, and descriptive literature relating to the products is subject to copyright protection. Certain trademarks of the Company have been registered.

Other Consents. In addition to the licensing agreements, a major supply contract, a capital lease of a major item of equipment, and the real property lease require consents of the other parties for any change in control of the Company and such consents will be a condition to closing.

Employee Benefits and Pension Plans. The Company has employee benefit, vacation, health, bonus, and other similar plans, including a 401(k) plan.

Post-Closing Adjustment. Buyer will prepare a balance sheet of the Company as of the closing date and the purchase price will be adjusted (up or down), on a dollar-for-dollar basis, based on the difference between shareholders' equity as of the closing date and shareholders' equity reflected on the interim balance sheet.

Employment and Noncompetition Agreements. The Continuing Principal Shareholder will sign an employment agreement. All Sellers will be bound by the noncompetition provisions of the Model Agreement.

Sellers' Indemnification; Escrow. Buyer will require that all Sellers jointly and severally indemnify Buyer with respect to their representations and obligations under, and any certificates delivered by them pursuant to, the Model Agreement. A portion of the sales proceeds will be held in escrow by a third party escrow agent to secure Sellers' indemnification obligations.

Stock Purchase Agreement

by

_____

and

_____

Dated _____

Table of Contents

Index of Defined Terms

Term	Defined at Page:	Found in Section(s):
Encumbrance	17	3.2, 3.3, 3.6, 3.11, 3.16, 3.17, 3.19, and 3.22
End Date	17	2.3 and 10.1
Environment	17	Definitions of "Environmental Law," "Hazardous Activity," "Release," and "Threat of Release" in Section 1.1
Environmental, Health, and Safety Liability	18	3.19 and 11.3
Environmental Law	18	Definition of "Environmental, Health, and Safety Liability" in Section 1.1
Equity Security	20	3.3, 3.16, 3.24, 5.6, and 8.9
ERISA	20	3.13
Escrow Agent	20	2.2, 2.4, and 12.1
Escrow Agreement	20	2.2, 2.4, 11.7, and 12.1
Escrow Funds	20	2.2 and 2.4
Exchange Act	20	Definitions of "Equity Security" and "Related Person" in Section 1.1 and in Sections 3.5 and 7.1
Facilities	20	3.19 and 11.3
Financial Statements	21	3.4, 3.8, and 3.9
GAAP	21	3.4 and 3.5
Governmental Authorization	23	3.2 and 3.14
Governmental Body	23	Definitions of "Order," "Person," "Proceeding," "Tax," and "Tax Return" and in Sections 3.2, 3.11, 3.14, 3.15, 3.21, 3.22, 3.27, and 6.1
Hazardous Activity	24	3.19, 8.7, and 10.3
Hazardous Material	25	3.19 and 10.3
HSR Act	28	2.3, 5.4, 6.1, and 11.1
Indemnified Person	28	11.8 and 11.9
Indemnifying Person	28	11.8 and 11.9
Independent Accountants	28	2.6
Intellectual Property Assets	28	3.16 and 3.22
Interim Balance Sheet	28	3.4, 3.6, 3.8, 3.9, 3.10, and 3.11
Interim Balance Sheet Date	28	3.4 and 3.8
Interim Shareholders' Equity	28	2.5
Invention Disclosures	28	3.22
IRS	28	3.11 and 3.13
Knowledge	28	3.15, 3.19, 3.20, 3.21, 3.22, 4.4, 10.1, and 10.6

Term	Defined at Page:	Found in Section(s):
Knowledge of Sellers	30	3.11, 3.15, 3.18, 3.19, 3.20, 3.21, 3.22, 3.26, and 3.29
Leased Real Property	30	3.6
Legal Requirement	30	Numerous sections
Loss	30	3.27, 11.2, 11.3, 11.4, and 11.8
Major Suppliers	31	3.26
Major Customers	31	3.26
Marks	31	3.22
Material Adverse Change	31	3.12, 7.1, and 8.12
Material Consents	34	5.4 and 8.3
Net Names	34	3.22
Objection Notice	34	2.6
Occupational Safety and Health Law	34	Definition of "Environmental, Health, and Safety Liability" in Section 1.1
Order	35	3.2, 3.15, 3.19, 3.20, 4.2, 7.7, and 8.5
Ordinary Course of Business	35	3.6, 3.8, 3.9, 3.10, 3.16, 3.17, 5.2, and 5.7
Organizational Documents	37	3.1, 3.2, 3.16, and 4.2
Owned Real Property	37	3.6
Patents	37	3.22
Permitted Encumbrances	37	3.6
Person	38	Numerous sections
Plan	38	3.13
Proceeding	38	3.11, 3.15, 3.21, 3.22, 4.4, 7.5, and 10.9
Promissory Notes	38	2.4, 2.6, and 3.2
Purchase Price	38	2.2, 8.9, and 12.5
Real Property	38	3.6 and 5.1
Record	38	3.4, 3.5, 3.11, 5.1, 5.2, and 7.3
Related Person	38	3.24, 5.4, 5.6, 6.1, 8.6, 8.8, and 8.11
Release	40	1.1
Representative	40	2.6, 3.23, 3.25, 3.28, 4.5, 5.1, 5.3, 5.6, 5.9, 6.1, 7.3, 11.2, and 12.1
Securities Act	40	2.3, 3.2, 3.3, 3.24, and 4.3
Seller(s)	41	Numerous sections
Sellers' Closing Documents	41	3.2
Sellers' Releases	41	2.4 and 7.4
Sellers' Representative	41	2.2 and 2.3

Term	Defined at Page:	Found in Section(s):
Shares	41	2.1, 2.2, 2.4, 3.3, 4.3, 7.1, 8.5, and 9
Software	41	3.22 and 7.4
Subsidiary	41	Definition of "Acquired Company" in Section 1.1 and in Sections 3.3 and 11.9
Tax	41	3.2, 3.11, 3,17, 3.20, 3.21, and 10.9
Tax Return	41	3.11
Third Party	41	3.6, 3.22, 8.9, and 11.8
Third-Party Claim	41	11.3, 11.8, and 11.9
Threat of Release	42	Definition of "Environmental Law" in Section 1.1
Trade Secrets	42	3.22

Stock Purchase Agreement

        This Stock Purchase Agreement ("Agreement") is made as of _____ by _____, a _____ corporation ("Buyer"), and those individuals who have executed the signature page to this Agreement (collectively, "Sellers" and individually, a "Seller").

COMMENT

The transaction covered by the Model Agreement is the purchase and sale of shares of the Company, and the parties are the Buyer and Sellers. It is not necessary that the Company be a party, but Buyer might prefer to add the Company so that Buyer could have more direct control over the Company's performance of certain pre-closing activities. If the Company were to be a party, a number of changes in the Model Agreement would be necessary to, among other things, make it clear that Sellers would have no claims against the Company by virtue of its representations and covenants, that Buyer may look to Sellers directly for breaches of the representations and obligations of both Sellers and the Company, and that breaches by the Company will not limit Sellers' liability.

SELLERS' RESPONSE

Sellers may not object to the Company being a party, and might even suggest that it be made a party. Some Sellers might feel more comfortable in having the Company make representations about which they may have limited or no knowledge, even though they will ultimately stand behind those representations.

RECITALS

Sellers desire to sell, and Buyer desires to purchase, all issued and outstanding shares (the "Shares") of capital stock of _____, a _____ corporation (the "Company"), for the consideration and on the terms set forth in this Agreement.

The parties, intending to be legally bound, agree as follows:

1. Definitions and Usage

PRELIMINARY NOTE

It is useful, both to reduce the length of other sections and to facilitate changes during negotiations, to list in a separate section of the acquisition agreement all defined terms that appear in more than one section of the agreement. The drafters of the Model Agreement believe that it is advisable, however, to avoid including substantive requirements in the definitions section of an agreement (such as covenants, representations, or mechanical requirements). Such requirements generally are better located in the appropriate section of the agreement.

A common dilemma in drafting definitions is whether to include long lists of terms with similar, but slightly different meanings. *See, e.g.,* the definition of "Encumbrance." If the goal is to draft a comprehensive, all-inclusive definition, the tendency is to list every term that comes to mind. If too many terms are listed, however, the absence of a particular term may be accorded more significance than intended, even if phrases such as "without limitation" or "any other" are used. *See* commentary to Section 1.2(a). Long lists of terms with similar meanings also perpetuate a cumbersome and arcane style of drafting that many lawyers and clients find annoying at best and confusing at worst. The Model Agreement generally resolves this dilemma in favor of short lists of terms that are intended to have their broadest possible meanings.

There are alternative methods of handling definitions in acquisition agreements. They may be placed at the end of the document as opposed to the beginning; they may be placed in a separate ancillary document referred to in the agreement; or they may be incorporated in the earliest section of the agreement where they appear followed by initial capitalization of those defined terms when used in subsequent sections of the agreement. There are proponents for each of these alternatives, and each of them may be preferable in certain circumstances. The drafters of the Model Agreement believe that reference generally is easier if most of the principal definitions are in one place, except where terms with relatively brief definitions are used in only one section, in which case those terms are defined in the section where they are used. The Model Agreement does not attempt to incorporate definitions from the various agreements and documents that are exhibits or ancillary to the Agreement. It is preferable where possible to use defined terms consistently in the acquisition agreement, its exhibits, and ancillary documents.

1.1 DEFINITIONS

For purposes of this Agreement, the following terms have the meanings specified or referred to in this Section 1.1:

"Acquired Companies"—the Company and its Subsidiaries, collectively, and "Acquired Company" means any one of the Acquired Companies.

"Adjoining Property"—as defined in Section 3.19(e).

"Adjustment Amount"—as defined in Section 2.5(a).

"Agreement"—as defined in the first paragraph of this Agreement.

"Applicable Contract"—any Contract (a) under which any Acquired Company has or could acquire any rights, (b) under which any Acquired Company has or could become subject to any obligation or liability, or (c) by which any Acquired Company or any assets owned or used by it is or could become bound.

COMMENT

For a discussion of the scope of this definition and examples of the types of contracts that could be included within this term, *see* commentary to Section 3.2.

SELLERS' RESPONSE

Seller may object to use of the word "could" in each of the clauses in the definition. Words such as "could reasonably be expected to" are a possible variant.

"Balance Sheet Date"—as defined in Section 3.4.

"Breach"—any breach of, or any inaccuracy in, any representation or warranty or breach of, or failure to perform or comply with, any covenant or obligation in or of the Contract in question, or any event that with the passing of time or the giving of notice, or both, would constitute such a breach, inaccuracy, or failure.

COMMENT

The definition of "Breach" is broad, enabling Buyer to discover potential issues with respect to Applicable Contracts.

SELLERS' RESPONSE

Sellers may seek to limit this definition by, for instance, introducing materiality qualifiers.

"Business Day"—any day other than (a) Saturday or Sunday or (b) any other day on which national banks in _____ are generally permitted or required to be closed.

COMMENT

The blank in the definition of Business Day is usually filled in with the city where the closing will occur (to assure that funds can be transferred at closing) and may also include the locations of other parties or the institutions that are providing funding for the transaction.

"Buyer"—as defined in the first paragraph of this Agreement.

"Buyer Group"—as defined in Section 5.1.

"Buyer Indemnified Persons"—as defined in Section 11.2.

"Buyer's Closing Documents"—the Promissory Notes and the Escrow Agreement.

"Cleanup"—all actions to clean up, remove, treat, or in any other way address the presence, Release, or Threat of Release of any Hazardous Material whether or not any expense incurred in connection with such action constitutes a capital expenditure.

"Closing"—as defined in Section 2.3.

"Closing Balance Sheet"—as defined in Section 2.6(a).

"Closing Date"—the date on which the Closing occurs.

COMMENT

The date is determined by application of Section 2.3.

"Closing Date Shareholders' Equity"—as defined in Section 2.5(a).

"Closing Payment"—as defined in Section 2.2.

"COBRA"—as defined in Section 3.13(d).

"Code"—the Internal Revenue Code of 1986.

"Company"—as defined in the Recitals of this Agreement.

"Confidential Information"—as defined in Section 7.3(a).

"Consent"—any approval, consent, ratification, waiver, or other authorization.

"Contemplated Transactions"—the transactions contemplated by this Agreement.

COMMENT

See commentary to Section 3.2.

"Contract"—any agreement, contract, lease, consensual obligation, promise, commitment, or undertaking (whether written or oral and whether express or implied), whether or not legally binding.

COMMENT

This definition includes all obligations, however characterized, whether or not legally binding. Buyer will want the definition of Contract to be broad. For example, Buyer may want to know about statements an Acquired Company has made to its distributors that the Acquired Company will generally grant credit returns for unsold products when the Acquired Company introduces a replacement product. Buyer may also want the definition to identify established practices of the Acquired Companies that may constitute a course of dealing or usage of trade. Similarly, Buyer may want the definition to encompass "comfort letters" confirming an Acquired Company's intention to provide financial support to a Subsidiary or other Related Person and assurances to employees regarding compensation, benefits, and tenure, whether or not such letters or assurances are legally binding. A representation that certain specified Contracts are legally binding is included in Section 3.17(b)(i).

SELLERS' RESPONSE

Sellers may respond by objecting to including implied contracts, contracts that are not legally binding, and oral contracts.

"Copyrights"—as defined in Section 3.22(a)(iii).

"Disclosure Letter"—the disclosure letter delivered by Sellers to Buyer concurrently with the execution and delivery of this Agreement.

COMMENT

The form and content of the Disclosure Letter (sometimes called a disclosure schedule) should be negotiated and drafted concurrently with the negotiation and drafting of the Model Agreement. The Disclosure Letter is an integral component of the acquisition documentation and should be prepared and reviewed as carefully as the Model Agreement itself. Buyer or Sellers may prefer to attach multiple schedules or exhibits to the Model Agreement instead of using a disclosure letter.

The Disclosure Letter will usually provide exceptions to representations made by Sellers. Accuracy is critical because inaccuracy can trigger a breach of relevant representations. The Buyer's first draft of an acquisition agreement can omit exceptions to representations and references to a disclosure letter, thereby shifting the burden to Seller to add language in the representations that provides for exceptions.

See commentary to Section 3.2; M&A Process 233–40.

"Employee Plan"—as defined in Section 3.13(a).

"Encumbrance"—any charge, claim, community or other marital property interest, condition, equitable interest, lien, option, pledge, security interest, mortgage, right of way, easement, encroachment, servitude, right of first option, right of first refusal, or similar restriction, including any restriction on use, voting, transfer, receipt of income, or exercise of any other attribute of ownership.

COMMENT

The definition of "Encumbrance" is broad because Buyer wants to determine whether there are any potential issues with respect to title to the Shares or to the assets of the Acquired Companies.

SELLERS' RESPONSE

Sellers may seek to limit this definition by, for instance, introducing materiality qualifiers.

"End Date"—as defined in Section 10.1(d).

"Environment"—soil, land surface and subsurface strata, surface waters (including navigable and nonnavigable inland and ocean waters), groundwaters, drinking water supply, stream sediments, ambient air (indoor air), plant and animal life, and any other environmental medium or natural resource.

COMMENT

The term "Environment" appears in the definitions of "Environmental Law," "Hazardous Activity," "Release," and "Threat of Release" in Section 1.1. This definition comes primarily from the United States Comprehensive Environmental Response, Compensation, and Liability Act ("CERCLA"), 42 U.S.C. §§ 9601–9626, 9651–9657. It is intended to cover all environmental media and has been modified to include a reference to indoor air, which is not covered under CERCLA, but may be subject to regulation under other environmental statutes.

"Environmental, Health, and Safety Liability"—any Loss, obligation, or other responsibility resulting from or arising under an Environmental Law or an Occupational Safety and Health Law.

COMMENT

This definition is broad in scope.

SELLERS' RESPONSE

Sellers will likely want to limit their responsibilities under the representations and indemnification provisions that use this and other related definitions, and the logical first step in doing so is to narrow the definition. Sellers may want to add a materiality qualification either to the entire definition (for example, by limiting the definition to "material" losses, as that term would be further defined, or to losses in excess of a specified amount) or to specified environmental matters.

"Environmental Law"—any Legal Requirement that provides for or relates to:

(a) advising appropriate authorities, employees, or the public with respect to the use of any Hazardous Material, the Release or Threat of Release of Hazardous Material, violation of discharge or emission limits or other prohibitions, or any Hazardous Activity or any activity, such as resource extraction or construction, that could have a significant effect on the Environment;

(b) preventing or reducing to acceptable levels the Release of Hazardous Material into the Environment;

(c) reducing the quantities, or minimizing or controlling the hazardous characteristics, of Hazardous Material that are generated;

(d) assuring that products are designed, formulated, packaged, and used so that they do not present an unreasonable risk to human health or the Environment when used or disposed of;

(e) protecting the Environment;

(f) reducing the risks involved in the transportation of Hazardous Material;

(g) the cleanup of Hazardous Material that has been Released, preventing its Release, or addressing the Threat of Release, or paying the costs of such actions; or

(h) making a Person compensate any other Person for damage done to its health or property or the Environment or permitting self-appointed

representatives of the public interest to recover for injuries done to public assets or resources.

COMMENT

A short form of this definition is: "Legal Requirements designed to minimize, prevent, remedy, or impose penalties for, the consequences of actions that damage or threaten the Environment or public health and safety." Buyers often group occupational, safety, and health laws within the definition of Environmental Law with the result that all such matters are covered by representations as to Environmental Laws and are subject to what are often longer survival periods applicable to the representations.

A broad definition of "Environmental Law" is important to Buyer for several reasons. For example, Buyer may be a public company or may in the future want to become a public company. Securities and Exchange Commission (SEC) disclosure rules relating to environmental issues use a broad definition that includes federal, state, and local laws regulating the discharge of materials into the environment or otherwise enacted primarily to protect the environment. *See* SEC Regulation S-K, Item 103, Instruction 5. Therefore, comprehensive disclosures from Sellers will help Buyer meet its disclosure requirements under federal securities law.

In addition, a separate "Environmental Law" definition is necessary when there are separate environmental representations and indemnifications. If Buyer relies upon the representations in Sections 3.14, 3.15, and 3.19 and the general indemnification provisions of Section 11.3, care should be taken to determine whether the additional elements addressed here are adequately covered.

Some states, such as Connecticut and New Jersey, require that certain filings be made, and possibly environmental investigation and remedial measures be taken, prior to the transfer of property in the state from one "owner" or "operator" to another. *See, e.g.,* Connecticut Transfer Act, CONN. GEN. STAT. ANN. § 22a-134a; Industrial Site Recovery Act, N.J. STAT. ANN. § 13:1K-6 *et seq.,* formerly known as the Environmental Cleanup Responsibility Act or "ECRA." The requirements are generally triggered by a "change of control" of the owner or operator, including the purchase of its stock. New Jersey regulations require the filing of a "cleanup plan" to be implemented by the owner or operator. Generally, a seller will be responsible for implementing the cleanup plan, although that responsibility may be assumed by the buyer. In New Jersey, the state environmental agency has the ability to void a sale if no cleanup plan or "negative declaration" has been filed, and significant fines can be levied for failure to comply with the regulations. Buyer should identify such regulations and require that their compliance be a condition to the closing. If Buyer assumes the cleanup responsibility, it may want to negotiate for an adjustment to the purchase price or a right to terminate the Model Agreement if its due diligence reveals the plan to be too costly.

SELLERS' RESPONSE

Sellers may seek to limit these definitions to exclude areas such as occupational health and safety and materials not considered hazardous under CERCLA. Such limitations may be acceptable to Buyer depending upon the nature of the Acquired Companies' businesses.

Sellers may also want to limit their exposure in this definition and/or in the environmental indemnity in Section 11.3 to laws in effect on the date of the Model Agreement. *See* commentary to the definition of "Legal Requirement" in Section 1.1 and commentary to Section 11.3.

"Equity Security"—in respect of any Person, (a) any capital stock or similar security, (b) any security convertible into or exchangeable for any security described in clause (a), (c) any option, warrant, or other right to purchase or otherwise acquire any security described in clauses (a), (b), or (c), and (d) any "equity security" within the meaning of the Exchange Act.

COMMENT

Clause (d) incorporates by reference the Exchange Act definition. The definition in the Model Agreement encompasses rights that may convert into, or otherwise become, shares of stock or other types of securities.

"ERISA"—the Employee Retirement Income Security Act of 1974.

"Escrow Agent"—as defined in the Escrow Agreement.

"Escrow Agreement"—as defined in Section 2.4(a)(vii).

"Escrow Funds"—as defined in Section 2.2(c).

"Exchange Act"—the Securities Exchange Act of 1934.

"Facilities"—any real property owned or operated or formerly owned or operated by any Acquired Company and any buildings, plants, structures, or equipment (including motor vehicles, tank cars, and rolling stock) owned or operated or formerly owned or operated by any Acquired Company.

COMMENT

Buyer wants a broad definition of Facilities as the term is used in representations of Seller. Buyer will seek to include facilities formerly owned by any Acquired Company because CERCLA liability extends to prior owners of a facility. If such formerly owned facilities are not so included, Buyer can consider conducting an environmental investigation of these facilities, but this may be impossible for facilities no longer owned by an Acquired Company.

SELLERS' RESPONSE

Sellers may attempt to limit their responsibilities to existing facilities or to those for which Buyer can demonstrate a real basis for concern based on their character and use or that of the adjoining property. At the least, Sellers may want to include only facilities in existence during their ownership of the Acquired Companies and propose that representations concerning other facilities be limited by a knowledge qualification. If Buyer is prepared to accept any such limitations, it may prefer to do so in a more nuanced fashion in representations or indemnification provisions rather than in the definition itself.

"Financial Statements"—as defined in Section 3.4.

"GAAP"—generally accepted accounting principles in the United States.

COMMENT

GAAP refers to the accounting principles generally accepted in the United States used by nongovernmental entities in the preparation of financial statements presented in conformity with GAAP. The reference to GAAP in acquisition agreements is customary.

GAAP Hierarchy. In 1992, the American Institute of Certified Public Accountants (AICPA) issued Statement on Auditing Standards No. 69, "The Meaning of 'Present Fairly in Conformity With Generally Accepted Accounting Principles' in the Independent Auditor's Report." Statement 69 identified the sources of accounting principles and established a framework for selecting the principles to be used in the preparation of financial statements of nongovernmental entities that are presented in conformity with GAAP (GAAP hierarchy). The GAAP hierarchy set forth the different levels of authority attributed to various accounting pronouncements. In 2008, the Financial Accounting Standards Board (FASB) issued Statement of Financial Accounting Standards No. 162, "The Hierarchy of Generally Accepted Accounting Principles." Statement 162 did not change the GAAP hierarchy. Rather, it was moved from the auditing literature to the accounting literature to convey more clearly its application by entities (rather than auditors) in preparing their financial statements.

FASB Accounting Standards Codification. On June 30, 2009, the FASB issued Statement of Financial Accounting Standards No. 168, "The *FASB Accounting Standard Codification* and the Hierarchy of Generally Accepted Accounting Principles—a replacement of FASB Statement No. 162." Statement 168 established the *FASB Accounting Standards Codification* (FASB ASC) as the source of authoritative non-SEC accounting principles recognized by the FASB to be used in the preparation of financial statements of nongovernmental entities (public and nonpublic) that are presented in conformity with GAAP. The FASB ASC does not change the existing accounting pronouncements, but only reorganizes them so that all applicable authoritative pronouncements are accessible by topic. What it does change is the different levels of authority previously attributed to the accounting pronouncements in the GAAP hierarchy. All of the guidance contained in the FASB ASC now carries an equal level of authority. Accounting guidance is authoritative if included in the FASB ASC or nonauthoritative if not included, except that the rules and interpretative releases of the SEC are considered sources of authoritative GAAP for public reporting companies.

Statement 168 became effective for financial statements issued for interim and annual periods ending after September 15, 2009. The FASB will issue Accounting Standards Updates, which are not authoritative in their own right but will update the FASB ASC and provide background information about the guidance and the basis for the changes made.

Applying GAAP. The requirement that financial statements be prepared in accordance with GAAP should provide some comfort to a buyer. However, it is important to understand that GAAP does not convey a single set of rules that similarly apply in all circumstances. In particular:

- GAAP requires many estimates. Estimates are necessarily subjective and subject to professional judgments that in some cases can produce different reporting depending on the facts and circumstances, e.g., fair values and reserves for doubtful accounts.

- GAAP permits different accounting methods in specified circumstances, e.g., inventory valuation (FIFO, LIFO, or weighted average cost), depreciation (straight line or accelerated methods), and accounting for repairs and small tools (capitalize or expense). The accounting method used can substantially affect reported results.

- GAAP is not static. It is subject to change, depending on the projects on the FASB's standard-setting agenda at any point in time and the timing of the projects (when the FASB expects to finalize and make effective updates to the FASB ASC).

A buyer may want to examine the target's historical financial statements to obtain an understanding of the critical accounting estimates and alternative accounting methods used to ensure consistency in application from year to year. A buyer may also want to determine the timing of FASB standard-setting projects that are in process and the extent to which any new guidance arising from those projects might impact the target's financial reporting.

International Accounting Standards. In international transactions, a buyer should be aware that there can be important differences between GAAP standards and accounting standards used in other countries. For example, the International Financial Reporting Standards (IFRS) might be applied in the preparation of a target's financial statements. These standards, which have been adopted by the International Accounting Standards Board (IASB), are permitted or required in the preparation of financial statements in many countries. The IASB and FASB have agreed to seek convergence on certain topics and are working cooperatively in the development of new standards. In November 2009, these Boards issued a joint statement describing their plans and milestone targets for completing the major projects in 2011. The SEC has also released for comment a roadmap for the transition by U.S. public companies to using IFRS. The convergence of these accounting standards, should that ultimately occur, will likely impact certain provisions of the Model Agreement, such as the financial statement representation in Section 3.4 and the purchase price adjustment in Sections 2.5 and 2.6, as well as Ancillary Document D—Earnout Agreement.

"Governmental Authorization"—any (a) Consent, license, registration, or permit issued, granted, given, or otherwise made available by or under the authority of any Governmental Body or pursuant to any Legal Requirement; or (b) right under any Contract with any Governmental Body.

"Governmental Body"—any:

(a) nation, state, county, city, town, borough, village, district, or other jurisdiction;

(b) federal, state, local, municipal, foreign, multinational, or other government;

(c) governmental or quasi-governmental authority of any nature (including any agency, branch, department, board, commission, court, tribunal, or other entity exercising governmental or quasi-governmental powers);

(d) body exercising, or entitled or purporting to exercise, any administrative, executive, judicial, legislative, police, regulatory, or taxing authority or power, whether local, national, or international; or

(e) official of any of the foregoing.

COMMENT

Although presumably encompassed by the words "other jurisdiction," "other government," and the like, Buyer may want the definition of "Governmental Body" to make specific reference to the political or governmental entities that exist in the jurisdictions in which the Acquired Companies are located or do business (such as commonwealths, provinces, and parishes).

"Hazardous Activity"—the distribution, generation, handling, importing, management, manufacturing, processing, production, refinement, Release, storage, transfer, transportation, treatment, or use of Hazardous Material and any other act, business, operation, or activity that increases the danger, or poses a risk of harm, to the Environment.

COMMENT

The latter portion of this definition, beginning with "and any other act," is quite expansive.

SELLERS' RESPONSE

Sellers may seek to limit this definition to activities that pose only environmental risks or that are regulated by environmental laws.

"Hazardous Material"—any substance, material, or waste that is or will foreseeably be regulated by any Governmental Body, including any material, substance, or waste that is defined or classified as a "hazardous waste," "hazardous material," "hazardous substance," "extremely hazardous waste," "pollutant," "restricted hazardous waste," "contaminant," "toxic waste," "pollutant," or "toxic substance" under any provision of Environmental Law, including petroleum, petroleum products, asbestos, presumed asbestos-containing material or asbestos-containing material, urea formaldehyde, or polychlorinated biphenyls.

COMMENT

The definition includes petroleum because many state and federal laws exclude it from coverage under their Superfund-type provisions or other requirements, even though it can cause environmental problems. The definition also includes asbestos. In certain circumstances, carefully defined exceptions or threshold quantities may be used to limit materials governed by environmental law. For example, exceptions could be provided for such materials with clauses such as "not more than usually present in dwellings for routine consumer and household use;" asbestos might be limited to friable asbestos; or polychlorinated biphenyls might be limited to those in excess of a specified concentration.

An alternate definition that favors the approach of referring to specific laws is as follows:

> "Hazardous Material"—includes any of the following under federal law and implementing regulations, as well as state and local counterparts to such provisions: (i) "hazardous substance," "pollutants," or "contaminant" (as defined in Sections 101(14) and (33) of the Comprehensive Environmental Response, Compensation, and Liability Act ("CERCLA"), including any element, compound, mixture, solution, or substance that is or may be designated pursuant to Section 102 of CERCLA (42 U.S.C. §§ 9601(14), (33), 9602)); (ii) substance that is or may be designated pursuant to Section 311(b)(2)(A) of the Federal Water Pollution Control Act, as amended (33 U.S.C. §§ 1251, 1321(b)(2)(A)) ("FWPCA"); (iii) hazardous waste having the characteristics identified under or listed pursuant to Section 3001 of the Resource Conservation and Recovery Act, as amended (42 U.S.C. §§ 6901, 6921) ("RCRA") or

having characteristics that may subsequently be considered under RCRA to constitute a hazardous waste; (iv) substance comprising or containing petroleum, as that term is defined in Section 9001(8) of RCRA (42 U.S.C. §§ 6901, 6991); (v) oil as that term is defined in Section 1001(23) of the Oil Pollution Act (33 U.S.C. § 2701(23)); (vi) toxic pollutant that is or may be listed under Section 307(a) of FWPCA; (vii) hazardous air pollutant that is or may be listed under Section 112 of the Clean Air Act, as amended (42 U.S.C. §§ 7401, 7412); (viii) imminently hazardous chemical substance or mixture with respect to which action has been or may be taken pursuant to Section 7 of the Toxic Substances Control Act, as amended (15 U.S.C. §§ 2601, 2606); (ix) hazardous material under the Hazardous Materials Transportation Law (49 U.S.C. §§ 5101, 5201(2)); (x) air contaminant under regulations set forth at 29 C.F.R. Part 1910 Subpart Z implementing the Occupational Safety and Health Act (29 U.S.C. §§ 651 *et seq.*); (xi) extremely hazardous substance under Section 329(3) of the Emergency Planning and Community Right-to-Know Act (42 U.S.C. §§ 11001, 11049(3)); and (xii) source, special nuclear, or by-product material as defined by the Atomic Energy Act of 1954, as amended (42 U.S.C. § 2011 *et seq.*); as well as (x) asbestos, asbestos-containing material, or urea formaldehyde or material that contains it; (y) waste oil and other petroleum products; and (z) any other toxic materials, contaminants, or hazardous substances or wastes pursuant to any Environmental Law.

Listing CERCLA and the substances designated pursuant to CERCLA (*see* 42 U.S.C. §§ 9601(14) & (33)) includes all substances designated by RCRA, the Clean Air Act, the Clean Water Act, and the Toxic Substance Control Act (43 U.S.C. § 9602(14)).

SELLERS' RESPONSE

Sellers may seek to impose a de minimis exemption or some sort of threshold trigger before a material is included in the definition. In addition, Sellers will likely object to the definition's inclusion of substances that in the future could be determined to be hazardous, and attempt to limit their responsibilities to substances that are considered hazardous at the date of signing the Model Agreement or the date of the closing. If Sellers' representations are so limited, Buyer might consider seeing that the representations, and the definition, are updated through the closing.

"HSR Act"—the Hart-Scott-Rodino Antitrust Improvements Act of 1976.

COMMENT

The HSR Act requires that the parties to a proposed acquisition subject to the Act give prior notice of the proposed acquisition to the Federal Trade Commission (FTC) and the Assistant Attorney General in charge of the Antitrust Division of the Department of Justice (DOJ), and delay consummation of the acquisition until expiration (or early termination) of the specified waiting period. The purpose of the

HSR Act is to allow the government an opportunity to evaluate the anticompetitive aspects of a proposed acquisition and to seek to enjoin its consummation in appropriate circumstances. Subject to certain statutory exemptions, the HSR Act's premerger notification filing and waiting period requirements apply to acquisitions in which a party is engaged in commerce or in any activity affecting commerce, and the acquisition itself, and in certain cases the parties to the acquisition, satisfy certain size requirements.

Absent an exemption, the HSR Act requires the submission of an HSR filing for a proposed acquisition if: (i) the value of the proposed transaction exceeds $253.7 million (all dollar amounts are as announced by the FTC in January 2010) or (ii) the value of the proposed transaction exceeds $63.4 million, and, in general, the annual net sales (worldwide) or total assets of one party to the transaction is $126.9 million or more and, for the other party, is $12.7 million or more. 15 U.S.C. § 18a(a)(2)(A)-(B). For purposes of the foregoing test, the relevant party is the "ultimate parent entity" of the party to the proposed transaction, i.e., the entity or individual that controls the party to the transaction and is controlled by no other entity. In applying the dollar thresholds, the ultimate parent entity is deemed to include all entities that it controls. The dollar thresholds are adjusted annually to reflect the change in the gross national product for the previous federal fiscal year (which begins on October 1). The FTC has indicated that it will publish revised thresholds in the Federal Register early in the calendar year, with the new thresholds becoming effective 30 days after such publication.

Once filings have been made, the parties must wait for the expiration of a mandatory 30-day waiting period before completing the acquisition. The parties can consummate the acquisition upon expiration of the 30-day waiting period unless the government determines that further investigation is necessary and requires submission of additional information and documents relevant to the acquisition (the "Second Request"). The parties may also request early termination of the waiting period, which may be granted if the transaction does not present any substantive antitrust issues. If the government issues a Second Request, the mandatory waiting period is generally extended another 30 days, which commences when both parties have substantially complied with the Second Request (the DOJ and the FTC interpret "substantial compliance" to mean full compliance—it may take several months to comply with a Second Request). During the waiting period, the agency may terminate the investigation (and the waiting period), file suit in federal court challenging the acquisition, or negotiate a restructuring that would address the substantive issue and allow the acquisition to proceed as restructured. When the FTC and DOJ negotiate such a settlement, they virtually always insist that it be embodied in an enforceable court or administrative order. Unless the government obtains an order from a federal district court enjoining the acquisition, the parties can consummate the acquisition upon expiration of the HSR waiting period.

The government may grant early termination of any waiting period either sua sponte or upon the written request of any person filing notification. *See* 16 C.F.R. § 803.11. Early termination is effective upon notice to any requesting person by telephone. The government must give such notice as soon as possible after a request is made (and confirm the notice in writing) and must publish its decision to grant early termination in the Federal Register, which prevents the parties from keeping the existence of the acquisition confidential. The FTC also makes this information available on its website (www.ftc.gov) and on a prerecorded telephone line.

Filings are made by each party on a Notification and Report Form, which includes a description of the proposed acquisition, a description of the parties, copies of their most recent regularly prepared financial statements, copies of studies or evaluations conducted by the parties in connection with their analysis of the acquisition's competitive effects, detailed revenue information, lists of subsidiaries, shareholders and shareholdings, and lists of geographic overlaps in competing products or services. All information filed pursuant to the HSR Act is confidential and exempt from disclosure under the Freedom of Information Act, except as may be relevant to any administrative or judicial action or proceeding. *See* 15 U.S.C. § 18a(h).

The form may be downloaded from the FTC's website. The buyer must pay a filing fee at the time of the filing. The amount of the fee is based upon a graduated scale applied to the value of the voting securities or assets to be held as a result of the transaction. The filing fees are $45,000 for transactions with a value greater than $63.4 million but less than $126.9 million; $125,000 for transactions with a value of $126.9 million or greater but less than $634.4 million; and $280,000 for transactions with a value of $634.4 million or greater. These filing fees dollar thresholds are also adjusted annually, as discussed above. The parties may agree to allocate responsibility for the cost of the filing fee (*see* Section 12.1).

Failure to comply with any provisions of the HSR Act may cause the imposition of a civil penalty of up to $16,000 per day, subject to further annual increases. *See* 15 U.S.C. § 18a(g). Any device used to avoid the requirements of the HSR Act will be disregarded, and the HSR Act will be applied to the substance of the acquisition. *See* 16 C.F.R. § 801.90. There have been over 30 instances in which civil penalties have been imposed under the HSR Act, in most cases for consummating a transaction without making a filing. The penalties paid have ranged from a low of $122,000 (United States v. Lonrho, PLC, 1988-2 Trade Cas. 68,232 (D.D.C. July 18, 1988)) to a high of $5.6 million (United States v. Mahle GmbH, 1997-2 Trade Cas. 71,868 (D.D.C. June 24, 1997)). In 2001, the FTC imposed $4 million in civil penalties on a company for submitting an incomplete HSR filing in 1997. (Federal Trade Commission v. The Hearst Trust, The Hearst Corp. and First Data Bank, Inc., Civ. No. 1:01CV00734 (D.D.C. April 5, 2001)). *See also* FTC Press Release, "FTC Charges Hearst Trust with Acquiring Monopoly In Vital Drug Information Market" (available at http://www.ftc.gov/opa/2001/04/hearst.shtm) and FTC Press Release, "The Hearst Corporation Settles Charges of Filing Incomplete Pre-merger Report" (Oct. 11, 2001) (available at http://www.ftc.gov/opa/2001/10/hearst.shtm). Further, because the incomplete HSR filing inhibited the FTC's antitrust analysis and resulted in clearance being granted when it otherwise would not have been, the FTC required the same company to divest the acquired business and disgorge $19 million of profits obtained as a result of its unlawful acquisition. FTC Press Release, "Hearst Corp. To Disgorge $19 Million and Divest Business to Facts and Comparisons to Settle FTC Complaint" (Dec. 14, 2001) (available at http://www.ftc.gov/opa/2001/12/hearst.shtm). In most cases, the government and the parties negotiate an amount below the full daily penalty accrued.

Additionally, the FTC and the DOJ have indicated an intention to investigate the competitive implications of transactions that do not require HSR notification and a number of acquisitions that did not meet the thresholds requiring premerger notification under the HSR Act have become the subject of antitrust enforcement actions.

A leading treatise on the HSR Act is AXINN, FOGG, STOLL, & PRAGER, ACQUISITIONS UNDER THE HART-SCOTT-RODINO ANTITRUST IMPROVEMENTS ACT (1998). Summaries of certain FTC informal interpretations of the HSR Act and regulations have been collected in SECTION OF ANTITRUST LAW, AMERICAN BAR ASSOCIATION, PREMERGER NOTIFICATION PRACTICE MANUAL (1991). Other useful websites relating to HSR include those of the Antitrust Division of the Department of Justice (www.usdoj.gov/atr), the American Bar Association Section of Antitrust Law (www.abanet.org/antitrust/) and the American Antitrust Institute (www.antitrustinstitute.org). Many of these websites contain links to other relevant websites.

"**Indemnified Person**"—as defined in Section 11.8(a).

"**Indemnifying Person**"—as defined in Section 11.8(a).

"**Independent Accountants**"—as defined in Section 2.6(d).

"**Intellectual Property Assets**"—as defined in Section 3.22(a).

"**Interim Balance Sheet**"—as defined in Section 3.4.

"**Interim Balance Sheet Date**"—as defined in Section 3.4.

"**Interim Shareholders' Equity**"—as defined in Section 2.5(a).

"**Invention Disclosures**"—as defined in Section 3.22(c)(i).

"**IRS**"—the United States Internal Revenue Service or any successor agency, and, to the extent relevant, the United States Department of the Treasury.

"**Knowledge**"—

(a) **An individual will be deemed to have Knowledge of a particular fact or other matter if:**

    (i)   **that individual is actually aware of that fact or matter; or**

(ii)   **a prudent individual could be expected to discover or otherwise become aware of that fact or matter in the course of conducting a reasonably comprehensive investigation regarding the accuracy of any representation or warranty in this Agreement.**

(b) **A Person (other than an individual) will be deemed to have Knowledge of a particular fact or other matter if any individual who is serving, or who has at any time served, as a director, officer, partner, manager, executor, or trustee of that Person (or in any similar capacity) has, or at any time had, Knowledge of that fact or other matter (as set forth in clauses (a)(i) and (ii) above).**

COMMENT

The term "Knowledge" is often used with respect to the representations of Sellers. *See* "'Knowledge' Qualifications" in preliminary note to Article 3. Therefore, Buyer may seek to include a broad definition of "Knowledge." Buyer might exclude a definition in its entirety because some courts will not require actual belief to find that Sellers have "knowledge." Rather, it would be generally sufficient to demonstrate that Sellers are familiar with, and aware of, information that is contrary to the statement. *See, e.g.*, Lambert v. Weyerhaeuser Co. (*In re* Paragon Trade Brands, Inc.), 324 B.R. 797, 821–22 (Bankr. N.D. Ga. 2002), *rev'd on other grounds*, CA No. 1:05-CV-1144-JEC (N.D. Ga. Sept. 26, 2007).

If Buyer agrees to a knowledge qualification, the next issue is whose knowledge is relevant. Buyer will seek to have the group of people be as broad as possible to ensure that this group includes those who are the most knowledgeable about the specific representation being qualified and to include constructive and actual knowledge. Depending upon the circumstances, such as the size of the company, the number of employees, and the subject matter of the representations, Buyer may want to further expand the scope of this definition to include the knowledge of all employees of the Acquired Companies (including nonofficer employees).

The parties must also determine the level of investigation to be built into the definition of "Knowledge." Some acquisition agreements define knowledge as actual knowledge without any investigation requirement, while others (like the Model Agreement) define it to require some level of investigation by the applicable party.

Ultimately, the issue is allocation of risk—whether Buyer or Sellers should bear the risk of the unknown. Buyer will often argue that Sellers have more knowledge of, and are in a better position to investigate, the Acquired Companies' businesses and therefore should bear the risk. Also, the broader the group and the greater the required degree of investigation by the people in the group, the greater will be the risk retained by Sellers.

SELLERS' RESPONSE

Representations are not limited by "knowledge" unless expressly so stated. *See* Ivize of Milwaukee, LLC v. Compex Litigation Support LLC, 2009 WL 1111179 (Del. Ch. Apr. 27, 2009). Therefore, Sellers will attempt to use knowledge qualifications to limit many of their representations. There is no standard practice for determining which representations, if any, should be qualified by knowledge. Sellers often argue that that they should not bear the risk because they have made all information they have about the Acquired Companies available to Buyer, and Buyer is acquiring the Acquired Companies as an ongoing enterprise with the possibility of either unexpected gains or unexpected losses. Resolution of this issue usually involves much negotiation.

Sellers may also seek to narrow the definition of "Knowledge" to apply only to knowledge of a specific list of persons, rather than to a broad group as Buyer desires. At the least, Sellers may want to limit the persons to whom knowledge applies to current directors or officers and eliminate any references to former directors or officers.

"Knowledge of Sellers"—Knowledge of any Seller or any Acquired Company.

COMMENT

This term is used in the knowledge qualifications in Article 3 of the Model Agreement, so that they refer not only to the knowledge of the individual Sellers, but also to the knowledge of the Acquired Companies. By virtue of the final sentence of the definition of "Knowledge," each reference to the knowledge of the Acquired Companies encompasses the knowledge of all of their current and former directors and officers. *See* commentary to definition of "Knowledge" in Section 1.1.

"Leased Real Property"—as defined in Section 3.6(b).

"Legal Requirement"—any constitution, law, ordinance, principle of common law, code, rule, regulation, statute, act, treaty, or order of general applicability of any Governmental Body, including rules and regulations promulgated thereunder.

COMMENT

This definition is not limited to laws in effect on the date of the Model Agreement. As a result, when this definition is used in representations that contemplate future events or circumstances (such as the "compliance with laws" representations in Section 3.14), it includes laws (and amendments to existing laws) passed after the Model Agreement is signed.

"Loss"—any cost, loss, liability, obligation, claim, cause of action, damage, deficiency, expense (including costs of investigation and defense and reasonable

attorneys' fees and expenses), fine, penalty, judgment, award, assessment, or diminution of value.

COMMENT

The term "Loss" is used instead of the term "Damages" to avoid judicial construction that the term includes a requirement that the Loss arise from a breach of duty. *See* The Hartz Consumer Group, Inc. v. JWC Hartz Holdings, Inc., Index No. 600610/03 (N.Y. Sup. Ct. Oct. 27, 2005), *aff'd*, 33 A.D.3d 555 (N.Y. App. Div. 2006). The definition of "Loss" sets forth a broad range of matters that connote harm to a Person; limitations as to how a Loss may arise in a given context are left to the provisions that use the defined term.

See commentary to Section 11.2.

"Major Suppliers"—as defined in Section 3.26.

"Major Customers"—as defined in Section 3.26.

"Marks"—as defined in Section 3.22(a)(i).

"Material Adverse Change"—with respect to an Acquired Company, any event, change, development, or occurrence that, individually or together with any other event, change, development, or occurrence, is materially adverse to its business, condition (financial or otherwise), assets, results of operations, or prospects.

COMMENT

The term "Material Adverse Change" ("MAC") is often used interchangeably with the phrase "Material Adverse Effect" ("MAE") in practice, and the comments that follow apply to either term.

Buyers generally prefer a broad MAC provision such as the one used in the Model Agreement. A broadly drafted MAC provision is thought to provide buyers with greater protection, as it gives buyers greater flexibility to terminate or renegotiate an acquisition agreement in the event of unforeseen adverse events that are not described in the agreement. However, a general definition can give rise to a dispute based on the specific circumstances that evolve in a particular transaction and a drafter representing a buyer may find that a MAC definition tailored to the specific circumstances of the transaction provides better protection for buyer's interests than a general MAC definition.

Buyers should further be aware that courts have construed MAC provisions, including those drafted in generic terms, in favor of sellers. In *In re* IBP, Inc. S'holders Litig., 789 A.2d 14 (Del. Ch. 2001), the court indicated that an event must have serious negative implications for the target's overall earning potential in the long term to be considered a material adverse change. In Hexion Specialty Chemicals, Inc. v. Huntsman Corp., C.A. No. 3841-VCL, slip op. (Del. Ch. Sept. 29, 2008), the court stated that in order for a material adverse change to occur, there must be an adverse change "consequential to the company's long-term earnings power over a commercially reasonable period"—i.e., "years, not months"—such that if poor earnings are to result in a material adverse change, it "must be expected to persist significantly into the future." The *Huntsman* court noted that, absent clear contract language to the contrary, the burden of proving that a material adverse effect has occurred falls on the party invoking the clause. The Huntsman court observed that demonstrating a material adverse effect is a significantly high burden and that as of September 29, 2008 (the date the case was decided), Delaware courts have never found a material adverse effect to have occurred in the context of a merger agreement. Courts have further indicated that litigation initiated by a third party against one of the parties to the applicable agreement would not trigger a MAC provision if there has not been an adverse judgment that would have a material adverse effect on the business. *See* Frontier Oil Corp. v. Holly Corp., 2005 WL 1039027 (Del. Ch. 2005) (suggesting that the buyer would have to show that the seller was likely to incur substantial damages in a lawsuit brought against its subsidiary to invoke the MAC clause); *see also* S.C. Johnson & Sons, Inc. v. Dow Brands, Inc., 167 F. Supp. 2d 657 (D. Del. 2001) (holding that a third party's patent infringement suit against the buyer regarding a patent acquired in the merger did not constitute a material adverse change when there had been no adverse final judgment preventing the buyer from using the patent).

There is no clear, bright-line rule establishing what constitutes a material adverse change or effect. Case law suggests that an event that is likely to have only a small impact on a seller's overall earning potential will probably not be considered a material adverse change. At least one court found that a reported 50% decline in the target's earnings over two consecutive quarters might constitute a material adverse development. *See* Raskin v. Birmingham Steel Corp., C.A. No. 11365, 10 (Del. Ch. Dec. 4, 1990); *see also* Genesco, Inc. v. The Finish Line, Inc., No. 07-2137-99-II(III) (Tenn. Ch. Dec. 27, 2007) (suggesting that target's reported 54% decline in earnings in the first three quarters of 2007 would constitute a material adverse change, but for the application of an exception in the definition). Other cases, however, have determined otherwise. For example, the *Frontier* court held that a seller's expenses in defending litigation brought against its subsidiary would not trigger the MAC provision when the defense costs were estimated as approximately 50% of the seller's overall value.

Case law guidance indicates that the applicable MAC analysis is both quantitative and qualitative. As an example, the *IBP* court held that a reported 64% decline in the target's earnings in two consecutive quarters relative to the same period the previous year did not constitute a material adverse change. In the *IBP* case, the court based its decision on the cyclical nature of the target's business and the fact that the buyer knew of the target's volatile earnings from its review of the target's financial statements, stating that a MAC provision must be read in the larger context in which the parties are transacting. The *IBP* decision suggests that courts will consider whether the buyer could have foreseen the event that caused it to invoke the MAC provision in determining whether the buyer has met its burden. The *IBP* decision also indicates that the nature of the buyer may be significant, suggesting that a substantial decline in earnings in one quarter could constitute a material adverse change to a short-term buyer, but not to a long-term investor.

Given the lack of a bright-line rule for what constitutes a material adverse change, Buyer may want to include specific, easily calculable or discernable closing conditions. Examples might be that the revenues for a designated period shall not have declined by more than a specified dollar amount or that there shall not have been a loss of business of more than a specified dollar amount from any of the major customers listed.

SELLERS' RESPONSE

Sellers will want to minimize Buyer's ability to walk away from or renegotiate the agreement based on developments unfavorable to the Acquired Companies. In this regard, Sellers will try to limit the definition of MAC to restrict the events or occurrences that could trigger the MAC condition. For example, Sellers may seek to limit a MAC to "financial condition or results of operations" in order to require a more global harm to the Acquired Companies (rather than one measured potentially against particular aspects of the business or items on its financial statements). Sellers may also seek to limit the forward-looking nature of the condition (that is, taking into account anticipated changes in the Acquired Companies' business). For example, Sellers might ask that the word "prospects" be deleted from the definition, arguing that it is too vague and unfairly requires Sellers to predict the future.

One way Sellers may further narrow MAC provisions is by requesting exceptions ("carve-outs") to the MAC definition. A common carve-out protects against developments caused by general economic conditions or industry conditions. Sellers who are concerned about "external" conditions can benefit when carve-outs for general economic conditions or industry conditions are expressly included in the Model Agreement, as these carve-outs can protect Sellers where Buyer could otherwise have been justified in invoking a MAC provision. Courts may be reluctant to allow Sellers to claim protection from changes in the industry when the agreement does not include a carve-out for industry conditions. *See* Pittsburgh Coke & Chemical Co. v. Bollo, 421 F. Supp. 908, 930 (E.D.N.Y. 1976). Buyer will often require that a carve-out for industry conditions contain an exception when changes resulting from industry conditions have disproportionately affected the target relative to other companies in the industry. Sellers may seek to specify certain items that would not constitute a MAC even if they do occur. Other common carve-outs sought by Sellers to limit the scope of MAC provisions include exceptions for events or changes resulting from the transaction itself (although proof that the transaction caused the event or change is often an issue), including developments caused by the announcement of the transaction, or by the execution, delivery, and performance of the acquisition agreement. For example, Sellers might request that the following carve-outs be added to the end of the definition of Material Adverse Change:

; provided, however, that in no event shall any of the following constitute a Material Adverse Change: (i) any change resulting from conditions affecting the industry in which an Acquired Company operates or from changes in general business or economic conditions, provided such conditions do not have a disproportionate effect on the Acquired Company; (ii) any change resulting from the announcement or pendency of any of the transactions contemplated by this Agreement; or (iii) any change resulting from compliance by Sellers or an Acquired Company with the terms of, or the taking of any action contemplated or permitted by, this Agreement.

There is a tendency by some lawyers to read clause (iii) of the suggested carve-out as relating to specific actions contemplated or permitted by the Model Agreement—for example, if the Model Agreement calls for the sale of a particular asset, the buyer should not be able to argue that such a sale is a MAC. However, clause (iii) of the carve-out is potentially much broader for two related reasons. First, since the Model Agreement requires that the Company operate in the ordinary course of business between signing and Closing, clause (iii) would exclude from the MAC definition the consequences of any action taken in the ordinary course of business, no matter how ill-conceived the action or catastrophic the consequences. Second, since the Model Agreement could be construed as "permitting" any action not prohibited by the agreement, a similar argument could be made as to the consequences of any action that did not violate an express covenant.

Sellers may also seek to narrow the scope of a MAC provision by changing "an Acquired Company" to "the Acquired Companies" and including the language "taken as a whole" in the definition so that harm to the Acquired Companies' businesses as a whole is necessary to trigger the MAC clause. *See* commentary to Section 3.12.

See KLING & NUGENT § 11.04[9].

"Material Consents"—as defined in Section 8.4.

COMMENT

The commentary to Section 8.4 provides a further discussion of Material Consents.

"Net Names"—as defined in Section 3.22(a)(vii).

"Objection Notice"—as defined in Section 2.6(c).

"Occupational Safety and Health Law"—any Legal Requirement designed to promote safe and healthful working conditions and to reduce occupational safety and health hazards, including the Occupational Safety and Health Act, and any program, whether governmental or private (such as those promulgated or sponsored by industry associations and insurance companies), designed to promote safe and healthful working conditions.

COMMENT

The definition includes private programs because some industries have been more extensively regulated in this area by their insurers than by the government. Such requirements may be introduced into any legal proceeding to establish a known hazard and negligence by management, and hence are an independent source of liability for the Acquired Companies.

SELLERS' RESPONSE

Sellers will try to limit this open-ended definition to laws and regulations, with the latter often incorporating those industry programs and standards by reference.

"Order"—any order, injunction, judgment, decree, ruling, assessment, or arbitration award of any Governmental Body or arbitrator.

COMMENT

The definition of "Order" is broad.

SELLERS' RESPONSE

Seller may object that including the word "assessment" makes the definition far too broad.

"Ordinary Course of Business"—an action taken by a Person will be deemed to have been taken in the Ordinary Course of Business only if that action:

(a) is consistent in nature, scope, and magnitude with the past practices of such Person and is taken in the ordinary course of the normal, day-to-day operations of such Person; and

(b) does not require authorization by the board of directors of such Person (or by any Person or group of Persons exercising similar authority) and does not require any other separate or special authorization of any nature.

COMMENT

An important consideration in drafting this definition is the relevant standard for distinguishing between major and routine matters: the past practices of the Acquired Companies, common practice in the Acquired Companies' industries, or both. In one of the few cases that have interpreted the term "ordinary course of business" in the context of an acquisition, the jury was allowed to decide whether fees paid in connection with obtaining a construction loan, which were not reflected on the company's last balance sheet, were incurred in the ordinary course of business. *See* Medigroup, Inc. v. Schildknecht, 463 F.2d 525 (7th Cir. 1972).

In *Medigroup* the trial judge defined "ordinary course of business" as "that course of conduct that reasonably prudent men would use in conducting business affairs as they may occur from day to day," and instructed the jury that the past practices of the company being sold, not "the general conduct of business throughout the community," was the relevant standard.

The Model Agreement definition distinguishes between major and routine matters based on the historic practices of the Acquired Companies and on the need for board or other approval. As an alternative, parties may use the definition from the analysis of "ordinary course of business" in bankruptcy, which examines both the past practice of the debtor and the ordinary practice of the industry. *See, e.g., In re* Roth American, Inc., 975 F.2d 949 (3d Cir. 1992); *In re* Yurika Foods Corp., 888 F.2d 42 (6th Cir. 1989); *In re* Dant & Russell, Inc., 853 F.2d 700 (9th Cir. 1988); *In re* Hills Oil & Transfer, Inc., 143 B.R. 207 (Bankr. C.D. Ill. 1992); *In re* Johns-Manville Corp., 60 B.R. 612 (Bankr. S.D.N.Y. 1986). Therefore, parties may want to use the practices of the industry in its definition. No standard, however, can eliminate all ambiguity regarding the need for consultation between Buyer and Sellers. In doubtful cases, Sellers may want to consult with Buyer and obtain its approval.

Buyer should be aware that its knowledge of transactions that the Acquired Companies plan to enter into before the closing may expand the scope of this definition. The court in *Medigroup* stated:

> [i]f a buyer did not know the selling corporation had made arrangements to construct a large addition to its plant, "the ordinary course of business" might refer to such transactions as billing customers and purchasing supplies. But a buyer aware of expansion plans would intend "the ordinary course of business" to include whatever transactions are normally incurred in effectuating such plans.

Thus, Buyer should monitor its knowledge of Sellers' plans for operating the Acquired Companies before the Closing, and if Buyer knows about any plans to undertake projects or enter into transactions different from those occurring in the past practice of the Acquired Companies and other companies in the same industries, Buyer may want specifically to exclude such projects or transactions, and all related transactions, from the definition of "Ordinary Course of Business."

SELLERS' RESPONSE

Sellers may seek to limit the definition by omitting clause (b) as overly broad (i.e., because any action requires authorization by someone, clause (b) has the effect of removing all actions from "Ordinary Course of Business").

"Organizational Documents"—(a) the articles or certificate of incorporation and the bylaws of a corporation; (b) the certificate of formation and limited liability company agreement, operating agreement, or like agreement of a limited liability company; (c) the partnership agreement and any statement of partnership of a general partnership; (d) the limited partnership agreement and the certificate of limited partnership of a limited partnership; (e) any charter or agreement or similar document adopted or filed in connection with the creation, formation, or organization of a Person; and (f) any amendment to or restatement of any of the foregoing.

"Owned Real Property"—as defined in Section 3.6(a).

"Patents"—as defined in Section 3.22(a)(ii).

"Permitted Encumbrances"—(a) Encumbrances for Taxes and other governmental charges and assessments (except assessments for public improvements levied, pending, or deferred against Owned Real Property) that are not yet due and payable, (b) Encumbrances of carriers, warehousemen, mechanics, and materialmen and other like Encumbrances arising in "the Ordinary Course of Business" (provided lien statements have not been filed or such Encumbrances otherwise perfected), (c) statutory Encumbrances in favor of lessors arising in connection with any property leased to any Acquired Company, and (d) Encumbrances disclosed in the Financial Statements.

COMMENT

Buyer and Sellers will want to identify Permitted Encumbrances because Buyer will generally seek to take only those encumbrances on real and personal property of which it is aware. Because Permitted Encumbrances will likely be exceptions to representations as to the quality of title to specified assets, Buyer wants a limited definition. Buyer may also need to consider its own loan agreement covenants to ensure that any permitted encumbrances it assumes are also permitted in its loan agreement.

Many of the Permitted Encumbrances are encumbrances that Sellers cannot eliminate. For example, a mechanics lien is included because it is an inchoate lien established by statute for the purpose of securing payment for work performed and materials furnished in constructing a building or other structure and cannot be completely removed other than by passage of time. Other Permitted Encumbrances, such as Encumbrances reflected in the Financial Statements as set forth in clause (d) of the definition, are included because Buyer is generally willing to proceed with the stock purchase subject to certain encumbrances of which it is aware.

SELLERS' RESPONSE

Seller will negotiate to provide for a broad definition of Permitted Encumbrances.

"Person"—an individual, partnership, corporation, business trust, limited liability company, limited liability partnership, joint stock company, trust, unincorporated association, joint venture, other entity, or a Governmental Body.

"Plan"—as defined in Section 3.13.

"Proceeding"—any action, arbitration, mediation, audit, hearing, investigation, litigation, or suit (whether civil, criminal, administrative, judicial, or investigative) commenced, brought, conducted, or heard by or before, or otherwise involving, any Governmental Body or arbitrator.

"Promissory Notes"—as defined in Section 2.2(b).

"Purchase Price"—as defined in Section 2.2.

"Real Property"—as defined in Section 3.6(b).

"Record"—information that is inscribed on a tangible medium or that is stored in an electronic or other medium.

COMMENT

The Model Agreement definition of "Record" is derived from the definition of "Record" in Article 1 of the Uniform Commercial Code (UCC).

"Related Person"—

(a) With respect to an individual:

    (i)   each other member of such individual's Family;

    (ii)   any Person that is directly or indirectly controlled by such individual or any one or more members of such individual's Family;

    (iii) any Person in which members of such individual's Family hold (individually or in the aggregate) a Material Interest; and

    (iv) any Person with respect to which one or more members of such individual's Family serves as a director, officer, partner, manager, executor, or trustee (or in a similar capacity).

(b) With respect to a Person other than an individual:

(i)   any Person that directly or indirectly controls, is directly or indirectly controlled by, or is directly or indirectly under common control with, such specified Person;

(ii)   any Person that holds a Material Interest in such specified Person;

(iii)   each Person that serves as a director, officer, partner, manager, executor, or trustee of such specified Person (or in a similar capacity);

(iv)   any Person in which such specified Person holds a Material Interest; and

(v)   any Person with respect to which such specified Person serves as a general partner, manager, or a trustee (or in a similar capacity).

(c) For purposes of this definition:

(i)   "control" (including "controlling," "controlled by," and "under common control with") means the possession, direct or indirect, of the power to direct or cause the direction of the management and policies of a Person, whether through the ownership of voting securities, by contract, or otherwise, and shall be construed as such term is used in the rules promulgated under the Exchange Act;

(ii)   the "Family" of an individual includes (A) the individual, (B) the individual's spouse, (C) any other natural person who is related to the individual or the individual's spouse within the second degree, and (D) any other natural person who resides with such individual; and

(iii)   "Material Interest" means direct or indirect beneficial ownership (as defined in Rule 13d-3 under the Exchange Act) of voting securities or other voting interests representing at least 10% of the outstanding voting power of a Person or Equity Securities representing at least 10% of the outstanding equity interests in a Person.

COMMENT

The main purpose of the representations concerning relationships with related persons (*see* Section 3.24) is to identify "sweetheart" deals benefiting the Acquired Companies (which may disappear after the Closing), transactions with related persons on terms unfavorable to the Acquired Companies (which Buyer may not be able to terminate after the Closing), and possibly diverted corporate opportunities.

Thus, Buyer will want a broad definition of "Related Person." For individuals, the Model Agreement definition focuses on relationships with and arising from members of an individual's family; depending on the circumstances, a broader definition may be necessary to capture other relationships. In the definition of "Material Interest," the appropriate percentage of voting power or equity interests will depend upon the circumstances. The objective is to identify the level of equity interest in a related person that may confer a significant economic benefit; this may be an interest well short of control of the related person. Tax and accounting considerations may also be relevant to determining the appropriate percentage.

With respect to family relationships, a person related within the second degree refers to a person within two relationships to the family member. For example, a person's parents and children are within one degree. It follows that a person's brothers or sisters, grandchildren and grandparents are within two degrees. To determine the identification of family members within the second degree, however, the law of the applicable jurisdiction should be reviewed. As an alternative to using "second degree," the parties may want to specify the familial relationship to which the definition of Related Person applies or incorporate a statutory definition.

Some Buyers may want to broaden "spouse" to include domestic partners.

The definition of "Material Interest" includes beneficial interests in trusts.

SELLERS' RESPONSE

As an example of the breadth of this definition, an "other natural person who resides with such individual" could include an au pair and other household employees. Sellers will, therefore, want to narrow the definition.

"Release"—any release, spill, emission, leaking, pumping, pouring, dumping, emptying, injection, deposit, disposal, discharge, dispersal, leaching, or migration on or into the Environment, or into or out of any property.

COMMENT

This definition is a short version of the CERCLA definition found at 42 U.S.C. § 9601(22).

SELLERS' RESPONSE

Sellers may object to the inclusion of leaching because the Acquired Companies may not be able to observe or control such events. However, because federal law may impose liability for such activities on the Acquired Companies and because such matters are hard to evaluate, Buyer may resist modifications to this definition.

"Representative"—with respect to a particular Person, includes any director, officer, manager, employee, agent, consultant, advisor, accountant, financial advisor, or legal counsel of such Person.

"Securities Act"—the Securities Act of 1933.

"Seller(s)"—as defined in the first paragraph of this Agreement.

"Sellers' Closing Documents"—the releases specified in Section 2.4(a)(v), the Escrow Agreement, and each other document to be executed or delivered by any Seller at the Closing.

"Sellers' Releases"—as defined in Section 2.4.

"Sellers' Representative"—as defined in Section 12.5(a).

"Shares"—as defined in the Recitals of this Agreement.

"Software"—as defined in Section 3.22(a)(v).

"Subsidiary"—with respect to any Person (the "Owner"), any corporation or other Person of which securities or other interests having the power to elect a majority of that corporation's or other Person's board of directors or similar governing body, or otherwise having the power to direct the business and policies of that corporation or other Person (other than Equity Securities or other interests having such power only upon the happening of a contingency that has not occurred) are held by the Owner or one or more of its Subsidiaries; when used without reference to a particular Person, "Subsidiary" means a Subsidiary of the Company.

"Tax"—any income, gross receipts, license, payroll, employment, excise, severance, stamp, occupation, premium, property, environmental, windfall profit, customs, vehicle, airplane, boat, vessel or other title or registration, capital stock, franchise, employees' income withholding, foreign or domestic withholding, Social Security, unemployment, disability, real property, personal property, sales, use, transfer, value added, concession, alternative, add-on minimum and other tax, fee, assessment, levy, tariff, charge, or duty of any kind whatsoever and any interest, penalty, addition, or additional amount thereon imposed, assessed, or collected by or under the authority of any Governmental Body or payable under any tax-sharing agreement or any other Contract.

"Tax Return"—any return (including any information return), report, statement, schedule, notice, form, declaration, claim for refund, or other document or information filed with or submitted to, or required to be filed with or submitted to, any Governmental Body in connection with the determination, assessment, collection, or payment of any Tax or in connection with the administration, implementation, or enforcement of or compliance with any Legal Requirement relating to any Tax.

"Third Party"—a Person that is not an Acquired Company or a party to this Agreement.

"Third-Party Claim"—any claim against any Indemnified Person by a Third Party, whether or not involving a Proceeding.

"Threat of Release"—a reasonable possibility of a Release that could require action (including triggering notification or reporting under Environmental Law) in order to prevent or mitigate damage to the Environment that could result from such Release.

"Trade Secrets"—as defined in Section 3.22(a)(vi).

1.2. USAGE

(a) In this Agreement, unless expressly stated otherwise:

   (i)   the singular includes the plural and vice versa;

   (ii)   reference to any Person includes such Person's successors and assigns, if applicable, but only if such successors and assigns are permitted by this Agreement, and reference to a Person in a particular capacity excludes such Person in any other capacity;

   (iii) reference to a gender includes the other gender;

   (iv)   reference to any agreement, document, or instrument means such agreement, document, or instrument as amended or modified and in effect from time to time in accordance with its terms;

   (v)   reference to any Legal Requirement means that Legal Requirement as from time to time in effect, including any amendment, modification, codification, replacement, or reenactment of such Legal Requirement;

   (vi)   reference to any section or other provision of any Legal Requirement means that provision of such Legal Requirement as from time to time in effect, including any amendment, modification, codification, replacement, or reenactment of such section or other provision;

   (vii) "hereunder," "hereof," "hereto," and words of similar import refer to this Agreement as a whole and not to any particular Article, Section, or other provision of this Agreement;

(viii) **"including" (and with correlative meaning "include") means including without limiting the generality of any description preceding such term;**

(ix) **"or" is used in the inclusive sense of "and/or";**

(x) **"any" means "any and all";**

(xi) **with respect to the determination of any period of time, "from" means "from and including" and "to" means "to but excluding";**

(xii) **a reference to a document, instrument, or agreement also refers to all addenda, exhibits, or schedules thereto;**

(xiii) **a reference to a "copy" or "copies" of any document, instrument, or agreement means a copy or copies that are complete and correct; and**

(xiv) **a reference to a list, or any like compilation (whether in the Disclosure Letter or elsewhere), means that the item referred to is complete and correct.**

COMMENT

Clauses (iv), (v), (vi), (viii), (ix), (x), (xii), and (xiii) of Section 1.2(a) are designed to eliminate the need for repetitive and cumbersome use of (a) the phrase "as amended" after numerous references to statutes and rules, (b) the phrase "including, but not limited to," or "including, without limitation," in every instance in which a broad term is followed by a list of items encompassed by that term, (c) "and/or" where the alternative and conjunctive are intended, (d) a list of all possible attachments or agreements relating to each document referenced in the Model Agreement, and (e) the phrase "complete and correct" after references to copies of documents. The Model Business Corporation Act, Section 1.40(12), contains a similar definition: "'Includes' denotes a partial definition." In certain jurisdictions, however, the rule of *ejusdem generis* has been applied to construe the meaning of a broad phrase to include only matters that are of a similar nature to those specifically described. *See, e.g.*, Forward Indus., Inc. v. Rolm of N.Y. Corp., 506 N.Y.S.2d 453 (App. Div. 1985) (requiring the phrase "other cause beyond the control" to be limited to events of the same kind as those events specifically enumerated); *see also* Buono Sales, Inc. v. Chrysler Motors Corp., 363 F.2d 43 (3d Cir. 1966), *cert. denied*, 385 U.S. 971 (1966); Thaddeus Davids Co. v. Hoffman-LaRoche Chem. Works, 166 N.Y.S. 179 (App. Div. 1917). Clause (xi) provides a rule for counting days in determining a period of time. Practices vary in this regard, but practitioners generally find that some specific rule will be helpful in applying time periods under the agreement involved.

(b) Unless otherwise specified in this Agreement, all accounting terms used in this Agreement will be interpreted, and all accounting determinations under this Agreement will be made, in accordance with GAAP.

COMMENT

See commentary to the definition of "GAAP" in Section 1.1.

(c) This Agreement was negotiated by the parties with the benefit of legal representation, and any rule of construction or interpretation otherwise requiring this Agreement to be construed or interpreted against any party as having been drafted by it will not apply to any construction or interpretation of this Agreement.

COMMENT

Section 1.2(c) is meant to neutralize any presumption that ambiguities in contracts are to be construed against the drafter or the party who caused the uncertainty to exist. This presumption normally is applied only when other rules of construction fail to eliminate the uncertainty. In City of Hope Nat'l. Med. Center v. Genentech, 43 Cal. 4th 375 (2008), the court, in construing a jury instruction, recognized that a jury might find it more difficult or even impossible to determine which party caused the particular ambiguity to exist where a contract was arrived at by negotiation, but this does not make the underlying rule irrelevant or inappropriate.

(d) The headings contained in this Agreement are for convenience of reference only, shall not be deemed to be part of this Agreement, and shall not be referred to in connection with the construction or interpretation of this Agreement.

COMMENT

See STARK ch. 21.

2. Sale and Transfer of Shares; Closing

PRELIMINARY NOTE

Article 2 of the Model Agreement describes the form and economic terms of the transaction. It specifies that stock of the Company will be delivered and the purchase price for that stock, and includes a provision for a post-closing adjustment to the purchase price. It also provides for the closing of the transaction and specifies the closing deliveries.

Often in the purchase of a private company, the buyer or seller desires that the assets held by the target be adjusted in some respect. For example, the seller may have used the target to pursue businesses or interests outside of the primary business of the target, and the buyer (or seller) might propose that the assets and liabilities of such side businesses or interests be separated from the target before the closing. Conversely, assets used in the target's business (particularly real property) may be held individually by the seller, and the seller (or buyer) may require that those assets be contributed to the target or acquired or leased separately. In the case of the sale of a subsidiary, the intangible or other property used in the business might be owned elsewhere in the consolidated group. *See* Appendix A—The Purchase of a Subsidiary. An acquisition agreement may include provisions requiring certain alterations of the target prior to closing, but no such provision appears in the Model Agreement.

2.1 SHARES

Subject to the terms and conditions of this Agreement, and in reliance upon the representations, warranties, and covenants contained in this Agreement, at the Closing, Buyer shall purchase the Shares from Sellers, and Sellers shall sell and transfer the Shares to Buyer, free and clear of any Encumbrance.

COMMENT

Section 2.1 provides for the purchase and sale of the "Shares" from Sellers to Buyer at the Closing "free and clear of any Encumbrance." The Model Agreement anticipates closing at a later time, rather than a concurrent signing and closing.

Many of the words in Section 2.1 are arguably not required. For example, the clause "Subject to the terms and conditions of this Agreement, and in reliance upon the representations, warranties, and covenants contained in this Agreement . . ." is perhaps unnecessary because the Model Agreement should be read as a whole. Also, the phrase "free and clear of any Encumbrance" should be unnecessary given the identical representation contained in Section 3.3 and the general operation of Article 8 of the UCC discussed below. Nevertheless this type of language is customarily included in many stock purchase agreements without objection from sellers.

The actual documents to be delivered at the Closing to accomplish the purchase and sale of the Shares and the other Contemplated Transactions are listed in Sections 2.4(a) and (b), but the legal context for the transfer of the Shares is described here.

The Shares. The word "Shares" is defined in the Recitals as all issued and outstanding shares of capital stock of the Company. Purchase of the Shares would be sufficient to transfer the entire ownership of the Company, and allow Buyer to control its business and assets, including its wholly owned subsidiaries. Buyer would normally want to acquire all outstanding shares of an entity, rather than leaving a minority interest outstanding. However, in certain contexts such as an acquisition by a private equity firm, Buyer may want management to retain or acquire equity in the Company.

Options, Warrants, and Convertible Securities. The purchase of all the capital stock would not eliminate other outstanding securities of the target. For example, if the target has options or warrants outstanding, a buyer may propose that these be exercised or extinguished in some way in connection with the purchase. Many options and warrants contain provisions that allow them to be eliminated in connection with a sale or change in control of the issuer, usually upon the payment of some consideration; however, some options and warrants do not. Therefore, it is important to review the provisions of any options or warrants, and the provisions of any plans pursuant to which they may have been granted. If they do not contain such a provision, or the provision is inapplicable in the circumstances, then the buyer or seller must negotiate with the holders of the options or warrants for their surrender and those holders, in effect, become additional sellers, or the transaction may need to be restructured. Similar issues arise in connection with any outstanding debt securities of the target that are convertible into capital stock. If the target has outstanding options, warrants, or convertible securities, this Section would usually be modified to include the purchase of those interests, or their elimination would be added elsewhere as a condition of closing. The Fact Pattern indicates that the Company has no such securities, and Section 3.3(b) of the Model Agreement contains a representation that no such interests exist.

Multiple Classes of Stock. Section 2.2 contemplates that the purchase price will be allocated among Sellers as set forth in Schedule 2.2 (presumably pro rata). When a target has multiple classes of stock having different voting and economic preferences, however, it may be preferable to modify this Section to specify the allocation of the purchase price among the various classes (retaining Schedule 2.2 as a means of specifying the further allocation among individual holders within those classes). The Model Agreement does not contemplate multiple classes of stock.

Uncertificated Shares. Clause (i) of Section 2.4(a) contemplates that the Shares are represented by certificates that are delivered at the Closing. Use of shares in uncertificated form, the usual default standard for noncorporate entities such as limited liability companies, has become more common. The language of Section 2.1 is not affected by whether the Shares are in certificated or uncertificated form, although clause (i) of Section 2.4(a) would need to be modified if they are uncertificated. *See* commentary to Section 2.4.

Encumbrances. Section 3.3(a) contains a representation that the Shares are free of any Encumbrances. However, since Buyer will be deemed to have notice of any restrictions placed on a certificate representing the Company's securities, Buyer may insist that it review outstanding certificates. If any legends are discovered on the certificates, they must be addressed. Often shareholder or other agreements restrict the transfer of shares so either specific consent to the transfer or termination of the agreement prior to closing may be required. Outstanding stock is often pledged as security for a loan so Buyer will need to be assured that either the loan is paid off or, if it is not paid off, the consent of the lender is obtained.

Shares Held in a Representative Capacity. Some Sellers may be trusts or estates. While that should not be an obstacle to their participation in the sale, the trust instruments should be reviewed, and the procedures required by applicable law for an executor or other estate representative to sell stock should be understood. That circumstance will also usually lead to additional deliveries that are required at the Closing, such as copies of trust instruments or any necessary orders from the probate court. Buyer will want to confirm that any required approval cannot be challenged after the Closing. In addition, Article 3 might be modified to add appropriate representations as to the authority of any representative holders to sell their Shares and enter into the Model Agreement.

Application of the Uniform Commercial Code. Article 8 of the UCC, which has now been adopted in all 50 states, the District of Columbia, and two U.S. possessions, pertains to the issuance and transfer of securities. References to the sections below are to the UCC unless otherwise indicated.

The UCC covers the effect of delivery and indorsement (the UCC spelling of that word) of a certificate representing securities. It also deals separately with uncertificated securities. With respect to stock interests in corporations, the internal corporate law by which the corporation was created will govern the initial issuance of securities. The UCC will cover the transfer and required registration of transfer of those interests.

Article 8 pertains only to a security (Section 8-102(a)(15)), which is broadly defined. Section 8-103(a) provides that a share issued by a corporation, business trust, joint stock company, or similar entity is a security, while Section 3-103(c) provides that an interest in a partnership or limited liability company is not, except in certain circumstances. Therefore, to the extent the target may be a limited liability company or partnership, the discussion below may not apply.

The Model Agreement contains a governing law provision in Section 12.12. Section 1-301(c) provides ". . . an agreement by parties to a domestic transaction that any or all of their rights and obligations are to be determined by the law of this State or of another State is effective, whether or not the transaction bears a relation to the State designated . . . ." Under Article 8, the law of the jurisdiction where the target is organized governs most matters pertaining to the issuer. *See* § 8-110(a) and (d). That law would govern the validity of the Shares and the registration of transfer. Because the Company is not a party to the Model Agreement, the Company's obligations under the UCC would not seem to be affected by the governing law provision in Section 12.12 of the Model Agreement. Section 8-110(c) provides that the local law of the jurisdiction in which a security certificate is located at the time of delivery governs whether an "adverse claim" can be asserted against the person to whom the certificate is delivered. The Model Agreement contemplates that the Closing will occur at the offices of Buyer's attorneys, which may be in a different state than the governing law selected under Section 12.12 and the state of incorporation of the Company. Unless the person asserting an "adverse claim" happens to be a party to the Model Agreement, it would appear that the governing law selection in Section 12.12 of the Model Agreement would not vary the result of Section 8-110(c).

Section 1-302(a) provides, "Except as otherwise provided in subsection (b) or elsewhere in [the UCC], the effect of provisions of [the UCC] may be varied by agreement." Hence, it is permissible for the provisions of the Model Agreement to vary the default rules provided by Article 8 as between the parties. The Model Agreement does not explicitly say that it supersedes other rules, and Section 12.11 of the Model Agreement provides that the remedies are cumulative and not alternative. Lawyers might argue that, under traditional contract interpretation principles, the intention of the parties to provide some remedies with respect to the subject matter of Article 8 implies that the representations in Article 3 of the Model Agreement and associated remedies are intended to be exclusive. We have assumed that that is not the case in the discussion below.

Section 8-202 deals with the rights of a purchaser for value (as Buyer would be) without notice as against the Company. Because Buyer is purchasing all the outstanding Shares of the Company, additional rights gained by operation of Article 8 may only be theoretical. Buyer takes subject to the terms of the Shares stated on the certificate or incorporated by reference (Section 8-202(a)). If Buyer takes for value and without notice of a defect in validity, the security becomes valid in the hands of Buyer (Section 8-202(b)). A forged certificate, however, is a complete defense for the issuer, even against a purchaser for value without notice (Section 8-202(c)). A restriction on transfer imposed by the issuer is ineffective against a person without knowledge of the restriction unless it is noted conspicuously on the certificate (Section 8-204(1)). Of course, because of Buyer's due diligence activities, as contrasted by the usual purchase of securities in the open market, Buyer may be aware of some of the stated problems. Special rules apply to the overissue of a security (Section 8-210), but that means in excess of the amount the issuer has the corporate power to issue (as authorized by its charter), not the issuance of securities in excess of what has been authorized by the board of directors.

Article 2 of the Model Agreement contemplates the physical delivery of certificates representing the Shares accompanied by an indorsement under the UCC. Section 8-303 defines a protected purchaser as a purchaser who gives value (as Buyer would), does not have notice of any adverse claim, and obtains control of the security (which would happen at the Closing). Section 8-105(a) of the UCC defines notice broadly, including actual knowledge and if "the person is aware of facts sufficient to indicate that there is a significant probability that the adverse claim exists and deliberately avoids information that would establish the existence of the adverse claim." Buyer may in fact have notice of an adverse claim because of its due diligence activities. A protected purchaser acquires all rights in the security that the transferor had and takes free of any adverse claim. Section 8-102(a)(i) defines an adverse claim as a claim that a third party has a property interest in a security and that it is a violation of its rights for another person to hold the security. The current concept of a "property interest" is much more limited than in prior versions of Article 8. *See* the Official Comment to § 8-102(a)(1).

Under Section 8-108(a), a person transferring a certificated security to a purchaser for value warrants to the purchaser, among other things, the genuineness of the certificate, the lack of any adverse claim, the nonviolation of any restriction on transfer, and that the "transfer is otherwise effective and rightful." Buyer would be a purchaser for value. Arguably Buyer would have a claim against a Seller if this warranty were untrue.

Under Section 8-306, a guarantor of a signature of an indorser warrants certain things, including the genuineness of the signature and legal capacity. It is customary in some areas of the commercial world for issuers and transfer agents to demand the signature guaranty of a bank or securities broker on a stock certificate presented for registration of transfer, so that the issuer has a claim against the guarantor in the event of certain problems with the indorsement. While some acquisition agreements require a signature guaranty, the Model Agreement does not, on the basis that the protection afforded by a signature guaranty is not great enough to justify imposing on multiple Sellers the burden of obtaining signature guaranties, and further complicating the closing process. Some buyers have suggested that if there are many sellers, that is when a signature guaranty is most useful.

SELLERS' RESPONSE

The language of the Model Agreement is probably unobjectionable based upon the Fact Pattern, but Sellers will need to confirm that the language works in their particular circumstances. For example, Sellers agree to transfer the Shares "free and clear of any Encumbrance." If there are encumbrances, a determination would have to be made as to whether Buyer is to take title subject to those encumbrances or otherwise how they are to be removed. To the extent that there are multiple classes of stock or other outstanding securities other than the Shares, the parties will need to agree on how to deal with them.

2.2 PURCHASE PRICE

The purchase price for the Shares (the "Purchase Price") is _____ dollars ($_____), plus or minus the Adjustment Amount. At the Closing, Buyer shall deliver as payment on account of the Purchase Price: (a) _____ dollars ($_____) (the "Closing Payment"), which will be allocated among Sellers as set forth on Schedule 2.2, and which shall be paid by wire transfer to Sellers' Representative pursuant to written wire transfer instructions delivered to Buyer by Sellers' Representative at least three (3) Business Days prior to the Closing; (b) promissory notes executed by Buyer and payable to each Seller, in the principal amounts set forth on Schedule 2.2 (collectively, the "Promissory Notes"), in the form of Exhibit 2.2(b); and (c) _____ dollars ($_____) paid by wire transfer to the Escrow Agent pursuant to the Escrow Agreement (the "Escrow Funds"). The Adjustment Amount shall be paid by Sellers or Buyer, as the case may be, in accordance with Section 2.5.

COMMENT

Amount and Form of Payment. The amount a buyer is willing to pay for a target depends on numerous factors, including the target's past, current and expected performance, industry, stage of development, intellectual property, financial condition, and the efficiencies or "synergies" that the buyer can achieve by combining the buyer's operations with those of the target, as well as industry trends and market conditions. A discussion of modern valuation theories in acquisition transactions is found in Thompson, *A Lawyer's Guide to Modern Valuation Techniques in Mergers and Acquisitions*, 21 J. CORP. L. 457 (Spring 1996). *See also* RISIUS, BUSINESS VALUATION: A PRIMER FOR THE LEGAL PROFESSIONAL (2007); DICKIE, FINANCIAL STATEMENT ANALYSIS AND BUSINESS VALUATION FOR THE PRACTICAL LAWYER (1998); M&A PROCESS 124–33.

The form of payment negotiated by the parties also depends on various factors, including the buyer's cash position, the tax consequences to the parties, and perhaps the buyer's desire for setoff rights against deferred payments (discussed in "Promissory Notes" in the commentary below). The method of payment may include some combination of cash, debt, and stock and may also have a contingent component based on the target's future performance. For example, if the buyer does not have sufficient cash or wants to reduce its initial cash outlay, the buyer could require that a portion of the purchase price be paid by a note. This method of payment, together with an escrow arrangement for indemnification claims (and often for payment of the adjustment amount or "true-up"), is reflected in Section 2.2. If the method of payment includes a debt component, issues such as security, subordination, and supporting covenants must be negotiated. Similarly, if the method of payment includes a stock component, issues such as valuation, registration rights, restrictions on resale, and other covenants will have to be negotiated. *See* Appendix B—Receipt of Stock of a Public Company as Purchase Consideration; M&A PROCESS 155–57.

Earnouts. If the buyer and the seller cannot agree on the value of the target, they may make a portion of the purchase price contingent on the target's performance post-acquisition. The contingent portion of the purchase price (often called an "earnout") is commonly based on the target's earnings (or other agreed-upon criterion, such as sales) over a specified period of time after the closing. Although an earnout may bridge a gap between the buyer's and the seller's views of the value of the target, constructing an earnout raises many issues, including how earnings will be determined, the formula for calculating the payment amount and how that amount will be paid (cash or stock), how the earnout will be taxed, how the target will be operated and who will have the authority to make major decisions, and the effect of a sale of the buyer or the target during the earnout period. Resolving these issues may be more difficult than agreeing on a fixed purchase price and typically requires extensive negotiation. While the Model Agreement does not contemplate an earnout, a form of Earnout Agreement is attached as Ancillary Document D with related commentary. If there were an earnout, the first sentence in Section 2.2 might state: "The consideration for the Shares (the 'Purchase Price') is _____ dollars ($_____), plus or minus the Adjustment Amount plus the Earnout Amount, if any." For more information about earnouts in general, *see* M&A PROCESS 147–151; KLING & NUGENT §17.03; Fuerst, San Filippo IV & Ornstein, *Earn-Outs; Bridge the Gap, With Caution*, 12 M&A L. Rep. 581 (BNA June 15, 2009); Gunderson, *Seller Beware: In an Earnout, the Buyer Has Doubts, the Seller Has Hopes,* 14 BUS. LAW TODAY 49 (March/April 2005); SECTION OF BUSINESS LAW, EARNOUTS IN BUSINESS ACQUISITIONS—A PRACTICAL SOLUTION OR A TRAP FOR THE UNWARY? (2005).

Purchase Price Adjustment. The Model Agreement assumes that the parties have agreed to a fixed price, subject only to an adjustment based on changes in the Company's consolidated shareholders' equity between the date of the Interim Balance Sheet and the Closing Date (Sections 2.5 and 2.6). Other methods are possible and sometimes negotiated. For example, MAPA includes an adjustment based on working capital rather than shareholders' equity. *See* commentary and sellers' response to Section 2.5.

Manner of Payment. The Model Agreement provides for payment to be made to Sellers' Representative, rather than to each individual Seller. This provision is for Buyer's convenience, to avoid the challenge of coordinating multiple wire transfers at the Closing. Similarly, the Model Agreement provides in Section 2.4(b) that the Promissory Notes are to be delivered to Sellers' Representative, rather than to each individual Seller. These provisions place on Sellers' Representative the responsibility of coordinating delivery to each individual Seller of his or her Promissory Note and share of the cash purchase price. *See* Section 12.5 and commentary with respect to Sellers' Representative.

The Model Agreement provides for payment by wire transfer as is customary in most substantial transactions. In some circumstances, the parties may choose to have payment made by bank cashier's or certified check for various reasons, including the size of the transaction. While all three forms of payment are commonly used and should be acceptable to Sellers, the parties should be aware of certain differences in Buyer's ability to stop payment and in the availability of the funds for use by Sellers.

A certified check is a check of the drawer that contains the drawee bank's certification on its face. As a result of the bank's certification, the drawee bank's liability is substituted for that of the drawer. A cashier's check is a check drawn by a bank on itself. Thus, a cashier's check is the primary promissory obligation of the drawee bank. Although there have been a few cases involving banks that stopped payment on certified and cashier's checks at the request of customers, courts generally have held that the customer has no right to stop payment. *See* CLARK, THE LAW OF BANK DEPOSITS, COLLECTIONS AND CREDIT CARDS ¶ 3.06 (Rev. Ed. 1999) ("CLARK").

Except for a wire transfer of federal funds, there is no difference among a cashier's check, a certified check, and a wire transfer in terms of the availability of funds. For cashier's checks, certified checks, and wire transfer of clearinghouse funds, a bank into which such checks are deposited or into which such wire transfers are sent is required to make the funds available to the payee or beneficiary no later than the business day following the deposit or receipt of the transfer. For wire transfers of federal funds, a bank is required to make the funds available immediately on the date of receipt of the transfer. Therefore, if Sellers want immediate use of the funds, the acquisition agreement should specify that payment will be made by a wire transfer of immediately available funds. *See* CLARK ¶¶ 7.01–.25. If Buyer is a foreign firm, Sellers may want to specify that payments will made in U.S. dollars. It is often useful, where multiple wire transfers are involved, for the parties to agree to a detailed funds flow schedule prior to Closing.

Promissory Notes. Exhibit 2.2(b) to the Model Agreement contains the form of Buyer's nonnegotiable Promissory Notes to be delivered to Sellers. The Promissory Notes bear interest, are subject to prepayment without penalty, and may be accelerated following the occurrence of an event of default.

The Promissory Notes are neither subordinated to the rights of other creditors of Buyer nor secured by a security interest in favor of Sellers. Whether such features are included depends on the provisions of Buyer's credit agreements and other factors. For example, a credit agreement may limit Buyer's ability to incur debt or grant liens, may contain negative or affirmative covenants restricting the type of debt Buyer may incur, and may require that Buyer's obligation to Sellers be subordinate to its obligation to senior lenders. When a promissory note is subordinated with regard to payment, the parties must specify the degree of subordination. A full subordination prohibits any payment of interest or principal until all senior debt is paid in full. Alternatively, the parties may agree to prohibit subordinated payments only when an event of default has occurred with respect to the senior debt, or in the event of a bankruptcy or reorganization proceeding involving Buyer, and may limit the period during which payments are blocked.

A seller who is in a strong bargaining position may request collateral to secure a buyer's note, especially if the buyer is weak financially, and the protection of a credit agreement containing both affirmative and negative covenants. The collateral could be a pledge of all or a portion of the shares of the target or assets of the target or buyer. The details of any understanding are usually included in the acquisition agreement, and the forms of documents are often attached as exhibits. Sellers might also request a third-party guaranty or other credit enhancement device.

To provide additional protection with respect to claims against Sellers, the Promissory Notes are subject to setoff rights by Buyer and are nonnegotiable to protect its setoff rights. *See* commentary to Section 11.7.

Escrow Agreement. Buyers often seek to have a fund available from which they can satisfy claims against sellers following the closing, particularly where recovery involves more than one person. One technique is to retain a portion of the purchase price in an escrow account for a specified period following the closing. This provides a source of recovery that is not dependent upon the solvency of the seller or the buyer's ability to find the seller (or the seller's assets) for purposes of commencing litigation or executing any judgment that may be obtained.

The Model Agreement provides that a portion of the purchase price will be paid to the Escrow Agent pursuant to the Escrow Agreement (Exhibit 2.4(a)(vii)), which provides a fund to assist Buyer in realizing on any successful indemnification claims that it may have under the Model Agreement. *See* commentary to Article 11 and to Exhibit 2.4(a) (vii). An escrow agreement could also be used to facilitate payment of the purchase price adjustment amount. Where, as in this case, part of the purchase price is being paid by a promissory note, consideration should be given to whether a buyer needs both an escrow and a right of setoff on the note. *See* commentary to Section 11.7.

Buyer's proposal of an escrow will, if accepted by Sellers, often lead to a proposal by Sellers that recourse to the funds held in escrow be Buyer's exclusive post-closing remedy and that the liability of Sellers therefore be capped at the amount held in escrow. Another possible response to Buyer's request for an escrow could be Sellers' request for some form of its own security against a Buyer default. In addition, Buyer must recognize that the existence of an escrow fund does not mean that those funds will be immediately available to Buyer in the event of a claim. Institutional escrow agents are generally unwilling to submit themselves to any risk resulting from the conflicting demands by buyers and sellers, even if the escrow agreement would expressly permit a release of escrowed funds prior to the conclusive determination of any claim. Accordingly, the typical institutional escrow agreement provides that the escrow agent may freeze and retain the funds at issue until conflicting demands are resolved by agreement of the parties or a nonappealable court order. If Buyer wishes to ensure that it will have access to funds pending resolution of a disputed claim, it should consider retaining a portion of the purchase price or requiring that the indemnification and other monetary obligations of Sellers be secured by a letter of credit that may be drawn in the event of a claim.

In some circumstances, Sellers' interests in an escrow fund may constitute a security for purposes of federal and state securities laws. *See* KLING & NUGENT § 16.04.

Not all acquisitions, particularly those between corporations, provide for an escrow.

Factors affecting the size of an escrow are the creditworthiness of the seller, the likelihood that a claim will be made, and the exclusiveness of the escrow (that is, whether claims against sellers are permitted in the event that the escrow fund is depleted).

The length of the escrow period also varies. Some negotiate for a decreasing level of the escrow on an annual basis, with the excess being released to the seller. If the escrow secures both the indemnification obligation and the purchase price adjustment, it is more likely to have early release provisions.

Allocation. Acquisition agreements often specify the allocation of the purchase price between the shares being purchased and the consideration for any other agreements, such as noncompetition covenants, or they specifically provide that none of the consideration is allocated to the noncompetition covenants. The Model Agreement does not do so and therefore leaves open the question of how it will be treated for tax purposes. *See* Wood, *Noncompete vs. Stock Payments: Evergreen Issue*, 15 M&A TAX REP. No. 9 (April 2007); commentary to Section 7.2.

Installment Sale Treatment. Sellers in most circumstances will want to be assured that the deferred payments (those they do not receive at the closing) will be subject to installment sale treatment so that, to the extent there is taxable gain, that gain will only be taxed when the cash is actually received. The Promissory Notes, the Adjustment Amount, the Escrow Funds, and any earnout would represent such deferred payments. Not all promissory notes allow installment sale treatment. *See* Gerson and Alioto, *The Taxation of Escrow Funds*, 15 M&A TAX REP. No. 12 (July 2007); 16 M&A TAX REP. No. 1 (Aug. 2007).

Cash-Free, Debt-Free. Sometimes the letter of intent, particularly if a private equity fund is the buyer, will specify that the shares are to be purchased on a "cash-free, debt-free" basis. That should not be taken literally, but means that the purchase price will be adjusted for debt and cash on the books or that debt must be paid on Closing. It often means that the buyer must use its cash to pay off indebtedness. The Model Agreement does not contain such a provision.

Subchapter S. Subchapter S corporations often are accorded special treatment in acquisitions. *See* commentary to Section 3.11.

SELLERS' RESPONSE

Prior to the preparation of an acquisition agreement, the parties may have agreed to a purchase price and its method of payment in some nonbinding manner, such as a letter of intent. Sometimes, however, the method of payment is not discussed, and the seller is surprised to find upon the delivery of the first draft of the acquisition agreement a provision for promissory notes as part of the consideration, and a previously unmentioned escrow for part of the cash purchase price. The terms of the promissory notes may also be a surprise, offering deep subordination rather than a senior credit.

Sellers usually prefer that the purchase price be paid in all cash at the closing; however, escrows and promissory notes are frequently proposed by buyers, and it is common for the acquisition agreement to contain provisions for either an escrow, or promissory notes with setoff rights, to protect the buyer's ability to collect post-closing indemnification payments. It is less common for an acquisition agreement to contain both. When choosing between an escrow and promissory note, a seller generally would choose an escrow, because an escrow removes the deferred purchase price from the buyer's control, and into the hands of the escrow agent, which gives the buyer greater incentive to settle any indemnification claims that the sellers dispute. Therefore, in the case where, as in the Model Agreement, Buyer requests both an escrow and promissory notes, Sellers might assert that the promissory notes are unnecessary, because Buyer is adequately protected by the Escrow Agreement. Where sellers agree to an escrow, they may insist that the amount of the escrow is also the cap on their indemnification obligation.

Sellers might ask that the wire transfer be of "immediately available funds." If Buyer had proposed payment by check, Sellers might negotiate for a wire transfer.

Sometimes an escrow agreement also provides that the escrow funds can be used to pay any post-closing purchase price adjustment that the seller may owe. That will usually benefit the seller because the purchase price adjustment is usually paid before any post-closing indemnification claims are made. Therefore, if a portion of the escrow fund is paid out to satisfy seller's purchase price adjustment payment, the buyer is left with a reduced escrow amount to secure the seller's indemnification obligations. The Escrow Agreement under the Model Agreement secures only indemnification claims under Article 11 of the Model Agreement. Thus, Sellers might suggest that the Escrow Agreement be revised to allow the Escrow Funds to be used to pay any post-closing purchase price adjustment that the Sellers may owe under Sections 2.5 and 2.6. On the other hand, the Sellers might refrain from making that suggestion to avoid the Buyer's likely counterproposal, which would be to agree to Sellers' suggestion only if the amount of the Escrow Funds is increased.

If an earnout has been proposed, Sellers will want to understand the methodology and require that the target will be operated in a manner to best assure that the earnout is paid.

2.3   CLOSING

Subject to Article 10, the purchase and sale (the "Closing") provided for in this Agreement will take place at the offices of [Insert name of Buyer's attorneys] at [Insert address] commencing at 10:00 a.m. (local time) on _____ or at such other date and time as Buyer and Sellers' Representative may otherwise agree, provided that on or prior to that date all conditions set forth in Articles 8 and 9 have been satisfied or waived. If all conditions set forth in Articles 8 and 9 are not satisfied or waived by _____, subject to Article 10, the Closing will take place upon the earlier of (a) five (5) Business Days following notice given by Buyer stating that all conditions set forth in Articles 8 and 9 have been satisfied or waived (other than conditions to be satisfied on the Closing Date), and (b) the End Date. The Closing will be deemed to be effective as of the close of business on the Closing Date [the Business Day prior to the Closing Date] for tax and accounting purposes.

COMMENT

Depending on the nature of the acquisition and the desire of the parties to complete the acquisition within a certain time frame, there are many ways to set the date of the closing. Section 2.3 of the Model Agreement provides that the Closing will take place on a specific date, subject to the closing conditions having been met or waived, unless Buyer and Sellers' Representative agree otherwise. If the Closing does not occur by the specified date because the conditions are not satisfied, the Closing Date may be set after all the closing conditions have been met or waived, subject to the termination rights provided in Article 10. *See* M&A PROCESS ch. 14.

By specifying a date in Section 2.3, the parties have fixed the earliest date that the Closing is required to occur. Use of a specified date provides certainty and motivation. This may be necessary in certain circumstances, such as when Buyer wants to complete its due diligence investigation or must obtain financing, although these circumstances could also be addressed, although with very different substantive consequences, by making these types of events conditions to closing and requiring that the closing occur a certain number of days after their satisfaction. A party may wish to specify a particular closing date if it suspects that the other party may be motivated to delay the closing. For example, a buyer that uses a calendar year may not want to close in mid-December to avoid unnecessary costs, such as preparation of a short-period tax return or interim financial statements for an unusual period of time. A seller wishing to close as soon as possible and sensing the buyer's possible desire to delay would want to include an early closing date. The reverse might be true when a seller desires to close a transaction after the end of its current tax year to defer the tax consequences of the transaction. Although the specific date chosen often takes into account the delays anticipated to satisfy the condition to closing which the parties expect will take the longest amount of time, the setting of a fixed earliest date for closing is to deal with matters that are not conditions. Conditions that typically take a relatively long time to satisfy include termination of the waiting period under the HSR Act (if applicable), receipt of regulatory approvals (when the buyer or target is in a regulated industry), and receipt of all (or certain specified) other third-party consents (e.g., those required under change-of-control provisions in various agreements). When there is doubt about which condition will take the longest time to satisfy, the parties might agree not to set a specific date and agree to close within a stipulated period after the satisfaction of the last condition or certain specified conditions. The parties should keep in mind, however, that the satisfaction of some conditions may be influenced by a party, even though the acquisition agreement contains provisions (such as Sections 5.7 and 6.3) requiring both parties to use their best efforts to satisfy all conditions to the closing of the transaction.

Section 2.3 does not provide that failure to consummate the acquisition at the time and place specified gives either party an independent right to terminate the Model Agreement. Rather, the Model Agreement provides in Section 10.1 that either party may terminate the agreement if the Closing has not taken place by a specified "drop-dead" date. The inclusion of a drop-dead date assures both parties that they will not be bound by the Model Agreement (and, in particular, by pre-closing covenants) for an unreasonable time. This date could be placed in the closing section. It is typically placed in the termination provision, however, to keep all termination rights in a single section. *See* commentary to Section 10.1.

There are also tax, accounting, and practical considerations in scheduling the closing. The parties should be aware of time constraints when transferring funds by wire. The time of the closing should be set with that in mind and pre-closing activities need to be carefully coordinated so that the closing occurs on time. For example, if a buyer is paying the purchase price in funds that are not immediately available (*see* the commentary to Section 2.2), seller will not want to close on a Friday (especially the Friday before a three-day weekend) because the seller would not have use of the funds over the weekend. If the buyer is paying the purchase price by a wire transfer of immediately available funds, the seller should know the time by which its bank must receive the funds in order to invest the funds overnight. The amount the seller could lose through not having use of the funds for a few days depends on the purchase price, but may be substantial. In some cases, accounting and computer system issues may require that the closing occur on the last business day of a month or other fiscal period. Further, if a physical inventory will be performed shortly before closing, the parties will want to schedule the closing on a day and at a time to permit this physical inventory with minimal disruption of the business. Often it is necessary to close at the end of an accounting period to assure that the books can be closed.

Section 2.3 contemplates the place of Closing will be the offices of Buyer's attorneys. Although Buyer's attorneys often insert in the first draft their offices as a place of closing, the actual place is usually negotiable. For example, if Buyer is obtaining financing for the transaction, a logical place may be where the closing of the financing is to take place, especially if the financing transaction is more complicated than the stock purchase, which can be relatively simple insofar as closing documents are concerned. Also, if many Sellers reside in a single geographical location differing from the location of Buyer's attorneys, the office of Sellers' attorneys might be a better choice for the Closing. Furthermore, despite the designation of a place for closing, many closings are being held remotely, with closing documents being exchanged electronically or by telecopier.

The last sentence of Section 2.3 specifies when the Closing is effective for tax and accounting purposes—at the close of business on the Closing Date. Alternatively, the close of business on the preceding Business Day may be selected. The same alternative should be selected in Section 2.6. Absent language specifying an effective time, the Closing would normally be effective when payment for the Shares is made, at the consummation of the Closing. A noon closing would be difficult to effectuate for accounting purposes, so the parties might deem the transaction effective at the close of business on that day. In other circumstances the parties might desire an early morning closing and to make it effective as of the close of business on the prior day. The addition of the words "for tax and accounting purposes" is to avoid unintended consequences such as an early shifting to the Buyer of the risk of loss.

SELLERS' RESPONSE

In their preliminary negotiations, the parties may not have contemplated a specific closing date. At best there may be vague references to an anticipated closing date. Sellers will need to determine whether the specificity of the Model Agreement and the mechanism that effectively allows Buyer to fix a closing date if the original date is not met, will be acceptable. Other alternative means of fixing the closing date might be considered, such as closing within a specified number of days after a major contingency has been satisfied. MAPA uses such an alternative means of fixing the closing date.

2.4 CLOSING OBLIGATIONS

At the Closing:

(a) Sellers shall deliver to Buyer:

    (i)   certificates representing the Shares, endorsed in blank (or accompanied by stock powers executed in blank) and otherwise in proper form for transfer;

(ii)   the Organizational Documents of each Acquired Company filed with any Governmental Body in connection with its organization, duly certified as of a recent date by the Secretary of State or other appropriate authority of the jurisdiction of its incorporation or organization, together with a certificate dated as of the Closing Date from the Secretary of each Acquired Company to the effect that no amendments to such Organizational Documents have been filed since the date referred to above;

(iii)   the Organizational Documents of each Acquired Company not filed with a Governmental Body in connection with its organization, certified as of the Closing Date by the Secretary of each Acquired Company;

(iv)   certificates dated as of a date not more than five (5) days prior to the Closing Date as to the good standing of each Acquired Company [and payment of applicable state Taxes], issued by the appropriate Governmental Body of the jurisdiction of the Acquired Company's organization and each jurisdiction in which the Acquired Company is licensed or qualified to do business as a foreign entity as specified in Part 3.1 of the Disclosure Letter;

(v)   releases in the form of Exhibit 2.4(a)(v) executed by Sellers;

(vi)   an employment agreement in the form of Exhibit 2.4(a)(vi), executed by _____ and the Company;

(vii)   an escrow agreement in the form of Exhibit 2.4(a)(vii), executed by Sellers (the "Escrow Agreement"); and

(viii) the certificate referred to in Section 8.3.

(b) Buyer shall deliver to Sellers' Representative (or in the case of the Escrow Funds, to the Escrow Agent):

(i)   the Closing Payment;

(ii)   the Promissory Notes;

(iii)   the Escrow Funds;

(iv)   the Escrow Agreement, executed by Buyer and the Escrow Agent; and

(v)   the certificate referred to in Section 9.3.

COMMENT

Acquisition agreements are not self-effectuating. That is, the actual transfer of an ownership interest takes place by virtue of the delivery of one or more additional documents. The usual reason for that is the lapse of time between the signing of an acquisition agreement and the actual transfer of an ownership interest brought about by the need to arrange financing, perform due diligence, obtain regulatory approvals, and deal with a host of other matters. But even when a transaction is closing concurrently with the execution and delivery of the acquisition agreement, the actual transfer is normally accomplished pursuant to the delivery of various documents.

Many acquisition agreements list the documents to be exchanged at the closing so that the parties have a checklist. The Model Agreement does not separately list those documents because the principal documents to be delivered at the closing are identified in Articles 2, 8, and 9. In general, documents within the power of Sellers to deliver are contained in Section 2.4(a) (similarly with respect to Buyer's deliverables in Section 2.4(b)), while documents depending upon third-party action or other matters beyond the control of the parties are included as conditions to closing in Articles 8 and 9.

The parties should be aware of the distinction between deliveries to be treated as covenants, the breach of which will afford the nonbreaching party a right to damages, and deliveries to be treated as conditions, the breach of which will give the nonbreaching party the right to terminate the acquisition agreement (i.e., a "walk right"), but not a right to damages. In Section 2.4, the parties covenant to make certain deliveries. Therefore, if Sellers fail to deliver the certificates for the Shares or Buyer fails to make the specified payments, the nonbreaching party can pursue its remedies. In contrast, if Sellers fail to deliver the legal opinion or consents (or other documents reasonably requested by Buyer) contemplated by Article 8, Buyer would have the right to terminate the Model Agreement, but it would not have the right to damages unless Sellers breached their covenant in Section 5.7 to use their best efforts to obtain these documents. If, however, Sellers had covenanted in Section 2.4 to deliver a particular consent (because, for example, a party related to Sellers was the landlord under a lease with one of the Acquired Companies that required a consent), Sellers' failure to deliver that consent (regardless of the efforts used) would give Buyer a right to damages as well as the right to terminate. *See* discussion regarding Section 2.4(a)(iv) below under Sellers' response, preliminary note to Article 8 and Sellers' response to Section 8.6.

An item normally contemplated by an acquisition agreement is a so-called "bring down" certificate. The certificate confirms a condition to closing that the representations and warranties be correct as though made on the date of closing. *See* commentary to Sections 8.1 and 8.3.

Shares. The Shares are crucial to the transaction and the delivery of certificates is required by Section 2.4(a)(i). If the Shares are in uncertificated form, instruments of transfer would be delivered as well as instructions to the Company and any other requisites for registration of the transfer required by the bylaws of the Company.

Organizational Documents and Good Standing Certificates. The documents required by clause (ii) are within the control of Sellers in that secretaries of state routinely issue these documents, given sufficient time. The good standing and tax payment certificates in clause (iv) are somewhat more problematic, but since Sellers have represented that the Acquired Companies are in good standing and that all Taxes have been paid, those certificates should be readily obtainable. The parties should be cognizant, however, that in some states tax clearance certificates are simply not given and that other states require a long lead time.

Releases. A release is to be delivered by each Seller, which also covers Related Persons. One of the objectives in obtaining the releases is to effect a clean break from the prior owners. In this regard, one might consider the interrelationship between the releases and certain of the representations in the Model Agreement, such as the absence of claims by Related Persons (including severance arrangements), and the existence or absence of any claims for indemnification under the Acquired Companies' Organizational Documents or by contract. By reviewing the representations, the Disclosure Letter, and the scope of the form of release, Buyer should be in a better position to assess the potential for post-closing liability arising from pre-closing events, thereby evaluating some of the risk of the transaction. The releases to be signed by Sellers (Exhibit 2.4(a)(v)) may sometimes carry unexpected consequences. Buyers have an expectation that once the purchase price is paid, the sellers will not attempt to benefit themselves by making additional claims against the target. On the other hand, a general release will also release rights to which the sellers may have a legitimate claim. For example, sellers normally expect to be protected against director and officer liability, particularly if D&O insurance is in place. Signing the release might in fact release that protection. *See* commentary to Exhibit 2.4(a)(v)—Release.

Employment Agreement. The employment agreement required by Section 2.4(a)(vi) is to be signed by a Seller, not a third party such as an employee who is not a Seller. *See* Appendix C—Considerations Regarding Employment Agreements in Connection With Sale of Stock. Although the Model Agreement contemplates that any employment agreements with key employees of the Company would be delivered pursuant to Section 8.6(c), as a condition of closing rather than a required delivery, buyers will sometimes include deliveries of important items, such as employment agreements from key employees who are not sellers, in the required delivery section of the acquisition agreement.

Escrow Agreement. The Escrow Agreement is discussed in the commentary to Section 2.2 and a form is provided in Exhibit 2.4(a)(vii). The Model Agreement requires Buyer to deliver the Escrow Agent's signature because the Escrow Agent is normally selected by Buyer.

Stamp Taxes. Some states impose a tax upon the sale of stock, including New York. The tax is paid by buying stamps, which must be affixed to the certificate representing the stock. While the tax is rebateable, the additional procedure of buying the stamps is one more thing to arrange for before the closing. If the certificates are to be delivered in New York, the closing document would need to reflect the stamps. Section 12.1(b) provides that stamp and other transfer taxes will be paid by Sellers.

Buyer's Deliverables. Buyer's deliveries follow from what has been agreed to as the form of payment of the Purchase Price discussed above.

SELLERS' RESPONSE

Sellers' Deliverables. The Model Agreement requires certified Organizational Documents of each Acquired Company (usually the secretary of state as to articles of incorporation and the secretary as to bylaws) and good-standing certificates of the state of organization of each Acquired Company and each jurisdiction in which it does business. That could require dozens or even hundreds of certificates. Few buyers read certified articles of incorporation and bylaws at the closing, so their required delivery may be a remnant of historical practice. Buyer undoubtedly reviewed the charter documents in connection with due diligence so what should take place at the closing is an assurance that what Buyer reviewed has not been changed. That can be easily accomplished through delivery of a so-called long-form good-standing certificate, which would list the date of the last amendment to the articles of incorporation, and a similar certificate from the secretary, which would list any amendments to the bylaws. Sellers' counsel might suggest that only articles and bylaws of the Company be delivered.

Tax clearance certificates are not available in all jurisdictions and may take an extended amount of time to obtain in other jurisdictions. To the extent that one or more of the Acquired Companies is insignificant, a tax clearance certificate should not be required. Good-standing certificates might be unavailable or there might be long lead times to obtain them. Sellers may want to delete clause (iv) of Section 2.4(a), bearing in mind the discussion above with respect to the distinction between deliveries treated as covenants and those treated as conditions as well as the risk of a possible condition failure over something relatively minor.

While the concept of a release is probably not troubling to most Sellers, its scope would need to be reviewed and negotiated, as noted above.

Although Section 2.4(a)(vi) of the Model Agreement is a covenant to deliver an employment agreement of a Seller, sellers' counsel should be aware that, as noted above, buyers will sometimes include deliveries of important items, such as employment agreements from key employees who are not sellers, in the required delivery section of the acquisition agreement. Sellers should carefully consider whether to take the risk of agreeing to such covenants. For example, even though sellers may believe that the employee in question is loyal and willing to sign an employment agreement, they should realize that they are incurring potential personal liability if the employee for any reason refuses to sign. Even if, as in the case of the Model Agreement, the employee is a Seller, the other Sellers should realize that they all have joint and several liability if he or she refuses to sign the employment agreement.

Sellers might contend that the delivery of a clean "bring down" certificate at Closing as required by Section 2.4(a)(viii) should be removed as a closing deliverable covenant and only be a condition of closing (*see* Section 8.3), since the accuracy of the representations and warranties as of the Closing Date can be adversely affected by matters beyond the control of the Sellers and that therefore Sellers should not be subjected to a breach of covenant liability as a result. *See* commentary to Section 11.2(a) re indemnification even if the covenant is deleted.

Buyer's Deliverables. Because Buyer is paying a portion of the Purchase Price with Promissory Notes, Sellers might require various certificates parallel to what Buyer is requesting. In this regard, Sellers might be guided by the closing documents specified in a typical bank loan agreement—after all, they are extending credit to Buyer.

2.5   ADJUSTMENT AMOUNT AND PAYMENT

    (a) The "Adjustment Amount" will be the difference, if any, between (i) the consolidated shareholders' equity of the Company and its Subsidiaries as of the Closing Date, as shown on the Closing Balance Sheet (the "Closing Date Shareholders' Equity"), and (ii) _____ dollars ($_____) (the consolidated shareholders' equity of the Company and its Subsidiaries as shown on the Interim Balance Sheet) (the "Interim Shareholders' Equity"). If the Closing Date Shareholders' Equity is less than the Interim Shareholders' Equity, the Adjustment Amount shall be paid by Sellers to Buyer. If the Closing Date Shareholders' Equity is greater than the Interim Shareholders' Equity, subject to Section 11.7, the Adjustment Amount shall be paid by Buyer to Sellers.

    (b) If the Adjustment Amount or, after giving effect to Section 11.7, any portion of the Adjustment Amount is to be paid by Buyer to Sellers, the Adjustment Amount or such portion thereof shall be paid by Buyer by wire transfer to Sellers' Representative pursuant to wire transfer instructions provided to Buyer by Sellers' Representative prior to the due date for the payment set forth in Section 2.5(c). If the Adjustment Amount is to be paid by Sellers to Buyer, the Adjustment Amount shall be paid by Sellers by wire transfer to Buyer pursuant to wire transfer instructions provided by Buyer to Sellers' Representative prior to the due date for the payment set forth in Section 2.5(c).

(c) **All payments under this Section 2.5 shall be made together with interest at the rate set forth in the Promissory Notes, which interest will begin accruing on the Closing Date and end on the day before the payment is made. Within three (3) Business Days after the Closing Balance Sheet and Adjustment Amount become binding on the parties pursuant to Section 2.6, Sellers or Buyer, as the case may be, shall make the payment provided for in this Section 2.5.**

COMMENT

The Model Agreement contains a purchase price adjustment mechanism (also known as a "true-up") to modify the Purchase Price in the event of a change in the shareholders' equity of the Company during the period between the date of the Interim Balance Sheet and Closing. In most acquisitions, the purchase price is determined, at least in part, on the basis of the financial condition of the target. The purchase price adjustment mechanism permits the parties to ensure the actual purchase price accurately reflects the target's financial condition on the Closing Date. It may serve to benefit either buyer or seller since it is usually negotiated as a mutual provision. Not all acquisition agreements contain purchase price adjustments. When they are utilized, however, they require careful review and may involve extensive negotiation. *See* M&A PROCESS 144–46; KLING & NUGENT § 17.02; Freeland & Burnett, *2008 Survey of Private Company Purchase Price Agreements*, 13 M&A LAW. 12 (June 2009); Freeland & Burnett, *Reevaluating Purchase Price Adjustments From a Seller's Perspective*, 13 M&A LAW. 10 (July/Aug. 2009); Freeland & Burnett, *A Buyer's Guide to Purchase Price Adjustments*, 13 M&A LAW. 9 (Sept. 2009).

The Model Agreement uses shareholders' equity (the difference between assets and liabilities) of the Company and its Subsidiaries on a consolidated basis at the effective time of Closing, and provides that the Purchase Price may be increased or decreased. The amount of the adjustment depends on measuring Closing Date Shareholders' Equity against a negotiated target amount, which in the case of the Model Agreement is the amount of shareholders' equity shown on the Interim Balance Sheet. Other alternative measurement dates are possible. For example, if in the negotiations Sellers assert that the shareholders' equity of the Acquired Companies should increase by $1 million between the date of the Interim Balance Sheet and the Closing Date, then Buyer may in turn argue that the Purchase Price has been determined based on that representation. In that case, Buyer might take the position that the Closing Date Shareholders' Equity should be measured against the shareholders' equity set forth on the Interim Balance Sheet, plus $1 million, because otherwise the Adjustment Amount would be $1 million and Buyer would have paid an additional $1 million when the net worth is only what the parties expected it to be. On the other hand, if the Acquired Companies were expected to operate at a loss prior to the anticipated closing date, or the Company paid or was expected to pay dividends to the Sellers, a deduction from the shareholders' equity shown on the Interim Balance Sheet, or using an Interim Balance Sheet from an earlier time, may be appropriate.

The metric of the purchase price adjustment depends upon the structure of the transaction and the nature of the target's business. There are a number of yardsticks available to use as the basis of a post-closing adjustment, with working capital and shareholders' equity being the most common. In some cases, more than one metric might be employed. For example, in a retail business, variations in both sales and inventory might be tracked.

The purchase price may be subject to an upward or downward adjustment or both and may be adjusted dollar-for-dollar or by an amount equal to some multiple of changes in the metric. The parties may choose to place limits on the amount of the purchase price adjustment. The purchase price adjustment provision can also contain a de minimis window or "collar" (i.e., a range within which neither party pays a purchase price adjustment amount).

In drafting purchase price adjustments, careful consideration should be given to the potential for overlap with the indemnification provisions of the acquisition agreement. Matria Healthcare Inc. v. Coral SR LLC, 2007 WL 763303 (Del. Ch. 2007), involved a claim based on a customer complaint that could be characterized as a misrepresentation or a balance sheet item. The merger agreement provided that any matter constituting a purchase price adjustment could not be the basis of an indemnification claim based on breach of a representation. The court held that the potential claim should have been reflected on the balance sheet and therefore needed to be presented to the accountants dealing with the purchase price adjustment, but observed: "One may doubt that this is what the parties intended; the Court, however, cannot read the Merger Agreement otherwise." In Brim Holding Co., Inc. v. Province Healthcare Co., 2008 WL 2220683 (Tenn. Ct. App. 2008), the court held that the seller was required to indemnify the buyer for the amount paid to settle litigation against the target, despite the fact that the settlement amount had been specifically reserved for on the closing balance sheet and operated to decrease the purchase price of the company in a post-closing working capital adjustment. The court held that the indemnification provision had no connection to the working capital adjustment provision. To avoid the possibility of such "double recovery," a seller could consider including in the working capital adjustment provision a statement to the effect that amounts reserved for in the closing date balance sheet cannot also be the subject of indemnification claims.

A similar issue, usually affecting the buyer, involves whether the financial statements used in the purchase price adjustment should be conformed to the representations with respect to financial statements made by the seller in the acquisition agreement. As is discussed in the commentary to Section 2.6(a), unless specific language to the contrary is contained in the acquisition agreement, breaches of the seller's financial statement representations (such as deviations from GAAP) will likely be ignored in the application of the purchase price adjustment provisions.

Section 2.5(b) provides that any payments of the Adjustment Amount are to be made by wire transfer. For a discussion of wire transfers, *see* commentary to Section 2.2. Section 11.7 is broad enough to allow Buyer a setoff against the Promissory Notes if Sellers fail to pay the adjustment amount, although it may prefer cash in hand rather than the reduction of a future obligation. As discussed in the commentary to Section 2.2, the parties could also agree to place a portion of the Purchase Price in escrow to facilitate payment of the Adjustment Amount.

Section 2.5(c) provides that the Adjustment Amount is to bear interest from the Closing Date. The interest rate is a matter of negotiation. A short-term rate such as that specified by a bank's prime rate may be appropriate. Since the Adjustment Amount will be paid within a few months, it would normally bear a lower interest rate than the Promissory Notes, which are probably longer-term instruments. In fact, if Buyer believes that it will be making an additional payment because in all likelihood shareholders' equity will continue to grow, it might not propose any payment of interest. The timing of the payment depends on when the Closing Balance Sheet and Adjustment Amount become binding on the parties, as provided in Section 2.6(c) and (e).

SELLERS' RESPONSE

Because of the purported neutrality of this provision, Sellers may be lulled into a sense of complacency. Among the points that Sellers might consider, however, are the appropriateness of the proposed metric and the initial measurement date, whether there are nuances or adjustments that should be taken into account and the relationship between the purchase price adjustment and other remedies.

Sellers will have to examine other expected events to determine how they would affect the outcome under the proposed language. For example, assume that the target is a Subchapter S corporation that regularly pays dividends used by the shareholders to meet their tax obligations. The payment of a dividend will decrease shareholders' equity. If Buyer has agreed that dividends may be paid, Buyer could recoup the amount of the dividends through the purchase price adjustment, which may not be what was intended (although it may indeed be what was intended since the dividend replaces a provision for tax that would have been taken into account). If working capital is used as the metric, even greater care is required. For example, the use of cash to buy a capital asset (which will inure to the benefit of Buyer) will reduce working capital and therefore reduce the purchase price. A working capital adjustment may produce unintended results if cash is used to pay down long-term debt. On the other hand, a net book value adjustment has built-in downward pressure from depreciation and amortization of fixed assets, which may in some cases be significant.

The dates chosen for the interim balance sheet (or other target amount) will also have an effect on the purchase price adjustment. In a cyclical business, working capital may vary significantly over a period of a few months. Often, when the acquisition agreement is about to be executed, a newer balance sheet will be available than the one used in negotiating the purchase price, in which case using the amount of shareholders' equity or working capital shown on the latest balance sheet may not be appropriate. On the other hand, the latest annual balance sheet also may not be appropriate, because year-end working capital may not be what is expected at the time of closing. To take into account issues such as these, some parties simply negotiate the dollar amount of the targeted closing date shareholders' equity or working capital, and include that dollar amount in the acquisition agreement in lieu of an amount from a prior balance sheet.

As noted above, Sellers in particular will want to consider the relationship between the purchase price adjustment and the indemnification provisions, and whether use of the purchase price adjustment precludes further claims based on components used to calculate the Adjustment Amount, particularly current items such as accounts receivable and inventories.

2.6   ADJUSTMENT PROCEDURE

(a) **Buyer shall prepare a consolidated balance sheet of the Acquired Companies as of the close of business on the Closing Date [the Business Day prior to the Closing Date] (the "Closing Balance Sheet"). The Closing Balance Sheet shall be prepared using the accounting principles, policies, and practices set forth on Exhibit 2.6(a). Buyer shall deliver the Closing Balance Sheet and the determination of the Adjustment Amount to Sellers' Representative within ninety (90) days following the Closing Date.**

(b) **Upon execution of such access letters as may be reasonably required by Buyer, Sellers' Representative and its Representatives shall, during reasonable business hours, be given reasonable access to (and copies of) all Buyer's and its Representatives' books, records, and other documents, including work papers, worksheets, notes, and schedules, used in preparation of the Closing Balance Sheet and the determination of the Adjustment Amount, for the purpose of reviewing the Closing Balance Sheet and determination of the Adjustment Amount, in each case, other than certain work papers that Buyer considers proprietary, such as internal control documentation, engagement planning, time control and audit sign off, and quality control work papers.**

(c) **If within 30 days following delivery of the Closing Balance Sheet and the determination of the Adjustment Amount to Sellers' Representative, Sellers' Representative has not given Buyer notice of an objection as to any amounts set forth on the Closing Balance Sheet or the determination of the Adjustment Amount (which notice shall state in reasonable detail the basis of Sellers' Representative's objections and Sellers' proposed** adjustments (the "Objection Notice")), the Closing Balance Sheet and the determination of the Adjustment Amount as prepared by Buyer will be final, binding, and conclusive on the parties.

(d) If Sellers' Representative timely gives Buyer an Objection Notice and if Sellers' Representative and Buyer fail to resolve the issues raised in the Objection Notice within 30 days after giving the Objection Notice, Sellers' Representative and Buyer shall submit the issues remaining in dispute for resolution to [name of individual] in the [location] office of [name of accounting firm] (or, if [name of individual or name of accounting firm] is providing services to Buyer or a Seller or is otherwise unable or unwilling to serve in such capacity, a recognized national or regional independent accounting firm mutually acceptable to Buyer and Sellers' Representative) (the "Independent Accountants").

(e) The parties shall negotiate in good faith in order to seek agreement on the procedures to be followed by the Independent Accountants, including procedures with regard to the presentation of evidence. If the parties are unable to agree upon procedures within 10 days of the submission to the Independent Accountants, the Independent Accountants shall establish such procedures giving due regard to the intention of the parties to resolve disputes as promptly, efficiently, and inexpensively as possible, which procedures may, but need not, be those proposed by either Buyer or Sellers' Representative. The Independent Accountants shall be directed to resolve only those issues in dispute and render a written report on their resolution of disputed issues with respect to the Closing Balance Sheet and the resulting Adjustment Amount as promptly as practicable, but no later than 60 days after the date on which the Independent Accountants are engaged. The determination by the Independent Accountants will be based solely on written submissions of Buyer, on the one hand, and Sellers' Representative, on the other hand, and will not involve independent review. Any determination of the Closing Balance Sheet or the Adjustment Amount by the Independent Accountants will not be outside the range established by the amounts in (i) the Closing Balance Sheet and the determination of the Adjustment Amount proposed by Buyer, and (ii) Sellers' Representative's proposed adjustments thereto. Such determination will be final, binding, and conclusive on the parties as of the date of the determination notice sent by the Independent Accountants.

(f) If issues are submitted to the Independent Accountants for resolution:

(i) Sellers' Representative and Buyer shall execute any agreement required by the Independent Accountants to accept their engagement pursuant to Section 2.6(d);

(ii) Sellers' Representative and Buyer shall promptly furnish or cause to be furnished to the Independent Accountants such work papers and other documents and information relating to the disputed issues as the Independent Accountants may request and are available to that party or its accountants or other Representatives, and shall be afforded the opportunity to present to the Independent Accountants, with a copy to the other party, any other written material relating to the disputed issues;

(iii) The determination by the Independent Accountants, as set forth in a report to be delivered by the Independent Accountants to both Sellers' Representative and Buyer, will include the revised Closing Balance Sheet and Adjustment Amount, reflecting the changes required as a result of the determination made by the Independent Accountants; and

(iv) Sellers and Buyer shall each bear one-half of the fees and costs of the Independent Accountants; provided, however, that the engagement agreement referred to in Section 2.6(f)(i) above may require the parties to be bound jointly and severally to the Independent Accountants for those fees and costs, and in the event Sellers or Buyer pay to the Independent Accountants any amount in excess of one-half of the fees and costs of its engagement, the other party(ies) agree(s) to reimburse Sellers or Buyer, as applicable, upon demand, to the extent required to equalize the payments made by Sellers and Buyer with respect to the fees and costs of the Independent Accountants.

COMMENT

Preparation of the Closing Balance Sheet. In order to minimize the potential for disputes with respect to the determination of the Adjustment Amount, the Model Agreement specifies the manner and procedures by which the calculation is to be made. As described in the commentary to Section 2.3, the effective date should be stipulated, typically the Closing Date or the day prior to the Closing Date. The Model Agreement requires that the Closing Balance Sheet be prepared in accordance with the accounting principles, policies, and practices set forth on Exhibit 2.6(a). This requires the parties to negotiate and confirm in writing on Exhibit 2.6(a) the method of preparation of the Closing Balance Sheet. Often such an exhibit will require that the closing balance sheet be prepared in a manner consistent with the interim financial statements to which the closing balance sheet will be compared. Such an exhibit will usually also require that the closing balance sheet be prepared in accordance with GAAP and a manner consistent with the annual financial statements delivered to the buyer prior to the execution of the acquisition agreement. The parties should consider describing the historical accounting practices of the Company on this exhibit, especially where those practices deviate from GAAP. Both Buyer and Sellers should also be aware of the flexibility permitted by GAAP (*see* commentary to the definition of "GAAP" in Section 1.1) and the resulting need for specificity. For example, GAAP allows a multitude of acceptable practices for valuing inventory. This exhibit might also include the method of valuation of significant line items for purposes of the Closing Balance Sheet, such as inventory and accounts receivable. For cost, timing, and other reasons, the parties may elect to prepare a less comprehensive Closing Balance Sheet for the limited purpose of determining the Adjustment Amount. Because the provisions of an exhibit such as is required by Section 2.6(a) are transaction-specific, and can vary significantly based on such factors as the industry of the Company, the past accounting practices of the Company, and the sophistication of the parties, the Model Agreement does not contain an example of Exhibit 2.6(a).

A frequent belief is that balance sheet items are objectively determined. Often, rather than listing the specific principles to be applied, there is merely a recitation of general principles with a statement that GAAP controls. Unfortunately, this may not provide sufficient guidance in reaching agreement on the calculation of amounts, particularly those requiring judgment. While sometimes, because of an abundance of goodwill and competency, the parties are able to make this final determination with ease, too often the process becomes contentious, often involving individuals not involved in the negotiation of the agreement and not necessarily familiar with the M&A process. Further, when dealing with a buyer that is a large organization, it is impossible to anticipate the culture and instructions given to internal personnel asked to prepare a closing balance sheet.

Unless specific language to the contrary is contained in the acquisition agreement, breaches of the seller's financial statement representations (such as deviations from GAAP) will likely be ignored in the application of the purchase price adjustment provisions, and the buyer may be precluded from basing the closing balance sheet on GAAP if the interim balance sheet does not conform to GAAP. For example, in the case entitled In the Matter of Westmoreland Coal Company, 794 N.E.2d 667 (N.Y. 2003), the acquisition agreement contained a representation by the seller that the financial statements provided to the buyer were prepared in accordance with GAAP, and also contained post-closing adjustment provisions based on closing date asset valuations, which were required to be prepared by the seller on a basis consistent with those financial statements. The buyer claimed a post-closing adjustment of the purchase price on the basis that certain of the seller's closing date asset valuations did not comply with GAAP. The seller argued that, because the closing date asset values were prepared in a manner consistent with the financial statements previously delivered to the buyer, the exclusive remedy available to the buyer was to claim a breach of the seller's representation (which was subject to litigation as opposed to being resolved under the purchase price adjustment provisions, and was also subject to an indemnification "basket"). The court held that the buyer's valuation objections should be resolved under the indemnification provisions and not under the purchase price adjustment provisions of the agreement. *See also* OSI Systems, Inc. v. Instrumentarium Corp., 892 A.2d 1086 (Del. Ch. 2006).

Because preparation of a closing balance sheet is not a science, parties frequently seek to have their own accountants prepare the closing balance sheet. Section 2.6 of the Model Agreement provides that Buyer will prepare the Closing Balance Sheet. Sellers may argue that they are in a better position to do this. Regardless of the party preparing the closing balance sheet and making the initial determination of shareholders' equity, acquisition agreements typically allow the other party to object to the initial determination, accompanied by an explanation of the objection, and contain provisions establishing dispute resolution procedures to resolve any such objection. The Model Agreement follows this format.

The Model Agreement provides that the Closing Balance Sheet and the Adjustment Amount (which is a simple subtraction) be delivered by Buyer within 90 days after the Closing Date. The precise time will be negotiated and may depend on the circumstances. For example, if the closing occurs close to Buyer's year end, a longer period may be negotiated if Buyer's accounting personnel need to be committed to other tasks.

Sellers' Review. In order to properly evaluate Buyer's preparation of the Closing Balance Sheet, Section 2.6(b) provides Sellers certain access rights to records and personnel. Despite this wording, independent accountants hired by Buyer may condition access to their papers on Sellers' execution of exculpation or indemnification letters.

Sellers' Reply. The Model Agreement affords Sellers 30 days to respond. The time is always negotiated and 30 days may not be adequate. If Sellers provide an Objection Notice, the procedure jumps to the next provision (Section 2.6(d)); otherwise the Closing Balance Sheet and Adjustment Amount become final, triggering the payment process set forth in Section 2.5(b) and (c).

Third-Party Dispute Resolution. The first sentence of Section 2.6(d) provides that, if the parties have failed to resolve the dispute within 30 days after Sellers' Representative gives an Objection Notice, the matter will be submitted to Independent Accountants. The party to which the dispute is to be submitted is designated as an accounting firm. Consideration might be given to broadening this to include consultants, so that the parties have more flexibility. For example, valuation firms or other consultants might be perfectly capable of dealing with the issues presented by the financial statements and calculation of the purchase price adjustment. Some practitioners may argue that there is an implied covenant to negotiate in good faith in the 30-day period. Even if there is no requirement to negotiate, the parties may believe it is in their own self interest to do so because they incur additional expenses and lose control of the process once the Independent Accountants are engaged. As a result, differences are often settled during this window period.

The Model Agreement provides for dispute resolution by Independent Accountants previously agreed to by the parties, and the qualifications of an alternate if the designated accountants are unable or unwilling to serve. If the parties are unable to agree on the alternate, court action may be required.

The Process Followed by the Independent Accountants. The procedure to be followed and the scope of authority given for resolution of disputes concerning the post-closing adjustments vary in acquisition agreements. The rules of engagement need to be approved. Unlike arbitration, where various organizations have standard rules that may be incorporated by reference, there is no particular framework specifying the procedures to be used by the accountants under an acquisition agreement dispute resolution procedure. Section 2.6(e) requires that the parties negotiate in good faith toward this end. Ideally, the accountants would be engaged and these procedures agreed to before the acquisition agreement is signed. But in practice, parties rarely want to go through such an exercise until it becomes necessary.

In order to provide guidance to the Independent Accountants, Section 2.6(e) attempts to confine them to "the issues in dispute" and requires a written report. The phrase "issues in dispute" in Section 2.6(e) limits the inquiry of the Independent Accountants to the specific unresolved items. It is sometimes not possible, however, to determine what issues truly are in dispute. Some parties will react to a proposed adjustment amount with a host of objections, some which they believe to be more serious than others, and will then offer to drop the less serious objections in the settlement negotiations. But in the usual process of negotiation, all objections are normally preserved until there is a settlement, and, therefore, if there is no settlement, the "issues in dispute" may include such "throwaway" objections. To address this issue, some acquisition agreements attempt to control unsubstantiated claims by awarding costs against the advocates of unsupportable positions.

Section 2.6(e) also attempts to limit the scope of review by the Independent Accountants by requiring that they base their determination solely on "written submissions of Buyer, on the one hand, and Sellers' Representative, on the other hand," and not on independent review. Furthermore, Section 2.6(f)(ii) requires only that the Sellers' Representative and Buyer furnish to the Independent Accountants such work papers and other documents and information relating to the disputed issues as the Independent Accountants may request and are available to that party or its accountants or other Representatives. The Independent Accountants, however, may desire broader rights so as to more fully understand the issues in dispute and the underlying facts and data. Such broader rights could include granting the Independent Accountants access to electronic data, key management and accounting personnel, the actual company site, and the accounting/financial systems of the Acquired Companies. Therefore, in addition to the parties' respective closing balance sheets, written submissions and work papers, some acquisition agreements contain provisions granting broader investigatory rights to the Independent Accountants. In negotiating and drafting these provisions, the parties should weigh the sometimes competing goals of thoroughness and reaching a speedy resolution.

The procedure set forth in Section 2.6 does not explicitly provide for the accountants to act as arbitrators, and there is no separate arbitration provision governing disputes under the Model Agreement. *See* Appendix E—Alternative Dispute Resolution for an arbitration provision with commentary. Section 2.6, however, provides that the determination by the accountants is to be "final, binding and conclusive" on the parties. The issue of whether this determination will be binding on the parties is often addressed in the context of a motion to compel arbitration or to enforce the determination by one of the parties to the acquisition agreement. The court in Talegen Holdings, Inc. v. Fremont General Corp., 1998 WL 513066 (S.D.N.Y. 1998), stated that, "Courts have consistently found that purchase price adjustment dispute resolution provisions such as the one at issue here constitute enforceable arbitration agreements." The clauses providing for dispute resolution mechanisms need not expressly provide for arbitration in order for a court to determine that the parties have agreed to arbitration.

The parties might consider parameters on the submission of issues in dispute to the Independent Accountants. For example, they could agree that, if the amount in dispute is less than a specified amount, they will split the difference and avoid the costs of the accountants' fees and the time and effort involved in resolving the dispute. The parties may also want to structure an arrangement for the payment of amounts not in dispute.

Certain Procedures. Section 2.6(f) requires that the parties execute any agreement required by the Independent Accountants to accept their engagement. Many accounting firms, as a prerequisite to accepting a dispute resolution engagement, require the execution of an engagement agreement containing provisions designed to protect the accounting firm. Absence of a provision such as Section 2.6(f) could allow one party to thwart the dispute resolution provisions of Section 2.6 by refusing to execute the engagement agreement. Such engagement agreements often include provisions limiting the liability of the accounting firm to matters of gross negligence or willful misconduct, and indemnification of the accounting firm for liability and expenses incurred if the accounting firm is made a party in any litigation resulting from the engagement. Such agreements also often contain provisions obligating the parties jointly and severally for the fees charged by the accounting firm for the engagement. As this is inconsistent with the requirement of Section 2.6(f)(iv) that the parties share equally the fees of the Independent Accountants, that Section provides that, in the event either party pays to the Independent Accountants any amount in excess of 50% of the fees and costs of the engagement, the other party will reimburse the paying party to the extent required to equalize the payments made by Sellers and Buyer.

Section 2.6(f)(iii) makes it clear that the Independent Accountants are to furnish the final details of the Adjustment Amount, since that final determination drives the payments to be made pursuant to Section 2.5.

SELLERS' RESPONSE

In reviewing this detailed procedure, Sellers might be tempted to believe that it appears to be fair and well calibrated. Sellers should remember that it will be applied by persons not familiar with either the Company or the negotiations.

Access to workpapers prepared by independent accountants has become a contentious issue as they attempt to protect themselves from liability. Access will usually be conditioned on providing exculpation or indemnification letters.

There may be a significant advantage to sellers that comes with the preparation of the initial balance sheet. While buyers often insist on their right to do so, sellers have a strong motivation to prepare the balance sheet. While buyers might argue that in a stock purchase they are "buying" the personnel associated with the target's accounting function, that really does not mean that they are buying the expertise necessary for the preparation of any set of financial statements, particularly if the sellers have been the officers of the target and will not be employed on a continuing basis. The preparation of any set of financial statements uses techniques, not just principles. Often what is most important is the consistent application of those methodologies, which may not be known to the buyer. Sellers normally have good arguments as to why they should prepare the closing balance sheet.

If sellers are not successful in negotiating the right to prepare the closing balance sheet, they might consider a mock exercise to determine how the buyer might prepare the closing balance sheet and how sellers would respond. The relationship of the purchase price adjustment provisions with other provisions in the acquisition agreement should be considered. For example, acquisition agreements sometimes provide a separate tax indemnification, which goes beyond simply indemnification for a breach of the tax representation. A component of the closing balance sheet may very well be an estimate of a tax liability. If high, the estimate will result in a reduction in the price, and if it turns out that that estimate was erroneously high, there will be no further benefit to the seller. On the other hand, if the estimate is low, the seller, through the tax indemnification provisions, might have responsibility for the taxes. To avoid this possibility, the tax provision could be excluded from the adjustment mechanism or a bilateral mechanism in the tax indemnification provisions might be constructed, so that the seller could benefit from an overestimation of tax liability on the closing balance sheet. This may suggest that Exhibit 2.6(a) might specify a mechanism for calculating certain amounts even though it has not been used historically.

Too often in the rush to close a transaction, the details of Sections 2.5 and 2.6, particularly Exhibit 2.6(a), are referred to the accountants, who think in amorphous, global terms such as "GAAP" and may not understand how these provisions will be applied once the acquisition is closed.   Similarly, the lawyers may not understand the accounting details. As a result, some sellers are surprised after the closing, not only by the procedure and the resulting purchase price adjustment, but also at how they failed to understand the implications of the purchase price adjustment provisions prior to the execution of the acquisition agreement. To avoid such surprises, sellers should understand the importance of the purchase price adjustment procedures, and that these procedures will always be applied— they are never theoretical. Sellers and their accountants should take the time to arrive at an in-depth understanding of these procedures.

3. Representations and Warranties of Sellers

PRELIMINARY NOTE

Sellers' representations and warranties are Sellers' formal description of the Acquired Companies and their businesses. Representations are statements of past or existing facts and warranties are promises that existing or future facts are or will be true. The technical difference between the two has proven unimportant in acquisition practice. *See* FREUND 153. Separating them explicitly in an acquisition agreement is a drafting nuisance, and the legal import of the separation may have little significance when interpreting an agreement. *See* Reliance Finance Corp. v. Miller, 557 F.2d 674, 682 (9th Cir. 1977). While both terms are used in drafting acquisition agreements, a distinction is often made in litigation between claims based on misrepresentations and claims based on breaches of warranty. *See* West & Benton, *Contracting to Avoid Extra-Contractual Liability—Can Your Contractual Deal Ever Really Be The "Entire" Deal?*, 64 BUS. LAW. 999 (Aug. 2009). The commentary to the Model Agreement generally refers only to representations, although the Model Agreement follows common practice and uses both words.

The scope of representations in an acquisition agreement will vary based upon factors such as the nature of the target's business, the relative bargaining power of the parties, the business context, and the size of the transaction.

The Model Agreement contains 29 illustrative representations of Sellers. While broad-ranging, these representations are generally limited to matters Sellers either know or can verify. Some representations may cover matters that Sellers cannot confirm to a certainty. In those instances, the representations serve a risk allocation function.

The representations do not cover everything Buyer would like to verify. For example, Buyer would like to have assurances with respect to the future performance of the Acquired Companies, but the Model Agreement representations do not provide it. Even if a seller provides financial projections to a buyer, an acquisition agreement will seldom contain any representation regarding them, other than that the underlying assumptions are reasonable. Sellers generally will not be asked to represent or warrant that the projected future results will be realized.

Purposes of Sellers' Representations. Sellers' representations serve four overlapping purposes.

First, they are a device for obtaining disclosure about the Acquired Companies before the signing of the Model Agreement. A thorough Buyer's draft elicits information about the Acquired Companies and their businesses relevant to Buyer's decision to buy the Company. This information is obtained not only through negotiation of the representations, but also through disclosures in the Disclosure Letter. For example, many of the representations in the Model Agreement, like those in Sections 3.3 (capitalization; subsidiaries), 3.6 (real and personal property), 3.13 (employee benefits), 3.17 (contracts) and 3.22 (intellectual property assets), provide that lists of items covered by those Sections be included in the Disclosure Letter. The Disclosure Letter also provides other information as exceptions to various representations. *See* commentary to definition of "Disclosure Letter" in Section 1.1, and commentary to Section 12.3.

Second, there may be areas covered by representations in which Sellers' knowledge and examination will not provide certainty. For example, Sellers represent in Section 3.22(c)(iv) that the Company's products do not infringe any third-party patents. Sellers might view this as an impossible statement to make. In these instances, the representation serves to allocate the risk of the unknown, with Buyer taking the position that Sellers, based upon their experience with the Company, are in a better position to bear that risk.

Third, Sellers' representations provide a foundation for Buyer's right to terminate the acquisition before or at the closing. *See* commentary to Sections 8.1 and 10.1. After the signing and before closing, Buyer usually continues its due diligence investigation of the Acquired Companies. In the Model Agreement, detailed Sellers' representations provide Buyer, on its subsequent discovery of a breach, the right not to proceed with the acquisition (commonly called a "walk right"). *See* Section 8.1 and related commentary.

Fourth and finally, Sellers' representations provide a basis for Buyer's right to a remedy if it discovers after the Closing that Sellers have breached one or more of the representations. *See* Section 11.2 and related commentary.

Bare representations, if false, may also support claims in tort and for federal securities act violations. *Cf.* U.C.C. § 2-313. *See* KLING & NUGENT § 11.01[1].

"Adverse Effect" Language. The importance of the content and detail of Sellers' representations are essential to the bargain. As noted above, Sellers' representations provide the basis for both Buyer's walk rights in Section 10.1 and Buyer's remedies in Section 11.2 and at law.

Consider, for example, the following simplified version of Sellers' litigation representation: "There is no lawsuit pending against the Company that will have an adverse effect on the Company." The phrase "that will have an adverse effect on the Company" should provide adequate protection to Buyer in the context of a post-closing indemnification claim against Sellers. If there is a previously undisclosed lawsuit against the Company that has an adverse effect on the Company (for example, because a judgment is ultimately rendered against the Company in the lawsuit or because the cost of defending the suit will have an adverse financial impact on the Company), Buyer will be able to recover damages from Sellers because of Sellers' breach of the litigation representation (Section 11.2(a)). The quoted phrase, however, may not adequately protect Buyer if it becomes aware of the lawsuit prior to closing and Buyer as a result seeks to terminate the acquisition. To terminate the acquisition without incurring any liability to Sellers, Buyer will have to demonstrate, on or prior to the scheduled closing, that the lawsuit "will have an adverse effect on the Company" (Section 10.1). This may be more difficult since the ultimate outcome of the suit is unknown, but Buyer may take that position based upon, for example, the nature of the suit, Buyer's own assessment, or the projected defense costs.

Buyer might be tempted to reword the litigation representation so that it covers lawsuits that "could reasonably be expected to have" an adverse effect on the Company (as distinguished from lawsuits that definitely "will" have such an effect). However, while this change in wording should expand the scope of Buyer's walk rights, it may actually limit Buyer's indemnification rights—even if the lawsuit ultimately has an adverse effect on the Company. Sellers may be able to avoid liability to Buyer by showing that, as of the Closing Date, it was unreasonable to expect that the lawsuit would have such an effect.

To protect both its indemnification rights and its walk rights in the context of undisclosed litigation, Buyer may propose that the litigation representation be reworded to cover any lawsuit "that may have an adverse effect" on the Company. If Sellers object to the breadth of this language, Buyer may propose, as a compromise, that the litigation representation be reworded to cover lawsuits "that will, or could reasonably be expected to, have an adverse effect" on the Company. This illustrates that in drafting "adverse effect" representations, Buyer will need to consider the degree of certainty required to trigger a breach of the representations. The possibilities range from "will have an adverse effect," which would require the highest degree of certainty, to "may" or "might" at the other end of the spectrum.

The approach in Section 3.15 is to request a list of all pending or threatened Proceedings, so that Sellers are not forced to make judgments as to materiality or adverse effect that would affect their disclosures. Section 3.15 then requires Sellers' representation that none of the disclosed pending or threatened Proceedings "will or could reasonably be expected to result in an adverse consequence to any Acquired Company or in any Acquired Company incurring Losses of $_____ or more or becoming subjected to any Order."

The Model Agreement generally avoids qualifying representations by materially adverse effect or adverse effect. The defined term "Material Adverse Change" is not used to qualify representations in part because negotiation may result in that term itself being subject to a number of qualifications that might be inappropriate when applied to a particular representation.

Incorporating Specific Time Periods. Representations that focus on specific time periods require careful drafting due to the expectations of the "bring down" clauses in Section 8.1 (focusing on the accuracy of Sellers' representations). For example, consider the representation in Section 3.14(a)(iii), which states that no Acquired Company has received notice of any alleged legal violation. In some acquisition agreements, this representation is worded differently, stating that no notice of an alleged violation has been received at any time during a specified time period (such as a five-year period) "prior to the date of this Agreement." If the representation was drafted in this manner, Buyer would not have a walk right or an indemnification right if an Acquired Company received notice of a significant alleged violation between the signing and the closing. The representation would remain accurate as of the Closing Date, because the notice would not have been received "prior to" the date of the Merger Agreement. In contrast, if the representation in Section 3.14(a)(iii) was drafted to state that "since" a specified date no Acquired Company had received such notice, the representation would be materially inaccurate as of the Closing Date because the notice of the alleged violation would have been received "since" the date specified in Section 3.14(a)(iii). Therefore Buyer would have a walk right pursuant to Section 10.1, provided the alleged violation is material.

Buyer may consider a number of factors in determining how many years to reach back in a representation. Chief among them is relevance. Buyer usually should only ask for past information it needs to assess the current state of the Company. A time period may be chosen because it mirrors the applicable statute of limitations or because it will permit Buyer to discern patterns of conduct or issues. Whatever time frame is chosen, Buyer should be prepared to articulate the reasoning behind it.

Incorporating Specific Dates. Representations can also be made as to facts as they exist as of a specified date. While the accuracy of representations in an acquisition agreement generally may be determined as of the date of the agreement, as of the closing, or both, the accuracy of these representations will depend upon whether the facts are as represented as of the date specified.

"Knowledge" Qualifications. Sections 3.13, 3.15, 3.19, 3.20, 3.21, and 3.22 contain knowledge qualifications. The addition of knowledge qualifications to Sellers' representations in Article 3 can significantly limit Buyer's post-closing indemnification rights by shifting to Buyer the risks of unknown facts. However, such qualifications should not affect Buyer's walk rights under Section 10.1. If, prior to the closing, Buyer learns of a fact (not already known to Sellers) that is inconsistent with a representation containing a knowledge qualification, Buyer could simply disclose this fact to Sellers. Sellers will thus acquire knowledge of the fact, and the representation will be inaccurate. *See* commentary to definition of "Knowledge" in Section 1.1, and commentary to Sections listed above.

"Materiality" Qualifications. In general, Sellers' representations in the Model Agreement do not contain materiality qualifications. Rather, the issue of materiality is addressed in the remedies sections. Section 8.1(a) specifies that only material breaches of representations give Buyer the ability not to close. Section 8.1(b) covers the few representations that contain their own materiality qualifications. *See* "Absence of Materiality Qualification in Section 8.1(b)" in commentary to Section 8.1(b). The indemnification provisions replace a general and open-ended materiality qualification with a quantified "threshold" in Section 11.6(a) under which Sellers have no liability for breaches of a specified amount, subject to certain exceptions.

Sellers may object to the absence of materiality qualifications in their representations by arguing that, in light of the comprehensive and detailed nature of the representations, it is unrealistic to expect that every representation will be accurate in all respects.

Buyer may respond by pointing out that, given the limited purposes served by Sellers' representations, Sellers should not be concerned about the presence of immaterial inaccuracies in these representations. Under the Model Agreement, the principal remedies available to Buyer for a breach of Sellers' representations are Buyer's walk rights and indemnification rights, neither of which may be exercised if the breach is not material. Also, to exercise its indemnification rights on the basis of a breach by Sellers, Buyer must be able to demonstrate that it was actually damaged by the breach (*see* Section 11.2).

Overlap of Representations. It is in the Buyer's interests to draft the representations as broadly as possible, even if some of them cover virtually the same subject matter. For example, Section 3.14 deals generally with compliance with Legal Requirements, while compliance with law is also covered in many of the specific representations, such as those in Sections 3.11 (taxes), 3.19 (environmental matters), and 3.20 (employees and consultants). The difficulty that courts have in reconciling some of these general and specific representations is discussed in "Judicial Limitations on Enforcement—Judicial Interpretation" in preliminary note to Article 11, where the addition of language to the effect that each of the representations be given independent significance is discussed.

SELLERS' PERSPECTIVE

A seller would prefer an acquisition agreement with no representations. This would afford the seller more certainty regarding closing and limit the possibility of post-closing liability. Since an agreement without representations is generally unrealistic, a seller may instead work to narrow the scope of the representations. It may attempt to limit them to matters as to which it has a high degree of confidence. A seller may also request that pertinent time frames be shortened, and seek liberal use of knowledge and materiality qualifiers. It may further seek to limit the representation to matters over a specific dollar threshold.

Where a buyer uses words that tend to expand the scope of representations, such as "might," "may" or "could," sellers often propose more limiting language such as "will," "would," or "are reasonably likely to." Since these typical responses would be applicable to a number of representations in the Model Agreement, the "Sellers' Response" commentary to individual representations omits reference to them.

A seller's strategy with respect to the representations will depend upon several factors, including its degree of operational involvement in the target, the structure of the acquisition agreement, and the limitations on its liability for indemnification that it is able to negotiate.

Sellers might also want to propose language to the effect that certain general representations, such as that in Section 3.14 (compliance with Legal Requirements), will have no application to matters covered by certain designated more detailed representations (e.g., environmental matters or employee benefits) which Sellers may argue should be exclusive as to their subject matter.

Sellers, jointly and severally, represent and warrant to Buyer as follows:

COMMENT

The Fact Pattern provides for multiple Sellers. Under this lead-in clause, Sellers are making the representations in Article 3 "jointly and severally." This is desirable for Buyer because if there is a breach of a representation, Buyer can seek to enforce its remedies against any or all of Sellers. *See* "Joint and Several Liability of Sellers" in commentary to Section 11.2.

By virtue of the lead-in clause, Sellers are making their representations on the date of the Model Agreement. Section 8.1(a) and (b) contains a "bring down" clause, whereby Sellers' representations are "brought down" to the Closing Date to determine their accuracy as of that date, and Section 8.3 provides for Sellers' delivery of a closing or "bring down" certificate, whereby Sellers confirm the accuracy of the representations as of the Closing Date. The "bring down" clause and delivery of a "bring down" certificate are intended to protect Buyer from significant changes in the business of the Acquired Companies by affording it with the right to refuse to close the acquisition or, if it is closed, with the right to seek indemnification. Otherwise, the accuracy of the representations would be tested only at signing or, in some cases, as of dates specified in the representations.

If the "bring down" certificate makes no mention of a representation that has become untrue between signing and closing, and Buyer subsequently discovers the inaccurate representation, whether or not Sellers knew about it prior to the Closing, Buyer would be entitled to seek indemnification under Section 11.2(a) based on the inaccurate "bring down" certificate. Where, however, Sellers disclose to Buyer prior to the Closing that a representation has become untrue and delivers a supplement to the Disclosure Letter and a qualified "bring down" certificate, Sellers would have no liability for indemnification if Buyer chooses to close.

In some acquisition agreements, buyers provide that the representations are made by the seller both as of the date of the agreement and as of the closing, and in a few instances only as of the closing. This automatic reaffirmation of the accuracy of the representations on and as of the closing is intended to preserve the buyer's right to indemnification where a representation of the seller becomes untrue between signing and closing, even if the seller fails to deliver a "bring down" certificate or delivers a qualified certificate. For a discussion of judicial decisions that may affect this result, however, see "Judicial Limitations on Enforcement" in preliminary note to Article 11. The right to close and then claim indemnification under these circumstances would be in addition to the buyer's right to terminate the acquisition agreement. The buyer might threaten to terminate as leverage to renegotiate the price or terms of the transaction. If the buyer chooses not to close, the seller would have no liability for a representation that became untrue after signing because the closing has not occurred.

Another approach does not rely on a seller's "bring down" certificate would be to have the seller make "continuous" representations that must remain true at every moment from the signing until closing or termination. A provision of this nature would be unusual, because it would create liability for the seller for a representation that becomes untrue after signing, even if the buyer chooses not to close.

SELLERS' RESPONSE

Sellers may be concerned about making their representations in Article 3 "jointly and severally." For a discussion of this subject, see "Joint and Several Liability of Sellers" in commentary to Section 11.2.

If Buyer were to provide in the lead-in clause that Sellers' representations are made as of the Closing Date, that could subject Sellers to liability for events beyond their control. For example, if there were a major hurricane a short time after signing that constitutes the destruction or loss of an asset under Section 3.16(e), Buyer would retain the right to close and immediately bring a lawsuit demanding that Sellers indemnify it against any losses resulting from Sellers' breach. The parties should be aware, however, that some courts might not enforce Buyer's right to "close and sue" in this situation. See "Judicial Limitations on Enforcement" in preliminary note to Article 11.

Although Buyer may argue that it is entitled to the benefit of the original bargain struck when it signed the Model Agreement—notwithstanding the subsequent occurrence of events beyond Sellers' control—to many Sellers this is simply an untenable position. They will insist that if a representation becomes untrue after signing and before closing, and Sellers disclose the breach in a supplement to the Disclosure Letter or the "bring down" certificate delivered pursuant to Section 8.3, Buyer's only choices would be to either close and waive the breach or to terminate under Section 10.1. Further, if Article 3 were to contain a lead-in clause to the effect that Sellers' representations would be continuously true from signing until closing or termination, Buyer would also have the right to "walk and sue" over the destruction caused by the hurricane, which Sellers might find even more objectionable.

3.1   ORGANIZATION AND GOOD STANDING

(a) **Part 3.1 lists, for each Acquired Company, its legal name, its type of legal entity, its jurisdiction of organization, and each jurisdiction in which it is qualified to do business as a foreign entity. Each Acquired Company is duly organized, validly existing, and in good standing under the laws of its jurisdiction of organization, with full power and authority to conduct its business as it is being conducted, to own or use its assets, and to perform all its obligations under Applicable Contracts. Each Acquired Company is duly qualified to do business as a foreign entity and is in good standing under the laws of each jurisdiction that requires such qualification.**

(b) **Sellers have delivered to Buyer copies of the Organizational Documents of each Acquired Company. No Acquired Company is in default under or in violation of any of its Organizational Documents.**

(c) **No Acquired Company has conducted business under or otherwise used, for any purpose or in any jurisdiction, any legal, fictitious, assumed, or trade name other than the names listed in Part 3.1.**

COMMENT

Buyer wants assurance that the Acquired Companies have been properly organized and have authority to operate their respective businesses.

The first sentence of Section 3.1(a) calls for a listing of certain facts regarding each Acquired Company. The second sentence provides assurance that each Acquired Company has been properly organized and has the necessary authority to operate its business. The third sentence covers qualification as a foreign corporation in jurisdictions where an Acquired Company is doing business.

Buyers will sometimes ask that the representation regarding authority to conduct business apply not only to the business as currently conducted, but also to the business as "proposed to be conducted." This may be appropriate where the target has started to, or is proposing to, expand into a new line of business or sellers are otherwise emphasizing future prospects of the business through the use of a forward-looking business plan or projections, but may not be appropriate in other circumstances.

Because most states provide for qualification only of foreign corporations, limited partnerships, and limited liability companies, the representation in the last sentence applies only to those entities. Requiring a list of foreign jurisdictions does not limit or expand the breadth of the previous sentence, but does help force Sellers to give proper attention to this matter. The failure to be qualified as a foreign corporation where otherwise required can have significant adverse consequences, including the inability to access the courts of the jurisdiction in question or to enforce contractual rights. In some states (notably Alabama), there is limited or no ability to cure such failure after the fact. *See, e.g.,* ALA. CONST., art. XII, § 232; ALA. CODE § 10-2B-15.02. Failure to qualify may also have state tax implications, and closing could be delayed while back tax returns are prepared and processed.

By virtue of the usage provision in clause (xiii) of Section 1.2(a), the first sentence of Section 3.1(b) is Sellers' representation that they have delivered "complete and correct" copies of the Organizational Documents of each Acquired Company. In the second sentence of Section 3.1(b), Sellers represent that no Acquired Company is in default of its Organization Documents. This subsection covers existing defaults, as contrasted with clause (i) of Section 3.2(b), which covers violations caused by the Contemplated Transactions.

If Buyer is concerned that an Acquired Company might be an inadvertent "investment company" (for example, if an Acquired Company's assets include significant investment assets and ownership is widespread), Buyer should seek a representation such as: "None of the Acquired Companies is an 'investment company' within the meaning of the Investment Company Act of 1940."

The representation in Section 3.1(c) concerning the conduct of the business under other names is intended to help determine whether additional due diligence will be required under other names for lien searches, trademark searches, domain names, or predecessor companies. In appropriate circumstances (e.g., where the Acquired Companies have gone through a series of organic changes over time), Buyer may expand this Section to require additional disclosure regarding the background of the Acquired Companies and their predecessors.

See MANUAL ON ACQUISITION REVIEW 11.20.

SELLERS' RESPONSE

Sellers may request that the representation concerning the Acquired Companies' power and authority be qualified by a reference to "corporate" power and authority. Use of the word "corporate" narrows the representation to mean that each Acquired Company is authorized to conduct its business under applicable business corporation laws and its charter and bylaws and that such action is not *ultra vires*. When the word "corporate" is omitted, the term "power and authority" can be interpreted to mean "full power and authority" under all applicable laws and regulations, a much broader representation that is also covered in part by other sections of the Model Agreement. Where the target is a limited liability company or other noncorporate entity, the term "limited liability company" or other appropriate modifier can be substituted for "corporate."

Seller may also request that the representation concerning qualification of each Acquired Company as a foreign corporation in other jurisdictions contain an exception for jurisdictions in which "the failure to be so qualified would not constitute a Material Adverse Change," on the theory that Buyer should not be concerned about immaterial failures to qualify. *See* "'Materiality' Qualifications" in preliminary note to Article 3 and commentary to the definition of "Material Adverse Change" in Section 1.1.

3.2 ENFORCEABILITY AND AUTHORITY; NO CONFLICT

(a) **This Agreement has been duly executed and delivered by each Seller and constitutes the legal, valid, and binding obligation of each Seller, enforceable against each Seller in accordance with its terms. Upon the execution and delivery of Sellers' Closing Documents by each Seller party thereto, each Sellers' Closing Document will constitute the legal, valid, and binding obligation of such Seller, enforceable against such Seller in accordance with its terms. Each Seller has the absolute and unrestricted right, power, authority, and capacity to execute and deliver, and to perform its obligations under, this Agreement and each Sellers' Closing Document to which it is a party.**

(b) **Except as set forth in Part 3.2(b), neither the execution and delivery of this Agreement nor the consummation or performance of any Contemplated Transaction will, directly or indirectly (with or without notice or lapse of time):**

   (i) **contravene, conflict with, or violate (A) any Organizational Document of any Acquired Company, or (B) any resolution adopted by the board of directors or the shareholders (or Persons exercising similar authority) of any Acquired Company;**

   (ii) **contravene, conflict with, or violate, or give any Governmental Body or other Person the right to challenge any Contemplated Transaction, or to exercise any remedy or obtain any relief under, any Legal Requirement or any Order to which any Acquired Company or any Seller, or any assets owned or used by any Acquired Company, could be subject;**

   (iii) **contravene, conflict with, violate, result in the loss of any benefit to which any Acquired Company is entitled under, or give any Governmental Body the right to revoke, suspend, cancel, terminate, or modify, any Governmental Authorization held by any Acquired Company or that otherwise relates to the business of, or any assets owned or used by, any Acquired Company;**

      (iv)   **cause Buyer or any Acquired Company to become subject to, or to become liable for payment of, any Tax;**

      (v)   **cause any assets owned or used by any Acquired Company to be reassessed or revalued by any Governmental Body;**

      (vi)   **Breach, or give any Person the right to declare a default or exercise any remedy or to obtain any additional rights under, or to accelerate the maturity or performance of, or payment under, or cancel, terminate, or modify, any Applicable Contract or any Contract to which any Seller or any Acquired Company is a party;**

      (vii)   **result in the imposition or creation of any Encumbrance upon, or with respect to, any assets owned or used by any Acquired Company; or**

      (viii)   **result in, or give any other Person the right or option to cause or declare: (A) a loss of any Intellectual Property Asset, (B) the release, disclosure, or delivery of any Intellectual Property Asset by or to any escrow agent or other Person, or (C) the grant, assignment, or transfer to any other Person of any license, Encumbrance, or other right or interest under, to, or in any Intellectual Property Asset.**

(c)   Except as set forth in Part 3.2(c), no Seller or Acquired Company is or shall be required to give notice to, or obtain Consent from, any Person in connection with the execution and delivery of this Agreement or the consummation or performance of any Contemplated Transaction.

COMMENT

Section 3.2(a) contains Sellers' representation that the Model Agreement and, once executed, Sellers' Closing Documents are or will be legal obligations of Sellers that are enforceable against Sellers. If Sellers are unable or unwilling to make this fundamental representation, Buyer might question whether to go forward with the Contemplated Transactions.

Section 3.2(b) contains Sellers' "no conflict" representation. The purpose of this representation is to assure Buyer that, except as disclosed by Sellers in the Disclosure Letter, the acquisition will not violate (or otherwise trigger adverse consequences under) any legal or contractual requirements applicable to Sellers or the Acquired Companies.

The purpose served by the "no conflict" representation differs from that served by the more general representations concerning legal requirements, governmental authorizations, orders, and contracts (*see* Sections 3.14, 3.15, and 3.17), which alert

Buyer to violations and other potential problems not connected with the acquisition itself. The "no conflict" representation focuses specifically on violations and other potential problems that would be triggered by completing the Contemplated Transactions.

The term "Contemplated Transactions" is defined broadly in Section 1.1 to include not only the sale of the shares to Buyer at the Closing, but also the performance of the Employment Agreement, Buyer's exercise of control over the Acquired Companies, and various other actions that may be taken after the Closing Date. The use of an expansive definition of the term "Contemplated Transactions" makes the scope of the "no conflict" representation broader. The "no conflict" representation relates both to requirements binding upon the Acquired Companies and to requirements binding upon Sellers. Requirements binding upon Buyer are separately covered by Buyer's "no conflict" representation in Section 4.2 and the closing condition in Section 8.10.

The phrase "with or without notice or lapse of time," in the introduction to the "no conflict" representation, requires Sellers to disclose any "potential" or "unmatured" violations or defaults (circumstances that, although not technically constituting a current violation or default, could become a violation or default if a specified grace period elapses or if a formal notice of violation or default is delivered) that may be caused by the Contemplated Transactions.

Clause (ii) of Section 3.2(b) focuses specifically on Legal Requirements and Orders that might be contravened by the Contemplated Transactions. The broad language of this provision requires disclosure not only of legal violations, but also of other adverse legal consequences that may be triggered by the Contemplated Transactions. For example, the "Exon-Florio" regulations (31 C.F.R. § 800.101–702), provide for the submission of notices to the Committee on Foreign Investment in the United States in connection with acquisitions of U.S. companies by "foreign persons." Because the filing of an "Exon-Florio" notice is voluntary, the failure to file such a notice is not a regulatory violation. However, the filing of such a notice shortens the time period within which the President can exercise divestment authority and certain other legal remedies with respect to the acquisition described in the notice. Thus, the failure to file such a notice affords the President a continuing right to challenge the Contemplated Transactions. Clause (ii) of Section 3.2(b) alerts Buyer and Section 4.2(b)(ii) alerts Sellers to the existence of regulatory provisions of this nature. As part of their due diligence, Sellers may want to ascertain whether Buyer is a "foreign person" and within the coverage of the Exon-Florio regulations.

The parties may face a troublesome dilemma if both Buyer and Sellers are aware of a possible violation of law that might occur as a consequence of the Contemplated Transactions. If the possible violation is not disclosed in the Disclosure Letter, Sellers will bear the risks associated with any violation. But if Sellers elect to disclose the possible violation in the Disclosure Letter, they may be providing a discoverable "road map for a lawsuit by the government or a third party." *See*

KLING & NUGENT § 11.04[7][3]. Therefore, care is required in crafting disclosures of this type.

Clause (iii) addresses the possible revocation of Governmental Authorization. It overlaps to some extent with clause (ii). Clause (iii) is included because a Governmental Authorization may become subject to revocation without any statutory or regulatory violation actually having occurred.

Clauses (iv) and (v) are important because, under some laws and regulations regarding transfer taxes and property tax assessments, a change in the control or stock ownership of a corporation that owns property may be treated as a sale of the property by the corporation. *See, e.g.*, CAL. REV. & TAX. CODE § 64(c) (treating a change in control of the stock ownership of a corporation as a sale of real property owned by the corporation). For examples of statutory provisions that may be violated (or that may provide for the revocation of Governmental Authorizations) as a consequence of a change in control or a change in the stock ownership of a corporation, *see* BLUMBERG & STRASSER, THE LAW OF CORPORATE GROUPS; PROBLEMS OF PARENT AND SUBSIDIARY CORPORATIONS UNDER STATUTORY LAW SPECIFICALLY APPLYING ENTERPRISE PRINCIPLES (1992 & Supp. 2002). In connection with clause (iv), Sellers should consider whether any documentary stamp tax or similar taxes may be imposed with respect to the transfer of the Shares.

Clause (vi) deals with contractual defaults and other contractual consequences that may be triggered by the Contemplated Transactions under Applicable Contracts or Seller Contracts. Normally, the sale of a corporation's outstanding stock by its shareholders to a third party does not constitute a violation of a standard anti-assignment clause in a lease or other contract to which the corporation is a party. *See, e.g.*, Baxter Pharm. Prods., Inc. v. ESI Lederle Inc., 1999 Del. Ch. LEXIS 47 (Del. Ch. 1999); Dennis' Natural Mini-Meals, Inc. v. 91 Fifth Ave. Corp., 568 N.Y.S.2d 740 (N.Y. App. Div. 1991). In some contracts, however, the anti-assignment provision is broad enough to encompass a change in control or a transfer of the stock of a contracting party. *See, e.g.*, Associated Cotton Shops, Inc. v. Evergreen Park Shopping Plaza of Delaware, Inc., 170 N.E.2d 35 (Ill. App. 1960); *In re* Ames Dep't Stores, Inc., 127 B.R. 744 (Bankr. S.D.N.Y. 1991). Moreover, at least one court has found that a change of control of the licensee corporation violated the anti-assignment clause of an intellectual property license. *See,* SQL Solutions v. Oracle Corp. 1991 WL 626458 (N.D. Cal. 1991). Clause (vi) alerts Buyer to the existence of any such contracts. In addition, change of control provisions may be imposed by law. For example, the buyer of an investment advisory business must comply with the requirements of Section 205(a)(2) of the Investment Advisers Act of 1940 and, to the extent mutual fund clients are involved, Section 15(a)(4) of the Investment Company Act of 1940, both of which restrict the ability of advisers to "assign" (defined in the Investment Advisers Act to include the transfer of a controlling block of the assignee's voting securities) advisory contracts.

Even if a contract does not expressly characterize a change in control of a party as a "breach," "default," or "violation" by that party, the contract may nonetheless require a party undergoing a change in control to make a substantial cash payment (as in the case of a "golden parachute" employment agreement) or may otherwise provide for the exercise of various remedies by the other party or the grant of additional rights (such as increased payments owed under a lease or license). Clause (vi) thus refers not only to events constituting a breach, default, or violation of a contract, but also to events that would allow a party to the contract to exercise certain other rights.

Clause (vi) applies to "Applicable Contracts," the definition of which extends both to contracts to which an Acquired Company is a party and to contracts under which an Acquired Company has any rights or by which an Acquired Company may be bound. The inclusion of the latter types of contracts may be important to Buyer. For example, Buyer will want to know if an Acquired Company's rights under a promissory note or a guaranty given by a third party and held by the Acquired Company would be terminated or otherwise impaired as a result of the acquisition. Because such a promissory note or guaranty would presumably be signed only by the third-party maker or guarantor (and not by the Acquired Company as payee or beneficiary), the Acquired Company might not be a party to the note or guaranty.

Other examples of contracts that may be caught by the expansive definition of "Applicable Contract" include the following:

- contracts under which an Acquired Company is a third-party beneficiary;
- contracts under which a party's rights or obligations have been assigned to or assumed by an Acquired Company;
- contracts containing obligations that have been guaranteed by an Acquired Company;
- recorded agreements or declarations that relate to real property owned by an Acquired Company and that contain covenants or restrictions "running with the land;"
- contracts entered into by a partnership in which an Acquired Company is a general partner; and
- letters of credit.

In clause (vii), Sellers represent that neither the execution of the Model Agreement nor the consummation of the Contemplated Transactions will result in the creation of any Encumbrance on any asset of any Acquired Company. "Encumbrance" is broadly defined in Section 1.1.

Clause (viii) focuses on the impact of the Model Agreement and the Contemplated Transactions on the Intellectual Property Assets of the Acquired Companies. In clause (viii), Sellers represent that adverse consequences such as loss, disclosure, or compulsory licensing, will not befall any Intellectual Property Asset as a result of the Contemplated Transactions.

Section 3.2(c) requires that Sellers list in Part 3.2(c) of the Disclosure Letter any notices or consents that are required from a Person in connection with the Contemplated Transactions. The term "Person" is broadly defined and includes individuals, partnerships, corporations, other entities, and Governmental Bodies. Some of the required consents listed on Part 3.2(c) of the Disclosure Letter may be sufficiently important to justify giving Buyer (and, in some cases, Sellers) the right not to close if they are not ultimately obtained. *See* Sections 8.4 and 9.4 and related commentary.

SELLERS' RESPONSE

Sellers may seek an exception to the representation in the first sentence of Section 3.2(a) to the extent that enforceability is limited by bankruptcy, insolvency, moratorium, or similar laws affecting creditors' rights and remedies or by equitable principles. Such an exception is generally found in legal opinions regarding enforceability. Sellers may take the position that, without this qualification, the representation is simply untrue. Buyer may respond, however, that the exception would be inappropriate because Sellers should be willing to state without equivocation that the Model Agreement is binding. Ultimately, however, this is not a major issue to have a prolonged fight over.

The language in the third sentence of Section 3.2(a) regarding the "absolute and unrestricted right, power, authority, and capacity," is broad in its application and would encompass matters such as legal capacity as well as restrictions under third-party contracts or court orders.

The term "Contemplated Transactions" used in Section 3.2(b) is defined broadly in Section 1.1. Sellers may argue for a narrower definition of the term and may also seek to clarify that the "no conflict" representation does not extend to laws, contracts, or other requirements that are adopted or otherwise take effect after the Closing Date. In addition, Sellers may seek to clarify that the "no conflict" representation applies only to violations arising from Sellers' consummation of the Contemplated Transactions and not to violations arising from actions taken by, or circumstances particular to, Buyer or its affiliates.

Sellers may object to the use of the language "contravene" and "conflict" in each of clauses (i)–(iii) of Section 3.2(b) as being too broad or vague and, in lieu thereof, propose more concrete words such as "result in a breach or violation." Similarly, Sellers may argue that the representation that no person has the "right to challenge any Contemplated Transaction" is too broad when such statement is divorced from any qualification regarding the likely outcome or impact of such a challenge.

Sellers may object to clause (vi) of Section 3.2(b) as being too broad. For instance, it is possible to construe the definition of Applicable Contracts as including agreements entered into by third parties to which Seller or an Acquired Company is not a party. A lessor under an equipment lease with an Acquired Company may itself have granted a security interest in the leased equipment and the lender's security agreement would be a Contract by which assets used by an Acquired Company are or could become bound.

3.3 CAPITALIZATION OF COMPANY AND SUBSIDIARIES

(a) **The authorized Equity Securities of the Company consist of _____ shares of common stock, par value $_____ per share, of which _____ shares, constituting the Shares, are issued and outstanding. Sellers are the owners (of record and beneficially) of all of the Shares, free and clear of all Encumbrances, including any restriction on the right of any Seller to transfer the Shares to Buyer pursuant to this Agreement. The assignments, endorsements, stock powers, or other instruments of transfer to be delivered by each Seller to Buyer at the Closing will be sufficient to transfer such Seller's entire interest in the Shares (of record and beneficially) owned by such Seller. Upon transfer to Buyer of the certificates representing the Shares, Buyer will receive good title to the Shares, free and clear of all Encumbrances. Part 3.3(a) lists Sellers and the number of Shares held by each Seller.**

(b) **Part 3.3(b) lists for each Subsidiary its authorized Equity Securities, the number and type of Equity Securities issued and outstanding, and the identity of each owner (of record and beneficially) of such Equity Securities and number of shares held by each holder. All outstanding Equity Securities of each Subsidiary are owned of record and beneficially by one or more of the Acquired Companies, free and clear of all Encumbrances. All the outstanding Equity Securities of each Acquired Company have been duly authorized and validly issued, and are fully paid and nonassessable. Except as set forth in Part 3.3(b), there are no shareholder or other Contracts relating to any Equity Security of any Acquired Company, including the sale, voting, or transfer thereof. No outstanding Equity Security or other security of any Acquired Company was issued in violation of the Securities Act or any other Legal Requirement. No Acquired Company has any outstanding subscription, option, warrant, call or exchange right, convertible security, or other Contract or other obligations in effect giving any Person (other than another Acquired Company) the right to acquire (whether by preemptive rights or otherwise) any Equity Security of any Acquired Company.**

(c) **No Acquired Company owns, or is a party to or bound by any Contract to acquire, any Equity Security or other security of any Person or any direct or indirect equity or ownership interest in any other business. No Acquired Company is obligated to provide funds to or make any investment (whether in the form of a loan, capital contribution, or otherwise) in any other Person.**

COMMENT

Section 3.3 elicits information about the number of outstanding shares of the Company and each Subsidiary so that Buyer can verify that it is acquiring all the outstanding shares of the Company and, indirectly, a 100% ownership interest in each Subsidiary. The definition of "Equity Security" in Section 1.1 includes not only shares, but convertible securities and options and warrants to purchase shares. The representation is also designed to provide assurances to Buyer that no other party has any right to acquire any Equity Securities of the Company. Buyer will want to know the number of authorized shares to ensure that the outstanding shares were validly issued and, if the Company has any outstanding warrants, options, or convertible securities, that there are sufficient shares authorized to cover such securities. The Model Agreement contemplates that the Company has a relatively simple capitalization and one which does not include any outstanding options, warrants, or convertible securities. If a more complicated capital structure were present, Buyer may require more detailed representations designed to elicit specific information and also address such issues as dilution and pre-closing exercise of convertible securities.

Section 3.3(a) refers to the Shares as being owned of record and beneficially by Sellers free and clear of any Encumbrances. References to "marketable" title should be avoided since this term applies primarily to real estate, not securities. "Beneficial ownership" is a concept found both in state law and in Rule 13d-3 under the Exchange Act (17 C.F.R. § 240.13d-3). Since securities are often held of record in the name of a nominee, disclosure of beneficial ownership provides information with respect to the real parties in interest. The representation with respect to beneficial ownership identifies anyone other than Sellers who holds a beneficial interest in the Shares. Although the Sellers in the Model Agreement Fact Pattern are individuals, if the Seller is a corporation which is part of a consolidated group, there may be a direct parent, several intermediate holding companies, and an ultimate parent. All such entities have beneficial ownership. Buyer should investigate which of these various entities have significant assets and can provide meaningful indemnification. If the direct parent has little or no assets, Buyer may seek to bind another entity further up the chain. Although the term "Encumbrances" includes the concept of "community property interests," this can be easily overlooked. In certain jurisdictions, particularly community property states, Buyer should consider requiring that the spouses of individual Sellers consent to the Merger Agreement and Contemplated Transactions.

Section 3.3 should be read in conjunction with Section 8.9, which provides as a closing condition that no person claims to own or have the right to acquire shares in any of the Acquired Companies.

Section 3.3(b) provides information with respect to the Equity Securities of the Subsidiaries (i.e., the Acquired Companies other than the Company). It provides assurance that all such Equity Securities are owned by other Acquired Companies and are duly authorized and issued. It also provides assurance that there are no outstanding rights to buy any Equity Securities of any Subsidiary. Section 3.3(b) also states that no Equity Security of any Acquired Company was issued in violation of the Securities Act or other Legal Requirements. This representation is with respect to the Shares and the shares of the Subsidiaries.

Section 3.3(c) is designed to elicit information regarding minority investments that the Company may have in other entities and to determine whether there are any obligations of the Company or its Subsidiaries in respect of such minority investments (e.g., the obligation to respond to capital calls).

See MANUAL ON ACQUISITION REVIEW 20–29.

SELLERS' RESPONSE

Sellers may want to specify that the information being elicited in Section 3.3 is as of a given date, such as the date of the Model Agreement. This may be acceptable if the issuance of any additional shares between the date of the Model Agreement and the closing is prohibited, thus rendering this representation correct at all relevant times.

The definition of "Encumbrance" in Section 1.1 is broad. Sellers may request that the text in Sections 3.3(a) and (b) be changed to "free and clear of any adverse claim" as defined in UCC Section 8-102(a)(1). Section 8-102(a)(1) defines "adverse claim" as a claim that someone has a property interest in a security and that it is in violation of the rights of the claimant for another person to hold, transfer, or deal in the security.

Sellers may object to the sentence in Section 3.3(b) stating that no Equity Security was issued in violation of the Securities Act or any other Legal Requirement. The definition of "Legal Requirement" in Section 1.1 is broad and, depending on how much time has passed since the issuance of the Equity Securities in question, it may be difficult for Sellers to identify all of the Legal Requirements that applied at the time of issuance. Sellers might also argue that this representation does Buyer little practical good, since technical violations in the distant past have little chance of adversely affecting Buyer's title to the Shares.

Sellers should determine whether record and beneficial ownership, in fact, vest in the same person. For example, if shares are held in a trust, the trust may have record ownership, but the trustee may be the beneficial owner by reason of having the right to vote and dispose of the shares.

3.4   FINANCIAL STATEMENTS

Sellers have delivered to Buyer: (a) audited consolidated balance sheets of the Company and its Subsidiaries as at _____ (the "Balance Sheet Date") and as at _____, and the related audited consolidated statements of income, changes in shareholders' equity, and cash flows for each of the _____ fiscal years ended on such dates, including the notes thereto, together with the report thereon of the Company's independent public accountants, (collectively, the "Audited Financial Statements"), and (b) an unaudited consolidated balance sheet (the "Interim Balance Sheet") of the Company and its Subsidiaries as at _____ (the "Interim Balance Sheet Date"), and the related unaudited consolidated statements of income, changes in shareholders' equity, and cash flows for the _____ months then ended, certified by the chief financial officer of the Company (collectively, the "Unaudited Financial Statements", and together with the Audited Financial Statements, the "Financial Statements"). The Financial Statements (i) fairly present the consolidated financial condition and the results of operations, changes in shareholders' equity, and cash flows of the Company and its Subsidiaries as at the respective dates of, and for the periods referred to in, the Financial Statements, and (ii) were prepared in accordance with GAAP, subject, in the case of the Unaudited Financial Statements, to normal recurring year-end adjustments (the effect of which will not, individually or in the aggregate, be material) and the absence of notes (that, if presented, would not differ materially from those included in the Audited Financial Statements). The Financial Statements reflect the consistent application of GAAP throughout the periods involved, except as disclosed in the notes to the Audited Financial Statements. No financial statements of any Person other than the Acquired Companies are required by GAAP to be included or reflected in the Financial Statements. The Financial Statements were prepared from, and are consistent with, the accounting Records of each Acquired Company. Sellers have also delivered to Buyer copies of all letters from the Company's auditors to the Company's board of directors or audit committee thereof during the 36 months prior to the date of this Agreement, together with copies of all responses thereto.

COMMENT

This representation, which requires the delivery of specified financial statements of the Acquired Companies and provides assurances regarding their quality, is common in acquisition agreements. Financial statements are key tools in evaluating businesses. The most recent balance sheet included in such financial statements also provides a baseline for the Adjustment Amount (*see* Section 2.5(a)) to the Purchase Price.

The representation requires the delivery of (1) audited consolidated annual financial statements for a period of years ending with the most recently completed fiscal year, and (2) unaudited consolidated financial statements as of the end of an interim period subsequent to the last audited financial statements. The determination of which financial statements should be required will depend upon factors such as availability, relevance to Buyer's evaluation of the acquisition, and the burden and expense on Sellers that Buyer wishes to impose and Sellers are willing to bear. Frequently, where the target is closely held and does not have any external obligation to provide audited financial statements (e.g., pursuant to bank covenants), audited financial statements will not be available. Similarly, where the target has been operated as part of a larger enterprise and does not have a history of independent financing transactions, separate audited financial statements may not exist and, although the auditors that expressed an opinion concerning the entire enterprise's consolidated financial statements will, of necessity, have considered the financial statements of the Acquired Companies, such consideration may not have been sufficient for the expression of an opinion regarding the financial statements of the Acquired Companies by themselves. This occurs most frequently when the target does not represent a major portion of the entire enterprise, so that the materiality judgments made in the audit of the enterprise's financial statements are not appropriate for an examination of the Acquired Companies' financial statements. *See* Appendix A—The Purchase of a Subsidiary. Although it is not unusual for a buyer to require a seller to cause the target's auditors to do the necessary additional work to express an opinion on one recent set of financial statements, it may not be practical to seek this comfort for earlier periods. In the absence of audited financial statements, the representation concerning the accuracy of the Acquired Companies' books and records (Section 3.5) is critical because these books and records are Buyer's main tool for assessing the financial health of the Acquired Companies (under Section 5.1, Buyer has a right to inspect these books and records).

Buyer may also request audited or unaudited consolidating financial statements, which contain separate financial statements for each of the Acquired Companies and the eliminations necessary to produce the consolidated financial statements. Consolidating financial statements can be valuable from a due diligence perspective as they separately report the assets, liabilities, and profitability of each Acquired Company, along with all related intercompany transactions (e.g., loans, and receivables). Accordingly, among other things, they can (i) indicate which Acquired Companies are the most profitable (and thus worthy of due diligence focus), (ii) provide a window (and an appropriate subject for more targeted due diligence) into product-line profitability (at least where different Acquired Companies sell different products), and (iii) signal the degree of integration/synergy between the various Acquired Companies. If consolidating statements are not already available, Sellers are likely to object to the additional accounting or audit work required to produce them and contend that Buyer should be concerned about the financial aspects of the Acquired Companies as a whole, not individual entities. If Buyer insists on receiving consolidating financial statements, Buyer should be prepared to demonstrate to Sellers the relevance of that information to Buyer's evaluation of the acquisition. In such cases, the parties will need to agree who will bear the cost of the added accounting service, and may need to adjust the anticipated closing date to accomplish the task.

If Buyer is a public reporting company under the Exchange Act, it may have additional public reporting obligations that would necessitate obtaining, on a timely basis, audited fiscal year-end financial statements and unaudited interim financial statements of the Company that satisfy the requirements of SEC Regulation S-X. When other than in the ordinary course of business, Buyer must file a current report on Form 8-K and provide the information required by Item 2.01 and the financial statements and other financial information required by Item 9.01. An acquisition is deemed to involve a significant amount of assets if the net book value of the assets or the amount paid exceeds 10% of the total assets of the public company and its consolidated subsidiaries, or it involves a business that is significant as determined under Rule 11-01 of Regulation S-X. A buyer that is a public company may also seek representations as to the registration of the Company's auditors with the Public Company Accounting Oversight Board and as to the auditors' independence, including disclosure of any nonaudit services they may have performed for the Acquired Companies.

The type and extent of financial statements of an acquired business required for inclusion in Form 8-K are, depending on the size of the reporting company, set forth in Rule 3-05(b) or Rule 8-04(b) of SEC Regulation S-X. Since some of this financial information, particularly the pro forma information, may not be available at closing, it may be filed by an amendment to Form 8-K not later than 71 days after the date that the initial report was required to be filed. This financial information may also be required for subsequent registration statements on Form S-1 that Buyer may be filing. For a discussion of the requirements of the Securities Act and the Exchange Act as applied to acquisitions by public companies, *see* KLING & NUGENT §§ 5.02, .03. *See* Appendix B—Receipt of Stock of a Public Company as Purchase Consideration.

The financial statement representation does not attempt to characterize the auditors' report. Buyer's counsel should determine at an early stage whether the report contains any qualifications regarding conformity with GAAP, the audit having been in accordance with generally accepted auditing standards (GAAS), or fair presentation being subject to the outcome of contingencies. Any qualification in the auditors' report should be discussed with Buyer's accountants.

In some jurisdictions, auditors cannot be held liable for inaccurate financial reports to persons not in privity or near privity with the auditors, except in limited circumstances. For a detailed discussion regarding auditor liability standards and cases, *see* Feinman, *Liability of Accountants for Negligent Auditing; Doctrine, Policy and Ideology*, 31 FLA. ST. U.L. REV. 17 (2003). If the audited financial statements were prepared in the ordinary course, Buyer probably will not satisfy the requirements for pursuing auditors' liability in those jurisdictions in the absence of a "reliance letter" from the auditors addressed to Buyer. Requests for reliance letters are relatively unusual in acquisitions, and accounting firms are increasingly unwilling to give them.

Section 3.4 states that the Financial Statements "fairly present" the consolidated financial condition, results of operations, changes in shareholders' equity and cash flows of the Company and its Subsidiaries. It then states separately that the Financial Statements were prepared in accordance with GAAP. Financial statement representations sometimes state that the financial statements "fairly present . . . in accordance with GAAP." The Model Agreement separates the two concepts. Section 601 of SEC Regulation S-K requires that the principal executive officer and principal financial officer of a reporting company certify that the financial statements "fairly present" without a GAAP qualifier. In the view of the SEC, this reflects congressional intent to provide assurances as to the accuracy and completeness of the financial statements that are broader than the requirements of GAAP. Exchange Act Rel. No 34-46427 (2002). If Buyer is a public company, this representation may provide important comfort. *See* United States v. Simon, 425 F.2d (2d Cir. 1969), holding that compliance with GAAP does not immunize from prosecution for securities law violations an accountant who consciously chooses not to disclose known material facts relating to improper corporate officer activity.

Section 3.4 contains Sellers' representation that GAAP has been applied on a consistent basis in the preparation of the Financial Statements. If inconsistent accounting principals were used between the periods reported upon in the Financial Statements, it could skew the results and Buyer's understanding of them.

Section 3.4 also contains Sellers' representation that there is no other entity whose financial statements must be included or reflected in the Financial Statements. Where one entity holds a significant investment in another, even if less than a majority, GAAP requires that investment to be reflected in the owner's financial statements.

The last sentence of Section 3.4 requires Sellers to deliver copies of the so-called "management letters" issued to the Company by its accountants over the past 36 months. These letters critique the Company's accounting practices and controls and may provide insight to Buyer.

See Manual on Acquisition Review ch. 5.

SELLERS' RESPONSE

Sellers may request a financial statement representation that mirrors the language in the report of its independent accountants to the effect that the financial statements "fairly present in all material respects . . . . in conformity with GAAP." Buyer may resist this formulation, arguing first, that GAAP already includes materiality principles and that to add the qualifier would result in a double materiality qualifier. Buyer may also contend that the financial statements are the responsibility of the Company, and Sellers should bear the attendant risk and be held to a higher standard than its independent accountants. In addition, Buyer may resist the materiality qualifier because of the "threshold" provision in Section 11.6(a). *See*

"'Materiality' Qualifications" in preliminary note to Article 3, and commentary to Section 11.6.

Sellers may seek to limit the number of years covered by the financial statement representation, arguing that older financial statements have little relevance in assessing the present financial condition and operations of the Company. Requests for three to five years of financial statements are typical.

3.5   Books and Records

(a) **The books of account and other Records of each Acquired Company, all of which have been made available to Buyer, are complete and correct, represent actual, bona fide transactions, and have been maintained in accordance with sound business practices and the requirements of Section 13(b)(2) of the Exchange Act (whether or not any Acquired Company is subject to that Section). The Acquired Companies have implemented and maintain a system of internal control over financial reporting (as defined in Rules 13a-15(f) and 15d-15(f) under the Exchange Act) sufficient to provide reasonable assurance regarding the reliability of financial reporting and the preparation of financial statements for external purposes in accordance with GAAP, including that (i) transactions are executed in accordance with management's general or specific authorizations, (ii) transactions are recorded as necessary to permit preparation of financial statements in conformity with GAAP and to maintain asset accountability, (iii) access to assets is permitted only in accordance with management's general or specific authorization, and (iv) the recorded accountability for assets is compared with the existing assets at reasonable intervals and appropriate action is taken with respect to any differences.**

(b) **The minute books of each Acquired Company contain complete and correct Records of all meetings held of, and actions taken by written consent of, the holders of voting securities, the board of directors or Persons exercising similar authority, and committees of the board of directors or such Persons of such Acquired Company, and no meeting of any such holders, board of directors, Persons, or committee has been held, and no other action has been taken, for which minutes or other evidence of action have not been prepared and are not contained in such minute books. Each Acquired Company has at all times maintained complete and correct Records of all issuances and transfers of its Equity Securities. At the Closing, all such minute books and Records will be in the possession of the Company and located at [specify location(s)].**

COMMENT

The books of account of the Acquired Companies are the basis of the financial statements. If the books of account are inaccurate or incomplete, the information provided to the Company's auditors (or Buyer's auditors) will be suspect and the financial statements will be of little value to Buyer. Therefore, Buyer may seek to go behind the financial statements by requesting representations concerning the quality of the Acquired Companies' recordkeeping. Such representations are especially important when separate audited financial statements have not been prepared for the Acquired Companies, such as when the Acquired Companies are subsidiaries or divisions of a larger enterprise. Buyer may want to inquire about these matters by requesting Sellers to deliver copies of management letters and other reports received from the Acquired Companies' auditors over a specified period of time.

Section 13(b)(2) of the Exchange Act was added by the Foreign Corrupt Practices Act and applies only to public companies; the parenthetical phrase that follows the reference to that Act is necessary if that portion of the representation is to have any meaning in the case of private companies. Section 13(b)(2) requires the maintenance of books and records that "in reasonable detail, accurately and fairly reflect the transactions and dispositions of the assets of the issuer." It further requires the issuer to devise and maintain a system of internal accounting controls sufficient to provide assurances that transactions are being executed in accordance with management authorizations, recorded so as to maintain accountability and permit preparation of financial statements.

The Sarbanes-Oxley Act of 2002 imposed a number of requirements on public companies, including Section 404 and related rules that require them to maintain internal controls over financial reporting. Exchange Act Rules 13a-15(f) define "internal control over financial reporting" as a process designed to provide reasonable assurances regarding the reliability of financial statements in accordance with GAAP, including policies and procedures that:

- pertain to the maintenance of records that in reasonable detail accurately and fairly reflect the transactions and dispositions of the assets of the issuer;
- provide reasonable assurance that transactions are recorded as necessary to permit preparation of financial statements in accordance with GAAP, and that transactions are being made only in accordance with authorizations of management and directors of the issuer; and
- provide reasonable assurance regarding prevention or timely detection of unauthorized acquisition, use, or disposition of the issuer's assets.

Representations regarding internal controls have become increasing important, not only to buyers that are public companies, but to private buyers as well. The private buyer may contemplate going public or may face inquiries on internal controls from bank or institutional investors. For a discussion of these and other requirements of the Sarbanes-Oxley Act of 2002 and related rules of the SEC as they pertain to public companies, *see* KING & NUGENT § 5.10. These requirements will suggest other areas of due diligence that might be undertaken by a buyer and may suggest other representations that might be requested.

The portion of the representation relating to minute books could be troublesome to Sellers if the Acquired Companies are closely held and have conducted their affairs informally. It is in those instances, however, that this representation might be most important to Buyer.

See MANUAL ON ACQUISITION REVIEW ch. 2.

SELLERS' RESPONSE

Sellers may seek to eliminate or limit representations regarding its books and records to avoid giving financial representations that extend beyond those of Section 3.4. Sellers may argue that immaterial inaccuracies in the Acquired Companies' books and records should not give rise to damages unless they result in a breach of the financial statement representation.

Sellers may also object to the statement that all its Records have been made available to Buyer. Given the broad definition of Records and the number of Records that are generated in operating a business, Sellers may argue that it is both impossible and unnecessary to make all Records available to Buyer.

Sellers might seek to delete the references to Exchange Act Section 13(b)(2) and Rules 13a-15(f) and 15d-15(f) because the Company is not subject to the Exchange Act and does not have internal controls that rise to the level of those requirements.

Sellers might also object to the representation in Section 3.5(b), because the Company is privately held and its governance may have been far more informal than this representation would indicate. Alternatively, Sellers might seek time limitations with respect to the representations in Section 3.5(b).

3.6   REAL AND PERSONAL PROPERTY

(a) **Part 3.6(a) lists all real estate owned by each Acquired Company (the "Owned Real Property"), including the legal description, street address, and any tax parcel identification number of each property, and the Acquired Company that owns such property. Sellers have delivered to Buyer copies of the deeds and other instruments by which any Acquired Company acquired the Owned Real Property and copies of all title insurance policies, opinions, abstracts, and surveys in the possession of Sellers or any Acquired Company relating to the Owned Real Property.**

(b) Part 3.6(b) lists all real estate leased by any Acquired Company as a lessee, sub-lessee, or assignee (the "Leased Real Property" and, together with the Owned Real Property, the "Real Property"), including a description of the premises leased and the Acquired Company that leases the same. All Leased Real Property is leased pursuant to valid written leases listed in Part 3.17(a). Such leases contain the entire agreement between the landlord of each of the leased premises and the Acquired Company, and there is no other Contract between the landlord and any Acquired Company affecting such Leased Real Property. No Acquired Company leases Real Property as a lessor or sub-lessor.

(c) The Owned Real Property and the Acquired Companies' interests in the Leased Real Property are owned by the respective Acquired Companies free and clear of all Encumbrances, variances, or limitations of any nature, other than Permitted Encumbrances and as set forth in Part 3.6(c). All buildings, plants, and structures owned by any Acquired Company lie wholly within the boundaries of the Real Property in question and do not encroach upon the property of, or otherwise conflict with the property rights of, any other Person. There are no buildings, structures, fixtures, or other improvements primarily situated on adjoining property that encroach on any part of the Real Property. Each parcel of Real Property abuts on, and has direct vehicular access to, a public road or has access to a public road via a permanent, irrevocable, appurtenant easement benefiting such Real Property and constituting a part thereof. Certificates of occupancy are in full force and effect for each location of Real Property, and the uses thereof being made by the Acquired Companies do not violate any applicable zoning, subdivision, land use, or other Legal Requirement. No Third Party has a right to acquire any interest in the Owned Real Property or in the Acquired Companies' interests in the Leased Real Property. There is no existing or proposed plan to modify or realign any street or highway or any existing or proposed eminent domain Proceeding that would result in the taking of all or any part of any parcel of Real Property or that would prevent or hinder the continued use of any such parcel as used by the Acquired Companies. None of the Real Property is located within a flood plain for flood insurance purposes.

(d) The Acquired Companies own all tangible personal property reflected as owned in the Interim Balance Sheet (other than inventory sold since the Interim Balance Sheet Date in the Ordinary Course of Business), free and clear of all Encumbrances, other than Permitted Encumbrances and as set forth in Part 3.6(d). All the tangible personal property purchased or otherwise acquired by the Acquired Companies since the Interim

Balance Sheet Date (other than inventory acquired and sold since the Interim Balance Sheet Date in the Ordinary Course of Business) is owned by the Acquired Companies free and clear of all Encumbrances, other than Permitted Encumbrances and as set forth in Part 3.6(d). A copy of the fixed asset register of each Acquired Company has been delivered to Buyer. Each such register contains a complete and correct list of the fixed assets of the applicable Acquired Company as of the date specified.

COMMENT

Owned Real Property. Buyer will need correct legal descriptions to confirm that title is vested in the relevant Acquired Company and to identify any encumbrances. The street address will be needed in many jurisdictions to confirm zoning, land use, and building code compliance. The tax parcel identification number can be used to confirm that real estate taxes have been paid on the property and also whether the property is a separately taxed parcel. If the real property to be acquired is part of a larger tax parcel, the failure of the owner of the remainder of the parcel to pay its portion of the taxes could result in a lien against the acquired real estate. In acquisitions involving significant real property, or real property intended for development, Buyer should consider seeking a representation concerning the Acquired Companies' history of zoning and other land use disputes and perhaps more detailed representations regarding access to the property, availability of utilities and the like. If the Acquired Companies own no real property, the first statement can be changed to a representation to that effect and much of the rest can be omitted.

Leased Real Property. It may be important for Buyer to review the real estate leases to ascertain whether consents to transfer are necessary, to understand landlord and tenant rights and obligations going forward (including renewal options, termination options, and future rent increases) and to confirm that the Contemplated Transactions will not result in a termination or alteration of the leases. If any Acquired Company is a landlord under any leases, representations should be added to address those as well.

Title and Encumbrances. Section 3.6(c) seeks representations regarding Encumbrances and other matters that could adversely impact the value or use of Owned or Leased Real Property. Section 3.6(c) also recites several common title issues, seeking Sellers' representation that they do not affect the real property. If the Acquired Companies do not already have title insurance on the Owned Real Property, Buyer may want to consider requiring it as a closing condition, since it may ameliorate risks related to title and Encumbrances.

Tangible Personal Property. Section 3.6(d) contains Sellers' representations that the Acquired Companies have title to their tangible personal property (whether reflected on the Interim Balance Sheet or acquired thereafter), free and clear of all

Encumbrances other than "Permitted Encumbrances," as defined in Section 1.1, and those specifically disclosed. The principal intangible assets of the Acquired Companies, accounts receivable, and Intellectual Property Assets, are covered in Section 3.8 and 3.22, respectively.

Section 3.6(d) calls for Sellers to deliver fixed asset registers for the Acquired Companies. Although the transaction is structured as a purchase of Shares, it is a means by which Buyer is seeking to acquire control over the business and assets of the Acquired Companies. This subsection provides Buyer with a list of the personal property assets owned by each Acquired Company in a format that should be readily available.

Liens on personal property typically would be in the form of security interests and other liens in favor of a creditor. In addition to obtaining this representation, Buyer would typically conduct UCC searches, federal and tax lien searches, judgment, bankruptcy, and, perhaps, litigation searches.

See MANUAL ON ACQUISITION REVIEW ch. 4.

SELLERS' RESPONSE

Sellers may object to the level of detail required by Part 3.6(a), arguing that much of the information has already been delivered to Buyer in due diligence. Sellers may seek to limit the second sentence of Section 3.6(a) to materials in the possession of the Acquired Companies, since some of the listed items may not exist or be available.

Sellers may want to limit Part 3.6(b) to a listing of the address of each leased property, arguing that Buyer can obtain the property descriptions from the Leases, copies of which have already been provided in due diligence.

With respect to Section 3.6(c), Sellers may want to schedule all items shown on the updated title report and may also request an exception for minor imperfections of title, if any, none of which are substantial in amount, materially detract from the value, or impair the use of the property in question or impair the operations of any Acquired Company. This might be accomplished by amending the definition of "Permitted Encumbrances" in Section 1.1. Sellers should also consider whether exceptions are necessary for existing use and other restrictions, including environmental matters that may restrict the use or development of the property. Acquisition agreements will often include separate representations concerning environmental matters, such as in Section 3.19, but disclosure of environmental restrictions may be necessary here as well. Finally, Sellers may object to providing some of these representations, contending that Buyer should instead rely on the title report, particularly if it will be obtaining financing and will be purchasing an owner's policy while the lender obtains a mortgagee title insurance policy.

Similarly, with respect to personal property, Sellers may request an exception for Encumbrances that do not materially adversely detract from the value of such property or affect its use or operation by the Acquired Companies.

Depending on the facts, Sellers may want to expand the exception in Section 3.6(d) beyond inventory to also include obsolete or surplus equipment.

3.7   CONDITION AND SUFFICIENCY OF ASSETS

(a) **The buildings, plants, structures, and equipment owned or leased by the Acquired Companies are structurally sound, in good operating condition and repair, and adequate for the uses to which they are being put, and none of such buildings, plants, structures, or equipment is in need of maintenance or repairs other than ordinary, routine maintenance that is not material in nature or cost.**

(b) **The assets owned and leased by each Acquired Company constitute all the assets used in connection with the business of such Acquired Company. Such assets constitute all the assets necessary for such Acquired Company to continue to conduct its business following the Closing as it is being conducted.**

COMMENT

The representation in Section 3.7(a) seeks comfort regarding the condition of the Acquired Companies' tangible assets. Buyer does not want to face unexpected expenses for repair or replacement of the Acquired Companies' assets.

The purpose of the representation in Section 3.7(b) is to confirm that the Acquired Companies own, or have adequate rights to use, all assets necessary to continue operating the business in the same manner after the Closing as before. Section 3.7(b) can be especially significant when the Acquired Companies are closely held or are part of a larger enterprise. In a closely held company, the shareholders sometimes claim ownership of assets used by the company. Where the target is a subsidiary of a larger company, it may have shared resources with other companies in the group, so that it does not own all the assets used in its business. Section 3.24 also provides Buyer with information regarding claims by Sellers and others of ownership of assets used by the Acquired Companies.

See MANUAL ON ACQUISITION REVIEW ch. 4.

SELLERS' RESPONSE

Sellers may object to representing in Section 3.7(a) as to the condition of the plant and equipment of the Acquired Companies, contending that Buyer should rely on its own inspection of the assets. Sellers may assert that the breakdown of equipment sometimes is simply the nature of the business and that they should not be held accountable for such events. Sellers may also argue that "good operating condition and repair," in addition to being subjective, is too high a standard. Sellers may request that "good" be replaced with "adequate."

Sellers may object to Section 3.7(b) as vague and subjective. Sellers may also view this representation as problematic if, for example, employees sometimes use their own tools or supplies in performing their duties.

3.8   ACCOUNTS RECEIVABLE

All accounts receivable of each Acquired Company, whether or not reflected on the Interim Balance Sheet, represent valid obligations arising from sales actually made or services actually performed in the Ordinary Course of Business. The accounts receivable of each Acquired Company are current and collectible net of the reserve shown on the Interim Balance Sheet (which reserve is adequate and calculated consistent with past practice in the preparation of the Financial Statements). Subject to such reserve, each of the accounts receivable either has been or will be collected in full, without any setoff, expense, or other reduction, within 90 days after the day on which it first becomes due and payable. There is no contest, claim, defense, or right of setoff, other than returns in the Ordinary Course of Business, with respect to any account receivable. Part 3.8 lists and sets forth the aging of all accounts receivable as of the Interim Balance Sheet Date.

COMMENT

Typically, the term "accounts receivable" denotes trade debtors' accounts; other receivables are separately designated and recorded as special receivables. Accounts receivable due within one year are classified as "current assets" on the balance sheet. Accounts receivable are assets that Buyer expects will become cash in short order. The receivables may well be critical to Buyer's assessment of the Acquired Companies and their valuation. Therefore, it is not surprising that Buyer may seek stringent assurances regarding the accounts receivable.

The representation concerning accounts receivable provides line-item support to the more general representations regarding the financial statements as a whole. The purchase price adjustment provided for in Section 2.5 of the Model Agreement also provides Buyer with some comfort, since fluctuations in the accounts receivable will be taken into account in determining the change in shareholders' equity between the Interim Balance Sheet Date and the Closing Date.

Section 3.8 begins with an assurance that the Acquired Companies' accounts receivable represent valid obligations arising from sales actually made or services actually performed by the Acquired Companies. This is essentially an anti-fraud provision and should be construed as a representation that the accounts receivable reflected on the Company's balance sheets and in the books of account are genuine and not fabricated.

Assurances of collectibility should take into account any established reserve for uncollectible accounts. Such a reserve (also known as an allowance for doubtful accounts or a bad debt reserve) estimates the proportion of the accounts receivable that is not expected to be collected.

Methods of providing a buyer assurances regarding the collectibility of accounts receivable include: (i) a representation of collectibility, net of the corresponding reserve, backed by the Sellers' indemnification obligations, or (ii) an agreement that Sellers will purchase all pre-closing accounts receivable that remain unpaid after a specified period (such as 90 days) elapses after their creation.

In Section 3.8, Sellers warrant that the aggregate amount of the accounts receivable will be "current and collectible" as of the Closing, net of the reserve for uncollectible accounts. The representation further provides that each account will be collected in full, subject to the reserve, without set-off, within 90 days after the date on which it first becomes payable. The indemnification provisions of Article 11 provide that Sellers will be responsible to Buyer for any breach of this representation (Section 11.2(a)). Buyer should keep in mind that Sellers' indemnification obligations may be subject to limitations such as thresholds that must be achieved and time periods during which claims for indemnification must be made (Sections 11.5 and 11.6).

Courts have placed various interpretations on contractual representations concerning the collectibility of accounts receivable. *See, e.g.*, Metro-Goldwyn-Mayer, Inc. v. Ross, 509 F.2d 930 (2d Cir. 1975); Forms, Inc. v. American Standard, Inc., 546 F. Supp. 314 (E.D. Penn. 1982); *see also* Resort Car Rental Sys., Inc. v. Chuck Ruwart Chevrolet, Inc., 519 F.2d 317 (10th Cir. 1975); REA Express, Inc. v. Interway Corp., 410 F. Supp. 192 (S.D.N.Y.), *rev'd*, 538 F.2d 953 (2d Cir. 1976); Rocky Mountain Helicopters v. Air Freight, 773 P.2d 911 (Wyo. 1989). An acquisition agreement could indicate the mechanism for establishing the amount of the reserves for uncollectible accounts (whether by reference to particular financial statements, receivables schedules, or the Acquired Companies' books and records). *See* Armco Inc. v. Glenfed Financial Corp., 746 F. Supp. 1249 (D.N.J. 1990); Carolet Corp. v. Garfield, 157 N.E.2d 876 (Mass. 1959).

See MANUAL ON ACQUISITION REVIEW ch. 5.

SELLERS' RESPONSE

Sellers may request that Section 3.8 be deleted in its entirety, arguing that Buyer receives adequate assurance on the accounts receivable from the financial statement representation in Section 3.4. Sellers may also seek assurance that no "double-dipping" will occur if uncollectible receivables result in a post-closing purchase price adjustment pursuant to Section 2.5.

Sellers may resist providing assurances regarding collectibility by arguing that Buyer should conduct a thorough pre-closing investigation of the status of the receivables. Similarly, Sellers may assert that the acquisition is the sale of a going concern and that the possibility of uncollectibility of genuine accounts receivable is simply a risk of doing business that should be transferred to Buyer at the closing.

Purchase of Uncollected Accounts by Sellers. An alternative method of providing assurances of collectibility is Sellers' guaranty that after a stipulated period of time, they will purchase the uncollected receivables from the Acquired Companies at the net amount that has not been collected. Typically, such a guaranty requires that Sellers purchase accounts that remain uncollected, net of applicable reserves, after the passage of the predetermined period of time from the creation of the accounts. In deciding whether to use the purchase method, the parties should keep in mind that the quality of Buyer's post-closing collection efforts will affect Sellers' purchase obligations and that Sellers' collection efforts after the assignment could interfere with Buyer's conduct of the newly acquired business, especially with ongoing customer relations.

A sample accounts receivable purchase provision that could be added to Article 7 is set forth below. Where such a provision is used, certain adjustments to the purchase price will be necessary. For example, if there is no buy-back because all accounts receivable are collected, the purchase price provisions should provide a mechanism for payment to Sellers of the held-back amount.

ACCOUNTS RECEIVABLE PURCHASE

(a)   Buyer shall have the right, by written notice (the "Receivables Notice") to Sellers given on or after 90 days following the Closing Date (the "Repurchase Date"), to require Sellers to purchase for cash and without recourse, within five days of the date of the Receivables Notice, all of the Accounts Receivable of the Acquired Companies reflected on the books and records of the Acquired Companies on the Closing Date that are at the Repurchase Date uncollected [net of the reserve reflected on the Closing Balance Sheet] for a purchase price equal to their aggregate face value, and Sellers shall purchase and pay for such Accounts Receivable as provided herein.

(b)   At the Closing, Buyer shall deduct $_____ from the amount otherwise payable pursuant to Section ____ and place it in an account (the "Holdback Account"). The repurchase price of the receivables shall first be paid in whole or in part by reducing the amount in the Holdback Account. Sellers hereby acknowledge and agree that if the repurchase price of the uncollected Accounts Receivable exceeds the amount in the Holdback Account, Sellers shall, without further demand from Buyer, pay to Buyer an amount equal to the difference between the total repurchase price of the uncollected receivables and the amount in the Holdback Account. On the date 180 days after the Closing, Buyer shall close the

Holdback Account and pay any balance remaining in the Holdback Account to Sellers.

(c)   Buyer shall cause the Acquired Companies to execute and deliver to Sellers all instruments as shall be reasonably necessary to effectively vest in Sellers all of the right, title, and interest of the Acquired Companies with respect to any uncollected Accounts Receivable purchased by Sellers pursuant to this subsection, without representation or recourse.

If the parties use the purchase method, they should consider how to allocate the reserve for uncollectible accounts. Buyers may want to allocate the reserve to individual accounts. Sellers, however, may counter that their repurchase obligation should begin only when the entire reserve has been exhausted. The parties should also agree on specific procedures for reassignment of uncollected accounts to Sellers. In particular, they should decide whether Sellers will be allowed to set off amounts that Buyer owes the account debtor. *See* Hilton v. CET/DDT Corp., 1990 WL 6312 (Tenn. Ct. App. 1990).

Collection Efforts. In each of the alternatives discussed above, the quality of the Acquired Companies' collection efforts will affect Sellers' post-closing liability for uncollected accounts. Thus, Sellers may want to specify the required post-closing collection efforts, policies, and procedures. In particular, Sellers might insist that the Acquired Companies cannot simply allow the accounts to age and thereby force Sellers to respond in damages or compromise Sellers' ability to pursue collection after repurchasing the accounts. *See* Kominsky, *A Primer on Acquisition Hold Harmless Clauses*, 34 Prac. Law. 27 (1988). When procedures are established, the Acquired Companies are typically required to use best efforts to collect in the ordinary course of business, but are not required to resort to collection agencies or litigation. Buyer, in return, can negotiate for the option of bringing suit for collection of delinquent receivables and charging Sellers for any collection and litigation costs. In this case, Sellers may seek assurances that they will be notified of material proceedings and afforded the opportunity to participate.

The parties may want to outline the parameters of the Acquired Companies' ability to settle or compromise accounts. Although it is usually impractical to require that the Acquired Companies clear individual returns of merchandise with Sellers, Sellers may want to prohibit the Acquired Companies from forgiving large outstanding accounts to foster good relations with continuing customers and charging Sellers with the remaining deficiencies.

The parties may also want to specify procedures to be followed upon receipt of payments on accounts. This issue is of particular concern with respect to ongoing relationships with regular customers. Sellers may insist that the Acquired Companies be required to apply payments to the invoices of pre-closing accounts before applying such payments to current, post-closing invoices. Buyer could respond that if a customer disputes one invoice but pays another, the customer has not paid the disputed invoice, even though it was sent before the closing. Sellers may demand some formal method of monitoring the allocation of payments to invoices to ensure an equitable payment process and to prevent collusion with the customer in paying certain invoices and disputing others.

A related concern involves the customer that is a questionable credit risk because it is unable to make current payments without continued business with the Acquired Companies, presumably on similar credit terms. *See* MCGAFFEY, BUYING, SELLING AND MERGING BUSINESSES 39 (2d ed. 1989). Sellers will prefer to give the customer every opportunity to make payments on the account, but Buyer may not want to risk extending new credit to facilitate payment of old credit, only to end up with a new uncollectible account.

Finally, complex issues arise if all or a portion of the accounts receivable are secured by collateral. The acquisition agreement might specify which party has the right of repossession, during what time periods, and whether the other party has any interest or right to the collateral that must be respected by the repossessing party. In addition, the parties might decide whether the repossessing party has any obligation to repossess and possibly to sell the collateral before charging the other party with any deficiency, and whether the repossessing party must act within established time constraints.

As an alternative to a buy-back, the parties may negotiate an additional discount to be applied to the net value of the accounts receivable shown on the most recent balance sheet. The purchase price would be reduced by the amount of the discount, and the entire risk of noncollectibility would shift to the buyer at the closing. In such cases, old accounts are typically discounted more than new accounts.

3.9 INVENTORIES

All inventories of each Acquired Company, whether or not reflected on the Interim Balance Sheet, consist of a quality and quantity usable and, with respect to finished goods, saleable, in the Ordinary Course of Business. No Acquired Company is in possession of any goods not owned by such Acquired Company. Except as set forth in Part 3.9, the inventories (other than goods in transit) of each Acquired Company are located on the premises of an Acquired Company. All inventories are valued at the lower of cost or [market] [net realizable] value on a [first-in, first-out] [last-in, first-out] basis consistent with past practice used in the preparation of the Financial Statements. The reserve for obsolescence with respect to inventories [as adjusted for the passage of time,] is adequate and calculated consistent with past practice. Inventories that were purchased after the Interim Balance Sheet Date were purchased in the Ordinary Course of Business at a cost not exceeding market prices prevailing at the time of purchase for items of similar quality and quantity. The quantities of each item of inventory are not excessive, but are reasonable for the continued operation of each Acquired Company in the Ordinary Course of Business.

COMMENT

A manufacturing company's inventory can generally be classified into three broad categories: raw materials, work in process, and finished goods. The Model Agreement representation covers all three categories and provides that all inventory is useable and all finished goods are saleable in the Ordinary Course of Business.

Buyer may want to add a satisfactory physical inventory (and perhaps the existence of minimum or maximum inventory levels) as a condition to its obligations to close. In some circumstances, Buyer may require lists of inventory and a breakdown among raw materials, work in process, and finished goods.

In examining the inventory values shown on the Acquired Companies' financial statements, Buyer should be mindful of valuation methodology under GAAP. Under GAAP, inventories are usually valued at the lower of cost or market value. A critical factor in calculating financial statement income and the balance sheet value of inventories is the assumption of inventory flow used in inventory accounting. Acceptable methods under GAAP include First In, First Out (FIFO), Last In, First Out (LIFO), and average cost. Buyer should understand the reason for any recent change in the method used by the Acquired Companies because variations in the method used may require restating the Financial Statements to make for meaningful comparisons of inventory values between compared periods.

Under any method of accounting for inventory flow, inventory valuation is somewhat subjective. Buyer should attempt to determine whether inventory values have been overstated or understated. Overstatement or understatement may occur because, within the boundaries of GAAP, different kinds of costs can be included either in the cost of goods sold or in general administrative and selling expenses, and if such costs are included in the cost of goods sold, such inclusion will affect the stated value of the inventory and the amount of income reported by the Acquired Companies. In addition, the preparer of the financial statements must make judgments about the realizable value of obsolete items and the point at which goods in inventory become obsolete. Because of such variables involving inventories, Buyer may request a post-closing purchase-price adjustment based upon changes in inventory values after a specified period of time, which affords an opportunity to work with the purchased inventories after the sale but prior to the final settlement of accounts. It is also important when the LIFO method is used that the policy for valuing new inventory items be consistently applied.

Whether Buyer should seek comfort beyond the financial statement representations will depend upon the relative importance of the inventories to the Acquired Companies' businesses. Buyer may want to review the Acquired Companies' internal records if significant amounts of finished goods are consigned. Consigned goods are assets owned by one firm, but kept at another location. If significant finished goods are consigned, Buyer may want to specify the location of major inventory stocks. Even without significant consigned inventory, Buyer's first draft might include a representation concerning the location of inventories.

In acquisitions where the assets of the Acquired Companies will be used as collateral, Buyer's lender will typically require specific inventory representations from the borrower. If Buyer will use borrowed funds to pay the purchase price, Buyer may want to ask Sellers to make inventory representations similar or equivalent to those expected to be made by Buyer to its lender.

Some industries present special concerns when the acquisition agreement includes provisions requiring inventory verification prior to the closing or a post-closing purchase-price adjustment. Special methods are used to estimate inventory values in industries with significant natural resource inventories, such as gas, oil, and timber, and Buyer may want the additional comfort of an independent confirmation of inventory values in such circumstances. In service industries, Buyer may want to expand the inventory representation to address unbilled services or time in order to provide for a minimum level of revenue from unbilled amounts as of a specific date.

The representation that inventories are recorded at the lower of cost or market value assumes that the Acquired Companies do not have significant operations in countries with high inflation. In severely inflationary economies, nonmonetary inventories are valued at current replacement cost or restated historical cost. Acquisitions in such countries will require more specialized representations with regard to inventory and other pertinent matters.

The fourth sentence of Section 3.9 focuses on the Company's reserve for obsolescence. Buyer wants to know that the reserve is adequate, i.e., that the inventory of the Acquired Companies is not becoming obsolete at a faster or higher rate, and that the method of calculating the reserve has not changed.

The fifth sentence of Section 3.9 covers inventory acquired since the date of the Interim Balance Sheet to assure that such inventory was purchased in the ordinary course of business at market prices. The last sentence provides assurance that the Acquired Companies are not accumulating excess amounts of inventory that might need to be written down or disposed of at a discount.

See MANUAL ON ACQUISITION REVIEW ch. 5.

SELLERS' RESPONSE

Sellers may argue for deletion of this representation on the grounds that inventory is covered by the financial statement representation in Section 3.4. If the Acquired Companies record reserves for obsolescence, Sellers may request that the first sentence of Section 3.9 be qualified by reference to that reserve. Sellers may argue that the representation as to the adequacy of the reserve for obsolescence should be deleted because of the subjectivity incumbent in valuing inventory. Sellers may also request that the last sentence be deleted because it requires Sellers to predict future business conditions.

3.10   NO UNDISCLOSED LIABILITIES

Except as set forth in Part 3.10, no Acquired Company has any liability or obligation of any nature (whether known or unknown and whether absolute, accrued, contingent, or otherwise) other than liabilities or obligations to the extent shown on the Interim Balance Sheet and current liabilities incurred in the Ordinary Course of Business since the date of the Interim Balance Sheet.

COMMENT

This representation assures Buyer that it has been informed of all liabilities, including "contingent" liabilities, of the Acquired Companies. The reference to "liability or obligation of any nature . . ." makes this representation extremely broad. Nonetheless, Buyer should not overestimate the protection that this representation provides. Although the representation extends to "contingent" liabilities, as well as to other types of liabilities that are not required under GAAP to be shown as such on a balance sheet, the representation focuses exclusively on existing liabilities. It does not cover liabilities that may arise in the future from past events or existing circumstances. Indeed, a number of judicial decisions involving business acquisitions have recognized this distinction and have therefore narrowly construed the term "liability" (or "contingent liability"). For example, in Climatrol Indus. v. Fedders Corp., 501 N.E.2d 292 (Ill. App. 1986), the court concluded that a company's defective product did not represent a "contingent liability" of the company unless the defective product had actually injured someone. The court stated:

> As of [the date of the closing of the acquisition in question], there was no liability at all for the product liability suits at issue herein, because no injury had occurred. Therefore, these suits are not amongst the liabilities . . . whether accrued, contingent or otherwise, which exist[ed] on the Closing Date, which defendant expressly assumed.

Earlier in its opinion, the court noted:

> Other courts have sharply distinguished between "contingencies" and "contingent liabilities." A contingent liability is one thing, a contingency the happening of which may bring into existence a liability is another, and a very different thing. In the former case, there is a liability which will become absolute upon the happening of a certain event. In the latter there is none until the event happens. The difference is simply that which exists between a conditional debt or liability and none at all.

See also Godchaux v. Conveying Techniques, Inc., 846 F.2d 306 (5th Cir. 1988) (an employer's withdrawal liability under ERISA comes into existence not when the employer's pension plan first develops an unfunded vested liability but when the employer actually withdraws from the pension plan; therefore, there was no

113

breach of a warranty that the employer "did not have any liabilities of any nature, whether accrued, absolute, contingent, or otherwise"); East Prairie R-Z School Dist. v. U.S. Gypsum Co., 813 F. Supp. 1396 (E.D. Mo. 1993) (cause of action for property damage based upon asbestos contamination had not accrued at time of assumption of liabilities); Grant-Howard Assocs. v. Gen. Housewares Corp., 482 N.Y.S.2d 225 (1984) (there is no contingent liability from a defective product until the injury occurs).

In DCV Holdings v. ConAgra, Inc., 2005 WL 698133 (Del. Super. Ct. 2005), *aff'd*, 889 A.2d 954 (Del. 2005), several of the target's managers pled guilty post-closing to an antitrust conspiracy that existed prior to the closing. The buyer sued the sellers claiming, inter alia, that the antitrust liability had accrued prior to the closing and, since it had not been disclosed, constituted a breach of both the "no undisclosed liabilities" representation and the "compliance with law" representation. As to the former, the court acknowledged that the term "liabilities" in the "no undisclosed liabilities" representation could be interpreted to include both liabilities existing at the time of closing and potential liabilities unknown at the time of closing. The court examined extrinsic evidence of the parties' negotiation of the representation. It found that buyer's initial draft of the purchase agreement contained additional language that "there is not existing a condition or situation which could be reasonably expected to result in any such liabilities or obligations," and that the sellers had negotiated for the deletion of that language, indicating that the parties did not intend for the sellers to accept liability for unforeseen future events. Accordingly, the court found that there had been no breach of the "no undisclosed liabilities" representation.

The court went on to hold as a matter of law that the "compliance with law" representation in the purchase agreement controlled the issue of whether sellers were required to indemnify the buyer for damages arising from the antitrust conspiracy because, unlike the "no undisclosed liabilities" representation which referred to "liabilities" generally, this representation specifically addressed compliance with law. The court noted that the "compliance with law" representation was qualified by sellers' knowledge. The court reasoned that to hold the sellers liable under the general "no undisclosed liabilities" representation would render the specific provisions of the "compliance with law" representation, including the knowledge qualifier, meaningless. Because it was undisputed that the sellers had no knowledge of the antitrust conspiracy at the time of closing, the court held that sellers were not liable to indemnify buyer for damages.

Even though the terms "liability" and "contingent liability" may be narrowly construed, other provisions in the Model Agreement protect Buyer against various contingencies that may not actually constitute "contingent liabilities" as of the Closing Date. For example, the Model Agreement contains representations that no event has occurred that may result in a future Material Adverse Change in the business of an Acquired Company (Section 3.12); that no undisclosed event has occurred that may result in a future violation of law by an Acquired Company (Section 3.14); that Sellers have no knowledge of any circumstances that may serve as a basis for the commencement of a future lawsuit against an Acquired Company (Section 3.15); and that no undisclosed event has occurred that would constitute a future default under any of the contracts of the Acquired Companies (Section 3.17). In addition, the Model Agreement requires Sellers to indemnify Buyer against liabilities that may arise in the future from products manufactured by the Acquired Companies prior to the Closing Date (Section 11.2(e)).

If Buyer seeks even broader protection against undisclosed contingencies, it might consider proposing a definition of the term "liability" that expressly includes not only "contingent" liabilities, but also "unmatured," "unaccrued," "unliquidated," "unasserted," "conditional," "secondary," "potential," "disputed," and other similar categories of liabilities. Buyer might also consider expanding the scope of Sellers' indemnity obligations under Section 11.2 so that Sellers are obligated to indemnify Buyer not only against future product liabilities, but also against other categories of liabilities that may arise after the Closing Date from circumstances existing before the Closing Date.

See MANUAL ON ACQUISITION REVIEW ch. 5.

SELLERS' RESPONSE

Sellers may seek to narrow the scope of this representation by limiting the types of liabilities that must be disclosed. For example, Sellers might request that the representation extend only to "liabilities of the type required to be reflected as liabilities on a balance sheet prepared in accordance with GAAP." Buyer will likely object to this request, arguing that the accounting standards for accruing and reflecting liabilities on a balance sheet under GAAP are relatively restrictive compared to the standards for disclosing liabilities in the notes to the financial statements. Buyer may contend that the potential impact of all types of liabilities on the Acquired Companies, regardless of whether they are sufficiently definite, require them to be reflected in the financial statements. Buyer should also be mindful of the impact that so-called "off-balance sheet arrangements" can have on the financial condition of a company. *See* Item 303 of SEC Regulation S-K.

Sellers may also seek to limit this representation to undisclosed liabilities that could have a material adverse effect on the Acquired Companies.

3.11 TAXES

(a) Filed Returns and Tax Payments

(i) **Each Acquired Company has filed or caused to be filed on a timely basis all Tax Returns that were required to be filed by or with respect to it, either separately or as a member of a group of corporations, pursuant to applicable Legal Requirements.**

115

(ii)   No Acquired Company has requested any extension of time within which to file any Tax Return, except as to a Tax Return that has since been timely filed.

(iii)   All Tax Returns filed by (or that include on a consolidated basis) any Acquired Company are complete and correct and comply with applicable Legal Requirements.

(iv)   Each Acquired Company has paid, or made provision for the payment of, all Taxes that have or could have become due for all periods covered by any Tax Return or otherwise, including pursuant to any assessment received by Sellers or any Acquired Company, except such Taxes, if any, that are listed in Part 3.11(a) and that are being contested in good faith by appropriate Proceedings and for which adequate reserves have been provided in the Interim Balance Sheet.

(v)   Each Acquired Company has withheld or collected and paid to the proper Governmental Body or other Person all Taxes required to be withheld, collected, or paid by it.

(vi)   Part 3.11(a) lists each Tax Return filed by any Acquired Company since _____, and Sellers have delivered to Buyer copies of all such Tax Returns.

(vii)   No claim has ever been made by any Governmental Body in a jurisdiction where any Acquired Company does not file Tax Returns that it is or could be subject to taxation by that jurisdiction, nor is there any reasonable basis for such a claim.

(b) Audited or Closed Tax Years

(i)   Except as set forth in Part 3.11(b), all Tax Returns of each Acquired Company have been audited by the IRS or other Governmental Body or are closed by the applicable statute of limitations for all taxable years through _____.

(ii)   Part 3.11(b) lists all audits of all Tax Returns, including a description of the nature and, if completed, the outcome of each audit since [date]. Sellers have delivered copies of any reports, statements of deficiencies, or similar items with respect to such audits. Part 3.11(b) describes all adjustments to any Tax Return filed by or with respect to any Acquired Company for all taxable years since _____, and the resulting deficiencies proposed by the IRS or other Governmental Body. Part 3.11(b) lists all deficiencies proposed as a result of such audits, all of which have been paid or, as set forth in Part 3.11(b), have been settled or are being contested in good faith by appropriate Proceedings. Except as set forth in Part 3.11(b), to the Knowledge of Sellers, no Governmental Body will assess any additional taxes for any period for which Tax Returns have been filed.

(iii)   Except as set forth in Part 3.11(b), no Tax Return of any Acquired Company is under audit by the IRS or other Governmental Body, and no notice of such an audit has been received by any Acquired Company. To the Knowledge of Sellers, there are no threatened Proceedings for or relating to Taxes, and there are no matters under discussion with the IRS or other Governmental Body with respect to Taxes. Except as set forth in Part 3.11(b), no issues relating to Taxes have been raised in writing by the IRS or other Governmental Body during any pending audit, and no issues relating to Taxes have been raised in writing by the IRS or other Governmental Body in any audit that could recur in a later taxable period. Except as set forth in Part 3.11(b), there is no proposed Tax assessment against any Acquired Company.

(iv)   Except as set forth in Part 3.11(b), no Proceedings are pending before the IRS or other Governmental Body with respect to the Taxes of any Acquired Company.

(v)   Except as set forth in Part 3.11(b), no Seller or Acquired Company has given or been requested to give waivers or extensions (or is or would be subject to a waiver or extension given by any other Person) of any statute of limitations relating to the payment of Taxes of any Acquired Company or for which any Acquired Company could be liable.

(vi)   Except as set forth in Part 3.11(b), no Encumbrance for Taxes exists with respect to any assets of any Acquired Company, except statutory liens for Taxes not yet due.

(c) Accruals and Reserves

The charges, accruals, and reserves with respect to Taxes on the accounting Records of each Acquired Company are adequate and are at least equal to that Acquired Company's liability for Taxes and to the Acquired Companies' liability for Taxes on a consolidated basis, respectively.

(d) **Status of Acquired Companies**

    (i)   No Acquired Company is, or within the five-year period preceding the date of this Agreement has been, an "S corporation" within the meaning of Section 1361(a)(1) of the Code.

    (ii)   No Acquired Company has been a member of any affiliated group of corporations (other than a group of which the Company is the common parent) which has filed a combined, consolidated, or unitary income Tax Return with any Governmental Body. No Acquired Company is liable for the Taxes of any Person (other than another Acquired Company) under Treasury Regulation Section 1.1502-6 or any similar provision of any applicable Legal Requirement, as a transferee or successor, by contract, or otherwise.

(e) **Miscellaneous**

    (i)   There is no tax sharing agreement, tax allocation agreement, tax indemnity obligation, or similar agreement, arrangement, understanding, or practice, oral or written, with respect to Taxes that will require any payment by any Acquired Company.

    (ii)   No Acquired Company is a party to any Contract that could result separately or in the aggregate in any payment (A) of an "excess parachute payment" within the meaning of Section 280G of the Code, or (B) that would not be deductible as a result of the application of Section 404 of the Code.

    (iii)   No Acquired Company is required to include in income any adjustment pursuant to Section 481 of the Code by reason of a voluntary change in accounting method initiated by any Acquired Company, and the IRS has not proposed any such change in accounting method.

    (iv)   No Seller is a foreign person within the meaning of Section 1445(f)(3) of the Code. No Acquired Company has been a United States real property holding corporation within the meaning of Section 897(c)(2) of the Code during the applicable period specified in Section 897(c)(1)(A)(ii).

    (v)   Except as set forth in Part 3.11(e), no Acquired Company has received, been the subject of, or requested a written ruling of a Governmental Body relating to Taxes, and no Acquired Company has entered into a Contract with a Governmental Body relating to Taxes that would have a continuing effect after the Closing Date.

(vi)   **Each Acquired Company has disclosed on its federal income Tax Returns all positions taken by it that could give rise to substantial understatement of federal income Tax within the meaning of Section 6662 of the Code.**

(vii)   **No Acquired Company has ever distributed stock of another Person or had its stock distributed by another Person, in a transaction that purported or was intended to be governed in whole or in part by Code Section 355 or Code Section 361.**

(viii) **No Acquired Company has participated in any "reportable transaction" as defined in Treasury Regulation Section 1.6011-4(b).**

COMMENT

The representations in Section 3.11 require Sellers to provide relevant information regarding the Acquired Companies' tax positions and history.

Section 3.11(a) contains Sellers' basic tax representations—that the Acquired Companies have filed all their Tax Returns, paid all their Taxes, and honored their obligations with respect to withholding and sales taxes. Section 3.11(a)(vii) states that no Acquired Company has received any notice from any jurisdiction in which it does not currently file Tax Returns, claiming that the Acquired Company is subject to taxation in that jurisdiction.

Section 3.11(b) provides Buyer with information regarding which tax years have been audited, which are still open to being audited in accordance with the relevant statute of limitations, and whether any tax years are currently being audited. Buyer may consider requesting a jurisdiction-by-jurisdiction schedule of such audits.

Section 3.11(c) relates to the adequacy of the Acquired Companies' accruals and reserves for Taxes. GAAP requires accruals for taxes to be paid on income earned in a period. It also requires "deferred tax liabilities" to be recorded. These are temporary differences in tax basis and amounts recorded for financial accounting purposes that will eventually result in taxable amounts. If tax liabilities have been underaccrued, the Acquired Companies may become liable for unexpected tax liabilities.

In Section 3.11(d)(i), Sellers represent that no Acquired Company is, or for five years has been, an "S corporation" (i.e., a corporation that has made an election to be subject to Subchapter S of the Code) within the meaning of Section 1361(a)(1) of the Code. Since Sellers are all individuals, it is possible that the Company might be an S corporation, assuming that the Sellers are U.S. individuals, estates, permitted trusts, or tax-exempt organizations, and the other requirements to make the election are met. If the Company is an S corporation, its acquisition by a buyer that is not eligible to continue as an S corporation will terminate the S election as of the Closing. Once the election is terminated, the Company may be foreclosed from making a new S election for five years. However, if Buyer is an S corporation, it might be able to make a qualified subchapter S subsidiary (Q Sub) election with respect to the Company, provided Buyer acquires all of the stock of the Company and the Company is a domestic corporation and is not an "ineligible corporation" as defined in Section 1361(b)(2) of the Code.

If the Company is an S corporation and an election is made under Section 338(h)(10) of the Code, the transaction will be treated for corporate law purposes as a stock acquisition but for tax purposes as if the Acquired Companies had sold all their assets and then distributed the proceeds to the shareholders of the Company in liquidation. The purchase price for the assets reflects the price paid for the stock and the liabilities of the Acquired Companies. The allocation of that price among the categories of acquired assets is based upon their relative fair market values. The amount of gain or loss, and the character of the gain or loss as capital or ordinary, would be determined on an asset-by-asset basis. The tax on any gain for an S corporation would be incurred at the shareholder level, except that any "built-in gain" on assets held on the effective date of an S corporation election and on the date of the sale of stock would be taxed at the corporate level unless at least 10 years have elapsed since the effective date of the election (or, if less, the period since the date the S corporation was formed). In determining the impact of a Section 338(h)(10) election, however, any state and local taxes must also be considered.

If an election under Section 338(h)(10) is to be made, Buyer will want to be assured that the Company is an S corporation. The following is an example of a representation to replace Section 3.17(d)(i) that not only confirms that conclusion, but specifically negates the existence of facts that could disqualify the Company from being treated as an S corporation:

> The Company made a valid election under Subchapter S of the Code to which all persons who were shareholders on the date of such election gave their (and if necessary each shareholder's spouse gave his or her) consent, and such election became effective on _____(the "Subchapter S Effective Date"). On and following the Subchapter S Effective Date and through the date hereof, the Company has been eligible for and entitled to be treated under Subchapter S of the Code, and has met the following requirements: (A) the only authorized and outstanding capital stock of the Company has been common stock; (B) no person other than the Sellers (or his or her spouse) has been the record or beneficial owner of any common stock (or any interest therein) at any time; (C) no such owner or his or her spouse has been a nonresident alien within the meaning of Section 1361(b)(1)(C) of the Code or a dual-resident taxpayer within the meaning of Treasury Regulations § 301.7701(b)-7(a)(1); (D) the Company has not been an "ineligible corporation" within the meaning of Section 1361(b)(2) of the Code; (E) the Company has not issued or entered into any restricted stock, deferred compensation or profit-sharing plans, call

options, warrants or similar instruments with respect to its stock, stock appreciation rights, convertible debt instruments, stock-based employee incentive plans, or other similar obligations or arrangements; (F) the Company has not issued or entered into any indebtedness other than indebtedness which constitutes "straight debt" within the meaning of Section 1361(c)(5) of the Code and Treasury Regulations § 1.1361-1(1)(5); (G) neither the Company nor any of its shareholders has entered into any binding agreements relating to rights to distributions and liquidation proceeds in respect of the common stock; (H) the Company has not acquired the assets of any other corporation in a transaction described in Section 381(a) of the Code; and (I) the Company has not owned any stock (including any instrument or interest that constitutes stock for U.S. federal income purposes) of any entity (other than the other Acquired Companies, which are each qualified S subsidiaries under Section 1361(b)(3) of the Code) and has not entered into any partnership, joint venture, marketing, or other similar contract or arrangement with any person. The Company and Sellers are eligible to make an election under Section 338(h)(10) of the Code and any comparable election under any applicable state law.

If Buyer requires such a representation, it may also seek to exclude such representation from any ceiling on indemnification. *See* commentary—Exceptions or "Carve-outs"—to Section 11.6.

If a Section 338(h)(10) election is contemplated, covenants would ordinarily be added to Article 7 or contained in a separate Article setting forth the procedure for making the election and for determining the allocation of the deemed purchase price after the closing. *See* preliminary note to Article 7.

In Section 3.11(d)(2), Sellers represent that no Acquired Company has been a member of an affiliated group of corporations (other than a group of which the Company is the common parent), which has filed a combined, consolidated, or unitary return. This representation is requested because if an Acquired Company were a member of another group, it could be jointly and severally liable for the tax obligations of the other group for the period it was a member of that group. Additional due diligence with respect to such other group or specific unlimited indemnification may be needed. *See* Appendix A—The Purchase of a Subsidiary.

Section 3.11(e)(i) provides Buyers with assurance that no Acquired Company is subject to any tax sharing agreement or similar arrangement that could make the Acquired Company responsible for additional tax-related obligations. Affiliates sometimes enter into tax sharing agreements in order to reallocate tax obligations between or among them.

Section 3.11(e)(ii) requires disclosure of arrangements that the target may be unable to deduct for tax purposes. In some cases, the Company may have agreed not only to pay a generous severance payment, but also an additional "gross up" amount to cover the resulting taxes to the employee. Code Section 280G denies a corporate deduction for excessive compensatory remuneration (a "parachute payment") In addition, Code Section 4999 imposes a 20% excise tax on the parachute payment, which the disqualified person is obligated to pay, and the corporation has a withholding obligation to the extent the payment constitutes a wage under Code Section 3401. A disqualified person is an employee or independent contractor and is an officer, shareholder, or highly compensated individual. Parachute payments are defined as meeting the following four conditions: (a) they are compensatory, (b) they are to or for the benefit of a disqualified person, (c) they are in connection with change in ownership or control of the corporation, and (d) they involve an amount at least three times the disqualified person's base amount. In the case of a private corporation, the application of these Code Sections can be avoided if a parachute payment is approved by the shareholders and certain requirements pertaining to that approval are met. *See* Appendix C—Considerations Regarding Employee Agreements in Connection with Sale of Stock.

Section 404 of the Code limits the deductibility of certain payments to retirement and deferred compensation plans. Section 162(m) of the Code limits the deductibility of compensation payments over $1 million made to certain officers of publicly traded companies.

Section 481 of the Code may require an adjustment to taxable income where the taxpayer makes a change in its method of accounting, such as a change in its method of depreciation. Section 3.11(e)(iii) assures Buyer that no such adjustments are looming.

Section 3.11(e) (iv) refers to Section 1445 of the Code, which imposes a withholding obligation on the buyer where the target is a "United States real property holding corporation." The definition of U.S. real property holding corporation in Section 897(c)(2) includes any corporation if (a) the fair market value of its U.S. real property interests equals or exceeds 50% of (b) the fair market value of (i) its U.S. real property interests, (ii) its interests in real property located outside the United States, plus (iii) any other of its assets which are used or held for use in a trade or business. Generally, there is no withholding obligation on a stock purchase of a business interest. However, Section 1445 requires the buyer to deduct and withhold seller's tax when the acquired business interest fits within the definition of a U.S. real property holding corporation under Section 897(c)(2). If Section 1445 is applicable, the buyer must deduct and withhold from the purchase price a tax equal to 10% of the amount realized by the seller on the sale or exchange. Two conditions must be met to impose the Section 1445 withholding obligation on the buyer of a corporation: (1) the seller must not be a U.S. person (Section 1445(f)(3)) and (2) the buyer must be acquiring stock in a U.S. real property holding corporation.

Section 3.11(e)(v) seeks information with respect to tax rulings obtained or requested by the Acquired Companies and tax-related agreements entered into with any Governmental Body that will continue in effect after the Closing. In the area of transfer pricing, for example, taxpayers sometimes enter into a written agreement with the IRS relating to their transfer pricing methods.

In Section 3.11(e)(vi), Sellers represent that the Acquired Companies have complied with Section 6662 of the Code. Section 6662 imposes a 20% penalty on substantial understatements of income tax (in general, an understatement of 10% or more). Under Section 6662, the amount of the understatement is reduced to the extent the relevant facts relating to the taxpayer's position with respect to the understated item are adequately disclosed.

Section 3.11(e)(vii) refers to Section 355 of the Code, which permits tax-free distributions of securities of controlled corporations subject to certain conditions. Section 355 is subject to a number of limitations and exceptions (such as a subsequent acquisition) which can make the transaction taxable. Thus, if the target has been involved in such a transaction as either the distributing or controlled corporation, Buyer may want to review that transaction carefully.

Section 3.11(e)(viii) refers to reportable transactions of a type that the IRS determines as having a potential for tax avoidance or evasion and includes many transactions considered by the IRS to be corporate tax shelters. Buyer may want to know whether the Acquired Companies have been involved in these types of transactions.

See MANUAL ON ACQUISITION REVIEW ch. 6.

SELLERS' RESPONSE

Sellers may ask to limit the number of years covered by Section 3.11(a), reasoning that years beyond the applicable statute of limitations are irrelevant. Sellers may seek to have the phrase "on a timely basis" deleted from Section 3.11(a)(i), arguing that so long as the Tax Returns have been filed and any late-filing penalties paid, whether or not the Tax Returns were timely filed, is irrelevant.

Seller may ask that Section 3.11(a)(iv) be limited to payment of Taxes shown to be due on a Tax Return, since that representation, coupled with the Section 3.11(a)(i) representation that all required Tax Returns have been filed, would afford Buyer all the protection it needs. Seller may also argue that this Section is overly broad and vague.

Seller may also seek to have Section 3.11(a)(vii) limited to claims made to an Acquired Company in writing. Otherwise, "claims" may include public pronouncements and oral statements made by officials of various tax authorities. In addition, Sellers may seek to delete the language that there is no "reasonable basis" for such a claim as being overly broad.

If the Company is an S corporation and Buyer requests that the Sellers join in making a Section 338(h)(10) election, Sellers may require that Buyer gross up the purchase price for the amount of additional taxes to Sellers associated with that election. As in the case of an actual sale of assets, the availability of a step-up in the tax basis of the acquired assets for Buyer in this "deemed asset" sale may justify a higher purchase price for Sellers.

Sellers may request that the second sentence of Section 3.11(d)(ii) be deleted on the basis that it is too broad and vague, or that it be narrowed to liability under Treasury Regulation Section 1.1502-6, which provides that each member of a consolidated group remains severally liable for the group's federal tax liability.

3.12   NO MATERIAL ADVERSE CHANGE

Since the Balance Sheet Date, no Acquired Company has suffered any Material Adverse Change and no event has occurred, and no circumstance exists, that can reasonably be expected to result in a Material Adverse Change.

COMMENT

Section 3.12 provides that since the date of the Company's last audited consolidated balance sheet, no Acquired Company has suffered a "Material Adverse Change." "Material Adverse Change" is defined in Section 1.1 to include changes that are materially adverse to the business (financial and otherwise), assets, results of operations, or prospects of any Acquired Company. See commentary to the definition of "Material Adverse Change" in Section 1.1 for a discussion of judicial decisions interpreting the terms "material adverse change" and "material adverse effect" in representations and conditions.

While the Model Agreement generally avoids the use of materiality qualifiers (*see* "'Materiality' Qualifications" in preliminary note to Article 3), this representation is traditionally qualified by materiality. It would be impractical to ask Sellers to represent that nothing adverse has occurred.

For a discussion of the advisability of including a separate "no material adverse change" condition in an acquisition agreement, *see* the commentary to Section 8.12. For a discussion of the implications of various methods of drafting a phrase such as "that may result in such a material adverse change," *see* "'Adverse Effect' Language" in preliminary note to Article 3.

In addition to Section 3.12, which deals generally with Material Adverse Changes affecting the Acquired Companies, Section 3.16 deals with several specific changes and events that are considered significant (though not necessarily adverse) for the Acquired Companies. Section 3.16 requires disclosure of such changes and events that occur after the Balance Sheet Date.

SELLERS' RESPONSE

Sellers would prefer to make this representation on behalf of all Acquired Companies as a whole, rather than with respect to each Acquired Company. Buyer, however, may want to know if any particular Acquired Company has suffered serious recent setbacks so that it can judge the significance of these problems for the entire acquisition. Similarly, if significant lines or segments of an Acquired Company's business are conducted in divisions (rather than subsidiaries), Buyer may request this representation for one or more of those divisions.

Sellers may request that Section 3.12 refer to the date of the Interim Balance Sheet rather than of the Balance Sheet, so as to limit the period covered by this representation.

3.13   EMPLOYEE BENEFITS

(a) **Part 3.13(a) lists each "employee benefit plan" as defined by Section 3(3) of ERISA, all specified fringe benefit plans as defined in Section 6039D of the Code, and all other bonus, incentive-compensation, deferred-compensation, profit-sharing, stock-option, stock-appreciation-right, stock-bonus, stock-purchase, employee-stock-ownership, savings, severance, change-in-control, supplemental-unemployment, layoff, salary-continuation, retirement, pension, health, life-insurance, disability, accident, group-insurance, vacation, holiday, sick-leave, fringe-benefit, or welfare plan, and any other employee compensation or benefit plan, policy, practice, or Contract (whether qualified or nonqualified, effective or terminated, written or unwritten) and any trust, escrow, or other Contract related thereto that (i) is maintained or contributed to by any Acquired Company and (ii) provides benefits to, or describes policies or procedures applicable to, any current or former director, officer, employee, or service provider of any Acquired Company, or the dependents of any thereof, regardless of how (or whether) liabilities for the provision of benefits are accrued or assets are acquired or dedicated with respect to the funding thereof (each, an "Employee Plan"). Part 3.13(a) identifies as such any Employee Plan that is (x) a plan intended to meet the requirements of Section 401(a) of the Code or (y) a plan subject to Title IV of ERISA. Other than the Acquired Companies, no corporation or trade or business has ever been controlled by, controlling, or under common control with any Seller within the meaning of Section 414 of the Code or Section 4001(a)(14) or 4001(b) of ERISA.**

(b) **Sellers have delivered to Buyer copies of (i) the documents comprising each Employee Plan (or, with respect to an Employee Plan which is unwritten, a detailed written description of eligibility, participation,** benefits, funding arrangements, assets, and any other matters that relate to the obligations of any Acquired Company thereunder); (ii) all trust agreements, insurance contracts, or any other funding instruments related to each Employee Plan; (iii) all rulings, determination letters, no-action letters, or advisory opinions from the IRS, the United States Department of Labor, or any other Governmental Body that pertain to each Employee Plan and any open requests therefor; (iv) the most recent actuarial and financial reports (audited and/or unaudited) and the annual reports filed with any Governmental Body with respect to each Employee Plan during the current year and each of the three preceding years; (v) all Contracts with third-party administrators, actuaries, investment managers, consultants, or other independent contractors that relate to each Employee Plan; and (vi) all summary plan descriptions, summaries of material modifications and memoranda, employee handbooks, and other written communications regarding each Employee Plan.

(c) Except as set forth in Part 3.13(c), all amounts owed by any Acquired Company under the terms of any Employee Plan have been timely paid in full. Except as set forth in Part 3.13(c), each Employee Plan that provides health or welfare benefits is fully insured, and any incurred but not reported claims under each such Employee Plan that is not fully insured have been properly accrued. Each Acquired Company has paid in full all required insurance premiums, subject only to normal retrospective adjustments in the Ordinary Course of Business, with regard to each Employee Plan.

(d) Each Acquired Company has complied with the applicable continuation requirements for each Employee Plan, including (i) Section 4980B of the Code (as well as its predecessor provision, Section 162(k) of the Code) and Sections 601 through 608, inclusive, of ERISA ("COBRA") and (ii) any applicable state Legal Requirements mandating welfare benefit continuation coverage for employees.

(e) The form of each Employee Plan is in compliance with the applicable terms of ERISA, the Code, and any other applicable Legal Requirement, including the Americans with Disabilities Act of 1990, the Family Medical Leave Act of 1993, and the Health Insurance Portability and Accountability Act of 1996, and each Employee Plan has been operated in compliance with such Legal Requirements and the written Employee Plan documents. No Acquired Company and no fiduciary of an Employee Plan has violated the requirements of Section 404 of ERISA. Each required report and description of an Employee Plan (including IRS Form 5500 Annual Reports, Summary Annual Reports and Summary Plan Descriptions, and Summaries of Material Modifications) have been (to the extent required) timely filed with the IRS, the United States Department of Labor, or other Governmental Body and distributed as required, and all notices required by ERISA or the Code or any other Legal Requirement with respect to each Employee Plan have been appropriately given. No Acquired Company has any unfunded liability with respect to any deferred compensation, retirement, or other Employee Plan.

(f) Each Employee Plan that is intended to be qualified under Section 401(a) of the Code has received, or is based on a form of plan that has received, a favorable determination letter from the IRS, which is current, taking into account the Tax laws referred to as "GUST." To the Knowledge of Sellers, no circumstance exists that could result in revocation of any such favorable determination letter. Each trust created under any such Employee Plan has been determined to be exempt from taxation under Section 501(a) of the Code, and, to the Knowledge of Sellers, no circumstance exists that could result in a revocation of such exemption. No Employee Plan is intended to meet the requirements of Code Section 501(c)(9). No circumstance exists that could give rise to a loss of any intended tax consequence or to any Tax under Section 511 of the Code with respect to any Employee Plan.

(g) There has never been any Proceeding relating to any Employee Plan and, to the Knowledge of Sellers, no such Proceeding is threatened. To the Knowledge of Sellers, no event has occurred or circumstance exists that could give rise to or serve as a basis for the commencement of any such Proceeding. No Acquired Company and no fiduciary of an Employee Plan has engaged in a transaction with respect to any Employee Plan that could subject any Acquired Company or Buyer to a Tax or penalty imposed by either Section 4975 of the Code or Section 502(l) of ERISA or a violation of Section 406 of ERISA. Neither the execution and delivery of this Agreement nor the consummation or performance of any Contemplated Transaction will, directly or indirectly (with or without notice or lapse of time), result in the assessment of a Tax or penalty under Section 4975 of the Code or Section 502(l) of ERISA or result in a violation of Section 406 of ERISA.

(h) Neither the execution and delivery of this Agreement nor the consummation or performance of any Contemplated Transaction will, directly or indirectly (with or without notice or lapse of time), obligate any Acquired Company to pay any separation, severance, termination, or similar benefit to, or accelerate the time of vesting for, change the time of payment to, or increase the amount of compensation due to, any director, employee, officer, former employee, or former officer of any

Acquired Company. There is no Contract providing for payments that could subject any Person to liability under Section 4999 of the Code.

(i) Other than the continuation coverage requirements of COBRA, no Acquired Company has any obligation or potential liability for benefits to employees, former employees, or their dependents following termination of employment or retirement under any Employee Plan.

(j) Neither the execution and delivery of this Agreement nor the consummation or performance of any Contemplated Transaction will, directly or indirectly (with or without notice or lapse of time), result in an amendment, modification, or termination of any Employee Plan. No written or oral representation has been made to any employee or former employee of any Acquired Company promising or guaranteeing any employer payment or funding for the continuation of medical, dental, life, or disability coverage for any period of time beyond the end of the current plan year (except to the extent of coverage required under COBRA). No written or oral representation has been made to any employee or former employee of any Acquired Company concerning the employee benefits of Buyer.

(k) No Acquired Company contributes to, has any obligation to contribute to, or has any liability with respect to, any "employee pension benefit plan" within the meaning of Section 3(2) of ERISA that is a "defined benefit plan" within the meaning of Section 3(35) of ERISA.

(l) No Acquired Company contributes to, has any obligation to contribute to, or has any liability with respect to, a "multiemployer plan" within the meaning of Section 3(37) of ERISA or Section 414(f) of the Code or a plan that has two or more contributing sponsors, at least two of whom are not under common control within the meaning of Section 413(c) of the Code.

(m) Except as set forth in Part 3.13(m), no Employee Plan is subject to Section 409A of the Code. Each Employee Plan subject to Section 409A of the Code ("Deferred Compensation Plan") complies in all material respects with Section 409A of the Code. No Acquired Company has (i) granted to any Person an interest in any Deferred Compensation Plan that is, or upon the lapse of a substantial risk of forfeiture with respect to such interest will be, subject to the Tax imposed by Section 409A(a)(1)(B) or (b)(4)(A) of the Code, or (ii) materially modified any Deferred Compensation Plan in a manner that could cause an interest previously granted under such plan to become subject to the Tax imposed by Section 409A(a)(1)(B) or (b)(4) of the Code.

COMMENT

The representations in Section 3.13 elicit information regarding the Acquired Companies' employee benefit plans, both to assure that Buyer is aware of all existing plans and that it has been informed of all existing or potential liabilities related to those plans. Buyer will want to know the type and level of benefits to which the Acquired Companies' employees are accustomed, whether they are to be continued, terminated, or modified. Any reduction in benefits may reduce costs and increase operating profits, but may have a negative impact on employee morale. If Buyer terminates the employee benefit plans of the Acquired Companies and replaces them with Buyer's plans, for uniformity or other reasons, Buyer should carefully consider the relative costs of replacement plans and the resulting impact (positive or negative) on both profitability and employee morale.

A threshold consideration is whether Buyer will be able to freely terminate or modify the employee benefit plans of the Acquired Companies. For most types of plans, this is simply a question of reviewing the plans in advance, and Section 3.13 is designed to assist by requiring the Sellers to provide the relevant documents. If the employee benefit plan is insured, Buyer will want to know whether a plan termination may trigger a penalty, a market value adjustment, or other event which may cause an impairment of plan assets when Buyer terminates the plan.

In practice, most plans are unilaterally terminable by the plan sponsor. However, there are some situations in which Buyer may not be able to terminate a plan, so careful review of the plans is important.

Many rules applicable to employee benefits appear in both ERISA and the Code. For example, the vesting, benefit accrual, and minimum funding rules are set forth in ERISA Sections 203, 204, and 302, and Code Sections 411(a), 411(b), and 412, and the COBRA continuation of coverage provisions appear in both ERISA Section 601 *et seq.* and Code Section 4980B. The two statutes sometimes use different words to label the same or similar concepts, such as "party in interest" (ERISA Section 3(14)) and "disqualified person" (Code Section 4975(e)(2)). Conversely, the two statutes sometimes assign different meanings to a particular word; for example, the definition of "plan" in ERISA Section 3(3) differs from the definition in Code Section 4975(e)(1). Some rules are found only in one statute or the other. Notably, the termination rules for Title IV Plans and the withdrawal liability provisions applicable to multiemployer plans are found only in Title IV of ERISA.

Buyer should be concerned about the Acquired Companies' benefit plans since such plans have the potential to spawn significant liabilities. The main potential employee benefit liabilities include:

- minimum funding liability;
- termination liability for single-employer pension plans;
- withdrawal liability for multiemployer pension plans;

- Pension Benefit Guaranty Corporation ("PBGC") insurance premium liability;

- liability for retiree medical benefits;

- disqualification of a qualified plan;

- liability for failure to file, disclose, or notify;

- excise taxes;

- liability for failure to comply with the Health Insurance Portability and Accountability Act; and

- liability for violation of fiduciary duties.

The first four categories arise almost exclusively from defined benefit pension plans subject to Title IV of ERISA and impose joint and several liability on the plan sponsor and its ERISA Affiliates.

ERISA Affiliate. Generally, entities which are part of a "controlled group," including noncorporate entities, are jointly and severally liable for some, but not all, pension obligations, principally delinquent contributions, excise taxes for failure to make minimum required contributions to a pension plan, delinquent PBGC premiums, and underfunding on plan termination. *See* ERISA §§ 302(c)(I1)(B), 4001(b), 4007, 4041(c)(2)(B), 4062(a), 4068(a), 4001(a)(14); Code §§ 412(c)(11)(B), 4971(e). Similarly, all members of the controlled group (within the meaning of Code Sections 414(b) and (c)) of a contributing employer to a multiemployer plan are jointly and severally liable for that employer's withdrawal liability. ERISA defines a "controlled group" to include any group consisting of a "person" and all other persons under common control with such person within the meaning of Code Section 414. *See* ERISA § 4001(a)(14). The term "person" is defined by ERISA to include, among other entities, an individual, a partnership, a joint venture, or a corporation. A "parent-subsidiary" controlled group exists where there is at least 80% ownership measured, in the case of a corporation, by either voting rights or the value of all outstanding stock. Treas. Reg. § 1.414(c)-2(b). A "brother-sister" controlled group exists where: (i) at least 80% of each trade or business is owned by the same five or fewer individuals; and (ii) at least 50% is owned by the same five or fewer individuals counting only the lowest percentage held by that individual in each entity. Treas. Reg. § 1.414(c)-2(c). In determining whether an individual's stock may be taken into account for purposes of the 80% ownership test, the individual must own stock in each member of the purported controlled group. *See* Vogel Fertilizer Co. v. U.S., 455 U.S. 16 (1982). A "controlled group" generally includes affiliated service organizations under Code Section 414(m) and other related persons described in regulations under Code Section 414(o). Prop. Treas. Reg. §§ 1.414(m)-5, 1.414(o)-l. Buyer should determine whether an Acquired Company has liability arising from a plan established or maintained (or, in the case of a multiemployer plan, contributed to) by a related entity that is not being acquired.

It is important to determine if the Acquired Companies are part of a "controlled group," and, if so, whether the Acquired Companies have become jointly and severally liable for any liability with respect to any ERISA Affiliate's employee benefit plans. Although the Acquired Companies will cease to be a member of certain controlled groups after the acquisition, the Acquired Companies will remain jointly and severally liable for those liabilities that arose prior to the acquisition while the companies were members of the "controlled group."

Requirements to Report, Disclose, and Notify. Both ERISA and the Code impose requirements that various parties file and distribute reports and give various notices, and both impose sanctions for failure to meet these requirements. *See, e.g.,* ERISA §§ 101 *et seq.,* 502(c)(2), 4071; Code §§ 6047(d), 6058(a), 6652, 6692.

Excise Taxes. The Code imposes excise taxes for (i) failure to meet funding standards (Code § 4971); (ii) engaging in prohibited transactions (Code § 4975); (iii) making nondeductible contributions to a plan (Code § 4972); (iv) failing to distribute excess in a timely manner (Code § 4979); and (v) receiving reversions of excess assets (Code § 4980). The Code also imposes an excise tax on certain parachute payments (Code §§ 280G, 4999).

The Secretary of Labor may assess a civil penalty against a party in interest that engages in a prohibited transaction. *See* ERISA § 502(i). There are also penalties for failing to provide continuation of coverage in accordance with ERISA Sections 601 *et seq.* and Code Section 4980B.

Other Benefit Obligations. The term "other benefit obligations" covers arrangements with persons who are not employees, such as directors, that are not legally binding, but which Buyer may feel compelled to continue or that are not plans, such as a practice of entering into consulting agreements with retired directors. *See* 29 C.F.R. § 2510.3-1. The Acquired Companies' arrangements with present and former executives may not have been handled by the department that deals with other employee relationships, and may therefore require special due diligence efforts by Buyer.

Sections 3.13(a) and (b) require Sellers to furnish a complete list of employee benefit plans and all relevant documents, including plans, governmental reports, and actuarial studies which will enable Buyer to understand and assess the Acquired Companies' benefit plans. Since employee benefit plans are not always as well documented as the law might require, these provisions also require Sellers to furnish any employment manuals and policies, summary plan descriptions, or similar materials that may establish informal employee benefit plan arrangements. If the Acquired Companies do not sponsor one or more of the potential categories of employee benefit plans, Sellers can simply satisfy the provisions of Section 3.13(a) and (b) by indicating "none" or "not applicable" on Part 3.13(a) on a plan-by-plan basis.

Section 3.13(c) seeks assurance that the Acquired Companies have paid all contributions required under all employee benefit plans and, with respect to insured plans, that all premiums have been paid.

COBRA requires employers to give notice to terminating employees regarding their right to continue health care coverage. In Section 3.13(d), Sellers represent that the Acquired Companies have complied with their obligations under COBRA.

Section 3.13(e) covers several areas. First, it requires Sellers to represent that the Employee Plans comply as to form with various applicable Legal Requirements. Section 404 of ERISA imposes fiduciary duties on plan administrators, including the duty to act as a "prudent man" and to diversify the plan investments. Section 3.13(e) contains Sellers' representation that no plan fiduciary has breached Section 404. Lastly, Section 3.13(e) states that all required reports relating to the Employee Plans, including Form 5500 Annual Reports, have been filed and all required notices have been given.

Section 401(a) of the Code defines certain types of pension and profit sharing plans as "qualified plans." These plans must meet a number of criteria established by the IRS in order to be "qualified." While advance IRS approval is not required, it is customary and desirable. Thus, in Section 3.13(f) Sellers represent that all Employee Plans intended to qualify under Section 401(a) have received determination letters from the IRS, and that those letters are current, taking into effect changes in Legal Requirements, including "GUST," which refers to an IRS program for review of prototype plans that required amendment to account for a number of changes in the Legal Requirements impacting Employee Plans. Section 3.13(f) also contains Sellers' representations that all trusts created under any Employee Plan are tax exempt and that no "VEBAs" (voluntary employee benefit associations) have been established under Code Section 501(c)(9) for the benefit of employees of any Acquired Company.

In Section 3.13(g), Sellers represent that there have been no Proceedings relating to the Employee Plans, that none are threatened, and that no events have occurred that could lead to Proceedings. Sellers also represent that no taxes have been incurred under Section 4975 of the Code or Section 502(i) of ERISA. Section 4975 imposes excise fees on "prohibited transactions," which are defined to include use of plan assets for a fiduciary's own account and transferring plan assets to or for the benefit of persons who are not plan beneficiaries. Section 502(i) of ERISA permits the U.S. Department of Labor to assess a 20% civil penalty against plan fiduciaries involved in prohibited transactions.

Sections 3.13(h) and (j) cover the effects of the Contemplated Transactions on the employee benefit arrangements of the Acquired Companies. Section 3.13(h) requires disclosure of severance or other compensation arrangements that would be triggered by the Contemplated Transactions. Section 3.13(j) provides assurance that the Contemplated Transactions will not trigger changes in any employee benefit plan of an Acquired Company and that no promises have been made regarding continuation of any Acquired Company's benefit plans.

Sections 3.13(k) and (l) respectively state that no Acquired Company has a defined benefit pension plan or contributes to a "multiemployer plan." Defined benefit plans are subject to substantial regulation. Multiemployer plans are union-sponsored plans to which a number of employers contribute. If the target has a defined benefit pension plan or has contributed to a multiemployer plan, additional representations may be required.

Section 3.13(m) relates to Section 409A of the Code. Section 409A regulates deferred compensation plans. Section 409A and the related Treasury Regulations broadly define "deferred compensation" as any compensation to which an employee has a legal right during a taxable year but which is payable in a later year. Section 409A restricts when deferred compensation plans can be paid, prohibits acceleration of distributions, and limits the employee's ability to change the time and form of payment. Noncompliance with Section 409A can subject the employee to immediate taxation of deferred amounts, excise taxes, and interest assessments.

See Manual on Acquisition Review ch. 11.

SELLERS' RESPONSE

Section 3.13 is very detailed and, depending on the types of employee benefit plans of the Acquired Companies, might be more extensive than the circumstances warrant. Sellers might simply disclaim the existence of certain types of plans in the representations, which could serve to shorten the representation. Sellers may also seek to make Section 3.13 the exclusive set of representations on the subject of employee benefits. Sellers may contend that the last sentence of Section 3.13(a) is overly broad and that the pertinent question is not whether the Company was ever a member of a controlled group, but rather whether the Company and any of its ERISA Affiliates ever engaged in certain activities that could trigger joint and several liability with regard to certain employee benefit plans. Sellers may limit disclosure of past proceedings in Section 3.13(g) to those brought since a specified date.

3.14   Compliance with Legal Requirements; Governmental Authorizations

(a) **Except as set forth in Part 3.14(a):**

   (i)   **each Acquired Company has at all times been in compliance with each Legal Requirement that is or was applicable to it or the conduct of its business or the ownership or use of any of its assets;**

133

(ii)   no event has occurred or circumstance exists that (with or without notice or lapse of time) (A) could constitute or result in a violation by any Acquired Company of, or a failure on the part of any Acquired Company to comply with, any Legal Requirement, or (B) could give rise to any obligation on the part of any Acquired Company to undertake, or to bear all or any portion of the cost of, any remedial action;

(iii)   no Acquired Company has received any notice or other communication (whether oral or written) from any Governmental Body or any other Person regarding (A) any actual, alleged, or potential violation of, or failure to comply with, any Legal Requirement, or (B) any actual, alleged, or potential obligation on the part of any Acquired Company to undertake, or to bear all or any portion of the cost of, any remedial action; and

(iv)   no proposed Legal Requirement could have an adverse consequence on any Acquired Company or could require an expenditure of $_____ or more by any Acquired Company to comply with such Legal Requirement.

(b) Part 3.14(b) lists each Governmental Authorization that is held by any Acquired Company or that otherwise relates to the business of, or to any assets owned or used by, any Acquired Company. Each Governmental Authorization listed in Part 3.14(b) is valid and in full force and effect. Except as set forth in Part 3.14(b):

(i)   each Acquired Company has at all times been in compliance with each Governmental Authorization;

(ii)   no event has occurred or circumstance exists that could (with or without notice or lapse of time) (A) constitute or result, directly or indirectly, in a violation of, or a failure on the part of any Acquired Company to comply with, any Governmental Authorization listed in Part 3.14(b), or (B) result, directly or indirectly, in the revocation, suspension, cancellation, termination, or modification of any Governmental Authorization;

(iii)   no Acquired Company has received any notice or other communication (whether oral or written) from any Governmental Body or any other Person regarding (A) any actual, alleged, or potential violation of, or failure to comply with, any Governmental Authorization, or (B) any actual, proposed, or potential revocation, suspension, cancellation, termination, or modification of any Governmental Authorization; and

(iv)   **all applications required to have been filed for the renewal or reissuance of the Governmental Authorizations listed in Part 3.14(b) have been duly filed on a timely basis with the appropriate Governmental Bodies, and all other filings required to have been made with respect to such Governmental Authorizations have been duly made on a timely basis with the appropriate Governmental Bodies.**

(c)   **The Governmental Authorizations listed in Part 3.14(b) constitute all Governmental Authorizations necessary to permit each Acquired Company lawfully to continue to conduct its business in the manner in which it conducts such business and to own and use its assets in the manner in which it owns and uses such assets.**

COMMENT

Section 3.14(a) contains Sellers' "compliance with laws" representation. This representation requires disclosure of past, current, and potential violations of Legal Requirements by the Acquired Companies. It covers:

- general compliance (clause (i));
- potential or "unmatured" violations (clause (ii)); and
- violations asserted by Governmental Bodies and other parties (clause (iii)).

For a discussion of the significance of the phrase "with or without notice or lapse of time" (which appears in clause (ii) of Section 3.14(a)), *see* commentary to Section 3.2.

Although clause (iii) of Section 3.14(a), which requires disclosure of notices received from Governmental Bodies and third parties concerning actual and potential violations, overlaps to some extent with clauses (i) and (ii), clause (iii) is not redundant. Clause (iii) requires disclosure of violations that have been asserted by other parties. Sellers are required to disclose such asserted violations pursuant to clause (iii), even if there is some uncertainty or dispute over whether the asserted violations have actually been committed.

The references in clauses (ii) and (iii) to "remedial action" are included because, under some statutory and regulatory provisions, an Acquired Company may become subject to significant monetary or other obligations without necessarily having committed a "violation" of the provision in question.

The parties should recognize that if information regarding an actual or potential legal violation is included in Sellers' Disclosure Letter, this information may be discoverable by adverse parties in the course of litigation involving the Acquired Companies and may also have to be reported to a Governmental Body. Accordingly, it is important to use care in preparing the descriptions included in Part 3.14 of the Disclosure Letter. *See* commentary to Section 3.2.

The representation in Section 3.14(b) relating to governmental licenses and permits of the Acquired Companies is crucial in regulated industries. In these industries, the availability and transferability of licenses and permits often affect the viability of the acquisition.

Section 3.14(c) contains Sellers' representation that the government licenses and permits that Sellers have disclosed constitute all the licenses and permits that are required to operate the business of each Acquired Company. Buyer may discover that an Acquired Company was operating without the proper authorization and faces fines or other penalties. Together with the representation concerning the sufficiency of the Acquired Companies' assets (Section 3.7), this representation gives Buyer some comfort that all the essential elements of the businesses will be present and operational after the Closing.

Other representations in Article 3 address the Acquired Companies' compliance with specific Legal Requirements. *See, e.g.*, Sections 3.11 (tax laws), 3.13 (ERISA), 3.19 (environmental laws), and 3.21 (labor laws). In light of the holding in DCV Holdings v. ConAgra, Inc., 2005 WL 698133 (Del. Super. Ct. 2005), *aff'd*, 889 A.2d 954 (Del. 2005), that a specific "compliance with law" representation trumps a general "no undisclosed liabilities" representation, Buyer may want to consider adding language to limit the overlap between Section 3.14 and certain other representations in Article 3, including those that cover specific areas of law. *See* commentary to Section 3.10. Such a provision might read as follows:

> Nothing contained in this Section 3.14 shall be construed as a representation or warranty with respect to:
>
> (i)   any Legal Requirement or Governmental Authorization that is the subject matter of a specific representation or warranty contained in this Article 3, or
>
> (ii)   the matters referenced in Sections 3.4 , 3.10, 3.12, or 3.29.

See Manual on Acquisition Review chs. 12, 13.

SELLERS' RESPONSE

Section 3.14(a) requires disclosure of past violations of Legal Requirements. Sellers may contend that no business operates in strict compliance with all laws and that Section 3.14(a) should include a materiality qualifier. Sellers may also argue that Buyer should not be concerned about historical violations that have been cured and are no longer pending. Buyer may respond by pointing out that it has a legitimate concern that the Acquired Companies' operations have not been based on, and do not involve a pattern of, violations. In addition, without this provision, Sellers might be able to circumvent the representation by altering the

Acquired Companies' operations immediately prior to the signing in order to bring the Acquired Companies into temporary compliance with applicable Legal Requirements. The parties may compromise on this point by selecting a relatively recent date to mark the beginning of the period with respect to which disclosure of past violations is required.

Sellers could request time limitations in clauses (i), (ii), and (iii) of Section 3.14(a), arguing that older violations are irrelevant.

Sellers may ask that oral notices be deleted from clause (iii), arguing that oral comments made in passing by a governmental inspector may not be reported to management of the Acquired Companies and are likely irrelevant if they do not lead to written notice of a violation.

Sellers might object to clause (iv) in its entirety, since they may not monitor legislative proposals.

Similarly, Sellers could request time limitations in clauses (i), (ii), (iii), and (iv) of Section 3.14(b), and deletion of the oral notice reference in clause (iii).

3.15 LEGAL PROCEEDINGS; ORDERS

(a) Except as set forth in Part 3.15(a), since _____ there has not been, and there is not pending or, to the Knowledge of Sellers, threatened, any Proceeding:

    (i)   by or against any Acquired Company or that otherwise relates to or could affect the business of, or any assets owned or used by, any Acquired Company; or

    (ii)   by or against any Seller that relates to the Shares; or

    (iii)   that challenges, or that could have the effect of preventing, delaying, making illegal, imposing limitations or conditions on, or otherwise interfering with, any Contemplated Transaction.

To the Knowledge of Sellers, no event has occurred or circumstance exists that could give rise to or serve as a basis for the commencement of any such Proceeding. Sellers have delivered to Buyer copies of all pleadings, correspondence, and other documents relating to each pending or threatened Proceeding listed in Part 3.15(a). None of the pending or threatened Proceedings listed in Part 3.15(a), individually or in the aggregate, will or could reasonably be expected to result in an adverse consequence to any Acquired Company or in any Acquired Company incurring Losses of $_____ or more or being subjected to any Order.

(b) Except as set forth in Part 3.15(b):

(i) there is no Order to which any Acquired Company, or any assets owned or used by any Acquired Company, is subject; and

(ii) no Seller is subject to any Order that relates to the business of, or any assets owned or used by, any Acquired Company.

(c) Except as set forth in Part 3.15(c):

(i) each Acquired Company has at all times been in compliance with each Order to which it, or any assets owned or used by it, is or has been subject;

(ii) no event has occurred or circumstance exists that could constitute or result in (with or without notice or lapse of time) a violation of, or failure to comply with, any Order to which (A) any Acquired Company, or any assets owned or used by any Acquired Company, is subject, or (B) any Seller is subject that relates to the business of, or any assets owned or used by, any Acquired Company; and

(iii) no Acquired Company or Seller has, at any time received any notice or other communication (whether oral or written) from any Governmental Body or any other Person regarding any actual, alleged, or potential violation of, or failure to comply with, any Order to which (A) any Acquired Company, or any assets owned or used by any Acquired Company, is subject, or (B) any Seller is subject that relates to the business of, or any assets owned or used by, any Acquired Company.

COMMENT

Section 3.15(a) contains Sellers' representations concerning pending and potential Proceedings. The term "Proceedings" is defined in Section 1.1 to include not only lawsuits, but arbitrations, mediations, and administrative actions. Section 3.15(a) requires disclosure of Proceedings that may affect the Acquired Companies or the consummation of the Contemplated Transactions.

Buyer would usually evaluate each disclosed Proceeding to determine the probability of an adverse determination and the magnitude of the potential damages. However, if Buyer reviews privileged materials relating to legal proceedings in which the Acquired Companies are involved, there may be a waiver of the attorney-client privilege (*see* commentary to Section 5.1). For each disclosed Proceeding, Buyer might determine whether the potential liability requires some additional changes to the Model Agreement. Among other things, Buyer and Sellers might agree on the manner in which all such Proceedings will be conducted up to and after the

Closing, such as who will designate lead counsel and who is empowered to effect a settlement.

Section 3.15(b) contains Sellers' representations concerning the existence of Orders to which the Acquired Companies are subject. "Order" is defined in Section 1.1 to include not only judicial orders, but orders of other Governmental Bodies. Section 3.15(c) focuses on violations of those Orders.

For a discussion of the significance of the phrase "with or without notice or lapse of time" (which appears in clause (ii) of Section 3.15(c)), *see* commentary to Section 3.2.

Clause (iii) of Section 3.15(c), which requires disclosure of notices received from Governmental Bodies and third parties concerning actual and potential violations, overlaps to some extent with clauses (i) and (ii), but clause (iii) is not redundant. Clause (iii) requires disclosure of violations that have been asserted by other parties. Sellers are required to disclose such asserted violations pursuant to clause (iii), even if the Acquired Company denies the alleged violation.

The parties should recognize that if information regarding an actual or potential violation of an Order is included in Sellers' Disclosure Letter, this information may be discoverable by adverse parties in the course of litigation involving the Acquired Companies and may also have to be reported to a Governmental Body. Accordingly, it is important to use care in preparing the descriptions included in Part 3.15 of the Disclosure Letter. *See* commentary to Section 3.2.

Representations concerning litigation typically require the seller to represent that "to its knowledge, no proceeding involving the target has been threatened." The word "threatened" connotes action that a prudent person would expect to be taken based either upon receipt of an oral threat of litigation, a written demand letter threatening litigation, or notice of an impending investigation or audit. When the term "threatened" is used in conjunction with a knowledge qualification, a buyer will normally insist that the seller's knowledge be based upon some inquiry or process of investigation, whereas the seller may attempt to limit its knowledge of threatened action to the actual knowledge of the seller and perhaps the target's senior management (or a limited number of designated officers) without any independent investigation. *See* commentary to the definition of "Knowledge" in Section 1.1.

Since the concept of "threatened" is limited, Section 3.15(a) requires Sellers to represent that no event has occurred that could result in a Proceeding. For example, assume that a significant industrial accident had recently occurred at an Acquired Company's plant. No Proceedings have yet been filed or "threatened," but the nature of the accident is such that it would require disclosure under Section 3.15(a).

See Manual on Acquisition Review ch. 7.

SELLERS' RESPONSE

As stated above, Sellers may voice concern over the effect the document delivery requirements of Section 3.15(a) may have upon claims of attorney-client privilege relating to such documents.

Sellers may seek to limit the scope of Section 3.15(a) in several respects. For example, Sellers may point out that the representations in Section 3.15(a) are so broad that they require Sellers to disclose an acquisition-related lawsuit in which Buyer is the only named defendant. Sellers might request that these representations be limited to legal proceedings in which Sellers or the Acquired Companies are actually named as parties or are otherwise directly involved. In making this request, Sellers could remind Buyer that they are not proposing to modify Buyer's ability to terminate the Model Agreement under Section 10.1 in the event of certain lawsuits against Buyer.

Sellers may also point out that the last sentence of Section 3.15(a) effectively requires Sellers to bear the litigation risks associated with each Proceeding disclosed by Sellers in the Disclosure Letter, including routine lawsuits brought against the Acquired Companies in the normal course of operations, since even these lawsuits could have adverse consequences. Sellers might insist that the parties determine, on a case-by-case basis, which of the disclosed Proceedings should remain Sellers' responsibility and which should become Buyer's responsibility following the Closing.

Sellers may ask that the reference to oral notices in clause (iii) of Section 3.15(c) be deleted, arguing that oral comments made in passing by a government inspector or other person may not have been reported to management, and if they were significant, would have matured into a written notice of violation.

Sellers may object to the provision in clauses (i) and (ii) of Section 3.15(c) that requires disclosure of past violations, arguing that Buyer should not be concerned about historical violations that have been cured and are no longer pending. Buyer may respond by pointing out that it has a legitimate concern that the Acquired Companies' operations have not been based on, and do not entail a pattern of, violations that Buyer will be unwilling to continue. In addition, without this provision, Sellers might be able to circumvent the representation by altering the Acquired Companies' operations immediately prior to the signing in order to bring the Acquired Companies into temporary compliance with applicable Orders. The parties may compromise on this point by selecting a relatively recent date to mark the beginning of the period with respect to which disclosure of past violations is required.

3.16   ABSENCE OF CERTAIN CHANGES AND EVENTS

Except as set forth in Part 3.16, since the Balance Sheet Date, each Acquired Company has conducted its business only in the Ordinary Course of Business, and there has not been any:

(a) issuance of or change in the authorized or issued Equity Securities of any Acquired Company; purchase, redemption, retirement, or other acquisition by any Acquired Company of any Equity Security of any Acquired Company; or declaration or payment of any dividend or other distribution or payment in respect of the Equity Securities of any Acquired Company;

(b) amendment to the Organizational Documents of any Acquired Company;

(c) other than any payments by an Acquired Company of bonuses, salaries, benefits, or other compensation in the Ordinary Course of Business, payment, increase or decrease by any Acquired Company of any bonus, salary, benefit, or other compensation to any holder of an Equity Security, director, manager, officer, employee, or consultant or entry into or amendment of any employment, severance, bonus, retirement, loan, or other Contract with any holder of any Equity Security, director, manager, officer, employee, or consultant;

(d) adoption of, amendment to, or material increase or decrease in the payments to or benefits under any Employee Plan;

(e) damage to or destruction or loss of any asset owned or used by any Acquired Company, whether or not covered by insurance;

(f) entry into, modification, termination, or expiration of, or receipt of notice of termination of, any Applicable Contract listed in Part 3.17(a);

(g) sale (other than sales of inventory in the Ordinary Course of Business), lease, other disposition of, or imposition of an Encumbrance on any asset owned or used by any Acquired Company;

(h) release or waiver of any claim or right of any Acquired Company with a value in excess of $_____;

(i) change in the accounting methods used by any Acquired Company;

(j) capital expenditure (or series of related capital expenditures) by any Acquired Company either involving more than $_____ or outside the Ordinary Course of Business;

(k) capital investment in, loan to, or acquisition of the securities or assets of, any Person (or series of related capital investments, loans, and acquisitions) by any Acquired Company either involving more than $_____ or outside the Ordinary Course of Business or acquisition (by merger, exchange, consolidation, acquisition of Equity Securities or assets, or otherwise) of any Person by any Acquired Company;

(l) note, bond, debenture, or other indebtedness for borrowed money issued, created, incurred, assumed, or guaranteed (including advances on existing credit facilities) involving more than $_____ individually or $_____ in the aggregate by any Acquired Company;

(m) Contract by any Acquired Company or any Seller to do any of the foregoing; or

(n) other material occurrence, event, action, failure to act, or transaction outside the Ordinary Course of Business involving any Acquired Company.

COMMENT

This representation seeks information about actions taken by the Acquired Companies or other events affecting the Acquired Companies since the date of the most recent annual balance sheet. It alerts Buyer to changes that have occurred and would not be reflected in that balance sheet. For example, if employee benefits have been significantly increased, the future cost of such benefits will be greater than is reflected in the balance sheet. In addition, this provision requires disclosure of actions taken by an Acquired Company in anticipation of the acquisition.

In addition to alerting Buyer to changes, this representation, in combination with Section 5.2, serves another purpose. Section 5.2(l) provides that Sellers will not take any action of the nature described in Section 3.16 during the period between the date of signing the Model Agreement and the Closing.

The date in the first sentence of Section 3.16 could be either the date of the target's most recent annual balance sheet, which may be audited, or the date of the most recent interim balance sheet, which generally would not be audited. The Model Agreement uses the Balance Sheet Date because Buyer will have a higher degree of confidence from audited financial statements than from unaudited statements. Finally, in addition to the matters covered by this representation, which usually are important to Buyer, there may be other specific matters that pose special risks to Buyer, and Buyer may want to include those matters in this representation.

SELLERS' RESPONSE

The lead-in to Section 3.16 requires Sellers to represent that, except as set forth in Part 3.16 of the Disclosure Letter, since the Balance Sheet Date, the affairs of the Acquired Companies have been conducted only in the Ordinary Course of Business. Given the definition "Ordinary Course of Business" in Section 1.1, this is a broad representation that, depending on the Balance Sheet Date, may require extensive disclosure by Sellers. The representation is not limited to disclosure regarding the listed items, but requires disclosure of any action taken outside of the Ordinary Course of Business since the Balance Sheet Date. Sellers may question whether the Ordinary Course of Business standard is too vague. Sellers may also seek to limit the time period in question so that it commences with the Interim Balance Sheet Date.

Sellers should be wary of Section 3.16 since it will be "brought down" to the Closing Date. If any of the events covered by this Section occur between signing and the Closing, whether voluntarily or involuntarily, it could give Buyer a right not to close. Moreover, by virtue of Section 5.2, voluntarily taking an action described in Section 3.16 would constitute a breach of covenant that could provide Buyer with both a right not to close and an action for damages.

Sellers might request that certain provisions of Section 3.16 be deleted as covered by other representations in the Model Agreement. For example, in Section 3.1(b), Sellers represent that there have been no amendments to the Organizational Documents of the Acquired Companies. Since the Buyer could determine for itself whether they have been amended, Section 3.16(b) is arguably unnecessary. Similarly, since Section 3.17 calls for extensive disclosure with respect to Applicable Contracts, the information requested in Section 3.16(f) may not provide additional benefit to Buyer.

Sellers might ask that threshold dollar amounts be inserted in certain clauses of Section 3.16, such as clauses (c), (e), and (g), so that Sellers are not required to disclose items involving immaterial amounts.

Sellers may request that clause (i) be revised to exempt changes in accounting methods required by GAAP.

Sellers might seek to delete clause (n) in its entirety as being overly broad and vague and also unnecessary, given the lead-in to Section 3.16 and the number of specific representations requested of Sellers.

3.17   CONTRACTS

(a) Part 3.17(a) lists, and Sellers have delivered to Buyer a copy of, each Applicable Contract:

   (i)   involving the performance of services, delivery of goods or materials, or payments by one or more Acquired Companies of an amount or value in excess of $_____;

   (ii)   involving the performance of services, delivery of goods or materials, or payments to one or more Acquired Companies of an amount or value in excess of $_____;

   (iii) that was not entered into in the Ordinary Course of Business;

   (iv)   affecting the ownership of, leasing of, title to, use of, or any leasehold or other interest in, any real or personal property (except personal property leases and installment and conditional sales agreements having a value per item or aggregate payments of less than $_____ and with remaining terms of less than one year);

   (v)   with respect to Intellectual Property Assets, including Contracts with current or former employees, consultants, or contractors regarding the ownership, use, protection, or nondisclosure of any of the Intellectual Property Assets;

   (vi)   with any labor union or other employee representative of a group of employees relating to wages, hours, or other conditions of employment;

   (vii) involving any joint venture, partnership, or limited liability company agreement involving a sharing of profits, losses, costs, Taxes, or other liabilities by any Acquired Company with any other Person;

   (viii) containing covenants that in any way purport to restrict the right or freedom of any Acquired Company or any other Person for the benefit of any Acquired Company to (A) engage in any business activity, (B) engage in any line of business or compete with any Person, or (C) solicit any Person to enter into a business or employment relationship, or enter into such a relationship with any Person;

   (ix)   providing for payments to or by any Person based on sales, purchases, or profits, other than direct payments for goods;

(x)   containing an effective power of attorney granted by any Acquired Company;

(xi)   containing or providing for an express undertaking by any Acquired Company to be responsible for consequential, special, or liquidated damages or penalties or to indemnify any other party;

(xii)   for capital expenditures in excess of $_____;

(xiii) involving payments to or from an Acquired Company that are not denominated in U.S. dollars;

(xiv)   involving the settlement, release, compromise, or waiver of any material rights, claims, obligations, duties, or liabilities;

(xv)   relating to indebtedness of any Acquired Company in excess of $_____;

(xvi)   relating to the employment of any employee of any Acquired Company;

(xvii) relating to a distributor, reseller, OEM, dealer, manufacturer's representative, broker, finder's, sales agency, advertising agency, manufacturing, assembly, or product design and development relationship with an Acquired Company;

(xviii) under which any Acquired Company has loaned to, or made an investment in, or guaranteed the obligations of, any Person in excess of $_____;

(xix)   relating to any bond or letter of credit;

(xx)   containing any obligation of confidentiality or nondisclosure between any Acquired Company and any other Person for the benefit of any Acquired Company or such other Person; and

(xxi)   constituting an amendment, supplement, or modification (whether oral or written) in respect of any of the foregoing.

(b) Except as set forth in Part 3.17(b):

(i)   each Applicable Contract listed in Part 3.17(a) is in full force and effect, and is valid and enforceable in accordance with its terms;

(ii)   the completion or performance of each Applicable Contract for the sale of goods or services by an Acquired Company listed in Part 3.17(a) will not result in less than normal profit margins to such Acquired Company; and

      (iii)   the completion or performance of each Applicable Contract listed in Part 3.17(a) will not result in an adverse consequence to any Acquired Company.

(c) Except as set forth in Part 3.17(c):

      (i)   each Acquired Company has been in compliance with each Applicable Contract since the effective date of such Applicable Contract;

      (ii)   each other Person that has any obligation or liability under any Applicable Contract has been in compliance with such Applicable Contract since the effective date of such Applicable Contract;

      (iii)   no event has occurred or circumstance exists that (with or without notice or lapse of time) could result in a Breach of, or give any Acquired Company or other Person the right to declare a default or exercise any remedy under, or accelerate the maturity or performance of or payment under, or cancel, terminate, or modify, any Applicable Contract;

      (iv)   no event has occurred or circumstance exists under or by virtue of any Applicable Contract that (with or without notice or lapse of time) would cause the creation of any Encumbrance affecting any assets owned or used by any Acquired Company; and

      (v)   no Acquired Company has given to, or received from, any other Person any notice or other communication (whether oral or written) regarding any actual, alleged, or potential Breach of any Applicable Contract.

(d) There is no renegotiation of, attempt to renegotiate, or outstanding rights to renegotiate any Applicable Contract with any Person, and no Person has made written demand for such renegotiation.

(e) Each Applicable Contract relating to the sale, design, manufacture, or provision of products or services by an Acquired Company has been entered into in the Ordinary Course of Business and without the commission of any act alone or in concert with any other Person, or any consideration having been paid or promised, in violation of any Legal Requirement.

COMMENT

Section 3.17 requires Sellers to provide a complete list of the Acquired Companies' contracts that meet specified criteria and to advise Buyer of any pending, asserted, or potential defaults under these contracts. Contracts are generally major assets of the target as well as potential sources of significant liabilities. In either case, representations regarding those contracts are important. The list of contracts in Section 3.17(a) is expansive. The types of contracts to be listed will vary depending on the nature of the target's business. For examples of the types of contracts that may fall within the broad scope of the definition of "Applicable Contract," *see* commentary to Section 3.2.

In Section 3.17(b), Sellers represent that each Applicable Contract is effective and enforceable, and that the performance of the Applicable Contract will result in a normal profit and will not result in any adverse consequence to an Acquired Company.

Section 3.17(c) contains Sellers' representation that both the Acquired Companies and the counterparties to the Applicable Contracts are in compliance with the Applicable Contracts, and that no breach of an Applicable Contract has occurred or been alleged. The representation in Section 3.17(c) does not address whether any listed contract is subject to termination at the option of a third party upon consummation of the Contemplated Transactions; that issue is covered by Section 3.2(b).

For a discussion of the significance of the phrase "with or without notice or lapse of time" (which appears in Section 3.17(c)), *see* Section 3.2.

See Manual on Acquisition Review ch. 3.

SELLERS' RESPONSE

Many of the clauses in Section 3.17(a) are not qualified by materiality or other thresholds. As a result, Sellers may object to the breadth of the required disclosure, especially when they are required to provide complete and accurate copies of each contract in Part 3.17(a) of the Disclosure Letter. Many large businesses would find providing complete and accurate copies of many routine contracts a daunting if not impossible task. Sellers may also object to the scope of the definition of Applicable Contract. *See* commentary and sellers' response to Section 3.2.

Sellers might request that clause (iii) of Section 3.17(a) regarding contracts outside the Ordinary Course of Business be deleted as vague and unnecessary, given the number of specific types of contracts that must be disclosed.

Sellers might ask that the reference to "or any other Person for the benefit of any Acquired Company" in clauses (viii) and (xx) of Section 3.17(a) be deleted since it requires disclosure of contracts to which no Acquired Company is a party, and requires Sellers to make the representations in Sections 3.17(b) and (c) with respect to those contracts.

Seller may also ask that clause (xiv) of Section 3.17(a) be limited to settlement agreements and releases, since compromises and waivers could encompass many aspects of contracts, such as contractual limitations on damages and remedies.

Sellers could object to clause (xvi) of Section 3.17(a) because "relating to employment" makes it quite broad. Sellers might ask that it be limited to employment contracts.

Sellers may object to Section 3.17(b) in several respects. In clause (i) of Section 3.17(b), Sellers effectively represent that each Applicable Contract is enforceable not only against the Acquired Company, but the counterparty as well. Sellers may ask that the representation be limited to the Acquired Companies or that the representation with respect to counterparties be qualified by knowledge. Sellers may contend that clauses (ii) and (iii) require Sellers to predict the future, which they do not control, particularly since Buyer will own the Acquired Companies, and that the terms "normal profit margins" and "adverse consequence" are vague and devoid of any commonly accepted meaning. Rather than being forced to essentially guarantee future events, Sellers may seek a "reasonably expected to" standard.

Sellers might ask that reference to oral notice in clause (v) of Section 3.17(c) be deleted. Sellers may also request that Section 3.17(e) be deleted because it is vague and its subject matter is covered by Sections 3.14(a) and 3.23.

3.18   INSURANCE

(a) **Sellers have delivered to Buyer:**

   (i)   **copies of all policies of insurance (and correspondence relating to coverage thereunder) to which any Acquired Company is a party, an insured, or a beneficiary, or under which any Acquired Company, or any director, officer, or manager of any Acquired Company in his or her capacity as such, is or has been covered at any time since _____, a list of which is included in Part 3.18(a);**

   (ii) **copies of all pending applications for policies of insurance; and**

   (iii) **any written statement by the auditor of any Acquired Company or any consultant or risk management advisor provided to or in the possession of an Acquired Company with regard to the adequacy of its coverage or its reserves for actual or potential claims.**

(b) **Part 3.18(b) sets forth:**

(i) any self-insurance or retention arrangement by or affecting any Acquired Company, including any reserves established thereunder;

(ii) any Contract, other than a policy of insurance, for the transfer or sharing of any risk by any Acquired Company; and

(iii) all obligations of any Acquired Company to third parties with respect to insurance coverage (including such obligations under leases and service agreements) and identifying the policy under which such coverage is provided.

(c) Part 3.18(c) sets forth for each Acquired Company for the current policy year and each of the preceding _____ policy years by year:

(i) a summary of the loss experience under each policy of insurance;

(ii) a statement describing each claim under a policy of insurance for an amount in excess of $_____, which sets forth:

(A) the name of the claimant;

(B) a description of the policy by insurer, type of insurance, and period of coverage; and

(C) the amount and a brief description of the claim; and

(iii) a statement describing the loss experience for all claims that were self-insured, including the number and aggregate cost of such claims.

(d) Except as set forth in Part 3.18(d):

(i) all policies of insurance to which any Acquired Company is a party, an insured, or a beneficiary or that provide coverage to any Seller in such Seller's capacity as a shareholder of the Company, any Acquired Company, or any director, officer, or manager of an Acquired Company in such capacity:

(A) are valid, outstanding, and enforceable;

(B) are issued by an insurer that is financially sound and reputable;

(C) taken together, provide adequate insurance coverage for the assets and the operations of each Acquired Company [for all risks normally insured against by a Person carrying on the same business or businesses as such Acquired Company] [for all risks to which such Acquired Company is normally exposed];

(D) are sufficient for compliance with applicable Legal Requirements and all Applicable Contracts to which any Acquired Company is a party or by which it is bound;

(E) will continue in full force and effect following the consummation and performance of the Contemplated Transactions; and

(F) do not provide for any retrospective premium adjustment or other experience-based liability on the part of any Acquired Company;

(ii) since _____, no Seller or Acquired Company has received:

(A) any refusal of insurance coverage or any notice that a defense will be afforded with reservation of rights; or

(B) any notice of cancellation or any other indication that any policy of insurance is no longer in full force or effect or will not be renewed or that the issuer of any policy of insurance is not willing or able to perform its obligations thereunder;

(iii) each Acquired Company has paid all premiums due, and has otherwise performed its obligations, under each policy of insurance to which it is a party or that provides coverage to it or to any of its directors, officers, or managers, in their capacity as such;

(iv) each Acquired Company has given notice to the insurer of all insured claims; and

(v) no Acquired Company and no Seller has received any notice of any, and to the Knowledge of Sellers there are no, planned or proposed increases in the premiums or any other adverse change in the terms of any policy of insurance covering any Acquired Company, any Seller in such Seller's capacity as a shareholder of the Company, or any officer, director, or manager of an Acquired Company in his or her capacity as such.

(e) No Acquired Company has provided any information to any insurer in connection with any application for insurance that could result in (i) cancellation of any insurance policy or bond for the benefit of such Acquired Company or (ii) denial of coverage for a risk otherwise covered by any such insurance policy or bond.

(f) Part 3.18(f) describes the manner in which the Company insures or self-insures with respect to workers' compensation liability. Part 3.18(f) lists each incident or claim that creates or could create a workers' compensation liability of any Acquired Company since _____, and the related disposition and accrual with respect to such incident or claim. No Acquired Company has received any notice that, and no Acquired Company has any reason to believe, based on its incident or claim experience that, its workers' compensation insurance premiums or expenses will increase in the next 12 months, or, if self-insured, that it will not be permitted to continue to self-insure without increase in any related bonds, letters of credit, or other form of financial security.

COMMENT

This representation seeks information and assurances regarding the adequacy of the Acquired Companies' insurance coverage and their exposure to uninsured risks. Buyer will often examine the present and prospective cost of the Acquired Companies' insurance, the availability of continued coverage following the acquisition, and whatever insight that the loss runs or claims history may give into matters such as the Acquired Companies' quality control and safety programs. In addition to traditional property and casualty insurance policies, many corporations have large self-insured retentions and complicated retrospective premium programs and may participate in captive insurance programs. Buyer will want to understand these alternative risk-transfer mechanisms in evaluating the insurance program of the Acquired Companies.

Buyer may want to continue some or all of the Acquired Companies' existing policies, especially for coverages that may be difficult or expensive to obtain. If Buyer wants to continue the Acquired Companies' insurance policies, it should verify that the policies are issued to the Acquired Companies. Under the Fact Pattern, this should not present an issue. If, however, a buyer is purchasing the stock of a subsidiary of another company, it may find that the insurance is provided under a group umbrella policy issued to the parent company that will terminate as to the subsidiary upon sale. *See* Appendix A—The Purchase of a Subsidiary.

In clause (i)(B) of Section 3.18(d), Sellers represent that all the insurance policies held by the Acquired Companies are issued by "financially sound and reputable" insurers. Buyer may in addition wish to review the financial soundness of those insurers. Various agencies rate insurers, including A.M. Best Co., Moody's Investors Service, and Standard & Poor's.

Additional provisions may be needed if the Acquired Companies' businesses are covered under policies that also insure other businesses of Sellers. To the extent that the Acquired Companies have significant exposure to uninsured risks, the parties may allocate those risks in the Model Agreement.

Workers' compensation liability can be a significant expense in some industries and jurisdictions. Section 3.18(f) elicits information on claims history and prospective workers' compensation expense.

See MANUAL ON ACQUISITION REVIEW ch. 8.

SELLERS' RESPONSE

Sellers may argue that Section 3.18(d)(iii) imposes impractical requirements with respect to third- party insurance coverage obligations, particularly if the Acquired Companies have numerous contracts and equipment leases.

Sellers may object to clause (i)(C) of Section 3.18(d), arguing that there is no objective means of measuring the adequacy of insurance coverage and that Buyer must make its own assessment. Sellers might request that the words "or any other indication" be removed from clause (ii)(B) of Section 3.18(d), reasoning that it is too vague and that the representation should be limited to written notice from the insurers.

Sellers may contend that the second sentence of Section 3.18(f) is overly broad and requires Sellers to engage in speculation. Sellers may also ask that the phrase "and no Acquired Company has any reason to believe" be deleted from the third sentence of Section 3.18(f), reasoning that belief is too amorphous a standard and that because it refers to future periods, it should be limited to matters of which an Acquired Company has been notified.

3.19   ENVIRONMENTAL MATTERS

Except as set forth in Part 3.19:

(a) **Each Acquired Company has at all times complied with all Environmental Laws.**

(b) **No Seller or Acquired Company or any other Person for whose conduct any of them is or could be held responsible has received any Order, notice, or other communication (written or oral) relating to any actual, alleged, or potential violation of or failure to comply with any Environmental Law, or any actual or potential Environmental, Health, and Safety Liability.**

(c) **There are no pending or, to the Knowledge of Sellers, threatened claims or Encumbrances resulting from any Environmental, Health, and Safety Liability or arising under or pursuant to any Environmental Law, with respect to or affecting any of the Facilities or any other asset owned or used by any Acquired Company or in which it has or had an interest.**

(d) No Seller or Acquired Company, or any other Person for whose conduct any of them is or could be held responsible, has any Environmental, Health, and Safety Liability, and no event has occurred or circumstance exists that (with or without notice or lapse of time) could result in any Acquired Company or any other Person for whose conduct any of them is or could be held responsible (i) having any Environmental, Health and Safety Liability or (ii) violating any Environmental Law.

(e) There is no Hazardous Material present on or under the Facilities or, to the Knowledge of Sellers, any geographically, geologically, hydraulically or hydro-geologically adjoining property ("Adjoining Property"). No Seller, Acquired Company, any other Person for whose conduct any of them is or could be held responsible, or, to the Knowledge of Sellers, any other Person, has permitted or conducted, or is aware of, any Hazardous Activity conducted with respect to the Facilities or any other asset in which any Acquired Company has or had an interest.

(f) None of the Facilities and, to the Knowledge of Sellers, no Adjoining Property, contains any (i) above-ground or underground storage tanks or (ii) landfills, surface impoundments, or disposal areas.

(g) Sellers have delivered to Buyer copies of all reports, studies, analyses, or tests initiated by or on behalf of or in the possession of Seller or any Acquired Company pertaining to the environmental condition of, Hazardous Material or Hazardous Activity in, on, or under, the Facilities or any Adjoining Property, or concerning compliance by any Acquired Company or any other Person for whose conduct any of them is or could be held responsible, with Environmental Laws.

COMMENT

Statutes such as CERCLA and similar state statutes, which are the primary basis for environmental liability, impose strict and retroactive liability. Consequently, Buyer will not want to limit these representations to violations of environmental laws, but will also want Sellers to represent that there are no past or present actions or conditions that could form the basis of an environmental claim against the Acquired Companies or anyone for whose actions the Acquired Companies may be liable. This representation is included in Section 3.19(d).

An important issue for a buyer in a stock acquisition is the potential liability of the target relating to its predecessors and subsidiaries, in respect of properties they no longer own or businesses they no longer operate (such as divisions that have been spun off), and in respect of prior agreements to indemnify and assume environmental liabilities. Consequently, the representations include any person or entity for whose conduct Sellers or any Acquired Company is or could be held responsible.

Section 3.19(e) addresses off-site locations to account for liabilities that arise under CERCLA and analogous state statutes, even if the Acquired Companies have taken all actions in a lawful manner.

In many transactions, the buyer will resist any attempt by the seller to qualify or otherwise weaken the environmental representations. Among other reasons, the buyer may be or become a public company with a responsibility to make environmental disclosures that will require its understanding of all pending and threatened matters. For example, SEC Regulation S-K, Item 103, requires disclosure of a pending administrative or judicial proceeding, or known to be contemplated by the government, arising under environmental laws to which the registrant or its subsidiary is a party, or to which any of their property is subject, if "[a] governmental authority is a party to such proceeding and such proceeding involves potential monetary sanctions, unless the registrant reasonably believes that such proceeding will result in no monetary sanctions, or in monetary sanctions, exclusive of interest and costs, of less than $100,000." Obviously, the registrant must have the information necessary to make such an assessment, and Buyer will want to be aware of these issues prior to the Closing.

Buyer should be aware of any relevant information already in the possession of the Acquired Companies or Sellers. Such information enables Buyer, if a public company, to anticipate environmental disclosure issues, including cost estimates.

In defending the breadth and definitiveness of the environmental representations, Buyer may contend that these representations are a risk-sharing mechanism and that Sellers' knowledge or lack thereof is irrelevant.

See MANUAL ON ACQUISITION REVIEW ch. 9.

SELLERS' RESPONSE

Sellers may request a time limitation in Section 3.19(a) such as "Since ____, each Acquired Company has complied," arguing that possible violations beyond the applicable statute of limitations are irrelevant.

The concept of "any other Person for whose conduct any of them [Seller or Acquired Company] is or could be held responsible" is repeated throughout Section 3.19. Seller may ask that this language be eliminated or redrafted to be more specific. For example, if Buyer is concerned about predecessor entities, the language could be replaced with a reference to those entities.

Section 3.19(b) refers to "other communication (written or oral)." Sellers may ask that this language be eliminated on the ground that they should only be responsible for written notices.

Sellers may request that Section 3.19(c) be limited to assets in which an Acquired Company currently has an interest, since it may be difficult to determine if claims or Encumbrances have resulted from assets in which it no longer has an interest.

Section 3.19(e) may raise multiple objections from Sellers. Sellers may object to the broad definition of "Hazardous Material" in Section 1.1 which requires them to "foresee" what substances might be regulated in the future. Sellers may request that the reference to "Adjoining Property" be eliminated, because of the impracticality of determining the environmental condition of property in which any of those listed do not have an interest.

Sellers may challenge the risk-sharing thrust of these representations and argue that they should be more knowledge-based.

3.20   EMPLOYEES AND CONSULTANTS

(a) Part 3.20(a) lists the following information for each employee of each Acquired Company, including each employee on leave of absence or layoff status: employer, name, job title, date of hiring, date of commencement of employment, details of leave of absence or layoff, rate of compensation, bonus arrangement, and any change in compensation or bonus since _____, vacation, sick time, and personal leave accrued as of _____, and service credited for purposes of vesting and eligibility to participate under any Employee Plan.

(b) Part 3.20(b) lists the following information for every independent contractor, consultant, or sales agent of each Acquired Company: name, responsibilities, date of engagement, and compensation. Each such independent contractor, consultant, or sales agent qualifies as an independent contractor in relation to such Acquired Company for purposes of all applicable Legal Requirements, including those relating to Taxes, insurance, and employee benefits.

(c) Except as set forth in Part 3.20(c), to the Knowledge of Sellers, (i) no director, officer, or other key employee of any Acquired Company intends to terminate such Person's employment with such Acquired Company, and (ii) no independent contractor, consultant, or sales agent intends to terminate such Person's arrangement with any Acquired Company.

(d) Part 3.20(d) lists the following information for each retired employee or director of any Acquired Company, or their dependents, receiving benefits or scheduled to receive benefits from any Acquired Company in the future: name, pension benefits, pension option election, retiree medical insurance coverage, retiree life insurance coverage, and other benefits.

(e) Part 3.20(e) states the number of employees terminated or laid off by any Acquired Company since _____, and contains a list of the following information for each employee of an Acquired Company who has been terminated or laid off, or whose hours of work have been reduced by more than 50% by an Acquired Company, in the six months prior to the date of this Agreement: (i) the date of such termination, layoff, or reduction in hours; (ii) the reason for such termination, layoff, or reduction in hours; and (iii) the location to which the employee was assigned.

(f) No Acquired Company has violated the Worker Adjustment and Retraining Notification Act or any similar state or local Legal Requirement.

(g) To the Knowledge of Sellers, no director, officer, employee, agent, consultant, or independent contractor of any Acquired Company is bound by any Contract or subject to any Order that purports to limit the ability of such director, officer, employee, agent, consultant, or independent contractor (i) to engage in or continue or perform any conduct, activity, duties, or practice relating to the business of any Acquired Company or (ii) to assign to any Acquired Company any rights to any invention, improvement, or discovery. No former or current employee of any Acquired Company is a party to, or is otherwise bound by, any Contract that in any way adversely affected, affects, or could affect the ability of any Acquired Company to continue to conduct its business as conducted.

COMMENT

Section 3.20 solicits information with respect to three groups: employees, independent contractors, and retirees. Buyer's interest in the latter is limited to retirees who are receiving benefits from an Acquired Company. It provides Buyer with insight as to the compensation and benefit costs of the Acquired Companies.

The employment relationship between an employee and employer in the United States generally is on an "at-will" basis; that is, it can be terminated at any time without notice by either party for any reason or for no reason. The nature and obligation of that relationship can change, however, if the parties have entered into an employment contract for a fixed period of time or if the employee is covered by a collective bargaining agreement with a union. Furthermore, in some states, an employment contract can be implied from personnel policies or employee handbooks. In addition, most states have carved out statutory and judicial exceptions to the employment-at-will doctrine, including public policy exceptions. For example, federal and state civil rights laws protect employees against termination based on race, sex, religion, and other protected categories. Some jurisdictions also have laws that protect "whistleblowers" (i.e., employees who report violations of law by their employers) from termination or other retaliation. Buyer may therefore wish to review applicable state law to determine its effect on the employment-at-will relationship.

Section 3.20(a) requires that a significant amount of information concerning employees be set forth in the Disclosure Letter. Buyer should be cognizant of any legislation in the jurisdiction in which the Acquired Companies operate protecting the privacy or confidentiality of employee records or information. For example, there may be statutes protecting medical information, Social Security numbers, and other categories of information. The target may also have a published policy regarding employee records, and Sellers will want to handle disclosure in a manner consistent with that policy. Buyer may want to consider whether employee information should be shared in a more discrete, controlled fashion, since it is often the case that Buyer may want the information to be reviewed by a large number of people within Buyer's organization and Buyer may want to keep information such as salary and benefits confidential.

Section 3.20(b) requires disclosure of certain information regarding independent contractors retained by the Acquired Companies. If any of these relationships are memorialized in written contracts, they will be disclosed pursuant to Section 3.17.

Section 3.20(c) requires Sellers to provide information regarding employees and consultants who intend to resign. If key employees or consultants have indicated such an intention, it may impact Buyer's willingness to complete the acquisition or its view on the value of the Acquired Companies.

Section 3.20(e) and (f) relate to the Worker Adjustment and Retraining Notification Act, or "WARN Act." If an Acquired Company has recently terminated a number of employees or if an Acquired Company or Buyer is considering the possibility of terminating a number of employees in the near future, Buyer may want to consider the implications of the WARN Act. The WARN Act generally requires that a "covered employer" provide 60 days advance notice of a "plant closing" or "mass layoff" to affected employees, bargaining representatives, and local government officials. A "covered employer" under the WARN Act is an employer with (a) 100 or more employees (excluding part-time employees) or (b) 100 or more employees (whether or not part-time) who, in the aggregate, work at least 4,000 hours per week (excluding overtime hours). The WARN Act defines part-time employees as those who are employed for an average of fewer than 20 hours per week or who have been employed fewer than six of the 12 months preceding the date on which notice is required. 29 U.S.C. § 2101 (a)(8).

The WARN Act requires that a covered employer provide advance notice of a "plant closing" in which 50 or more full-time employees experience an "employment loss" during any 30-day period. A "plant closing" is a temporary or permanent shutdown of a single site of employment or one or more facilities or operating units within a single site of employment. An "employment loss" includes: (a) a termination of employment other than a discharge for cause or a voluntary departure or retirement, (b) a layoff exceeding six months, and (c) reductions of more than 50% of an employee's working hours during each month of a six-month period. The WARN Act also requires that a covered employer provide advance notice of a "mass layoff." A mass layoff includes situations in which: (1) at least one-third of the full-time employees at a single site during any 30-day period experience an employment loss where at least 50 full-time employees are laid off; and (2) at least 500 employees at a single site during any 30-day period experience an employment loss. 29 U.S.C. §§ 2101 (a)(2)(3).

The WARN Act contains a somewhat vague provision relating to the sale of a business. Generally, a seller is responsible for providing notices up to and including the effective date of the sale and the buyer is responsible for giving notices thereafter. Despite that provision, however, potential problems for a buyer may arise when the seller, prior to the effective date of the sale, has laid off a number of employees insufficient to trigger the WARN Act but that, when combined with the number of employees laid off after the Closing, total a sufficient number to trigger WARN Act obligations with respect to employees laid off. For this reason, Buyer should be aware of all employees of the Acquired Companies who have suffered an employment loss within 90 days prior to the Closing Date and consider seeking indemnification for actions of the Acquired Companies that may trigger (or contribute to the triggering of) WARN Act liability.

Many states, and some local governments, have enacted similar statutes relating to plant closings and mass layoffs.

Section 3.20(g) solicits information with respect to contracts with third parties, such as previous employers, that may limit the business activities of an employee or consultant or require an employee or consultant to assign intellectual property rights. Agreements protecting confidential information, requiring assignments of intellectual property (both during and post employment), and sometimes containing restrictive covenants such as noncompete and nonsolicitation provisions, have proliferated. Buyer will want information regarding these agreements to assure that an Acquired Company's employees are in compliance.

See MANUAL ON ACQUISITION REVIEW ch. 11.

SELLERS' RESPONSE

Sellers may seek to limit the amount of information regarding employees and independent contractors that is disclosed in the Disclosure Letter out of concern for employee privacy or the potential damage to the Acquired Companies that might result if that information became widely available. Sellers' concern regarding employee privacy may stem from Legal Requirements or from the Company's published policy. This may raise a practical issue on how to provide Buyer with a verifiable body of responsive information in another form.

If the Acquired Companies have a relatively large number of employees and/or independent contractors, Sellers may, from practical necessity, seek to conform the information requested by this representation to the manner in which the Acquired Companies maintain records and also seek to limit the level of detailed disclosure required for each employee.

Sellers may want to limit each of subsections (a), (b), and (c) of Section 3.20 by adding the phrase "as of the date of this Agreement." Sellers cannot control whether an employee or consultant terminates between signing and Closing, and the announcement of the pending transaction may hasten the departure of some. If the representations in subsections 3.20(a), (b) and (c) are "brought down" to the Closing, and employees leave in the interim, Sellers will have breached those representations.

3.21   LABOR DISPUTES; COMPLIANCE

(a) **Each Acquired Company has at all times complied with all Legal Requirements relating to employment practices, terms, and conditions of employment, equal employment opportunity, nondiscrimination, sexual harassment, immigration, wages, hours, benefits, collective bargaining and similar requirements, the payment of Social Security and similar Taxes, and occupational safety and health. No Acquired Company is liable for the payment of any Taxes, fines, penalties, or other amounts, however designated, for failure to comply with any of the foregoing Legal Requirements.**

(b) **Except as set forth in Part 3.21(b):**

   (i) **no Acquired Company is or has been a party to any collective bargaining agreement or other labor contract;**

   (ii) **since _____, there has not been, there is not pending or existing, and, to the Knowledge of Sellers, there is not threatened, any strike, slowdown, picketing, work stoppage, employee grievance process, organizational activity, or other labor dispute involving any Acquired Company;**

   (iii) **to the Knowledge of Sellers, no event has occurred or circumstance exists that could provide the basis for any work stoppage or other labor dispute;**

       (iv)   **since _____, there has not been, and there is not pending or, to the Knowledge of Sellers, threatened against or affecting any Acquired Company any Proceeding relating to the alleged violation of any Legal Requirement pertaining to labor relations or employment matters, including any charge or complaint filed with the National Labor Relations Board or any comparable Governmental Body;**

       (v)   **no application or petition for an election or for certification of a collective bargaining agent is pending;**

       (vi)   **since _____, there has not been, and there is not pending or, to Sellers' knowledge, threatened, any lockout of any employees by any Acquired Company; and**

       (vii)   **since _____, there has not been, and there is not pending or, to the Knowledge of Sellers, threatened, against any Acquired Company any charge of discrimination or sexual harassment filed with the Equal Employment Opportunity Commission or similar Governmental Body, and no event has occurred or circumstances exist that could provide the basis for any such charge.**

COMMENT

Section 3.21 requires disclosure regarding the labor relations of the Acquired Companies and their compliance with labor-related Legal Requirements. The degree of detail of these representations will vary depending upon the nature and extent of the Acquired Companies' businesses. In this regard, Buyer should be mindful that the matters included in Section 3.21(a) are covered more generally in Section 3.14 regarding compliance with Legal Requirements. If any Acquired Company operates abroad, Buyer may want to include specific representations concerning compliance with the labor laws and practices of the applicable foreign jurisdictions.

If the Acquired Companies conduct some operations that are subject to collective bargaining agreements and some operations that are not subject to such agreements, Buyer may want to analyze in detail the Acquired Companies' collective bargaining agreements and their different operations to determine whether such operations may be continued and integrated with Buyer's operations without significant labor disputes. If Buyer is already involved in a similar business, Buyer may also want to consider the impact of union/nonunion operations on its existing operations.

Some states have special labor relations agencies. If an Acquired Company's business falls within the jurisdictional reach of such a statute, Buyer may want to obtain an understanding of the statutory framework, not only to seek appropriate representations, but also to understand how that framework will affect its conduct of the business following the acquisition.

Section 3.21(b) states that there have been no proceedings instituted or threatened in respect of an employee grievance. Virtually all collective bargaining agreements, as well as the nonunion employment policies and practices of many companies, provide procedures for handling employee grievances. Often the disclosure and description of grievances are burdensome and produce information almost meaningless for a buyer. Buyer may want to obtain an understanding of the Acquired Companies' grievance procedures and collective bargaining agreements in order to define the level of significance to which grievances must rise before disclosure is required. Buyer should be aware, however, that a large number of pending grievance proceedings, immaterial in any single case, could be symptomatic of deeper problems with the employee relations of the Acquired Companies.

If any Acquired Company is or has been a party to labor contracts or collective bargaining agreements, Buyer may want to obtain copies at an early stage in the negotiations to ascertain their expiration dates and to gain an understanding of the contracts and their impact on Buyer's operation of the businesses following the Closing.

Buyer may also want to consider any potential liability for the Acquired Companies' failure to comply with state, federal, and local employment discrimination laws. In particular, Buyer may want to require disclosure of any pending or potential discrimination charges or complaints that might arise from the Acquired Companies' actions. Most federal employment discrimination laws prohibit employers with 15 or more employees from discriminating against employees in protected categories, including, race, sex, age, disability, religion, and national origin. Many states have enacted similar employment discrimination laws.

See MANUAL ON ACQUISITION REVIEW ch. 11.

SELLERS' RESPONSE

Sellers may argue that Section 3.21(a) and clause (iv) of Section 3.21(b) be deleted, since the matters are already covered by Sections 3.14 and 3.15. Sellers may also ask that Section 3.21(a) be limited as to time, arguing that violations, known or unknown, beyond the applicable statute of limitations are irrelevant.

3.22   INTELLECTUAL PROPERTY ASSETS

(a) Definition of Intellectual Property Assets

The term "Intellectual Property Assets" means all intellectual property owned, licensed (as licensor or licensee), or used by an Acquired Company, including:

(i)   the name of each Acquired Company, assumed, fictional, business and trade names, registered and unregistered trademarks, service marks, and logos, and trademark and service mark applications (collectively, "Marks");

(ii)   patents, patent applications (collectively, "Patents"), and Invention Disclosures;

(iii)   registered and unregistered copyrights in both published works and unpublished works (collectively, "Copyrights");

(iv)   all rights in mask works (as defined in Section 901 of the Copyright Act of 1976);

(v)   software (including firmware and other software embedded in hardware devices), software code (including source code and executable or object code), subroutines, interfaces, including APIs, and algorithms (collectively "Software");

(vi)   all know-how, trade secrets, confidential or proprietary information, customer lists, technical information, data, process technology, plans, drawings, inventions, and discoveries, whether or not patentable (collectively, "Trade Secrets"); and

(vii)   all rights in Internet websites, Internet domain names, and keywords held by an Acquired Company (collectively "Net Names").

(b) **Nature of Intellectual Property Assets**

(i)   The Intellectual Property Assets owned by each Acquired Company, together with the Intellectual Property Assets licensed by that Acquired Company and listed in Part 3.17(a)(v), are all those used in or necessary for the conduct of the business of such Acquired Company as it is being conducted. One or more Acquired Companies is the owner of each of the owned Intellectual Property Assets, free and clear of any Encumbrance, and has the right to use them without payment to any Person. No Acquired Company is bound by, and none of the owned Intellectual Property Assets is subject to, any Contract that in any way limits or restricts the ability of any Acquired Company to use, exploit, assert, or enforce any such Intellectual Property Asset anywhere in the world.

(ii)   All former and current employees or independent contractors of each Acquired Company have executed written Contracts with that Acquired Company that assign to that Acquired

Company all rights to any inventions, improvements, discoveries or information, and works of authorship of such employee or independent contractor relating to the business of that Acquired Company.

(iii)   No funding, facilities, or personnel of any Governmental Body, any educational institution, or any other Person (other than an Acquired Company) were used, directly or indirectly, to develop or create, in whole or in part, any owned Intellectual Property Asset.

(iv)   Since _____, no Acquired Company has assigned or otherwise transferred any interest in, or agreed to assign or otherwise transfer any interest in, any Intellectual Property Asset to any other Person, except pursuant to nonexclusive licenses in the Ordinary Course of Business.

(v)   No Acquired Company is or ever was a member or promoter of, or a contributor to, any industry standards body or other organization that could require or obligate any Acquired Company to grant or offer to any other Person any license or right to any Intellectual Property Asset.

(c) Patents

(i)   Part 3.22(c) lists all Patents and invention disclosures relating to inventions conceived or reduced to practice by one or more officers, employees, independent contractors, or other parties with whom any Acquired Company may have collaborated in connection with developments on behalf of such Acquired Company's business ("Invention Disclosures"), including the name of the Acquired Company that owns or uses such Patent or Invention Disclosure.

(ii)   All Patents are in compliance with all applicable Legal Requirements (including payment of filing, examination, and maintenance fees, and proofs of working or use), are valid and enforceable, and are not subject to any maintenance fees, taxes, or actions falling due within 90 days after the Closing Date. No Invention Disclosure describes any invention that has been publicly disclosed or offered for sale, creating a bar to filing patent applications within 90 days after the Closing.

(iii)   No Patent has been or is involved in any interference, reissue, reexamination, or opposition Proceeding, and, to the Knowledge of Sellers, no such Proceeding is threatened. To the Knowledge of Sellers, there is no potentially interfering patent or patent application of any Person with respect to any Patent.

(iv) No Patent is or has been infringed or has been challenged or, to the Knowledge of Sellers, no such challenge is threatened. None of the products manufactured or sold, or any process or know-how used, by any Acquired Company infringes or is alleged to infringe any patent or other proprietary right of any other Person.

(v) All products made, used, or sold under the Patents have been marked with the proper patent notice.

(d) Marks

(i) Part 3.22(d) lists all Marks, including the name of the Acquired Company that owns or uses such Mark.

(ii) Except as set forth in Part 3.22(d), all Marks have been registered with the United States Patent and Trademark Office and foreign countries where any of the Acquired Companies do substantial business related to the goods or services associated with such Marks, are in compliance with all applicable Legal Requirements (including the timely post-registration filing of affidavits of use and incontestability and renewal applications), are valid and enforceable, and are not subject to any maintenance fees, taxes, or actions falling due within 90 days after the Closing Date.

(iii) No Mark has been or is involved in any dispute, opposition, invalidation, or cancellation Proceeding and, to the Knowledge of Sellers, no such Proceeding is threatened.

(iv) To the Knowledge of Sellers, there is no potentially interfering trademark or trademark application of any Person with respect to any Mark.

(v) No Mark is or has been infringed or has been challenged and, to the Knowledge of Sellers, no such challenge is threatened. None of the Marks used by any Acquired Company infringes or is alleged to infringe any trade name, trademark, or service mark of any Person.

(vi) All products and materials containing a registered Mark bear the proper federal registration notice where permitted by law.

(e) Copyrights

(i)   Part 3.22(e) lists all registered Copyrights and all material unregistered Copyrights used in connection with the products or services provided by any Acquired Company, including the name of the Acquired Company that owns or uses such Copyright.

(ii)   All registered Copyrights are in compliance with all applicable Legal Requirements, and all the Copyrights listed in Part 3.22(e) are valid and enforceable, and are not subject to any maintenance fees, taxes, or actions falling due within 90 days after the Closing Date.

(iii)   No Copyright listed in Part 3.22(e) is or has been infringed or has been challenged, and, to the Knowledge of Sellers, no such challenge is threatened. None of the subject matter of any Copyright infringes or is alleged to infringe any copyright of any Person or is a derivative work based upon the work of any other Person.

(iv)   All works encompassed by the Copyrights listed in Part 3.22(e) have been marked with the proper copyright notice.

(f) Trade Secrets

(i)   The documentation relating to each Trade Secret is current, accurate, and sufficient in detail and content to identify and explain it and to allow its full and proper use without reliance on the knowledge or memory of any individual.

(ii)   Each Acquired Company has taken all reasonable precautions to protect the secrecy, confidentiality, and value of each Trade Secret (including the enforcement by each Acquired Company of a policy requiring each employee or contractor to execute proprietary information and confidentiality agreements substantially in such Acquired Company's standard form, and all current and former employees and independent contractors of each Acquired Company have executed such an agreement).

(iii)   No Trade Secret is part of the public knowledge or literature or has been used, divulged, or appropriated either for the benefit of any Person (other than an Acquired Company) or to the detriment of any Acquired Company. No Trade Secret is subject to any adverse claim or has been challenged, and, to the Knowledge of Sellers, no such challenge is threatened. No Trade Secret infringes or is alleged to infringe any intellectual property right of any Person.

(g) Software

All Software owned, licensed, or used by any Acquired Company (other than commonly available, noncustomized third-party software licensed to an Acquired Company for internal use on a nonexclusive basis) is listed in Parts 3.22(c), (e), or (f) or 3.17(a)(v). Each Acquired Company has all rights necessary to use all copies of all Software used by such Acquired Company.

(h) Net Names

(i) Part 3.22(h) lists all Net Names, including the name of the Acquired Company that owns or uses such Net Name.

(ii) All Net Names have been registered in the name of an Acquired Company and are in compliance with all applicable Legal Requirements.

(iii) No Net Name has been or is involved in any dispute, opposition, invalidation, or cancellation Proceeding and, to the Knowledge of Sellers, no such Proceeding is threatened.

(iv) To the Knowledge of Sellers, there is no domain name application pending of any other Person which would or would potentially interfere with or infringe any Net Name.

(v) No Net Name is or has been infringed or has been challenged and, to the Knowledge of Sellers, no such challenge is threatened. No Net Name infringes or is alleged to infringe the trademark, copyright, or domain name of any other Person.

COMMENT

Section 3.22(a) defines "Intellectual Property Assets" broadly to include all intellectual property owned, licensed, or used by the Acquired Companies, including trademarks, patents, copyrights, and trade secrets.

Section 3.22(b)(i) contains Sellers' representation that the owned and licensed Intellectual Property Assets constitute all the intellectual property used in, or necessary for, the conduct of the business of the Acquired Companies. In addition, Sellers represent that owned Intellectual Property Assets are free and clear of Encumbrances and restrictions on their use.

Section 3.22(b)(ii) requires Sellers to represent that all current and former employees and consultants of the Acquired Companies have signed a written contract assigning their rights in Intellectual Property Assets to an Acquired Company. While an employer may own certain inventions developed by its employees and may own the copyrights in works authored by its employees, it is good practice to obtain written assignments of intellectual property rights from employees and essential to obtain them from independent contractors.

If there is a general representation that all the Acquired Companies' contracts are valid and binding and in full force and effect and that neither party is in default (*see* Section 3.17), a separate representation is not needed in this Section. If there is no general representation regarding contracts, or if it is limited in some way, Buyer should consider including such a representation in this Section, especially if an Acquired Company licenses intellectual property that is important to its business.

Section 3.22(b)(iii) requires Sellers to represent that no government program or university was involved in the development of any owned Intellectual Property Assets. Government or university sponsorship of research can raise special issues regarding the ownership of the resulting intellectual property. For example, the Bayh-Dole Act (35 U.S.C. §§ 200-12) permits universities to retain ownership of patentable inventions developed with federal funds if certain conditions are met. The federal government, however, retains a nonexclusive right to practice the invention. Section 3.22(b)(iii) identifies any Intellectual Property Assets generated in this manner so that the appropriate due diligence can be undertaken.

Section 3.22(b)(iv) requires disclosure of intellectual property that the Acquired Companies have disposed of within a specified time period. This gives Buyer an opportunity to assess technology that is no longer in the portfolio and therefore unavailable for future exploitation.

Section 3.22(b)(v) requires disclosure regarding the Acquired Companies' involvement in any industry standards organization, since use of technology as an industry standard could legally, contractually, and/or ethically preclude the Acquired Companies' enforcement of the Intellectual Property Asset involved or require the Acquired Companies to license that Intellectual Property Asset to its competitors.

Whether Buyer will want to include each of the representations in Sections 3.22(c)-(h) depends upon the existence and importance of the various types of Intellectual Property Assets in a particular transaction. For example, patents and trade secrets can be the key asset of a technology-driven manufacturing company, whereas trademarks and copyrights could be important to a service company. Below are descriptions of the main categories of intellectual property and how they are treated in the Model Agreement.

See Manual on Acquisition Review ch. 10.

Patents. There are three types of U.S. patents. A "utility patent" may be granted for "any new and useful process, machine, manufacture, or composition of matter, or any new and useful improvement thereof." 35 U.S.C. § 101. Patents also may be granted for new varieties of plants (other than tuber or plants found in an uncultivated state) (a "plant patent"). Ch. 15, 35 U.S.C. §§ 161–64. Finally, a patent may be granted for a new, original, and ornamental design for an article of manufacture (a "design patent"). Ch. 16, 35 U.S.C. §§ 171–73.

In the United States, the patenting process begins with the filing of a patent application in the Patent and Trademark Office (PTO). Except under certain limited conditions, the inventor (or the inventor's patent attorney) must file the application. A patent application or a patent may be assigned by the owner, whether the owner is the inventor or a subsequent assignee.

The term "patent" as used in the definition of "Intellectual Property Assets" would include utility, plant, and design patents as well as any pending patent applications, and covers those granted by the United States as well as foreign jurisdictions.

Section 3.22(c) requires disclosure of information that will enable Buyer to determine whether an Acquired Company has patents for the technology used in its business and how long such patents will remain in force. It will also enable Buyer to conduct its own validity and infringement searches, which Buyer may want to do if Sellers' representations are subject to a knowledge qualification or if the patents are essential to Buyer.

In Section 3.22(c)(ii), Sellers represent that the Acquired Companies' patents are valid. For a patent to be valid, the invention or discovery must be "useful" and "novel" and must not be "obvious." Very few inventions are not "useful." Well-known examples of inventions that are not "useful" are perpetual motion machines and illegal devices (such as drug paraphernalia). In order to qualify as "novel," the invention must be new. A patent cannot be granted for an invention already made by another person, even if the person seeking the patent made the invention independently. An invention is "obvious" if the differences between the invention sought to be patented and the prior art are such that the subject matter of the invention as a whole would have been obvious at the time the invention was made to a person having ordinary skill in the art to which the subject matter pertains.

To determine conclusively that an invention is "novel" and not "obvious" requires knowledge of all prior art. It is difficult even to identify all prior art relevant to the invention, much less to make judgments about what would have been obvious to a person having reasonable skill in such art. Thus, although Sellers may, in good faith, believe that Acquired Companies' patents are valid, those patents are subject to challenge at any time. If someone can establish that the invention covered by a patent does not meet these three criteria, the patent will be invalid.

Buyer can determine that the terms of the Company's patents have not expired and that all necessary maintenance fees have been paid. In general, the term of a utility or plant patent is 20 years from the date of application.

Although U.S. patents are creatures of federal law, the question of ownership of a patent is controlled by state law. In many states, an invention made by an employee is not necessarily the property of the employer. A buyer may want to verify, therefore, that the target has perfected title to all patents or patent applications for inventions made by its employees. In addition, the target should have written agreements with its employees providing that all inventions, patent applications, and patents awarded to employees will be transferred to the target to the full extent permissible under state law.

A U.S. patent has no extraterritorial effect; that is, a U.S. patent provides the patent owner the right to exclude others from making, using, or selling the invention only in the United States. Thus, the owner of a U.S. patent can prevent others from making the patented invention outside the United States and shipping it to a customer in the United States and from making the invention in the United States and shipping it to a customer outside the United States. The patent owner cannot, however, prevent another from making the invention outside the United States and shipping it to a customer also outside the United Sates. If the Acquired Companies have extensive foreign business, Buyer can seek assurances that important foreign markets are protected, to the greatest extent possible, under the intellectual property laws of the applicable foreign jurisdictions. If there are extensive foreign patents and patent applications pending, Buyer's due diligence may become quite involved and time-consuming.

More than 125 countries, including the United States, are parties to the Patent Cooperation Treaty which is administered by the World Intellectual Property Organization ("WIPO"). This Treaty provides for the filing of international patent applications that can cover a number of countries. The decision to grant a patent, however, remains the purview of the authorities in each country.

Section 3.22(c)(ii) contains Sellers' assurances that the Acquired Companies' patents are enforceable. Failure to disclose to the PTO relevant information material to the examination of a patent application can result in the patent being unenforceable. In addition, misuse of a patent (for example, use that results in an antitrust violation) can result in the patent being unenforceable. Finally, because patent rights vary in each jurisdiction, representations can confirm the enforceability of foreign patents separately in each jurisdiction.

Even the grant of a patent does not provide assurance that using the invention will not infringe another person's patent. For example, a patent could be granted for an improvement to a previously patented device, but the practice of the improvement might infringe the claims of the earlier patent on the device. In Section 3.22(c)(iv), Sellers represent that the products sold by the Acquired Companies do not infringe any third-party patents.

Section 3.22(d)(v) covers patent marking. If an Acquired Company is selling products covered by a patent without proper marking of the patented product or the product made using a patented process, damages cannot be collected for infringement of the patent unless or until actual notice of infringement is given to the infringer.

Trademarks. A trademark is a word, name, symbol, or slogan used in association with the sale of goods or the provision of services (the latter are sometimes referred to as "service marks"). Generally, all trademarks are created under the common law through use of the mark in offering and selling goods or services. A trademark that is not registered is commonly referred to as an "unregistered mark" or a "common law mark." The term "trademark" as used in the definition of "Intellectual Property Assets" includes both registered and unregistered marks.

The owner of a trademark can prevent others from using confusingly similar marks and, in some instances, can recover damages for infringement.

Although trademark registration systems are maintained at both the state and federal levels, trademarks need not be registered at either level. State registrations are of little value to businesses that operate in more than one state or whose markets are defined by customers from more than one state.

Two of the major benefits of registration at the federal level are "constructive use" and "constructive notice." The owner of a federal registration is deemed to have used the mark in connection with the goods or services recited in the registration on a nationwide basis as of the filing date of the application. Therefore, any other person who first began using the mark after the trademark owner filed the application is an infringer regardless of the geographic areas where the trademark owner and the infringer use their marks. Federal registration also provides constructive notice to the public of the registration of the mark as of the date of issuance of the registration. Because of the importance of federal registration, the representation in Section 3.22(d)(ii) seeks assurance that the Acquired Companies have taken all steps necessary to maintain the registrations of their federally registered marks.

An application for federal registration of a trademark is filed in the PTO. The PTO maintains two trademark registers: the Principal Register and the Supplemental Register. The Supplemental Register is generally for marks that cannot be registered on the Principal Register. The Supplemental Register does not provide the trademark owner the same rights as those provided by the Principal Register, and it provides no rights in addition to those provided by the Principal Register. If Buyer learns that an important mark is on the Supplemental Register, Buyer can ask why it was not registered on the Principal Register.

After a trademark has been registered with the PTO, the owner should file two affidavits or declarations to protect its rights. An affidavit or declaration of "incontestability" may be filed during the sixth year of registration of a mark to strengthen the registration by marking it "incontestable." An affidavit or declaration of "continuing use" must be filed with the PTO during the sixth year of registration; otherwise, the PTO will automatically cancel the registration at the end of the sixth year. Cancellation of a registration (or abandonment of an application) does not necessarily mean that the trademark owner has abandoned the mark and no longer has rights in the mark; proving abandonment of a mark requires more than merely showing that an application has been abandoned or that a registration has been canceled. Nevertheless, because of the benefits of federal registration, the representations in Section 3.22(d)(ii) require the Acquired Companies to have timely filed continuing use affidavits (as well as incontestability affidavits, which are often combined with continuing use affidavits) for all of their trademarks.

Federal registrations issued on or after November 16, 1989, have a term of 10 years; registrations issued prior to that date have a term of 20 years. All federal registrations may be renewed if the mark is still in use when the renewal application is filed. Registrations may be renewed repeatedly. An application for renewal must be filed during the one-year period immediately preceding the expiration date of the current term (whether an original or renewal term), and within the six months (grace period) following such expiration date.

Generally, the owner of a common law mark can prevent others from using a mark that is likely to be confused with the owner's mark only in the trademark owner's "trading area," i.e., where the goods and/or services are similar. Thus, the owner of a common law mark may find that, upon expanding use of the mark outside that area, another person has established superior rights in that area and can stop the trademark owner's expansion.

Rights in a trademark can be lost through nonuse or through unauthorized use by others. In an extreme example of the latter, long use of a mark by the public in referring to the type of goods marketed by the trademark owner and its competitors can place the trademark into the public domain. Therefore, Buyer may want to determine whether the Acquired Companies are using the marks that are of primary interest to Buyer and whether any others using those marks for similar goods or services are doing so under a formal license agreement.

The trademark owner must ensure a certain level of quality of the goods or services sold with the mark. Thus, a license agreement must provide the licensor with the right to "police" the quality of the goods or services sold with the mark. The licensor must actually exercise this right because failure to do so works an abandonment of the mark by the licensor. Similarly, an assignment of a mark without an assignment of the assignor's "goodwill" associated with the mark constitutes an abandonment of the mark, unless the mark is the subject of an intent-to-use trademark application, for which the assignor has not yet used the mark in commerce prior to the assignment date. In the latter case, a valid assignment is made if "to a successor to the business of the applicant, or portion thereof, to which the mark pertains, if that business is ongoing and existing."

Notwithstanding the representation in Section 3.22(d)(iv), Buyer may want to retain a search firm to conduct a trademark search to ensure that there are no potentially interfering trademarks or trademark applications. A trademark search and analysis of the results should be much less costly than a patent search and analysis.

A mark need not be identical to another mark or be used with the same goods or services of the other mark to constitute an infringement. Rather, a mark infringes another mark if there is a likelihood of confusion between the two. Several factors are examined to determine whether there is a likelihood of confusion between two marks, including the visual and phonetic similarities between the marks, the similarities between the goods or services with which the marks are used, the nature of the markets for the goods or services, the trade channels through which the goods or services flow to reach the markets, and the media in which the goods or services are advertised.

A U.S. trademark registration has no extraterritorial effect. Therefore, if the Acquired Companies have foreign operations or significant export sales, Buyer will want to review the status of the Acquired Companies' trademarks in foreign markets.

The United States and over 70 other countries are parties to the Madrid Protocol which is administered by WIPO. The Madrid Protocol provides for the filing of "international applications" that can result in "international registrations" of trademarks. It is still up to each participating country, applying its own laws, to determine whether the mark will be protected in that country.

Copyrights. "[C]opyright protection subsists . . . in original works of authorship fixed in any tangible medium of expression . . . from which they can be perceived, reproduced, or otherwise communicated." 17 U.S.C. § 102(a). Works of authorship that can be protected by copyright include literary works, musical works, dramatic works, pantomimes and choreographic works, pictorial, graphic and sculptural works, motion pictures and other audiovisual works, architectural works, and sound recordings. *See* 17 U.S.C. § 102(a)(1)-(8). Computer software is considered a "literary work" and can be protected by copyright. Ideas, procedures, processes, systems, methods of operation, concepts, principles, and discoveries cannot be copyrighted. *See* 17 U.S.C. § 102(b). The copyright in a work subsists at the moment of creation by the author; registration of the copyright with the United States Copyright Office is not necessary. The term "Copyrights" as used in the definition of "Intellectual Property Assets" includes all copyrights, whether or not registered. It might be impossible, however, for Sellers to identify all of the copyrighted material owned by an Acquired Company. Therefore, Section 3.22(e) (i) limits disclosure to certain copyrighted materials actually used in the business.

Section 3.22(b) provides assurances to Buyer that the Acquired Companies actually have title to the copyrights for works used by the Acquired Companies. Such assurances are important because the copyright in a work vests originally in the "author," who is the person who created the work unless the work is a "work made for hire." *See* 17 U.S.C. § 201 (a)-(b). A work can be a "work made for hire" in two circumstances: (a) when it is created by an employee in the course of employment or (b) when it is created pursuant to a written agreement that states that the work will be a work made for hire and the work is of a type listed within the definition of "work made for hire" (17 U.S.C. § 101).

Although rights in a copyright may be assigned or licensed in writing, the transfer of copyrights in a work (other than a "work made for hire") may be terminated under certain conditions. *See* 17 U.S.C. § 203. If an Acquired Company owns copyrights by assignment, Buyer may seek assurance that the assignment cannot be terminated during the foreseeable useful life of the copyrighted work.

Buyer can verify that the terms of the Acquired Companies' copyrights have not expired. The term of copyright for works created on or after January 1, 1978, is as follows:

(a)   The life of the author plus 70 years after the author's death.

(b)   For joint works created by two or more authors "who did not work for hire," the life of the last surviving author plus 70 years after the death of the last surviving author.

(c)   For anonymous works, pseudonymous works and "works made for hire," 95 years from the date of first publication or 120 years from the year of creation of the work, whichever expires first.

The term of copyright for works under copyright protection prior to January 1, 1978, is complex and beyond the scope of this commentary.

Although it is not necessary to register a copyright with the United States Copyright Office for the copyright to be valid, there are benefits such as the right to obtain statutory damages, attorneys' fees, and costs in a successful copyright infringement action if the copyright in the work has been registered and a notice of copyright has been placed on the work. Indeed, registration is a prerequisite to bringing an infringement suit with respect to U.S. works and certain foreign works.

While U.S. copyrights and registrations have no extraterritorial effect, international treaties, such as the Berne Convention, provide for international protection of copyrighted works. More than 160 countries are parties to the Berne Convention. Each contracting country agrees to provide copyright protection to works originating in the other contracting countries. If the Acquired Companies have foreign operations or significant export sales of copyrighted materials, such as software, Buyer may want to determine the status of copyright protection in the countries involved.

Trade Secrets. Trade secret protection traditionally arose under common law, which remains an important source of that protection. Now, however, a majority of the states have adopted some version of the Uniform Trade Secrets Act, which defines and protects trade secrets. Moreover, the misappropriation of trade secrets is punishable as a federal crime under the Economic Espionage Act of 1996 (18 U.S.C. §§ 1831–39). Trade secrets relate to information that provides a commercial advantage to the trade secret owner relative to its competitors and, thus, need not be just technical information. Trade secrets can include customer lists, recipes, or anything of value to a company, provided that it is secret, substantial, and valuable. One common type of trade secret is "know-how": a body of information that is valuable to a business and not generally known outside the business. The term "trade secret" as used in the definition of "Intellectual Property Assets" includes both common law and statutory trade secrets of all types, including know-how.

As part of the disclosure required by Section 3.22(f)(i), Buyer may want a list of all the Acquired Companies' trade secrets and the location of each document that contains a description of the trade secret. Although such an inventory would assist the parties in identifying the trade secrets, it may be difficult or impossible to create. Buyer could ask Sellers to identify key trade secrets, which would enable Buyer to determine whether information regarded by Buyer as important is treated by Sellers as proprietary. Sellers, however, may be reluctant to disclose trade secrets to Buyer prior to either the Closing or a firm commitment by Buyer to proceed with the acquisition. Moreover, Buyer's receipt of this information can place it in a difficult position if the acquisition fails to close and Buyer subsequently wants to enter the same field or develop a similar product or process. In these circumstances, Buyer risks suit by the Acquired Companies for theft of trade secrets, and Buyer may have the burden of proving that it developed the product or process independently of the information it received from the Acquired Companies, which may be difficult.

Because the validity of trade secrets depends in part upon the efforts made to keep them secret, the representation in Section 3.22(f)(ii) provides assurances to Buyer that the Acquired Companies treated their trade secrets as confidential. Important methods of maintaining the confidentiality of trade secrets include limiting access to them, marking them as confidential, and requiring that everyone to whom they are disclosed agrees in writing to keep them confidential. In particular, Buyer may want to verify that the Acquired Companies have treated valuable know-how in a manner that gives rise to trade secret protection, such as through the use of confidentiality agreements. In the case of software, Buyer can determine whether the software is licensed to customers under a license agreement that defines the manner in which the customer may use the software or, instead, is sold on an unrestricted basis. Buyer may want to also investigate any other procedures used by the Acquired Companies to maintain the secrecy of its trade secrets. Buyer may want to determine whether agreements exist that govern the disclosure and use of trade secrets by employees and consultants of the Acquired Companies and others who need to learn of them.

Software. If an Acquired Company is involved in software development or distribution (and this can include software "embedded" in a product) or if custom software is important to the operation of an Acquired Company's business, Buyer may want to consider including a representation in the Model Agreement that focuses exclusively on Software. Set forth below is an example of such a representation that could be substituted for Section 3.22(g):

    (i)   Part 3.22(g) lists all Software owned, developed (or being developed), used, marketed, distributed, licensed, or sold by any Acquired Company (other than commonly available, noncustomized third-party software licensed to an Acquired Company for internal use on a nonexclusive basis) and identifies which is owned, licensed, leased, or otherwise used, as the case may be. The Software listed in Part 3.22(g) is either:

(A) owned by an Acquired Company;

(B) in the public domain or otherwise available to the Acquired Companies without the license, lease, or consent of any third party; or

(C) used under rights granted to an Acquired Company using such Software pursuant to a written Contract with a third party, which written Contract is listed in Part 3.22(g).

(ii) No Acquired Company's use of any Software violates the rights of any Person.

(iii) All Software was developed by:

(A) employees of the Acquired Companies within the scope of their employment;

(B) independent contractors as "work made for hire," as that term is defined under Section 101 of the U.S. copyright laws or analogous law of another country, pursuant to written Contracts; or

(C) independent contractors who have assigned their entire right, title, and interest in and to such Software to the Acquired Companies pursuant to written Contracts.

(iv) The Acquired Companies have all rights necessary to use all copies of all Software (including off-the-shelf Software) used by an Acquired Company.

(v) None of the Software:

(A) contains any bug, defect, or error that materially and adversely affect the use, functionality, or performance of such Software or any product or system containing, or used in conjunction with, such Software; or

(B) fails to comply with any applicable warranty or other contractual commitment relating to the use, functionality, or performance of such Software or any product or system containing, or used in conjunction with, such Software.

(vi) No Software contains any "back door," "drop-dead device," "time bomb," "Trojan horse," "virus," or "worm" (as such terms are commonly understood in the software industry) or any other code designed or intended to have, or capable of performing, any of the following:

      (A) disrupting, disabling, harming, or otherwise impeding in any manner the operation of, or providing unauthorized access to, a computer system or network or other device on which such code is stored or installed; or

      (B) damaging or destroying any data or file without the user's consent.

  (vii) No source code for any Software listed in Part 3.22(g) has been delivered, licensed, or made available to any escrow agent or other Person who is not, as of the date of this Agreement, an employee of an Acquired Company. No Acquired Company has any duty or obligation (whether present, contingent, or otherwise) to deliver, license, or make available the source code for any such Software to any escrow agent or other Person who is not, as of the date of this Agreement, an employee of an Acquired Company. No event has occurred, and no circumstance or condition exists, that (with or without notice or lapse of time) will, or could reasonably be expected to, result in the delivery, license, or disclosure of any source code for any such Software to any other Person who is not, as of the date of this Agreement, an employee of an Acquired Company.

  (viii) No Software listed in Part 3.22(g) is subject to any "copyleft" or other obligation or condition (including any obligation or condition under any "open source" license such as the GNU Public License, Lesser GNU Public License, or Mozilla Public License) that:

      (A) could require, or could condition the use or distribution of such Software on, the disclosure, licensing, or distribution of any source code for any portion of such Software; or

      (B) could otherwise impose any limitation, restriction, or condition on the right or ability of any Acquired Company to use or distribute any such Software.

Subsection (i) of the alternative software representation requires identification of all software owned or used by the Acquired Companies other than standard "off-the-shelf" software.

Subsection (v) requires disclosure regarding "bugs" and similar defects in the Acquired Companies' software. This information can be important by providing Buyer an indication of how much effort and expense will be required to resolve problems with the software and satisfy warranty obligations.

Subsection (vi) addresses any "harmful code" which resides in the software. These types of codes could result in claims by users of the software and can be difficult to isolate and remove, especially if the programmer ceases to be employed by the Acquired Companies.

Subsection (vii) relates to the source code of the Acquired Companies' software. For most software companies, the source code for their products is among their most valuable trade secrets. Section (g) requires disclosure that will allow Buyer to determine whether the source code is, and can continue to be, maintained as a trade secret.

Subsection (viii) relates to "open source" software licenses. "Open source" software is software that is freely available in source code form, usually over the Internet, under the terms of a standard license. There are several different types of open source licenses, some of which impose significant limitations or conditions on subsequent distribution of the software by the licensee. The most restrictive conditions, known as "copyleft" provisions, require that whenever the licensee incorporates, or links in particular ways, the open source software into or with another software program and distributes the other program, the source code for the other program must also be made available at little or no charge. Thus, open source code can contaminate a proprietary software product and undermine the proprietary nature of the source code for the product. Not all open source licenses have this effect. Some impose no, or relatively harmless, conditions on the licensee, and hence Sellers may want to limit clause (B) in Subsection (viii) to "any material limitation, restriction, or condition."

Net or Domain Names. Internet domain names may be obtained through a registration process. The registrars are private companies accredited by the Internet Corporation for Assigned Names and Numbers (ICANN), a technical coordination body charged with ensuring the stability of the system of assigning Internet domain names. Internet domain name registration is a process separate and independent of trademark registration, but registering another's trademark as a domain name for the purpose of selling it to the trademark owner ("cybersquatting") or diverting its customers ("cyberpiracy") may be actionable as unfair competition, trademark infringement, or dilution or under Section 43(d) of the Lanham Act (the Anticybersquatting Consumer Protection Act). Domain name disputes may also be resolved under the ICANN Rules for Uniform Domain Name Dispute Resolution.

Even in a stock transaction, Buyer may want to determine the transferability of the domain name registrations of the Acquired Companies, if Buyer intends to change registrars or to change the administrative or technical contacts on the registration. Only the registered holder or named administrative contact can authorize a transfer, so Buyer may want to check that the Acquired Company is the registered holder and that one of its employees is the administrative contact of record. Domain name holders sometimes permit IT consultants and others to be named registered holder or administrative contact and can complicate transfer.

Mask Works. Mask works are related to semiconductor products and are protected under 17 U.S.C. Section 901 *et seq.* Because this technology is unique to the microchip industry, the Model Agreement does not contain a separate representation concerning mask works.

SELLERS' RESPONSE

Sellers may object to the representation called for in Section 3.22(b)(i) as too subjective and may ask Buyer to draw its own conclusion as to whether the Intellectual Property Assets are sufficient to operate the business of the Acquired Companies.

If it has not been the practice of the Acquired Companies to require employees and independent contractors to execute assignments of intellectual property, Sellers will object to the representation in Section 3.22(b)(ii). Buyer will then need to assess the potential for adverse consequences to the Acquired Companies' Intellectual Property Assets in the absence of such assignments.

Sellers may argue that the benefit to Buyer of the representation in Section 3.22(b)(iv) is not worth the effort required by Sellers to retrace history.

Given the broad scope of materials that are protected by copyright, Sellers may object to the requirement in Section 3.22(e)(i) that unregistered copyrights be listed, even though it is qualified by materiality. Buyer may be unwilling to accommodate Sellers' objection, recognizing that relatively few copyrighted works are registered.

Each of subsections (c)(iv), (d)(v), (e)(iii), (f)(iii), and (h)(iv-v) contains a representation that Intellectual Property Assets of the Acquired Companies are not infringed by, and do not infringe, the intellectual property of any third party. Sellers may argue that, given the proliferation of intellectual property protection claims and the complexity of determining infringement, it is impossible for Sellers to say with certainty that the Intellectual Property Assets of the Acquired Companies do not infringe or are not being infringed. Therefore, Sellers may request that each of these subsections be deleted, or, in the alternative, that they be qualified by Knowledge.

3.23 Compliance with the Foreign Corrupt Practices Act and Export Control and Antiboycott Laws

No Acquired Company and no Representative of any Acquired Company in its capacity as such has violated the Foreign Corrupt Practices Act or the anticorruption laws of any jurisdiction where the Company does business. Each Acquired Company has at all times complied with all Legal Requirements relating to export control and trade sanctions or embargoes. No Acquired Company has violated the antiboycott prohibitions contained in 50 U.S.C. Sections 2401 *et seq.* or taken any action that can be penalized under Section 999 of the Code.

COMMENT

Section 3.23 deals with certain Legal Requirements that might apply to the activities and operations of the Acquired Companies. While the matters covered in this Section are also covered by Section 3.14, if an Acquired Company has foreign operations or export sales, Buyer may want these matters covered with specificity.

The purpose of the representations in the first sentence of Section 3.23 is to determine whether an Acquired Company may be in violation of the Foreign Corrupt Practices Act ("FCPA") (15 U.S.C.§§ 78dd-1 *et seq.*) or other anticorruption laws in the jurisdictions where the Acquired Company may operate. Buyer may wish to include this representation if any Acquired Company conducts business outside the United States, especially with foreign governments or entities owned or controlled by foreign governments. Companies dealing with foreign governments or government-owned entities using agents who are either government officials or closely related to or aligned with government officials may be particularly vulnerable to FCPA liability.

The FCPA's antibribery provisions prohibit bribery of any foreign official by any "domestic concern," including any individual, corporation, partnership, association, joint stock company, business trust, unincorporated organization, or sole proprietorship. The legislative history of the FCPA confirms the intent of Congress to exempt foreign subsidiaries of U.S. parent companies (even if they are acting at the direction of their U.S. parent company) from the antibribery provisions so long as the foreign subsidiary does not fall within the FCPA's statutory definition of "domestic concern" or "issuer." "Issuer" means an issuer of securities registered pursuant to Section 12 of the Exchange Act or an issuer required to file reports pursuant to Section 15(d) of that Act. 15 U.S.C. § 78m(b)(2). While the antibribery provisions of the FCPA do not prohibit "grease payments" made to expedite or secure the performance of "routine government action," such as obtaining permits, licenses, or documents or facilitating shipments through customs (15 U.S.C. §§ 78dd-l(b), -2(b)), they are prohibited by the anticorruption laws of other countries. Penalties for violating the antibribery provisions of the FCPA include fines of up to $2 million for corporations and fines of $250,000 and/or imprisonment for up to five years for individuals. 15 U.S.C. § 78dd-2(g). Fines imposed against individuals may not be paid directly or indirectly by their companies. Therefore, companies are prevented from indemnifying their officers and employees against liability under the FCPA. 15 U.S.C. §§ 78ff(c)(3), dd-2(g)(3).

FCPA also imposes recordkeeping requirements on public companies that are discussed in the commentary to Section 3.5. These requirements are enforced by the SEC.

In its due diligence, Buyer may want to review any business practices, ethics, conflicts-of-interest, or similar policies of the Acquired Companies, the reports and questionnaires that may have been periodically submitted by employees pursuant to these policies and details relating to breaches of these policies, and actions taken in response to any such breaches. In addition to requiring disclosure of these policies, Buyer may want to include representations that the policies have been in place for a given period of time and that there have been no breaches other than as described in the Disclosure Letter. *See* Krakoff, Parkinson & Balsanek, *FCPA Due Diligence in the Context of Mergers and Acquisitions,* 4 BLOOMBERG CORP. L.J. 101 (2009).

The second sentence of Section 3.23 provides assurances that the Acquired Companies have complied with U.S. export control and trade sanctions laws. The Export Administration Act ("EAA") and the Export Administration Regulations ("EAR") restrict exports of commercial tangible and intangible goods and technical data by regulating (a) direct exports of goods and technology from the United States, (b) re-exports of U.S.-origin commodities and technical data from one foreign country to another, (c) exports and re-exports from a foreign country of foreign products containing U.S.-origin parts and components, and in some cases (d) exports and re-exports from a foreign country of foreign products developed based on U.S.-origin technical data, regardless of the products' actual origin. The export control laws apply to products that fall within the above categories for their entire existence, no matter how many times they are resold, and violations carry potentially serious criminal and civil penalties for manufacturers and their employees.

These laws apply to U.S. persons when such persons are exporting goods, software, or technology from the United States. The laws also have an extraterritorial reach that makes them apply to any controlled items that are re-exported by non-U.S. persons. "U.S. persons" include U.S. citizens and resident aliens (regardless of where they are located), U.S. corporations, partnerships, and other legal entities, their foreign branches, and anyone while in the United States. A company involved in exporting U.S. goods, software, or technology will need to know the export control classification number of each item so that it can determine if an export license is required to export that item to a specific destination. If an Acquired Company is a foreign company and uses U.S. goods, software, or technology in the manufacture of its goods or the provision of its services, it needs to know if any of the re-export provisions of the export laws will impact its ability to sell its products outside its home country without a re-export license from the United States. These licensing requirements are country-specific.

The export of military products is governed by the Arms Export Control Act ("AECA") and the International Traffic in Arms Regulations ("ITAR"). U.S. companies that manufacture, export, sell, or broker items (including parts and components) on the U.S. Munitions List are required to register with the Department of State, Directorate of Defense Trade Controls ("DDTC"). With very few exceptions, licenses are required to export any defense article, defense service, or related technical data. The DDTC policy for determining if a product is a defense article is very broad. For example, if an Acquired Company makes a product for the commercial market and is then asked to modify, adapt, or configure it for a military application, the modified, adapted, or configured version of the product may very likely be a defense article that would require a license for export. If an Acquired Company is selling to U.S. or foreign defense contractors, it may be subject to the ITAR. Also, a number of countries are subject to a U.S. arms embargo, so Buyer may want to see where the products were shipped.

For purposes of these requirements, disclosing technical data to a foreign national is considered an export to the home country of the foreign national and may require a license prior to disclosure. This includes foreign employees working in the United States pursuant to a visa. For Buyer, this means that it needs to understand what technologies the Acquired Company has, whether those technologies are controlled under either the EAR or the ITAR, and which foreign nationals have access.

The Trading with the Enemy Act ("TWEA"), the International Emergency Economic Powers Act ("IEEPA") and the Foreign Assets Control Regulations prohibit transactions with countries, entities, or persons that are subject to U.S. sanctions. TWEA prohibits "persons subject to the jurisdiction of the United States" from selling goods, technology, or services to Cuba and in some cases North Korea without a license. This law applies extraterritorially to the subsidiaries of U.S. companies. Country-based sanctions under IEEPA prohibit U.S. persons from most transactions with Iran and Sudan. The export laws also prohibit most sales of U.S.-origin items to Syria and North Korea. List-based sanctions prohibit targeted transactions with targeted companies, entities, or individuals. Most of the sanctions regulations also prohibit U.S. persons from helping non-U.S. persons to conduct business that the U.S. person could not otherwise conduct. Buyer should determine if an Acquired Company has a compliance program in place to identify transactions with sanctioned countries, companies, entities, and individuals, as civil and criminal penalties apply to both entities and individuals. These laws are complex and companies must be very careful to avoid running afoul of their prohibitions on evasion, circumvention, and facilitation.

The last sentence of Section 3.23 addresses statutes and regulations that prohibit and penalize U.S. companies and taxpayers for taking actions in support of foreign economic boycotts. In particular, the representation addresses the antiboycott prohibitions of the EAA and related penalties imposed under the Code.

The intention of the representation is to require Sellers to reveal any relationships that the Acquired Companies may have with parties that engage in prohibited boycotts, and any contracts (or other transaction documents such as purchase orders, letters of credit, or shipping documents) of the Acquired Companies that contain boycott provisions. If Buyer acquires an Acquired Company that has contracts that contain boycott provisions (or that has agreed to boycott terms in other transaction documents such as purchase orders, letters of credit, or shipping documents), then, under Section 999 of the Code, as soon as the Acquired Company becomes a part of Buyer's consolidated group, Buyer may lose certain tax benefits related to foreign operations, including certain foreign tax credits and tax benefits associated with foreign sales corporations and domestic international sales corporations. In addition, if an Acquired Company performs a contract in violation of the EAA or fails to report a reportable boycott request, it may be subject to civil penalties (fines and the denial of export privileges) and criminal fines and imprisonment. Under the Code, if one member of a "controlled group" participates in or cooperates with a foreign boycott, all operations of the controlled group in all boycotting countries will be presumed tainted by participation in the boycott unless it can be established that the operation in which the participation was found is "separate and identifiable" from other operations.

See MANUAL ON ACQUISITION REVIEW ch. 14.

SELLERS' RESPONSE

Sellers might want Section 3.23 to be deleted in its entirety because compliance with laws, which would include any antiboycott and export control laws, is covered by Section 3.14. Sellers might ask that Section 3.23 be limited in time, arguing that disclosing violations beyond the applicable statute of limitation achieves no purpose.

Section 3.23 is sometimes drafted so that de minimis payments and expenses under a certain dollar amount, e.g., $100, do not fall within the scope of the representation regarding compliance with the FCPA.

3.24   RELATIONSHIPS WITH RELATED PERSONS

No Seller and no Related Person of any Seller or of any Acquired Company has, or since _____ has had, any interest in any asset owned or used by any Acquired Company. No Seller and no Related Person of any Seller or of any Acquired Company is, or since _____ has been, a Related Party of or the owner (of record or beneficially) of any Equity Security or any other financial or profit interest in, a Person that has (a) had business dealings or a material financial interest in any transaction with any Acquired Company or (b) engaged in competition with any Acquired Company, other than ownership of less than one percent of the outstanding capital stock of a Person that is listed on any national or regional securities exchange. Except as set forth in Part 3.24, no Seller or any Related Person of any Seller or of any Acquired Company is a party to any Applicable Contract with, or has any claim or right against, any Acquired Company.

COMMENT

This representation assures that Sellers and any Related Person, such as a relative of a Seller or an entity in which a Seller has a significant interest (*see* definition of "Related Person" in Section 1.1), have no interest in property used in the Acquired Companies' businesses and no conflicting business interests. Such relationships are not unusual in privately owned businesses. If they do exist, Sellers can describe them in the Disclosure Letter. Buyer can then determine whether it will require that any of those interests or relationships be "unwound" at or prior to the Closing.

SELLERS' RESPONSE

Sellers may request that the representation be revised to exclude Sellers' rights to any pre-closing compensation or other distributions that they currently receive from the Acquired Companies.

3.25   SECURITIES LAW MATTERS

(a) **Each Seller is acquiring its Promissory Note for its own account and not with a view to its distribution within the meaning of Section 2(11) of the Securities Act. Each Seller is an "accredited investor" as such term is defined in Rule 501(a) under the Securities Act.**

(b) **Each Seller confirms that Buyer has made available to such Seller and its Representatives the opportunity to ask questions of the officers and management employees of Buyer and to acquire such additional information about the business and financial condition of Buyer as such Seller has requested, and all such information has been received.**

COMMENT

The definition of "security" under the Securities Act includes "any note." Thus, the United States Supreme Court has held that a promissory note is presumed to be a "security." This presumption can be rebutted, however, by a showing that the note bears a strong "family resemblance" to one of the instruments that the courts have found not to be securities. *See* Reves v. Ernst & Young, 492 U.S. 56 (1990). The motivation of the parties to the transaction, the plan of distribution, and the reasonable expectations of the investing public are examined to determine if the presumption has been rebutted. If the maker's motivation in issuing the note is to raise money, and the holder's motivation is profit, the note is likely a security. A note exchanged to "facilitate the purchase or sale of a minor asset," to correct the maker's cash flow difficulties or for "some other commercial purpose" is less likely to be deemed a security.

Thus, a question exists whether a note representing seller financing constitutes a "security" for purposes of the Securities Act. Nonetheless, the Model Agreement treats the Promissory Note as a "security" that has not been registered under the Securities Act. This representation is intended to support a claim that the issuance of the Promissory Note is exempt from the registration requirements of the Securities Act.

Section 4(2) of the Securities Act exempts from the registration requirements "transactions by an issuer not involving any public offering," generally referred to as "private placements." The U.S. Supreme Court has held that the Section 4(2) exemption must be interpreted in light of the statutory purpose of the Securities Act to "protect investors by promoting full disclosure of information thought necessary to informed investment decisions" and that its applicability "should turn on whether the particular class affected need the protection of the Act." *See* SEC v. Ralston Purina Co., 346 U.S. 119 (1953). Subsequent court opinions have enumerated a number of more specific factors to be considered in determining whether a transaction involves a "public offering," including the following:

(a) the number of offerees (there is no number of offerees that always make an offering either private or public; 25 to 35 is generally considered consistent with a private offering, but the sophistication of the offerees is more important; an offer to a single unqualified investor can defeat the exemption, and an offering to a few hundred institutional investors can be exempt);

(b) offeree qualification (each offeree should be sophisticated and able to bear the economic risk of the investment; a close personal, family, or employment relationship should also qualify an offeree);

(c) manner of offering (the offer should be communicated directly to the prospective investors without the use of public advertising or solicitation);

(d) availability of information (each investor should be provided or otherwise have access to information comparable to that contained in a registration statement filed under the Securities Act); commonly investors are furnished a "private offering memorandum" describing the issuer and the proposed transaction); and

(e) absence of redistribution (the securities must come to rest in the hands of qualified purchasers and not be redistributed to the public; securities sold in a private placement generally may be replaced privately, sold pursuant to SEC Rule 144 under the Securities Act (17 C.F.R. § 230.144), or sold to the public pursuant to a registration statement filed and effective under the Securities Act; the documentation of a private placement normally includes contractual restrictions on subsequent transfers of the securities purchased).

See Schneider, *The Statutory Law of Private Placements*, 14 Rev. Sec. Reg. 869 (1981); ABA Committee on Federal Regulation of Securities, *Integration of Securities Offerings: Report of the Task Force on Integration*, 41 Bus. Law. 595 (1986); Fletcher, *Sophisticated Investors Under the Federal Securities Laws*, 1988 Duke L.J. 1081 (1988).

SEC Regulation D under the Securities Act contains several exemptions from the registration requirements of the Securities Act. Under Rule 506 of Regulation D, which provides an exemption under Section 4(2) of the Securities Act, there is no limitation on the dollar amount of securities that may be offered and sold, and the offering can be sold to an unlimited number of "accredited investors" (generally institutions, individuals with a net worth of over $1 million and officers, directors, and general partners of the issuer) and to a maximum of 35 nonaccredited investors (there is no limit on the number of offerees so long as there is no general advertising or solicitation). Each of the purchasers, if not an accredited investor, must (either alone or through a "purchaser representative") have such knowledge and experience in financial matters as to be capable of evaluating the risks and merits of the proposed investment. It is not uncommon in acquisitions for one or more purchaser representatives to be appointed on behalf of the nonaccredited shareholders of the target. Such a representative must satisfy (or the buyer must reasonably believe that the representative satisfies) the requirements in Rule 501(h). Unless the offering is made solely to accredited investors, purchasers must generally be furnished with the same level of information that would be contained in a registration statement under the Securities Act. Section 3.25 contains a representation that each Seller is an "accredited investor." If Sellers are unable to make this representation, it may greatly increase Buyer's compliance burden under Regulation D. One advantage of Regulation D is that it preempts state Blue Sky laws.

In addition, resale of the securities must be restricted and a Form D notice of sale must be filed with the SEC. An offering which strictly conforms to the Regulation D requirements will be exempt even if it does not satisfy all the judicial criteria applicable to Section 4(2) exemption. However, because Regulation D does not purport to be the exclusive means of compliance with Section 4(2), a placement that conforms to the judicial criteria also may be exempt from registration under Section 4(2) of the Securities Act.

Section 3(a)(11) of the Securities Act exempts from registration "any security which is a part of an issue offered and sold only to persons resident within a single State or Territory, where the issuer of such security is a person resident and doing business within, or if a corporation, incorporated by and doing business within, such State or Territory." Consequently, there are two principal conditions to the intrastate offering exemption: (a) that the entire issue of securities be offered and sold exclusively to, and come to rest in the hands of, residents of the state in question (an offer or sale to a single nonresident will render the exemption unavailable to the entire issue), and (b) that the issuer be organized under the laws of and doing substantial business in the state. Rule 147 under the Securities Act, provides specific standards for determining whether an offering is intrastate within the meaning of Section 3(a)(11).

SELLERS' RESPONSE

Sellers may request that Section 3.25(b) be amended to state that nothing in that Section affects Sellers' ability to rely on Buyer's representations in Article 4.

3.26   CUSTOMERS AND SUPPLIERS

Part 3.26 lists for each of the ___ years ending _____ the names of the respective customers that were, in the aggregate, the _____ largest customers in terms of dollar value of products or services, or both, sold by each Acquired Company ("Major Customers"). Part 3.26 also lists for each such year, the names of the respective suppliers that were, in the aggregate, the _____ largest suppliers in terms of dollar value of products or services, or both, to each Acquired Company ("Major Suppliers"). Except as set forth in Part 3.26, no Major Customer or Major Supplier has given any Acquired Company notice (written or oral) terminating, canceling, reducing the volume under, or renegotiating the pricing terms or any other material terms of any Applicable Contract or relationship with any Acquired Company or threatening to take any of such actions, and, to the Knowledge of Sellers, no Major Customer or Major Supplier intends to do so.

COMMENT

Section 3.26 provides Buyer with information regarding the largest customers and suppliers of each Acquired Company. The number of customers or suppliers Sellers will be asked to list will depend on the nature of the business of the Acquired Companies. If the business of an Acquired Company deals with "mission critical" suppliers that are not high volume, Buyer may want to expand the scope of Section 3.26 to cover those suppliers.

If the Acquired Companies have a relatively small number of stable customer and supplier relationships, covering two years and listing the top 10 may be sufficient. Otherwise, Buyer may want to see a clearer picture of the evolution of the customer and/or supplier mix, and may draft Section 3.26 to cover a longer period and a larger sample of customers and/or suppliers.

SELLERS' RESPONSE

Sellers may ask that the third sentence of Section 3.26 be limited to matters as to which an Acquired Company has received written notice, arguing that they cannot possibly know everything that is discussed between employees of an Acquired Company and those of its customers and suppliers.

Moreover, depending on the nature of the business, fluctuations in volume or even threats of renegotiation may be regular occurrences. In that case, Sellers may request that specific elements of the second sentence be deleted.

3.27   PRODUCT LIABILITIES AND WARRANTIES

(a)   Except as set forth in Part 3.27(a), no Acquired Company has incurred any Loss as a result of any defect or other deficiency (whether of design, materials, workmanship, labeling, instructions, or otherwise) with respect to any product designed, manufactured, sold, leased, licensed, or delivered, or any service provided by any Acquired Company, whether such Loss is incurred by reason of any express or implied warranty (including any warranty of merchantability or fitness), any doctrine of common law (tort, contract, or other), any other Legal Requirement, or otherwise. No Governmental Body has alleged that any product designed, manufactured, sold, leased, licensed, or delivered by any Acquired Company is defective or unsafe or fails to meet any product warranty or any standards promulgated by any such Governmental Body. No product designed, manufactured, sold, leased, licensed, or delivered by any Acquired Company has been recalled, and no Acquired Company has received any notice of recall (written or oral) of any such product from any Governmental Body. No event has occurred or circumstance exists that (with or without notice or lapse of time) could result in any such liability or recall.

(b) Except as set forth in Part 3.27(b), no Acquired Company has given to any Person any product or service guaranty or warranty, right of return, or other indemnity relating to the products manufactured, sold, leased, licensed, or delivered, or services performed, by any Acquired Company. Each Acquired Company has legally excluded liability for all special, incidental, punitive, and consequential damages to any customer, dealer, or distributor of any Acquired Company or customer of any such dealer or distributor.

COMMENT

Section 3.27(a) elicits the history of the Acquired Companies with respect to product liability. While some information regarding product liability may be disclosed elsewhere in Sellers' representations, for example Section 3.15, this Section covers in depth an area that could pose significant risk of liability and economic loss for the Acquired Companies. The first sentence requires information about product liabilities resulting from injury to consumers or others. It also requires information with respect to warranty liabilities in the form of product repairs, replacements, and refunds.

The second sentence of Section 3.27(a) requires disclosure of any allegations by a government agency regarding the products of the Acquired Companies. In the United States, the Consumer Product Safety Commission has jurisdiction over many, but by no means all, products. Food and drugs, for example, are regulated by the U.S. Food and Drug Administration, while automobiles and other motor vehicles are regulated by the U.S. Department of Transportation. These agencies can order product recalls and manufacturers sometimes voluntarily recall their products.

The last sentence of Section 3.27(a) solicits information regarding occurrences that could result in product liabilities. The applicability of Section 3.27(a) is fact-specific and will depend on the nature of the business of the Acquired Companies. Also, in allocating liability between Sellers and Buyer, it may be difficult to determine whether a particular item was made before or after the Closing.

The first sentence of Section 3.27(b) requires Sellers to disclose all the express product warranties and indemnities any Acquired Company has provided to customers. This would require disclosure of standard "limited warranties" as well as other express warranties given by an Acquired Company. Indemnity provisions, including patent indemnities, must also be listed. Where an Acquired Company is not conscientious about its contracting practices, the customers' terms and conditions embodied in its purchase order forms, including warranties and indemnities, may become part of the contract and would need to be disclosed. In its due diligence, Buyer can review the Acquired Companies' history of warranty claims and its warranty reserves.

In the last sentence of Section 3.27(b), Sellers represent that the Acquired Companies have contractually excluded consequential damages and certain other damages in all contracts with customers, dealers, and distributors.

If Sellers are unable to make some or all of the representations in Section 3.27, it will serve to highlight potential risks to the Acquired Companies that Buyer must assess.

SELLERS' RESPONSE

Sellers may seek a time limitation in the first sentence of Section 3.27(a), arguing that old product liability claims, which may involve products the Acquired Company no longer manufactures, are of no relevance, and that detailing every warranty return or repair in company history is burdensome, if not impossible. Buyer may not agree to a time limit with respect to products liability disclosure if the products in question are still in use.

Sellers may request that the last sentence of Section 3.27(a) be deleted, arguing that it requires Sellers to predict future events and makes Sellers responsible for what some would regard as Ordinary Course of Business events.

In light of the "battle of forms" provisions in Section 2-207 of the UCC and Article 19 of the United Nations Convention on Contracts for the International Sale of Goods, it may be difficult for the Acquired Companies to ascertain their warranty and indemnity obligations with precision.

Sellers may request that the last sentence of Section 3.27(b) be deleted. Even if the Acquired Companies routinely exclude these damages in their contracts, Sellers may be unable to represent that the exclusions are effective in every jurisdiction in which the Acquired Companies sell products or services.

3.28   BROKERS OR FINDERS

No Seller or Acquired Company, and none of their respective Representatives, has incurred any obligation or liability, contingent or otherwise, for any brokerage or finder's fee or agent's commission or other similar payment in connection with this Agreement or the Contemplated Transactions.

COMMENT

Various intermediaries offer services to facilitate acquisitions, including valuation, finders, and brokerage services, as well as negotiation, due diligence, and closing assistance. The representation contained in Section 3.28 assures Buyer that neither Sellers nor the Acquired Companies have engaged or become obligated to compensate any such intermediaries. If Sellers indicate that such an obligation has been incurred, the Model Agreement should specify whether Sellers or Buyer (including the Acquired Companies) will accept payment responsibility. If an Acquired Company assumes this obligation, there may be tax consequences (e.g., whether the payments would be deemed a constructive dividend).

SELLERS' RESPONSE

Sellers may ask that the reference to Representatives be deleted, arguing that Sellers have limited information regarding what their Representatives may do and, so long as the Acquired Companies have no liability, Buyer has little need to know.

3.29   DISCLOSURE

No representation or warranty or other statement made by any Seller in this Agreement, the Disclosure Letter, any supplement to the Disclosure Letter, the certificate delivered pursuant to Section 8.3, or otherwise in connection with the Contemplated Transactions contains any untrue statement of material fact or omits to state a material fact necessary to make the statements in this Agreement or therein, in light of the circumstances in which they were made, not misleading.

COMMENT

Section 3.29 contains a so-called "10b-5 representation" (named after Rule 10b-5 under the Exchange Act). It is intended to assure Buyer that the representations and disclosure made by Sellers in connection with the Contemplated Transactions do not contain any material misstatements or omissions.

Unlike the federal securities law after which this representation was patterned, Section 3.29 is contractual in nature and does not require Sellers' knowledge or scienter, require Buyer's reliance upon the facts misrepresented or omitted, or permit Sellers to assert a defense that they could not have known about the misstatement or omission even with the exercise of reasonable care (as provided by Section 12(2) of the Securities Act). Section 3.29 therefore imposes a higher disclosure standard upon Sellers. It covers not only the representations in the Model Agreement, but all other representations and statements made by a Seller in connection with the Contemplated Transactions.

This representation is intended to fill any disclosure gaps and cover a fact or circumstance that might have fallen outside the scope of other Article 3 representations.

SELLERS' RESPONSE

Sellers may argue that Section 3.29 is unduly broad and should be either deleted or limited to the representations in the Model Agreement and the certificates delivered at the Closing, because it is unreasonable to ask Sellers to be responsible for every oral statement made and every document delivered in the course of the acquisition process. Buyer may respond that it should not bear the risk of any inaccuracies in the information delivered to Buyer in connection with its investigation of the Acquired Companies.

Sellers may request that Section 3.29 be replaced by a disclaimer stating that Sellers are making no representations, express or implied, other than those expressly set forth in Article 3. Another formulation that might be requested by Sellers would be a "nonreliance clause" such as the following:

> Buyer acknowledges and agrees that in entering into this Agreement it has not relied and is not relying on any representations, warranties, or other statements whatsoever, whether written or oral, by Sellers or any Person acting on their behalf, other than those expressly set forth in this Agreement, and that it will not have any right or remedy arising out of any representation, warranty or statement not set forth in this Agreement.

For a discussion of nonreliance and related clauses, *see* West & Benton, *Contracting to Avoid Extra-Contractual Liability— Can Your Contractual Deal Ever Be the "Entire" Deal?*, 64 Bus. Law. 999 (Aug. 2009).

4. Representations and Warranties of Buyer

PRELIMINARY NOTE

The Model Agreement contains 29 representations by Sellers, but only a few representations by Buyer. In an acquisition in which the purchase price is paid at the closing in cash, the seller is interested primarily in the buyer's due organization, the power of the buyer, the authority of the buyer's agents to execute a binding acquisition agreement, and the buyer's obligations to finders or brokers. Questions as to a buyer's ability to pay the purchase price may be better addressed by the seller's due diligence than by representations. Where a buyer is borrowing to pay part of the purchase price, however, a seller may seek a representation regarding the buyer's financing commitments. In some circumstances, a seller may desire assurances that the buyer is in a position to pay the cash portion of the purchase price at closing. In addition to due diligence regarding this question, the seller may request a representation such as the following: "Buyer presently has, and will have at Closing, all funds or financing in place necessary to pay and deliver to Sellers the Purchase Price as contemplated hereby." The buyer, however, may be unwilling to do more than simply describe the nature of its financing arrangements and may insist that financing be a condition to its obligation to close. *See* Section 8.11 and related commentary.

If a buyer is issuing shares of its stock in exchange for the stock of the target, the seller is investing in the buyer. Accordingly, the seller might request representations of the buyer that resemble those made by the seller to the buyer. In the case of a stock-for-stock transaction involving two companies of roughly equal size, financial strength, and stability, the representations may be virtually the same for each party. *See* Appendix B—Receipt of Stock of a Public Company as Purchase Consideration.

Where a significant amount of the purchase price is to be represented by a promissory note or payment is otherwise deferred, a seller is placed in the role of lender to the buyer. The notes representing a portion of the purchase price most often are unsecured. Accordingly, the seller usually performs a credit analysis of the buyer to confirm that it is financially able to make timely payments of the debt service. Depending upon the size of the note in relation to the size of the overall transaction, the seller may insist on receiving certain representations as well as covenants from the buyer. The representations may cover the buyer's financial statements, the ranking of the notes in the buyer's debt hierarchy, the absence of contingent or undisclosed liabilities that could affect the buyer's ability to pay, the absence of any material adverse change in the buyer's business, accounts receivable and inventories, and the absence of liens and encumbrances on the buyer's assets. These representations can form the basis for additional covenants concerning collateral, financial covenants and ratios, and the like. For example, if the buyer's note is to be secured, additional representations concerning the collateral may be appropriate.

A buyer will most likely resist providing these representations. It may argue that the note is an insignificant amount of the total purchase price or contend that the seller is needlessly complicating a simple, straightforward transaction. Nevertheless, whenever the seller is investing in and/or lending to the buyer, the seller may be justified in demanding the protections it believes are appropriate under the circumstances.

Buyer represents and warrants to Sellers as follows:

4.1   ORGANIZATION AND GOOD STANDING

Buyer is a corporation duly organized, validly existing, and in good standing under the laws of the State of _____ .

COMMENT

This representation parallels that given by Sellers in the second sentence of Section 3.1. If Buyer does not have proper corporate existence under the laws of the jurisdiction in which it purports to be organized or is not in good standing in that jurisdiction, Buyer does not have the basic foundation to enter into the Model Agreement. Absent significant noncash consideration, a seller typically has no real interest in other matters covered by Section 3.1 concerning the buyer, such as whether it is qualified to do business in foreign jurisdictions.

See commentary to Section 3.1.

4.2   ENFORCEABILITY AND AUTHORITY; NO CONFLICT

(a) The execution, delivery, and performance by Buyer of this Agreement and Buyer's Closing Documents have been duly authorized by all necessary corporate action. This Agreement has been duly executed and delivered by Buyer and constitutes the legal, valid, and binding obligation of Buyer, enforceable against Buyer in accordance with its terms. Upon execution and delivery of Buyer's Closing Documents by Buyer, each of Buyer's Closing Documents will constitute the legal, valid, and binding obligation of Buyer, enforceable against Buyer in accordance with its terms. Buyer has the absolute and unrestricted right, power, and authority to execute and deliver this Agreement and

Buyer's Closing Documents and to perform its obligations under this Agreement and Buyer's Closing Documents.

(b) Except as set forth in Part 4.2, neither the execution and delivery of this Agreement nor the consummation or performance of any Contemplated Transaction will directly or indirectly (with or without notice or lapse of time):

(i)   contravene, conflict with, or violate (A) any Organizational Document of Buyer, or (B) any resolution adopted by the board of directors or the shareholders of Buyer;

(ii)   contravene, conflict with, or violate, or give any Governmental Body or other Person the right to challenge any Contemplated Transaction, or to exercise any remedy or obtain any relief under, any Legal Requirement or any Order to which Buyer, or any assets owned or used by Buyer, is subject; or

(iii) Breach, or give any Person the right to declare a default or exercise any remedy or to obtain any additional rights under, or to accelerate the maturity or performance of, or payment under, or to cancel, terminate, or modify, any Contract to which Buyer is a party.

(c) Except as set forth in Part 4.2, Buyer is not required to give notice to or obtain Consent from any Person in connection with the execution and delivery of this Agreement or the consummation or performance of any Contemplated Transaction.

COMMENT

This representation mirrors Section 3.2 with certain exceptions. As in Section 3.1, absent significant noncash consideration, Sellers would have little interest in knowing about the other matters covered by Section 3.2(b).

See commentary to Section 3.2.

4.3   INVESTMENT INTENT

Buyer is acquiring the Shares for its own account and not with a view to their distribution within the meaning of Section 2(11) of the Securities Act.

COMMENT

The stock of a privately owned corporation is a "security" as defined in Section 2(a)(i) of the Securities Act. *See* Landreth Timber Co. v. Landreth, 471 U.S. 681 (1985).

Section 5 of the Securities Act provides that it is illegal to sell a security unless a registration statement is effective or an exemption from registration is available.

The Securities Act contains no express statutory exemption that permits the resale of shares by persons who are affiliates or controlling persons of the issuer. Therefore, the marketplace and the courts have created the so-called "4(1-1/2)" exemption, which derives its name from the interplay between Sections 4(1) and 4(2) of the Securities Act.

Section 4(1) of the Securities Act exempts transactions by a person other than an issuer, underwriter, or dealer. Section 2(11) of the Securities Act defines an "underwriter" as "any person who has purchased from an issuer with a view to, or offers or sells for an issuer in connection with, the distribution of any security." It further states that as used in the definition, "issuer" includes any person directly or indirectly controlling, controlled by, or under common control with the issuer. Therefore, affiliates involved in the distribution of an issuer's securities cannot avail themselves of the Section 4(1) exemption.

Section 4(2) of the Securities Act exempts transactions by issuers not involving any public offering. *See* commentary to Section 3.25. It does not exempt sales by controlling persons.

To avail themselves of the "4(1-1/2)" exemption, neither Sellers nor Buyer can be involved in a "distribution" of securities within the meaning of Section 2(11). While Section 2(11) does not define "distribution," it is considered the equivalent of a public offering. *See* Ackerberg v. Johnson, 892 F.2d 1328 (8th Cir. 1989). Accordingly, Section 4(2) considerations are applied to determine whether the parties are involved in a "distribution."

Presumably, Sellers have held the Shares for some time. They are selling to a single purchaser and the representation in Section 4.3 assures Sellers that Buyer is not purchasing the Shares with a view to a "distribution." Therefore, Sellers can take the view that Buyer is not an "underwriter" as defined in Section 2(11) of the Securities Act, and that the transaction is in fact exempt.

SELLERS' RESPONSE

Given the emphasis on disclosure under U.S. securities laws, Sellers, in addition to the representation above, may seek something along the following lines to document the performance of their disclosure obligations:

> Buyer confirms that Sellers have made available to Buyer and its Representatives the opportunity to ask questions of the officers and management employees of the Acquired Companies and to acquire such additional information regarding the business and financial condition of the Acquired Companies as Buyer has requested, and all such information has been received.

While the inclusion of this language would not preclude a claim by Buyer under the securities laws, Buyer may nonetheless reject such language, arguing that it might create a basis upon which Sellers might later refute any indemnity claim of Buyer for breach of Sellers' representations. Sellers may counter by suggesting additional language disclaiming any intention to impair Buyer's indemnification rights.

4.4   CERTAIN PROCEEDINGS

There is no Proceeding pending against Buyer that challenges, or could have the effect of preventing, delaying, making illegal, imposing limitations or conditions on, or otherwise interfering with, any Contemplated Transaction. To Buyer's Knowledge, no such Proceeding has been threatened.

COMMENT

This Section is similar to Sellers' representation in Section 3.15(a)(iii).

In making this representation, Buyer must be concerned with potential, rather than actual, barriers to the Contemplated Transactions. This might apply if there are any actions threatened by third parties, such as regulatory proceedings, shareholder suits, or claims by creditors or competitors, seeking to undermine Buyer's efforts to acquire the Company. Given the somewhat broad definition of "Knowledge" in Section 1.1, Buyer would be expected to undertake a reasonable inquiry to determine if any Proceedings are threatened.

See commentary to Section 3.15.

SELLERS' RESPONSE

If Sellers are accepting a significant amount of noncash consideration, they may ask for a representation that more closely resembles Section 3.15.

4.5   BROKERS OR FINDERS

Neither Buyer nor any of its Representatives has incurred any obligation or liability, contingent or otherwise, for any brokerage or finder's fee, agent's commission, or other similar payment in connection with this Agreement or the Contemplated Transactions.

COMMENT

This Section mirrors Sellers' representation in Section 3.28. *See* commentary to Section 3.28.

5. Covenants of Sellers Prior to Closing Date

PRELIMINARY NOTE

Articles 3 and 4 contain the representations made by the parties to one another. Consistent with current practice, the Model Agreement segregates the representations in Articles 3 and 4 from the covenants to be performed under Articles 5, 6, and 7, and from the conditions to the parties' obligations to complete the acquisition in Articles 8 and 9. The Model Agreement bifurcates the covenants into those that must be performed prior to closing (Articles 5 and 6), and those that primarily relate to the obligations of the parties post-closing (Article 7). The Model Agreement provides that Sellers will cause the Acquired Companies to perform those obligations under Article 5 that would otherwise be imposed directly on the Acquired Companies if they were parties to the Model Agreement.

A breach of the covenants in Article 5, like a breach of any other covenant under basic principles of contract law, may result in liability by the Sellers to the Buyer. Section 11.2(b) provides that Sellers are obligated to indemnify Buyer for any breach of any covenant, although the effect of Section 12.11 is that indemnification pursuant to Article 11 is not the exclusive remedy available to Buyer for breach of a covenant under the Model Agreement (*see* commentary to Sections 11.2 and 12.11). Furthermore, Section 12.16 provides that Buyer may be entitled to equitable relief in situations that may include a breach of a covenant under Article 5. Additionally, a material breach of a covenant in Article 5 could result in the termination of the Model Agreement by Buyer pursuant to Section 10.1(b).

Sellers will want to limit the right of access and investigation afforded to Buyer to what is reasonable under the circumstances, and will also require that the covenants under this Article do not unduly restrict the ability of the Acquired Companies to conduct business in the ordinary course during the period between the signing of the Model Agreement and the Closing Date. Given the remedies available to Buyer for a Seller breach of a covenant under the Model Agreement, including the covenants under Article 5, Sellers will want to ensure that the scope of the obligations they have assumed is reasonable and that they are confident of their ability to satisfy such obligations.

5.1   ACCESS AND INVESTIGATION

Prior to the Closing Date, and upon reasonable notice from Buyer, each Seller shall, and shall cause each Acquired Company to, (a) afford Buyer and its Representatives and prospective lenders and their Representatives (collectively, "Buyer Group") full and free access, during regular business hours, to each Acquired Company's personnel, assets, Contracts, and Records, (b) furnish Buyer Group with copies of all such Contracts and Records as Buyer may reasonably request, (c) furnish Buyer Group with such additional financial, operating, and other relevant data and information as Buyer may reasonably request, and (d) otherwise cooperate and assist, to the extent reasonably requested by Buyer, with Buyer's investigation of the business, condition (financial or otherwise), assets, results of operations, or prospects of each Acquired Company. In addition, Buyer shall have the right to have the Real Property and the tangible personal property of each Acquired Company inspected by Buyer Group, at Buyer's sole cost and expense, including the performance of subsurface or other intrusive testing.

COMMENT

Section 5.1 provides Buyer Group with access to the Acquired Companies' personnel, assets, Contracts, and Records so that Buyer can continue its investigation of the Acquired Companies through the Closing Date. This right of access provides Buyer with the opportunity to confirm the accuracy of Sellers' representations and verify the satisfaction of the other conditions to Buyer's obligation to complete the acquisition, such as the absence of a Material Adverse Change with respect to each Acquired Company. Buyer may also want to learn more about the business operations of the Acquired Companies in order to make appropriate post-closing plans, including the integration of Buyer's and the Acquired Companies' product lines, marketing strategies, and administrative functions.

The access right provided in Section 5.1 extends to Buyer Group, which includes prospective lenders to Buyer and their Representatives. A prospective lender to Buyer may want to engage, and secure the advice of, environmental consultants, asset appraisers, and other consultants before making a definitive lending commitment.

The access right in subsection (a) is accompanied by the rights in subsection (b) to obtain copies of Contracts and Records, which may include licenses, certificates of occupancy, and other permits issued in connection with the ownership, development, or operation of the Real Property, and in subsection (c) to obtain other relevant data and information not yet reduced to writing or data storage. Section 5.1(d) requires Sellers to comply with Buyer's reasonable requests for cooperation and assistance that may not be specifically covered elsewhere in Section 5.1. The last sentence of Section 5.1, although likely already covered by Section 5.1(d), specifically allows site visits by Buyer, and provides that any on-site testing of the Real Property for environmental contamination may be intrusive in nature.

During its due diligence investigation, Buyer is likely to have access to extensive information concerning the Acquired Companies. If, during the period between signing and Closing, the information reveals a material inaccuracy in any of Sellers' representations as of the date of the Model Agreement, Buyer has several options. If the inaccuracy results in the inability of Sellers to satisfy the applicable closing condition in Section 8.1, Buyer can decide to terminate the Model Agreement under Section 10.1 and pursue its remedies as permitted by Section 10.2. Buyer may, however, want to complete the acquisition despite the inaccuracy and later pursue any available indemnification rights (and any available claim for damages) based on the inaccuracy of Sellers' representation (*see* discussion under those scenarios in Appendix D wherein Sellers would be required to indemnify Buyer after the Closing with respect to a breach of Sellers' representations disclosed prior to the Closing). As discussed in the commentary to Section 11.1, however, this latter course of action is not without uncertainty. Therefore, it sometimes happens that Buyer, following its discovery of a material inaccuracy in any of Sellers' representations, brings the discovery to Sellers' attention and attempts to obtain some concession (such as an adjustment to the purchase price, or a specially tailored indemnification) which, if not granted by Sellers, may result in Buyer terminating the Model Agreement and, if applicable, pursuing the remedies afforded by Section 10.2 (*see* commentary to Section 10.2). In return for granting such a concession, Sellers will obtain an amendment of the applicable representation to cure the inaccuracy.

SELLERS' RESPONSE

Sellers may have an interest in limiting the right of access afforded to Buyer and its Representatives under clause (a). For example, Sellers may argue that the phrase "reasonable access" be used in lieu of the phrase "full and free access" in clause (a), or Sellers may wish to include the following clause immediately before clause (b): "... provided that such right of access is exercised in a manner that does not unreasonably interfere with the operations of any Acquired Company."

Sellers may also negotiate certain limitations on the scope of Buyer's investigation. For example, Sellers may have disclosed that an Acquired Company is involved in a material third-party dispute or is the subject of a governmental investigation. While Buyer clearly has a legitimate interest in ascertaining as much as it can about the dispute or investigation, Sellers and Buyer should exercise caution in granting access to certain information so as to avoid any resulting loss to an Acquired Company of its attorney-client privilege. *See* King, *The Common Interest Doctrine and Disclosures During Negotiations for Substantial Transactions*, 74 U. Chi. L. Rev. 1411 (2007). While the parties might be able to claim the "joint defense doctrine" to protect an existing attorney-client privilege in circumstances where it can be successfully claimed that the Acquired Company and Buyer have a common legal interest, reliance on this exception can create serious exposure for the parties, particularly Sellers if the transaction is not completed.

Special considerations may also apply when the target and the buyer are competitors. Sellers may be reluctant to share sensitive information with a competitor until they are certain that the transaction will close. The business risk inherent in exchanging information with a buyer that is a competitor may be mitigated by limiting the competitively sensitive information to that which is truly needed for the buyer's due diligence and integration planning, and by delaying the delivery of such information until the need for the information is clear and the seller's confidence in closing is high. For example, the agreement could provide that access to sensitive customer contracts will only be provided on an agreed-upon date on which the parties expect to have more certainty. Sellers may also want to restrict or at least delay release of detailed personnel information.

Moreover, the parties will want to consider the extent to which sharing of information prior to closing may raise antitrust concerns. *See* ABA Section of Antitrust Law, FTC Practice and Procedure Manual, 98–102 (2007); Naughton, *Gun-Jumping and Pre-Merger Information Exchange: Counseling the Harder Questions*, 20 Antitrust 66 (Summer 2006). Great caution should be exercised with respect to any exchange of information regarding open contract bids, bidding or pricing practices, actual pricing or specific marketing plans, and other comparable information. Exchanges of information among competitors can give rise to allegations that there exists an agreement between the parties in restraint of trade.

The parties can further mitigate the antitrust and competitive risks by conducting ongoing due diligence in more competitively sensitive areas through third-party intermediaries that are subject to confidentiality obligations. These third-party intermediaries can either provide the information to Buyer on an aggregated basis or assess it and advise their client of the implications of the information reviewed, without revealing the specific details of the sensitive information in a manner that raises antitrust concerns or conveys competitively sensitive information to their client. This will allow confirmatory due diligence to proceed while shielding the two competitors from access to information presenting the greatest antitrust risk.

Given the various concerns regarding the disclosure of certain information to Buyer during the due diligence process, Sellers may wish to include the following language at the end of the first sentence of Section 5.1: "…subject at all times in each of the above cases to (i) compliance with applicable antitrust laws and regulations relating to the exchange of information, (ii) compliance with applicable laws protecting the privacy of employees and personnel files, and (iii) appropriate limitations on the disclosure of information to maintain the attorney-client privilege."

Sellers may also want confidentiality agreements for third parties such as a lender.

Sellers are likely to resist subsurface or other intrusive testing by Buyer Group. Such activities could disclose the existence of one or more adverse environmental situations, which Sellers or Buyer or those conducting the testing will likely be obligated to report to a governmental agency. A test boring could exacerbate or create an adverse environmental situation by carrying an existing subsurface hazardous substance into an uncontaminated subsurface area or water source. Sellers would ordinarily not be in privity of contract with Buyer's Representative conducting the testing nor would communications and information received from such Representative ordinarily be protected by an attorney-client privilege available to Sellers or the Acquired Companies. In addition, if the deal is abandoned, Sellers will likely need to disclose the test results to the next prospective buyer.

Sellers may want to seek indemnification from Buyer in the event the Closing does not occur with respect to any claim, damage, or expense arising out of inspections and related testing conducted on behalf of Buyer, including the cost of restoring the property to its original condition, the removal of any liens against the Real Property, and compensation for any impairment to the Acquired Companies' use and enjoyment of the same. In addition, upon termination, Sellers may wish to have Buyer confirm payment for all work performed and deliver to Sellers copies of all the surveys, tests, reports, and other materials produced for Buyer. Buyer may resist this indemnity particularly if the deal does not close due to a perceived failure on the part of Sellers.

5.2   OPERATION OF THE BUSINESSES OF THE ACQUIRED COMPANIES

Prior to the Closing Date, each Seller shall, and shall cause each Acquired Company to:

    (a) conduct the business of such Acquired Company only in the Ordinary Course of Business;

    (b) use its best efforts to preserve intact the current business organization of such Acquired Company, keep available the services of the officers, employees, and agents of such Acquired Company, and maintain its relations and goodwill with suppliers, customers, landlords, creditors, employees, agents, and others having business relationships with such Acquired Company;

    (c) confer with Buyer prior to implementing operational decisions of a material nature;

    (d) report to Buyer at such times as Buyer may reasonably request concerning the status of the business, condition (financial or otherwise), assets, results of operations, or prospects of such Acquired Company;

    (e) make no material changes in management personnel of such Acquired Company;

(f) maintain the assets owned or used by such Acquired Company in a state of repair and condition that complies with Legal Requirements and Contracts and is consistent with the requirements and normal conduct of the business of such Acquired Company;

(g) keep in full force and effect, without amendment, all material rights relating to the business of such Acquired Company;

(h) comply with all Legal Requirements applicable to, and all Applicable Contracts of, such Acquired Company;

(i) continue in full force and effect the insurance coverage under the policies set forth in Part 3.18 or substantially equivalent policies;

(j) except as required to comply with ERISA or to maintain qualification under Section 401(a) of the Code, not amend, modify, or terminate any Employee Plan and, except as required under the provisions of any Employee Plan, not make any contributions to or with respect to any Employee Plan;

(k) maintain all records of such Acquired Company consistent with past practice; and

(l) take no action, or fail to take any reasonable action within its control, as a result of which any of the changes or events listed in Section 3.16 would be likely to occur.

COMMENT

The covenants in Section 5.2 are often referred to as "operating covenants." Generally, a buyer has an interest in assuring that the business of the target will be substantially the same at closing as it was on the date the purchase agreement was signed. Accordingly, Section 5.2(a) requires Sellers to operate the Acquired Companies only in the "Ordinary Course of Business" (defined in Section 1.1). This provision prohibits Sellers from taking certain actions that could adversely affect the value of the Acquired Companies or frustrate Buyer's expectations regarding the condition and operations of the Acquired Companies.

Beyond the "Ordinary Course of Business" limitation, Section 5.2 sets out a number of specific items that Sellers must cause the Acquired Companies to do or refrain from doing between signing and the Closing.

The covenants contained in each of the clauses of Section 5.2, with the exception of (e) and (l), are all "affirmative" in nature, each requiring Sellers to, or to cause the Acquired Companies to, take certain actions or to maintain certain practices. Many of these requirements are within the Ordinary Course of Business but the clauses (other than (a)) are more specific and are intended to cause the parties to focus on certain areas of the operations of the Acquired Companies. The subjects addressed are commonly of concern to Buyer and could cause pre-closing disagreement between Buyer and Sellers.

Section 5.2(b) introduces the use of a "best efforts" standard. Often, the use of an absolute standard or duty with respect to future performance is not reasonable. While certain activities and affirmative covenants can be absolute, those which are not entirely within the control of Sellers are more appropriately qualified by the best efforts standard. *See* commentary to Section 5.7 for a discussion of the meaning of "best efforts."

When the Model Agreement is signed, Buyer typically wants to become involved in material decisions concerning the Acquired Companies. The parties to the transaction should be mindful of antitrust concerns and, in particular, the risk that such involvement by Buyer may be viewed as a premature transfer of operational control over the Acquired Companies before expiration of the HSR waiting period and, as such, a violation of the HSR Act as well as a potential violation of Section 1 of the Sherman Act. *See* U.S. v. Computer Associates International, Inc., 2002 U.S. Dist. LEXIS 23039 (D.D.C. 2002). Section 5.2(c) and (d) require Sellers to, and to cause the Acquired Companies to, confer with Buyer on operational matters of a material nature prior to their implementation and report to Buyer at such times as Buyer may reasonably request on the status of, among other things, the business and financial condition of each Acquired Company. The reach of clause (c) is broader than that of clause (a), as it requires Sellers and the Acquired Companies to affirmatively confer with Buyer on these operational matters prior to their implementation, even if they involve discussions on matters arising in the Ordinary Course of Business. On matters falling within this category, however, Buyer has only a right of conferral, and Sellers and the Acquired Companies retain the right to make decisions in their discretion. Sellers have the obligation to take the initiative in conferring with Buyer under clause (c) and in reporting to Buyer under clause (d). For example, if the Acquired Companies are retail companies, clause (c) would require Sellers to confer with Buyer about large purchases of seasonal inventory, even though this would fall within the Ordinary Course of Business. The decision whether to purchase the inventory, however, would remain with the Acquired Companies. Because the affirmative covenant does not limit Sellers from making the decision, Buyer may seek to include a "negative covenant" in the Agreement to limit Sellers' right to make material decisions from the time of signing until the Closing.

Section 5.2(e) requires that no material change be made with respect to the management personnel of each Acquired Company. A material change that results from a decision by a member of management to leave the employ of an Acquired Company, for example, would not be covered under this provision. The departure might constitute a breach of the Sellers' representations as of the Closing Date under Sections 3.12 or 3.20(c). Assuming that the departure is material or might constitute a Material Adverse Change, a closing condition would not be satisfied as a consequence.

The covenants in Section 5.2(f) require that the assets owned or used by the Acquired Companies be maintained in accordance with applicable legal and contractual requirements as well as in a manner consistent with the normal conduct of the business. However, Buyer should note that these covenants do not require Sellers to, or to cause the Acquired Companies to, acquire, lease, or sell assets to meet any changing needs of the Acquired Companies.

Section 5.2(g) requires that the material rights of the Acquired Companies be kept in full force and effect. These could include rights under contracts, intellectual property agreements, and governmental authorizations, among others.

Section 5.2(i) creates the obligation to keep in full force and effect insurance coverage under existing or substantially equivalent policies. These covenants may require, for example, that Sellers or the Acquired Companies take the necessary steps to review the insurance coverage and determine what may be required to preserve such rights or coverage up to the Closing Date.

The covenants in Section 5.2(h) deal with compliance with Legal Requirements and contractual obligations of the Acquired Companies. Noncompliance by an Acquired Company with a material Contract could obviously be harmful to the business or diminish its value to Buyer.

Section 5.2(j) imposes a negative covenant on Sellers to not amend, modify, or terminate, or to make any contributions to, any Employee Plan, unless required under Legal Requirements or any Employee Plan. Buyer will not want Sellers or the Acquired Companies to do anything that might increase the liabilities of the employer under any Employee Plan since the date of signing, nor will Buyer want Sellers or the Acquired Companies to take any actions which may, for instance, create concern among the employees of any Acquired Company as to how they will be affected by the change of control resulting from the transaction.

Buyer also has an interest in having the books and records of each of the Acquired Companies maintained in a manner consistent with past practice (Section 5.2(k)). Note that the defined term "Record" is purposefully not used because the term "records" is self explanatory.

As mentioned above, Section 5.2(l) incorporates a number of specific actions or occurrences by reference to Section 3.16. However, Section 5.2(l), unlike Section 3.16, only applies to actions within the control of Sellers or the Acquired Companies. As a result, even though certain changes and events described in Section 3.16 may not be within the control of Sellers or the Acquired Companies for purposes of the representations provided for Buyer's benefit, the obligations of Sellers and the Acquired Companies pursuant to Section 5.2(l) are not as onerous. Note that Section 5.7, operating in conjunction with Section 8.1, requires Sellers to use their best efforts so that the representations in Section 3.16 are accurate as of the Closing Date as if made on the Closing Date. Thus, Sections 5.2 and 5.7 overlap to some degree.

SELLERS' RESPONSE

Many of the operating covenants will cover practical and unique operational activities and, as a result, negotiation will often require significant input from Sellers and others, including management, who have detailed knowledge of the Acquired Companies.

Section 5.2(a) requires that the Acquired Companies conduct their business only in the "Ordinary Course of Business" between the date of the Agreement and the Closing Date. It may not always be clear, however, whether certain activities constitute the "Ordinary Course of Business." In fact, not all companies conduct their business in the ordinary course with any degree of consistency. Accordingly, Sellers might consider adding a list of specific activities to Section 5.2(a) that would be considered to be in the Ordinary Course of Business so that Sellers and Buyer may share the same understanding as to those activities. Sellers should also consider whether there are any activities outside the Ordinary Course of Business that have been committed to by Sellers or in which Sellers would like to engage prior to Closing that would necessitate an exception to this covenant.

Sellers might argue that the best efforts requirement in Section 5.2(b) is too onerous and should be reduced to a lesser standard, such as "commercially reasonable efforts." *See* commentary to Section 5.7. Also, the nature and extent of the obligation to keep available the services of the officers, employees, and agents of the Acquired Companies, as well as the precise purpose of this requirement, could be clarified and limited. As drafted, Sellers could not terminate anyone, even for cause. It could also require Sellers to offer incentives to employees to remain employed. Finally, Sellers might object to the obligation to maintain relations and goodwill as set forth in Section 5.2(b), as this covenant could be interpreted as unfairly limiting the ability of the Acquired Companies to deal with suppliers, customers, creditors, and others as they deem necessary in the circumstances.

While it is not unusual for a seller to agree to provide certain reports to a buyer regarding the target between signing and closing, the covenant in Section 5.2(d) that Sellers "report to Buyer at such times as Buyer may reasonably request concerning the status of the business, condition (financial or otherwise), assets, results of operations, or prospects" of an Acquired Company may be too general in terms of the scope and frequency of the reports required of Sellers. Sellers may want to agree with Buyer on specific reports that will satisfy Buyer's information needs and that Sellers will be able to reasonably provide, as well as the timing for providing such reports.

Certain of Sellers' covenants under Section 5.2 depend on whether the action taken by Sellers is "material" or refer to decisions of a "material" nature, as in Section 5.2(c) or to "material" rights, as in Section 5.2(g). The use of the word "material" in covenants of this type is common but may result in lack of certainty as to its intended meaning. For example, it is not clear from the text whether the firing of a vice president would necessarily constitute a "material change in management personnel." To avoid this potential ambiguity, Sellers may wish to define which actions are "material," for instance, by further specifying the categories of management personnel that are subject to the covenant (e.g., personnel who rank as senior vice presidents or higher) or in other instances by specifying dollar amount thresholds for materiality. Furthermore, with respect to those covenants in Section 5.2(f) requiring the maintenance of assets in compliance with Legal Requirements and Contracts, in Section 5.2(h) dealing with compliance with Legal Requirements and Applicable Contracts, and in Section 5.2(j) covering Employee Plans, Sellers might argue that the obligations should be qualified by materiality so that the covenants of Sellers are not unreasonable or onerous.

The reference to "records" in Section 5.2(k) is broad and may be problematic for Sellers. Sellers may want to limit this covenant to cover only such information as the parties can agree is important to the business of the Acquired Companies.

Because many companies are not accustomed to operating under such restrictions, Sellers may have to implement new procedures so that the restrictions will be honored. Depending on the nature of the restricted activity, Sellers might consider taking the necessary steps so that the appropriate persons within the Acquired Companies (such as directors, officers, and employees) are aware of the obligations imposed on the Acquired Companies and that procedures are implemented and monitored at appropriate levels. Sellers might also want to negotiate the covenants under Section 5.2 to allow Sellers to operate the business of each Acquired Company in a manner that is consistent with its past business practices so that Sellers are not placed in a situation where a typical business operation requires Buyer's consent. Otherwise, failure to receive such consent could force Sellers to decide between breaching a covenant under the Model Agreement or risking harm to the business. Sellers might argue that the covenants in Section 5.2(c), for example, place unnecessary restrictions on the ability of the Acquired Companies to make timely decisions on operational matters which, although of a material nature, are nonetheless part of the Ordinary Course of Business. As a result, Sellers may seek to remove such contractual restrictions.

5.3 FILINGS AND NOTIFICATIONS; COOPERATION

As promptly as practicable after the date of this Agreement, and in any event within the applicable time period prescribed by Legal Requirements, each Seller shall, and shall cause each Acquired Company and each of their Related Persons to, make all filings and notifications required by Legal Requirements to be made by them in connection with the Contemplated Transactions (including all filings under the HSR Act). Each Seller shall, and shall cause each Acquired Company and each of their Related Persons to, cooperate with Buyer, its Related Persons, and their respective Representatives (a) with respect to all filings and notifications that Buyer or its Related Persons elect to make or shall be required by Legal Requirements to make in connection with the Contemplated Transactions,

(b) in identifying and obtaining the Governmental Authorizations required by Buyer to own and operate each Acquired Company from and after the Closing Date, and (c) in obtaining all Consents identified in Exhibit 9.4 (including taking all actions requested by Buyer to cause early termination of any applicable waiting period under the HSR Act).

COMMENT

Section 5.3 works in conjunction with Section 6.1, which sets forth Buyer's filing and notification requirements. The purpose of Section 5.3 is to require Sellers to make all necessary filings as promptly as practicable and to cooperate with Buyer in obtaining all consents and approvals from Governmental Bodies and private parties (including, for example, lenders) that are necessary to complete the acquisition and operate the Acquired Companies after the Closing. Because of the inevitable timing issues involved in this process, it would be helpful for Sellers and Buyer to assess prior to signing any potential problems in obtaining these consents and approvals in a timely fashion.

The need for governmental approvals, such as permits and licenses, is more likely to arise in an acquisitions of assets. Even in stock acquisitions, however, governmental notifications or approvals may be necessary. The HSR Act, if applicable, provides that the acquisition cannot be consummated until the filings are made and the waiting period expires or is terminated. *See* commentary to the definition of "HSR Act" in Section 1.1.

The HSR Act requires Sellers and Buyer (or their ultimate parent entities) to make separate filings. Accordingly, Sections 5.3 and 6.1 impose mutual filing obligations on Sellers and Buyer and provide that each party will cooperate with the other in connection with these filings. There may be circumstances, however, in which it is appropriate to give one party control over certain aspects of the approval process. For example, Section 5.3 gives Buyer control over the decision to request early termination of the waiting period under the HSR Act.

Responsibility for Buyer's HSR Act filing fee is allocated equally between Buyer and Sellers in Section 12.1(a).

If the parties' operations or ownership are such that Buyer concludes that certain filings or notifications that are not required by a Legal Requirement as a technical matter are nevertheless useful to Buyer as a business matter, specific language should be added to this Section requiring the desired filings or notifications be made by Sellers or the Acquired Companies as applicable.

SELLERS' RESPONSE

Sellers might request that their obligation in the second sentence of Section 5.4 to cooperate with Buyer be qualified by a "reasonableness" standard. In addition,

Sellers should consider putting specific limits on the types of filings and notifications that Buyer may elect to make in connection with the Contemplated Transactions in order to control the dissemination of Sellers' confidential information as well as potential damage to the business of the Acquired Companies in the event the proposed transaction does not close. Sellers might also request that Buyer be responsible for all fees and costs incurred by Sellers in cooperating with Buyer with respect to filings and notifications that are not required by law.

5.4 NOTICE

(a) **Prior to the Closing Date, each Seller shall promptly provide notice to Buyer of any Breach of any representation or warranty of Sellers or any fact or circumstance that would or would reasonably be likely to cause or constitute a Breach of any such representation or warranty had that representation or warranty been made as of the time of the occurrence of such fact or circumstance. Should any such Breach relate to the Disclosure Letter, each Seller shall promptly deliver to Buyer a supplement to the Disclosure Letter. No such notice or delivery will be deemed to have cured any Breach of any representation or warranty or affect any right or remedy of Buyer under this Agreement.**

(b) **Prior to the Closing Date, each Seller shall promptly provide notice to Buyer of any Breach of any covenant of Sellers in this Article 5 or any fact or circumstance that could make the satisfaction of any condition in Article 8 impossible or unlikely and of all corrective actions undertaken, or to be undertaken, by such Seller with respect thereto. No such notice will be deemed to have cured any Breach of any covenant or affect any right or remedy of Buyer under this Agreement.**

COMMENT

Section 5.4(a) requires each Seller to notify Buyer if it discovers that a representation of Sellers would have been breached had it been made at that time, or if an occurrence since the date the Model Agreement was signed would or would reasonably be likely to cause such a breach. Where a breach of a representation relates to the Disclosure Letter, Section 5.4 requires each Seller to provide a supplement to the Disclosure Letter. Section 5.4(b) also requires each Seller to notify Buyer if it discovers that a covenant of Sellers in Article 5 has been breached or if an occurrence since the date the Agreement was signed renders the satisfaction of the closing conditions in Article 8 impossible or unlikely. This notification is not simply for Buyer's information. Section 8.1 makes the accuracy of Sellers' representations at signing and at the Closing Date a condition to Buyer's obligation to complete the acquisition. Likewise, Section 8.2 makes it a condition to Buyer's obligation to complete the acquisition that all the covenants that each Seller is required to perform at or prior to the Closing have been performed in all material respects.

Sellers' disclosure of an inaccurate representation or a failure to comply with a covenant does not cure the resulting breach of that representation or covenant or affect any remedy of Buyer. *See* Appendix D, scenarios 5 and 9. Depending on the seriousness of the matter disclosed by Sellers, Buyer may decide to terminate the acquisition or cease incurring expenses until Buyer decides, on the basis of further evaluation and perhaps price concessions from Sellers, to proceed with the acquisition. Section 5.4 notwithstanding, if Buyer proceeds with the acquisition after Sellers shall have disclosed a real or anticipated breach, Buyer's remedies for this breach could be affected. *See* commentary to Section 11.1(b).

SELLERS' RESPONSE

This Section requires continuous diligence and, if the business is of any significant size, can quickly become burdensome. Sellers may suggest that requiring "each" Seller to take these actions, which would be duplicative, is not necessary. Changing the references from "each Seller" to "Sellers" should accomplish this goal. Alternatively, Sellers might propose that notice from any of the Sellers or the Sellers' Representative is all that is necessary to give Buyer the necessary notice.

With respect to the last sentence of Section 5.4 (a) and (b), Sellers may object to permitting Buyer to close and seek indemnification for a breach of a representation or covenant that has been disclosed prior to the Closing. *See* commentary to Section 11.1(b). Rather, Sellers may argue that delivery of pre-closing notice should eliminate Buyer's right to seek post-closing indemnification for a breach of the representation or covenant, and that, upon receipt of notice, Buyer should be required to elect either to terminate the acquisition promptly or to proceed with the closing.

5.5   PAYMENT OF INDEBTEDNESS BY RELATED PERSONS

Each Seller shall cause all indebtedness owed to an Acquired Company by any Seller or any Related Person of any Seller to be paid in full prior to Closing.

COMMENT

Closely held companies frequently make loans to a shareholder or to an affiliate of a shareholder. It is for this reason that the representation concerning Related Persons in Section 3.24 forces Sellers to disclose any such loans.

If Buyer is inclined to allow loans by an Acquired Company to a Seller or any Related Person of a Seller to remain outstanding after the Closing, Buyer may wish to require that, at the time of the Closing, the terms of such loans be modified, if necessary, to reflect terms more commonly found in loans between parties dealing at arm's length. Buyer should also be aware that, in such circumstances, it may be difficult to collect that indebtedness. For example, if there is a post-closing dispute involving a claim by Buyer for indemnification pursuant to the Model Agreement based on an alleged breach of a representation of Sellers, the borrower may be less inclined to pay amounts owing under the loan promptly if it is involved in a dispute with Buyer, and any indemnification obligation as a result of a breach under the Model Agreement may potentially cause the borrower no longer to be in a position financially to meet its obligations under the loan.

SELLERS' RESPONSE

A Seller to whom an Acquired Company may have made a loan that is outstanding at the time of negotiation of the Model Agreement may wish to argue that the terms of the loan are similar to those of an arm's-length transaction and that the loan should not have to be repaid except in accordance with its terms. In any event, Sellers may want to make it clear that the obligation to pay any existing indebtedness is that of the individual Seller to whom such obligation applies, rather than a joint obligation.

5.6 EXCLUSIVE DEALING

Until this Agreement shall have been terminated pursuant to Section 10.1, no Seller shall, and each Seller shall cause each Acquired Company and each of their respective Representatives not to, directly or indirectly, solicit, initiate, encourage, or entertain any inquiries or proposals from, discuss or negotiate with, provide any nonpublic information to, or consider the merits of any inquiries or proposals from any Person (other than Buyer) relating to any business combination transaction involving any Seller or Acquired Company, however structured, including the sale of the business or assets (other than in the Ordinary Course of Business) of any Acquired Company, or any Equity Security of any Acquired Company, or any merger, consolidation, or similar transaction or arrangement. Each Seller shall notify Buyer of any such inquiry or proposal within 24 hours of receipt thereof by any Seller, Acquired Company, or any of their respective Representatives.

COMMENT

Section 5.6 is commonly referred to as a "no-shop" provision. This provision is intended to prevent another buyer from interfering with the acquisition during the period between the signing of the Model Agreement and the Closing and to give Buyer information regarding any competing offers. A "no-shop" provision may be unnecessary because the Agreement is a legally binding undertaking of Sellers to consummate the acquisition, subject only to the satisfaction of the various closing conditions. Thus, each Seller is liable for damages if it breaches the Agreement to pursue a transaction with another buyer, and the other buyer may be liable for tortious interference with the signed Model Agreement. Nonetheless, Buyer has a legitimate interest in preventing Sellers from seeking to obtain a better offer, and the "no-shop" provision may provide a basis for Buyer to obtain injunctive relief if appropriate.

Section 5.6 is not qualified by a "fiduciary-out" exception, which is an exception to these prohibitions that permits a board of directors, in the exercise of its fiduciary duty, to take certain actions, such as dealing with competing bidders. In a stock acquisition of a closely held company, a "fiduciary out" exception is not appropriate because Sellers own all the outstanding stock and have provided the only required approval by executing the Model Agreement.

SELLERS' RESPONSE

Sellers might argue that they should not be required to notify Buyer of any inquiry or proposal that is unsolicited and therefore does not result from a breach by any Seller of its obligations under this Section 5.6. Moreover, the imposition of a deadline by which a Seller must notify Buyer makes this obligation more onerous to Sellers.

Sellers might argue that the list of persons included in the term "Representatives," together with the provision making Sellers strictly liable for actions of their Representatives, is too broad. Sellers could point out that while they can control, and will accept liability for actions of, their officers and directors, they should not be strictly liable for actions of all their employees, many of whom will not even be aware of the restrictions contained in Section 5.6, or for actions of certain independent contractors.

Buyer, in turn, could argue that this change would limit the effectiveness of the "no-shop" provision by possibly permitting Sellers to use one of their nonofficer employees or professional advisors to take an action that their officers and directors are prohibited from taking.

5.7   BEST EFFORTS

Each Seller shall use its best efforts to cause the conditions in Article 8 (other than Section 8.11) to be satisfied.

COMMENT

Section 5.7 establishes a contractual obligation of each Seller to use his or her "best efforts" to cause the conditions in Article 8 to Buyer's obligation to complete the acquisition to be satisfied. If the Closing does not occur because one of the conditions in Article 8 is not satisfied, each Seller may have liability to Buyer for breach of this covenant if he or she has not used best efforts to cause the condition to be satisfied. *See* preliminary note to Article 8. The contractual obligation created by Section 5.7 does not extend to Section 8.11 (which sets forth Buyer's obligation to obtain financing as a condition of closing in favor of Buyer), as Sellers are not in a position to cause this condition to be satisfied, and while Section 5.9 requires that Sellers cooperate with Buyer with respect to Buyer's arranging of financing of the acquisition, this covenant only extends to what is reasonably required by Buyer. *See also* commentary to Section 5.9.

Section 5.7, for example, requires each Seller to use best efforts with respect to the accuracy of the representations as of the Closing Date, as if made on that date, because Section 8.1 makes accuracy a condition to Buyer's obligation to complete the acquisition. Section 5.7 also requires each Seller to use best efforts to obtain all the Material Consents (as listed in Exhibit 8.4), because Section 8.4 makes this a condition to Buyer's obligation to complete the acquisition. The term "best efforts" also appears in Sections 5.2 and 6.3.

Because "best efforts" duties apply most often to sellers, a high standard of what constitutes "best efforts" generally favors buyers. Buyers will therefore often omit a definition of best efforts in their first draft and, consistent with this practice, the Model Agreement does not define "best efforts." Sellers, however, would generally seek to include a definition to specify and limit the extent of effort required.

"Efforts" clauses are commonly used to qualify the level of effort required in order to satisfy an applicable covenant or obligation. An absolute duty to perform covenants or similar obligations relating to future actions will often be inappropriate or otherwise not acceptable to one or more parties to the agreement, as, for instance, when a party's ability to perform depends upon events or third-party acts beyond that party's control. In such circumstances, parties typically insert "efforts" provisions.

There is a general sense of a hierarchy of various types of efforts clauses that may be employed. Although formulations may vary, if the agreement does not contain a definition of the applicable standard, some practitioners ascribe the following meanings to these commonly selected standards:

- *Best efforts:* the highest standard, requiring a party to do essentially everything in its power to fulfill its obligation (for example, by expending significant amounts or management time to obtain consents).

- *Reasonable best efforts:* somewhat lesser standard, but still may require substantial efforts from a party.

- *Reasonable efforts:* still weaker standard, not requiring any action beyond what is typical under the circumstances.

- *Commercially reasonable efforts:* not requiring a party to take any action that would be commercially detrimental, including the expenditure of material unanticipated amounts or management time.

- *Good faith efforts:* the lowest standard, which requires honesty in fact and the observance of reasonable commercial standards of fair dealing. RESTATEMENT (SECOND) OF CONTRACTS § 205, cmt a. Good faith efforts are implied as a matter of law. RESTATEMENT (SECOND) OF CONTRACTS § 205.

Interpretation of Standards Varies. Although practitioners may believe there are differences between the various efforts standards, courts have been inconsistent both in interpreting these clauses and in perceiving distinctions between them. With respect to "best efforts," for example, case law provides little guidance for its interpretation. *See* Farnsworth, *On Trying to Keep One's Promises: The Duty of Best Efforts in Contract Law*, 46 U. Pitt. L. Rev. 1 (1984). Some courts have held that "best efforts" is equivalent to "good faith" or a type of "good faith." *See, e.g.,* Gestetner Corp. v. Case Equip. Co., 815 F.2d 806 (1st Cir. 1987); Western Geophysical Co. of Am. v. Bolt Assocs., Inc., 584 F.2d 1164 (2d Cir. 1978); Kubik v. J. & R. Foods of Or., Inc., 577 P.2d 518 (Or. 1978). Other courts view "best efforts" as a more exacting standard than "good faith." *See, e.g.,* Bloor v. Falstaff Brewing Corp., 601 F.2d 609 (2d Cir. 1979); Aeronautical Indus. Dist. Lodge 91 v. United Tech. Corp., 230 F.2d 569 (2d Cir. 2000); Grossman v. Lowell, 703 F. Supp. 282 (S.D.N.Y. 1989); *In re* Heard, 6 B.R. 876 (Bankr. W.D. Ky. 1980). The standard is not definable by a fixed formula but takes its meaning from the circumstances. *See, e.g.,* Triple-A Baseball Club Ass'n v. Northeastern Baseball, Inc., 832 F.2d 214 (1st Cir. 1987), *cert. denied*, 485 U.S. 935 (1988); Joyce Beverages of N.Y., Inc. v. Royal Crown Cola Co., 555 F. Supp. 271 (S.D.N.Y. 1983); Polyglycoat Corp. v. C.P.C. Distribs., Inc., 534 F. Supp. 200 (S.D.N.Y. 1982). The "standard industry practice" may also provide guidance as to whether efforts are sufficiently "best." *See* Pink, *Divining the Meaning of "Best Efforts,"* CAL. LAW. 41 (Jan. 2008); citing Zilg v. Prentice-Hall, 717 F.2d 671 (1983), *cert. denied*, 466 U.S. 938 (1983). *See* Miller, Note, *Best Efforts?: Differing Judicial Interpretations of a Familiar Term*, 48 ARIZ. L. REV. 615 (2006).

Furthermore, case law offers little support for the position that "reasonable best efforts," "reasonable efforts," or "commercially reasonable efforts" will be interpreted as separate standards less demanding than "best efforts." *See, e.g.,* Herrmann Holdings Ltd. v. Lucent Technologies Inc., 302 F.2d 552 (5th Cir. 2002); In re IBP, Inc. Shareholders Litigation, 789 A.2d 14 (Del. Ch. 2001). The majority of courts seem to analyze the various types of efforts clauses as having essentially the same meaning or effect; all of the clauses are generally subject to a facts and circumstances analysis and require the parties to act diligently, reasonably, and in good faith. *See, e.g.,* Triple-A Baseball Club v. Northeastern Baseball, 832 F.2d 214 (1st Cir. 1987); *In re* Chateaugay Corp. v. LTV Aerospace and Defense Co., 198 B.R. 848 (S.D.N.Y. 1996). In Hexion Specialty Chemicals, Inc. v. Huntsman Corp., C.A. No. 3841-VCL, slip op. (Del. Ch. Sept. 29, 2008), the court equated "reasonable best efforts" to actions that are "commercially reasonable." The court noted that such a clause does not require a party to ignore its own interests or "spend itself into bankruptcy," but it does require that the interests of the other party be taken into account. Regardless of the standard selected, where a party takes actions such as using financial resources, hiring competent people, or demonstrating a commitment toward completing the contract condition, and where there is a reasonable explanation for not taking further action, courts have been reluctant to speculate that such efforts are insufficient. *See, e.g.,* Castle

Properties v. Lowe's Home Centers, Inc., 2000 Ohio App. LEXIS 1229 (Mar. 20, 2000). On the other hand, courts have found a breach of an efforts obligation where a party failed to take the initial steps that would obviously be required to achieve a stated objective, engaged in minimal effort, or was nonresponsive to third parties who were considered necessary in order to effectuate a transaction. *See, e.g.,* Satcom Int'l Group PLC v. Orbcomm Int'l Partners, L.P., 2000 U.S. Dist. LEXIS 7739 (S.D.N.Y. June 6, 2000). In the event parties to an agreement omit an applicable standard, courts have nevertheless generally implied a duty to use reasonable efforts. *See, e.g.,* Chabria v. EDO Western Corp., 2007 WL 582293 (S.D. Ohio Feb. 20, 2007). In that regard, a court may also impose a duty to use best efforts based on the facts and circumstances of the agreement.

Some courts have held that "best efforts" language is too vague and unenforceable unless the parties have indicated the level of performance required by the provision. This minority approach, which generally has been taken in Illinois, Texas, and, to some extent, New York, holds that such a provision is too vague and indefinite to be commercially binding in the absence of objective criteria by which to judge whether the proper effort has been made. *See, e.g.,* Kraftco Corp. v. Kolbus, 274 N.E.2d 153 (Ill. App. 3d 1971); Beraha v. Baxter Health Care Corp., 956 F.2d 1436 (1992); Pinnacle Books, Inc. v. Harlequin Ent. Limited, 519 F. Supp. 118 (S.D.N.Y. 1981).

Defining Desired Standards. Given the uncertainty in the courts' interpretation of efforts clauses, parties may want to consider expressing more precisely their expectations, specifying exactly what measures are or are not required to be taken. The parties can set guidelines, numerical (e.g., specific dollar amount) or otherwise, to facilitate the court's determination of what is required and whether such requirements were met. Some attorneys, particularly those representing a seller, prefer to use the term "commercially reasonable efforts" rather than "best efforts." A sample definition of "commercially reasonable efforts" that takes the approach of stating a limitation including a specific dollar amount follows:

> For purposes of this Agreement, "commercially reasonable efforts" will not be deemed to require a Person to undertake extraordinary or unreasonable measures, including the payment of amounts in excess of $_____, or other payments with respect to any Contract that are significant in the context of such Contract (or significant on an aggregate basis as to all Contracts).

SELLERS' RESPONSE

The use of the term "best efforts" in the Model Agreement could require Sellers to spend money or take other burdensome actions to satisfy the conditions in Article 8, even where one or more of the conditions may be qualified by a "materiality" standard.

As noted above, "best efforts" applies most often to Sellers in the Model Agreement; a high standard of what constitutes best effort favors Buyer. An attempt is made in some acquisition agreements, including MAPA, to define "best efforts," such as the following:

> "Best Efforts"—the efforts that a prudent Person desirous of achieving a result would use in similar circumstances to achieve that result as expeditiously as possible; provided, however, that a Person required to use Best Efforts under this Agreement will not be thereby required to take actions that would result in a material adverse change in the benefits to such Person of this Agreement and the Contemplated Transactions or to dispose of or make any change to its business, expend any material funds, or incur any other material burden.

This definition requires more than good faith but stops short of requiring a party to subject itself to economic hardship. Alternatively, Sellers may request limitations on their "best efforts" obligation along the lines set forth for Buyer in Section 6.3, which provides that Buyer "shall not be required to dispose of or make any change to its business, expend any material funds, or incur any other material obligation."

Some attorneys, particularly those representing a seller, prefer a different or less rigorous standard, such as "commercially reasonable efforts," "good faith efforts," or "reasonable efforts." The following is an example of a provision that might be added to Section 1.2:

> (xv) reference to "commercially reasonable efforts" will not be deemed to require a Person to undertake extraordinary or unreasonable measures, including the payment of amounts in excess of normal and usual filing fees and processing fees, if any, or other payments with respect to any Contract that are significant in the context of such Contract (or significant on an aggregate basis as to all Contracts).

Before negotiating for the use of a different or less rigorous standard, Sellers might evaluate which standard best serves their interest under the Model Agreement. Because the required actions will be different in each transaction, that decision can be made by Sellers in light of their estimation of the particular actions they will need to take. For example, Sellers may prefer that Section 5.7 remain an unqualified "best efforts" obligation, and request removal of the qualifications for Buyer under Section 6.3.

5.8   FINANCIAL INFORMATION

Sellers shall deliver to Buyer within _____ days after the end of each month a copy of each Acquired Company's [describe the nature of the financial information required] for such month prepared in a manner and containing information consistent with such Acquired Company's current practices.

COMMENT

Section 5.8 requires Sellers to deliver to Buyer monthly financial information for each Acquired Company, among other things, to enable Buyer to monitor the performance of the Acquired Companies during the period prior to the Closing Date and provide Buyer with financial information that will likely be useful in arranging for the financing needed by Buyer to consummate the Contemplated Transactions and fund the working capital of each Acquired Company. This provision also supplements the notification provisions of Section 5.4.

SELLERS' RESPONSE

Sellers may want to coordinate this Section with the normal financial reporting practices of the Acquired Companies so that no additional burdens are placed on the Acquired Companies.

5.9   FINANCING COOPERATION

Each Seller shall, and shall cause each Acquired Company, their Related Persons, and their respective Representatives to, cooperate with Buyer with respect to Buyer's arranging of financing of the Contemplated Transactions, as Buyer may reasonably request.

COMMENT

Section 5.9 requires each Seller to cooperate with Buyer with respect to Buyer's arranging of the financing of the Contemplated Transactions. *See* commentary to Section 8.11. Section 5.7 does not impose on Sellers the obligation to use "best efforts" to cause Buyer's financing to be consummated. Nevertheless, the cooperation of Sellers and the Acquired Companies can be essential in satisfying the requirements of lenders. Therefore, buyers commonly include a provision such as Section 5.9 in the acquisition agreement.

SELLERS' RESPONSE

Sellers might ask that the obligation to cooperate pursuant to this Section 5.9 be conditioned upon Buyer's request not unreasonably interfering with the ongoing operations of each Acquired Company and Related Person to whom such obligation extends. Sellers may also argue that Buyer should bear the expense of this cooperation. Moreover, the language of Section 5.9 might describe more precisely the nature of the cooperation that would be required. Where Buyer is unable to provide greater precision as to the nature of the cooperation required, Sellers may argue that this covenant should be removed in its entirety, on the basis that the legitimate interests of Buyer are already adequately covered through the right of access and investigation afforded pursuant to Section 5.1.

6. Covenants of Buyer Prior to Closing Date

PRELIMINARY NOTE

As is the case with the covenants in Article 5, a breach of the covenants in Article 6 may result in liability by the breaching party (in this case, Buyer) to the nonbreaching party (in this case, Sellers). Section 11.4(b) provides that Buyer is obligated to indemnify Sellers for any breach of any covenant, which would include a covenant in Article 6, just as Section 11.2(b) provides that Sellers are obligated to indemnify Buyer for any breach of any covenant in Article 5. Additionally, a material breach of a covenant in Article 6 could result in the termination of the Model Agreement by Sellers pursuant to Section 10.1(c).

Buyer's covenant in Section 6.1 is to make all filings and notifications that are required under applicable laws to consummate the acquisition. Although Sellers make a similar covenant in Section 5.3, such filings including all filings under the HSR Act are generally Buyer's obligation, and therefore the primary significance of Section 5.3 is that it requires Sellers to cooperate with Buyer in making such filings. Buyer's other covenants in Article 6, to provide notice of a breach of a representation or covenant of Buyer (Section 6.2) and to use best efforts to cause the conditions in Section 9 to be satisfied (Section 6.3), are less onerous than Sellers' covenants under Article 5 because the underlying representations and conditions are of more limited scope.

Sellers may request other pre-closing covenants of Buyer. For example, under Section 8.11, Buyer's obligation is conditioned upon having obtained the financing it deems necessary to close the Contemplated Transactions and to fund the working capital requirements of each Acquired Company. Sellers may require not only a representation concerning the status of Buyer's financing when the Model Agreement is signed, but also a covenant regarding the financing. This could take the form of a covenant of Buyer to use its best efforts to obtain the financing required by Section 8.11 upon the terms disclosed to Sellers or in a financing commitment attached as an exhibit, or a provision such as the following:

> Buyer shall promptly negotiate and enter into agreements containing the terms specified in the Lender Commitment (as defined) and such other terms as are commercially reasonable to Buyer, and will obtain the financing thereunder subject to the satisfaction of the terms and conditions thereof; provided, however, that the conditions contained therein are substantially the same as the conditions set forth in the Lender Commitment.

The foregoing provision is more favorable to Sellers. It specifies before signing what terms Buyer will need to accept in the Lender Commitment in order to obtain the financing. Buyer's willingness to accept even a best efforts covenant will depend on how confident it is in obtaining the financing it has negotiated and the status of the credit markets.

6.1 Filings and Notifications; Cooperation

As promptly as practicable after the date of this Agreement, and in any event within the applicable time period prescribed by Legal Requirements, Buyer shall, and shall cause each of its Related Persons to, make all filings and notifications required by Legal Requirements to be made by them in connection with the Contemplated Transactions (including all filings under the HSR Act). Buyer shall, and shall cause each of its Related Persons to, cooperate with each Seller, each Acquired Company, their Related Persons and their respective Representatives (a) with respect to all filings and notifications that any Seller, any Acquired Company, or their Related Persons shall be required by Legal Requirements to make in connection with the Contemplated Transactions and (b) in obtaining all Material Consents; provided, however, that Buyer shall not be required to dispose of or make any change to its business, expend any material funds, or incur any other material obligation in order to comply with this Section 6.1.

COMMENT

Section 6.1 generally mirrors Section 5.3. Section 6.1 requires Buyer to make (or cause to be made) all filings required to consummate the acquisition. The HSR Act requires a filing to be made by Buyer's "ultimate parent entity." Accordingly, if Buyer were a subsidiary of another company, that company may be required to make the HSR Act filing.

Section 6.1 also requires Buyer to cooperate with Sellers in obtaining all Material Consents that Sellers must obtain to complete the transaction; however, Section 6.1 is qualified by the concluding proviso, which works in conjunction with the concluding proviso in Section 6.3, to protect Buyer from becoming obligated to undertake potentially detrimental actions. *See* commentary to Section 6.3.

SELLERS' RESPONSE

Sellers might insist on an obligation of Buyer to do more than just "make filings and notifications required by Legal Requirements," since in many cases a "filing" or "notification" is only the first step in a process that ultimately requires a consent, order, or permit from a Governmental Body. Thus, Sellers might insist that Buyer obligate itself to follow through with the entire process required to obtain a required consent, order, or permit.

To achieve these objectives, Sellers may want to consider proposing various additions to Section 6.1. The following provision would require that Buyer actively seek necessary consents, approvals, or permits required pursuant to a Legal Requirement:

> Buyer shall take all steps necessary to prosecute such filings and applications with diligence and shall diligently oppose any objection to, appeals from, or petitions to reconsider approvals, in order that preliminary orders and final orders pursuant to such Legal Requirements may be obtained as soon as practicable.

Without this type of provision, Buyer could merely respond that the required application or filing had been made, but not pursue the ultimate goal of obtaining the necessary consent, approval, or permit.

Sellers may also have a concern arising from the fact that many types of governmental filings will require information about the Contemplated Transactions, Sellers, and the Acquired Companies. Sellers have an interest to ensure that all this information is accurate, and so they may want the right to review the information that is to be filed with a Governmental Body. The following provision addresses these concerns:

> Subject to applicable Legal Requirements relating to the exchange of information, Sellers will have the right to review in advance and, to the extent practicable, Buyer shall consult with Sellers about all information relating to Sellers or any Acquired Company that appears in any filing made with, or other written materials submitted to, any Governmental Body in connection with the Contemplated Transactions.

At a minimum, Sellers could seek this covenant with respect to information relating to the Company or Sellers. This can be a real issue for HSR Act filings, which can cover unrelated buyer group information.

Sellers may also want Buyer to keep them abreast of its progress in preparing and making the requisite filings and obtaining any required consent, approval, or permit, so they will know as early as practicable whether any issues are being raised that might delay or derail the Contemplated Transactions. It is possible that Sellers can offer assistance with a particular Governmental Body if Buyer is experiencing a problem. A provision such as the following may also assist in maintaining Buyer's focus on the Contemplated Transactions, especially if it is involved in other transactions:

> Buyer shall keep Sellers informed of the status of matters relating to the completion of the Contemplated Transactions, including promptly furnishing Sellers with copies of any notice or other communication received by Buyer from any Governmental Body with respect to the Contemplated Transactions. Buyer shall promptly advise Sellers upon receiving any communication from any Governmental Body whose

consent, approval, or permit is required for consummation of the Contemplated Transactions that causes Buyer to believe that there is a reasonable likelihood that approval of a Governmental Body will not be obtained or that receipt of any such approval will be delayed beyond [anticipated closing date].

If a filing under the HSR Act will be required (as is contemplated in the Fact Pattern), Sellers may consider proposing a separate provision such as the following, which details the obligations of Buyer:

> As promptly as possible, Buyer shall prepare and make the filings required by the HSR Act with the required Governmental Authorities no later than the [10th] Business Day following the date of this Agreement. Buyer shall request early termination of the waiting period required by the HSR Act, cooperate with Sellers to the extent reasonably necessary to assist in making reasonable supplemental presentations to the applicable Governmental Body, and, if requested by a Governmental Body, respond to inquiries and requests for additional information. Buyer undertakes to litigate in good faith any judicial action brought by a Governmental Body seeking the entry of an injunction (preliminary or permanent) to enjoin, in whole or in part, the Contemplated Transactions.

In certain situations, the following provision may also be appropriate:

> Buyer shall use its best efforts (i) to lift or rescind any injunction or restraining order or other order resulting from any Proceeding adversely affecting the ability of the parties to consummate the Contemplated Transactions, and (ii) to defend any litigation seeking to enjoin, prevent, or delay the consummation of the Contemplated Transactions or seeking damages.

The above language may be particularly important in view of Buyer's "litigation out" in Section 8.8. Sellers could argue that if Buyer is going to retain the "litigation out," it should also have the obligation to mitigate the situation. Buyer may well be unwilling to assume the burden of litigating an antitrust case with the government and resist this provision.

If Sellers are aware that the transaction may give rise to antitrust concerns, Sellers may be unwilling to allow Buyer to terminate the Model Agreement in the face of what Sellers may determine to be a reasonable divestiture requirement. Therefore, Sellers may request that the proviso in Section 6.1 be qualified through provisions setting forth some level of divesture that Buyer would be obligated to undertake if requested by the FTC or DOJ, so that Buyer could terminate the Model Agreement only if the required divestiture exceeded the specified level. Buyer would probably resist this request on the basis that the inclusion of such language may itself trigger a divestiture request to the specified level, because the agreement must be provided to the FTC pursuant to Section 4(c) of the HSR application form. Buyer would argue that Sellers should rely on Buyer's nonbinding, verbal representations that Buyer will agree to a reasonable level of divestiture, but that it would be unreasonable for Buyer to "tip its hand" to the authorities, who otherwise may not require as much a divestiture as Buyer may be willing to suffer. The FTC and DOJ deny that such a provision would have this effect. This tension between Sellers' desire for transaction certainty and Buyer's desire to have a free hand in negotiations with the FTC or DOJ is highly fact-specific and must be resolved on a case-by-case basis.

6.2   NOTICE

(a) Prior to the Closing Date, Buyer shall promptly provide notice to Sellers of any Breach of any representation or warranty of Buyer or any fact or circumstance that would or would reasonably be likely to cause or constitute a Breach of any such representation or warranty had that representation or warranty been made as of the time of the occurrence of such fact or circumstance. No such notice will be deemed to have cured any Breach of any representation or warranty or affect any right or remedy of Sellers under this Agreement.

(b) Prior to the Closing Date, Buyer shall provide notice to Sellers of any Breach of any covenant of Buyer in this Article 6 or any fact or circumstance that could make the satisfaction of any condition in Article 9 impossible or unlikely and of all corrective actions undertaken, or to be undertaken, by Buyer with respect thereto. No such notice will be deemed to have cured any Breach of any covenant or affect any right or remedy of Sellers under this Agreement.

COMMENT

Section 6.2 mirrors Sellers' obligations under Section 5.4. Section 6.2(a) requires Buyer to notify Sellers if it discovers that a representation of Buyer would have been breached had it been made at that time, or if an occurrence since the date the Model Agreement was signed would or would reasonably be likely to cause or constitute such a breach. Section 6.2(b) similarly requires Buyer to notify Sellers if it discovers that a covenant of Buyer in Article 6 has been breached or if an occurrence since the date the Model Agreement was signed renders the satisfaction of the closing conditions in Article 9 impossible or unlikely. This notification is not simply for Sellers' information. Section 9.1 conditions Sellers' obligation to complete the acquisition upon the accuracy of Buyer's representations when the Model Agreement is signed and on the Closing Date. Likewise, Section 9.2 makes it a condition to Sellers' obligation to complete the acquisition that all the covenants that Buyer is required to perform at or prior to the Closing have been performed in all material respects.

With respect to Sellers' disclosure of an inaccurate representation or a failure to comply with a covenant, *see* commentary to Section 5.4. The requirements of Section 6.2 are burdensome, but not as burdensome as Section 5.4 is upon Sellers.

6.3   BEST EFFORTS

Buyer shall use its best efforts to cause the conditions in Article 9 to be satisfied; provided, however, that Buyer shall not be required to dispose of or make any change to its business, expend any material funds, or incur any other material obligation in order to comply with this Section 6.3.

COMMENT

Section 6.3 establishes "best efforts" as an affirmative contractual obligation of Buyer. Unlike Sellers' "best efforts" covenant in Section 5.7, Buyer's obligation under Section 6.3 is qualified by the proviso, which works in conjunction with the proviso in Section 6.1, to protect Buyer from becoming obligated to undertake potentially detrimental actions, as might occur when a Governmental Body or third party imposes conditions on the granting of a required consent or approval. *See* commentary to Section 5.7.

The provisos at the end of Sections 6.1 and 6.3 make it clear that Buyer's obligations are limited to lawful efforts to persuade officials to grant approvals. Buyer retains sole discretion to determine, for example, whether to dispose of one of its existing businesses to obtain antitrust approval. The provisos at the end of Sections 6.1 and 6.3 have no counterparts in Sections 5.3 and 5.7 because Sellers would not expect to be asked to dispose of a line of business in order to obtain approval to consummate the Contemplated Transactions. The provisos in Sections 6.1 and 6.3 can be important in transactions that give rise to antitrust concerns, because the usual requirement of the FTC or the DOJ to cure the anticompetitive effects of a transaction is divestiture. They are intended to allow Buyer to negotiate a divestiture plan with the FTC or DOJ, without being constrained by any obligation under the Model Agreement to Sellers.

SELLERS' RESPONSE

Sellers might argue that the provisos in Sections 6.1 and 6.3 limiting Buyer's obligations be deleted, so as to achieve symmetry with Sections 5.3 and 5.7. If Sellers are successful in negotiating additional covenants of Buyer in Section 6.1 (*see* commentary to Section 6.1), then Sellers may suggest the inclusion of an exception to the proviso in Section 6.3 (such as "except as otherwise provided in Section 6.1" or "except as otherwise provided in this Agreement").

7. Post-Closing Covenants

PRELIMINARY NOTE

In the purchase of a business, a buyer will demand from the seller various covenants or agreements to be performed after the closing. A buyer's need for these is generally greatest in a sale of assets or of stock of a subsidiary. In a sale of assets, covenants may be needed in the acquisition agreement to deal with employee benefits, payment of taxes, payment of retained liabilities, and further assurances. In a sale of a subsidiary, administrative support for the subsidiary often comes from elsewhere within the seller's organization, and a transitional services agreement is sought when the buyer is not prepared or equipped to perform similar services immediately after the acquisition. Similarly, the buyer may need a supply arrangement where raw materials or components have been provided to the target by the seller or its other subsidiaries. *See* Appendix A—The Purchase of a Subsidiary.

The Fact Pattern contemplates the sale of stock by Sellers who are individuals. Under these circumstances, the types of covenants and agreements requested of Sellers will be fewer in number than in an asset sale or in the sale of stock of a subsidiary by a corporate parent. A question may arise as to whether the requested covenants or agreements should be included as covenants in the Model Agreement or addressed in separate agreements. When an agreement must be in a particular form, has differing terms, or expires at a different time, a separate agreement may be preferable. Examples would be employment agreements and leases. In the Fact Pattern, an employment agreement is requested of only one Seller, so this would likely call for a separate agreement. Often sellers own real property occupied by the target. Sometimes a buyer will require that the property be contributed to the target.

Sellers, whether individuals or entities, will frequently be asked to enter into noncompetition and confidentiality agreements. These agreements basically are in support of the goodwill that a buyer is purchasing and assure that the seller will do nothing to harm or diminish the value of the business being purchased. These can be included as covenants in the acquisition agreement or can be separate agreements delivered at the closing. One factor influencing the placement is whether the covenants affect all sellers in the same or a similar manner. If, for example, noncompetition agreements are to be signed by fewer than all sellers or the duration or scope varies among the sellers, separate agreements may be more appropriate. Even when all sellers are entering into noncompetition agreements, a buyer may request separate agreements rather than including covenants within the acquisition agreement.

The types of covenants that apply generally to Sellers (such as those restricting competition, requiring cooperation in business relationships and proceedings, and maintaining confidentiality) are reflected in Article 7. In some cases, such as Section 7.1(b), Sellers and Buyer are mutually obligated. Certain of these covenants, such as Sections 7.2(b) and (c), begin immediately upon signing the Model Agreement.

The circumstances may warrant the addition of other post-closing covenants. For example, the commentary to Section 11.2(d) contains an example of a stand-alone provision that deals with tax indemnification and related matters, including the filing of tax returns. Some of the covenants in that provision could be added to Article 7, and the portion dealing with cooperation and access to records could be integrated into Section 7.1. If the Company is an S corporation, it is likely that post-closing covenants will be required. As an S corporation, the Company will file information returns showing income and losses, but Sellers will report their allocable share of the income and losses on their own tax returns and will be responsible for payment of the income taxes. This will have an impact on, among other things, the allocation of income and loss and tax liabilities between the parties and the filing of tax returns, which can be covered in the post-closing covenants. In addition, if an election under Section 338(h)(10) of the Code is to be made, as discussed in commentary to Section 3.11, the procedure for filing the election and the allocation of the Purchase Price to reflect the "deemed" sale of assets would also normally be dealt with in post-closing covenants. These could be added to Article 7 or contained in a separate article, such as Article 13 that is included in Exhibit 2 (Alternative Provisions) to Appendix A—The Purchase of a Subsidiary. The sale of a subsidiary out of a consolidated group presents many of the same tax considerations as the sale of an S corporation, including the ability to make an election under Section 338(h)(10) of the Code. In addition, this may require an adjustment to the tax indemnification provisions in Section 11.2(d).

If any of the covenants are crafted as separate agreements, execution and delivery would likely be a closing deliverable under Article 2 or, if persons other than Sellers are involved, a closing condition under Article 8 or Article 9.

See Kling & Nugent § 13.04; M&A Process 229–30.

7.1   Cooperation and Proceedings; Access to Records

(a) **After the Closing, each Seller shall cooperate with Buyer and its counsel and make itself and its Representatives available to Buyer and the Acquired Companies in connection with the institution or defense of any Proceeding, whether existing, threatened, or anticipated, involving or relating to the Contemplated Transactions, Buyer, any Seller, or any Acquired Company, including providing testimony, Records, and other information.**

COMMENT

Section 7.1(a) obligates Sellers to assist Buyer in connection with Proceedings (which would include litigation and governmental proceedings), whether already existing, threatened, or merely anticipated. Seller must provide Records as well as testimony and other information.

The commentary to Section 11.2(d) contains an example of a stand-alone provision that deals with tax indemnification and related matters, including cooperation with respect to Proceedings. If that provision were to be included in the Model Agreement, it should be coordinated with Section 7.1(a) to avoid duplication and inconsistencies.

SELLERS' RESPONSE

This obligation applies not only to Sellers, but also to their Representatives, over which Sellers may have no control. Sellers may therefore wish to insert a best efforts standard as to the cooperation of the Representatives or direct the Buyer's requests to the Representatives. Sellers may also wish to narrow the scope of the cooperation requirement to Proceedings actually commenced, and to Records, testimony, or other information that relates directly to those Proceedings. Sellers further may want to require advance notice by Buyer, reimbursement of their fees and expenses, and a reciprocal commitment of cooperation from Buyer.

> **(b) Each Seller and Buyer will make available to the other any Records in the nonrequesting party's custody or control for the purpose of preparing any financial statement or Tax Return or preparing for or defending any tax-related examination of the requesting party or any Acquired Company by any Governmental Body. The party requesting such Records will reimburse the nonrequesting party for the reasonable out-of-pocket costs and expenses incurred by the nonrequesting party. The nonrequesting party will afford access to such Records during normal business hours, upon reasonable advance notice given by the requesting party, and subject to such reasonable limitations as the nonrequesting party may impose to delete competitively sensitive or privileged information.**

COMMENT

Each party is obligated to furnish Records to the others in connection with the preparation of financial statements, tax returns, or a governmental audit (which is also contemplated by subsection (a), since "Proceeding" is defined to include a governmental audit). The party providing the Records will be reimbursed for its reasonable out-of-pocket costs and expenses. The obligation subjects access to the Records to reasonable advance notice and limitations.

In a typical situation, the Company would have maintained all the tax-related Records. Nevertheless, Sellers may have copies of some historical Records that might have been destroyed by the Company. This subsection might be more to the advantage of Sellers, particularly where the Company is an S corporation for tax purposes and the Records are needed for preparation or an audit of Sellers' tax returns.

The commentary to Section 11.2(d) contains an example of a stand-alone provision that deals with tax indemnification and related matters, including access to records, and includes references to Tax Returns and tax-related examinations. If that provision were to be included in the Model Agreement, it should be coordinated with Section 7.1(b) to avoid duplication and inconsistencies.

SELLERS' RESPONSE

Sellers may wish to expand the scope of Section 7.1(b). For example, if Sellers have retained real estate used by the Acquired Companies, the Acquired Companies' records may be pertinent to Sellers.

Sellers may also favor the addition of a provision providing access to, and the retention of, tax records, such as that contained in subsection (d) of the example in commentary to Section 11.2(d). *See also* commentary to Section 11.8 with respect to tax audits and other Proceedings.

7.2   NONCOMPETITION, NONSOLICITATION, AND NONDISPARAGEMENT

COMMENT

A buyer will often request noncompetition covenants from the shareholders of the target. In addition, except in jurisdictions where such an agreement would clearly be unenforceable, a buyer will often request noncompetition agreements from certain nonowner employees of the target. The permissible scope of a noncompetition agreement under the applicable state law may be different for shareholders and nonowner employees and, accordingly, consideration might be given to using separate forms of noncompetition agreements, keeping in mind that the nonowner employees will not be parties to the acquisition agreement. In considering whether to seek noncompetition agreements from nonowner employees, there is the possibility that they will refuse to sign such an agreement and will seek employment elsewhere. Securing noncompetition agreements from entirely passive shareholders may be of no significance to a buyer and often is not requested.

If a shareholder will be entering into an employment agreement, as assumed in the Fact Pattern, a noncompetition covenant can be added to the employment agreement in addition to or in place of the one in the Model Agreement. To take advantage of the relatively more favorable regard in which courts hold noncompetition covenants given by shareholders as compared to those given by nonowner employees, it may be helpful to include noncompetition covenants from the employee shareholders in the Model Agreement, regardless of whether they are also included in the employment agreement. In a transaction involving multiple jurisdictions with varying standards for enforceability of noncompetition covenants, separate forms may be appropriate in different jurisdictions. These agreements do not necessarily supplant similar covenants appearing in employment agreements. For instance, an employment agreement might have a noncompetition period that extends for a specified period following termination of employment, while the noncompetition agreement for a seller will usually extend for a specified period following closing.

Tax consequences flow from the manner in which noncompetition covenants are documented. With respect to the specific allocation of the purchase price to the noncompetition covenant, *see* "Allocation" in commentary to Section 2.2. Whether or not separately provided for, the amount of the purchase price allocated to a covenant not to compete is amortizable for federal tax purposes by the buyer over a 15-year period. The same amount is includible in income of the seller as ordinary income in accordance with the applicable tax accounting method. Sellers will generally prefer that none of the purchase price be allocated to the noncompetition covenant because it must be reported as ordinary income rather than capital gain. Because a noncompetition covenant is amortizable over a 15-year period, the incentive for a buyer to insist that part of the purchase price be allocated to the noncompetition covenant is reduced. Nevertheless, except where the stock purchase is treated for tax purposes as an asset purchase from an S corporation, it is still advantageous to the buyer to allocate part of the purchase price to a noncompetition covenant, because the portion allocated to the stock purchase cannot be amortized.

Various nontax issues are raised in connection with attempting to assign a value to noncompetition covenants. If some active shareholders are asked to execute noncompetition covenants and other passive shareholders are not, the active shareholders may feel that the amounts allocated to the noncompetition covenants should be paid to them and not divided in accordance with their equity ownership. Buyers may also be concerned that the value assigned to a noncompetition covenant could be used to limit the liability of shareholders in the event of a breach.

Legal Limitations on Enforceability

General. Noncompetition covenants are agreements in restraint of trade and historically have not been favored by the courts. The courts are more prone, however, to enforce these covenants if they are reasonable in geographic scope and duration and are necessary to protect important business interests such as trade secrets and goodwill. *See* Wilson v. Electro Marine Sys., Inc., 915 F.2d 1110 (7th Cir. 1990) (applying New York and Illinois law).

The question of enforceability is a local one, and the laws of each relevant jurisdiction should be examined both to advise the client regarding whether a noncompetition covenant is likely to be enforced and to structure the covenant in such a way as to maximize its chances of being enforced (which, depending upon the applicable law of the states in question, may require revisions to Section 7.2). Examples of cases from all 50 states in both the sale-of-business and employment context can be found in Committee on Employment Rights and Responsibilities, ABA Section of Labor and Employment Law, Covenants Not to Compete: A State-By-State Survey (6th ed. BNA 2008) as supplemented annually. *See also* Filipp, Covenants Not to Compete (3d ed. Supp. 2009). A complete discussion of the enforceability of noncompetition covenants is beyond the scope of this commentary.

Some states have statutes that deal specifically with the subject, and some states without a statute have extensive case law. Even in states that do not prohibit post-employment noncompetition covenants outside the context of a sale of a business, covenants given in connection with a sale are more likely to be enforced or to have a greater enforceable scope and duration than those given by a nonowner employee. This is because a noncompetition covenant given to a buyer serves to preserve the value of the goodwill that the buyer has purchased. Courts also may be more disposed to enforce covenants in the sale of business context because the seller has more bargaining power than a nonowner employee and is receiving consideration other than wages. *See* Blake, *Employee Agreements Not to Compete*, 73 Harv. Law Rev. 625 (1960); Note, *The Validity of Covenants Not to Compete: Common Law Rules in Illinois Law*, 1978 Ill. L. Forum 249; O'Sullivan v. Conrad, 358 N.E.2d 926 (1976); Business Records Corp. v. Lueth, 981 F.2d 957 (7th Cir. 1992). In California, for example, noncompetition covenants given by employees are generally not enforceable after termination of employment and, hence, buyers should be aware that they may be unable to restrict competition by departing employees of the target. If, however, employees are also owners and enter into the noncompetition covenant in connection with sale of shares of a corporation, covenants may be enforceable with certain limitations. *See* Cal. Bus. & Prof. Code §§ 16600-602.

Approaches to Unreasonable Noncompetition Covenants. Some states adhere to a strict version of the "blue pencil" doctrine, permitting a court only to strike grammatically severable, unreasonable provisions from an otherwise reasonable covenant (i.e., the court uses a blue pencil to strike the unreasonable provision(s) leaving the reasonable provision(s) in effect). If a court in these states finds that editing other than simply deleting the offensive words would be required, it will hold the entire covenant to be unenforceable. The states that have followed this strict "blue pencil" doctrine include Arizona, West Virginia, Indiana, and North Carolina. *See, e.g.,* Valley Medical Specialists v. Farber, 982 P.2d 1277 (Ariz. 1999); Reddy v. Community Health Foundation of Man, 298 S.E.2d 906 (W. Va. 1982); Central Indiana Podiatry, P.C. v. Krueger, 882 N.E.2d 723 (Ind. 2008); Hartman v. W.H. Odell and Associates, Inc., 450 S.E.2d 912 (N.C. App. 1994). For an example of a covenant drafted to survive strict "blue pencil" treatment, *see* commentary to Section 7.2(a)(i).

Many states follow a less strict form of "blue penciling" to reform a covenant ancillary to the sale of a business so as to render it reasonable. Covenants will be enforced only to the extent necessary to protect the interests of the buyer and may be narrowed by judicial ruling. *See, e.g.,* Wells v. Wells, 400 N.E.2d 1317 (1980) (covenant with an unlimited duration is unreasonable, but the court narrowed the covenant to a 52-month duration). In these states, the court will go beyond merely striking unreasonable language, and will actually add a new or different term or rework the existing terms. Among the states that have followed this approach are Illinois, Massachusetts, Minnesota, New Jersey, New York, and Pennsylvania. *See, e.g.,* Joy v. Hay Group, Inc., 2003 WL 22118930 (N.D. Ill. 2003); L.G. Balfour Co. v. McGinnis, 759 F. Supp. 840 (D.D.C. 1991) (applying Massachusetts law); Klick v. Crosstown State Bank of Ham Lake, Inc., 372 N.W.2d 85 (Minn. Ct. App. 1985); Solari Industries, Inc. v. Malady, 264 A.2d 53 (N.J. 1970); BDO Seidman v. Hirshberg, 712 N.E.2d 1220 (N.Y. 1999); Hillard v. Medtronic, Inc., 910 F. Supp. 173 (M.D. Pa. 1995).

Often a provision is inserted to allow a court to reform a covenant that it regards as unreasonable in duration, geographic area, or business scope, even though it might otherwise not rewrite the covenant on its own initiative. *See* Section 7.2(e).

In certain states, courts will not employ the "blue pencil" doctrine (strict or reformation) at all and will find a covenant with unreasonable terms to be unenforceable, even in spite of the inclusion of a severability clause in the contract. Georgia, Virginia, and Wisconsin have followed this approach. *See, e.g.,* Allied Informatics, Inc. v. Yeruva, 554 S.E.2d 550 (Ga. App. 2001); Better Living Components, Inc. v. Coleman, 2005 WL 771592 (Va. Cir. Ct. 2005); General Medical Corp. v. Kobs, 507 N.W.2d 381 (Wis. Ct. App. 1993) (summarizing the requirements of Wis. Stat. § 103.465 governing noncompetition covenants between employers and employees). In these states, the drafting strategy for a buyer may be different because excessive zeal may result in complete rejection of the covenant where a more modest covenant might have survived and be satisfactory to the buyer.

Conflicts of Law. Conflicts of law issues relevant to agreements for a sale of a business are addressed generally in the commentary to Section 12.12. Conflicts of law issues are particularly significant in connection with noncompetition covenants, as courts are particularly likely to depart from a contractual choice of law.

Although the laws of most states place some restrictions on enforceability of noncompetition covenants, the degree of hostility to these covenants and the nature of the limitations vary from state to state. Hence, the question of what law applies to the noncompetition covenant is often of great importance. Under Section 187(2) of Restatement (Second) of Conflict of Laws, the law chosen by the parties to govern their contractual rights and duties will be respected unless (a) the chosen state has no substantial relationship to the parties or the transaction, or (b) the application of law of the chosen state would be contrary to a fundamental public policy of a state that has a materially greater interest than the chosen state in the determination of the particular issue. Because a number of states have very strong public policies regarding noncompetition covenants, application of this standard may well lead a court to apply the law of a state other than the chosen state to deny enforcement of a noncompetition covenant, even in circumstances in which the contractual choice of law would otherwise be upheld for purposes of the acquisition agreement or other documents. *See, e.g.,* Davis v. Ebsco Indus., Inc., 150 So. 2d 460 (Fla. Dist. Ct. App. 1963) (noncompetition covenant in the sale of a business, although valid under New York law, which was the law chosen in the agreement, was not enforced as to sales within Florida because of public policy); *cf.* MedX v. Ranger, 780 F. Supp. 398 (E.D. La. 1991) (federal court applying Louisiana law upholds contractual choice of Florida law in noncompetition covenant given in the sale of a business, reasoning that, although Louisiana had a strong public policy against noncompetition covenants, the Louisiana exception for noncompetition covenants in the sale of a business for up to two years from closing showed that there was no strong public policy, thus permitting application of Florida law even after the two-year limit in Louisiana); Webcraft Technologies Inc. v. McCaw, 674 F. Supp. 1039 (S.D.N.Y. 1987) (New York courts would likely uphold New Jersey choice of law in noncompetition agreement by employee because New York and New Jersey policies were not so seriously in conflict).

Consequently, Buyer may want to suggest a choice of forum (Section 12.13) that is likely to sustain its view or a choice of law (Section 12.12) that will be respected in the circumstances. Consideration might be given to a bifurcated choice of law between the Model Agreement and Section 7.2 or other post-closing covenants, or the post-closing covenants might be placed in a separate agreement with a different governing law, keeping in mind the possible increased burden of bifurcating.

SELLERS' RESPONSE

Joint and Several Liability. Sellers must be mindful that Section 12.4 imposes joint and several liability under the Model Agreement. Imposing liability on all Sellers for violation by an individual Seller for post-closing covenants may be inappropriate. In contrast to pre-closing covenants, where the time period is short and violation of the covenants could dramatically damage the business, liability for a breach of post-closing covenants by one Seller with no continuing relationship to the other Sellers and no control by them may be harsh. Sellers may therefore insist that certain post-closing covenants be contained in individual agreements or that Section 12.4 be revised to remove joint and several liability for post-closing covenants.

Assignment. Section 12.9 permits Buyer to "assign any of its rights and delegate any of its obligations under this Agreement to any Subsidiary of Buyer and, after the Closing, to the purchaser of all or a substantial part of the equity securities or business of the Acquired Companies . . . ." Sellers will want to consider the interplay between Section 12.9 and the covenants in Article 7. An assignment may enlarge the scope of the restrictions imposed on Sellers. If Buyer is a small player in the software business and sells to a large software company, Sellers may be restricted in ways they did not anticipate. If portions of the businesses of the Acquired Companies are sold to several entities, duties may be owned by Sellers to each of them.

   (a) For a period of _____ years after the Closing Date:

   (i)   No Seller shall, directly or indirectly, engage, invest in, own, manage, operate, finance, control, advise, render services to, guarantee the obligations of, be employed by, be associated with, or in any manner be connected with any Person engaged in any business that any Acquired Company conducts as of the Closing Date [in any geographic area in which any Acquired Company conducts such business]; provided, however, that any Seller may acquire or otherwise own less than __% of the outstanding capital stock of a Person that is listed on any national securities exchange [or which is registered under Section 12(g) of the Exchange Act].

COMMENT

The ability of Buyer to secure a meaningful but enforceable noncompetition agreement from Sellers often can be a critical element of an acquisition. Buyer's benefit of the bargain could be significantly diminished if it cannot limit Sellers' ability to compete with the Acquired Companies. This is especially true for the acquisition of a small company where the principal shareholders have intimate knowledge, experience, and contacts within the industry served by the business being sold. Buyer will likely want to assure that its investment will not be adversely affected by direct or indirect competition from Sellers for some reasonable period.

The Model Agreement does not attempt to define a competing business, choosing instead to encompass any business in which any of the Acquired Companies are engaged as of the Closing Date. In some cases, Buyer also may request a restriction against Sellers engaging in any business planned by the Acquired Companies at the time of execution of the Model Agreement. Buyer may ask for restrictions against Sellers engaging in other unrelated lines of business in which Buyer, but not the target, is then engaged. Aside from being hard to justify as being part of the purchase of the Company's good will, the latter prohibition likely would be resisted by Sellers since it bears no relationship to the business being acquired by Buyer and enforceability may be questionable.

The duration of the noncompetition covenant will vary depending both upon negotiating leverage and what is more likely to be enforceable. In those cases where the covenant is being given by someone who is a shareholder but also will serve as an employee after the acquisition, the period requested by a buyer frequently is the longer of a specified number of years after the closing or a number of years after termination of employment.

A buyer in a jurisdiction that follows the strict "blue pencil" doctrine permitting the court only to strike grammatically severable, unreasonable provisions from an otherwise reasonable covenant, might write this covenant as follows: "No Seller shall . . . (i) in an area within 100 miles from where any Acquired Company conducts such business, (ii) within the State of New York, within the State of New Jersey, within the Commonwealth of Pennsylvania, (iii) within the states of the northeastern United States, consisting of the States of New York, Pennsylvania, New Jersey, Maryland, and Delaware, (iv) within the continental United States, and (v) within the world." The technique is to list the components so that the court can literally strike a component while leaving an intelligible sentence.

The Model Agreement permits (as an exception to the noncompetition covenant) ownership of up to a specified percentage of the stock of a company that is listed on a national securities exchange. A percentage is usually selected so as to exclude those not in a position to influence the company's management or policies and thus would properly fall outside the purpose of the restriction. The bracketed language would include a broader range of publicly held companies, as so-called "12(g) companies" may be very small. The percentages of ownership for each category of company may differ.

SELLERS' RESPONSE

Sellers may insist on greater precision as to the nature of involvement, the type of business as to which their activities are restricted, and the scope of the geographical restriction. The covenant is very broadly written, prohibiting involvement with any business, as an employee, owner, or otherwise, that an Acquired Company conducts on the Closing Date. For example, an Acquired Company might be engaged in a small way in the widget business from which it derives 1% of its revenues. Under Section 7.2(a)(i), any Seller would be prohibited from, among other things, rendering services to or otherwise being associated with any widget business. Without including the bracketed language as to geographic areas, the restriction is worldwide. That may be unreasonable where the Acquired Companies have operated on a local level with no prospects of expansion. Even if the bracketed language is included, it might be clarified. Sellers may seek to have the geographical areas specifically designated. Sellers might also seek to reduce the duration of the covenant that will be included in Section 7.2 if it is perceived to be unreasonable or they might want to temper it so that some activities (investment but not active involvement in a business) are either permitted or subject to a shorter duration. Sellers might attempt to carve out specific activities in which they would be permitted to engage.

> **(ii)** **No Seller shall, directly or indirectly, (A) cause, induce, or attempt to cause or induce any employee, agent, or independent contractor of any Acquired Company to terminate such relationship; (B) in any way interfere with the relationship between any Acquired Company and any of its employees, agents, or independent**

contractors; or (C) hire, retain, employ, or otherwise engage or attempt to hire, retain, employ, or otherwise engage as an employee, independent contractor, or otherwise, any employee, agent, or independent contractor of any Acquired Company.

COMMENT

Nonsolicitation restrictions, such as those in subsections (ii) and (iii), offer protections that complement the noncompetition covenants, particularly regarding the prohibition of Sellers from attempting to interfere with any relationship among employees, customers, suppliers, or other third parties and the Acquired Companies. These protections are in many cases equally important to Buyer and often are a substantial part of the overall goodwill being acquired. However, they may be subject to some of the same concerns as to enforceability as noncompetition covenants. This restriction can be more of an issue in the sale of a wholly owned subsidiary where employees of the subsidiary have a relationship with the parent or its affiliates.

SELLERS' RESPONSE

Sellers would probably tailor their response to the circumstances. If Sellers contemplate hiring a trusted employee of the Acquired Companies to work for some of them after the Closing or if they own other businesses that may want to solicit employees, they would need to carve that out of this provision.

> (iii) **No Seller shall, directly or indirectly, (A) solicit, induce, or otherwise cause, or attempt to solicit, induce, or otherwise cause, any customer, supplier, licensor, licensee, or any prospective customer, supplier, licensor, or licensee that has been contacted or targeted for contact by any Acquired Company on or before the Closing Date, or any other person engaged in a business relationship with any Acquired Company, to (1) terminate, curtail, or otherwise modify its relationship with any Acquired Company or (2) engage in business with a competitor of any Acquired Company, or (B) interfere in any way with the relationship between any Acquired Company, and any of its customers, suppliers, licensors, licensees, or any such prospective customers, suppliers, licensors, or licensees, or any other Person engaged in a business relationship with any Acquired Company.**

COMMENT

This provision is worded very broadly. This might be a particular concern to Buyer if the Acquired Companies have under development and have been promoting new products with customers, but will not begin to sell them until after the Closing.

SELLERS' RESPONSE

If any of the Sellers intend to engage in a business, this would be of concern, and they would need to understand the operation of this provision. This restriction will be applicable regardless of whether a Seller in any way is engaged in a competing business.

> **(b) No Seller shall make any disparaging statement, either orally or in writing, regarding Buyer, any Acquired Company, the business, products, or services thereof, or any of their respective shareholders, directors, officers, employees, or agents.**

COMMENT

By this covenant, each Seller binds itself to avoid making any "disparaging statement" about Buyer, the Acquired Companies, or their business. The persons to whom the remarks may be made are not limited. This covenant is designed to protect Buyer from adverse comments, whether before or after the Closing.

SELLERS' RESPONSE

Sellers might insist that this subsection be deleted in its entirety because of its vagueness and because it seems to reach ordinary banter. Otherwise, Sellers may seek to limit its duration (perhaps the length of the noncompetition covenant), or its effect by including materiality or intent standards.

> **(c) For a period from the date of this Agreement until two years after the Closing Date, within 10 days after any Seller entering into an employment, consulting engagement, independent contractor engagement, partnership, or other business association with any Person, each such Seller shall advise Buyer of the identity and address of such Person. Buyer may notify each such Person that such Seller is bound by this Section 7.2 and may furnish each such Person with a copy of applicable provisions of this Agreement.**

COMMENT

This subsection is intended to provide Buyer some means of enforcing the covenants in Section 7.2. Each Seller is required to inform Buyer of normal commercial relationships that the Seller enters into and permits Buyer to notify those persons that Seller is bound by Section 7.2 and furnish the applicable provisions of the Model Agreement. Often a new employer or other party would be willing to honor these restrictions, but it cannot honor what it does not know.

SELLERS' RESPONSE

Sellers will argue that they intend to abide by their covenants, and that Buyer's attempt to provide a compliance mechanism is overkill. Sellers may be concerned that Buyer's notification may not be understood and could interfere with a proper business relationship. This could particularly affect those Sellers who are not involved in the business of the Acquired Companies, and creates a possibility that Buyer would disclose the pending transaction to persons who are not bound by any confidentiality obligation where there is less need to do so. Therefore, Sellers may insist that this provision be removed.

> **(d) Each Seller agrees that this Section 7.2, including the provisions relating to duration, geographical area, and scope, is reasonable and necessary to protect and preserve Buyer's and the Acquired Companies' legitimate business interests and the value of the Shares and the Acquired Companies, and to prevent an unfair advantage from being conferred on any Seller.**

COMMENT

This provision extracts acknowledgments from Sellers affecting the enforceability of the noncompetition covenant. Courts may not require it as a condition to enforceability, but it might be helpful to be able to point to a specific acknowledgement of the parties' intent.

An alternative formulation is as follows:

> Sellers acknowledge that (a) the business of the Acquired Companies prior to Closing is [national] [international] in scope; (b) its products and services related to such business are marketed throughout the [United States] [world]; (c) the Acquired Companies' business prior to Closing competes with other businesses that are or could be located in any part of the [United States] [world]; (d) Buyer has required that Seller make the covenants set forth in this Section 7.2 as a condition to Buyer's purchase of the Shares; (e) the provisions of this Section 7.2 are reasonable and necessary to protect and preserve the Acquired Companies' business from and after the Closing; and (f) the Acquired Companies would be irreparably damaged if Sellers were to breach the covenants set forth in this Section 7.2.

> **(e) If any provision of this Section 7.2 would be held to be excessively broad as to duration, geographical area, scope, activity, or subject, for any reason, such provision shall be modified, by limiting and reducing it, so as to be enforceable to the extent allowed by applicable Legal Requirements.**

237

COMMENT

Although courts in many jurisdictions will reform overly broad provisions so as to allow enforcement and to further the parties' intent, some jurisdictions will invalidate the entire covenant. Conversely, restrictions that are drafted too narrowly, although enforceable, may result in Buyer facing unanticipated competition in markets where it does business, or within certain business segments. This could result in a significant loss of value to Buyer.

This savings clause is intended to invite a court to "blue pencil" or reform the noncompetition covenant to render it enforceable and thus permit Buyer to draft a more comprehensive provision than it might otherwise seek if the only remedy for an overbroad provision was to strike it in its entirety. *See* commentary to this Section 7.2.

(f) Each Seller acknowledges that any Breach of this Section 7.2 would result in serious and irreparable injury to Buyer, Buyer could not be adequately compensated by monetary damages alone, and Buyer's remedy at law would not be adequate. Therefore, each Seller acknowledges and agrees that, in the event of a Breach by any such Seller, Buyer shall be entitled, in addition to any other remedy at law or in equity to which Buyer may be entitled, to equitable relief against such Seller, including temporary restraining orders and preliminary and permanent injunctions to restrain such Seller from such Breach and to compel compliance with the obligations of such Seller, and each Seller waives the posting of a bond or undertaking as a condition to such relief.

COMMENT

This provision may make it easier for Buyer to obtain injunctive relief against Sellers.

Section 12.16 relates generally to the enforcement of the Model Agreement, authorizing specific performance and injunctive relief. While Section 12.16 would be applicable to relief under this Section 7.2, Section 7.2(f) is intended, by its proximity and specificity, to relate to Section 7.2.

Often the posting of a bond is statutorily required when injunctive relief is granted, and this provision purports to waive that requirement. However, although some courts have held that the statutory requirement cannot be waived, the existence of this clause may permit the court to minimize the amount of the required bond.

SELLERS' RESPONSE

Sellers may wish to pare back the acknowledgments and agreements. For instance, in the first sentence Sellers may only want to acknowledge that a Breach *"could result in serious and irreparable injury"* and in the second sentence, "Buyer shall be entitled *to seek . . . ."* Seller may also wish to object to any waiver of the posting of a bond or undertaking as a condition to relief.

7.3 CONFIDENTIALITY

(a) **As used in this Section 7.3, the term "Confidential Information" includes any of the following information held or used by or relating to any Acquired Company:**

    (i) **all information that is a Trade Secret;**

    (ii) **all information concerning product specifications, data, know-how, formulae, compositions, processes, designs, sketches, photographs, graphs, drawings, samples, inventions and ideas, past, current, and planned research and development, current and planned manufacturing or distribution methods and processes, computer hardware, Software and computer software, database technologies, systems, structures and architectures; and**

    (iii) **all information concerning the business and affairs of any Acquired Company, including historical and current financial statements, financial projections and budgets, tax returns and accountants' materials, historical, current, and projected sales, capital spending budgets and plans, business plans, strategic plans, marketing and advertising plans, publications, client and customer and prospect lists and files, current and anticipated customer requirements, price lists, market studies, Contracts, the names and backgrounds of key personnel and personnel training techniques and materials, however documented.**

(b) **Each Seller acknowledges the confidential and proprietary nature of the Confidential Information and agrees that such Seller shall, except to the extent required for a Seller who is employed by an Acquired Company to fulfill his or her duties in the course of such employment, from and after the Closing: (i) keep the Confidential Information confidential and deliver promptly to Buyer, or immediately destroy at Buyer's option, all embodiments and copies of the Confidential Information that are in such Seller's possession; (ii) not use the Confidential Information for any reason or purpose; and (iii) without limiting the foregoing, not disclose the Confidential Information to any Person, except with Buyer's Consent.**

COMMENT

Information properly belonging to a target may be commingled with Sellers' personal information and regarded by Sellers as their own. Buyer has a legitimate concern about maintaining the confidentiality of this information.

Section 7.3(b) sets forth the post-closing requirement that Sellers indefinitely maintain the confidentiality of all Confidential Information, deliver to Buyer or destroy at Buyer's option any embodiments and copies of Confidential Information, not use any Confidential Information for any purpose, and not disclose any Confidential Information without Buyer's consent.

These provisions are intended to protect Buyer from the use or disclosure by Sellers of any Confidential Information that is proprietary to the Acquired Companies. It can be an important covenant to Buyer, which has a right to expect exclusive ownership and control over the Confidential Information. Note, however, that overly restrictive confidentiality agreements may be invalidated as being in restraint of trade. *See, e.g.,* Island Air, Inc. v. LaBar, 566 P.2d 972 (Wash. Ct. App. 1977).

It is often easier to prevent disclosures than to sue for breach. In addition to relying on a general covenant, Buyer might consider identifying Confidential Information in the hands of Sellers and crafting a covenant requiring Sellers to deliver the Confidential Information back to the Acquired Companies as a condition to closing.

See STARK ch. 13.

SELLERS' RESPONSE

The term "Confidential Information" includes information held or used by or relating to any Acquired Company. This would extend to information developed before or while a Seller is a shareholder of the Company, as well as information developed after a Seller's relationship with the Acquired Companies ends. Therefore, Sellers may wish to limit Confidential Information to information possessed by Sellers prior to the Closing Date.

Sellers may want to limit the time period during which the restriction will apply, rather than agreeing to an indefinite time period. Often the confidentiality agreements used when a target is in the process of being sold have a definite and rather short time period during which confidentiality is to be maintained on the theory that this type of information (other than perhaps information rising to the level of Trade Secrets) becomes stale over time.

Sellers cannot use the Confidential Information for any reason or purposes. This is a very broad restriction that goes beyond disclosure. For example, they might be prohibited from filing their own tax returns or providing their salary information to the extent they "use" Confidential Information. Sellers therefore may suggest that this requirement be conditioned by materiality, limited to some type of commercial use that might adversely affect the Acquired Companies, or qualified by specific carve-outs.

(c) Section 7.3(b) does not apply to that part of the Confidential Information that becomes generally available to the public other than as a result of a Breach of this Section 7.3 by any Seller. Confidential Information shall not be deemed "generally available to the public" merely because it is included or incorporated in more general information that is publicly available or because it combines features which individually may be publicly available.

COMMENT

Confidentiality agreements normally have an exclusion for information that otherwise becomes available to the general public. However, other normal exceptions to a confidentiality agreement, such as information that comes into the hands of the recipient without a breach of duty and independently developed information, have not been included since Sellers were once privy to this information. The second sentence makes it clear that information is not considered publicly available simply because certain elements may be publicly known. It may be the particular combination of elements that contain value and that the Buyer will want to maintain as confidential.

(d) If any Seller becomes compelled in any Proceeding to make any disclosure that is prohibited by this Section 7.3, such Seller shall, to the extent legally permissible, provide Buyer with prompt notice of such compulsion so that Buyer may seek an appropriate protective order or other appropriate remedy or waive compliance with the provisions of this Section 7.3. In the absence of a protective order or other remedy, such Seller may disclose that portion (and only that portion) of the Confidential Information that, based upon the opinion of such Seller's counsel, such Seller is legally compelled to disclose; provided, however, that such Seller shall use its best efforts to obtain written assurance that any Person to whom any Confidential Information is so disclosed shall accord confidential treatment to such Confidential Information.

COMMENT

Sellers are permitted to disclose Confidential Information if legally compelled to do so as part of a judicial or other proceeding, although in that event Sellers must notify Buyer to afford Buyer the opportunity to prevent disclosure if it so chooses, and must use their best efforts to obtain from the person to whom Confidential Information is disclosed an assurance that it will be kept confidential. To the extent that information may be produced to a court without a protective order, it may be public information.

SELLERS' RESPONSE

Sellers might object to the proviso in the last sentence of the subsection, requiring that they use best efforts to obtain written assurance that the information disclosed be treated confidentially. Since the Confidential Information would be disclosed in a court proceeding, best efforts could extend to obtaining a protective order, which is inconsistent with the first sentence of the subsection that makes obtaining such an order Buyer's obligation. Further, the requirement that Sellers obtain an opinion of counsel in responding, for example, to an ordinary subpoena, may be objectionable; as a compromise, requiring Sellers to obtain advice of counsel may be less objectionable.

Sellers may desire broader permission than contemplated in this subsection, such as being allowed to make any disclosure required by law.

> **(e) Nothing in this Section 7.3 will diminish the protections and benefits under applicable Legal Requirements to which any Trade Secret of any Acquired Company is entitled. If any information that an Acquired Company asserts to be a Trade Secret under applicable Legal Requirements is found by a court of competent jurisdiction not to be such a Trade Secret, such information will nonetheless be considered Confidential Information of that Acquired Company for purposes of this Section 7.3.**

COMMENT

This subsection is intended to protect Buyer from the disclosure of any Confidential Information by Sellers, notwithstanding that an Acquired Company might have lost a claim that the Confidential Information is a Trade Secret. Sellers thus cannot benefit from a third party's successful challenge of an Acquired Company's rights to a Trade Secret. *See* commentary to Section 3.22.

7.4 CUSTOMER AND OTHER BUSINESS RELATIONSHIPS

> **(a) After the Closing, each Seller shall cooperate with Buyer and the Acquired Companies in their efforts to continue and maintain for the benefit of Buyer and the Acquired Companies those business relationships of any Acquired Company and of such Seller relating to the business of any Acquired Company, including relationships with any customers, suppliers, licensors, licensees, lessors, employees, regulatory authorities, and others. Each Seller shall refer to Buyer and the Acquired Companies all inquiries and communications received by such Seller relating to any Acquired Company after the Closing.**

COMMENT

The seamless continuation of the business being acquired after the Closing requires the transition of relationships with third parties and is an important component of the goodwill being acquired. Section 7.4(a) sets forth Sellers' affirmative obligation to assist Buyer in maintaining these customer and other business relationships after the Closing. Without such an obligation, Sellers would have no obligation to assist with the post-closing transition of customers, employees, suppliers, or other third parties. In many cases, this assistance will be critical to Buyer, particularly where Sellers enjoy direct relationships with these third parties. Similarly, Sellers are required to refer to Buyer all inquiries and other communications relating to any Acquired Company, which also can be important to the continuation of the business.

SELLERS' RESPONSE

Sellers would want to understand the degree of cooperation that is contemplated or required by Section 7.4(a). This cooperation might not apply to Sellers not active in the business. If a Seller, other than one who remains employed after the Closing, will be required to spend a significant amount of time, he or she may want to be compensated for these efforts or at least be reimbursed for costs. It is not unusual for consulting agreements to be entered into making certain Sellers goodwill ambassadors and providing for compensation, in which case Sellers might ask that the first sentence be deleted and an appropriate agreement be added to the closing deliverables to be signed only by the appropriate Sellers. Sellers may want to limit the period of cooperation. Sellers may also want to clarify which inquiries and communications are required to be referred to the Acquired Companies, for example, limiting them to those relating to the business or affairs of the Acquired Companies.

(b) After the Closing, no Seller shall take any action, either directly or indirectly, that could diminish the value of any Acquired Company or interfere with the business of any Acquired Company.

COMMENT

Section 7.4(b) provides that Sellers must refrain from taking any direct or indirect action that could diminish the value of any Acquired Company or interfere with the business of any Acquired Company. This restriction expands upon that contained in Section 7.2(a)(iii) which expressly prevents Seller from interfering with any third-party relationships. Although in certain instances Buyer might have common law tort claims against a Seller for engaging in this activity, this subsection might impose liability without requiring Buyer to prove intent, thereby reducing its burden of proof.

SELLERS' RESPONSE

Sellers may object to the indefiniteness of this provision and ask to have it deleted. If the provision is not deleted, Sellers might insist that, while not precisely overlapping, the thrust of this provision should be covered by the noncompetition or nondisparagement provisions. Sellers might suggest that "materially" be inserted prior to "diminish" and "interfere," or they might insist that "could" in the second line be changed to "such Seller knows will." Sellers might suggest that "either directly or indirectly" be omitted.

8. Conditions Precedent to Buyer's Obligation to Close

PRELIMINARY NOTE

Articles 8 and 9 set forth, respectively, the conditions precedent to Sellers' and Buyer's obligations to close the acquisition. If any of the conditions in Article 8 or 9 are not satisfied, Buyer or Sellers, as the case may be, could decline to proceed with the acquisition. The failure of a condition may also give them the right, under certain circumstances, to terminate the Model Agreement pursuant to Article 10. A party's right to refuse to close an acquisition when a condition remains unsatisfied often is referred to as a "walk right" or an "out." Conditions such as these are only required when the closing is deferred, and would not be necessary if the closing occurs concurrently with signing the acquisition agreement. For a general discussion of closing conditions, *see* KLING & NUGENT ch. 14.

The interpretation of closing conditions, and in particular whether a buyer can properly claim a failure of a condition as justification for walking away from an acquisition, has been the subject of a number of court decisions. This litigation often centers around conditions relating to the accuracy of representations, such as Section 8.1, and the occurrence of a "material adverse effect" or "material adverse change," such as Section 8.12. *See, e.g.,* Hexion Specialty Chems., Inc. v. Huntsman Corp., 995 A.2d 715 (Del. Ch. 2008) (disappointing quarterly earnings); Genesco, Inc. v. The Finish Line, Inc., No. 07-2137 (Tenn. Ch. Dec. 27, 2007) (decline in financial performance); Frontier Oil Corp. v. Holly Corp., 2005 Del. Ch. LEXIS 57 (mass tort litigation); *In re* IBP, Inc. S'holders Litig., 789 A.2d 14 (Del. Ch. 2001) (write-offs relating to accounting problems, decline in financial performance, and asset impairment). *See* the definition of "Material Adverse Change" and related commentary in Section 1.1.

There is a fundamental difference between closing conditions, on the one hand, and representations and covenants, on the other. Although the accuracy of representations and performance of covenants by the parties also operate as closing conditions, some closing conditions are not based upon representations or covenants. If Sellers fail to satisfy any of these closing conditions, Buyer may have the right not to close the acquisition, but, unless there has also been a separate misrepresentation or breach of a covenant, Sellers will not be liable to Buyer for their failure to satisfy the condition. However, Sellers are obligated in Section 5.7 to use their best efforts to satisfy all the conditions in Article 8, other than Section 8.11, so they may be liable if they fail to use their best efforts to satisfy these conditions, even those that are not based upon representations or covenants of Sellers.

This difference can be illustrated by examining the remedies that may be exercised by Buyer if Sellers fail to obtain the Material Consents referred to in Section 8.4. Because obtaining each of the Material Consents is a condition to Buyer's obligation to close the acquisition, Buyer may elect not to close as a result of the failure to obtain any of the Material Consents. Assuming the Material Consents are all properly identified in the Disclosure Letter as exceptions to Sellers' representations in Section 3.2(c), there would be no misrepresentation, either when the Model Agreement is signed or at the Closing Date, for which Buyer can seek recovery. Furthermore, the delivery of the Material Consents is not an absolute covenant of Sellers. Accordingly, Sellers' failure to obtain the Material Consents will not, in and of itself, render Sellers liable to Buyer. Sellers could, however, be liable to Buyer under Section 5.7 if they failed to use their best efforts to satisfy the condition in Section 8.4, even though they lack the power to obtain the Material Consents without the cooperation of a third party. *See* commentary to Section 5.7. For a discussion of the relationship and interplay between representations, covenants, conditions, and indemnification provisions in acquisition agreements, *see* FREUND 153–72. *See also* M&A PROCESS 228–31.

Buyer's obligations to purchase the Shares and to take the other actions required pursuant to this Agreement to be taken by Buyer at the Closing are subject to the satisfaction, at or prior to the Closing, of each of the following conditions (any of which may be waived in whole or in part by Buyer):

COMMENT

The number and scope of the conditions to Buyer's obligations will depend upon the circumstances and the relative bargaining power of the parties. Article 8 includes conditions more numerous and broader in scope than those found in many acquisition agreements. Even so, it does not provide an exhaustive list. For example, a buyer may want to add a "due diligence out," making the buyer's obligation to purchase shares subject to satisfactory completion of its due diligence investigation relating to the business of the target. A buyer may find it difficult to persuade a seller to include such a condition because it would give the buyer a very broad "walk right" and in effect turn the acquisition agreement into an option to purchase the shares of the target. Such a condition has not been included in the Model Agreement because it is assumed that Buyer's due diligence has been completed by the time the Model Agreement is signed. When this is not the case or verification of some of the information provided in the due diligence investigation is still needed, a due diligence condition might be appropriate. For a discussion of "due diligence" conditions, *see* KLING & NUGENT § 14.10.

Other conditions often include meeting specified financial thresholds, such as revenues, EBITDA or net worth, or some other measures of financial performance, or divesting certain operations or assets. The commentary to Sections 8.5 and 8.6 suggest that certain Governmental Authorizations or the delivery of certain documents or agreements might also be added as stand-alone conditions to Buyer's obligation to close the acquisition.

Buyer may waive in whole or in part any of the conditions to its obligation to close the acquisition. *See* STARK § 16.06. Section 12.17 requires that any waiver be in writing signed by the party giving the waiver. This is an attempt to avoid a court determining that a condition is waived by conduct of the parties. *See, e.g.,* Merchant Wired LLC v. Transaction Network Services, Inc., Del. Super., C.A. No. 02C-08-244, Feb. 28, 2005 (seller permitted to go forward with a breach of contract lawsuit if it could show that the buyer—in writing or through conduct—either extended the closing deadline or waived a condition); *see also* STARK § 16.07. On the other hand, if Buyer proceeds with the acquisition with knowledge that a condition has not been satisfied, Buyer may have difficulty arguing that a waiver has not occurred. Buyer's acceptance of substitute performance under contract law may discharge Sellers from a claim under the indemnification provision in Section 11.2 for a misrepresentation that caused the condition not to be satisfied. *See* preliminary note to Article 11. Certain conditions, such as Section 8.5 requiring the receipt of Governmental Authorizations, can always be waived, but the failure to receive some Governmental Authorizations can result in liability or restrictions on future operations, or even having to unwind the transaction. Even if the Buyer had no knowledge that a condition was not met, it may have no effective remedy for the failed condition if it closes the acquisition.

SELLERS' RESPONSE

Each of the conditions in Article 8 provides Buyer the right to walk away from the acquisition and, under certain circumstances, terminate the Model Agreement pursuant to Article 10. Accordingly, Sellers' goal will be to limit these conditions to the greatest extent possible. Most problematic are the types of conditions over which Buyer has sole control and can exercise discretion. If Sellers are unsuccessful in eliminating these conditions, they might seek to narrow the scope or limit the time during which they can be exercised. For example, if Buyer insists on adding a "due diligence out," Sellers might require that Buyer limit its due diligence to certain matters or specify a date before the scheduled Closing Date by which Buyer must exercise its "due diligence out."

8.1   ACCURACY OF SELLERS' REPRESENTATIONS

(a) **Subject to Section 8.1(b), each of Sellers' representations and warranties in this Agreement will have been accurate in all material respects as of the date of this Agreement and will be accurate in all material respects as of the Closing Date as if then made, without giving effect to any supplement to the Disclosure Letter.**

(b) Each of Sellers' representations and warranties in Sections 3.2(a), 3.3, 3.4, 3.12, and 3.29, and each of the representations and warranties in this Agreement that contains an express materiality qualification, will have been accurate in all respects as of the date of this Agreement and will be accurate in all respects as of the Closing Date as if then made, without giving effect to any supplement to the Disclosure Letter.

COMMENT

Section 8.1 provides that Sellers' representations function as closing conditions. Thus, the inaccuracy of their representations provides Buyer with a possible basis for exercising a "walk right" and electing not to close the acquisition. Sometimes this provision is expanded to include representations contained in any certificate, document, or other writing delivered pursuant to the acquisition agreement, as well as those in the agreement itself. Even if not included in the condition, the accuracy of these certificates, documents, and other writings can be subject to indemnification, such as in Section 11.2(a). For a discussion of the pre-closing discovery of a misrepresentation or breach of a covenant, *see* M&A PROCESS 274–77.

Materiality Qualification in Section 8.1(a). Section 8.1(a) allows Buyer to refuse to complete the acquisition if each of Sellers' representations is not accurate in all material respects. Most of Sellers' representations do not contain a materiality qualification (*see* "'Materiality' Qualifications" in preliminary note to Article 3), so the addition of a materiality qualification in Section 8.1(a) prevents Buyer from using an immaterial breach of any of Sellers' representations as an excuse for electing not to close the acquisition. *See* Appendix D—Nine Hypothetical Scenarios (scenarios 4, 8, and 9).

Materiality under Section 8.1(a) is measured on an individual basis, so that the material inaccuracy of any representation may result in a failure of the condition. Buyer may prefer to provide that each representation individually, and all representations in the aggregate, must be accurate in all material respects, on the theory that this would aggregate nonmaterial inaccuracies to the point that they become material. The risk, however, is that a court might determine the test is really to be made only on an aggregate, rather than an individual, basis.

Absence of "Materiality" Qualification in Section 8.1(b). Certain of Sellers' representations may be so fundamental that Buyer will want to retain the ability to terminate the acquisition if they are inaccurate in any respect. Consider, for example, Sellers' representation in Section 3.3 that sets forth the capitalization of the Company and its Subsidiaries, including the number of Shares that are issued and outstanding and are owned by Sellers. Assume that Sellers own that number of shares, but Buyer discovers shortly before the Closing that a third party also owns shares. Buyer will likely consider it highly undesirable to acquire shares of a target that has even one minority shareholder, no matter how insignificant the percentage interest represented by those shares. Accordingly, Buyer would not want to give

Sellers an opportunity to argue that this representation is accurate in all material respects and therefore require that Buyer proceed with the acquisition. Section 8.9 also contains a condition as to the absence of a claim that a third party is the holder or beneficial owner of any Equity Security of any Acquired Company or is entitled to all or any portion of the Purchase Price.

A few of Sellers' representations (such as the "no Material Adverse Change" representation in Section 3.12 and the "disclosure" representation in Section 3.29) are dealt with separately in Section 8.1(b) because they already contain express materiality qualifications. Section 3.4 has been included because GAAP contains its own materiality standards. Therefore, these representations must be accurate "in all respects" (rather than merely "in all material respects"). While there is some disagreement among practitioners as to whether this is an actual or merely a theoretical concern, this provision is an effort to avoid weakening the condition through what is referred to as "double materiality" (i.e., a representation already containing a materiality qualification must be accurate in all material respects). For a further discussion of "double materiality" issues, *see* FREUND 245–46; KLING & NUGENT § 14.02[3].

In some agreements, a condition will contain a materiality qualification and then simply carve out as exceptions those representations that must be accurate "in all respects." An example of this formulation follows:

> Each of Sellers' representations and warranties in this Agreement will have been accurate in all material respects as of the date of this Agreement and will be accurate in all material respects as of the Closing Date as if then made, except to the extent that such representations and warranties are qualified by the terms "material" or "materially" [or by terms such as "material adverse effect" or "Material Adverse Change"], in which case such representations and warranties (as so written with such qualifications) shall be accurate in all respects as of the date of this Agreement and will be accurate in all respects as of the Closing Date, without giving effect in either case to any supplement to the Disclosure Letter.

Operation of the "Bring Down" Clause. Subsections (a) and (b) each contain two clauses, one focusing on the accuracy of Sellers' representations on the date of the Model Agreement, and the other as of the Closing Date. By virtue of this second clause—referred to as a "bring down" clause—Sellers' representations are "brought down" to the Closing Date to determine their accuracy as if made on that date. The "bring down" clause is intended to protect Buyer from significant changes in the business of the Acquired Companies by affording it with the right to refuse to close the acquisition or, if it is closed without taking an exception to the "bring down" certificate required by Section 8.3, with the right to seek indemnification. For a discussion of the significance of this clause, *see* commentary to the lead-in clause to Article 3.

The application of the "bring down" clause will depend on the wording of the particular representation. Consider, for example, the representation in Section 3.4 concerning the Acquired Companies' financial statements. This representation states that the Financial Statements "fairly present the consolidated financial condition . . . of the Company and its Subsidiaries as at the respective dates of . . . the Financial Statements." The "bring down" clause in Section 8.1 does not require, as a condition to Buyer's obligation to close, that these historical financial statements also fairly present the Acquired Companies' financial condition as of the Closing Date. The inclusion of the phrase "as at the respective dates" precludes the representation from being "brought down" to the Closing Date pursuant to Section 8.1(b) except to the extent related to the specific dates as noted. For a discussion of the "bring down" of representations that incorporate specific time periods, see "Representations Incorporating Specific Time Periods" in preliminary note to Article 3.

Effect of Disclosure Letter Supplements. Subsections (a) and (b) provide that supplements to the Disclosure Letter will have no effect for purposes of determining the accuracy of Sellers' representations. This ensures Buyer that its "walk rights" will be preserved notwithstanding any disclosures made by Sellers after the signing of the Model Agreement.

The importance of negating the effect of supplements to the Disclosure Letter can be illustrated by the following example. Assume that a material lawsuit is brought against the Company after signing and that Sellers promptly disclose the lawsuit to Buyer in a Disclosure Letter supplement as required by Section 5.4. Assume further that the lawsuit remains pending on the Closing Date. In these circumstances, the representation in Section 3.15(a) (which states that, except as disclosed in the Disclosure Letter, there are no legal proceedings pending against any Acquired Company) will be deemed accurate as of the Closing Date if the Disclosure Letter supplement is taken into account, but would be inaccurate if the supplement is not taken into account. Because Section 8.1 provides specifically that supplements to the Disclosure Letter are not to be given effect, Buyer may decide not to close and be able to terminate the Model Agreement. *See* Appendix D—Nine Hypothetical Scenarios (scenario 5).

SELLERS' RESPONSE

Materiality Qualification. Under Section 8.1(a), materiality is measured on an individual basis, so that the material inaccuracy of any representation will result in a failure of the condition. Sellers might try to make the condition much easier to satisfy by making an exception for the inaccuracy of representations that have not had a material adverse effect on the Acquired Companies taken as a whole. The following is an example of such a condition:

> Each of Sellers' representations and warranties in this Agreement will have been accurate in all respects as of the date of this Agreement and will be accurate in all respects as of the Closing Date as if then made, interpreted

without giving effect to any supplement to the Disclosure Letter, except where the failure of such representations and warranties to be accurate as of the date of this Agreement or as of the Closing Date would not, in the aggregate, have a materially adverse effect on the business, condition (financial or otherwise), assets, or results of operations of the Acquired Companies taken as a whole.

Another possibility is to define materiality as a specific dollar amount, which would operate akin to the indemnification "threshold" in Section 11.6. This might be satisfactory for those representations where materiality can be quantified, but not for those where quantification would be difficult.

Accuracy of Representations When Made. Although it is unlikely that Sellers would object to the inclusion of a standard "bring down" clause, they may object to the first clause in Section 8.1, which requires that Sellers' representations be accurate on the date of the Model Agreement. This clause permits Buyer to terminate the acquisition because of a representation that was materially inaccurate when made, even if the inaccuracy has been fully cured by the Closing Date, thus giving the Buyer a free "walk right" that may be used for some reason unrelated to the misrepresentation. If Sellers object, Buyer may point out that the elimination of this clause would permit Sellers to sign the acquisition agreement knowing that their representations were inaccurate at that time with the expectation that they will be able to cure the inaccuracies before the closing. This possibility could seriously undermine the disclosure function of Sellers' representations (*see* "Purposes of Sellers' Representations" in preliminary note to Article 3) and may compromise Buyer's due diligence function and procedure. *See* KLING & NUGENT § 14.02[1].

Operation of the "Bring Down" Clause. Sellers can attempt to make it clear that certain representations speak as of the date of the Model Agreement or some other specific date and are not to be "brought down" to the Closing Date. For example, they may be concerned that the representation in Section 3.17(a)(i) (which states that the Disclosure Letter lists all of the Applicable Contracts meeting specified criteria) would be rendered inaccurate as of the Closing Date if the Acquired Companies were to enter into any of these types of contracts as part of their routine business operations between signing and the Closing Date. Because Section 8.1 does not give effect to supplements to the Disclosure Letter, Sellers would not be able to eliminate Buyer's "walk right" in this situation simply by listing the new contracts in a Disclosure Letter supplement. To avoid Buyer having a "walk right" tied to routine actions taken in the normal course of the Acquired Companies' business operations, Sellers may want the representation in Section 3.17(a) to be introduced by the phrase "as of the date of this Agreement" so that it will not be "brought down" to the Closing Date. Buyer may respond that, if the new contracts are not really material, the representation in Section 3.17(a)(i) would remain accurate in all material respects and the condition would be satisfied.

To eliminate any possible uncertainty about the proper interpretation of the "bring down" clause where dates are specified, Sellers also may want to modify the clause to include a specific exception for representations made as of a particular date. The following shows how such an exception might be added to Section 8.1(a):

> Subject to Section 8.1(b), each of Sellers' representations and warranties in this Agreement will have been accurate in all material respects as of the date of this Agreement and will be accurate in all material respects as of the Closing Date as if then made (except to the extent such representations and warranties are as of a specified date, they need only be accurate in all material respects as of such specified date), without giving effect to any supplement to the Disclosure Letter.

A similar exception would also be added to Section 8.1(b).

Sellers may also request that the "bring down" clause be modified to clarify that Buyer will not have a "walk right" if any of their representations are rendered inaccurate as a result of an occurrence specifically contemplated by the Model Agreement. The requested modification entails inserting in Section 8.1 the words "except as contemplated or permitted by this Agreement" or some similar qualification. For example, announcement of the proposed acquisition by Buyer may cause some employees to leave and receive severance payments or customers to give notice of termination of their contracts, which may cause the representations in Section 3.16 to be inaccurate when brought down to the Closing Date. While Sellers might use this type of example to illustrate the appropriateness of the requested modification, Buyer could counter that such a deterioration in the business is precisely what the "bring down" of that representation is intended to avoid. Furthermore, it may be difficult to determine whether a particular inaccuracy arose as a result of something "contemplated" or "permitted" by the Model Agreement. *See* KLING & NUGENT § 14.02[4]. Buyer may argue that if Sellers are truly concerned, they should propose specific exceptions to their representations that Buyer can consider, rather than relying on a potentially overbroad qualification in the "bring down" clause. The qualification "permitted" by the Model Agreement is particularly dangerous for the Buyer, because it can be read as meaning "not prohibited."

Effect of Disclosure Letter Supplements. Sellers might attempt to convince Buyer that the accuracy of their representations at the Closing should take into account supplements to the Disclosure Letter, at least where the new information provided in the supplement does not constitute a material adverse change or arises in the ordinary course of business. In any event, if Buyer elects to close knowing the information provided in a supplement, Sellers may seek to have Buyer forfeit its right to bring a claim for indemnification. Even when supplements to the Disclosure Letter are not given effect for purposes of determining whether a buyer has a "walk right," they sometimes are given effect in determining whether a buyer has a right to indemnification after the closing. However, Section 11.2(a) of the Model Agreement provides for indemnification for a misstatement without giving effect to any supplement to the Disclosure Letter. For a discussion of this provision, *see* commentary to Section 11.2(a). The more severe problem for the Buyer is that permitting supplemental information to alter representations effectively guts the purpose of the "bring down."

Sections Designated in Section 8.1(b). Sellers may want to exclude certain portions of the Sections designated in Section 8.1(b), so they would have the benefit of the materiality qualification in Section 8.1(a). Consideration might be given in particular to certain portions of Sections 3.3 and 3.4.

8.2   SELLERS' PERFORMANCE

The covenants and obligations that each Seller is required to perform or to comply with pursuant to this Agreement at or prior to the Closing will have been duly performed and complied with in all material respects.

COMMENT

Under Section 8.2, Sellers' pre-closing covenants and obligations function as closing conditions. Thus, if Sellers breach any of their pre-closing covenants in a material respect, Buyer will have a "walk right" in addition to its right to sue and recover damages from Sellers because of the breach. This condition is closely related to the representations condition in Section 8.1, and sometimes is included as part of that condition. The condition also refers to obligations, because some practitioners feel that this better covers covenants that are outside the portion of the acquisition agreement that addresses pre-closing covenants.

Even though some of the covenants themselves might have materiality or similar qualifications, it is fairly typical to require compliance in "all material respects" in this closing condition. Nevertheless, a buyer might want to distinguish between those covenants that already have a materiality qualification or a performance standard that is less than absolute, and covenants that are so critical that absolute performance should be required in order to close the acquisition.

8.3   BRING DOWN CERTIFICATE

Buyer will have received a certificate executed by each Seller confirming (a) the accuracy of its representations and warranties as of the date of this Agreement and as of the Closing Date in accordance with Section 8.1 and (b) the performance of and compliance with its covenants and obligations to be performed or complied with at or prior to the Closing in accordance with Section 8.2.

COMMENT

Section 8.3 requires as a closing condition that each Seller deliver to Buyer a certificate confirming the accuracy of his or her representations as of the date of the Model Agreement and as of the Closing Date, and the performance of all of his or her covenants and obligations to be performed or complied with at or prior to the Closing. Sometimes the certificate will also confirm the satisfaction of the conditions to Buyer's obligation to close the acquisition.

As indicated by the title to this Section, this type of certificate is called a "bring down" certificate because its purpose is to confirm and "bring down" to the Closing the accuracy of representations and performance of pre-closing covenants. This Section works in conjunction with Section 5.4 that requires Sellers to inform Buyer of inaccuracies of their representations and failures to perform their covenants, and to provide any related supplements to the Disclosure Letter.

The failure of Sellers to deliver these certificates can itself give Buyer a "walk right." However, even if the certificates are delivered by Sellers without qualification, the conditions in Sections 8.1 and 8.2 will operate independently, so that Buyer can still claim that the inaccuracy of the representations or failure of performance of the covenants is justification to exercise a "walk right." Furthermore, if the condition in Section 8.2 is not satisfied, Sellers may still be liable for a breach of their pre-closing obligations. Although delivery of a "bring down" certificate is therefore not necessary to protect Buyer, its use is fairly typical. It will cause Sellers to be more careful and give them pause before signing a certificate they know to be false. Delivery of a false certificate can result in liability for fraud and possibly for breach of contract, as well as being the only basis for indemnification under Section 11.2(a) or (b).

SELLERS' RESPONSE

Sellers might want to insert a "knowledge qualification" with respect to the form of this certificate. Buyer might object on the basis that, like the representations and covenants themselves, it is not a question of what one knows, but rather who should bear the risk for any inaccuracy or breach and the relationship to the right to indemnification. These certificates will typically incorporate or track the language of Sections 8.1 and 8.2 so that the materiality standard in the certificates matches that in those Sections.

It is important to determine which parties should be signing certificates and whose representations and covenants are to be covered. For example, in ABRY Partners V, L.P. v. F&W Acquisition LLC, 891 A.2d 1032 (Del. Ch. 2006), the seller provided a "bring down" certificate that formed the basis for the buyer's ability to assert claims against the seller for representations made by the target. If any of Sellers' representations are inaccurate or there has been a breach of their covenants, they might include an exception in the certificates. From a buyer's standpoint, this then raises a question as to whether its acceptance of the certificates constitutes a waiver.

8.4 CONSENTS

Each of the Consents identified in Exhibit 8.4 (the "Material Consents") will have been obtained in form and substance satisfactory to Buyer and will be in full force and effect. Copies of the Material Consents will have been delivered to Buyer.

COMMENT

Under Section 8.4, Buyer's obligation to close the acquisition is conditioned upon obtaining the Consents that have been identified by the parties on Exhibit 8.4 and are defined as Material Consents. Similarly, Sellers' obligation to close the acquisition is conditioned in Section 9.4 upon obtaining the Consents that have been identified by the parties on Exhibit 9.4. Some Consents may be listed on both Exhibits 8.4 and 9.4 because of their importance to both Buyer and Sellers. For a discussion of consents required as closing conditions, *see* M&A PROCESS 260–61.

Several types of Material Consents might be so identified. Some Consents may be needed because of requirements applicable to the Acquired Companies. These Consents would be among those disclosed in the Disclosure Letter as exceptions to Section 3.2(b) and (c). Because that Section contains no materiality qualifications, some relatively insignificant Consents may be listed in the Disclosure Letter. Accordingly, Section 8.4 will only condition Buyer's obligation to close on obtaining those separately identified as Material Consents, which would generally be those that must be obtained in order to close the acquisition or the lack of which might have a Material Adverse Effect on the ability of the Acquired Companies to carry on their businesses, but could be an even stricter standard insisted upon by Buyer. An example might be a Consent required to be obtained from a third-party landlord under a significant lease containing a "change-in-control" provision. It is possible that Buyer may not have sufficient knowledge about the Acquired Companies' businesses to be comfortable in limiting the required Consents to those identified on Exhibit 8.4. In that case, Section 8.4 might be worded to require not only those Consents identified in Exhibit 8.4, but all other Consents, the failure to obtain which, individually or in the aggregate, could have a Material Adverse Effect on the Acquired Companies.

There may also be Consents that are needed because of legal requirements. Accordingly, there may be some overlap with the condition in Section 8.5 relating to Governmental Authorizations. For example, if applicable, HSR Act clearance may be listed on Exhibits 8.4 and 9.4, as well as being a Governmental Authorization covered by Section 8.5.

Finally, there may be Consents that are needed because of requirements applicable to Buyer and that are among those disclosed under Section 4.2(b) and (c). This might include, for example, a Consent required to be obtained by Buyer from a third-party lender under a loan agreement providing that the lender must approve any major acquisition by Buyer.

The condition in Section 8.4 does not overlap the "bring down" of Sellers' representation in Section 3.2(c). Assume, for example, that one of the Consents listed in the Disclosure Letter cannot be obtained by the scheduled Closing Date. In this situation, Buyer would not automatically have a "walk right" under the "bring down" clause in Section 8.1(a), because the representation in Section 3.2(c), which only identifies the consent as required would remain accurate as of the Closing Date. However, if the withheld Consent were included among those specifically identified as Material Consents, then Buyer would have a "walk right" under Section 8.4. In addition, Sellers are obligated pursuant to Section 5.7 to use their best efforts to cause the condition in Section 8.4 to be satisfied.

SELLERS' RESPONSE

Before executing the Model Agreement, Sellers must determine with Buyer which of the Consents identified under Sections 3.2 and 4.2 are significant enough to justify allowing Buyer to terminate the acquisition if they cannot be obtained, and only those Consents will be identified as Material Consents. To eliminate any later misunderstandings as to what will be required, it may be appropriate to describe, where practical, in or attach to Exhibit 8.4 a description of what documentation would be considered sufficient to satisfy Buyer with respect to some of the Material Consents. This might give Sellers greater comfort in satisfying their best efforts obligation under Section 5.7. If Sellers are unsuccessful with this approach, they could ask that this condition at least be qualified such that the Material Consents must be "in form and substance reasonably satisfactory" to Buyer in an attempt to avoid Buyer acting arbitrarily.

Sellers might object to the inclusion in Exhibit 8.4 of Consents that are needed because of requirements that are applicable to Buyer, because Buyer may have control over obtaining those Consents and use its failure to obtain them to walk away from the acquisition. Sellers may require that these Consents be obtained prior to signing, rather than risking a condition not being satisfied.

The parties often underestimate how difficult it may be to obtain the required consents in a timely manner. Third parties normally have no incentive to deliver their consents and may have concerns that the business relationship will be jeopardized with the proposed change in ownership. The strategy for obtaining these Material Consents must be carefully orchestrated with management of the Acquired Companies. While the parties seeking consents ordinarily bear their own costs, there may be circumstances in which they would negotiate for reimbursement of all or a portion of their costs by the other party. This could be covered in Section 12.1.

8.5   GOVERNMENTAL AUTHORIZATIONS

Buyer will have received such Governmental Authorizations as are necessary or which it considers desirable to allow Buyer to acquire and own the Shares and for the Acquired Companies and Buyer to own and operate the business of each Acquired Company from and after the Closing.

COMMENT

Section 3.14(b) requires Sellers to list all Governmental Authorizations relating to the business or assets of any Acquired Company, and Sellers represent in Section 3.14(c) that these are all the Governmental Authorizations necessary for continuation of the business and ownership and use of the assets in the same manner. This is a starting point for determining what Governmental Authorizations may be needed to satisfy the condition in Section 8.5. Some of the Governmental Authorizations listed will continue to apply to the Acquired Companies after the Closing without any further action, but some may require that transfers or new licenses, permits, or other authority be obtained due to the change in ownership or for other reasons. Examples are environmental licenses or permits pertaining to real property owned or operated by the Acquired Companies, which in some cases may require affirmation that no environmental conditions exist or that any outstanding conditions will be investigated and remediated. In addition, there are some Governmental Authorizations that would not be covered by Section 3.14, but may apply due to the nature of the transaction. Examples are compliance with the HSR Act (*see* commentary to Section 5.3) and the Exon-Florio regulations (*see* commentary to Section 3.2). Sometimes compliance with the HSR Act or Exon-Florio regulations are specifically referenced in this condition or are subject to separate conditions. The following is an example of such a condition pertaining to the HSR Act:

> Any waiting period under the HSR Act applicable to consummation of the Contemplated Transactions will have expired or been terminated, and no action will have been instituted by the United States Department of Justice or Federal Trade Commission challenging or seeking to enjoin consummation of the Contemplated Transactions, which action shall not have been withdrawn or terminated.

SELLERS' RESPONSE

Sellers may want to reword this Section so that the Governmental Authorizations must be "necessary" and to delete the clause regarding those that Buyer considers to be desirable. This would eliminate filings such as Exon-Florio, which is "voluntary." Sellers may also ask that the Governmental Authorizations be specifically identified in Section 8.5 or on an exhibit to avoid any later misunderstandings. *See also* commentary to Section 8.4. As an alternative, Sellers might try to make the condition broader by phrasing it such that the failure to obtain the Governmental

Authorizations must have a material adverse effect on ownership of the Shares or the business of the Acquired Companies or distinguish by state or municipal jurisdictions.

A similar condition might be added to Sellers' obligation to sell their Shares in Article 9 so that Sellers can choose not to close if there are any Governmental Authorizations that, if not received, might have an adverse impact on them following the Closing.

In connection with the HSR Act, in rare cases language is added to this condition or sometimes to the covenants in order, as a matter of risk allocation, to create limitations on the lengths that the parties must go to satisfy the U.S. Department of Justice or the Federal Trade Commission. This subject must be dealt with rather delicately since any divestitures or other actions that the parties agree to implement if needed to obtain clearance would be detailed in the acquisition agreement that is required to be filed under the HSR Act. *See* commentary to Section 6.1.

8.6 ADDITIONAL DOCUMENTS

Each of the items to be delivered pursuant to Section 2.4(a) and each of the following documents will have been delivered (or tendered subject only to Closing) to Buyer:

(a) an opinion of _____, dated the Closing Date, in the form of Exhibit 8.6(a);

(b) estoppel certificates executed on behalf of _____ and dated as of a date not more than five days prior to the Closing Date, each in the form of Exhibit 8.6(b);

(c) an executed copy of each of the agreements listed on Exhibit 8.6(c); and

(d) such other documents as Buyer may reasonably request, each in form and substance satisfactory to Buyer, and, if necessary, executed by each Seller or the relevant Acquired Company, for the purpose of:

(i) evidencing the accuracy of any of Sellers' representations and warranties;

(ii) evidencing the performance by each Seller of, or the compliance by each Seller with, any covenant or obligation required to be performed or complied with by such Seller;

(iii) evidencing the satisfaction of any condition referred to in this Article 8; or

(iv)   **otherwise facilitating the consumption or performance of any Contemplated Transaction.**

COMMENT

Section 8.6 provides that Buyer's obligation to close the acquisition is conditioned upon Sellers' delivery (or tender) to Buyer of certain items specified in Section 2.4(a) and documents described in this Section. Section 2.4(a) identifies various items that Sellers are to deliver at the Closing, including the Organizational Documents, good standing certificates, Sellers' releases, an employment agreement, and the Escrow Agreement. The performance of this covenant of Sellers in Section 2.4(a), like all of their covenants in the Model Agreement, is a condition to Buyer's closing obligation in Section 8.2, as well as being included in Section 8.6.

The items identified in Section 2.4(a) are generally executed by or under the control of Sellers. By contrast, the documents identified in Section 8.6 are generally executed by parties other than Sellers. Because Sellers cannot guarantee that these other parties will deliver these documents at the Closing, the delivery is not made an absolute covenant of Sellers, but rather is a closing condition. Pursuant to Section 5.7, however, Sellers are obligated to use their best efforts to cause the conditions, including the condition in Section 8.6, to be satisfied.

The first document that is required to be delivered is an opinion of counsel. The parties should consider whether the benefit of an opinion of counsel justifies the cost before requesting an opinion. Opinions have become less common, particularly in larger acquisitions. The language of the opinion will be negotiated by counsel and the resulting form is to be attached as Exhibit 8.6(a). For a discussion of legal opinions, *see* FREUND 304–21 (including advice regarding pending and threatened litigation); KLING & NUGENT § 14.09; M&A PROCESS 292. An annotated form of opinion is contained in Exhibit 9.5(a)—Opinion of Counsel to Seller.

The Fact Pattern states that the business is conducted from two sites, one of which is owned and the other is leased from an unrelated third party. Estoppel certificates have been added for the leased property in Section 8.6(b) with the form to be attached as an Exhibit. With respect to the owned real estate, Buyer might want to specify other documents to be delivered much like those that might be required in an asset purchase agreement, such as title insurance policies and surveys.

Section 8.6(c) contemplates that there may be agreements to be delivered other than those covered by Section 2.4(a). These may include employment and noncompetition agreements with key employees and other agreements with parties other than Sellers. For a discussion of ancillary agreements that may be required in connection with an acquisition, *see* M&A PROCESS 243–47.

Section 8.6(d) contemplates the delivery of additional documents as a condition to Buyer's obligation to close the acquisition. *See* M&A PROCESS 247. To the extent additional documents constitute agreements, they can be listed on Exhibit 8.6(c).

SELLERS' RESPONSE

Sellers might ask that this Section be deleted in its entirety, with any agreements or other documents being subject to separate conditions. The reference to the delivery of the items specified in Section 2.4(a) is unnecessary because that delivery is one of Sellers' covenants, the performance of which is covered by the condition in Section 8.2. However, unlike Section 8.6, Section 8.2 only requires compliance in all material respects. *See* the discussion regarding good standing certificates and tax clearance certification in sellers' response to Section 2.4.

Sellers may seek to avoid having to deliver an opinion of counsel as an unnecessary expense that adds little value, arguing that their representations and indemnification should afford sufficient protection for Buyer. If an opinion is still required, Sellers might seek to limit it to core issues (e.g., organization, authority, capitalization) and allow some leeway by providing that the opinion be "substantially" in the form attached. It is helpful to have the form attached as an exhibit to avoid later arguments over the language of the opinion and what would be appropriate qualifications. Sellers need to analyze the required opinion carefully, since each element becomes a closing condition without regard to materiality. One technique is to permit opining counsel to include exceptions in its opinion that conform to the qualifications applicable to the corresponding condition.

Sellers may wish to object to the delivery of estoppel certificates as a closing condition, particularly if the lease is not vital to the continued operation of the business. They might argue that all significant leases are required to be identified in the Disclosure Letter under Section 3.17(a) and Buyer will have an opportunity to review their terms. To the extent that leases are not so identified or the leases that are identified do not contain all the terms of the agreement with the landlords, Buyer could seek indemnification under Section 11.2, assuming that it had an indemnifiable loss arising from those facts.

Requiring the delivery of other agreements in Section 8.6(c) puts Sellers at risk and may provide key employees or other third parties with considerable leverage to extract concessions. It might be preferable if these agreements could be executed and delivered at the time of signing the Model Agreement, with effectiveness being conditioned on the Closing.

Sellers might demand that the catch-all provision in Section 8.6(d) be deleted as being too broad and uncertain in its application. If Buyer has anything particular in mind, it should be specifically identified in the condition rather than relying on an open-ended right to seek other documents.

8.7 ENVIRONMENTAL REPORT

Buyer will have received reports and other information, in form, scope, and substance satisfactory to Buyer, regarding environmental matters relating to the Facilities, which reports shall include, for each Facility, a report that conforms

to the ASTM Standard Practice for Environmental Site Assessments: Phase I Environmental Site Assessment Process, E 1527-05.

COMMENT

Liabilities arising from environmental problems can sometimes be enormous and could potentially dwarf the value of the properties and even the entire value of the target. In Section 3.19, Sellers make extensive representations regarding environmental matters. If these representations prove to be untrue, Buyer has the right to bring a claim for indemnification under Section 11.3. For Buyer, this remedy may be inadequate if Sellers do not have the financial resources to cover the liability that might be incurred. For this reason, in any acquisition that includes real estate, whether it involves the purchase of assets or stock, a buyer may insist upon a fairly broad provision such as Section 8.7 that requires as a condition to closing an environmental report and other information satisfactory to it regarding environmental matters. The language will differ depending upon the nature and significance of the real estate to the target's value and operations.

A buyer will often start with a Phase I assessment of potential environmental contamination. The assessment is usually based upon a site inspection and interviews, adjacent land use surveys, regulatory program reviews, aerial photo evaluations, and other background research. The scope is typically limited to existing data. If the Phase I investigation uncovers potential site contamination, the environmental consultant may suggest a Phase II assessment that may include drilling, soil sampling, setting up monitoring wells, and laboratory analysis and testing. The results of these investigations are reduced to writing in a detailed report containing the consultant's conclusions and recommendations. It should be noted that the retention agreements for environmental consultants often bar reliance by anyone other than the party commissioning the report. It is also common to include exculpation provisions protective of the environmental consultant, so that a buyer may not be able to hold the expert responsible for a failure to detect problems.

All this can take much more time than the parties initially estimate. Often, the environmental investigation has not been completed and the reports have not been issued by the time the parties sign an acquisition agreement. It is for this reason that Buyer will insist that its receipt of a satisfactory report be made a closing condition. Furthermore, Buyer will not want to be second-guessed when it comes to potentially ruinous environmental liabilities and will require, as in Section 8.7, that the report be "in form, scope, and substance satisfactory to Buyer."

SELLERS' RESPONSE

Sellers may argue, particularly if they have significant financial resources, that Buyer should rely on the representation and not insist on a condition. This closing condition can put Sellers in a difficult position. They may become aware of an environmental problem that was previously unknown to them, which could require remediation in order to minimize liability. In addition, any previously unknown environmental problems that are uncovered may have to be reported to the appropriate governmental authorities by the Company or the environmental consultant conducting the study. Accordingly, Sellers may be faced with a scenario where not only has Buyer walked away from the deal, but Sellers now face significant environmental remediation costs.

One approach would be for Sellers to commission an environmental study up front and deal with any problems before the Company is put up for sale. If they are unwilling to do so, another approach, depending on the circumstances, might be to limit Buyer to a Phase I assessment and force it to make its decision on the basis of that report without resorting to an intrusive investigation. Sellers would argue that an environmental site assessment report, coupled with the broad indemnification provision in Section 11.3, provide Buyer with adequate protection from potential environmental liability.

Sellers may suggest changes in the language, such as attempting to define "environmental matters" and inserting a reasonableness qualification to Buyer's having to be satisfied with the form, scope, and substance of the reports and other information. In RUS, Inc. v. Bay Industries, Inc., No. 01 Civ. 6133, 2004 WL 1240578 (S.D.N.Y. 2004), the court considered a condition in an acquisition agreement requiring the delivery of the results of a Phase I environmental assessment and that the buyer be "reasonably satisfied therewith." Although the consultant who prepared the report stated that he had found some items that would need more investigation, the court found that the issues raised were essentially minor, the language did not give the buyer the right to refuse to close in its sole discretion, and the evidence established that the "Phase 1 report would have been eminently satisfactory to a reasonable buyer acting in good faith."

8.8 NO PROCEEDINGS

Since the date of this Agreement, there will not have been commenced or threatened against Buyer, or against any Related Person of Buyer, any Proceeding (a) involving any challenge to, or seeking relief (monetary or otherwise) in connection with, any Contemplated Transaction or (b) that could have the effect of preventing, delaying, making illegal, imposing limitations or conditions on, or otherwise interfering with, any Contemplated Transaction.

COMMENT

This condition (sometimes called a "litigation out") is often the subject of considerable negotiation. It gives Buyer a "walk right" if any proceeding having a specified effect on the acquisition has been commenced or threatened against Buyer or a Related Person since the date of the Model Agreement. Litigation against an Acquired Company or relating to the business is separately covered by the "bring down" of Sellers' legal proceedings representation in Section 3.15(a) pursuant to Section 8.1(a). However, Sellers' representation in Section 3.15(a) is drafted very broadly and also extends to proceedings potentially affecting the acquisition or interfering with any Contemplated Transaction. Thus, the "bring down" of Section 3.15(a) to some extent overlaps Section 8.8.

The phrase "since the date of this Agreement" is included in Section 8.8 because it is normally considered inappropriate to permit a buyer to terminate an acquisition as a result of legal proceedings that were originally brought before an acquisition agreement is signed. Indeed, Buyer represents to Sellers in Section 4.4 that no such proceeding relating to the acquisition was at that time pending or threatened against Buyer. However, Buyer might want a "walk right" if, after the date of the Model Agreement, there is a significant adverse development in a proceeding that had been originally identified as pending against Buyer or a Related Person or if litigation was not disclosed on signing.

SELLERS' RESPONSE

Initially, Sellers may want to ask for a materiality qualification, arguing that lawsuits are often meritless and plaintiffs typically seek considerably more in terms of relief or damages than the facts might warrant. It may be difficult, however, to come to agreement on what could be considered material. Materiality will generally depend upon the type of proceeding (legal or equitable), the relief sought, and the likelihood of an adverse outcome.

The inclusion of "threatened" proceedings might be questioned. Sellers could ask that any threat at least be made in writing. Furthermore, Sellers might attempt to limit this condition to pending proceedings, suggesting the possibility that Buyer could be tempted to encourage a third party to simply threaten a lawsuit against Buyer as a way of providing Buyer a "walk right." Indeed, Sellers may take the position that Buyer should be required to purchase the Shares even if there is a significant pending lawsuit challenging Buyer's acquisition of the Shares—in other words, Sellers may seek to ensure that Buyer will not have a "walk right" unless a court issues an injunction prohibiting Buyer from purchasing the Shares. Alternatively, Sellers may try to limit Buyer's right to terminate the acquisition only if a Governmental Body has brought or threatened to bring a legal proceeding in connection with the acquisition, but not if a private party has brought or threatened to bring a proceeding; Sellers might also distinguish among governmental bodies or jurisdictions which are significant enough to justify providing a "walk right."

8.9   NO CLAIM REGARDING STOCK OWNERSHIP OR SALE PROCEEDS

   There will not have been made or threatened by any Third Party any claim asserting that such Third Party (a) is the holder or the beneficial owner of any Equity Security of any Acquired Company or (b) is entitled to all or any portion of the Purchase Price.

COMMENT

This condition can be critical to a buyer in a stock acquisition because it does not want to end up with less than total ownership of the target or have to deal with claims that a third party is entitled to an ownership interest or any of the purchase price. These same claims could also implicate Section 8.8, as well as the "bring down" of Sellers' capitalization representation in Section 3.3(a) and legal proceedings representation in Section 3.15. For a discussion of the rights of a purchaser for value under the UCC, *see* "Application of the Uniform Commercial Code" in commentary to Section 2.1.

Sellers should recognize that in a transaction that is structured as a stock purchase, a buyer will typically insist upon receiving certificates representing 100% of the shares. If Sellers anticipate that there may be difficulty in achieving delivery of the share certificates of certain minority stockholders (whether because of the potential for a dispute over their ownership, an uncooperative or unavailable stockholder, or otherwise), Sellers should consider restructuring the transaction as a merger. If the potential dispute relates not to the delivery of the share certificates but instead to who is entitled to the sale proceeds, the Sellers could suggest that Buyer escrow the sums in question so as not to impede the entire transaction.

SELLERS' RESPONSE

Sellers may object to the inclusion of this condition because it permits Buyer not to close the acquisition in the face of a meritless or trivial claim by a third party. Sellers may argue that even the use of the term "claim" is much too broad. Furthermore, the language covers a claim being made or threatened, which would presumably include a prior claim that has been withdrawn. The term "beneficial" may, under some circumstances, be too ambiguous. Buyer may respond that its "walk right" under Section 8.9 is triggered only by claims that relate to the Acquired Companies' equity or to the purchase price for the Shares—claims that go to the very heart of the acquisition—and that it may not be able to determine at the time of the Closing whether the claim has merit or is material. Thus, Buyer would argue, the mere existence of a claim should afford it the right not to close.

8.10 No Conflict

Neither the consummation nor the performance of any Contemplated Transaction will, directly or indirectly (with or without notice or lapse of time), contravene, conflict with, or violate, or cause Buyer or any Related Person of Buyer to suffer any adverse consequence under, (a) any applicable Legal Requirement or Order or (b) any Legal Requirement or Order that has been published, introduced, or otherwise proposed by or before any Governmental Body.

COMMENT

Section 8.10 allows Buyer not to close the acquisition if the consummation or performance of any Contemplated Transaction would conflict with or violate, or cause Buyer or any Related Person to suffer any adverse consequence under, an applicable or proposed Legal Requirement or Order. This Section supplements Sellers' "no conflict" representations in Section 3.2(b)(ii) and (iii) and their representations in Sections 3.14(a) and 3.15(c) relating to compliance with Legal Requirements and Orders, respectively, all of which operate as closing conditions pursuant to Section 8.1(a).

Buyer may exercise its "walk right" under Section 8.10 if closing the acquisition would cause it to "suffer any adverse consequence" under any applicable Legal Requirement, even though there might be no actual "violation" of the Legal Requirement in question.

SELLERS' RESPONSE

Sellers may initially ask that this condition be eliminated as being unnecessary because it is covered by the representations in Section 3.2. If it remains, they might attempt to introduce a materiality qualification to distinguish among the jurisdictions that are the source of a Legal Requirement and to delete the reference to a "proposed" Legal Requirement or Order. Sellers may also seek to limit the scope of Section 8.10 to Legal Requirements that are in effect on the scheduled Closing Date and that have been adopted or proposed since the date of the Model Agreement, arguing that Buyer should not be entitled to a "walk right" as a result of a Legal Requirement or Order that is no longer in effect at the scheduled Closing Date or was in effect (and that Buyer presumably knew to be in effect) at signing. Buyer may respond that, even if a particular statute was already in effect as of the signing, there may have been significant changes in its interpretation or enforcement, and that these changes should be sufficient to justify Buyer's refusal to close the acquisition. Indeed, Buyer may seek to expand the scope of Section 8.10 to ensure that it will have a "walk right" if any change in the interpretation or enforcement of a Legal Requirement or Order creates a mere risk that such an adverse consequence might occur or be asserted, even though there may be some uncertainty about the correct interpretation of the Legal Requirement or Order in question.

8.11 Financing

Buyer will have obtained, on terms and conditions satisfactory to it, the financing it deems necessary in order to close the Contemplated Transactions and to fund the working capital requirements of each Acquired Company.

COMMENT

Buyers who are making acquisitions may line up financing in advance in order to ease the process and make their eventual offer more competitive. For example, as part of its principal credit facility, a buyer may ask that its lender pre-approve certain types of acquisitions as long as the target satisfies certain criteria (e.g., size, profitability, or line of business). Not all buyers, however, will have the financial resources readily available to fund an acquisition at the time an acquisition agreement is signed, which would cause them to insist on a "financing out" such as that in Section 8.11. For a discussion of "financing outs," *see* KLING & NUGENT § 14.11[4].

Various layers of funding may be required by a buyer to finance the acquisition, including senior, mezzanine, or subordinated debt and equity. All these financing sources will have their own requirements pertaining to due diligence and documentation, and they often will influence a buyer in negotiating the terms of the acquisition agreement. For a discussion of financing contingencies and dealing with third-party funding sources, *see* M&A PROCESS 265–67. *See also* preliminary note to Article 4.

SELLERS' RESPONSE

A financing condition subjects Sellers to the actions of financing sources with which they probably have no relationship and with respect to which they have no or very limited visibility. There are any number of reasons why financial institutions or other financing sources might elect not to finance an acquisition, particularly during periods of economic downturn and tight credit markets, and Sellers generally are not in a position to influence them. The requirements imposed by Buyer's financing sources will undoubtedly be introduced from time to time by Buyer in its negotiations with Sellers over the terms of the Model Agreement.

If there is a financing condition, Sellers can take certain steps in an attempt to gain more certainty. For example, they can insist that Buyer secure a commitment letter (or a "highly confident" letter) and review the letter in order to satisfy, to the extent possible, conditions to the financing prior to signing the Model Agreement. They might also propose a relatively short time period in which the conditions must be satisfied or waived. Sellers could ask for a representation by Buyer concerning the status of its financing at the time the Model Agreement is signed, and a covenant requiring Buyer to use its best efforts to obtain the financing or setting forth the steps Buyer must take (with a timeline) to eliminate conditions to the commitment letter for the financing. They might insist that the financing be "reasonably satisfactory" to Buyer "acting in good faith," in an attempt to prevent Buyer from arbitrarily claiming that the condition was not met or using this as an excuse to refuse to close for reasons unrelated to the financing. Finally, they could ask that a "reverse termination fee" be paid by Buyer if the financing is not obtained. *See* commentary to Section 10.2.

Depending on the status of the credit markets, Sellers might require that Buyer put pressure on its potential financing sources to limit their financial contingencies and match them to the acquisition conditions, thereby gaining more certainty that funds will be available to close the transaction. Sellers may become much more involved in reviewing and commenting on the terms of the documents that are presented to Buyer. This would require that financing sources place more emphasis on their own due diligence, as well as their relationship with and trust of Buyer.

8.12   No Material Adverse Change

Since the date of this Agreement, no Acquired Company will have suffered any Material Adverse Change and no event will have occurred, and no circumstance will exist, that could result in a Material Adverse Change.

COMMENT

Section 8.12 gives Buyer a "walk right" if any Acquired Company has suffered a Material Adverse Change (commonly called a "MAC") since the date of the Model Agreement. Even when Buyer is successful in negotiating a broadly defined MAC condition, its ability to terminate the Model Agreement may be limited. Because the MAC standard may be so high and reliance on this standard so uncertain, Buyer might consider either substituting or adding some objective conditions dealing with areas of particular concern, such as maintaining a specified level of backlog or not sustaining a loss over a certain amount. For a discussion of case law dealing with a buyer's reliance on a MAC condition to terminate an acquisition agreement, *see* commentary to the definition of "Material Adverse Change" in Section 1.1. *See also* Kling & Nugent § 14.11[5].

Buyer also receives protection by virtue of Sellers' "no MAC" representation in Section 3.12, which is to be brought down to the Closing pursuant to Section 8.1(b). By having such a representation brought down to the Closing, it becomes an indirect MAC condition (sometimes called a "back door MAC"). However, there is a potentially significant difference between the representation in Section 3.12 and the condition in Section 8.12. While the representation in Section 3.12 focuses on the time period beginning on the Balance Sheet Date (the date of the most recent audited balance sheet (*see* Section 3.4)), the condition focuses on the period beginning on the date of the Model Agreement (which may be months after the Balance Sheet Date).

The following example illustrates the extra protection that Buyer might obtain by including such a condition. Assume that the business has improved between the Balance Sheet Date and the date of the Model Agreement, but has deteriorated significantly between the date of the Model Agreement and the scheduled Closing Date. Assume further that the net cumulative change in the business between the Balance Sheet Date and the scheduled Closing Date is not materially adverse (because the magnitude of the improvement between the Balance Sheet Date

267

and the date of the Model Agreement exceeds the magnitude of the deterioration between signing and the scheduled Closing Date). In this situation, Buyer might have a "walk right" by virtue of the separate condition in Section 8.12, but not if left to rely exclusively on the "bring down" of the representation in Section 3.12.

While the representation in Section 3.12 may, except for the difference in time periods, obviate the need for a closing condition, some practitioners believe that a buyer would have a stronger contractual basis for refusing to close if the acquisition agreement contains an express and unambiguous MAC closing condition.

SELLERS' RESPONSE

Notwithstanding the growing body of case law favoring sellers against buyers seeking to invoke MAC clauses, Section 8.12 is still likely to put Sellers in a difficult position because the determination of whether there has been a MAC is so subjective and the term is so vague. If Buyer claims that the condition has not been satisfied, Sellers can litigate the issue, let Buyer walk away from the acquisition or, if permitted to do so, renegotiate the price. Even if the case law may be in favor of Sellers, the costs of litigation can be so high and the effort so great that the other alternatives become more appealing. This Section and the related definition of MAC may therefore be the focus of intense negotiations.

If Section 8.12 is included in the Model Agreement, Sellers may seek to ensure that the "no MAC" representation in Section 3.12 speaks only as of the date of the Model Agreement and is not separately "brought down" to the scheduled Closing Date pursuant to Section 8.1(b) and the introductory clause to Article 3. This can be accomplished by replacing the phrase "Since the Balance Sheet Date" (which appears at the beginning of Section 3.12) with the phrase "From the Balance Sheet Date through the date of this Agreement" together with a specific exception for representations made as of a particular date (discussed in commentary to Section 8.1(b)).

Sellers might want either to delete or narrow the language in the latter portion of Section 8.12 as to the occurrence of an event or existence of circumstances that could result in a MAC. One possibility would be to insert "reasonably be expected to" after "could." Another approach would be to provide that a MAC not be suffered by the Acquired Companies taken as a whole, rather than by each Acquired Company separately. As discussed in the commentary to the definition of "Material Adverse Change" in Section 1.1, Sellers can attempt to add exceptions to that definition. Some may be broad, such as changes in general economic conditions, and others may be narrow, such as temporary changes in results of operations. These exceptions can further limit Buyer's ability to claim a failure of the condition.

9. Conditions Precedent to Sellers' Obligations to Close

PRELIMINARY NOTE

Article 9 sets forth the conditions precedent to Sellers' obligation to sell their Shares to Buyer. The failure to satisfy any of these conditions will give Sellers a walk right and the right, under certain circumstances, to terminate the Model Agreement under Section 10.1. *See* preliminary note to Article 8 regarding the relationship of representations, covenants, and conditions that is applicable as well to Article 9.

The structure of Article 9 is similar to the structure of Article 8, and there is a degree of symmetry between the two Articles. Specifically, Sections 9.1 through 9.4 correspond generally to Sections 8.1 through 8.4, and Section 9.5 corresponds generally to Section 8.6. In reality, however, the walk rights given to Sellers are much narrower than the walk rights given to Buyer. This reflects the view that, if Sellers receive the promised consideration for their Shares and any other ancillary agreements at the Closing, they will have received the full "benefit of the bargain" and, with few exceptions, should be unconditionally obligated to proceed with the acquisition.

Because of this symmetry between Articles 8 and 9, if Sellers are successful in negotiating some of the limitations to Buyer's conditions in Article 8, they probably will have to accept similar limitations in Article 9. This may not be a bad result since further limiting Buyer's walk rights is probably more important to Sellers than accepting additional limitations on their own walk rights. Buyer also will have somewhat of a dilemma in drafting Article 9 because the inclusion of limitations for its own benefit will bolster Sellers' argument that similar limitations should apply to the conditions in Article 8.

Sellers' obligations to sell the Shares and to take the other actions required pursuant to this Agreement to be taken by Sellers at the Closing are subject to the satisfaction, at or prior to the Closing, of each of the following conditions (any of which may be waived in whole or in part by Sellers' Representative):

COMMENT

See commentary to lead-in clause to Article 8 regarding waiver of conditions.

SELLERS' RESPONSE

Sellers might consider whether any of the conditions in Article 8 should be added to Article 9 for their protection and whether any other conditions might be appropriate. For example, because a portion of the purchase price is in the form of Promissory Notes, Sellers might request a condition to the effect that Buyer has suffered no material adverse change. *See* preliminary note to Article 4.

Many of the same considerations that apply to Sellers with respect to Article 8 will apply to Buyer in Article 9. This will particularly be the case where Buyer's representations and covenants are more extensive due, for example, to the purchase price consisting of some stock or notes of Buyer.

The introduction, as well as some of the conditions, to Article 9 gives authority to Sellers' Representative to act on behalf of Sellers. This can facilitate Buyer's efforts to deal with multiple Sellers, but may not be acceptable to Sellers. *See* commentary to Section 12.5.

9.1 ACCURACY OF BUYER'S REPRESENTATIONS

Each of Buyer's representations and warranties in this Agreement will have been accurate in all material respects as of the date of this Agreement and will be accurate in all material respects as of the Closing Date as if then made.

COMMENT

Section 9.1 provides that all of Buyer's representations function as closing conditions. Thus, they provide Sellers with a possible basis for exercising a walk right, but only if Buyer's representations are not accurate in all material respects. Unlike Sellers' representations, Buyer's representations do not contain materiality qualifications so the bifurcated approach taken in Section 8.1 is not necessary. The risk of not satisfying this condition falls less on Buyer because it has made fewer and less detailed representations. If its representations become more extensive and materiality qualifications are added, the same bifurcated approach may be appropriate.

9.2 BUYER'S PERFORMANCE

The covenants and obligations that Buyer is required to perform or to comply with pursuant to this Agreement at or prior to the Closing will have been duly performed and complied with in all material respects.

COMMENT

Under Section 9.2, all of Buyer's pre-closing covenants function as closing conditions. Thus, if Buyer's pre-closing covenants and obligations are not performed or complied with in all material respects, Sellers will have a walk right. Because Buyer's pre-closing covenants are less extensive than those of Sellers, Sellers' walk right under Section 9.2 is not as significant as Buyer's walk right under Section 8.2.

9.3   BRING DOWN CERTIFICATE

Sellers' Representative will have received a certificate executed by Buyer confirming (a) the accuracy of its representations and warranties as of the date of this Agreement and as of the Closing Date in accordance with Section 9.1 and (b) the performance of and compliance with its covenants and obligations to be performed or complied with at or prior to the Closing in accordance with Section 9.2.

COMMENT

Section 9.3 requires as a condition to Closing the delivery by Buyer of a "bring down" certificate like that required of Sellers in Section 8.3. Its purpose is to confirm and bring down to Closing the accuracy of Buyer's representations and performance of its pre-closing covenants. *See* commentary to Section 8.3.

9.4   CONSENTS

Each of the Consents identified in Exhibit 9.4 will have been obtained in form and substance satisfactory to Sellers' Representative and will be in full force and effect. Copies of such Consents will have been delivered to Sellers' Representative.

COMMENT

Under Section 9.4, Sellers' obligation to close the acquisition is conditioned upon obtaining the Consents that have been identified by the parties on Exhibit 9.4. The Consents listed on this Exhibit will probably include some of those identified on Schedule 4.2. They will not necessarily include those referred to as Material Consents in Section 8.4. *See* commentary to Section 8.4; FREUND 299. For example, assume that the Company is leasing a facility from a third party under a lease that requires the landlord's approval of any "change in control" such as will occur in the transfer of the Shares. If the receipt of the landlord's approval is a Material Consent required under Section 8.4, Buyer can refuse to close if it has not been obtained by the scheduled Closing Date. However, Buyer may decide that the facility covered by the lease is not sufficiently important to the Company's operations (and that the potential liability of the Company for failing to obtain the landlord's approval is not sufficiently great) to justify Buyer exercising its walk right under Section 8.4. In that case, Buyer may elect to waive the closing condition and close the acquisition.

In these circumstances, assuming that Sellers have not personally guaranteed the Company's obligations under the lease and that the landlord's remedies are limited to terminating the lease and recovering damages from the Company (and not from Sellers), Sellers arguably should not have a walk right if the landlord's approval is not obtained. Furthermore, assuming that the "change in control" provision of the lease is adequately disclosed as an exception to Sellers' representation in Section 3.2(c), that representation will not be rendered inaccurate by the failure to obtain the landlord's approval, and Sellers will not be liable to Buyer if it waives the closing condition. On the other hand, if Sellers might have continuing personal liability under the lease, they would want it to be listed on Exhibit 9.4 so that the acquisition could not be closed without the landlord's approval.

9.5   ADDITIONAL DOCUMENTS

Each of the items to be delivered pursuant to Section 2.4(b) and each of the following documents will have been delivered (or tendered subject only to Closing) to Sellers' Representative:

(a)   an opinion of _____, dated the Closing Date, in the form of Exhibit 9.5(a); and

(b)   such other documents as Sellers' Representative may reasonably request, each in form and substance satisfactory to Sellers' Representative, and, if necessary, executed by Buyer, for the purpose of:

    (i)   evidencing the accuracy of any of Buyer's representations and warranties;

    (ii)   evidencing the performance by Buyer of, or the compliance by Buyer with, any covenant or obligation required to be performed or complied with by Buyer;

    (iii)   evidencing the satisfaction of any condition referred to in this Article 9; or

    (iv)   otherwise facilitating the consummation or performance of any Contemplated Transaction.

COMMENT

Section 9.5 provides that Sellers' obligation to close the acquisition is conditioned upon Buyer's delivery to Sellers' Representative of certain specified documents. The same considerations will apply to Section 9.5 as apply to Section 8.6. For an annotated form of opinion, *see* Exhibit 9.5(a)—Opinion of Counsel to Buyer.

SELLERS' RESPONSE

Section 9.5 expands Buyer's obligation and provides Sellers an opportunity to seek additional assurances reasonably expected from this type of transaction.

9.6   NO LEGAL PROHIBITION

There will not be in effect any Legal Requirement or Order that prohibits the sale of the Shares by Sellers to Buyer or the consummation of any of the other Contemplated Transactions.

COMMENT

Sellers' walk right under Section 9.6 is considerably narrower than that of Buyer under Sections 8.8 and 8.10. For example, Sellers will not have a walk right merely because there is pending or threatened a Proceeding that challenges the acquisition; rather, Sellers can refuse to close under Section 9.6 only if there is an actual Legal Requirement or Order in place that prohibits the sale of Shares or the consummation of any of the other Contemplated Transactions.

SELLERS' RESPONSE

Sellers may want to broaden their walk right under this Section, particularly if any Proceeding, Legal Requirement, or Order could expose them to liability after the Closing.

10. Termination

PRELIMINARY NOTE

Under basic principles of contract law, the performance of a party's obligations under an agreement is excused if there is a material breach by the other party or if a condition precedent to the terminating party's obligation to perform can no longer occur. *See* RESTATEMENT (SECOND) OF CONTRACTS §§ 225(2), 237; 13 CORBIN ON CONTRACTS §§ 68.1, 68.2. An acquisition agreement does not require a special provision simply to confirm these principles. Article 10, however, serves several additional purposes. First, it provides that a nondefaulting party may terminate the Model Agreement whenever the satisfaction of a condition to that party's obligations becomes impossible, even though the date specified for satisfaction of the condition has not been reached. Second, it confirms that termination of the Model Agreement will not relieve a party from any liability for a breach and that certain obligations of the parties will survive termination. Third, it provides for a right of termination by a nondefaulting party merely because the Closing has not occurred by a specified date.

Often the same issues are addressed in multiple sections of an acquisition agreement. In negotiating and drafting an acquisition agreement, it is important to recognize the interrelationship and functions of these various sections. For example, the accuracy of the representations in Sections 3 and 4 of the Model Agreement serve as bases for determining the satisfaction of closing conditions in Sections 8.1 and 9.1 and may provide a right to terminate the Model Agreement under Section 10.1. Similarly, breaches of the pre-closing covenants in Sections 5 and 6 may give rise to the failure of closing conditions in Sections 8.2 and 9.2, and may also serve as bases for termination of the Model Agreement. Therefore, the final form of the representations, covenants, and closing conditions, including the limitations that have been negotiated, will have a direct impact on whether the Model Agreement can be terminated under Section 10.1. The ability to exercise the right of termination is important, because it will relieve a party of its obligations under the Model Agreement, except to the extent set forth in Section 10.2.

10.1   TERMINATION EVENTS

Subject to Section 10.2, by notice given prior to or at the Closing, this Agreement may be terminated as follows:

(a)   **by mutual consent of Buyer and Sellers;**

(b)   **by Buyer if a material Breach of any provision of this Agreement has been committed by any Seller;**

(c)   **by Sellers if a material Breach of any provision of this Agreement has been committed by Buyer;**

(d)   **by Buyer if satisfaction of any condition in Article 8 by _____ or such later date as the parties may agree upon (the "End Date") becomes impossible (other than through the failure of Buyer to comply with its obligations under this Agreement);**

(e)   **by Sellers if satisfaction of any condition in Article 9 by the End Date becomes impossible (other than through the failure of any Seller to comply with its obligations under this Agreement);**

(f)   **by Buyer if the Closing has not occurred on or before the End Date, unless Buyer is in material Breach of this Agreement; or**

(g)   **by Sellers if the Closing has not occurred on or before the End Date, unless Sellers are in material Breach of this Agreement.**

COMMENT

Clause (a) of Section 10.1 enables the parties to terminate the Model Agreement by mutual consent. It would seem that the parties always have this right, but its inclusion in Section 10.1 is an attempt to negate any suggestion that the consent of any third-party beneficiaries would be necessary for termination. Despite an express limitation of third-party beneficiary rights, such as in Section 12.10, there have been instances in which courts have nevertheless granted this status to third parties. *See* commentary to Section 12.10.

Clauses (b) and (c) provide that Buyer and Sellers have the right to terminate if the other is in material breach of any provision of the Model Agreement and the breach has not been waived. These clauses, in combination with Section 10.2, are intended to eliminate any requirement under the law of contracts that a party close the acquisition and then litigate over damages for a breach. They are intended to make clear that a nondefaulting party can terminate the Model Agreement if the other is in material breach and then litigate over the breach.

Clauses (d) through (g) provide the final bases for termination. Each of these clauses operates off a date, defined as the "End Date," that the parties agree is the deadline by which satisfaction of a condition either becomes impossible or the Closing has not occurred. This augments Section 2.3, which first specifies a date and time for the Closing (with the parties' right to change them), and then provides that if the conditions in Articles 8 and 9 have not been satisfied or waived as of that date, the Closing will take place on the earlier of five business days after notice by Buyer that those conditions have been satisfied or waived and the End Date. The significance of the parties not deviating from the End Date is the principal reason for the addition of a "time of essence" provision in Section 12.20.

Under clauses (d) and (e), Buyer or Sellers can terminate the Model Agreement if the satisfaction of a condition in Article 8 or Article 9, as the case may be, by the End Date becomes impossible, provided that the terminating party has complied with its obligations under the Model Agreement. Sometimes this is phrased in terms of a condition becoming incapable of fulfillment or of being satisfied, rather than becoming impossible. Satisfaction of the conditions in Articles 8 and 9 can become impossible without any party breaching the Model Agreement or being at fault. For example, the parties' obligations to close are conditioned upon the continued accuracy of their representations as of the Closing Date under Sections 8.1 and 9.1. The condition in Section 8.1 might fail due to outside forces over which the parties have no control, such as material damage to or destruction of the manufacturing facility of an Acquired Company that could not be rebuilt by the End Date. The party for whose benefit such a condition is provided should have the right to terminate its obligations under the Model Agreement once it becomes clear that satisfaction of the condition will be impossible, thus avoiding continuing time and expense. Impossibility is a high standard. Satisfaction of a condition, however, might look doubtful but not be impossible. For example, if material litigation arises after signing, it could be dismissed by the End Date so that the "bring- down" condition could be satisfied. Similarly, a Material Adverse Change sustained by an Acquired Company might be alleviated by the End Date. In that event, a party may not be able to terminate the Model Agreement under these clauses.

Clauses (f) and (g), on the other hand, permit Buyer or Sellers to terminate the Model Agreement if the Closing has not occurred by the End Date, provided that the terminating party is not in material breach. This is designed to provide an outside date beyond which a further investment of the parties' resources, and the continued distractions and uncertainties arising from the transaction, may not be justified. In some situations, such as those described toward the end of the prior paragraph, a party may have to wait until the End Date to exercise its right of termination.

Designation of the End Date, which is negotiated by the parties and is commonly referred to as the "drop-dead" date, sometimes will be fairly obvious from the circumstances of the acquisition and the nature of the approvals to be obtained and other conditions to be satisfied prior to the Closing. In other cases, it may be quite arbitrary or the parties may have differing views as to the period of time they wish to remain committed to the transaction. Among the factors that might be considered are the time that is anticipated to complete governmental reviews and obtain governmental approvals and consents from counterparties, the effect of covenants in the acquisition agreement on the ability of management to operate the business in the ordinary course, the potential impact on the operations of an extended delay in closing, and any contractual rights and limitations under any nonsolicitation covenant. Sometimes, provision is made for the "drop- dead" date to be automatically extended in order to provide additional time to satisfy certain of the conditions, such as review under the HSR Act, but even in those cases there is often a firm outside date.

Buyer might consider whether there are other events or circumstances that could be added to Section 10.1 as "termination events." These could be particular developments that would affect adversely the Acquired Companies or the acquisition itself, such as a decision in significant pending litigation or the passage of legislation pertaining to the industry. Sometimes, what otherwise would be included as conditions are expressed as rights of termination. Examples are the "financing out" contained in Section 8.11, a court or governmental body issuing an order enjoining the acquisition as covered in Section 8.8, or a "due diligence out" described in the commentary to Article 8. *See* M&A Process 269–71.

SELLERS' RESPONSE

If Buyer provides a notice of termination to Sellers under Section 10.1 and if Sellers disagree, Sellers' only remedy would be to commence litigation against Buyer and prove that the termination was improper. This can be a costly and lengthy process. For that reason, this leads quite often to renegotiation of the purchase price or simply conceding the issue and allowing termination. To lessen this risk, Sellers might try to negotiate for some limitations on the right of termination. They should be aware, however, that Buyer will undoubtedly want similar limitations on Sellers' right to terminate, but that should be less of a concern because Buyer's representations, covenants, and conditions are more limited.

There are several issues raised by the language in clause (b) that Sellers might raise. First, there is no definition of the term "material." Sellers can suggest adding a definition much like that discussed in the commentary to Section 8.1. Second, clause (b) refers to a material breach of "any provision" of the Model Agreement. Sellers can suggest that the breach must be only of a material provision, although an expansion in the definition of "material" might make that unnecessary.

Sellers could try to delete (b) and have Buyer rely on (d). Sellers could also suggest that Buyer should be unable to terminate the Model Agreement under clause (b) if any Breaches are cured before the scheduled Closing Date. The following is an example of a right to cure being added to clause (b):

> (b) by Buyer if a material Breach of any provision of this Agreement has been committed by any Seller, which Breach has not been waived

by Buyer and has not been cured within 10 Business Days following notice by Buyer to Sellers of such Breach;

A right to cure might be reasonable in some circumstances, but Buyer could be concerned with the ramifications of giving Sellers a blanket right to cure any Breaches regardless of their nature. Sometimes, the right to cure is worded so that it applies only when the Breach is curable through the exercise of commercially reasonable efforts or some similar formulation. Otherwise, giving the notice and providing a right to cure would be futile acts. Buyer may also require that the cure be subject to its reasonable satisfaction and that a similar right to cure be added to clause (c).

A right to cure may not be applicable without express language to that effect. In Annecca, Inc. v. Lexent, Inc., 307 F. Supp. 2d 999 (N.D. Ill. 2004), the court considered whether the failure to satisfy a minimum net worth condition could be relied upon by the buyer to terminate an acquisition agreement. The condition was not satisfied at the closing date, but the sellers argued that they had an express right to cure the deficiency. The court interpreted the net worth requirement as pertaining to the target's "preacquisition activities" that could not be cured by sellers' proposed capital contribution, stating that "[e]xpress conditions precedent must be literally performed—substantial compliance is not enough to compel the other party's performance of its resultant obligation."

The selection of a suitable "drop-dead" date can be important to Sellers. They will not want that date to be too soon, for fear of not having enough time to satisfy the closing conditions. On the other hand, they would not want the date to be too far out. For example, Section 5.2 of the Model Agreement contains a number of requirements and restrictions with respect to operation of the business of the Acquired Companies prior to the Closing. Most important, perhaps, is the ability to sell to someone else. If it appears that any of the closing conditions may not be satisfied, Sellers may want to have the ability to terminate the Model Agreement and to operate the business without these requirements and restrictions, and thus to eliminate the distractions and uncertainties arising from a significant transaction of this nature. This is illustrated by Henkel Corporation v. Innovative Brands Holdings, LLC, Case No. 3633 (Del. Ch., Aug. 26, 2008), where the buyer in an asset acquisition asserted that the seller had failed to satisfy the "material adverse change" condition, which permitted the buyer to waive the condition or terminate the agreement. It did neither and claimed that the seller therefore remained subject to a "no-shop" provision that precluded it from seeking other buyers. There was no "drop-dead" date specified for the benefit of the seller, so it feared that it would be constrained indefinitely. The court, in denying the seller's motion to dismiss the buyer's counterclaim for declaratory judgment, said it is unreasonable to believe that sophisticated parties would have agreed to an open-ended, unlimited period for making such a decision, and therefore the court would be required to determine from the facts a "reasonable" period within which the buyer would have to make a decision.

Clause (g) provides that Sellers can terminate the Model Agreement if the Closing has not occurred by the End Date, unless they are in material Breach of the Model Agreement. Otherwise, Sellers could be left not knowing whether Buyer will eventually close the acquisition and with no way of either terminating the Model Agreement or forcing action by Buyer without litigating the issue as in the *Henkel* case. As an alternative, albeit rarely invoked, they could request a provision to the effect that the Model Agreement will terminate automatically if Buyer does not exercise its right of termination or agree to a waiver or extension by a specified date, which might be fairly soon after the End Date. Sellers might also consider requesting removal of the exception regarding a Breach, arguing that Buyer can still pursue its remedies under Section 10.2.

Sellers might resist any attempt by Buyer to insert additional "termination events," depending upon their nature. Some termination events can turn what would otherwise be a binding agreement into an option due to the broad discretion given Buyer. Moreover, Sellers might want to add their own "termination events," such as being able to terminate the Model Agreement earlier than the scheduled Closing Date due to Buyer's inability to meet certain timelines in arranging its acquisition financing. *See* commentary to Section 8.11.

To facilitate the exercise of Sellers' right to terminate the Model Agreement, they may want to give this authority to Sellers' Representative. However, this is such a significant step that all Sellers may want to participate in the decision to terminate.

10.2 EFFECT OF TERMINATION

Each party's right of termination under Section 10.1 is in addition to any other right it may have under this Agreement (including under Section 12.16) or otherwise, and the exercise of a party's right of termination will not constitute an election of remedies. If this Agreement is terminated pursuant to Section 10.1, this Agreement will be of no further force or effect; provided, however, that (i) this Section 10.2 and Article 12 will survive the termination of this Agreement and will remain in full force and effect, and (ii) the termination of this Agreement will not relieve any party from any liability for any Breach of this Agreement occurring prior to termination.

COMMENT

Section 10.2 provides that a party's right of termination under Section 10.1 is in addition to any other right it may have under the Model Agreement, such as the right to enforce any provision of the Model Agreement under Section 12.16. More specifically, the exercise of the right of termination is not an election of remedies.

Section 10.2 further provides that if the Model Agreement is terminated pursuant to Section 10.1, it will be of no further force or effect. This would include any right of Buyer or Sellers to indemnification under Article 11. One exception is for Section 10.2 itself, so it is clear that it remains in existence. This would also preserve any termination fee, expense reimbursement, liquidated damages, or reverse termination fee provisions that, as discussed below, might be added to this Section. The exception for Article 12 acknowledges that the parties will have some continuing obligations, as for example, to pay their own expenses pursuant to Section 12.1. Buyer's obligation to maintain confidentiality with respect to the information it has received would continue to be subject to the Confidentiality Agreement by virtue of Section 12.7, which provides that the Model Agreement will supersede the Confidentiality Agreement only upon the Closing.

In some instances, a buyer may want to provide for specific consequences or remedies that will be available in the event of termination, rather than to rely on its general legal and equitable rights and remedies. Typically, a distinction would be made between a termination that is based upon the fault or breach by a party and a termination that is not based upon fault or a breach. Provision might be made for a termination fee, expense reimbursement, or liquidated damages, which are usually mutually exclusive.

The purpose of a termination fee, which is often called a "break-up" fee and is more common in acquisitions of public companies, is generally to compensate a buyer for the opportunity lost when it is unable to acquire the target. Payment of a termination fee can be triggered without a breach and does not necessarily foreclose the opportunity for a party to seek damages for the breach. It is usually based on a percentage of the purchase price, so the amount of the fee will be higher in larger acquisitions. The following is an example of such a provision:

> In the event that this Agreement is terminated by Buyer pursuant to [Section 10.1(d) or (f)], Sellers shall pay, or cause to be paid, to Buyer by wire transfer within _____ Business Days following such termination a fee in the sum of $_____. Upon payment of the foregoing fee, Sellers shall have no further liability to Buyer or its Affiliates with respect to this Agreement, the Contemplated Transactions, or otherwise, except for liability arising out of fraud or an intentional Breach of this Agreement.

Expense reimbursement is intended to make a buyer whole for its out-of-pocket expenses incurred in a failed transaction. The following is an example of a provision requiring reimbursement for out-of-pocket expenses, with optional wording for the reasonableness of the expenses and a cap on the amount of the reimbursement:

> In the event that this Agreement is terminated by Buyer pursuant to Section 10.1(b), Sellers shall pay, or cause to be paid, to Buyer by wire transfer promptly following notice by Buyer an amount equal to Buyer's documented out-of-pocket fees and expenses set forth in such notice [and reasonably] incurred by it in connection with this Agreement and

the Contemplated Transactions [in an aggregate amount not to exceed $_____].

Liquidated damage provisions are only triggered by a breach of an acquisition agreement and are intended to quantify damages for the breach. *See* STARK § 9.03[3][b]. They represent, in effect, the parties' best estimate of the injury that would be sustained in the event of a contractual breach in circumstances where a judicial determination of damages would otherwise be "uncertain or not easily susceptible of proof." S.H. Deliveries, Inc. v. TriState Courier & Carriage, Inc., 1997 WL 817883 (Del. Super. Ct. 1997). The following is an example of a liquidated damages provision, which is based on a Breach by Sellers and cuts off further liability of Sellers for the Breach, with an exception for fraud or an intentional Breach.

> In the event that this Agreement is terminated by Buyer pursuant to Section 10.1(b), Sellers shall pay, or cause to be paid, to Buyer by wire transfer within ____ Business Days following such termination the sum of $_____. Upon payment of the foregoing fee, Sellers shall have no further liability to Buyer or its Affiliates with respect to this Agreement, the Contemplated Transactions, or otherwise, except for liability arising out of fraud or an intentional Breach of this Agreement. Sellers and Buyer acknowledge and agree that the agreement to pay the foregoing amount is an integral part of the transactions contemplated by this Agreement and that, without that agreement, Buyer would not have entered into this Agreement, and further that any amounts payable hereunder do not constitute a penalty but rather are liquidated damages in a reasonable amount to compensate Buyer for its efforts and resources expended and its opportunities foregone while negotiating this Agreement and in reliance on this Agreement and on the expectation of the consummation of the Contemplated Transactions.

The latter portion of the provision is an example of language intended to conform to state law requirements, whereby a distinction is made between provisions that have been tailored to provide reasonable compensation in the event of a breach, and are therefore enforceable, and that are in the nature of a penalty for a breach, and are unenforceable. *See* Brazen v. Bell Atlantic Corp., 695 A. 2d 43 (Del. 1997) (determination of the reasonableness of a termination fee using a liquidated damages analysis). These requirements vary from state to state, and so the wording might have to be modified in order to address applicable state law concerns.

SELLERS' RESPONSE

While the Model Agreement can be terminated in the event of a "material" Breach, the proviso to Section 10.2 preserves the liability of a party for any Breach. Sellers may want to add a "materiality qualification" to that proviso. They might also try to limit their liability to an intentional action that the party knows will constitute a breach or fraud. Sellers may want to add a sentence making it absolutely clear that they are specifically relieved from liability for indemnification under Sections 11.2 and 11.3 arising from a Breach, unless the acquisition is closed.

Since a Breach of the Model Agreement by Sellers may be more likely than by Buyer, Sellers may be the ones negotiating for a liquidated damages provision as the exclusive remedy to limit their exposure for a termination arising out of their Breach. Whenever a termination fee, expense reimbursement, or liquidated damages provision is added, Sellers may want to make clear how this affects their exposure, if any, for a Breach in the event of termination.

Sellers may ask for a deposit by Buyer to be paid if there is a termination of the Model Agreement by Buyer without fault on the part of Sellers. In lieu of a deposit, they may negotiate for a "reverse termination fee," for reimbursement of their expenses, or for both if there is a termination of the Model Agreement by Buyer under certain circumstances. The wording for expense reimbursement could be modified from the language set forth above for Buyer.

Reverse termination fee provisions have been more common with buyers that are private equity firms and in highly leveraged transactions, but also have been used in transactions involving strategic buyers. Such a provision may provide for a fee based on a specified percentage of the purchase price if the agreement is terminated due to the failure of the buyer to obtain financing or to any failure of the buyer to close if required. It will typically be combined with a limitation of a seller's remedies and of a buyer's exposure, so that a buyer may not find it too objectionable. In United Rentals, Inc. v. RAM Holdings, Inc., 937 A.2d 810 (Del. Ch. 2007), the court found the language of an agreement ambiguous as to whether the remedy of specific performance was precluded by a provision for payment of a fee, but denied the plaintiff's petition for specific performance based on its failure to demonstrate that the common understanding of the parties permitted specific performance. If not already agreed to, a request for a reverse termination fee by Sellers may lead Buyer to ask that a termination fee be paid by them or that its expenses be reimbursed under specified circumstances. Sometimes these provisions are negotiated in tandem but the final provisions are not necessarily symmetrical.

The following is an example of a provision for a reverse termination fee triggered by a failure to obtain financing, which could be added as another termination event in Section 10.1:

> (h) by Sellers if the conditions to closing set forth in Article 8 (other than Sections 8.3 and 8.6) are satisfied on [the scheduled Closing Date set forth in Section 2.3] [the End Date] and proceeds of the financing contemplated by Section 8.11 (other than as a result of failure by Sellers to satisfy the conditions set forth in Sections 8.3 and 8.6) have not been received on or prior thereto.

In the event that this Agreement is terminated by Sellers pursuant to Section 10.1(h), Buyer shall pay, or cause to be paid, to Sellers by wire transfer within ____ Business Days following such termination a fee in the sum of $_____. Upon payment of the foregoing fee, Buyer shall have no further liability to Sellers or their Affiliates with respect to this Agreement, the Contemplated Transactions, or otherwise, except for liability arising out of fraud or an intentional Breach of this Agreement. In the event Buyer fails to pay the foregoing amount when the payment thereof is not the subject of a bona fide dispute, Sellers shall be entitled to seek and receive, in addition to the fee, interest thereon and costs of collection thereof (including reasonable attorneys' fees and expenses).

The date by which the conditions to closing must be satisfied could be the scheduled Closing Date, the End Date, or some other date agreed to by the parties. Payment of the fee under this condition is triggered by Sellers' election to terminate when the conditions have been satisfied, but there has been a failure by Buyer to receive proceeds from the financing. Sellers could still terminate under another condition and pursue other remedies to which they might be entitled. Some reverse termination fee provisions are also accompanied by an expense reimbursement provision.

When considering provisions that require performance by a buyer of its obligations under an acquisition agreement, and particularly monetary obligations, the type of buyer becomes important. For example, it may be that the buyer is a shell company that has been formed by a private equity firm or an operating company, in which case these provisions may be illusory unless the seller receives a guarantee of the obligations of the shell company or a solvent entity otherwise becomes responsible, at least to the extent of the shell company's monetary liabilities. The use of such a limited guarantee of the obligations of shell entities was explained by the court in United Rentals, Inc. v. RAM Holdings, Inc., 937 A.2d 810 (Del. Ch. 2007). In RUS, Inc. v. Bay Industries, Inc., 2004 WL 1240578 (S.D.N.Y. 2004), a parent was held liable where the court found that an acquisition subsidiary functioned merely as an extension of the parent, its actions were wholly controlled by the parent's officers and the parent did not respect the subsidiary as a separate entity. This analysis is fact-specific, so that the result reached by this court cannot necessarily be applied to other situations, and, in fact, the Delaware Chancery Court respected the separation of parent and acquisition entities in Alliance Data Systems v. Blackstone Capital Partners VL.P., 963 A.2d 746 (Del. Ch. 2009).

11. Indemnification; Payment; Reimbursement; Remedies

PRELIMINARY NOTE

Article 11 of the Model Agreement provides for indemnification and other post-closing monetary remedies. Generally, the buyer of a privately held company seeks to impose financial responsibility on the seller for breaches of the seller's representations in the acquisition agreement and for other specified matters that may not be the subject of representations. The conflict between the buyer's desire for that protection and the seller's desire not to have continuing responsibility for a business that it no longer owns often results in intense negotiation. Thus, there is no such thing as a set of "standard" indemnification provisions. However, there is a standard set of issues typically dealt with in the indemnification provisions of an acquisition agreement. Article 11 of the Model Agreement addresses these issues in a way that favors a buyer. The commentary identifies areas in which a seller may propose a different resolution.

If no remedy has been specified in a contract, the parties may nevertheless have a remedy for breach of the contract, and may have other equitable remedies, such as reformation or specific performance of the contract. There may be additional remedies arising upon the formation of the contract—tort or other tort-like remedies (e.g., fraud in the inducement). The fact that some remedies are specified in the Model Agreement does not imply that other remedies (both contractual and noncontractual) are limited or excluded; Section 12.11 of the Model Agreement makes that clear, but Sellers may seek to make the indemnification provisions the exclusive remedy. There may be limitations on these other remedies, and the language of the Model Agreement may not be sufficient to overcome such limitations (nor under some legal principles could it), such as cases that deny the buyer a remedy if it knew the falsity of a representation.

See STARK ch. 10.

Before the intricacies of indemnification are explored, an understanding of contract remedies and limitations on contract remedies may be helpful.

GENERAL CONTRACT REMEDIES

General contract remedies available to aggrieved buyers and sellers of businesses include recovery of damages for breach of contract, and equitable remedies of rescission, specific performance or injunctive relief, and reformation. These remedies are not dependent on any recital in the acquisition agreement of the right to sue or other specified remedy.

For the most part, a buyer is concerned about what happens when a transaction closes and it discovers some problem with the business. But if the transaction does not close, either justifiably or not, the agreement may give one party certain remedies. The parties may bargain for a termination fee (or reverse termination fee) in lieu of other remedies under the agreement. *See* commentary to Section 10.2. Upon the buyer's breach, the seller could sue for specific performance to compel the buyer to complete the transaction, could terminate the agreement and sue for damages, or could just sue for damages. In addition to remedies based in contract law, tort remedies may be available, such as a claim based in fraud that the buyer entered into the agreement without ever intending to honor it. The Model Agreement does not contain detailed provisions governing rights and remedies for a pre-closing breach. All remedies are preserved, including the remedies in Article 11. The application of Article 11 to a transaction that has not closed is explained in "The Transaction That Does Not Close" in this preliminary note.

If a transaction has closed, an aggrieved buyer may have the remedy of rescission, simply returning ownership of the target to the seller, and recovery of the purchase price paid. For example, ABRY Partners, V, L.P. v. F&W Acquisition, LLC, 891 A.2d 1032 (Del. Ch. 2006), involved a suit for rescission. But while rescission may be available in certain circumstances, it is not commonly granted in cases involving acquisitions.

Pre-closing covenants (such as the failure to contribute a significant property to the target) might also be enforced through specific performance or injunctive relief. Alternatively, a buyer who knows about a breach of a pre-closing covenant might assert it as a basis for not closing.

Damages should be an available remedy (absent some judicially imposed limitation) with respect to pre-closing breaches of representations, as well as breaches of covenants under the agreement. Damages must be the type recognized as recoverable in breach of contract actions. Many contracts outside the M&A context do not provide for specific remedies, but instead attempt to grant specific damages, such as liquidated damages, or deny some measure of damages, such as consequential or punitive damages.

For the most part, the remedy provisions of the Model Agreement generally and nominally apply to both parties (exceptions are Section 11.3 regarding Sellers' indemnification for environmental matters and Section 12.16 regarding specific performance). But usually it is Buyer who is seeking to assert some remedy. Therefore, although these remedies should be available to Sellers as well, the discussion below focuses on remedies available to Buyer.

PROTECTIONS INDEPENDENT OF REPRESENTATIONS: BUYER'S EXPANSION OF REMEDIES

Most post-closing claims under acquisition agreements relate to breaches of representations or covenants contained in those agreements. But a buyer in a stock purchase transaction might seek a stand-alone remedy not dependent on a breach of representations. For example, a seller may disclose a litigation matter regarding an alleged liability as an exception to its "no litigation" representation (Section 3.15). Because of its disclosures there is no breach of the representation, but a buyer might nevertheless want to be protected against the adverse effects of the disclosed litigation. In the acquisition agreement, the buyer might negotiate for an indemnification against loss arising from the disclosed litigation.

In a particular case, a buyer of stock might desire results that are functionally equivalent to those of an asset purchase, in which no liabilities or only specified liabilities of the target are assumed by the buyer. Such a buyer could employ any one of several approaches in the agreement. It might require a representation that, except as disclosed, the target has no liabilities, and require the seller to indemnify both the buyer and the target against all undisclosed liabilities. The agreement could require that the seller expressly assume any liabilities of the target other than disclosed or defined liabilities, and indemnify both the buyer and the target against any other liabilities. The agreement could simply provide that the seller indemnify both the buyer and the target against all pre-closing liabilities except for certain classes of defined pre-closing liabilities (characterized by some practitioners as an "our watch/your watch" provision, in this case holding the seller responsible for liabilities incurred while the target was owned by the seller). The first approach involves a contract claim for a breach of a representation, as to which all contract defenses are available. The second is a straightforward assumption of liability. The third is indemnification that is independent of representations, which may be subject to certain defenses that may be available as discussed in the commentary to Section 11.10.

In some cases, a seller may be willing to offer specific indemnification if facts diverge from the particular set of facts desired by the buyer. In the example above, the seller may suspect that the target is subject to some unknown liabilities, and might offer to indemnify the buyer against any adverse consequence of those unknown liabilities. The buyer is protected by the seller through what is simply a contractual allocation of risk.

In fact, acquisition agreements frequently offer protection not dependent on a breach of a representation. Certain indemnifications set forth in Section 11.2 of the Model Agreement extend to liabilities regardless of whether a representation has been breached. They attempt to protect against harm that may come to Buyer and that the Acquired Companies may incur apart from whether the representations are true. An example is found in Section 11.2(e) (an "our watch/your watch" indemnification related to goods manufactured or sold prior to the Closing Date). No representation in Article 3 of the Model Agreement specifically relates to this subject of the indemnification: it is purely an allocation of risk. Another example is found in Section 11.2(d) (the tax indemnification). While there are extensive representations in Section 3.11 relating to tax liabilities, Section 11.2(d) is intended to make the responsibility absolute. Whether or not there is a breach of Section 3.11, the Buyer intends through Section 11.2(d) to be protected against undisclosed pre-closing tax liabilities of the Acquired Companies. An intention to indemnify for matters not dependent on a breach of a representation, however, must be clear and unambiguous. *See* Hartz Consumer Group, Inc. v. JWC Hartz Holdings, Inc., Sup. Ct., N.Y. County, Nov. 9, 2005, Gammerman, J.H.O., Index No. 600610/03, *aff'd*, 33 A.D. 3d 555 (2006).

JUDICIAL LIMITATIONS ON ENFORCEMENT

Reliance. To be entitled to recovery for damages relating to a breach of a representation, proof of the breach and damages may not be enough. In some jurisdictions, a buyer must also prove its reliance on the misrepresentation. That is because some jurisdictions conflate an action for misrepresentation in a contract with the tort of deceit (and similar tort claims such as fraud in the inducement), which has always required the causal link of reliance. *See* West & Benton, *Contracting to Avoid Extra-Contractual Liability – Can Your Contractual Deal Ever Be the "Entire" Deal?*, 64 BUS. LAW. 999 (Aug. 2009).

Hendricks v. Callahan, 972 F 2d 190 (8th Cir. 1992), illustrates the principle that if a buyer acquires knowledge of a breached warranty before the closing, and nevertheless closes the transaction, then the buyer cannot recover for the breach because it has not relied on the warranty. That case, applying Minnesota law, held that a buyer's personal knowledge of an outstanding lien defeated a claim under either a property title warranty or a financial statement warranty even though the lien was not specifically disclosed or otherwise exempted from disclosure.

The court in CBS, Inc. v. Ziff-Davis Publishing Co., 553 N.E.2d 997 (N.Y. 1990), however, reached the opposite conclusion. In that case, a buyer discovered, during a pre-closing investigation, a possible inaccuracy in seller's warranties and then closed under an express reservation of rights. The seller had denied the existence of a breach and insisted on closing. After the closing, the buyer sued the seller for the alleged breach of the warranty. The New York Court of Appeals held that, in contrast to a tort action based on fraud or misrepresentation, which requires the plaintiff's belief in the truth of the information warranted, the critical question in a contractual claim based on an express warranty is "whether [the buyer] believed [it] was purchasing the [seller's] promise as to its truth." The court stated:

> The express warranty is as much a part of the contract as any other term. Once the express warranty is shown to have been relied on as part of the contract, the right to be indemnified in damages for its breach does not depend on proof that the buyer thereafter believed that the assurances of fact made in the warranty would be fulfilled. The right to indemnification depends only on establishing that the warranty was breached.

Although this dichotomy has not been completely resolved, the weight of authority favors the approach of the court in *Ziff-Davis*. *See* Power Soak Systems, Inc. v. Emco Holdings, Inc, 482 F. Supp. 2d 1125 (W.D. Mo. 2007); Cobalt Operating, LLC v. James Crystal Enterprises, LLC, 2007 WL 2142926 (Del. Ch. 2007), *aff'd*, 945 A.2d 594 (Del. 2008); Schwan-Stabilo Cosmetics GmbH & Co. v. PacificLink

International Corporation, 401 F.3d 28 (2d Cir. 2005); Pegasus Management Co., Inc. v. Lyssa, Inc., 995 F. Supp. 43 (D. Mass 1998); and American Family Brands, Inc. v. Giuffrida Enterprises, Inc., No. 96-7062, 1998 WL 196402 (E.D. Pa. 1998). *See also,* Johannes and Simonis, *Buyer's Pre-Closing Knowledge of Seller's Breach of Warranty,* 75 Wis. Law. 7 (July 2002) ("It is clear, however, that lack of reliance will not defeat [the purchaser's] warranty claim. The modern trend is that a buyer need not rely on a seller's express warranty in order to recover for the seller's subsequent breach of the express warranty.").

Doctrine of Substituted Performance. The doctrine of substituted performance can come into play when both parties recognize before the closing that the sellers cannot fully perform their obligations. The common law has long been that if a breaching party expressly conditions its substitute performance on a waiver, the nonbreaching party may not accept the substitute performance while at the same time retaining its right to sue under the original contract, even with an express reservation of rights. *See* United States v. Lamont, 155 U.S. 303 (1984); Restatement (Second) of Contracts § 278, comment a. Thus, if a seller offers to close on the condition that the buyer waive its right to sue on the seller's breach, under the common law the buyer must choose whether to close or to sue, but the buyer cannot close and then sue. Although the acquisition agreement may contain an express reservation of the buyer's right to close and sue (as does the Model Agreement in Sections 11.1(b) and (c)), there has been some uncertainty as to whether courts will respect such a provision and allow the buyer to close and sue under circumstances in which the doctrine of substitute performance could apply. The more widely accepted view, however, is that such provisions should be respected under the analysis adopted by the courts in *Ziff-Davis* and its progeny cited above.

Judicial Interpretation. Courts sometimes decline to enforce certain provisions of an agreement to limit the liability of the sellers, despite their plain meaning. The rationale is often that the language of the offending provisions conflicts with other provisions of the agreement. For example, in DCV Holdings, Inc. v. ConAgra, Inc., 2005 WL 698133 (Del. Super. Ct. 2005), *aff'd,* 889 A.2d 954 (Del. 2005), the buyer discovered after the closing that the target was subject to antitrust liability for pre-closing price-fixing, which could have constituted a breach of either the "no undisclosed liabilities" representation or the "compliance with laws" representation made by the seller in the acquisition agreement. The court held that the general "no undisclosed liabilities" representation was overridden by the "compliance with laws" representation, because the latter was more specific to the circumstances. Because the "compliance with laws" representation was qualified by knowledge, and there was no showing that the seller had knowledge of the price-fixing activities of the target's management, the court found no breach. In other words, a general representation on liabilities was held to yield to a specific representation on liabilities arising from noncompliance with law. *See* "Overlap of Representations" in preliminary note to Article 3. Acquisition agreements almost invariably contain numerous representations that overlap other representations, and specific representations that would be breached by factual circumstances that would also breach general representations. However, despite holdings such as that in *DCV Holdings*, acquisition agreements often do not contain a provision which states that redundancy of representations or overlap are intended. In an attempt to deal with this issue, consideration might be given by Buyer to the inclusion in Section 1.2 of a provision like the following:

> The parties intend that each representation, warranty, covenant, and agreement contained in this Agreement will have independent significance. The fact that any conduct or state of facts may be within the scope of two or more representations, warranties, covenants, or agreements contained in this Agreement, whether relating to the same or different subject matters and regardless of the relative levels of specificity, shall not be considered in construing or interpreting this Agreement.

Seller, on the other hand, might suggest language to the effect that certain specific representations will control over general representations, as suggested in preliminary note to Article 3.

Courts also use various presumptions to interpret provisions in a contract, such as construction against the drafter and the forthright negotiator principles. *See* RESTATEMENT (SECOND) OF CONTRACTS. *See also* United Rentals, Inc. v. Ram Holdings, Inc., 937 A.2d 810 (Del. Ch. 2007). Some of the "boilerplate" provisions in Article 12 and the usage provisions in Section 1.2 are designed to counteract these judicial constructions.

Burden of Proof. In most circumstances, the buyer would seek damages based upon a breach of contract. In that endeavor, it will incur the cost of litigation (although the cost might be recoverable from the seller) and bear the burden of proof. While perhaps inherent in the enforcement of legal obligations, these burdens may in fact discourage a buyer from seeking judicial recourse even if there clearly has been a breach and damages have resulted.

Damages. Even when a breach is clear, the measure of damages may not be so clear. While the buyer may believe it should get the benefit of the bargain (the difference between the value of the target as received and as promised), the courts, because of the uncertainty, may be inclined to award lesser damages. In any event, the buyer may be forced to incur the cost of proving its damages, including the hiring of experts.

Avoiding Judicial Limitations. There are provisions of the Model Agreement, and many other agreements, that attempt to avoid some of these judicial limitations. Section 12.11 attempts to preserve all remedies, even while the Model Agreement includes extensive indemnification remedies. Section 11.1(b) provides that, regardless of any investigation, and regardless of what Buyer knows, the right to indemnification or other remedies will not be affected. Section 11.10 seeks to avoid limitations on indemnification based on strict liability or negligence.

CONTRACT REMEDIES

Indemnification as the Exclusive Remedy. Parties typically negotiate extensively over the workings of the indemnification provisions, including inserting baskets and caps and negotiating specifically as to when claims must be brought. It might seem disingenuous for a buyer to assert that, despite the heatedly negotiated and finely constructed limitations on indemnification, it should be entitled to assert a simple contract remedy without those limitations. *See* commentary to Section 12.11. Further, if a particular state law requires reliance on the representation, couching the remedy as indemnification rather than general breach of contract may not avoid the result. A court might find that the expression of the remedy of indemnification excludes other remedies. *See* commentary to Section 11.1(b).

Rescission. Rescission is available for fraud or mistake, or in certain other instances. While this remedy is a theoretical possibility, it may be impossible to "unscramble the egg." Further, a buyer may only want to get a reduction in purchase price to reflect accurately the value of the target.

Reformation. While reformation of an acquisition agreement is available for fraud or mistake, it is rarely used as a remedy in an acquisition of stock. (The "blue pencil" doctrine, used to modify covenants not to compete, is discussed in Article 7.) Because acquisition agreements are often long and complex, courts will simply interpret the agreements rather than reform them. In Cerberus International, Ltd. v. Apollo Management, L.P., 794 A.2d 114 (Del. 2002), the Delaware Supreme Court reversed a grant of summary judgment involving calculation of a merger price. The court held reformation to be appropriate for mutual mistake and in cases of unilateral mistake, where one party is mistaken as to a material term and the other party knows of the mistake and remains silent; however, the plaintiff is generally required to prove each element of a reformation claim by clear and convincing evidence.

NONCONTRACT REMEDIES

When there is litigation involving an alleged breach of representation, plaintiffs often include other claims, such as fraud, violations of securities laws, and perhaps violations of state statutes. In some respects, these theories may be less desirable than breach of contract claims because additional elements must be established. For example, common law fraud and some securities laws violations require that the plaintiff prove the defendant acted with "scienter." Courts have applied varying degrees of skepticism to such claims, believing that parties writing elaborate contracts and being able to fend for themselves should be bound by those contracts. Often they find that an essential element of a fraud claim has not been met. For example, a frequent contract provision is that "buyer represents that it has not relied on any representations not contained herein." In dealing with noncontract claims, courts have found such language (or other indicia of buyer's state of mind) persuasive to establish that a buyer has not relied on extra-contract representations.

Securities Laws. Sellers may still be subject to post-closing liability under the antifraud provisions of the federal securities laws and under principles of common law fraud. The sale of the stock of a privately held company is a sale of securities for purposes of the federal securities laws. *See* Landreth Timber Co. v. Landreth, 471 U.S. 681 (1985). Under Section 14 of the Securities Act and Section 29 of the Exchange Act, remedies may not be waived. The actions of a corporate officer or other agent in negotiating a merger or sale may be imputed to the seller to establish the scienter required for a cause of action under the antifraud provisions of the federal securities laws and for common law fraud. *See* Reinfeld v. Riklis, 722 F. Supp. 1077 (S.D.N.Y. 1990).

Sellers sometimes attempt to defeat the reliance elements of a securities law claim by including "nonreliance" language in the transaction documents. For example, the confidentiality agreement and the offering memorandum by which the target is marketed may contain a provision which states that no representations are made except in the definitive acquisition agreement. The acquisition agreement itself might contain something such as the following: "Except for the representations and warranties contained in Article 3, neither Sellers nor any other Person make any express or implied representation or warranty on behalf of or with respect to Sellers, the business of the Acquired Companies, or the Shares, and Sellers hereby disclaim any representation or warranty not contained in Article 3." Merrill Lynch & Co. v. Allegheny Energy, Inc., 2003 WL 22795650 (S.D.N.Y. 2003). In light of a clause similar to this one, courts may find that it was not reasonable to rely on alleged oral representations. The court in AES Corp. v. The Dow Chemical Company, 325 F.3d 174 (3d Cir. 2003), held that a nonreliance provision was only evidence of nonreliance and identified five factors to be considered. The case was remanded to the trial court to consider these factors. On the other hand, in Poth v. Russey, 281 F. Supp. 2d 814 (E.D. Va. 2003), the court used an eight-factor test developed by the Fourth Circuit to hold that reliance on oral representations was unreasonable.

Fraud. As in the federal securities law area, the question arises whether a nonreliance clause can defeat a state common law fraud claim. In Consolidated Edison, Inc. v. Northeast Utilities, 249 F. Supp. 2d 387 (S.D.N.Y. 2003), the confidentiality agreement contained a disclaimer of reliance and the merger agreement barred reliance on any representations not set forth in the merger agreement. The trial court held that the buyer could not establish that it reasonably relied on oral representations.

Deceptive Trade Practices. Deceptive trade practices statutes, as adopted in most states, apply to consumer rather than commercial transactions. In states where their use is not limited to consumers, an aggrieved party may find their use helpful, sometimes including the availability of treble damages and recovery of attorneys' fees.

Blue Sky Laws. State Blue Sky laws may be available to a buyer for recovery. Some courts have rejected the "sale of business" doctrine in connection with the sale of stock by controlling stockholders. *See* Andrews v. Browne, 662 S.E.2d 58 (Va. 2008), following Landreth Timber Co. v. Landreth, 471 U.S. 681 (1985).

Negligent Misrepresentation. In his opinion in Corporate Property Associates 14 Inc. v. CHR Holding Corp., 2008 WL 963048 (Del. Ch. 2008), Vice Chancellor Strine explained:

> Thus, a negligent misrepresentation claim, like an equitable fraud claim, is in essence a fraud claim with a reduced state of mind requirement. Scienter is replaced by negligence, but the doctrine requires additional elements to compensate for this significant concession. The primary policy trade-off for the reduction in the state of mind required to recover is that the law pares down the class of potentially liable defendants to those with a pecuniary duty to provide accurate information.

Other courts have held that a negligent misrepresentation claim will lie only when the parties are in a "special relationship."

LIMITING REMEDIES

Generally, there is a tension in negotiating any contract. Sellers will attempt, in many subtle and unsubtle ways, to limit buyers' remedies, such as breach of contract and tort remedies. Buyers will naturally attempt to fend off such efforts by preserving all remedies and by expanding indemnification to provide protection beyond the representations.

The Outside Bounds to Limitations. Parties should understand that a remedy may be limited by agreement between the parties or by law. An example of the lengths to which sellers go in attempting to protect themselves by agreement can be found in ABRY Partners V, L.P. v. F&W Acquisition, LLC, 891 A.2d 1032 (Del. Ch. 2006). The buyer and seller were sophisticated private equity firms. The purchase agreement contained several robust exculpation, disclaimer, and nonreliance clauses, under which the buyer disclaimed all express or implied representations other than those expressly set forth in the agreement, agreed that the sale was "as is, where is," and agreed that indemnification (subject to a $20 million cap) under the agreement was buyer's exclusive remedy (except for specific performance or injunction as to covenants). Despite these contractual limitations, buyer sued to rescind the transaction, claiming that the seller knowingly made false financial statement representations in the agreement, and delivered a false "bring down" certificate at the closing. The court in *ABRY* held that the unambiguous liability limiting provisions of the agreement were invalid to the extent they purported to shield sellers from responsibility for lies in the express representations in the agreement. The court went on to state, however, that the burden of proof to overcome such provisions is very high: "This will require Buyer to prove that the Seller acted with an illicit state of mind, in the sense that the Seller knew that the representation was false and either communicated it to Buyer directly itself or knew that the Company had." *See* KLING & NUGENT ¶ 15.03[4] (criticizing *ABRY*).

Exceptions to Exculpation and Disclaimer Clauses. If the sellers are successful in negotiating one or more liability-limiting provisions, they often agree to remain fully liable for "willful" or "intentional" misconduct such as fraud or intentional misrepresentation. It may be that such an exception is required by negotiation—give the buyer something in respect of what the seller might regard as an unlikely occurrence. Perhaps drafters believe that broad exculpation might be unenforceable, and the exception is included to enhance the chances of having it upheld. Although some doubt exists, a complete disclaimer of liability should be enforceable, subject to the limits defined in *ABRY*. Some of the standards often used in the exceptions to exculpation clauses, such as "willful" and "fraudulent," are, however, ambiguous. For example, in Johnson & Johnson v. Guidant Corp., 2007 WL 2456625 (S.D.N.Y. Aug. 29, 2007) the court, in interpreting an exception for "willful and material breach" stated that "'willful' is a notoriously ambiguous word." *See also*, Hexion Specialty Chemicals, Inc. v. Huntsman Corp., 2008 WL 4457544 (Del. Ch. 2008) ("knowing and intentional" required a deliberate act, but not knowledge of the consequences of that act, and is not synonymous with "willful and malicious breach"); West & Lewis, *Contracting to Avoid Extra-Contractual Liability – Can Your Contractual Deal Ever Be the "Entire" Deal?*, 64 Bus. Law. 999 (2009). The parties might consider defining whatever term is used in an attempt to avoid this ambiguity.

The Transaction that Does Not Close

While the discussion in this preliminary note to Article 11 focuses largely on indemnification after a transaction has closed, the remedy in Article 11 by its terms applies equally where a transaction fails to close. Sellers often fail to consider what happens in this circumstance. If a breach of a representation were the basis for a buyer not closing a transaction, it would have a claim for indemnification for that breach. Under Section 10.2, termination does not preclude the exercise of other remedies, including normal contract remedies.

Normally, indemnification is considered to be a restitutional remedy. For example, if there is a lawsuit that should have been disclosed and was not, the remedy of indemnification would make the buyer whole—any damages awarded in the undisclosed lawsuit and the costs of defense would be ordered. If the pre-closing discovery of the undisclosed litigation is used by the buyer as the basis for terminating the agreement, it may then look to be compensated for the loss of the benefit of the bargain, not merely its out-of-pocket expenses. In such circumstances, the utility or value of an indemnification provision, rather than a breach of contract claim, is questionable. It may be possible to seek a "benefit of the bargain" measure of damages under the indemnification provisions, but it is not clear that a buyer would be successful.

In fact, many agreements (but not the Model Agreement) limit the availability of indemnification to transactions that close, preserving contract and noncontract remedies for transactions that have not closed. Due to uncertainty regarding the practical availability of contract damages for transactions that do not close, some buyers insist on a termination fee in the case of a transaction that does not close because of a seller breach. To be sure, there are a number of high-profile cases involving transactions that fail to close. Usually, the buyer seeks a declaratory judgment that a condition to closing has not been satisfied, while the seller seeks specific performance (or damages if that is not available). When a seller seeks damages for a transaction not closed, the measure of damages (the difference between what the buyer agreed to pay and what the seller is ultimately able to sell the target for) is clearer, but the issue of proof can be very difficult.

If the transaction does not close, the negotiated limits on indemnification in the Model Agreement, such as survival periods, thresholds, and caps, are not applicable. *See* Sections 11.5 and 11.6.

Escrow Agreement

Under the Fact Pattern, at the Closing, Buyer and Sellers will enter into the Escrow Agreement and will deposit a negotiated portion of the Purchase Price with the Escrow Agent. The Escrow Agreement will be available with respect to "Claims" (as defined in the Escrow Agreement) that Buyer may have against Sellers under Article 11 of the Model Agreement (but not for payment of the Adjustment Amount or other claims under the Escrow Agreement). Buyer would not be able to pursue claims under the Escrow Agreement for tort or tort-like claims outside the Model Agreement, or for contract claims that are not brought under Article 11. Further, Buyer need not proceed under the Escrow Agreement; rather, it could make claims against Sellers and simply ignore the Escrow Agreement.

Under the Escrow Agreement, no particular form or details are required for a Claim, although Buyer would probably want to supply enough detail to avoid the "Counter Notice" (as defined in the Escrow Agreement) from Sellers' Representative. If a Counter Notice is received, the Escrow Agent need only pay out the Escrow Funds upon joint written instructions or a final nonappealable order. If a Counter Notice is not given, the Escrow Agent is required to pay out the amount claimed. Buyer might suggest the following: "Except as provided in Section 3(a) of the Escrow Agreement, no action taken by any of the parties pursuant to the Escrow Agreement will be dispositive of Sellers' obligations under this Agreement."

How Article 11 is Organized

The organization of Article 11 is as follows.

- Section 11.1 provides that the parties' representations, warranties, covenants, and obligations survive the closing of the acquisition and are thus available as the basis for post-closing monetary remedies. It also attempts to negate defenses based on knowledge and implied waiver.
- Section 11.2 defines the matters for which Sellers will have monetary liability. It is not limited to matters arising from inaccuracies in Sellers' representations.

- Section 11.3 provides a specific monetary remedy for environmental matters. It is included as an example of a provision that deals specifically with contingencies that may not be adequately covered by the more general indemnification provisions. The types of contingencies that may be covered in this manner vary from transaction to transaction.

- Section 11.4 defines the matters for which Buyer will have monetary liability. In a cash acquisition, the scope of this provision is limited; indeed, it is often omitted entirely.

- Section 11.5 defines the time periods during which post-closing monetary remedies for breach of representation may be sought.

- Section 11.6 defines the levels of loss below (and above) which the Buyer may not have a post-closing monetary remedy against Sellers for breach of representation.

- Section 11.7 provides Buyer setoff rights against notes delivered as part of the Purchase Price and other amounts payable under the terms of the Model Agreement.

- Section 11.8 provides procedures to be followed in seeking monetary remedies for, and in the defense of, third-party claims.

- Section 11.9 provides the procedure for seeking monetary remedies for matters not involving third-party claims.

- Section 11.10 provides that any liability that might be imposed on Buyer under statute, regulation, or case law and that might otherwise adversely affect Buyer's right to indemnification will be overridden and disregarded in enforcing the indemnification provisions of Article 11.

The commentary in Article 11 uses the term "indemnification" to refer to indemnification, reimbursement, and other monetary remedies, without distinction. Throughout Article 11, the three-part phrasing of "indemnify and hold harmless . . . pay . . . or reimburse" is used. This is to make clear that, no matter how the obligation arises or the legal theory advanced, there is a right under Article 11 to receive a payment.

SELLERS' PERSPECTIVE

In reviewing Article 11 of the Model Agreement, there are four general points for Sellers to consider before proceeding to a section-by-section review.

First, the scope of Article 11 must be considered in conjunction with Sellers' representations set forth in Article 3, pre-closing covenants in Article 5, and other obligations of Sellers. It is difficult to know how much negotiating effort and capital to spend on Article 11 without understanding the scope of Sellers' liabilities and obligations in total and, more specifically, the risk that material damages will exist by virtue of a breach.

Second, albeit related, is Sellers' negotiating strategy for Article 11 as a whole. Often, there is so much to object to that it will be tempting to respond to Buyer's first draft of the indemnification provisions by discarding them and offering instead a substitute pro-seller version. Most negotiations, of course, do not allow that type of response. Therefore, depending upon the facts of the particular transaction, Sellers might consider not objecting to some points of lesser importance and concentrating on other issues of greater consequence in the indemnification provisions or elsewhere in the Model Agreement.

Third, Sellers and Buyer may disagree on the elements of indemnification such as liability (particularly for the unknown), duration of exposure, size of thresholds or deductibles, size of caps, and the existence of escrows. Where bargaining may break down and an impasse results, the parties might consider looking to representation and warranty insurance or environmental insurance, or both, as a way to deal with fundamental differences. Resort to insurance, the cost of which can be borne as the parties may negotiate, can bridge otherwise irreconcilable differences.

Fourth, Sellers should consider that Sections 11.2 and 11.3 impose joint and several liability on each Seller. Sellers should consider, among themselves, whether, as to particular provisions of Article 11, joint and several liability is fair and appropriate.

11.1 Survival; Remedies

GENERAL COMMENT

Section 11.1 embodies three concepts: (a) the obligations of the parties survive the closing, (b) the right to a remedy is unaffected by any investigation or information obtained, regardless of when obtained (the antidote to the *Hendricks* case discussed in "Judicial Limitations on Enforcement" in preliminary note to Article 11), and (c) a waiver of a condition to Closing does not affect the right to bring a claim (the antidote to the substituted performance doctrine). These concepts will be explored separately.

> **(a) All representations, warranties, covenants, and obligations in this Agreement, the Disclosure Letter, the supplements to the Disclosure Letter, and any certificate, document, or other writing delivered pursuant to this Agreement will survive the Closing and the consummation and performance of the Contemplated Transactions.**

COMMENT

The representations made by the sellers in acquisitions of private companies are typically intended to provide a basis for post-closing liability if they prove to be inaccurate. In acquisitions of public companies, the target's representations typically terminate at the closing and thus serve principally as information-gathering mechanisms, closing conditions, and a basis for liability if the closing does not occur. *See* "Purposes of Sellers' Representations" in preliminary note to Article 3.

In order to confirm that Sellers' representations are intended to provide a basis for post-closing liability, the Model Agreement includes an express survival clause to avoid the possibility that a court might import the real property law principle that obligations merge with the delivery of a warranty deed and hold that the representations merge with the sale of the Shares and thus cannot form the basis of a remedy after the closing. Secondary authorities and discussions by the courts might suggest that a survival clause is necessary for the representations to be enforced beyond the closing. That should not be the case, but no practitioner would want his or her transaction to be the one in which a court takes a different view. Although the typical contract provides that the representations survive, what is really meant, with respect to pre-closing breaches, is that a claim relating to the breach survives. If a representation has been breached, the breach could be used as the basis to terminate the contract. But there is no continuing representation. The representation that there is no litigation does not mean there is a continuing representation that would be applicable to litigation brought years after the closing. So what is meant by saying the representations "survive" is that a remedy is preserved after closing.

Sometimes the survival provision provides that the "representations survive for a period of x years," and goes on to say that, if a claim is made within x years, the representation survives until the matter is resolved. That formulation is what causes the courts the most trouble, in that it conflates survival with a privately ordered statute of limitations. The Model Agreement not only contains in Section 11.1 a provision that representations survive the closing, but includes separately in Section 11.5 time limits for bringing claims. This structure is intended to avoid the difficulties sometimes encountered with less precise language. *See* commentary to Section 11.5; KLING & NUGENT § 15.02[2].

SELLERS' RESPONSE

It is unusual, but not unprecedented, for the sellers' representations to terminate at the closing in some private sales. If sellers of a private company are numerous or include investors who have not actively participated in the target's business (such as venture capital investors in a development stage company), they may analogize their situation to that of the shareholders of a public company and argue that their representations should not survive the closing. Or sellers conducting an auction of a company that is sought-after by a number of buyers might have enough bargaining leverage to eliminate any post-closing liability.

Sellers might object to the survival of pre-closing covenants as distinct from covenants such as nondisclosure or noncompetition which by their terms are to operate after closing.

Sellers might also argue that representations, covenants, and obligations in any document or writing other than the Model Agreement should be governed by that other document or writing, not the Model Agreement.

> **(b) The right to indemnification, payment, reimbursement, or other remedy based upon any such representation, warranty, covenant, or obligation will not be affected by any investigation (including any environmental investigation or assessment) conducted or any Knowledge acquired at any time, whether before or after the execution and delivery of this Agreement or the Closing Date, with respect to the accuracy or inaccuracy of, or compliance with, such representation, warranty, covenant, or obligation.**

COMMENT

Section 11.1(b) makes it clear that Sellers and Buyer have expressly agreed that Buyer is not to be charged with any investigation conducted or any knowledge resulting from any investigation. If Buyer sues for fraud, perhaps the existence of an investigation is an element of whether there was justifiable reliance. But in a contract action, Buyer will want to rely on the representations made, with or without an investigation and no matter how superficially the investigation was conducted. Buyer is bargaining for the accuracy of the representations, and has, in part, offered a Purchase Price based on their accuracy.

While Buyer has presumably made a due diligence investigation and conditioned closing on the truth of the representations, the fact that there is a Closing does not mean that Buyer has waived its right to make a post-closing claim. In fact, prior to assuming control of the target, it is impossible to know its true state of affairs. Modern businesses are far too complex. To be sure, courts are skeptical when an investigation is made and problems are not uncovered. Witness the court's scathing remarks about "the six-million dollar due diligence team" in the trial court ruling in Merrill Lynch & Co., Inc. v. Allegheny Energy, Inc., 2005 WL 1663265 (S.D.N.Y. 2005), rev'd, 500 F.3d 171 (2d Cir. 2007).

To the extent that Section 11.2 contains stand-alone indemnifications unrelated to representations, such as the tax indemnification in Section 11.2(d), it is clear that Buyer has bargained for the absolute protection those clauses represent. In fact, Buyer may have bargained for such indemnification *because* it made an investigation and became aware of a problem. Therefore, knowledge is simply irrelevant to these stand-alone indemnifications.

Section 11.1(b) provides that knowledge of an inaccuracy by the indemnified party (or any investigation) is not a defense to the claim for indemnification. Thus, Buyer can assert an indemnification claim not only for inaccuracies first discovered after the closing, but also for inaccuracies disclosed or discovered before the closing. Section 11.1(b) emphasizes that when knowledge is acquired is irrelevant. While it is not clear whether a court would make this distinction, an untruth discovered prior to signing of an acquisition agreement could conceivably differ from an untruth discovered after the bargain is made, but before closing. Section 11.1(b) does not make such a distinction. Buyer is still entitled to receive the bargain negotiated, regardless of when the untruth is discovered.

As discussed in preliminary note to this Article 11, some courts have found that reliance, an element of the tort remedy of deceit, is also a required element of a contract claim based upon a breach of a representation. In their view, if a buyer knew that a representation as made was untrue, it could not have relied upon the representation and an essential element of the contract claim would not have been proven. To counter those judicial rulings, the right to indemnification is expressly preserved in the Model Agreement, despite knowledge or investigation. While a reservation of rights is not known to carry the day in any jurisdiction where reliance is required, the inclusion of such a clause has been cited favorably in other jurisdictions. *See, e.g.,* Cobalt Operating, LLC v. James Crystal Enterprises, LLC, 2007 WL 2142926 (Del. Ch. 2007), *aff'd*, 995 A.2d 594 (Del. 2008).

Buyer's principal rationale for its position is that it is entitled to rely on the representations made when the Model Agreement was signed—which presumably entered into Buyer's determination of the price that it is willing to pay—and that Sellers should not be able to limit Buyer's options to either waiving the breach or terminating the Model Agreement. Buyer can also argue that it has purchased Sellers' representations and the related right to indemnification and is entitled to a purchase price adjustment for an inaccuracy in those representations, regardless of Buyer's knowledge. In addition, Buyer can argue that any recognition of a defense based on Buyer's knowledge could convert each claim for indemnification into an extensive discovery inquiry as to the state of Buyer's knowledge, which could preclude Buyer from obtaining summary judgment regardless of how clear the breach.

SELLERS' RESPONSE

Sellers, in all earnestness, explain that they do not want to be "sandbagged" by buyers. They postulate that the buyer discovers a problem in due diligence, lets the seller represent to the contrary in the agreement without informing the seller that its representation is inaccurate, and then closes, only to make an indemnification claim for a breach of representation. Sellers may cast their argument as an appeal to "fairness"—that if they had known of the problem they could have remedied it or negotiated a price adjustment. *See* West & Shah, *Debunking the Myth of the Sandbagging Buyer: When Sellers Ask Buyers to Agree to Anti-Sandbagging Clauses, Who Is Sandbagging Whom?*, 11 M&A Law. 3 (Jan. 2007); Quaintance, *Can You Sandbag? When a Buyer Knows Seller's Reps and Warranties Are Untrue*, 5 M&A Law. 8 (March 2002). *See also* Vice Chancellor Strine's discussion of the "double liar" in ABRY Partners V, L.P. v. F&W Acquisition, LLC, 891 A.2d 1032 (Del. Ch. 2006).

This issue is often the subject of considerable negotiation. Sellers may argue that Buyer should be required to disclose a known breach of Sellers' representations before the Closing and waive it, renegotiate the price, or refuse to close. They may request a contractual provision requiring that Buyer disclose its discovery of an inaccuracy immediately and elect at that time to waive the inaccuracy or terminate the Model Agreement, precluding an indemnity claim for breaches known to it before closing. An example of such an anti-sandbagging provision follows:

> [Except as set forth in a Certificate to be delivered by Buyer at the Closing,] Buyer has no knowledge of any facts or circumstances that would serve as the basis for a claim by Buyer against Sellers based upon a breach of any of the representations and warranties of Sellers contained in this Agreement [or breach of any of Sellers' covenants or agreements to be performed by any of them at or prior to Closing]. Buyer shall be deemed to have waived in full any breach of any of Sellers' representations and warranties [and any such covenants and agreements] of which Buyer has knowledge at the Closing.

Buyer will likely object to an anti-sandbagging provision for the reasons discussed previously in the commentary. Even if Buyer is not willing to accept this provision, it may be willing to delete Section 11.1(b) as a compromise, so the Model Agreement is silent on the sandbagging issue.

If Buyer is willing to accept some limitation on its entitlement to indemnification based on its knowledge, it should carefully define the circumstances in which knowledge is to have this effect. For example, the Model Agreement could distinguish among knowledge that Buyer had before signing, knowledge acquired through Buyer's pre-closing investigation, and knowledge resulting from Sellers' pre-closing disclosures, and could limit the class of persons within Buyer's organization whose knowledge is relevant (for example, the actual personal knowledge of named senior officers having responsibility for the transaction).

Sellers might suggest that, where they specifically bring the inaccuracy of the representations to the attention of Buyer in written supplements, Buyer must either waive the breach and close, sue for breach, or renegotiate. In Gusmao v. GMT Group, Inc., 2008 WL 2980039 (S.D.N.Y. Aug. 1, 2008), the sellers claimed they had informed the buyer prior to closing of the facts that allegedly constituted a breach of warranty, and therefore the buyer had waived its right to rely on the sellers' warranties. The court found the critical issue to be not whether the buyer knew of, but whether the sellers had disclosed to the buyer, these facts. The court explained that if the buyer closed in the full knowledge and acceptance of facts disclosed by the sellers which would have constituted a breach of warranty, it would have waived its right to rely on the warranty unless it had expressly preserved its right. Buyers often find this proposal unacceptable on the grounds that it denies them the benefit of the bargain, and the other grounds set forth above. *See* Committee on Negotiated Acquisitions, *Purchasing the Stock of a Privately*

Held Company: The Legal Effect of an Acquisition Review, 51 Bus. Law. 479 (1996); Kling & Nugent § 15.02[2].

> **(c)** **The waiver of any condition relating to any representation, warranty, covenant, or obligation will not affect the right to indemnification, payment, reimbursement, or other remedy based upon such representation, warranty, covenant, or obligation.**

COMMENT

Section 11.1(c) states that the waiver of any condition to Closing relating to a representation, warranty, covenant, or obligation will not affect any right to indemnification based thereon. This provision is designed to avoid the effects of the substituted performance argument, discussed in preliminary note to this Article 11, and to take advantage of such cases as *Ziff-Davis* without the need for a specific reservation of rights. Whether it is effective has not been established by case law. This Section primarily relates to Section 8.1 of the Model Agreement, which makes the accuracy of Sellers' representations a condition precedent to the Buyer's obligation to close the transaction. Therefore, if Buyer has knowledge of a breach of one of Seller's representations prior to the Closing, the Buyer conceivably could be deemed to have waived Section 8.1 by closing, despite Section 12.17, which provides that waivers must be in writing. Buyer may be faced with a waiver of Section 8.1 under two circumstances. The first arises where Buyer discovers the untruth of a representation (or other breach) and does not bring it to the attention of Sellers. The second occurs where Sellers bring the untruth of a representation (or other Breach) to the attention of Buyer, either before Closing or by refusing to deliver the required certificate at Closing. In either case, this Section seeks to preserve Buyer's rights.

SELLERS' RESPONSE

Sellers may object to Section 11.1(c) and suggest that it be deleted in its entirety and the contrary be inserted. Sellers might insist that they should be required to close only when they understand what the financial consequences of the breach of representation may be.

11.2   Indemnification, Payment, and Reimbursement by Sellers

GENERAL COMMENT

Although, as noted under "Contract Remedies" in preliminary note to this Article 11, the inaccuracy of a representation or a breach of covenant that survives the closing may give rise to a claim for damages for breach without any express indemnification provision, it is customary in the acquisition of a privately held company for the buyer to be given a clearly specified right of indemnification for breaches of representations, warranties, covenants, and obligations, and against certain other liabilities. Although customary in concept, the scope and details of the indemnification provisions are often the subject of intense negotiation.

Indemnification provisions should be carefully tailored to the type and structure of the acquisition, the identity of the parties, and the specific business risks associated with the target. Adjustments may be required for a purchase from a consolidated group of companies, a foreign corporation, or a joint venture, because in each case there may be different risks and difficulties in obtaining indemnification. Still other adjustments will be required to address risks associated with the nature of the target's businesses and its past manner of operation.

The provisions of Section 11.2 are intended to operate independently of each other. Certain business risks and liabilities may not be covered adequately by the representations, the breach of which would be subject to indemnification, and instead may be covered by specific indemnification provisions such as in Section 11.2(d), (e), and (f). *See* "Protections Independent of Representations: Buyer's Expansion of Remedies" in preliminary note to this Article 11. The extent to which this type of provision is included varies depending on the circumstances of each acquisition and is often subject to negotiation. *See* KLING & NUGENT § 15.02[1][d]. Similar provisions may be included for indemnification for liabilities arising from disclosed contingencies affecting the target, which, as a result of their disclosure in the Disclosure Letter, would not give rise to a claim for breach of a representation (*see* Section 11.2(f)). A common example of such a specifically indemnified contingency is a lawsuit affecting the target that is disclosed in response to Section 3.15(a).

The indemnification provisions, which typically bear most heavily on sellers, often will be the most vigorously contested portion of an acquisition agreement. They provide the means of recourse for a buyer in the event the seller has not lived up to its end of the bargain. The points of conflict between the interests of buyers and the interests of sellers are many. *See* M&A PROCESS 231–32. With respect to the give and take in the negotiation of the indemnification provisions, *see* KLING & NUGENT ch. 15.

Some experts have asserted there is no distinction between "indemnify" and "hold harmless," while some drafters believe one phrase is more powerful than the other. *See, e.g.,* ADAMS, A MANUAL OF STYLE FOR CONTRACT DRAFTING §§12.134—146 (2nd ed. 2008). Both are customarily included. In Majkowski v. American Imaging Management Services, LLC, 913 A.2d 572 (Del. Ch. 2006), the court stated that, while modern authorities confirm that the terms "indemnify" and "hold harmless" have little, if any, different meanings, a distinction is sometimes made in litigation. It is also customary to include the trilogy of concepts (i) indemnify, (ii) pay, and (iii) reimburse, although all three may not be necessary to provide the clear assurance Buyer wants.

See STARK ch. 10.

GENERAL SELLERS' RESPONSE

While Sellers will be expected to respond to the details of the language Buyer has demanded, they should consider whether Buyer should be provided a remedy at all (after all, in public acquisitions no one suggests that shareholders have responsibility), and, if a remedy is provided, how it should be circumscribed.

In the absence of an explicit provision to the contrary, Sellers may be surprised to find that Buyer's remedies for inaccuracies in Sellers' representations and other breaches may not be limited to those provided by the indemnification and reimbursement provisions of the Model Agreement. Buyer may also have causes of action based on breach of contract, fraud and misrepresentation, negligent misrepresentation, federal securities laws, deceptive practices acts, and other federal and state statutory claims.

In particular, Section 11.2 is silent on the issue of exclusivity of remedy. Furthermore, Section 12.11 makes it clear that indemnification under Article 11 is *not* the exclusive remedy. Sellers have a strong interest in making the indemnification provisions the exclusive remedy. The parties are likely to spend significant time and effort negotiating the provisions of the Model Agreement limiting dollar amounts and time periods (Sections 11.5 and 11.6). Sellers want the assurance of knowing that there is a single document upon which they can rely in assessing their exposure, regardless of the nature or form which a claim may take (contract, tort, equity, fraud, securities fraud, or other). Sellers will argue that the parties will have totally wasted their time and effort in negotiating limits in Article 11 if they can be easily circumvented.

Buyer might consider conceding Sellers' argument to some extent by allowing the limitations in Sections 11.5 and 11.6 to apply whether Buyer casts its claim for indemnification under Article 11 or otherwise. This concession, however, would address only part of Sellers' stated desire for certainty. Sellers might assert that they do not want to face a claim that they engaged in a transaction tainted by common law misrepresentation, fraud, or securities fraud. Sellers, however, must face the fact that federal securities laws claims cannot be waived in advance. Other claims, including those based on common law fraud and state securities laws claims, may also survive an exclusivity clause under applicable state law.

Therefore, Sellers might advocate for several changes to the document. Sellers would want the language of Section 11.2 (or Section 12.11) to reflect the intent that the claim for indemnification under Article 11 is the exclusive remedy for any claim arising out of the transaction, except for breach of noncompetition or nondisclosure covenants. Sellers may suggest a clause as follows:

> [After the Closing,] the rights set forth in Sections 11.2, 11.3, and 11.4 will be the exclusive remedy for breach or inaccuracy of any of the representations and warranties contained in Articles 3 and 4 and will be in lieu of all other remedies available at law or in equity. Notwithstanding the foregoing, nothing in this Agreement will prevent any party from

bringing an action based upon fraud or willful misconduct by the other party in connection with this Agreement.

Although not itself an exclusive remedy provision, Sellers may want to add language (perhaps in Article 12) to the effect that Buyer has not regarded as material and has not relied upon any representations or other inducements except for those set forth in the Agreement. Sellers may suggest a clause as follows:

> Buyer has not relied on Sellers with respect to any matter in connection with Buyer's evaluation of the Company other than the representations and warranties of Sellers specifically set forth in Article 3, and Buyer acknowledges that Sellers are making no representations or warranties, express or implied, of any nature whatever with respect to the Company other than the representations and warranties of Sellers specifically set forth in Article 3.

These two provisions have separate effects. The first makes indemnification the exclusive contract remedy. It probably precludes a tort claim for innocent breaches of the representations, but preserves a tort claim for fraud or intentional breaches.

While an exception such as "fraud or willful misconduct" is often made and, in fact, may be volunteered by Sellers, such exceptions have been criticized as being too imprecise. *See* Johnson & Johnson v. Guidant Corp., 2007 WL 2456625 (S.D.N.Y. Aug. 29, 2007) (interpreting an exception for "willful and material breach" and stating that "'willful' is a notoriously ambiguous word"). *See also* West and Shah, *Debunking the Myth of the Sandbagging Buyer: When Sellers Ask Buyers to Agree to Anti-Sandbagging Clauses, Who Is Sandbagging Whom?*, 11 M&A Law. 3 at 6 (Jan. 2007). *See also* Kling & Nugent § 15.03[4].

The second provision has a different effect. It is an acknowledgement by Buyer that it has not relied on any representations outside of the Model Agreement. By inserting this clause, Sellers hope that a court will be convinced that all of their representations about the business outside the express representations in the Model Agreement (every conversation by Sellers about the business is arguably a representation about the business) were not reasonably relied upon, hence defeating an essential element of securities law claims and common law claims based on fraud. *See* "Noncontract Remedies" in preliminary note to this Article 11.

Sellers, jointly and severally, shall indemnify and hold harmless Buyer, the Acquired Companies, and their respective Representatives, shareholders, Subsidiaries, and Related Persons (collectively, the "Buyer Indemnified Persons") from, and shall pay to Buyer Indemnified Persons the amount of, or reimburse Buyer Indemnified Persons for, any Loss that Buyer Indemnified Persons or any of them may suffer, sustain, or become subject to, as a result of, in connection with, or relating to:

WHEN THE OBLIGATION TO INDEMNIFY BEGINS

COMMENT

The obligation to indemnify under Section 11.2 begins at the date of signing of the Model Agreement. Accordingly, Buyer is provided with a contractual indemnification remedy for breaches of representations, warranties, covenants, and obligations under the Model Agreement that occur from and after signing. As noted above, however, if the transaction does not close, the negotiated limits on indemnification in the Model Agreement, such as survival periods, thresholds, and caps, are not applicable. *See* "The Transaction That Does Not Close" in preliminary note to this Article 11. *See also* Sections 11.5 and 11.6.

SELLERS' RESPONSE

Sellers may logically argue that indemnification should not start until closing of the transaction because, until the transaction closes, Buyer will have suffered no loss or other damage. This change could be accomplished by adding the phrase, "From and after the Closing," at the beginning of the lead-in clause to Section 11.2. Alternatively, Sellers could request that the negotiated limits on indemnification in the Model Agreement, such as survival periods, thresholds, and caps, should be equally applicable to pre-closing indemnification claims.

JOINT AND SEVERAL LIABILITY OF SELLERS

COMMENT

Section 11.2 provides for joint and several liability of all Sellers. This is Buyer's opening position under the Fact Pattern because there is no dominant shareholder. Each Seller may be held liable for the entirety of damages, regardless of the amount of consideration received by that Seller and regardless of that Seller's lack of participation in, or knowledge of, the business. Among other reasons Buyer may seek broad relief is because of a concern that one or more Sellers may not be creditworthy or may put themselves beyond service of process.

Factors of creditworthiness may influence Buyer in selecting the persons from whom to seek indemnity. Buyer may seek indemnity (or a guaranty of indemnity) from an affiliate of Seller (for example, an individual who is the sole shareholder of a Seller that is a thinly capitalized holding company).

SELLERS' RESPONSE

Sellers may object to their obligations to indemnify being on a joint and several basis. Sellers will argue that such joint and several liability makes one shareholder, presumably the one with the most assets (or the most accessible assets), responsible for the entire obligation even though this shareholder receives only a portion of the proceeds. This result is particularly objectionable since, as shareholders, Sellers' risk of loss for other claims against the target is proportional and confined (in the absence of "veil-piercing" circumstances) to the value of their investment in their shares with no personal liability whatsoever. Sellers also might suggest that different liability be imposed on different Sellers, depending on the representations at issue. For example, Sellers might be jointly and severally liable for representations concerning the target, but only individually liable for the representations concerning their respective ownership of the stock being sold.

To the extent that an escrow has been negotiated that represents Sellers' maximum exposure or in other circumstances, joint and several liability may not be necessary.

Sellers' proposal would ordinarily be to substitute other language, which would achieve one of the following results:

- The optimum result for Sellers would normally be to have their liability for indemnity not be joint, but several, individual, and proportionate to each Seller's shareholdings. For example, if there are two equal shareholders, then each would be liable for 50% of each loss. At the very least, Sellers would normally insist on several and individual liability on such strictly personal matters as title to stock sold by an individual shareholder and, of course, personal performance of covenants such as the noncompete and nondisclosure.

- A less favorable alternative for Sellers is to allow joint and several liability, but to have any particular shareholder's liability capped at that Seller's individual share of the purchase price.

- In any scenario other than the optimum result referred to above, Sellers could seek an undertaking by Buyer to use best efforts to join all Sellers in any action in seeking indemnity and to provide that all Sellers submit to personal jurisdiction in the designated forum.

In any circumstance where Buyer has not agreed to across-the-board several/individual liability, Sellers should at least consider having a contribution agreement among themselves to deal with any disproportionate liability suffered by any individual Seller as a result of joint and several obligations. Sellers can divide up responsibility among themselves in any manner they wish. *See* Ancillary Document E—Contribution Agreement. Sellers may also consider placing a certain amount of the proceeds into a separate escrow account accessible only by themselves and that they established in order to fund any eventual liability which arises within an agreed-upon time frame.

INDEMNIFIED PERSONS

COMMENT

The persons indemnified may include virtually everyone involved on Buyer's side of the acquisition, including its directors, officers, and shareholders, who may become defendants in litigation involving the target or who may suffer a loss resulting from their association with problems at the target. It may be appropriate to include fiduciaries of Buyer's employee benefit plans if such plans have played a role in the acquisition, such as when an employee stock ownership plan participates in a leveraged buyout.

Both Buyer and the Acquired Companies are indemnified parties. The Acquired Companies are not parties to the Model Agreement, but some buyers may add the Company to the parties making the representations and covenants. In any Breach, Buyer will usually suffer only an indirect harm. For example, if the accounts receivable are less than represented, Buyer has only suffered an indirect injury, perhaps not cognizable. On the other hand, the Acquired Companies' receivables are depleted and Buyer may be protected if the deficiency in the receivables is restored by their equivalent value in cash.

In providing indemnification rights, Buyer should be aware of the risk of creating an artificial defense. In Katun Corp. v. Clark, 484 F.3d 972 (8th Cir. 2007), a target's CEO, several other officers, and the target had engaged in massive tax fraud; the CEO and the target pled guilty. Several months earlier the corporation had been sold to PNA Holdings, LLC. PNA and the target (Katun Corporation) sought indemnification from the selling shareholders. The representative of the sellers entered into a settlement agreement on behalf of the selling shareholders. Katun brought an action against the CEO for failure to pay his portion of the settlement. The district court granted the CEO's motion to dismiss on the basis that the indemnification was void as against public policy because it allowed the target to avoid responsibility for its illegal actions (in pari delicto). While the appellate court overturned the decision, recognizing that PNA was the harmed party, the case serves as a cautionary tale.

See KLING & NUGENT § 15.03[3].

SELLERS' RESPONSE

Sellers might object to some or all of the persons other than Buyer being within the defined class of "Buyer Indemnified Persons," all of whom would thereby have third-party rights under Section 12.10. Sellers might argue that they have dealt with Buyer and have reached conclusions about Buyer's fairness, objectiveness, and propensities. Sellers may not want to expose themselves to a large universe of adverse parties who were not privy to the negotiations. Sellers might argue that they may be precluded from raising counterclaims and defenses that would otherwise exist if these suits were brought not by Buyer, but by certain other "Buyer

Indemnified Persons." Sellers may particularly object to the indemnification of representatives, shareholders, and Related Persons.

The Sellers may ask how the indemnitees would be liable and why they would need this protection. To the extent there is any risk, indemnifying multiple parties, who have inconsistent positions and therefore require separate counsel, could be complicated, confusing, and expensive.

DEFINITION OF LOSS

COMMENT

Loss. The definition of "Loss" set forth in Section 1.1 is very broad and includes, among other things, losses unrelated to third-party claims. However, the common law definition of the term "indemnification" describes a restitutionary cause of action in which a plaintiff sues a defendant for reimbursement of payments made by the plaintiff to a third party. A court may hold, therefore, that a drafter's unadorned use of the term "indemnify" (usually coupled with "and hold harmless") refers only to compensation for losses due to third-party claims. *See* Pacific Gas & Electric Co. v. G.W. Thomas Drayage & Rigging Co., 442 P.2d 641 (Cal. 1968) (indemnity clause in a contract ambiguous on the issue; failure to admit extrinsic evidence on the point was error); *see also* Mesa Sand & Gravel Co. v. Landfill, 759 P.2d 757 (Colo. Ct. App. 1988), *rev'd in part on other grounds*, 776 P.2d 362 (Colo. 1989) (indemnification clause covers only payments made to third parties). *But see* Atari Corp. v. Ernst & Whinney, 981 F.2d 1025 (9th Cir. 1992) (limiting *Pacific Gas & Electric* and relying on Black's Law Dictionary; the term "indemnification" is not limited to repayment of amounts expended on third-party claims); Edward E. Gillen Co. v. United States, 825 F.2d 1155 (7th Cir. 1987). Modern usage and practice have redefined the term "indemnification" in the acquisition context to refer to compensation for all losses and expenses, regardless of source, caused by a breach of the acquisition agreement (or other specified events). The courts should respect express contract language that incorporates the broader meaning.

The Model Agreement also includes the requirement of Sellers to "pay" and "reimburse" Buyer Indemnified Persons. Reference to payment and reimbursement is intended to further avoid potentially troublesome case law regarding the implications of narrowly defining the word "indemnify."

The Model Agreement does not expressly include interest within the definition of Loss. Buyer may provide that damages include interest from the date Buyer first is required to pay any expense through the date the indemnification payment is received. Such a provision may be appropriate if Buyer expects to incur substantial expenses before Buyer's right to indemnification has been established and also lessens Sellers' incentive to dispute the claim for purposes of delay. If any indemnification is fully litigated to a judgment, state law may provide for pre-judgment interest in any event.

The amount to be indemnified is generally the dollar value of the out-of-pocket payment or loss. That amount may not fully compensate Buyer, however, if the loss relates to an item that was the basis of a pricing multiple. For example, if Buyer agreed to pay $10 million, which represented five times the target's earnings for the prior year, but it was discovered after the closing that annual earnings were overstated by $200,000, indemnification of $200,000 would not reimburse Buyer fully for its $1 million overpayment. The Model Agreement could specify the basis for the calculation of the purchase price (which may be vigorously contested by Sellers) and provide specifically for indemnification for overpayments based on that pricing methodology. Buyer should proceed cautiously in this area, since the corollary to the argument that it is entitled to indemnification based on a multiple of earnings is that any matter that affects the balance sheet, but not the earnings statement (for example, fixed asset valuation), should not be indemnified at all. Furthermore, raising the subject in negotiations may lead to an express provision excluding the possibility of determining damages on this basis. The inclusion of diminution in value as an element of damages gives a buyer flexibility to seek recovery on this basis without an express statement of its pricing methodology. In Cobalt Operating, LLC v. James Crystal Enterprises, Inc., 2007 WL 2142926 (Del. Ch. 2007), *aff'd*, 945 A.2d 594 (Del. 2008), the court looked very carefully at a claim based on a deficiency in represented cash flow and awarded a multiple. *See* KLING & NUGENT § 15.02[3].

Duty to Mitigate. The duty to mitigate is a principle of contract law requiring that a party exert reasonable efforts to minimize losses. RESTATEMENT (SECOND) OF CONTRACTS § 350; 11 CORBIN ON CONTRACTS § 57.11. While this principle is generally referred to as a duty, it is really a means by which a party breaching a contract can invoke a failure to mitigate as a defense to reduce the damages for which it otherwise might be liable. For example, in Vigortone AG Products, Inc. v. AG Products, Inc., 316 F.3d 641 (7th Cir. 2002), the court considered charges of fraud and breach of contract in the sale of a business. It appeared to the court that the buyer could have averted most of the loss by hedging contracts that it had inherited, in which case it would not be entitled to recover damages that it could readily have avoided. The decision of the lower court was reversed and this matter was left to be dealt with on remand.

SELLERS' RESPONSE

Loss. The definition of "Loss" may be found by Sellers to be exceedingly broad. Sellers can argue that "costs of investigation" should not be an element of damages, except perhaps in response to a Third-Party Claim. Sellers can object to being put in a position of financing a voluntary investigation by Buyer (a "fishing expedition") to find fault in order to make the case against Sellers, as opposed to some legally mandated investigation (for example, in the case of an environmental matter where there is an indication of a spill or discharge that Buyer is legally obligated to investigate).

Sellers may assert that incidental or consequential damages should be expressly excluded, as should punitive damages. It is one thing for Buyer to be entitled to compensatory or actual damages (i.e., damages that flow directly and immediately from the breach), but any damages other than compensatory damages are speculative and remote and will encourage contention between Buyer and Sellers. *See* West & Duran, *Reassessing the Consequences of "Consequential" Damage Waivers in Acquisition Agreements*, 63 Bus. Law. 777 (2008).

The inclusion of "reasonable attorneys' fees and expenses" may also be objectionable to Sellers, except perhaps in connection with the defense of a third-party action against Buyer. Sellers can argue that a well-financed Buyer could intimidate or take advantage of weaker Sellers by holding over their heads the threat of massive legal fees. Moreover, as in the case of expenses of investigation, Sellers would have the same objection to attorneys' fees that Buyer might incur in investigating nonthird-party claims and in developing the case against Sellers.

Sellers are likely to resist inclusion of "diminution of value" precisely to preclude a multiple-of-earnings theory. Sellers could argue that they have no control or influence on how Buyer makes its price determination, and that, if it were to have been the subject of open negotiations, Sellers would never have agreed to it.

Reduction by Tax Benefit and Insurance. Sellers often argue that the appropriate measure of damages is the amount of Buyer's out-of-pocket payment, less any tax benefit that Buyer receives as a result of the loss, liability, or expense. If this approach is accepted, the logical extension is to include in the measure of damages the tax cost to Buyer of receiving the indemnification payment (including tax costs resulting from a reduction in basis, and the resulting reduction in depreciation and amortization or increase in gain recognized on a sale, if the indemnification payment is treated as an adjustment of purchase price). These tax provisions are often highly complex and dependent on Buyer's particular tax status and administration of its tax affairs. Consequently, the entire issue of offsets against indemnification for tax benefits is often omitted.

Sellers may also argue that the Model Agreement should explicitly state that damages will be net of any insurance proceeds or payments from any other responsible parties. If Buyer is willing to accept such a limitation on the amount of its indemnification recovery, it may wish to consider seeking to be compensated for any cost it incurs due to its efforts to obtain insurance or other third-party recoveries, including those that may result from retrospective premium adjustments, experience-based premium adjustments, and indemnification obligations. Including insurance raises timing issues since insurance payments are often delayed, and are frequently subject to negotiations and disputes with the insurance carriers. *See* Kling & Nugent § 15.03[2].

Purchase Price Adjustment. The Model Agreement contains a purchase price adjustment mechanism in Sections 2.5 and 2.6. Sellers will often request a provision to the effect that the indemnification provisions do not require Sellers to compensate Buyer for matters already taken into account through the post-closing adjustment mechanism provided for elsewhere in the Agreement. This can be done by providing that the losses subject to indemnification for a matter that was also the subject of a post-closing adjustment are reduced by the amount of the corresponding purchase price reduction. *See* commentary to Section 2.5.

> **(a) any Breach of any representation or warranty made by Sellers in (i) this Agreement or the Disclosure Letter (without giving effect to any supplement to the Disclosure Letter), (ii) any supplement to the Disclosure Letter, (iii) the certificate delivered pursuant to Section 8.3 (without giving effect to the words "in all material respects" in Section 8.1(a)), or (iv) any other certificate, document, or other writing delivered by Sellers pursuant to this Agreement;**

SCOPE OF INDEMNIFICATION

COMMENT

The scope of the indemnification provisions is important. Buyer generally will want the indemnification provisions to cover breaches of representations in the Disclosure Letter, any supplements to the Disclosure Letter, and any other certificates delivered pursuant to the Model Agreement, but may not want the indemnification provisions to cover breaches of noncompetition agreements, service agreements, and similar agreements related to the acquisition, for which there would normally be separate breach of contract remedies, separate limitations (if any) regarding timing and amounts of any claims for damages, and arguably equitable remedies.

Section 11.2(a)(i) provides for indemnification for any breach of Sellers' representations in the Model Agreement (without giving effect to a supplement to the Disclosure Letter). Any qualification included as a supplement to the Disclosure Letter is not recognized and therefore cannot avoid or cure a Breach.

"BRING DOWN" OF REPRESENTATIONS TO CLOSING

COMMENT

Section 8.1(a) and (b) contains a "bring down" clause, whereby Sellers' representations are "brought down" to the Closing Date to determine their accuracy as of that date, and Sections 2.4(a)(viii) and 8.3 provide for Sellers' delivery of a closing or "bring down" certificate, whereby Sellers confirm the accuracy of the representations as of the Closing Date. If the "bring down" certificate makes no mention of a representation that has become untrue between signing and closing, and Buyer subsequently discovers the inaccurate representation, whether or not Sellers knew about it prior to the Closing, Buyer would be entitled to seek indemnification under Section 11.2(a) based on the inaccurate "bring down" certificate. Even where Sellers disclose to Buyer prior to the Closing that a representation has become untrue and deliver a supplement to the Disclosure Letter and a qualified "bring down" certificate, Sellers would have liability for indemnification if Buyer chooses to close. However, the size of the threshold or deductible that the parties negotiate will determine whether the Sellers have liability for an immaterial breach. *See* commentary to Section 11.6.

SELLERS' RESPONSE

Sellers may seek to exclude from the indemnity a Breach of the representations at the date of the Model Agreement if the Breach is disclosed by a supplement to the Disclosure Letter before the closing. This provides an incentive for Sellers to update the Disclosure Letter carefully. Seller can also argue that if the problem has been cleared up and the representations are true at the Closing, Buyer is getting what it bargained for. Buyer could counter that under those circumstances it does not get what it bargained for, namely a company that conformed in all respects to what was represented at signing.

Sellers may want to argue that an indemnifiable breach must be material (and, in some instances, defining materiality by virtue of a dollar threshold). If Buyer has allowed a reasonably sized threshold or deductible in Article 11, it will argue that the purpose of the threshold or deductible is to allow Sellers to have freedom from liability from breaches that in the aggregate are not material, and that separate materiality standards in Article 11 would constitute "double-dipping."

REPRESENTATIONS IN OTHER DOCUMENTS

COMMENT

Clauses (i) and (ii) of Section 11.2(a) extend indemnification to representations made in the Disclosure Letter and any supplement to the Disclosure Letter. While one does not think of Disclosure Letters as containing representations, they frequently do. Often in at attempt to characterize, put bounds around, or neutralize a particular disclosure, Sellers may characterize them in some way, e.g. "the cumulative effect of which would not be material" or "the Company's exposure would not exceed $50,000." Buyer is afforded protection if those statements prove to be incorrect.

Clause (iii) of Section 11.2(a) refers to the "bring down" certificate delivered pursuant to Section 8.3. If Sellers deliver certificates to the effect that the representations are true as though made on and as of the Closing Date, a new representation is being made and would be relied on by the Buyer. *See, e.g.,* ABRY Partners V, L.P., v. F&W Acquisition, LLC, 891 A.2d 1052 (Del. Ch. 2006), where buyer, attempting to rescind an acquisition agreement, alleged that the "bring down" certificate was false.

The Model Agreement provides in clause (iv) of Section 11.2(a) for indemnification for any inaccuracy in the representations and warranties made in certificates, documents, and other writings delivered pursuant to the Model Agreement.

SELLERS' RESPONSE

Sellers may complain that clause (iv) of Section 11.2(a) is too broad in that it appears to provide that representations may be contained in any "document . . . delivered by Sellers pursuant to this Agreement . . . ." As Sellers, it is necessary to control the disclosure process, in the sense of being able to produce reliable information in a careful and disciplined way. This is normally done by means of carefully crafted statements contained in the representations and related Disclosure Letter on which Sellers would concede that Buyer can rely. Even though limited to documents delivered pursuant to the Model Agreement, the language quoted may make Sellers responsible for statements that might be made in documents received and reviewed in a due diligence review, which are not likely to be vetted with the same care and discipline as the representations and Disclosure Letter.

Buyer may believe that it is entitled to this degree of protection, but Sellers can argue that if Buyer wants to be assured of a given fact, that fact should be included in the representations in the Model Agreement, and to demand that all documents provided by Sellers be factually accurate, or to require Sellers to correct inaccuracies in them, places unrealistic demands on Sellers and would needlessly hamper the due diligence process. Further, some of the documents delivered pursuant to the Model Agreement will have their own remedies.

> **(b) any Breach of any covenant or obligation of any Seller in this Agreement or in any certificate, document, or other writing delivered by any Seller pursuant to this Agreement;**

COMMENT

Section 11.2(b) provides indemnification for breach of a covenant, regardless of amount or materiality, and regardless of whether it occurs before or after the Closing. The limitations applicable for claims for breach of a representation in Sections 11.5 and 11.6 are not applicable to breach of a covenant. This Section also provides indemnification for a breach of covenant contained in any other writing delivered pursuant to the Model Agreement.

SELLERS' RESPONSE

Sellers may want Section 11.2(b) to be limited to breaches of covenants or obligations set forth in specified ancillary documents rather than in a broadly stated class of documents or other writings. Sellers may also object to a provision that purports to cover other agreements that may contain their own remedies. For example, an employment agreement is to be delivered by one Seller. That Seller might insist that he be sued under the very detailed remedies section of that agreement, rather than the Model Agreement.

To the extent that Sellers' argument is correct about representations in documents delivered in due diligence, they may be even more concerned about becoming liable under Section 11.2(b) for breach of covenants and obligations in those documents.

(c)   any claim by any Person for brokerage or finder's fees or commissions or similar payments based upon any agreement or understanding made, or alleged to have been made, by any such Person with any Seller or any Acquired Company (or any Person acting on their behalf) in connection with any Contemplated Transaction;

COMMENT

This provision protects Buyer against broker's fees for agreements made by any Seller or any Acquired Company. It also protects against all alleged agreements to pay such fees. Although there is a specific representation that no such agreement has been entered into, a Buyer is better protected by specific indemnification because the time and dollar limitations in Sections 11.5(a) and 11.6(a) do not apply.

SELLERS' RESPONSE

Seller may argue this is redundant since it is covered by a representation in Section 3.28 and the time and dollar limitations in Sections 11.5(a) and 11.6(a) are not applicable to a Breach of that representation.

(d)   (i) any Taxes of any Acquired Company not reflected on the Closing Date Balance Sheet relating to periods on or prior to the Closing Date, and (ii) any liability of any Acquired Company for Taxes of any other Person, as a transferee or successor, by Contract or otherwise;

COMMENT

This provision backs up the tax representation. Regardless of whether it is breached, Sellers are asked to indemnify against Taxes (broadly defined) not reflected on the Closing Date Balance Sheet. The Company is a C corporation. Therefore, it is likely that it has liabilities for Taxes. While a corporation operating at a loss may not have income taxes, virtually every company will be obligated for sales and use taxes, property taxes, and payroll taxes.

The clause also applies to liability for Taxes of a third person arising out of transferee liability. For example, the laws of some states impose successor liability in a purchase of assets outside the ordinary course of business. If the target had purchased assets and was subject to successor liability for the transferor's Taxes, clause (ii) would cover that exposure.

Acquisition agreements frequently contain stand-alone provisions that not only provide for indemnification with respect to taxes, but also identify the parties responsible for filing tax returns and making payments attributed to those returns, and provide for cooperation with respect to tax matters and for access to and the retention of tax records. The following is an example of such a stand-alone provision:

> ___. Tax Matters. The following provisions shall govern the allocation of responsibility for certain Tax matters following the Closing Date:
>
> (a) Tax Indemnification. Sellers, jointly and severally, shall indemnify Buyer Indemnified Persons from, and shall pay to Buyer Indemnified Persons the amount of, or reimburse Buyer Indemnified Persons for, any Loss that Buyer Indemnified Persons or any of them may suffer, sustain, or become subject to, as a result of, in connection with, or relating to (i) any Taxes of any Acquired Company not reflected on the Closing Date Balance Sheet relating to periods on or prior to the Closing Date, and (ii) any liability of any Acquired Company for Taxes of any other Person, as a transferee or successor, by Contract or otherwise. For purposes of this Section ___, in the case of any Taxes that are imposed on a periodic basis and are payable for a Tax period that includes (but does not end on) the Closing Date, the portion of such Taxes which relates to the portion of such Tax period ending on the Closing Date shall (x) in the case of any Taxes other than Taxes based upon or related to income, be deemed to be the amount of such Tax for the entire Tax period multiplied by a fraction the numerator of which is the number of days in the Tax period ending on the Closing Date and the denominator of which is the number of days in the entire Tax period, and (y) in the case of any Tax based upon or related to income, be deemed equal to the amount which would be payable if the relevant Tax period ended on the Closing Date. All determinations necessary to give effect to the foregoing allocations shall be made in a manner consistent with prior practice of the Acquired Companies.
>
> (b) Tax Periods Ending on or Before the Closing Date. Sellers shall prepare or cause to be prepared and file or cause to be filed any Tax Returns of the Acquired Companies for all Tax periods ending on or prior to the Closing Date which are filed after the Closing Date. Sellers shall permit Buyer to review and comment on each such Tax Return prior to filing. Sellers shall reimburse Buyer for Taxes of the Acquired Companies not reflected on the Closing Balance Sheet with respect to such periods within 15 days after payment of such Taxes by Buyer or the Acquired Companies; provided, however, that if the Closing Balance Sheet has not been determined to be final under Section 2.6, such 15-day period shall begin on the date that the Closing Balance Sheet becomes final.
>
> (c) Tax Periods Beginning Before and Ending After the Closing Date. Buyer shall prepare or cause to be prepared and file or cause to be filed any Tax Returns of the Acquired Companies for Tax periods which begin before the Closing Date and end after the Closing Date. Sellers shall

[pay the Taxes of the Acquired Companies] [reimburse Buyer for Taxes of the Acquired Companies with respect to such periods within 15 days after payment of such Taxes by Buyer or the Acquired Companies] in an amount equal to the portion of such Taxes as determined pursuant to subsection (a) of this Section ___ to the extent such portion of Taxes is not reflected on the Closing Balance Sheet; provided, however, that if the Closing Balance Sheet has not been determined to be final under Section 2.6, such 15-day period shall begin on the date that the Closing Balance Sheet becomes final.

(d) <u>Cooperation on Tax Matters</u>. Sellers and Buyer shall cooperate, and Buyer shall cause the Acquired Companies to cooperate, as and to the extent reasonably requested, in connection with the filing of Tax Returns and any Proceeding with respect to Taxes. Such cooperation shall include the retention and (upon request) the provision of Records and information which are reasonably relevant to any such Proceeding and making employees available on a mutually convenient basis to provide additional information and explanation of any material provided hereunder. Buyer and Sellers shall, and Buyer shall cause the Acquired Companies to, (i) retain all Records with respect to Tax matters and pertinent to the Acquired Companies relating to any taxable period beginning before the Closing Date until the expiration of the statute of limitations (and, to the extent notified by Buyer or Sellers, any extensions thereof) of the respective taxable periods, and to abide by all record retention agreements entered into with any Governmental Body, and (ii) to provide to the others reasonable written notice prior to transferring, destroying, or discarding any such Records and, if so requested, the Acquired Companies or Sellers, as the case may be, shall allow the others to take possession of such Records:

If such a provision were to be included, it should be coordinated with other provisions of the Model Agreement to avoid duplication and inconsistencies. For example, Section 7.1 (a) and (b) deals with cooperation with respect to Proceedings and access to records, and includes references to Tax Returns and tax-related examinations. Section 12.1(b) makes Sellers responsible for stamp, documentary, and other transfer Taxes, and for filing all related Tax Returns and other documentation.

SELLERS' RESPONSE

Sellers might object to Section 11.2(d) on the basis that the representations in Section 3.11 provide sufficient protection to Buyer with respect to Taxes, and that Section 11.2(d) is overreaching by Buyer because it is not subject to any threshold in Section 11.6 or the qualifications that were used in formulating the representations in Section 3.11.

Sellers might take issue with the breadth of subsection (d) because it fails to distinguish between Taxes in the nature of income taxes and Taxes that could be characterized as "operating taxes" (such as employment taxes, sales and use taxes, and ad valorem taxes), which, Sellers would argue, should not be singled out for treatment any differently from other operating expenses.

> **(e) any product shipped or manufactured by, or any services provided by, any Acquired Company, in whole or in part, prior to the Closing Date; or**

COMMENT

Because of the breadth of this provision, its use is often raised at the letter of intent stage.

Section 11.2(e) protects Buyer against certain liabilities related to products and services produced or rendered while Sellers were in charge of the business, a so-called "your watch/our watch" provision. It does not depend upon a breach of representation. While it does not relate to any liability of the Acquired Companies, it does relate to a very large category of liabilities associated with the customary activities of any manufacturing company (products shipped or manufactured or services provided). It could be expanded to products designed on Sellers' watch. Buyers could even seek this to apply to *any* liability originating on Sellers' watch, converting a stock purchase to the functional equivalent of an asset purchase between Sellers and Buyer. *See* Kling & Nugent § 15.02[1][f].

SELLERS' RESPONSE

In general, this type of provision is often objectionable to Sellers because it makes them liable for the risks of future post-closing business operations of the target while reserving for Buyer the rewards of post-closing operations. Sellers initially might argue that their responsibility for product liability should be limited to the representation in Section 3.27. Furthermore, this subsection is not limited to product liability, but also could include normal returns and allowances and warranty work, both business functions where commercial give and take govern rather than strict technical conformity determinations. *But see* Hartz Consumer Group, Inc. v. JWC Hartz Holdings, Inc., Sup. Ct., N.Y. County, Nov. 9, 2005, Gammerman, J.H.O., Index No. 600610/03, *aff'd*, 33 A.D.3d 555 (2006), holding that such a provision did not apply to customer returns. If this provision is to be retained, Sellers might want to expressly exclude these normal types of liabilities. In addition, they could argue that product liability, whether for products sold or products manufactured and to be sold, is an ordinary risk of doing business, just as returns and allowances for customers are a normal cost of doing business. Moreover, after the Closing, the target would probably carry insurance for product liability just as it did prior to the Closing.

Another reason to object is that Buyer controls when and how finished goods are released to the marketplace and this would extend indefinitely the risk of Sellers. Buyer, however, may argue that there is a purchase price adjustment and it should not be penalized because a claim against the target's operations arises subsequent to, rather than prior to, the resolution of the purchase price adjustment.

Sellers might want to exclude this liability up to any reserves included or reflected on the target's balance sheet. Also, it may be extremely difficult to track (in the absence of either batch or lot numbers) which products were sold or manufactured before or after the Closing.

Sellers might endeavor to negotiate a cutoff for claims made after a certain period of time to relieve Sellers of the necessity of maintaining insurance and the other costs and burdens of claim administration for an indefinite period.

Finally, Sellers could argue that any threshold or cap set forth in Section 11.6 should apply to Sellers' exposures for product liability.

(f) any matter disclosed in Part 11.2(f).

COMMENT

The regimen of the Model Agreement is to present a representation and to require that any exceptions be set forth in the Disclosure Letter. Hence, if litigation were pending against the Acquired Companies, by describing the existence of that litigation on the Disclosure Letter, Sellers avoid any responsibility. That may not be acceptable to Buyer, or Buyer may hold Sellers accountable when it is claimed that the litigation is not a problem.

Rather than "any matter disclosed in Part 11.2(f)," Buyer may attempt to develop specific language dealing with each matter, particularly since this Part may cover multiple matters.

SELLERS' RESPONSE

Where Sellers are to provide Buyer stand-alone indemnities to protect it from disclosed situations or situations of which Buyer becomes aware in its due diligence prior to the Closing, Sellers might consider whether:

- the retention by Sellers of the risks in question have been taken into account in pricing the transaction; and
- where appropriate, seek to retain control of the matters and assure the cooperation of Buyer regarding access to resources to successfully resolve the matters, such as the retention of records and the obligation of target employees to be examined and to testify.

11.3 **INDEMNIFICATION, PAYMENT, AND REIMBURSEMENT BY SELLERS—ENVIRONMENTAL MATTERS**

In addition to the provisions of Section 11.2, Sellers, jointly and severally, shall indemnify and hold harmless Buyer Indemnified Persons from, and shall pay to Buyer Indemnified Persons the amount of, or reimburse Buyer Indemnified Persons for, any Loss (including costs of any Cleanup) that Buyer Indemnified Persons or any of them may suffer, sustain, or become subject to, as a result of, in connection with, or relating to:

(a) any Environmental, Health, and Safety Liability arising out of or relating to:

    (i) (A) the ownership, operation, or condition at any time on or prior to the Closing Date of the Facilities, or (B) any Hazardous Material that was present on or at the Facilities at any time on or prior to the Closing Date; or

    (ii) (A) any Hazardous Material, wherever located, that was generated, transported, stored, treated, Released, or otherwise handled by any Acquired Company at any time on or prior to the Closing Date, or (B) any Hazardous Activity that was conducted by any Acquired Company or by any other Person for whose conduct they are or may be held responsible; or

(b) any bodily injury (including illness, disability, and death, and regardless of when any such bodily injury occurred or manifested itself), property damage (including trespass, nuisance, wrongful eviction, and deprivation of the use of real property), or other damage of or to any Person, including any employee or former employee of any Acquired Company, in any way arising from or allegedly arising from any Hazardous Activity conducted with respect to the Facilities or the operation of the Acquired Companies on or prior to the Closing Date or from Hazardous Material that was:

    (i) present on or prior to the Closing Date on or at the Facilities (or present on or at any other property, if such Hazardous Material emanated or allegedly emanated from any of the Facilities on or prior to the Closing Date), or

    (ii) Released by Sellers or any Acquired Company or any other Person for whose conduct they are or may be held responsible, at any time on or prior to the Closing Date.

Section 11.8 notwithstanding, Buyer shall be entitled (at its election) to control any Cleanup, any related Proceeding, and, except as provided in the following sentence, any other Proceeding with respect to which relief may be sought under this Section 11.3. The procedure described in Section 11.8, however, will apply to any Third-Party Claim solely for monetary damages relating to a matter covered by this Section 11.3.

COMMENT

This provision for indemnification for environmental matters supplements and largely overlaps the indemnification provided in Section 11.2(a), which addresses the accuracy of Sellers' representations (including those relating to environmental matters in Section 3.19). There are several reasons why Buyer may seek to include separate indemnification for environmental matters in addition to just relying on the general indemnification based on Sellers' representations. Environmental matters are often the subject of a risk allocation agreement with respect to unknown and unknowable liabilities, and Sellers who are willing to assume those risks may nevertheless be reluctant to make representations concerning factual matters of which they cannot possibly have knowledge. An indemnification obligation that goes beyond the scope of the representation implements such an agreement. In addition, the nature of, and the potential for disruption arising from, environmental cleanup activities often leads buyers to seek different procedures for handling claims with respect to environmental matters. Buyer will often believe it is more important to control the environmental cleanup and related proceedings than to control other types of third-party claims.

The effectiveness of contractual provisions such as indemnification in protecting Buyer against environmental liabilities is difficult to evaluate. Such liabilities may be discovered at any time in the future and are not cut off by any statute of limitations that relates to the date of release of hazardous materials. In contrast, a contractual provision may have an express temporal limitation, and in any event should be expected to decrease in usefulness over time as parties go out of existence or become difficult to locate (especially when Sellers are individuals). Buyer may be reluctant to assume that Sellers will be available and have adequate resources to meet an obligation that matures several years after the acquisition. The longer the period of time after the Closing that it takes to discover a problem may make it more difficult for Buyer to prove that the cause occurred prior to the Closing. In addition, environmental liabilities may be asserted by governmental agencies and third parties, which are not bound by the Model Agreement and are not bound to pursue only the indemnitor.

Finally, it is often difficult to assess the economic adequacy of an environmental indemnity. Even with an environmental audit, estimates of the cost of remediation or compliance may prove to be considerably understated years later when the process is completed, and Sellers' financial ability to meet that obligation at that time cannot be assured. These limitations on the usefulness of indemnification provisions may lead, as a practical matter, to the negotiation of a price reduction or an increased escrow of funds or letter of credit to meet indemnification obligations, in conjunction with some limitation on the breadth of the provisions themselves. Often, the amount of money saved by Buyer at the time of the Closing will be far more certain than the amount it may receive years later under an indemnification provision.

While a responsible party's liability to the government and third parties under CERCLA cannot be transferred to another party by contract (*see* 42 U.S.C. § 9607(e)), express contractual allocation has generally been held to be enforceable between the parties to a contract, and an indemnification provision would thus be enforceable between Buyer and Sellers. *See, e.g.,* Mardan Corp. v. CGC Music, Ltd., 804 F.2d 1454 (9th Cir. 1986). There is, however, some authority to the effect that indemnity agreements between potentially responsible parties under CERCLA are unenforceable. *See* CPC Int'l, Inc. v. Aerojet-General Corp., 759 F. Supp. 1269 (W.D. Mich. 1991); AM Int'l Inc. v. International Forging Equip., 743 F. Supp. 525 (N.D. Ohio 1990). There may also be limitations on the enforceability of indemnification provisions. *See, e.g.,* Section 11.10 and related commentary.

One consequence of treating an unknown risk through an indemnity instead of a representation is that Buyer may be required to proceed with the acquisition even if a basis for the liability in question is discovered prior to the closing, because the existence of a liability subject to indemnification will not by itself cause a failure of the condition specified in Section 8.1. The representations in Section 3.19 substantially overlap this indemnity in order to avoid that consequence.

The issue of control of cleanup and other environmental matters is often controversial. Buyer may argue for control based upon the greater than normal potential that these matters have for interference with business operations. Sellers may seek control based upon their financial responsibility under the indemnification provision.

If Sellers are unwilling to commit to such broad indemnification provisions, or if Buyer is not satisfied with such provisions because of specific environmental risks that are disclosed or become known through the due diligence process or are to be anticipated from the nature of the Acquired Companies' businesses, alternatives exist for resolving the risk allocation problems that may arise. For example, Sellers may ultimately agree to a reduction in the purchase price in return for deletion or limitation of their indemnification obligations or the parties may secure environmental liability insurance.

SELLERS' RESPONSE

Many acquisition agreements do not contain a separate provision for environmental indemnification, and often such indemnification is woven into the general indemnification section or is eliminated entirely by reliance on the representations or in express post-closing covenants that delineate exactly what must be done to remediate situations that have been identified through environmental due diligence. Whether separate indemnification is required depends on the nature of the target's business and its real property. For example, a software provider that has always leased its premises poses a lower risk of environmental liability than a large industrial enterprise. Although in the latter case, rather than being viewed as the ultimate disaster, an environmental claim may only constitute a routine cost of doing business.

Sellers are likely to have several concerns with the indemnification provisions in Section 11.3. Many of these concerns are discussed in the commentary to Section 3.19, such as the indemnification for third-party actions and with respect to substances that may be considered hazardous in the future or with respect to future environmental laws. Sellers may also be interested in having Buyer indemnify them for liabilities arising from the operation of the Acquired Companies' businesses after the Closing Date, although it is often difficult for Sellers to articulate the basis on which they may have liability for such matters.

Sellers may object to obligations regarding future environmental laws and concomitant liabilities arising from common law decisions interpreting such laws. From Buyer's perspective, however, the reference to future laws is needed to account for strict liability statutes such as CERCLA that impose liability retroactively. Sellers may insist that the representations in Section 3.19 clearly be limited to existing or prior laws.

Even if Sellers are willing to be responsible for environmental liability, they may reject the provision that allows Buyer to control any Cleanup. The usual remediation is done with the involvement of state or federal officials, so Buyer's ability to control matters should not be necessary to protect Buyer.

Sellers may object to indemnification for each type of "Environmental, Health, and Safety Liability," which may include such routine matters as OSHA liabilities.

11.4   INDEMNIFICATION, PAYMENT, AND REIMBURSEMENT BY BUYER

Buyer shall indemnify and hold harmless Sellers from, and shall pay to Sellers the amount of, or reimburse Sellers for, any Loss that Sellers or any of them may suffer, sustain, or become subject to, as a result of, in connection with, or relating to:

(a) any Breach of any representation or warranty made by Buyer in (i) this Agreement, (ii) the certificate delivered pursuant to Section 9.3, or (iii) in any other certificate, document, or other writing delivered by Buyer pursuant to this Agreement;

(b) any Breach of any covenant or obligation of Buyer in this Agreement or in any certificate, document, or other writing delivered by Buyer pursuant to this Agreement; or

(c) any claim by any Person for brokerage or finder's fees or commissions or similar payments based upon any agreement or understanding made, or alleged to have been made, by any such Person with Buyer (or any Person acting on its behalf) in connection with any Contemplated Transaction.

COMMENT

In general, indemnification by buyers is similar to that of sellers. The significance of a buyer's indemnity will depend to a large extent on the type of consideration being paid and, consequently, the breadth of its representations. In cash transactions, a buyer's representations are usually minimal and it generally runs little risk of liability for post-closing indemnification. While such a provision could be, and sometimes is, deleted entirely from the buyer's first draft, such a provision is often included in order to provide symmetry between the seller's and buyer's indemnification obligations. When stock or a promissory note is being delivered as some or all of the purchase consideration, sellers may demand more extensive representations and indemnification in their favor.

In a stock acquisition, a buyer would not be expected to indemnify sellers with respect to products manufactured or sold or services provided by the target after the closing. Sellers, as former owners of the target, would not have liability for the future operations. By contrast, a buyer, as acquirer of the stock of the target, would indirectly bear the consequences if the target experiences losses relating to the past conduct of the target. Thus, because indemnification for future matters would be superfluous, the indemnification provisions of Buyer in Section 11.4 do not mirror those of Sellers in Section 11.2. To the contrary, *see* KLING & NUGENT § 15.02[1][c].

SELLERS' RESPONSE

This Section is the counterpart to the indemnity by Sellers in Section 11.2. Any success by Sellers in limiting the scope of their indemnification obligations in Section 11.2 will be used by Buyer to similarly limit Sellers' corresponding rights under Section 11.4. Sellers will normally not object to reciprocal limitations, largely because in a transaction that has closed it is usually difficult to imagine Sellers suffering from a material indemnifiable breach by Buyer of its representations.

If a substantial portion of the consideration paid were in the form of equity or debt securities of Buyer, Sellers may seek broad representations comparable to those given by Sellers, including a schedule of exceptions to the Buyer's representations. In such a case, the buyer's indemnification would be closer to being a mirror image of the Sellers' indemnification, including stand-alone indemnities for specific matters.

If the seller has personally guaranteed obligations of the target, it might request the buyer to indemnify it against the consequences of nonperformance by the target or require releases at the closing.

Sellers sometimes ask a buyer to indemnify them against damages arising from the operation of the target subsequent to the closing. Buyers do not always object since they are assuming they will be responsible for all post-closing obligations of the business anyway and even if a Seller is sued on account of such post-closing obligations (usually unlikely), Buyer can address this issue by satisfying the obligations. Furthermore, if a seller requests indemnification for claims arising out of post-closing operations, the buyer may very well turn the table on the seller and demand a comprehensive pre-closing operation clause under Section 11.2 which might create much greater exposure to sellers. Sellers must carefully consider the consequences of what they seek because buyers will almost always seek comparable provisions.

11.5   TIME LIMITATIONS

(a) If the Closing occurs, Sellers shall have liability under Section 11.2(a) with respect to any Breach of a representation or warranty (other than those in Sections 3.1, 3.2, 3.3, 3.11, 3.13, 3.19, 3.24, or 3.28, as to which a claim may be made at any time), only if on or before the date that is three years after the Closing Date, Buyer notifies Sellers' Representative of a claim, specifying the factual basis of the claim in reasonable detail to the extent known by Buyer.

(b) If the Closing occurs, Buyer shall have liability under Section 11.4(a) with respect to any Breach of a representation or warranty (other than those in Sections 4.1, 4.2, and 4.5, as to which a claim may be made at any time), only if on or before the date that is three years after the Closing Date, Sellers notify Buyer of a claim specifying the factual basis of the claim in reasonable detail to the extent known by Sellers.

COMMENT

Acquisition agreements often specify the time period within which notice of a claim for indemnification for a breach of representation must be given (as distinguished from when a lawsuit must be commenced). Sellers want to eliminate uncertainty after a period of time, and buyers want a reasonable opportunity to discover any problems that would form the basis for an indemnification claim. The time period will vary depending on factors such as the type of business, the adequacy of financial statements, the buyer's plans for retaining existing management, its ability to perform a thorough investigation prior to the acquisition, the method of determination of the purchase price, and the relative bargaining strength of the parties. A two-year period may be sufficient for most liabilities because it will permit at least one post-closing audit (although audits are not necessarily intended to find breaches and auditors may not necessarily discover a breach) and because, as a practical matter, many hidden liabilities will be uncovered within two years. However, an extended or unlimited time period for certain representations, such as those relating to stock ownership, capitalization, products liability, taxes, ERISA, and environmental matters is often sought by buyer.

Section 11.5 provides for a limitations period only for representations covered by Section 11.2(a) and not for indemnification based on breach of covenant, finders' fees, tax liabilities, or other specified items covered by clauses (b) through (f). Therefore, those types of claims covered by clauses (b) through (f) should be subject to the statute of limitations pertaining to contracts, but that may be measured by when the cause of action accrued or the breach was discovered. Since the Model Agreement contains post-closing covenants, the lack of a limitations period is appropriate. However, Sellers might reasonably request a limitations period for pre-closing covenants.

The appropriate standard for some types of liabilities may be the period of time during which a private or governmental plaintiff could bring a claim for actions taken or circumstances existing prior to the closing. For example, indemnification for tax liabilities often extends for as long as the relevant statute of limitations for collection of the tax extends. If this approach is taken, the time limitation might be drafted to include extensions of the statute of limitations (which are frequently granted in tax audits), situations in which there are no statute of limitations (such as those referred to in Section 6501(c) of the Code), and a brief period after expiration of the statute of limitations to permit a claim for indemnification to be made if the tax authorities act on the last possible day.

Buyer might consider the relationship between the time periods within which a claim for indemnification may be made and the time periods for other post-closing transactions. For example, if there is an escrow, Buyer will want to have the escrow last until any significant claims for indemnification have been paid or finally adjudicated and would resist escrows that decrease over a period of time. Similarly, if part of the purchase price is to be paid by promissory note, or if there is to be an earnout pursuant to which part of the consideration for the shares is based on future performance, Buyer will want to be able to set off claims for indemnification against any payments that it owes on the promissory note or earnout (*see* Section 11.7).

Section 11.5 does not affect any statute of limitation for claims arising out of a failure to close the transaction. Section 11.5 and Section 11.6 are only operative if the Closing occurs. Section 11.7 describes a situation that only exists after the Closing. Other provisions of Article 11 are applicable whether or not there has been a Closing.

Enforcement of a contract is, of course, subject to commencing an action within the relevant statute of limitations or statute of repose, some of which are extremely long under state law. The applicable period of time may begin when the contract is breached or when the harm is discovered. Agreements between parties can toll the statutes. In proposing this Section, Buyer is acting contrary to its own interests because, while the Section is mutual, Sellers would be unlikely to have claims against Buyer. Buyer instead proposes the Section because it knows that Sellers will do so and such a provision has come to be expected.

Courts have struggled with private statutes of limitation, which are subject to state law limitations (either statutory or judicial) restricting the ability to contract (or extend) limitations periods. For example, in Western Filter Corp. v. Argan, Inc., 540 F.3d 947 (9th Cir. 2008), a provision in a stock purchase agreement that representations "shall survive the Closing for a period of one year" was held not to shorten the applicable statute of limitations, thus permitting litigation with respect to a claim to be filed by the buyer more than a year following the closing. The court explained that under California law, a stipulation shortening the statute of limitations must be clear and explicit, and the provision at issue was ambiguous. *See also* Herring v. Teradyne, Inc., 242 F. App'x 469 (9th Cir. 2007); Case Financial, Inc. v. Alden, 2009 Del. Ch. LEXUS 153 (Del. Ch. Aug. 21, 2009) (provision that representations "shall expire and terminate on the closing date" is a limitation on the time when a breach may occur and not the time when a claim may be brought). The court in *Western Filter* acknowledged that there were reported opinions holding that similar language shortened the statute of limitations, citing principally State Street Bank & Trust Co. v. Denman Tire Corp., 240 F.3d 83 (1st Cir. 2001). The wording of Section 11.5 is intended to avoid that ambiguity.

Sometimes the statute of limitations may not be tolled by the wording of the provision. For example, Section 11.5(a) purports to say that a claim may be made (notice given) "at any time" for breach of certain specified representations. In Herring v. Terradyne, Inc., 256 F. Supp. 2d 118 (S.D. Cal. 2002), *rev'd*, Herring v. Teradyne, Inc., 242 F. App'x 469 (9th Cir. 2007), the court said that a provision that the "representations . . . shall survive . . . indefinitely" meant that the applicable statute of limitations would govern from the date of breach. While the language of Section 11.5 (as to which a claim may be made at any time) differs, a court might hold that to mean "any time within the applicable statute of limitations."

Parties may want to provide that, despite the tolling by giving notice of claim, an action must be commenced by a date certain. They may want to explore whether, in fact, the statute of limitations may be extended.

Other defenses akin to laches may be asserted. *See* cases cited in KLING & NUGENT § 15.02[2] n. 29.

Section 11.5 provides for no time limits with respect to Sections 3.1 (organizational good standing), 3.2 (enforceability and authority; no conflict), 3.3 (capitalization), 3.11 (taxes), 3.13 (employee benefits) 3.19 (environmental), 3.24 (relationships with related persons), or 3.28 (brokers and finders). Some of these are common carve-outs or exceptions, but there is no rule or prevailing convention that is inviolable.

SELLERS' RESPONSE

Representations. A time limit for claims is common. Different time limits for different claims and different circumstances are also common. Sellers will normally endeavor to shorten the general time limit as much as possible. Buyer typically justifies the proposed time limit by reference to post-closing audit cycles (although audits are not generally regarded as being designed to disclose breaches of representations). Sellers may take the approach in any event that a normal fiscal year audit plus 60 or 90 days ought to suffice. Buyer's argument for unlimited or extended time periods is based upon, among other things, difficulty of discovery and the ever-expanding technology and regulations. Sellers will naturally resist perpetual exposure.

The capitalization representation, which deals in large part with Sellers' ownership of stock of the Company, should be a low-risk proposition for Sellers, and Sellers' efforts to eliminate time limits may raise suspicion on the part of Buyer. However, the last four sentences of Section 3.3(b) go beyond mere ownership and cover such things as compliance with securities laws, contract rights, and equity ownership by the Company, and therefore are candidates for some time limit.

One typical compromise on the time limits for taxes and employee benefits is the statute of limitations for tax matters (which will cover many of the employee benefit matters as well) plus a very short stub period (for example, 30 days) in case the IRS makes a last-minute claim. If Buyer goes along with this approach, it will want to allow for extensions, whereas Sellers will endeavor to put some limitation on the number of any such extensions.

Covenants. The Model Agreement provides no cutoff of claims arising under covenants, as opposed to representations. Sellers will often argue that pre-closing covenants should have a stated time limit contemporaneous with the time limits on representations. Sellers are often vigilant about putting limits on exposure to claims which will be crafted by litigators as covenant breaches when the time limits on representations have expired.

Other Provisions. Sellers may argue that Section 11.5 should also include a cutoff for claims under Sections 11.2(c)-(f), on the basis that Sellers are entitled to closure at some certain point in the future.

Nonindemnification Remedies. If the final agreement between the parties is that all remedies are preserved under Section 12.11, Sellers may want to add a cutoff by which other contract claims, tort claims, and statute-based claims can be brought.

11.6   CERTAIN LIMITATIONS ON AMOUNT

(a) **If the Closing occurs, Sellers shall have no liability with respect to claims under Section 11.2(a) until the aggregate of all Losses suffered by all Buyer Indemnified Persons with respect to such claims exceeds $_____; provided, however, that if the aggregate of all such Losses exceeds $_____, Sellers shall be liable for all such Losses. [If the Closing occurs, the aggregate liability of Sellers with respect to Losses for claims under Section 11.2(a) shall not exceed $_____.] However, this Section 11.6(a) will not apply to any Breach of which a Seller has Knowledge at any time at or prior to the date on which such representation and warranty was made or to any Breach of any representation or warranty in Sections 3.1, 3.2, 3.3, 3.11, 3.13, 3.19, 3.24, or 3.28.**

GENERAL COMMENT

This Section is not applicable to a claim for Breach of a representation if there is no Closing.

Section 11.6(a) provides Sellers with a margin of error or cushion with respect to Breaches of representations (but not other contractual obligations such as covenants). The formulation of the Model Agreement results in a "threshold" (as opposed to a true "deductible") that, once crossed, entitles the indemnified party to recover all damages, rather than merely the excess over the stated amount. The purpose of the "threshold" is to recognize that representations concerning an ongoing business are unlikely to be perfectly accurate and to avoid disputes over smaller amounts unless they accumulate to the extent of the "threshold." Often the term "basket" is used when referring to this limitation. Some lawyers believe "basket" means a threshold, while others believe it can mean either a "threshold" or a true "deductible." *See, e.g.,* FREUND 370.

At the other end of the spectrum, it has become common practice to provide for a maximum indemnification limit (a "cap"). Section 11.6(a) does not establish a cap, unless the bracketed clause is included.

In the Model Agreement, Sellers' representations are generally not subject to materiality qualifications, and the full dollar amount of damages caused by a breach must be indemnified, subject to the effect of the threshold established by this Section. This framework does not give rise to "double-dipping"—that is, the situation in which Sellers contend that the Breach exists only to the extent that it is material, and then the material Breach is subjected to the deduction of the threshold. If the Model Agreement as negotiated contains materiality qualifications to Sellers' representations, Buyer might consider a provision to the effect that such a materiality qualification will not be taken into account in determining the magnitude of the damages occasioned by the breach for purposes of calculating whether the threshold has been exceeded; otherwise, the individually immaterial items may be material in the aggregate, but not applied to the threshold. To accomplish this, Buyer could suggest the following provision: "For purposes of determining the Breach of any representation or warranty for purposes of Section 11.2(a) or the amount of Loss suffered by any Buyer Indemnified Persons, "materiality" and similar qualifications shall be ignored." These are sometimes referred to as "materiality scrape" provisions. *See* Caplan and Lefcort, *Seller Beware: Potential Pitfalls and Unintended Consequences of the Materiality Scrape,*" M&A LAW. (June 2008); LeClaire, Kemp, Kendall & Weidhaas, *Scraping By*, MERGERS & ACQUISITIONS (July 2008).

See KLING & NUGENT § 15.03[1].

SELLERS' RESPONSE

The first sentence of Section 11.6(a), which reflects a common practice of granting some limited measure of relief from financial responsibility for Breaches, is favorable to Sellers in only a limited respect in that it provides a conditional "threshold" (as opposed to a "deductible") allowance or forgiveness regarding any liability that Sellers may have for breaches of representations under Section 11.2(a). Buyer's rationale for this indulgence is a recognition of the inability to achieve perfect compliance with the stringent demands of representations. Buyer may be influenced by a sensible desire not to fight about minor matters unless they accumulate beyond the threshold. Sellers will want to accept this concept and enlarge upon it.

"Threshold" or "Deductible." Sellers may object to Section 11.6(a), apart from the amount of cushion provided, as not being a deductible and therefore illusory. Sellers will point out that a threshold formulation creates a greater likelihood of contentious post-closing relations between Buyer and Sellers since Buyer would have an incentive to focus on minor issues, thus defeating the purpose of the provision. By doing so Buyer can improve its chances of getting some money back from Sellers for routine run-of-the-mill "nicks and dents" that every business encounters.

Covenants. Sellers may also object to the narrow application of the relief to breaches of representations only. As drafted, the first sentence does not cover breaches of covenants, especially pre-closing covenants. Sellers may, therefore, request that the threshold apply to the covenants as well. Buyer might resist such a provision, arguing that while not always the case with representations, Sellers can control their conduct as it relates to covenants.

Double-Dipping. Buyer might agree that materiality and other dollar qualifiers in the text of representations will be given effect for purposes of determining whether closing conditions have been met, but not for purposes of determining the amount Buyer is entitled to recover from Sellers under the indemnity. Sellers may argue that such a suggestion overlooks the real (and imprecise) world of business operations, and that there must be room for flexibility at both the closing conditions stage and the indemnity stage.

The Amount of Relief. Sellers are, of course, interested in the largest amount of relief possible. There is no standard amount. In any event, the stated dollar amount of relief has to be judged in the light of the outcome of the "double-dipping" arguments.

De Minimis. Sellers may want to exclude from consideration for the threshold de minimis claims that are under a certain amount, often called a minibasket. Buyers may argue that such a provision is not common, as one threshold is generally viewed as sufficient to protect Sellers from small claims for minor breaches or problems based on pre-closing events.

Sellers' argument is that some matters are so insignificant that they are not even worth tracking, much less contesting. This threshold-beneath-the-threshold provides added assurance to Sellers that they will not be "nickel-and-dimed" by a Buyer seeking to meet the threshold with minor claims. The appeal to both sides would be that harmonious operations would best be served if neither side had an incentive to record and seek compensation for every little problem. Therefore, Sellers might be able to convince Buyer that such insignificance should be disregarded for all purposes of the Model Agreement. Sellers might urge that a de minimis provision should apply to all representations without exception, even the tax and employee benefits representations.

Buyer might be willing to give consideration to a de minimis provision, but may try to hold out for aggregation. Sellers might properly go along with an aggregation of de minimis losses linked by a single event or incident. Sellers may want to resist aggregating losses which are merely similar but not causally related. A de minimis provision could read as follows: "For purposes of this Section 11.6(a), any single Loss that is less than $_____ shall be disregarded; provided, however, that any series of Losses arising out of the same occurrence or recurring Losses of a similar nature shall be aggregated and treated as a single Loss."

EXCEPTIONS OR "CARVE-OUTS"

COMMENT

Buyer may want Sellers' obligation as to certain types of indemnities to be absolute and not subject to the threshold. The last sentence of Section 11.6(a) excepts from the threshold the representations made in Sections 3.1 (organization and good standing), 3.2 (enforceability and authority; no conflict), 3.3 (capitalization), 3.11 (taxes), 3.13 (employee benefits), 3.19 (environmental matters), 3.24 (relationships with related persons), and 3.28 (brokers or finders). The parties could negotiate different thresholds for different types of liabilities.

SELLERS' RESPONSE

Sellers should be prepared to accept some exceptions to the threshold. Typical candidates are the basic corporate representations, such as due incorporation and authority.

KNOWLEDGE EXCEPTION

COMMENT

The threshold provided in the Model Agreement does not apply to Breaches of which any Seller had knowledge. The rationale is that Sellers should not be allowed to avoid liability for behavior that is less than forthright.

SELLERS' RESPONSE

Sellers might be expected to take issue with a knowledge carve-out, which turns every alleged breach initially into a dispute as to whether there was a breach and then into a dispute as to knowledge. Sellers will argue that, rather than avoiding disputes, such a provision actually fosters them. Sellers may also be concerned that knowledge of any one Seller would affect all of them.

An argument by Sellers against this carve-out provision might attract the counterargument by Buyer that Sellers seek a license to engage in willful misrepresentations. If Sellers are unsuccessful in eliminating the knowledge-based carve-out entirely, they may want to argue that Buyer be required to prove that it was "actually known" by a higher standard of proof such as clear and convincing evidence or suggest a fraud exception.

THE CAP

COMMENT

While the Model Agreement provides a cap only as an alternative, in practice a cap is a common provision. Setting a cap is a significant deal point and is often addressed in the letter of intent. Like carve-outs from the threshold, it is common to provide for exceptions to the cap. One typical exception is for knowing misrepresentations. Buyers may also seek to deny the benefit of the cap by means of a carve-out for breach of fundamental representations such as corporate existence, due incorporation, due authorization, ownership of stock, and capitalization, on the basis that sellers have no excuse for those representations being inaccurate. In addition, buyers commonly insist that the cap does not apply to liabilities for taxes, environmental matters, or ERISA matters—for which they may have unlimited liability under applicable law. The cap provided in the Model Agreement applies only to indemnification for breaches of representations and does not apply to covenants and other indemnities. The amount of the cap varies based on bargaining power, risk, and other variables of the transaction.

SELLERS' RESPONSE

Sellers will often seek to limit their exposure by providing for a cap, which is frequently less than the purchase price. Depending on their bargaining position, sellers have sometimes been able to achieve caps that are a relatively small percentage of the purchase price, particularly when it is a "seller's market" or in an active auction. Their argument for a cap no higher than the purchase price is that they had limited liability as shareholders and should be in no worse position having sold the target than they were in when they owned it. As a practical matter, they might even have substantially reduced their exposure by terminating the target's business, liquidating its assets, and dissolving it. The amount of the economic value that Sellers could have extracted in this way can be argued with some force to be the cap. This argument may not be persuasive, particularly if Buyer views the target as a component of its overall business strategy, intends to invest additional capital, or is unwilling to see its subsidiaries' obligations dishonored.

Sellers that are private equity funds are usually required to distribute profits to individual investors shortly after the closing, so they frequently attempt to avoid post-closing liability or negotiate a cap that is significantly lower than the purchase price, with the amount of the cap being placed in escrow to satisfy all their indemnification obligations.

In many cases, sellers may just decide that unless they take away some minimum amount free and clear, and without risk of clawback, they will not sell. Between the two extremes, buyers and sellers should find some common ground, perhaps with some exceptions for matters that are basic (such as corporate existence and authority, ownership of stock) or special caps for categories of matters that are difficult to assess pre-closing (such as tax and ERISA).

(b) If the Closing occurs, Buyer shall have no liability with respect to claims under Section 11.4(a) until the aggregate of all Losses suffered by all Seller Indemnified Persons with respect to such claims exceeds $_____; provided, however, that if the total of all such Losses exceeds $_____, Buyer shall be liable for all such Losses. [If the Closing occurs, the aggregate liability of Buyer with respect to Losses for claims under Section 11.4(a) shall not exceed $_____.] However, this Section 11.6(b) will not apply to any Breach of which Buyer has Knowledge at any time at or prior to the date on which such representation and warranty was made or to any Breach of any representation or warranty in Section 4.1, 4.2, or 4.5.

COMMENT

In its first draft, a buyer often suggests a provision regarding relief in an amount below which it is not required to respond in damages to breaches of its representations, typically the same dollar amount as that used for the seller's threshold.

The bracketed alternative would probably be included as a matter of symmetry if Buyer allows Sellers a cap on liability.

SELLERS' RESPONSE

Every small victory Sellers may achieve in limiting their liability to Buyer under Section 11.6(a) may be matched by a commensurate defeat in limiting Buyer's liability to Sellers for Buyer's breach of its representations under Section 11.6(b). Since Buyer's liabilities under Section 11.6(b) would normally be largely theoretical in cash purchases (as opposed to transactions in which Buyer securities form part of the purchase consideration), Sellers would ordinarily be willing to accept comparable favorable limitations of Buyer's exposure under Section 11.6(b) as the price of relief under Section 11.6(a).

11.7 SETOFF RIGHT

Upon notice to Sellers' Representative specifying in reasonable detail the basis therefor, Buyer may set off any amount to which it claims to be entitled from any Seller, including any amounts that may be owed under this Article 11 or otherwise, against amounts otherwise payable under the Promissory Notes or any provision of this Agreement. The exercise of such right of setoff by Buyer in good faith, whether or not ultimately determined to be justified, will not constitute a default under this Agreement, the Promissory Notes, or any instrument securing any of the Promissory Notes, regardless of whether any Seller disputes such setoff claim, or whether such setoff claim is for a contingent or an unliquidated amount. Neither the exercise of, nor the failure to exercise, such right of setoff or give notice of a claim under the Escrow Agreement will constitute an election of remedies or limit Buyer in any manner in the enforcement of any other remedies that may be available to it.

COMMENT

Regardless of the clarity of an acquisition agreement regarding the allocation of risk and the buyer's right of indemnification, the buyer may nonetheless have difficulty enforcing the indemnity—especially against sellers who are individuals. To remedy this problem, buyers can place a portion of the purchase price in escrow, hold back a portion of the purchase price (often in the form of a note, an earnout, or payments under consulting or noncompetition agreements) with a right of setoff, or obtain other security (such as a letter of credit) to secure performance of the sellers' indemnification obligations. These techniques shift bargaining power in post-closing disputes from sellers to buyers and usually will be resisted by sellers.

The buyer may seek an express right of setoff against sums otherwise payable to the seller. The buyer obtains more protection from an express right of setoff against deferred payments due under a promissory note or purchase price adjustments than from a deposit of the same amounts in an escrow because the former leaves the buyer in control of the funds and thus gives the buyer more leverage in resolving disputes. The buyer may also want the setoff to apply against payments under employment, consulting, or noncompetition agreements (although state law may prohibit setoffs against payments due under such agreements). The comfort received by the buyer from an express right of setoff depends on the schedule of the payments against which it can be withheld. As in the case of an escrow, the suggestion of an express right of setoff often leads to discussions of exclusive remedies.

Rather than inviting counterproposals from the seller by including an express right of setoff in the acquisition agreement, the buyer's counsel may decide to omit such a provision and instead rely on the buyer's possible common law right of counterclaim and setoff. Even without an express right of setoff in the acquisition agreement or related documents such as a promissory note or an employment, consulting, or noncompetition agreement, the buyer can, as a practical matter, withhold amounts from payments due to the sellers under the acquisition agreement or the related documents on the ground that the buyer is entitled to indemnification for these amounts from the sellers. The question then is whether, if the seller sues the buyer for its failure to make full payment, the buyer will be able to counterclaim that it is entitled to set off the amounts for which it believes it is entitled to indemnification.

The common law of setoff (or recoupment) varies from state to state, and when deciding whether to include or forgo an express right of setoff, buyer's counsel should examine the law governing the acquisition agreement. State laws commonly condition the right of setoff on the fulfillment of certain requirements, such as a common transaction, mutuality of parties, and a liquidated amount. Buyer's counsel should determine whether the applicable requirements would be met in the context of a dispute under the acquisition agreement and related documents. For example, although a promissory note representing deferred purchase price payments would almost certainly be considered part of a common transaction with the acquisition, it is less certain that an employment, consulting, or noncompetition agreement would meet the common transaction requirement, even if a condition to the closing of the acquisition.

An express right of setoff might address the possible consequences of an unjustified setoff. Section 11.7 of the Model Agreement allows Buyer to set off amounts for which Buyer in good faith believes that it is entitled to indemnification from Sellers against payments due to Sellers under the promissory notes or the post-closing purchase price adjustment, without bearing the risk that, if Sellers ultimately prevail on the indemnification claim, they will be able to accelerate the promissory note or obtain damages or injunctive relief. Note that under the Model Agreement, setoff rights can be asserted independently of claims against the escrow.

See KLING & NUGENT § 15.06[2].

SELLERS' RESPONSE

Sellers may regard an express setoff provision as another attempt by Buyer to gain an advantage in the event of a post-closing dispute where Buyer has an obligation to make post-closing payments to Sellers. Sellers may challenge the fairness of allowing Buyer to set off a fixed payment obligation against a disputed claim of indemnification. Achieving removal of an express setoff provision such as that in Section 11.7, while helpful to Sellers, might not as a legal matter insulate them from a lawful setoff or recoupment by Buyer. The laws in some states are liberal in permitting buyers to set off or recoup in certain situations, but may not allow setoffs against wages. *See* Keon v. Saxton & Co., 257 NY 412 (N.Y. 1931); Dunn v. Ulvade Asphalt Paving Co., 175 NY 214 (N.Y. 1903); Kahn v. New York Times, 503 N.Y.S.2d 561 (App. Div. 1986).

Even if Sellers agree to express setoff rights, they may attempt to prohibit setoffs prior to definitive resolution of a dispute and to preserve customary provisions that call for acceleration of any payments due by Buyer if Buyer wrongfully attempts setoff. Sellers may seek to require that Buyer exercise its setoff rights on a pro rata basis in proportion to the amounts due to each Seller. They may also wish to specify the order of setoff and suggest that any setoff amounts be escrowed. If the promissory note is to be pledged to a bank (for example, as substitute collateral for a loan previously collateralized by a Seller's stock), the bank as pledgee will likely resist setoff rights, because of the possible diminution of the value of the note as collateral, and because the inclusion of express setoff rights would make the note nonnegotiable.

Regardless of how this debate turns out, Sellers should remain cognizant that if Buyer has post-closing payment obligations, it might as a practical matter withhold such payments in the event of post-closing indemnification disputes. Whether such withholding would be permitted under the law governing the agreement, and any other applicable legal conditions, will be the determining factors.

11.8 THIRD-PARTY CLAIMS

GENERAL COMMENT

This Section sets forth the procedures and obligations in the case where a Third Party makes a claim or brings an action against Buyer or an Acquired Company and Buyer in turn seeks to be indemnified by Sellers under the provisions of Section 11.2 or 11.3. This Section also applies when Sellers seek indemnity from Buyer for a Third-Party Claim under Section 11.4. Although on its face the language of Section 11.8 is neutral and does not overtly favor Buyer over Sellers, in operation it tends to favor Buyer, which is most often the Indemnified Person. For purposes of analyzing Section 11.8, wherever the Section uses the term "Indemnifying Person," one should think "Sellers"; whenever the Section uses the term "Indemnified Person," one should think "Buyer." An Indemnifying Person can expect to have some role in the defense of a Third-Party Claim asserted against the Indemnified

Person since the Indemnifying Person takes on characteristics of an insurer against such claims. The extent and implementation of that role, however, are matters for negotiation. Most buyers would prefer to control their own destiny in dealing with third-party claims, as they would any other contingency. It is certainly possible for this Section to be even more pro-Buyer and give Buyer almost total control in dealing with Third-Party Claims.

Under the Model Agreement, Section 11.8 applies to claims brought before the Closing as well as claims brought after the Closing. For example, if the sale of Shares would breach an agreement to which the Company is a party, Sellers would be obligated to indemnify Buyer against an action brought prior to the Closing by that third party.

This Section does not establish an independent duty to indemnify or to defend, but only establishes a procedure for dealing with Third-Party Claims when the indemnification provisions of Sections 11.2, 11.3, or 11.4 are triggered.

See KLING & NUGENT §§ 15.02[1][e], .05[3].

GENERAL SELLERS' RESPONSE

In general, a set of procedures (such as those provided in Section 11.8) can benefit Sellers. In the absence of such a set of procedures, Buyer might be free to preclude Sellers from dealing with Third-Party Claims (subject to duties of good faith and fair dealing).

The procedures set forth in Section 11.8 are designed to deal primarily with the normal types of claims that might result in litigation, even though the term "Proceedings" used in the definition of "Third-Party Claims" is much broader and would include, for example, audits by the IRS. However, because a routine tax audit might not be considered a claim until sometime later in the process, Sellers may want to suggest specific procedures for tax audits. To the extent that an audit could result in a liability for which Sellers would be responsible, they may want to control communications with the IRS or, at least, participate in formulating responses and proposals to the IRS. They may also want the right to approve any compromises or settlements during the audit. Tax audits often cover multiple periods, so Buyer might be inclined to compromise or settle matters to its advantage and to the disadvantage of Sellers relating to the earlier periods prior to Closing. There might also be other types of Proceedings with respect to which Sellers may want to suggest special procedures.

> (a) **A Person benefited by Section 11.2, 11.3 (solely to the extent provided in the last sentence of Section 11.3), or 11.4 (an "Indemnified Person") shall give notice of the assertion of a Third-Party Claim to Sellers' Representative or Buyer (an "Indemnifying Person"), as the case may be; provided, however, that no failure or delay on the part of an Indemnified Person in notifying an Indemnifying Person will relieve the**

> **Indemnifying Person from any obligation under this Article 11 except to the extent that the failure or delay materially prejudices the defense of the Third-Party Claim by the Indemnifying Person.**

COMMENT

Under the Model Agreement, while an Indemnified Person must give the Indemnifying Person notice of Third-Party Claims, failure to give such notice does not relieve an obligation of the Indemnifying Person unless the Indemnifying Person demonstrates that a failure materially prejudices the defense of the claim.

SELLERS' RESPONSE

Sellers may seek to require notice of threatened claims at the time when there may be the greatest prospects for resolution, as well as the best opportunities for investigation, preservation of evidence, and mitigation. Sellers might even go so far as to require that notice be given upon the happening of an occurrence (i.e., an event that Buyer should know will likely lead to a claim), but Buyer could object on the basis of a lack of certainty. Sellers might negotiate for a definite time limit by which the required notice must be given.

The last clause of Section 11.8(a) provides that Buyer's failure to notify will not relieve Sellers of their obligation except to extent Sellers demonstrate that the defense of the action is materially prejudiced. Sellers might regard the application of a prejudice standard as being too narrow, and might suggest the substitution of "resolution of the Third-Party Claim" for "defense of the Third-Party Claim." This sentence could be viewed as objectionable even with the substitution. Prejudice could be a very difficult issue to prove. If Sellers cannot get a provision that late notice is per se prejudicial, then there should be some attempt to define circumstances that are de facto prejudicial (e.g., a right to assert a defense lost). It is worth re-emphasizing that not allowing Sellers to intervene at the earliest stage of a potential Third-Party Claim, when the prospect of successful and less costly defense and resolution is the greatest, may be prejudicial to Sellers. Sellers may request that the term "adversely affected" be substituted for "prejudicial."

> **(b) (i) Except as provided in Section 11.8(c), the Indemnifying Person may elect to assume the defense of the Third-Party Claim with counsel satisfactory to the Indemnified Person by (A) giving notice to the Indemnified Person of its election to assume the defense of the Third-Party Claim and (B) giving the Indemnified Person evidence acceptable to the Indemnified Person that the Indemnifying Person has adequate financial resources to defend against the Third-Party Claim and fulfill its obligations under this Article 11, in each case no later than 10 days after the Indemnified Person gives notice of the assertion of a Third-Party Claim under Section 11.8(a).**

COMMENT

Section 11.8(b) provides that the Indemnifying Person may assume the defense, subject to being satisfied with the choice of counsel (Buyer would want to be assured of counsel's competence and absence of negative prior relationships, among other matters) and the requirement that the Indemnifying Person furnish evidence, acceptable to the Indemnified Person, of adequate financial resources to undertake the defense.

The Indemnified Person has the right to monitor the defense pursuant to Section 11.8(e).

SELLERS' RESPONSE

Consideration might be given to how this would work for multiple Sellers, particularly when there is joint and several liability. If one of the Sellers is wealthy, while others have far lesser means, maybe only the wealthy Seller can assume the defense. Sellers might also object that the requirement of "adequate financial resources" is unfair and may lend itself to abuse. Sellers' argument would be that Buyer must take Sellers as Buyer finds them. They might suggest that the evidence of financial resources be "reasonably acceptable." It might be reasonable, however, for Sellers to allow Buyer to have the right to step back into a case if, for example, counsel fees are not being paid and the defense of the action is thereby threatened.

Sellers may seek to modify the requirement that counsel be "reasonably satisfactory" or, alternatively, actually agree upon satisfactory counsel in the Model Agreement. Otherwise, Sellers may want to have their choice of counsel prevail. Sellers also may seek to require, in cases in which they do not assume the defense, that all Indemnified Persons be represented by the same counsel (subject to conflicts of interest).

Sellers may seek to modify the provision that the Indemnifying Person is bound by the Indemnified Person's defense or settlement of a proceeding if the Indemnifying Person does not give written notice that it is assuming such defense within 10 days after notice of the claim. Sellers may request a right to assume the defense of the proceeding at a later date or a requirement for advance notice of a proposed settlement, and a right to reject a settlement.

Sellers may be better served if the words "assume the defense" in the first sentence were revised to "control the defense or resolution." An alternative would be to say "exclusively assume."

How this Section works when an escrow is established or when Sellers' liability is capped should be carefully examined. Section 11.8 is procedural and does not extend or enlarge the financial obligation of the Indemnifying Persons, unlike a typical insurance policy in which the cost of defense may be in addition to policy limits. Sellers cannot use the escrow fund to pay counsel, and cannot be reimbursed from the escrow fund if they ultimately prevail in their defense (unless provided in the agreement, which would be unusual). If Sellers do not assume the defense, counsel fees incurred by Buyer in defense of the Third-Party Claim can be paid from the escrow.

(ii) **If the Indemnifying Person elects to assume the defense of a Third-Party Claim:**

(A) **it shall diligently conduct the defense and, so long as it diligently conducts the defense, shall not be liable to the Indemnified Person for any Indemnified Person's fees or expenses subsequently incurred in connection with the defense of the Third-Party Claim other than reasonable costs of investigation;**

(B) **the election will conclusively establish for purposes of this Agreement that the Indemnified Person is entitled to relief under this Agreement for any Loss arising, directly or indirectly, from or in connection with the Third-Party Claim (subject to the provisions of Section 11.6);**

(C) **no compromise or settlement of such Third-Party Claim may be effected by the Indemnifying Person without the Indemnified Person's consent unless (I) there is no finding or admission of any violation by the Indemnified Person of any Legal Requirement or any rights of any Person, (II) the Indemnified Person receives a full release of and from any other claims that may be made against the Indemnified Person by the Third Party bringing the Third-Party Claim, and (III) the sole relief provided is monetary damages that are paid in full by the Indemnifying Person; and**

(D) **the Indemnifying Person shall have no liability with respect to any compromise or settlement of such claims effected without its consent.**

COMMENT

This provision sets forth the ground rules for conducting the defense against Third-Party Claims, and is constructed from Buyer's point of view. It allows Sellers to participate in, and even control the management of the resolution, but imposes some limitations and conditions. The Model Agreement imposes strict limits on that right (no settlement without the Indemnified Person's consent unless it is fully released without cost to, or any finding of wrongdoing by, the Indemnified Person). Buyer will be concerned that any Third-Party Claim will affect its business.

Clause (B) provides that if the Indemnifying Person elects to assume the defense, such act conclusively determines that the Indemnified Person is entitled to indemnification, subject to any limitations on amount.

SELLERS' RESPONSE

While it is customary to obligate the Indemnifying Person to conduct the defense "diligently," Sellers may object because the phrase is ambiguous and want to understand when their defense is less than diligent. Perhaps a procedure could be formulated.

Under the language of clause (B), by assuming the defense, the Indemnified Person concedes that any Loss is covered by the indemnification (subject to the cap and basket or threshold). Sellers may find this objectionable since it deprives Sellers of their ability to reserve their rights, as an insurer might do in analogous circumstances. If upon investigation (and even litigation), it turns out that the Third-Party Claim does not fall within the scope of the indemnification obligation (e.g., where it is originally unclear when a product was made, but turns out to have been manufactured on Buyer's watch), it would just be an undeserved windfall to Buyer.

> (iii)   **If the Indemnifying Person does not assume the defense of a Third-Party Claim in the manner and within the period provided in Section 11.8(b)(i), or if the Indemnifying Person does not diligently conduct the defense of a Third-Party Claim, the Indemnified Person may conduct the defense of the Third-Party Claim at the expense of the Indemnifying Person and the Indemnifying Person shall be bound by any determination resulting from such Third-Party Claim or any compromise or settlement effected by the Indemnified Person.**

COMMENT

Under Section 11.8(b)(iii), Sellers would be bound by any adverse determination or settlement by Buyer where Sellers have not elected to assume the defense (or have not conducted the defense as provided in Section 11.8(b)(ii)).

SELLERS' RESPONSE

Sellers may want to clarify that any adverse determination does not obviate negotiated thresholds and caps. Sellers may request that any settlement by Buyers be both reasonable and made in good faith.

Sellers may suggest a provision that if Sellers reach a compromise with the third party, and that compromise is not consented to by Buyer, Sellers' indemnity obligation is capped at the compromise amount (subject, of course, to any other applicable deductibles, caps, or other limitations on Sellers' indemnity obligations). Sellers may also consider requesting a provision that requires Sellers' consent to any settlement (perhaps with a caveat that such consent may not be unreasonably withheld or delayed).

> **(c) Notwithstanding the foregoing, if an Indemnified Person determines in good faith that there is a reasonable probability that a Third-Party Claim may adversely affect it or any Related Party other than as a result of monetary damages for which it would be entitled to relief under this Agreement, the Indemnified Person may, by notice to the Indemnifying Person, assume the exclusive right to defend, compromise, or settle such Third-Party Claim.**

COMMENT

Section 11.8(c) permits the Indemnified Person to retain control of a proceeding that presents a risk of adverse consequences beyond monetary damages that would be borne by the Indemnifying Party. For example, Buyer may want to maintain control of a proceeding that could have an adverse effect on its business that would be difficult to measure as a monetary loss, or a proceeding that could result in adverse injunctive or other equitable relief or could have precedential effect. Buyer may even want to broaden its rights by changing "in good faith" to "in its absolute discretion" and by suggesting a lesser standard than "a reasonable probability."

SELLERS' RESPONSE

Sellers might find Buyer's ability to exclude Sellers from the resolution and defense of a Third-Party Claim for fear of consequences other than monetary damages to be too great a temptation to Buyer. The argument is that this ability is subject to potential abuse by Buyer. Sellers might find that Buyer's right to assume the defense and then to offer up a settlement in which Sellers would participate significantly could be disastrous.

Sellers might suggest an alternative provision in which Buyer's right to assume the defense is limited to Third-Party Claims seeking injunctive or similar relief that, if granted, would adversely affect the Acquired Companies.

Sellers could be expected to demand a right to consent to any determination or any compromise or settlement effected by Buyer by adding the following provision: "but the Indemnifying Person shall not be bound by any determination resulting from any compromise or settlement effected without its consent (which may not be unreasonably withheld or delayed)."

(d) **Notwithstanding the provisions of Section 12.13, Sellers consent to the nonexclusive jurisdiction of any court in which a Proceeding is brought against any Indemnified Person for purposes of determining any claim that an Indemnified Person may have under this Agreement with respect to such Proceeding or the matters alleged therein.**

COMMENT

Section 11.8(d) permits Buyer to assert its claim for indemnification in the same proceeding as the claims against an indemnified Person. Unlike the other provisions of Section 11.8, it does not bind Buyer when it is an Indemnifying Person since only Sellers consent to this provision. Buyer may determine that a particular court might not be a favorable forum for its claim. This provision may also facilitate economies of time and expense.

SELLERS' RESPONSE

Sellers and Buyer, in other provisions of the Model Agreement, have agreed to the substantive law governing the interpretation of the Model Agreement and to the jurisdiction and venue of the courts that will decide any claims between Buyer and Sellers. In this Section, Buyer proposes an exception in order to have the same court hear both the Third-Party Claim and the claim for indemnification to avoid inconsistent results. Sellers may consider resisting this provision by pointing out that leaving the judicial determinations to courts randomly selected by third parties might give rise to aberrational interpretations by courts not as well equipped as the negotiated forum specified in Section 12.13 to consider the contractual issues under the Model Agreement. Furthermore, it is possible that there could be inconsistencies among such jurisdictions, thus defeating the stated purpose of the provision. Because "Indemnified Persons" could be anyone, Sellers may face a claim for indemnification anywhere. In any event, Sellers might suggest that the provision be made mutual.

(e) **With respect to any Third-Party Claim subject to this Article 11:**

(i) **any Indemnified Person and any Indemnifying Person, as the case may be, shall keep the other Person fully informed of the status of such Third-Party Claim and any related Proceeding at all stages thereof where such Person is not represented by its own counsel; and**

(ii) **both the Indemnified Person and the Indemnifying Person, as the case may be, shall render to each other such assistance as they may reasonably require of each other and shall cooperate in good faith with each other in order to ensure the proper and adequate defense of any Third-Party Claim.**

COMMENT

Clause (i) of Section 11.8(e) mandates that an Indemnified and Indemnifying Person keep each other informed about the status of the Third-Party Claim. Note, however, this provision may not bind an Indemnified Person that is not Buyer or a Seller since it is not a party to the Model Agreement.

Clause (ii) of Section 11.8(e) mandates a similar duty of cooperation, and may suffer the same limitation as to nonparties.

SELLERS' RESPONSE

Sellers may want to condition any duty to indemnify on receipt of an undertaking from a nonparty with respect to the subject matter of Sections 11.8(e) and (f), or provide that Buyer will cause its related nonparties to perform the obligations under these Sections.

(f) In addition to Section 7.3, with respect to any Third-Party Claim subject to this Article 11, the parties shall cooperate in a manner to preserve in full (to the extent possible) the confidentiality of all Confidential Information and the attorney-client and work-product privileges. In connection therewith, each party agrees that:

   (i) it shall use its best efforts, in respect of any Third-Party Claim in which it has assumed or participated in the defense, to avoid production of Confidential Information (consistent with applicable law and rules of procedure); and

   (ii) all communications between any party and counsel responsible for or participating in the defense of any Third-Party Claim shall, to the extent possible, be made so as to preserve any applicable attorney-client or work-product privilege.

COMMENT

Section 11.8(f) imposes requirements on the parties to maintain confidentiality consistent with applicable law and attorney-client and work-product privileges. *See* commentary to Section 7.3.

(g) Any claim under this Article 11 for any matter involving a Third-Party Claim shall be indemnified, paid, or reimbursed promptly. If the Indemnified Person shall for any reason assume the defense of a Third-Party Claim, the Indemnifying Person shall reimburse the Indemnified Person on a monthly basis for the costs of investigation and the reasonable fees and expenses of counsel retained by the Indemnified Person. Buyer may elect in its discretion to have payment or reimbursement made from the Escrow Funds pursuant to the terms of the Escrow Agreement, by setoff against amounts otherwise payable under the Promissory Notes or otherwise pursuant to Section 11.7, or in any other manner.

COMMENT

Buyer will want to be paid or reimbursed promptly and, if it assumes the defense of the claim, it will want to be reimbursed currently for its costs of investigation and the fees and expenses of its counsel. In some agreements the first sentence of this section is worded such that a party has a specified amount of time after receiving notice to object to the claim, in the absence of which it is deemed to have accepted the claim, much like the way in which Section 3(a) of the Escrow Agreement operates. With respect to reimbursement for the costs of investigation and defense, it is arguable that this is not itself a Third-Party Claim and is covered by Section 11.9, but the second sentence is intended to make it clear that, in any event, reimbursement is to be made on a current basis.

SELLERS' RESPONSE

Sellers could decide whether they would prefer that Buyer proceed to recover Losses first from the Escrow Funds or by setoff against the Promissory Notes or otherwise, and request that the last sentence of Section 11.8(g) be revised accordingly. In addition to establishing the order for recovery by Buyer, they might request that Buyer be required to use its best efforts to recover Losses from the Escrow Funds and by offset against the Promissory Notes before attempting to recover any Losses from Sellers in any other manner.

11.9   OTHER CLAIMS

A claim under this Article 11 for any matter not involving a Third-Party Claim may be made by notice to Sellers' Representative or Buyer, as the case may be, and shall be indemnified, paid, or reimbursed promptly after such notice. Buyer may elect in its discretion to have payment or reimbursement made from the Escrow Funds pursuant to the terms of the Escrow Agreement, by setoff against amounts otherwise payable under the Promissory Notes or otherwise pursuant to Section 11.7, or in any other manner.

COMMENT

This Section emphasizes the parties' intention that indemnification remedies provided in the Model Agreement are not limited to Third-Party Claims. Some courts have implied such a limitation in the absence of clear contractual language to the contrary. *See* commentary to Section 11.2.

This provision does not control the procedure for settling claims. For instance, some acquisition agreements require information on the claim be presented in some detail and require that the seller respond in some fashion.

SELLERS' RESPONSE

Sellers may want information beyond a bare statement of the claim provided and may want some of the detail from Section 11.8 repeated. They may also request language acknowledging their right to contest Buyer's claim, so that its providing notice of a claim is not interpreted as a *fait accompli.*

Similar to Section 11.8(g), Sellers could decide whether they would prefer that Buyer proceed to recover Losses from the Escrow Funds or by setoff against the Promissory Notes or otherwise, and request that the last sentence of Section 11.9 be revised accordingly. In addition to establishing the order for recovery by Buyer, they might request that Buyer be required to use its best efforts to recover Losses from the Escrow Funds and by offset against the Promissory Notes before attempting to recover any Losses from Sellers in any other manner.

11.10   STRICT LIABILITY OR INDEMNITEE NEGLIGENCE

THE PROVISIONS IN THIS ARTICLE 11 SHALL BE ENFORCEABLE REGARDLESS OF WHETHER THE LIABILITY IS BASED UPON PAST, PRESENT, OR FUTURE ACTS, CLAIMS, OR LEGAL REQUIREMENTS (INCLUDING ANY PAST, PRESENT, OR FUTURE ENVIRONMENTAL LAW, OCCUPATIONAL SAFETY AND HEALTH LAW, OR PRODUCTS LIABILITY, SECURITIES, OR OTHER LEGAL REQUIREMENT) AND REGARDLESS OF WHETHER ANY PERSON (INCLUDING THE PERSON FROM WHOM RELIEF IS SOUGHT) ALLEGES OR PROVES THE SOLE, CONCURRENT, CONTRIBUTORY, OR COMPARATIVE NEGLIGENCE OF THE PERSON SEEKING RELIEF, OR THE SOLE OR CONCURRENT STRICT LIABILITY IMPOSED UPON THE PERSON SEEKING RELIEF.

COMMENT

Purpose of Section. Section 11.10 attempts to eliminate enforceability defenses asserted by an Indemnifying Person, such as the law applicable at the time of a claim, or the Indemnified Person's culpability. Accordingly, the Indemnified Person may seek to enforce a claim regardless of (a) the date on which the claim arises, (b) whether such claim is based on a law or regulation in effect at the time it arises, or (c) whether the Indemnified Person was either negligent in whole or in part, or even strictly liable (e.g., pursuant to a products liability claim). The Indemnifying Person, of course, may assert other defenses to its indemnification obligation, but it should not be able to avail itself of the unenforceability defense.

The Section is in all capital letters because some jurisdictions require that any risk-shifting provision be conspicuously presented.

These limitations on indemnification have arisen where parties to contracts, such as a construction contract, provide for indemnification against third-party claims when the indemnified party might have some culpability in the third-party claim. These limitations should not apply when indemnification is simply a contract remedy. However, Section 11.2(a) goes beyond contract remedies, and in any event Buyer would want to be protected against a court that may not make a distinction.

The purpose of this section is illustrated by Fina, Inc. v. ARCO, 200 F.3d 266 (5th Cir. 2000), in which the U.S. Court of Appeals for the Fifth Circuit invalidated an asset purchase agreement indemnification provision with respect to environmental liabilities. In *Fina*, the liabilities arose from actions of three different owners over a 30-year period during which both seller and buyer owned and operated the business and contributed to the environmental condition. The asset purchase agreement indemnification provision provided that the indemnitor "shall indemnify, defend and hold harmless [the indemnitee] . . . against all claims, actions, demands, losses or liabilities arising from the use or operation of the Assets . . . and accruing from and after closing." The court, applying Delaware law pursuant to the agreement's choice of law provision, held that the indemnification provision did not satisfy the Delaware requirement that indemnification provisions that require payment for liabilities imposed upon the indemnitee for the indemnitee's own negligence or pursuant to strict liability statutes such as CERCLA must be clear and unequivocal. The court explained that the risk-shifting in such a situation is so extraordinary that, to be enforceable, the provision must state with specificity the types of risks that the agreement is transferring to the indemnitor.

There are other situations in which an acquisition agreement may require indemnification where the buyer's action may contribute to the loss. For example, a defective product may be shipped prior to closing, but the buyer may fail to effect a timely recall, which could have prevented the liability, or an account receivable may prove uncollectible because of the buyer's failure diligently to pursue its collection or otherwise satisfy the customer's requirements.

This Section is intended to address court holdings, such as *Fina*, that indemnification is unenforceable because it does not contain specific words indicating that certain kinds of risks are intended to be shifted by the agreement.

Indemnification for Indemnitee's Own Negligence. Indemnities, releases, and other exculpatory provisions are generally enforceable as between the parties absent statutory exceptions for certain kinds of liabilities (e.g., Section 14 of the Securities Act and Section 29 of the Exchange Act), or judicially created exceptions (e.g., some courts as a matter of public policy will not allow a party to shift responsibility for its own gross negligence or intentional misconduct and negligence). *See* RESTATEMENT (SECOND) OF CONTRACTS § 195 cmt. b (1981) ("Language inserted by a party in an agreement for the purpose of exempting [it] from liability for negligent conduct is scrutinized with particular care and a court may require specific and conspicuous reference to negligence . . . . Furthermore, a party's attempt to exempt [itself] from liability for negligent conduct may fail as unconscionable.")

Assuming none of these exceptions is applicable, the judicial focus turns to whether the words of the contract are sufficient to shift responsibility for the particular liability. A minority of courts have adopted a literal enforcement approach under which a broadly worded indemnity for any and all claims is held to encompass claims from unforeseen events including the indemnitee's own negligence. The majority of courts closely scrutinize, and are reluctant to enforce, indemnification or other exculpatory arrangements that shift liability away from the culpable party and require that provisions having such an effect be "clear and unequivocal" in stating the risks that are being transferred to the indemnitor. *See* Conwell, *"Recent Decisions: The Maryland Court of Appeals,"* 57 MD. L. REV. 706 (1998). If an indemnification provision is not sufficiently specific, a court may refuse to enforce the purported imposition on the indemnitor of liability for the indemnitee's own negligence or strict liability, as in *Fina*.

The actual application of the "clear and unequivocal" standard varies from state to state and from situation to situation. Jurisdictions such as Florida, New Hampshire, Wyoming, and Illinois do not mandate that any specific wording be used in order for an indemnity to be enforceable to transfer responsibility for the indemnitee's negligence. *See* Hardage Enterprises v. Fidesys Corp., 570 So.2d 436 (Fla. App. 1990); Audley v. Melton, 640 A.2d 777 (N.H. 1994); Boehm v. Cody Country Chamber of Commerce, 748 P.2d 704 (Wyo. 1987); Neumann v. Gloria Marshall Figure Salon, 500 N.E. 2d 1011 (Ill. 1986). Jurisdictions such as New York, Minnesota, Missouri, Maine, North Dakota, and Delaware require also that reference to the negligence or fault of the indemnitee be set forth within the contract. *See* Gross v. Sweet, 458 N.Y.S.2d 162 (1983) (holding that the language of the indemnity must plainly and precisely indicate that the limitation of liability extends to negligence or fault of the indemnitee); Schlobohn v. Spa Petite, Inc., 326 N.W.2d 920 (Minn. 1982) (holding that indemnity is enforceable where "negligence" is expressly stated); Alack v. Vic Tanny Intern., 923 S.W.2d 330 (Mo. 1996) (holding that a bright-line test is established requiring that the words "negligence" or "fault" be used conspicuously); Doyle v. Bowdoin College, 403 A.2d 1206 (Me. 1979) (holding that there must be an express reference to liability for negligence); Blum v. Kauffman, 297 A.2d 48 (Del. 1972) (holding that a release did not "clearly and unequivocally" express the intent of the parties without the word "negligence"); Fina, Inc. v. ARCO, 200 F.3d 266, 270 (5th Cir. 2000) (applying Delaware law and explaining that no Delaware case has allowed indemnification of a party for its own negligence without making specific reference to the negligence of the indemnified party and requiring, at a minimum, that indemnity provisions demonstrate that "the subject of negligence of the indemnitee was expressly considered by the parties drafting the agreement"). Under the "express negligence" doctrine followed by Texas courts, an indemnification agreement is not enforceable to indemnify a party from the consequences of its own negligence unless such intent is specifically stated within the four corners of the agreement. *See* Ethyl Corp. v. Daniel Constr. Co., 725 S.W.2d 705 (Tex. 1987); Atlantic Richfield Co. v. Petroleum Personnel, Inc., 768 S.W.2d 724 (Tex. 1989).

In addition to requiring that the exculpatory provision be explicit, some courts require that its presentation be conspicuous. *See* Dresser Indus. v. Page Petroleum, Inc., 853 S.W.2d 505 (Tex. 1993) ("Because indemnification of a party for its own negligence is an extraordinary shifting of risk, this Court has developed fair notice requirements which . . . include the express negligence doctrine and the conspicuousness requirements. The express negligence doctrine states that a party seeking indemnity from the consequences of that party's own negligence must express that intent in specific terms within the four corners of the contract. The conspicuous requirement mandates that something must appear on the face of the [contract] to attract the attention of a reasonable person when he looks at it."); Alack v. Vic Tanny Intern. of Missouri, Inc., 923 S.W.2d 330, 337 (Mo. 1996). Although most courts appear not to have imposed a comparable "conspicuousness" requirement to date, some lawyers feel it prudent to put their express negligence words in all capital letters, bold face, or other conspicuous type.

Indemnification for Strict Liability. Concluding that the transfer of a liability based upon strict liability involves an extraordinary shifting of risk analogous to the shifting of responsibility for an indemnitee's own negligence, some courts have held that the clear and unequivocal rule is equally applicable to indemnification for strict liability claims. *See, e.g.,* Fina, Inc. v. ARCO, 200 F.2d 300 (5th Cir. 2000); Purolator Prod. v. Allied Signal, Inc., 772 F. Supp. 124 (W.D.N.Y. 1991); Houston Lighting & Power Co. v. Atchison, Topeka & Santa Fe Ry., 890 S.W.2d 455 (Tex. 1994); *see also* Parker and Savich, *Contractual Efforts to Allocate the Risk of Environmental Liability: Is There a Way to Make Indemnities Worth More Than the Paper They Are Written On?*, 44 Sw. L.J. 1349 (1991). In *Fina*, the court concluded that the broad clause in an asset purchase agreement did not satisfy the clear and unequivocal test in respect of strict liability claims because there was no specific reference to claims based upon strict liability.

In view of the judicial hostility to the contractual shifting of liability for strict liability risks, counsel may wish to include in the acquisition agreement references to additional kinds of strict liability claims for which indemnification is intended.

SELLERS' RESPONSE

The Section should be tailored to the specific circumstances of the parties to the transaction and the applicable laws of the various jurisdictions. While sellers may understand a buyer's desire to counter the holdings of cases like *Fina*, they may be unwilling to indemnify the buyer generally against its own negligence.

12. Miscellaneous

PRELIMINARY NOTE

While this Article is entitled "Miscellaneous," it is referred to by many lawyers as the "boilerplate" section. For an explanation of the term, *see* STARK 9. Usually the boilerplate section deals with contractual provisions that could be applicable to any type of agreement. These provisions often attempt to state or modify common law rules otherwise applicable to contracts (e.g., limitations on assignability). But the section may include other provisions of a general nature that do not fit elsewhere (e.g., expenses and public announcements). The Model Agreement provides a usage section (Section 1.2), which might be considered boilerplate, but is included as part of Article 1 to facilitate review of the Model Agreement.

While many consider the boilerplate section as merely mechanical and defining certain rules of the road (e.g., notices), it may in fact enlarge or contract the remedial provisions of the contract (e.g., waiver of jury trial). Practitioners have come to realize that boilerplate can be significant, and alternatives need to be understood and considered.

12.1 EXPENSES

(a) **Except as otherwise provided in this Agreement or the other documents to be delivered pursuant to this Agreement, each party will bear its respective fees and expenses incurred in connection with the preparation, negotiation, execution, and performance of this Agreement and the consummation and performance of the Contemplated Transactions, including all fees and expenses of its Representatives. Buyer will pay one-half and Sellers will pay one-half of (i) the HSR Act filing fee and (ii) the fees and expenses of the Escrow Agent under the Escrow Agreement. No Acquired Company has incurred, and Sellers will cause the Acquired Companies not to incur, any fees or expenses in connection with this Agreement and the Contemplated Transactions; provided, however, that to the extent such fees and expenses have been incurred by an Acquired Company, Sellers will reimburse the Acquired Company for such fees and expenses prior to the Closing. The obligation of each party to bear its own fees and expenses will be subject to any rights of such party arising from a Breach of this Agreement by another party.**

COMMENT

A buyer and seller often agree that fees and expenses will be paid by the party incurring them. The Model Agreement adopts this view with certain adjustments. Fees would include those of investment bankers, attorneys, accountants, experts on due diligence, and other consultants. There may be special circumstances where one party attempts to shift to the other the burden of fees, particularly if the transaction fails to close through some fault of either party. *See* commentary to Section 10.2.

Sections 3.28 and 4.5 of the Model Agreement contain representations of Sellers and Buyer to the effect that neither has incurred any obligation to any broker or finder in respect of the Contemplated Transactions. If either party had retained a broker or finder, the first sentence of Section 12.1(a) would require the party incurring the obligation to satisfy it.

The second sentence makes Sellers responsible for a portion of HSR fees. *See* commentary to definition of "HSR Act" in Section 1.1. While the legal obligation is imposed solely on the acquiring party under the HSR Act, the Model Agreement recognizes that, since HSR approval is a mutual condition, the parties often agree to allocate responsibility for the fees. The second sentence also divides responsibility for the escrow fees, although that would also be stated in the Escrow Agreement.

The third sentence may be contrary to what has actually occurred. The Company, rather than Sellers, may have entered into arrangements dealing with its sale. Although that is particularly true of investment banking arrangements, other fees may have been paid by the Company, particularly when its sale is initially being explored. The representation, if untrue, would be subject to indemnification under Section 11.2(a) or (b). When in fact the Company has incurred expenses, Section 12.1 provides that the Acquired Companies are to be reimbursed by Sellers.

The last sentence of Section 12.1(a) provides that the obligation to bear fees and expenses is subject to other rights resulting in a Breach, most generally when a court awards fees and expenses to the prevailing party.

See STARK ch. 12.

SELLERS' RESPONSE

While the general proposition is not troubling, Sellers may expect that the costs of sale will be borne by the Company, effectively shifting those expenses (without more) to Buyer. Because the Purchase Price is to be adjusted based on shareholders' equity in the Model Agreement, Buyer should not be concerned. To the extent such fees are expensed on or before closing, the costs of sale would reduce shareholders' equity and would be for the account of Sellers.

There may be some circumstances where Buyer would agree that some fees would be paid by the Company, such as attorneys' fees not exceeding some specified dollar amount. In that case, the purchase price adjustment mechanism of Section 2.5(a) would require adjustment to exclude such permitted payments.

Because the HSR fees are the legal responsibility of Buyer, Sellers could justifiably assert that they are to remain the responsibility of Buyer. Even if Sellers are willing to pay some portion of those fees, they might insist that it would be conditioned on successful HSR clearance. After all, the risk on HSR depends to a large extent upon Buyer's profile. Therefore, Sellers might negotiate to reimburse up to one-half of the fees, but only at the Closing. Escrow fees are so modest that their allocation is usually not worth contesting.

Even if Sellers intend to be responsible for the fees and expenses, the third sentence should be carefully reviewed. If the Company has paid any portion of fees and expenses, Sellers would not want to make a false representation. Sellers might also be concerned where counsel is being paid by the Company, subject to reimbursement. *See* M&A PROCESS 5–7, 19–20.

> **(b) All stamp, documentary, and other transfer Taxes (including any penalties and interest) incurred in connection with this Agreement, whether pertaining to the Shares or any assets and properties of the Acquired Companies, will be paid by Sellers. Each Seller will, at its own expense, file all necessary Tax Returns and other documentation with respect to all such Taxes.**

COMMENT

Section 12.1(b) makes Sellers responsible for all transfer Taxes arising from the transaction. Taxes payable with regard to the Shares, such as stamp taxes, while rare, are sometimes imposed. *See* commentary to Section 2.4. Taxes may also arise from the deemed sale of the underlying assets and properties of the Acquired Companies. *See, e.g.,* NEW YORK TAX LAW § 1400 *et seq.* (conveyance of real property includes sale of controlling interest in legal entity). This Section allocates these Taxes to Sellers.

SELLERS' RESPONSE

While Sellers may accept their responsibility for stamp and other transfer taxes on the Shares, and would be responsible for the personal income tax effects of the sale, they may object to being responsible for any local property transfer taxes arising from the transaction.

12.2   PUBLIC ANNOUNCEMENTS

> **Notwithstanding any confidentiality obligation to which Buyer is subject, any public announcement, including any press release, communication to employees, customers, suppliers, or others having dealings with the Acquired Companies, or**

similar publicity with respect to this Agreement or any Contemplated Transaction, will be issued, at such time, in such manner, and containing such content as Buyer determines.

COMMENT

Information about the transaction can have consequences on the Company's constituencies, particularly employees. The Model Agreement provides that Buyer will control the timing and content of public announcements. Section 12.2 will be negotiated in light of any confidentiality agreement in place. The Confidentiality Agreement set forth as Ancillary Document A is only binding on Buyer, although some confidentiality agreements are mutual. Section 12.7 provides that the Confidentiality Agreement is only superseded upon closing. Section 12.2 makes it clear that this Section, rather than the Confidentiality Agreement, now states the agreement of the parties with respect to its subject matter.

Buyer sometimes will negotiate for the additional right to visit with key customers or suppliers to obtain information concerning their relationship with the Company or to gain assurances that their relationship with the Company will continue as a part of its pre-closing access rights provided in Section 5.1. In that case, Buyer may want to add "and subject to Section 5.1."

If Buyer is a public company, the timing of a public announcement regarding the acquisition may be affected by federal securities laws, and Buyer may want to preserve the right to make any announcement required by law.

See STARK ch. 14.

SELLERS' RESPONSE

Sellers may suggest that control of public announcements be at least mutual. Sellers may want confidentiality of the Model Agreement and its signing to be mutual as well. Sellers may also suggest that they should be able to communicate with employees, customers, and suppliers so long as the name of Buyer is not revealed and other deal terms are kept confidential.

Sellers will be interested in restricting the ability of Buyer to make any announcement prior to closing to avoid the perception that the Company is damaged goods if the transaction does not close.

Sellers will also want to negotiate this provision in light of their best efforts obligation under Section 5.7. If Sellers will need to seek consents from customers and suppliers because of change of control provisions, they will want to at least be able to communicate effectively without interference from Buyer. This Section may effectively prevent compliance with Section 5.7 unless consents can be obtained without an explanation by Sellers of why they are seeking the consent. Both Buyer and Sellers have an interest in working out a methodology to obtain all necessary consents.

12.3   DISCLOSURE LETTER

(a) **In the event of any inconsistency between the statements in this Agreement and those in the Disclosure Letter (other than an exception expressly set forth as such in the Disclosure Letter with respect to a specifically identified representation or warranty), the statements in this Agreement will control.**

(b) **Notwithstanding anything to the contrary contained in the Disclosure Letter or any supplement to the Disclosure Letter, the statements in the Disclosure Letter, and those in any supplement thereto, relate only to the provisions in the Sections of this Agreement to which they expressly relate and not to any other provision in this Agreement.**

COMMENT

The Model Agreement provides for the delivery by Sellers of a Disclosure Letter containing lists called for by, and exceptions to, their representations in Article 3. No particular form is required for the Disclosure Letter, but standard practice is for listings and exceptions to respond to particular sections in the acquisition agreement, rather than being lumped together. *See* M&A Process 233–40; Houck & Rosenbloom, *Contract Schedules—The Stepchildren of Transactional Drafting*, 14 MERGERS & ACQUISITIONS LITIG. REP. 1 (2004).

Section 12.3(a) provides that the Model Agreement controls over any inconsistency between statements in the Disclosure Letter and in the Model Agreement. This is intended to counter the practice of some attorneys to include explanations or language with the disclosures of the lists and exceptions that are designed to modify their effect, thus arguably modifying the acquisition agreement unilaterally.

Section 12.3(b) provides that statements relate only to the provisions of the section of the Model Agreement to which they expressly relate and not to other provisions of the Model Agreement. Buyer will want to limit the effect of a disclosure to the specific representation in this manner, arguing that the implications of the disclosure cannot be properly evaluated in the absence of the context given by that representation. For example, Buyer may view differently a contract disclosed in response to a representation that calls for a list of material contracts and a contract disclosed in response to a representation concerning transactions with related parties. The latter situation increases the likelihood that the economic terms of the contract are not at arm's length. In particular, *see* the discussion and the court's resort to parol evidence in IBP, Inc. v. Tyson Foods, Inc., 789 A.2d 14 (Del. Ch. 2001). *See also* Ancillary Document C—Disclosure Letter.

SELLERS' RESPONSE

Sellers may argue that it is unfair for them to be penalized for a failure to identify each of the many representations in a long-form acquisition agreement to which a disclosed state of facts relates. Indeed, Sellers may prefer not to characterize the disclosures made in the Disclosure Letter by reference to any particular representation, but rather to qualify all representations by the Disclosure Letter (for example, Article 3 would begin "Sellers, jointly and severally, represent and warrant to Buyer except as otherwise set forth in the Disclosure Letter, as follows:").

A frequent compromise is to modify Section 12.3(b) by adding at the end "except to the extent that the relevance to such other representation and warranty is manifest on the face of the Disclosure Letter" or some similar exception.

Sellers may prefer to insert a provision such as the following in lieu of Section 12.3:

(a) Any disclosure under one part of the Disclosure Letter will be deemed disclosure under all parts of the Disclosure Letter and this Agreement. Disclosure of any matter in the Disclosure Letter will not constitute an expression of a view that such matter is required to be disclosed pursuant to this Agreement.

(b) The inclusion of any matter in the Disclosure Letter does not constitute a determination by Sellers that any such matter is material.

(c) The disclosure of any matter in the Disclosure Letter does not establish or imply a standard of materiality, a standard for what may be in the Ordinary Course of Business, or any other standard for purposes of this Agreement.

12.4 Nature of Sellers' Obligations

The liabilities of Sellers under this Agreement are joint and several. Sellers, jointly and severally, shall cause each Acquired Company to take, or refrain from taking, all actions as may be necessary or appropriate to implement this Agreement.

COMMENT

The Model Agreement provides that Sellers' obligations are joint and several. Sellers' liability for the representations in Article 3 and for indemnification in Sections 11.2 and 11.3 is stated to be joint and several, and this Section makes it clear that Sellers are jointly and severally liable for all obligations under the Model Agreement. Without such a provision, the liability of each Seller is less clear. In some cases it might be considered unduly harsh to make an insignificant shareholder liable for all of the obligations of the other shareholders.

SELLERS' RESPONSE

Sellers might object to this provision, contending that it poses great risk to the most creditworthy Sellers or those that are capable of being served, and because the potential for damage might far exceed a particular Seller's proceeds from sale of the Shares. Even if all Sellers were joined in a suit, there is risk to some Sellers should one or more other Sellers be in bankruptcy. Sellers might suggest that their liability be several, Buyer be contractually obligated to pursue all Sellers, or each Seller's liability be capped at the proceeds received. *See* "Joint and Several Liability of Sellers" in commentary to the lead-in to Section 11.2.

This provision must be coordinated with other provisions of the parties' bargain, such as the Escrow Agreement. Some of the concerns arising from joint and several liability can be addressed through a contribution agreement among Sellers. *See* Ancillary Document E—Contribution Agreement.

12.5 SELLERS' REPRESENTATIVE

(a) **Each Seller constitutes and appoints _____ as its representative (the "Sellers' Representative") and its true and lawful attorney in fact, with full power and authority in its name and on its behalf:**

   (i) **to act on such Seller's behalf in the absolute discretion of Sellers' Representative with respect to all matters relating to this Agreement, including execution and delivery of any amendment, supplement, or modification of this Agreement and any waiver of any claim or right arising out of this Agreement; and**

   (ii) **in general, to do all things and to perform all acts, including executing and delivering all agreements, certificates, receipts, instructions, and other instruments contemplated by or deemed advisable to effectuate the provisions of this Section 12.5.**

This appointment and grant of power and authority is coupled with an interest and is in consideration of the mutual covenants made in this Agreement and is irrevocable and will not be terminated by any act of any Seller or by operation of law, whether by the death or incapacity of any Seller or by the occurrence of any other event. Each Seller hereby consents to the taking of any and all actions and the making of any decisions required or permitted to be taken or made by Sellers' Representative pursuant to this Section 12.5. Each Seller agrees that Sellers' Representative shall have no obligation or liability to any Person for any action taken or omitted by Sellers' Representative in good faith, and each Seller shall indemnify and hold harmless Sellers' Representative from, and shall pay to Sellers' Representative the amount of, or reimburse Sellers' Representative for, any

Loss that Sellers' Representative may suffer, sustain, or become subject to as a result of any such action or omission by Sellers' Representative under this Agreement.

(b) Buyer shall be entitled to rely upon any document or other paper delivered by Sellers' Representative as being authorized by Sellers, and Buyer shall not be liable to any Seller for any action taken or omitted to be taken by Buyer based on such reliance.

(c) Until all obligations under this Agreement shall have been discharged (including all indemnification obligations under Article 11), Sellers who, immediately prior to the Closing, are entitled in the aggregate to receive more than 50% of the Purchase Price, may, from time to time upon notice to Buyer, appoint a new Sellers' Representative upon the death, incapacity, or resignation of Sellers' Representative. If, after the death, incapacity, or resignation of Sellers' Representative, a successor Sellers' Representative shall not have been appointed by Sellers within 15 Business Days after a request by Buyer, Buyer may appoint a Sellers' Representative from among the Sellers to fill any vacancy so created by notice of such appointment to Sellers.

COMMENT

Buyer, both before and after the Closing, would prefer to deal with one person under the Model Agreement, whether it be arranging the Closing or sorting out liabilities afterwards. Hence, Buyer is providing for the appointment of a Sellers' Representative for its convenience. Sellers, on the other hand, will want to assure that Sellers' Representative acts only within prescribed bounds. That could be accomplished within the Model Agreement, but no such limitations are included. The appointment of Sellers' Representative could be made outside the Model Agreement, but Buyer will want to be assured that the scope of the appointment satisfies its needs. Because this appointment may constitute a power of attorney, it may be subject to disclosure or other requirements under the laws of various jurisdictions. *See, e.g.,* N.Y. GEN. OBLIG. LAW § 5-150B (applicable to powers of attorney executed within New York State by an individual).

Section 12.5(a) assures that a Sellers' Representative will be appointed. It provides broad authority to act for Sellers under the Model Agreement and is irrevocable. As customary with powers of attorney, it provides that Sellers' Representative has no liability for actions taken or omitted in good faith. Buyer hopes that Sellers' Representative will act in a business-like fashion; in fact, Sellers' Representative would often have been active in the business. On the other hand, it does not compel Sellers' Representative to act, and in carrying out its responsibilities it may seek involvement by or direction from the other Sellers. In fact, Buyer may want to encourage the involvement of the other Sellers in an effort to avoid disputes among the Sellers that may impact Buyer.

Section 12.5(b) provides that Buyer will be entitled to rely on any document delivered by Sellers' Representative as being authorized by Sellers.

Section 12.5(c) provides a means of replacing Sellers' Representative and, if not availed of, a mechanism for Buyer to appoint a replacement.

SELLERS' RESPONSE

Sellers will not necessarily be unified in their response. While a controlling Seller (or one who has a large holding) may be amenable to the arrangement, minority holders may be concerned. Those holders would probably agree to having a designated person make minor decisions, but they may be reluctant about the lack of specificity in Section 12.5. Minority shareholders may want to curb the authority of the Sellers' Representative to make amendments to the Model Agreement or waivers of substantial rights, particularly in a way that affects shareholders in a nonuniform fashion. Similarly, minority shareholders may want to retain some recourse against Seller's Representative.

Even though a majority in interest is required to appoint a new Sellers' Representative, Section 12.5(c) does not suggest that collective action is required by Sellers on other matters. Minority shareholders might insist on a supermajority provision for some actions. At a minimum, Sellers may want more time than the 15 business days provided by the last sentence of Section 12.5(c).

12.6   FURTHER ASSURANCES

The parties will (a) execute and deliver to each other such other documents and (b) do such other acts and things as a party may reasonably request for the purpose of carrying out the intent of this Agreement, the Contemplated Transactions, and the documents to be delivered pursuant to this Agreement.

COMMENT

A further assurances provision is common in asset purchase agreements. Often there are permits, licenses, and consents that will be obtained as a routine matter after the Closing. The further assurances provision specifies that such routine matters will be accomplished. The use of a further assurances provision in a stock purchase agreement is less common. Unlike an asset purchase, where numerous documents could be required, a stock purchase requires the delivery of only stock certificates. Nevertheless, when a party is required to contribute assets or assume liabilities or there are a number of ancillary transactions, a further assurances clause may be meaningful. If a further assurance clause is to be included, Buyer may want to add language to avoid any interpretation that may require extraordinary efforts to close, as for example a divestiture required under the antitrust laws. *See* commentary to Section 6.3.

See STARK ch. 22.

SELLERS' RESPONSE

Sellers may be inclined to ignore this provision as routine without particular consequence. But perhaps it deserves more attention from Sellers. For example, if Buyer has waived a closing condition due to the failure of Sellers to obtain certain Consents and the Closing occurs, could this Section revive Sellers' obligation to obtain the Consents, even though that might be impossible? If Buyer has waived the condition, but wishes Sellers to pursue obtaining the Consents, it would be helpful to have a specific agreement at that time as to what efforts are required and how long this must be pursued.

12.7   ENTIRE AGREEMENT

This Agreement supersedes all prior agreements, whether written or oral, between the parties with respect to its subject matter (including any letter of intent and, upon the Closing, any confidentiality obligation to which Buyer is subject) and constitutes (along with the Disclosure Letter, the exhibits, and the other documents to be delivered pursuant to this Agreement) a complete and exclusive statement of the terms of the agreement between the parties with respect to the subject matter of this Agreement.

COMMENT

Section 12.7 provides that the Model Agreement supersedes all prior agreements, whether written or oral, between the parties relating to the subject matter of the Model Agreement, including the letter of intent. However, the Confidentiality Agreement is not to be superseded until the Closing (so that Buyer does not have a duty of confidentiality as to its own subsidiary). If any letter of intent itself contains confidentiality provisions or there are other agreements (such as a confidentiality agreement binding on Sellers) that are to survive the execution of the Model Agreement or the Closing, the parenthetical language will need to be adjusted.

Section 12.7 provides that the Model Agreement constitutes (along with specified other documents) a complete and exclusive statement of the terms of the agreement between the parties with respect to its subject matter. This means that additional purported oral agreements do not exist. An integration clause such as this should be respected by the courts. However, this clause will not preclude oral testimony as to the meaning of an ambiguous clause. *See* commentary to Section 1.2(c). It will also not prohibit testimony with respect to representations that were made to induce the contract. *See* "The Transaction That Does Not Close" in preliminary note to Article 11.

Consideration might be given to as to whether use of the term "subject matter" is ambiguous, particularly where the parties may have other agreements between them that do not relate to the transaction. In certain situations, Buyer might be more comfortable substituting "Contemplated Transactions" for "subject matter" where it appears in this Section.

See STARK ch. 18.

SELLERS' RESPONSE

While in general Sellers would be sympathetic with the general philosophy of this Section and in fact probably regard it as being to their advantage (generally it is Buyer that is claiming agreements made outside the Model Agreement), Sellers will want to carefully consider how it operates. For example, if the Confidentiality Agreement protects personal information of Sellers or affiliates of the Company, not just of the Company, they might not want that agreement to terminate at the Closing.

Like the Buyer, Sellers may also want to consider whether the term "subject matter" might cover other agreements that they would want to remain in effect after the Closing.

12.8 MODIFICATION

This Agreement may only be amended, supplemented, or otherwise modified by a writing executed by the Buyer and the Sellers' Representative.

COMMENT

Section 12.8 provides that the Model Agreement may be amended only by a written agreement between the parties. This section follows Section 2-209(2) of the UCC, which provides that "[a] signed agreement which excludes modification or rescission except by a signed writing cannot be otherwise modified or rescinded." Nevertheless, the courts find various rationales for enforcing oral modifications.

See STARK ch. 16.

SELLERS' RESPONSE

The Sellers' response concerning the authorization of Sellers' Representative to amend the Model Agreement is discussed in the commentary to Section 12.5.

12.9 ASSIGNMENTS AND SUCCESSORS

No party may assign any of its rights or delegate any of its obligations under this Agreement without the prior consent of the other parties, except that Buyer may assign any of its rights and delegate any of its obligations under this Agreement to any Subsidiary of Buyer and, after the Closing, to the purchaser

of all or a substantial part of the equity securities or business of the Acquired Companies and may collaterally assign its rights under this Agreement to any financial institution providing financing in connection with the Contemplated Transactions. Any purported assignment of rights or delegation of obligations in violation of this Section 12.9 will be void. Subject to the foregoing, this Agreement will apply to, be binding in all respects upon, and inure to the benefit of the heirs, executors, administrators, legal representatives, successors, and permitted assigns of the parties.

COMMENT

Absent an express provision to the contrary, contract rights are freely assignable. *See* RESTATEMENT (SECOND) OF CONTRACTS § 317(2); MURRAY, MURRAY ON CONTRACTS § 138 (3d ed. 1990). Of less certainty is whether contract duties may be delegated. *See* STARK § 3.04[2].

Assignment and Delegation. Section 12.9 requires the other party's consent before a party may assign its rights or delegate its obligations under the Model Agreement, with certain exceptions for the benefit of Buyer.

Buyer wants certainty, and any dealing by Sellers that expands its risk should be unacceptable. The analysis might be divided between pre-closing and post-closing. Sellers would probably have little interest in assignment or delegation pre-closing: they own the stock, and passage of title is essential to closing. There are pre-closing covenants that bind Sellers; those may be relevant to Buyer's receipt of stock in an ongoing business. The post-closing covenants (particularly covenants not to compete) are personal to Sellers; it is not certain how they would be delegated. Sellers may want to assign their rights to proceeds from the escrow and payments under any earnout.

On the other hand, Buyer's needs differ. Accordingly, Buyer has created three exceptions. The first allows an assignment of rights and delegation of duties to any Subsidiary. Buyers frequently effectuate transactions though subsidiaries, which may not have been organized when the Model Agreement is signed. The second allows an assignment of rights and delegation of duties to a purchaser of the business of the Company; the most obvious situation would be the assignment of the covenants not to compete, but would also include rights to indemnification. It would also include the delegation of duties (e.g., under an earnout). The third pertains to rights (but not the delegation of duties) to a lender, frequently required under credit arrangements.

Successors and Assigns. The last sentence of this Section expressly provides that the terms of the Model Agreement will be binding upon, and will inure to the benefit of, the heirs, executors, administrators, legal representatives, successors, and permitted assigns of the parties. It is not certain how this works. Courts differ as to whether this type of provision will bind an assignee to perform the obligations of the assignor. *See* STARK § 4.03[1]. It is difficult to see, however, how an assignee can be bound when not a party to the contract, without an express agreement to perform the assignor's obligations. *See* CORBIN ON CONTRACTS § 871. Even when an assignment of rights/delegation of duties is made with consent, the assignor/delegor is not relieved of liability, unless there is a novation. RESTATEMENT (SECOND) OF CONTRACTS § 318(3). If it is intended that an assignment relieve Buyer of its obligations, that should be made explicit.

SELLERS' RESPONSE

Sellers may want to specify that no assignment relieves Buyer from its obligations, and could do so by adding the following proviso at the end of the first sentence of Section 12.9: "; provided that no such assignment or delegation shall relieve Buyer from any of its obligations hereunder."

Sellers may object to the assignment of their continuing obligations under the Model Agreement, primarily the covenant not to compete, particularly if the alternative clause is selected, because there could be multiple assignees. Depending upon the wording of the noncompete, the assignment could actually increase the scope of the clause.

Banks and other funding sources typically are willing to finance a transaction only after conducting some due diligence on the target. In order to reduce the risks associated with a leveraged transaction, a lender may desire the right to proceed directly against Sellers for breaches of Sellers' representations, warranties, covenants, and obligations in the Model Agreement. Sellers may argue that their relationship with Buyer pertains only to the sale of the Company's stock, not to Buyer's financing, that they have no relationship with Buyer's lender, and that what Buyer must do to secure financing for the transaction is no concern of Sellers. Sellers may object on the ground that the lender does not have the same incentives and motivations to resolve disputes as Buyer. For example, Buyer may have a continuing relationship with Sellers (through employment agreements, consulting agreements, earnout agreements, and other contractual relationships), which may make Buyer more likely to take a softer approach with Sellers than would a lender. Further, in cases where Sellers have indemnification claims against Buyer, Buyer may be more willing to compromise on its own indemnification claims against Sellers. Sellers may argue, in short, that lenders have different motives than Buyer, and such motives work to Sellers' disadvantage. If, however, Buyer has a real need for financing and Sellers do not want to jeopardize the deal, Sellers should be prepared to make compromises.

Sellers may also want to specify that they can assign their rights to receipt of the Purchase Price arising in the future, such as payment of the post-closing adjustment under Section 2.5 or the release of funds from escrow.

12.10 NO THIRD-PARTY RIGHTS

Other than the Indemnified Persons and the parties, no Person will have any legal or equitable right, remedy, or claim under or with respect to this Agreement. This Agreement may be amended or terminated, and any provision of this Agreement may be waived, without the consent of any Person who is not a party to the Agreement.

COMMENT

It is well recognized that a contract may confer enforceable rights on a third-party beneficiary. *See* RESTATEMENT (SECOND) OF CONTRACTS § 302. If a third-party beneficiary has enforceable rights, modification or termination of the contract may be prohibited without consent of the third party. The rights of a third-party beneficiary may be specified or limited by the contract. FARNSWORTH, FARNSWORTH ON CONTRACTS § 10.8 (2d ed. 1998). The issue of third-party beneficiaries is a particular concern in acquisition agreements because of the broad constituencies that may be involved in the sale of a business. *See* American Bar Association, Section of Business Law, *Who Invited You? Third Party Beneficiary Issues in M&A Transactions* (Spring Meeting 2005).

The parties will be concerned that the rights of other parties may require that they be involved in the enforcement, amendment, or termination of the Model Agreement, or waiver of any rights thereunder. Section 12.10 expressly states that the parties do not create any rights, remedies, or claims on the part of any third parties, except upon assignment as permitted by Section 12.9 and other than Indemnified Persons. This is not a statement that there are no third-party beneficiaries; there may be incidental beneficiaries, and Indemnified Persons are specifically recognized. However, the second sentence provides that the Model Agreement may be amended or terminated, and any provision may be waived, without the consent of any person other than the parties.

See STARK 5.

If Article 11 has been negotiated to delete Indemnified Persons other than the parties from direct indemnification, that term would be deleted here. Even if there are Indemnified Persons beyond the parties, Buyer may prefer to be empowered to coordinate their rights. In that case, the term "Indemnified Persons" would be deleted and a sentence added, "Buyer shall enforce any legal or equitable right, remedy, or claim under or with respect to this Agreement for the benefit of Buyer Indemnified Persons."

SELLERS' RESPONSE

In some cases, Sellers may want certain provisions of the Model Agreement to benefit third parties upon the Closing. For example, if Buyer agrees to hire employees of the Company or to provide certain compensation and benefits to the employees, Sellers may want these promises to be enforceable by the employees. Buyer is likely to resist making the employees third-party beneficiaries so as not to subject itself to potential claims by numerous employees.

With respect to indemnification, Sellers may be concerned with many persons, each with separate counsel, defending or pursuing claims, all at Sellers' expense. They might suggest that Section 12.10 be better coordinated with Article 11.

12.11   REMEDIES CUMULATIVE

The rights and remedies of the parties are cumulative and not alternative.

COMMENT

The effect of Section 12.11 in relation to Article 11 is that a party may seek indemnification under Article 11 and pursue its remedies under common law or otherwise for breach of contract or other damages or relief. *See* STARK ch. 9.

If the parties have provided for a payment of a fee on termination, they would want to modify Section 12.11 to reflect the fact that payment of the termination fee is the sole remedy when applicable.

SELLERS' RESPONSE

Sellers may seek to exclude the provision in Section 12.11 providing that the rights of the parties in respect of the Model Agreement are cumulative, instead providing that the indemnification provided by Article 11 is Buyer's exclusive remedy for breach of the Model Agreement, arguing that any limitations on damages and the time for asserting claims that Sellers have succeeded in negotiating would be frustrated if Article 11 were not Buyer's exclusive remedy. Sellers would also deal with Section 12.16 (equitable relief), either limiting its effect or eliminating it entirely.

In fact, Sellers might suggest various limitations on remedies:

- Sellers might suggest that the remedies specified in the Model Agreement (indemnification) be exclusive, and that extra-contractual remedies be eliminated.
- Sellers might suggest that damages be capped at a fixed amount (often the amount deposited in escrow).
- Sellers might propose a reverse termination fee if Buyer refuses to close unjustifiably.
- Sellers might propose some limitation on damages.

See preliminary note to Article 10 and commentary to Article 11 regarding the effectiveness of these limitations.

Finally, Sellers might propose that certain forms of damages, such as incidental, consequential, punitive, and diminution in value, be excluded. *See* "Definition of Loss" in commentary to the lead-in clause to Section 11.2.

12.12   GOVERNING LAW

All matters relating to or arising out of this Agreement or any Contemplated Transaction and the rights of the parties (whether sounding in contract, tort, or otherwise) will be governed by and construed and interpreted under the laws of the State of _____ without regard to conflicts of laws principles that would require the application of any other law.

COMMENT

Section 12.12 is a selection of the law that will govern the contractual rights and obligations of the parties, perhaps including tort-based claims. *See* ABRY Partners V, L.P. v. F&W Acquisition LLC, 891 A.2d 1032, 1048 (Del. Ch. 2006). Without a choice of law provision, the court must determine the applicable substantive law to apply to the contract, using traditional conflict of laws analyses. The provision makes it clear that the selection is the internal law of a particular state.

RESTATEMENT (SECOND) OF CONFLICT OF LAWS § 187 provides:

§ 187. Law of the State Chosen by the Parties

(1) The law of the state chosen by the parties to govern their contractual rights and duties will be applied if the particular issue is one which the parties could have resolved by an explicit provision in their agreement directed to that issue.

(2) The law of the state chosen by the parties to govern their contractual rights and duties will be applied, even if the particular issue is one which the parties could not have resolved by an explicit provision in their agreement directed to that issue, unless either

(a) the chosen state has no substantial relationship to the parties or the transaction and there is no other reasonable basis for the parties' choice, or

(b) application of the law of the chosen state would be contrary to a fundamental policy of a state which has a materially greater interest than the chosen state in the determination of the particular issue and which, under the rule of § 188, would be the state of the applicable law in the absence of an effective choice of law by the parties.

(3)   In the absence of a contrary indication of intention, the reference is to the local law of the state of the chosen law.

Statutes Recognizing Choice of Law. Several states have enacted statutes enabling parties to a written contract to specify that the law of that state would govern the parties' relationship, notwithstanding the lack of any other connection to that state. *See, e.g.*, 6 Del. Code § 2708; N.Y. Gen. Oblig. Law § 5-1401. These statutes recognize that sophisticated parties may have valid reasons to choose the law of a given jurisdiction to govern their relationship, even if the chosen jurisdiction is not otherwise involved in the transaction. These statutes contain several requirements confining their use to sophisticated parties. The primary requirement is that the transaction involve a substantial amount.

The parties may wish to consider the use of one of these statutes in appropriate circumstances, perhaps to choose a neutral jurisdiction if the choice of law negotiation has become heated. Perhaps the most significant uncertainty is whether the choice of law based on such a statute would be respected by a court of a different jurisdiction (or a federal court hearing a diversity case).

Filling in the Blank. The choice may not be that difficult. If there are local Sellers and a local Buyer, the choice is often the law of that jurisdiction. On the other hand, even if the conflict of laws rules pose some risk that the choice of law will not be respected, the parties may choose a law that meets their expectations. Problems of enforceability of contracts under various judicial doctrines are discussed under "Judicial Limitations on Enforcement" in preliminary note to Article 11. Either party would probably prefer a jurisdiction in which the courts come closest to respecting the literal language of the Model Agreement without judicial exceptions to enforceability.

Application of the Uniform Commercial Code. *See* Application of the Uniform Commercial Code in commentary to Section 2.1 for a discussion of the interplay between the UCC and Section 12.12.

Scope of Provision. Section 12.12 specifies the law governing the rights of the parties (whether sounding in contract, tort, or otherwise), as well as the construction and interpretation of the Model Agreement. This is to address the decision in Benchmark Electronics, Inc. v. J. M. Huber Corp., 343 F.3d 719 (5th Cir. 2003), *modified*, 2003 U.S. App. LEXIS (5th Cir. Dec. 19, 2003), in which the court held that the language "governed by, and construed in accordance with, the internal laws of the State of New York" only dealt with claims arising from construction and interpretation of the agreement, and not claims of fraud and misrepresentation. *See* West & Benton, *Contracting to Avoid Extra-Contractual Liability—Can Your Contractual Deal Ever Be the "Entire" Deal?*, 64 Bus. Law. 999 (2009).

See Stark § 6.02.

12.13   JURISDICTION; SERVICE OF PROCESS

Except as otherwise provided in this Agreement, any Proceeding arising out of or relating to this Agreement or any Contemplated Transaction shall be brought in the courts of the State of _____, County of _____, or, if it has or can acquire jurisdiction, in the United States District Court for the _____ District of _____, and each of the parties irrevocably submits to the exclusive jurisdiction of each such court in any such Proceeding, waives any objection it may now or hereafter have to venue or to convenience of forum, agrees that all claims in respect of such Proceeding shall be heard and determined only in any such court, and agrees not to bring any Proceeding arising out of or relating to this Agreement or any Contemplated Transaction in any other court. Each party acknowledges and agrees that this Section 12.13 constitutes a voluntary and bargained-for agreement between the parties. Process in any Proceeding referred to in the first sentence of this Section or in Section 11.8(d) may be served on any party anywhere in the world, including by sending or delivering a copy of the process to the party to be served at the address and in the manner provided for the giving of notices in Section 12.18. Nothing in this Section 12.13 will affect the right of any party to serve legal process in any other manner permitted by law or at equity.

GENERAL COMMENT

Forum. Exclusive forum selection clauses are generally upheld by the courts if they have been freely bargained for, are not contrary to an important public policy of the forum, and are generally reasonable. *See* CASAD, JURISDICTION AND FORUM SELECTION § 4.17 (2d ed. 1999). A court in a forum other than the one selected may, in certain circumstances, elect to assert jurisdiction notwithstanding the parties' designation of another forum. In these situations, the court will determine whether the forum selection provision violates public policy of the forum state.

Some state statutes validate the parties' selection of a forum. For example, a California statute provides that actions against foreign corporations and nonresident persons can be maintained in California where the action arises out of or relates to an agreement for which a choice of California law has been made by the parties involving a transaction of not less than $1 million and containing a provision to submit to the jurisdiction of the California courts. CAL. CIV. PROC. CODE § 410.40. *See also* DEL. CODE tit. 6, § 2708(b); N.Y. GEN. OBLIG. LAW § 5-1402.

See STARK § 6.03.

Arbitration. Alternatively, the parties may specify arbitration for disputes under the Model Agreement. *See* STARK ch. 8 and numerous other publications, such as COMMERCIAL ARBITRATION AT ITS BEST: SUCCESSFUL STRATEGIES FOR BUSINESS USERS (ABA 2001). *See* Appendix E—Alternative Dispute Resolution for an arbitration provision with commentary.

COMMENT

Forum. Section 12.13 provides an exclusive forum for actions arising out of or relating to the Model Agreement or any Contemplated Transaction and also provides a method of securing personal jurisdiction.

Parties often seek to designate the forum of one's state of incorporation or principal place of business (or in the case of Sellers, residence). This attempt to gain the hometown advantage may not produce the best selection. For example, the court selected may have limited experience in business transactions or a crowded docket, perhaps prejudicial to Buyer. For an analysis of whether a forum selection clause is permissive or exclusive, *see* Action Corp. v. Toshiba America Consumer Prods., Inc., 975 F. Supp. 170 (D.P.R. 1997).

The Model Agreement also provides federal jurisdiction if the federal courts can acquire jurisdiction. While the provision allowing both federal and state jurisdiction is common, it is not required. If one is convinced that the state courts of a particular state understand acquisition agreements, it does not follow that the federal courts sitting in that state are similarly skilled.

The parties may not be able to confer jurisdiction on certain courts. For example, federal courts require either diversity jurisdiction or subject matter jurisdiction. If federal jurisdiction is desired, the state in which Buyer is incorporated may be significant in establishing complete diversity.

Forum vs. Venue. Some states specify particular venue (often counties) for bringing suit, which may not be varied by contract.

Service of Process. The last two sentences of Section 12.13 deal with service of process. Process may be served on any party anywhere in the world, an agreement that does not depend on long-arm statutes. Process may be served using the notice procedures of Section 12.18 (hand, overnight courier, or electronic), rather than traditional means of service of process. When litigation is contemplated, Buyer may prefer to rely on traditional means of serving process and a litigator might be consulted as to the effectiveness of this provision under applicable rules of the particular jurisdiction. The traditional means of service of process are preserved.

Alternatively, Buyer might propose, as to Sellers, the designation of an agent for service of process because of the number of Sellers, which could be either Sellers' Representative or a third-party service.

SELLERS' RESPONSE

Forum. Sellers may attempt to change the designation to a more convenient forum or simply to confer jurisdiction in the forum selected by Buyer without making it the exclusive forum. Sellers might respond with their hometown court, and the battle is joined. Objections frequently made by sellers include that they will be inconvenienced, will not have the continuous representation of their lawyers because they may need to hire local counsel, and will be subject to delays. How this argument is ultimately worked out is important. In selecting a forum, the choice of law (Section 12.12) is a consideration. While courts will apply the laws of other jurisdictions, they may not always do so properly and the law may be unclear due to conflicting precedent. In addition, conflict of law rules vary and courts may not respect the parties' choice of law.

Service of Process. Since Sellers are more likely to be the subject of claims by Buyer, they may be more concerned with the manner of serving process. Commencing litigation by the same means as notice (such as an e-mail) may not be desirable.

12.14   WAIVER OF JURY TRIAL

EACH PARTY, KNOWINGLY, VOLUNTARILY, AND INTENTIONALLY, WAIVES ITS RIGHT TO TRIAL BY JURY IN ANY PROCEEDING ARISING OUT OF OR RELATING TO THIS AGREEMENT OR ANY CONTEMPLATED TRANSACTION, WHETHER SOUNDING IN CONTRACT, TORT, OR OTHERWISE.

COMMENT

Buyer's circumstances may suggest whether it wants to include a jury-waiver provision. Conventional wisdom is that big corporations, fearing jury prejudice, want to avoid jury trials, while individuals would want a jury. But other judgments could be made. Buyer and Sellers might agree that the results of jury trials are too unpredictable. Alternatively, Buyer may suggest some form of alternative dispute resolution. *See* commentary to Section 12.13.

The Seventh Amendment to the U.S. Constitution guarantees the fundamental right to a jury trial. There is a strong presumption against the waiver of the right to a jury trial. Aetna Ins. Co. v. Kennedy, 301 U.S. 389 (1937) ("courts indulge every reasonable presumption against waiver"). Many states have a similar state constitutional provision. Nevertheless, jury-waiver clauses appear to be enforceable in many jurisdictions, although at least two states hold them unenforceable. *See* Grafton Partners L.P. v. Superior Court, 116 P.3d 479 (Cal. 2005); Bank South, N.A. v. Howard, 444 S.E.2d 799 (Ga. 1994). *See* STARK ch. 7.

Even where the Model Agreement is heavily negotiated, Buyer may anticipate a post-signing challenge to the jury-waiver clause, particularly if Sellers are financially distressed or not particularly sophisticated.

SELLERS' RESPONSE

Like Buyer, Sellers should consider the circumstances as to whether a jury trial would be preferable and the potential advantages of a form of alternative dispute resolution. The factors might include where the trial would take place, the likelihood of finding a jury sympathetic to Sellers' interests, the economics of conducting a trial, and the issues likely to be presented.

12.15   ATTORNEYS' FEES

In the event any Proceeding is brought in respect of this Agreement or any of the documents referred to in this Agreement, the prevailing party will be entitled to recover reasonable attorneys' fees and other costs incurred in such Proceeding, in addition to any relief to which such party may be entitled.

COMMENT

Section 12.15 provides for attorneys' fees in connection with the enforcement of the Model Agreement. This provision changes the general rule that a party in a legal proceeding is responsible for its own legal fees and is in addition to the legal fees provisions in Article 11 dealing with indemnification. It provides that attorneys' fees and costs will be available to the prevailing party. In determining whether to include this provision, Buyer might consider the same factors as set forth below for Sellers. *See* STARK § 12.08[3][d].

SELLERS' RESPONSE

Much like the waiver of a jury trial, Sellers might consider the circumstances before agreeing to this provision. The factors might include the type of disputes that might arise, the issues to be presented, the leverage gained by the prospect of recovering attorneys' fees and the potential disparity in the size of the fees that might be incurred by Buyer and Sellers.

12.16   ENFORCEMENT OF AGREEMENT

Sellers acknowledge and agree that Buyer would be irreparably harmed if any of the provisions of this Agreement are not performed in accordance with their specific terms and that any Breach of this Agreement by Sellers could not be adequately compensated in all cases by monetary damages alone. Accordingly, Sellers agree that, in addition to any other right or remedy to which Buyer may be entitled at law or in equity, Buyer shall be entitled to enforce any provision of this Agreement by a decree of specific performance and to obtain temporary, preliminary, and permanent injunctive relief to prevent Breaches or threatened Breaches, without posting any bond or giving any other undertaking.

COMMENT

This Section provides that Buyer is entitled to certain equitable remedies, namely specific performance and injunctive relief. Traditionally, equitable relief was available when the remedy at law (damages) was inadequate. The first sentence is an acknowledgment by Sellers that monetary damages would not be adequate. *See* STARK § 9.01[2][b].

Specific Performance. The RESTATEMENT (SECOND) OF CONTRACTS § 357(1) provides that, with certain exceptions, "specific performance of a contract duty will be granted in the discretion of the court against a party who has committed or is threatening to commit a breach of the duty." One of the exceptions is "if damages would be adequate to protect the expectation interest of the injured party." For specific performance to be granted, Buyer should be prepared to convince a court that the business being acquired is unique and damages would not be adequate to protect its interest. *See* Allegheny Energy, Inc. v. DQE, Inc., 171 F.3d 153 (3d Cir. 1999). A business is, in fact, unique, and courts have ordered performance of acquisition agreements. *See, e.g.*, Genesco, Inc. v. The Finish Line, Tenn. Ch. Ct. 07-2137 (December 27, 2007).

Specific performance may be available, whether or not the recitation supporting this type of relief is included. However, including the acknowledgement of the inadequacy of damages and the entitlement to equitable remedies is an attempt to estop Sellers from arguing the contrary.

If Buyer wants to deny the remedy of specific performance to Sellers, it should do so explicitly and avoid any potentially conflicting provisions. If, for example, Buyer has provided a reverse termination fee, it would want Sellers' sole remedy to be a suit for collection of the fee.

Injunction. Buyer may seek to enjoin a breach by Sellers of their covenants in the Model Agreement. An injunction may be the only way for Buyer to prevent irreparable injury to the goodwill purchased by Buyer. As in the case of specific performance, an injunction against a breach of contract duty can be granted in the discretion of the court. RESTATEMENT (SECOND) OF CONTRACTS § 357(2).

Providing for equitable remedies will not ensure that Buyer will be successful in obtaining the requested relief, but the acknowledgment of Buyer's right to equitable relief may be persuasive to a court that is considering the matter. Similarly, in granting an injunction, a court may have little or no discretion in requiring a bond or undertaking because of state statutes, but expressly negating the requirement of a bond in the Model Agreement may be helpful in convincing a court to minimize the amount of the bond to be posted by Buyer.

SELLERS' RESPONSE

It may be difficult for Sellers to argue that this provision should be deleted. An equitable remedy simply means a court would order what Sellers have already agreed to do.

In the Model Agreement, Buyer has not provided for a termination right without fault (which could be conditioned upon payment of a termination fee). Therefore, Sellers may request that the equitable remedies provision be made mutual. *See* United Rentals, Inc. v. RAM Holdings, Inc., 937 A.2d 810 (Del. Ch. 2007) (addressing relationship between specific performance and reverse termination fee), discussed in commentary to Section 10.2.

12.17   NO WAIVER

Neither any failure nor any delay by any party in exercising any right, power, or privilege under this Agreement or any of the documents referred to in this Agreement will operate as a waiver of such right, power, or privilege, and no single or partial exercise of any such right, power, or privilege will preclude any other or further exercise of such right, power, or privilege or the exercise of any other right, power, or privilege. To the maximum extent permitted by applicable Legal Requirements, (a) no claim or right arising out of this Agreement or any of the documents referred to in this Agreement can be waived by a party, in whole or in part, unless made in a writing signed by such party or Sellers' Representative on behalf of a Seller; (b) a waiver given by a party will only be applicable to the specific instance for which it is given; and (c) no notice to or demand on a party will (i) waive or otherwise affect any obligation of that party or (ii) affect the right of the party giving such notice or demand to take further action without notice or demand as provided in this Agreement or the documents referred to in this Agreement.

COMMENT

Section 12.17 attempts to limit the effect of certain common law doctrines that may limit remedies. *See* STARK §§ 16.06–.12.

The second sentence attempts to counteract judicial estoppel and election doctrines. The no-waiver provision also is intended to defeat arguments that the course of performance or course of dealing with respect to the acquisition agreement dictates the outcome of disputes between the parties and that any delay prejudices the rights of the delaying party.

The second sentence also attempts to preclude oral waivers. Despite this language, however, oral waivers may be enforced. *See* STARK §16.07. It also attempts to limit the effect of a waiver to the specific instance.

12.18 NOTICES

All notices and other communications required or permitted by this Agreement shall be in writing and will be effective, and any applicable time period shall commence, when (a) delivered to the following address by hand or by a nationally recognized overnight courier service (costs prepaid) addressed to the following address or (b) transmitted electronically to the following facsimile numbers or e-mail addresses, in each case marked to the attention of the Person (by name or title) designated below (or to such other address, facsimile number, e-mail address, or Person as a party may designate by notice to the other parties):

Sellers:

[Name of Sellers' Representative]
[Street]
[City, state, and zip code]
Fax no.:
E-mail address:

with a copy to:

_____
Attention:
[Street]
[City, state, and zip code]
Fax no.:
E-mail address:

Buyer:

_____
Attention:
[Street]
[City, state, and zip code]
Fax no.:
E-mail address:

with a copy to:

_____
Attention:
[Street]
[City, state, and zip code]
Fax no.:
E-mail address:

COMMENT

Section 12.18 specifies the form and effectiveness of any notices or other communications. The Model Agreement provides alternative means for giving notice and sending other communications: by hand, overnight courier, or electronically (facsimile or e-mail).

The Model Agreement does not provide for notice by registered or certified U.S. mail, the traditional means of giving notice, because notice by U.S. mail is no longer as common as it once was due to increasing reliance upon other more expeditious means of communication, such as facsimile and e-mail. No proof of delivery is required by the Model Agreement for any of the means of service. Nevertheless, the party giving notice must be prepared to prove that notice was actually sent or delivered by the specified means. If a notice is time-sensitive or especially critical, a party usually will take steps to ensure that it is personally delivered, with a signed receipt, or is sent by multiple methods so that adequate proof of the giving of notice can be presented if a dispute arises.

These provisions normally specify when notice is effective. Under the Model Agreement, notice is deemed given when sent by facsimile or e-mail or when delivered by hand or overnight courier. Buyer will ordinarily prefer that notice be deemed given when sent because it is more likely that it will be giving notices under the Model Agreement.

Many notice provisions designate a particular person by name or title to whose attention the notice is to be directed for a corporation or other entity. It may be better to use an attention line than to designate a person at the beginning of the address to avoid the argument that the notice has to be given to or received by that person.

The Model Agreement provides that copies of notices are to be sent to others (normally counsel). The notice provision suggests that these copies are mandatory, meaning that notice will not be deemed effective as to a party unless the copy is also given as required. Sometimes these are designated as a "courtesy copy." In some cases, the notice provision will state that sending or delivering the copy of the notice will not constitute the giving of notice to the party itself.

See STARK ch. 15.

SELLERS' RESPONSE

Sellers may feel uncomfortable in allowing notice to Sellers' Representative to suffice as notice to Sellers.

Sellers in particular will want to be sure that a notice in fact is received so that it can be acted upon in a timely manner. While use of facsimile and e-mail has become more widespread, there is a concern that these technologies are still unreliable. This concern about reliability to some extent can be alleviated by requiring confirmation of transmission, and Sellers might propose that. Most facsimile equipment will print a transmission report that confirms successful transmission and identifies the facsimile number and, in some cases, the party to which the notice has been sent. Sender can request a receipt in some e-mail programs. Third-party e-mail services can provide additional return receipt verification.

The application of this Section to any "communications" between the parties may appear overly broad. For example, Section 5.1 provides that certain information will be furnished to Buyer. It is not intended to apply to this type of communication, but only to those that are subject to a time period or otherwise have a particularly significant consequence if not delivered or transmitted. If Sellers have a concern, however, certain Sections of the Model Agreement might be excluded from the operation of Section 12.18.

12.19 SEVERABILITY

If any provision of this Agreement is held invalid or unenforceable by any court of competent jurisdiction, the other provisions of this Agreement will remain in full force and effect. Any provision of this Agreement held invalid or unenforceable only in part or degree will remain in full force and effect to the extent not held invalid or unenforceable.

COMMENT

Under Section 12.19, if a provision of the Model Agreement is held unenforceable, the remaining provisions are separated from the invalid or unenforceable provision and remain in effect. As to whether this language is effective, *see* STARK ch. 17.

The parties may also want to consider inserting a provision calling for judicial reformation to modify the invalid provision to achieve the parties' intention. This practice is common with respect to covenants not to compete and is adopted in Section 7.2(e). Buyer might also consider a more restrictive version that limits severability in circumstances where the effect of not enforcing the provision would deprive a party of a material benefit of its bargain. Such a provision might replace the first sentence of Section 12.19 with the following.

> If any provision of this Agreement is determined by any court of competent jurisdiction to be invalid, illegal, or incapable of being enforced by any rule of law or public policy, all other terms, conditions, and provisions of this Agreement shall nevertheless remain in full force and effect so long as the economic or legal substance of the transaction contemplated hereby is not affected in any manner materially adverse to any party.

In lieu of Section 12.19, Buyer may consider whether it would want to rescind the entire Model Agreement if a major, yet nonessential, provision is held to be invalid or unenforceable. For example, if a covenant not to compete is unenforceable, and the reason Buyer is entering into the transaction is to obtain the covenant not to compete, Buyer would most likely want to rescind the acquisition.

12.20   TIME OF ESSENCE

With regard to all dates and time periods set forth or referred to in this Agreement, time is of the essence.

COMMENT

If the parties to a contract, such as the Model Agreement, negotiate specific time periods or dates by which certain events have to occur, courts may not enforce them. The "time of the essence" provision in Section 12.20 is intended to make it clear the parties expect that these time periods and dates will be enforced and, if not adhered to, that they would provide grounds for termination. But since there can be many time periods for performance and the consequences of untimely performance are not specified, courts sometimes even ignore these provisions. *See* ADAMS, A MANUAL OF STYLE FOR CONTRACT DRAFTING (2d ed. 2008) §§12.394–.403.

If there are time periods or dates, such as the End Date in Section 10.1, that are particularly important, Buyer may want to be more direct and narrow the scope of the "time of the essence" provision or include it in the termination provisions, rather than having it apply generally by including it in Article 12. The following language is an example of such an approach:

> The parties acknowledge that the End Date in Section 10.1 is particularly important to them and that, if a party wishes to terminate this Agreement in accordance with that Section, that party will not be required to give the other party any time beyond the End Date to allow that party to satisfy any condition or perform any obligation under this Agreement.

SELLERS' RESPONSE

The desirability of this provision, from Sellers' perspective, depends on the nature of the parties' obligations prior to and after the Closing. If Sellers believe that they can materially satisfy their responsibilities on a timely basis, then they might accept this provision, as it may provide a spur for Buyer's performance (i.e., paying the purchase price). On the other hand, if Sellers have concerns about meeting their obligations, such as providing necessary third-party consents on a timely basis, they might reject this language.

12.21   COUNTERPARTS AND ELECTRONIC SIGNATURES

(a) This Agreement and other documents to be delivered pursuant to this Agreement may be executed in one or more counterparts, each of which will be deemed to be an original copy and all of which, when taken together, will be deemed to constitute one and the same agreement or document, and will be effective when counterparts have been signed by each of the parties and delivered to the other parties.

(b) A manual signature on this Agreement or other documents to be delivered pursuant to this Agreement, an image of which shall have been transmitted electronically, will constitute an original signature for all purposes. The delivery of copies of this Agreement or other documents to be delivered pursuant to this Agreement, including executed signature pages where required, by electronic transmission will constitute effective delivery of this Agreement or such other document for all purposes.

COMMENT

Section 12.21 permits execution in counterparts, common in acquisition agreements. It is included for the convenience of the parties and facilitates execution of the agreement when the signatories are not available at the same time or place. *See* STARK ch. 19. This Section does not alter the date specified on the initial page of the Model Agreement. The charter, bylaws, or board minutes authorizing the Model Agreement will determine which persons have the authority to execute the agreement on behalf of corporate parties.

The language with respect to delivery of copies and signature pages electronically recognizes the increasing trend to rely on electronic transmission for execution and delivery of acquisition agreements. In most cases, arrangements are made to exchange the original signed copies, but there is always the concern that this might for some reason not take place. The question then becomes whether one can rely on a signature that is only recreated by electronic transmission.

Like earlier cases dealing with telegrams and telexes, there is authority to the effect that the exchange of writings and acceptance by facsimile creates a binding contract. *See* Lackey v. Cagle's, Inc., 1998 WL 1037916 (N.D. Ala 1998). A facsimile signature can satisfy the statute of frauds. *See, e.g.,* N.Y. GEN. OBLIG. LAW § 5-701 (written text produced by telefacsimile constitutes a writing and any symbol executed or adopted by a party with the present intention to authenticate a writing constitutes a signing).

While language in the Model Agreement validating signature by electronic transmission may not be essential, it might be helpful to have authorized the practice of exchanging signature pages electronically if a dispute should arise.

IN WITNESS WHEREOF, the parties have executed and delivered this Agreement as of the date first written above.

BUYER: **SELLERS:**

_____   _____
                                              [1]

By:_____   _____

Name:_____   [2]

Title:_____   _____
                                              [3]

_____
[4]

_____
[5]

_____
[6]

_____
[7]

_____
[8]

NOTES

NOTES

NOTES

NOTES

NOTES

NOTES

NOTES

NOTES

NOTES

NOTES

NOTES

NOTES

NOTES

Notes

NOTES